THE MODERN WORLD AFTER COLONIALISM

Remaking the Social Sciences

Gurminder K. Bhambra, Ipek Demir,
Paul Robert Gilbert, Su-ming Khoo,
and Lucy Mayblin

First published in Great Britain in 2026 by

Bristol University Press
University of Bristol
1–9 Old Park Hill
Bristol
BS2 8BB
UK
t: +44 (0)117 374 6645
e: bup-info@bristol.ac.uk

Details of international sales and distribution partners are available at bristoluniversitypress.co.uk

© Bristol University Press 2026

DOI: 10.51952/9781529252149

British Library Cataloguing in Publication Data
A catalogue record for this book is available from the British Library

ISBN 978-1-5292-5211-8 hardcover
ISBN 978-1-5292-5212-5 paperback
ISBN 978-1-5292-5213-2 ePub
ISBN 978-1-5292-5214-9 ePdf

The right of Gurminder K. Bhambra, Ipek Demir, Paul Robert Gilbert, Su-ming Khoo and Lucy Mayblin to be identified as editors of this work has been asserted by them in accordance with the Copyright, Designs and Patents Act 1988.

All rights reserved: no part of this publication may be reproduced, stored in a retrieval system, or transmitted in any form or by any means, electronic, mechanical, photocopying, recording, or otherwise without the prior permission of Bristol University Press.

Every reasonable effort has been made to obtain permission to reproduce copyrighted material. If, however, anyone knows of an oversight, please contact the publisher.

The statements and opinions contained within this publication are solely those of the editors and contributors and not of the University of Bristol or Bristol University Press. The University of Bristol and Bristol University Press disclaim responsibility for any injury to persons or property resulting from any material published in this publication.

Bristol University Press works to counter discrimination on grounds of gender, race, disability, age and sexuality.

Cover design: Nicky Borowiec
Front cover image: Cover Art/Limma Ali
Bristol University Press uses environmentally responsible print partners.
Printed and bound in Great Britain by CPI Group (UK) Ltd, Croydon, CR0 4YY

Bristol University Press' authorised representative in the European Union is:
Easy Access System Europe, Mustamäe tee 50, 10621 Tallinn, Estonia,
Email: gpsr.requests@easproject.com

Contents

List of Worksheets   vi
Notes on Contributors   vii

Introduction: The Making of the Modern World – Colonialism and Empire   1
Gurminder K. Bhambra, Ipek Demir, Paul Robert Gilbert, Su-ming Khoo, and Lucy Mayblin

PART I   The Making of the Modern World
Edited by Gurminder K. Bhambra

1. The Haitian Revolution in the Making of the Modern World   17
Gurminder K. Bhambra
2. Understanding the Colonial Global Economy   30
Paul Robert Gilbert
3. Colonial Extraction and Dispossession   43
Su-ming Khoo
4. Enslavement, Indenture, and Resistance in the British Empire   57
Maria del Pilar Kaladeen
5. Enclosures and the Making of Modern Britain   70
Imogen Tyler
6. Decolonization in the Making of the Modern World   85
Deanndre Chen and Meera Sabaratnam

PART II   The Politics of Inequality
Edited by Paul Robert Gilbert

7. Class, Capitalism, and Colonialism   101
John Holmwood
8. The Grunwick Strike: Uncovering Migrant Women's Contributions to Struggles for Workers' Rights in the UK   114
Sundari Anitha
9. Staying Put in a Hostile Environment   127
Daniel Renwick
10. Exploring the Growth of 'Emergency' Charitable Food Aid in the UK   140
Kayleigh Garthwaite
11. Race, Colonialism, and Modern Slavery   153
Genevieve LeBaron and Ali Bhagat

| 12 | The UK's Elite: Colonial and Transnational Dynamics
Katie Higgins | 166 |

PART III Migration, Diaspora, and Asylum
Edited by Lucy Mayblin

13	Colonialism, Immigration, and the Making of British Citizenship *James Hampshire*	181
14	Asylum in Britain and the Legacies of Colonialism *Lucy Mayblin*	194
15	Diasporic Interventions: How Diasporas Have Shaped Modernity and Challenged the Global North *Ipek Demir*	207
16	Making Love, Making Empire: Family, Colonial Racism, and Border Controls *Joe Turner*	219
17	Populism, Migration, and the Politics of Racism *Karim Murji*	234
18	The British Migration–Citizenship Regime: From Decolonization to Brexit *Michaela Benson*	246

PART IV Multiculturalism and Anti-Racism
Edited by Ipek Demir

19	British Black Power *John Narayan*	263
20	(Un)archiving Black British Feminisms *Alexandra Wanjiku Kelbert*	275
21	Modes of Integration, Multiculturalism, and National Identities *Tariq Modood*	288
22	Anxieties of Multiculturalism: The Birmingham Trojan Horse Affair *John Holmwood*	302
23	Security and the War on Terror: Predict, Prevent, Police *Shereen Fernandez*	316
24	Policing, Racial Capitalism, and Abolition *Vanessa E. Thompson*	328

PART V The Environment
Edited by Su-ming Khoo

| 25 | Connected Sociologies of Pollution
Su-ming Khoo | 341 |

26	Extractivism, Anti-Extractivism, and Post-Extractivism in Latin America *Andrea Sempértegui*	356
27	A Global Green New Deal? Signatures of Continuing Colonial Violence *Harpreet Kaur-Spannos*	371
28	Political Ecology: Critical Reflections *Mitul Baruah*	385
29	Our Worlds of Palm Oil: A Tale of Colonialism, Consumerism, and Technology *Max Haiven*	399
30	Remaking Race in the Crucible of Climate Change *Andrew Baldwin*	412

Conclusion: Remaking the Social Sciences After Colonialism 424
Paul Robert Gilbert, Gurminder K. Bhambra, Ipek Demir, Su-ming Khoo, and Lucy Mayblin

Using the Lesson Plans for the Connected Sociologies Curriculum Project 432
Isabel Sykes

Index 440

List of Worksheets

1	The Haitian Revolution in the Making of the Modern World	28
2	Understanding the Colonial Global Economy	41
3	Colonial Extraction and Dispossession	55
4	Enslavement, Indenture, and Resistance in the British Empire	68
5	Enclosures and the Making of Modern Britain	82
6	Decolonization in the Making of the Modern World	96
7	Class, Capitalism, and Colonialism	111
8	The Grunwick Strike: Uncovering Migrant Women's Contributions to Struggles for Workers' Rights in the UK	125
9	Staying Put in a Hostile Environment	138
10	Exploring the Growth of 'Emergency' Charitable Food Aid in the UK	151
11	Race, Colonialism, and Modern Slavery	164
12	The UK's Elite: Colonial and Transnational Dynamics	175
13	Colonialism, Immigration, and the Making of British Citizenship	192
14	Asylum in Britain and the Legacies of Colonialism	204
15	Diasporic Interventions: How Diasporas Have Shaped Modernity and Challenged the Global North	217
16	Making Love, Making Empire: Family, Colonial Racism, and Border Controls	231
17	Populism, Migration, and the Politics of Racism	244
18	The British Migration–Citizenship Regime: From Decolonization to Brexit	258
19	British Black Power	273
20	(Un)archiving Black British Feminisms	286
21	Modes of Integration, Multiculturalism, and National Identities	299
22	Anxieties of Multiculturalism: The Birmingham Trojan Horse Affair	314
23	Security and the War on Terror: Predict, Prevent, Police	326
24	Policing, Racial Capitalism, and Abolition	337
25	Connected Sociologies of Pollution	353
26	Extractivism, Anti-Extractivism, and Post-Extractivism in Latin America	368
27	A Global Green New Deal? Signatures of Continuing Colonial Violence	383
28	Political Ecology: Critical Reflections	396
29	Our Worlds of Palm Oil: A Tale of Colonialism, Consumerism, and Technology	410
30	Remaking Race in the Crucible of Climate Change	422

Notes on Contributors

Sundari Anitha is Professor in the School of Sociological Studies, Politics and International Relations, University of Sheffield, UK.

Andrew Baldwin is Professor in the Department of Geography, University of Durham, UK.

Mitul Baruah is Associate Professor of Sociology and Anthropology and Environmental Studies in the Department of Environmental Sciences, Ashoka University, India.

Michaela Benson is Professor of Public Sociology in the School of Social Sciences, Lancaster University and Chief Executive of the Sociological Review, UK.

Ali Bhagat is Assistant Professor in the School Public Policy, Simon Fraser University, Canada.

Gurminder K. Bhambra is Professor of Historical Sociology in the Faculty of Social Sciences, University of Sussex, UK.

Deanndre Chen is a DPhil candidate in International Relations in the Department of Politics and International Relations, University of Oxford, UK.

Ipek Demir is Professor of Diaspora Studies and Director of the Centre for Racism and Ethnicity Studies at the University of Leeds, UK.

Shereen Fernandez is an LSE Fellow at LSE100 at the London School of Economics, UK.

Kayleigh Garthwaite is Associate Professor in the Department of Social Policy, Sociology and Criminology, University of Birmingham, UK.

Paul Robert Gilbert is Reader in Development, Justice and Inequality in the School of Global Studies, University of Sussex, UK.

Max Haiven is Associate Professor and Canada Research Chair in the Radical Imagination at Lakehead University, Canada.

James Hampshire is Professor of Politics in the School of Law, Politics and Sociology, University of Sussex, UK.

Katie Higgins is Lecturer in the School of Sociological Studies, Politics and International Relations, University of Sheffield, UK.

John Holmwood is Emeritus Professor of Sociology at the University of Nottingham, UK and Senior Researcher in the Centre for Science and Technology, Institute for Philosophy, Czech Academy of Science, Czech Republic.

Maria del Pilar Kaladeen is an Associate Fellow in the Institute of Commonwealth Studies, University of London, UK.

Harpreet Kaur-Spannos is a solicitor, has a PhD from the University of Warwick Law School, and is currently Senior Organizer for Greenpeace UK.

Alexandra Wanjiku Kelbert is Leverhulme Early Career Fellow in the Sarah Parker Remond Centre for the Study of Racism and Racialisation at UCL, UK.

Su-ming Khoo is Professor in Sociology at the University of Galway, Ireland and Visiting Professor in Critical Studies in Higher Education and Transformation at Nelson Mandela University, South Africa.

Genevieve LeBaron is Distinguished Professor of Global Supply Chain Governance and Director of the Centre for Public Policy Research, Simon Fraser University, Canada.

Lucy Mayblin is Senior Lecturer in Sociology and Co-Director of the Migration Research Group in the School of Sociological Studies, Politics and International Relations, University of Sheffield, UK.

Tariq Modood is Professor of Sociology in the School of Sociology, Politics and International Studies, and the founding (former) Director of the Centre for the Study of Ethnicity and Citizenship, University of Bristol, UK.

Karim Murji is Professor of Social Policy and Criminology in the School of Human and Social Sciences, University of West London, UK.

John Narayan is Senior Lecturer in European and International Studies at King's College London and Chair of the Institute of Race Relations, UK.

Daniel Renwick is a writer and videographer who has worked closely with the Grenfell community, UK.

Meera Sabaratnam is Associate Professor in International Relations and Fellow of New College, University of Oxford, UK.

Andrea Sempértegui is Assistant Professor of Politics and a Paul Garrett Fellow at Whitman College, US.

Isabel Sykes is Doctoral Researcher in Sociology in the Department of Social and Political Sciences, Brunel, University of London, UK.

Vanessa E. Thompson is Associate Professor and Distinguished Professor in Black Studies and Social Justice at Queen's University, Canada.

Joe Turner is Senior Lecturer in International Politics in the Department of Politics and International Relations, University of York, UK.

Imogen Tyler is Professor of Sociology in the School of Social Sciences, Lancaster University, UK.

Introduction: The Making of the Modern World – Colonialism and Empire

Gurminder K. Bhambra, Ipek Demir, Paul Robert Gilbert, Su-ming Khoo, and Lucy Mayblin

Objectives

- To set out the standard social scientific accounts of modernity and their failure to address world-historical processes of colonialism and empire.
- To discuss the significance of colonialism and empire to the making of the modern world.
- To point to how this would enable us to remake the social sciences (discussed at greater length in the Conclusion).
- To provide a summary of the different sections of the book and how they relate to the main themes.

Introduction

The Modern World After Colonialism: Remaking the Social Sciences starts from an understanding of the significance of colonial histories to the making of the modern world. It provides a number of chapters, organized in five parts, that rethink key social science topics and concepts from this perspective. While there have been many books calling for the curriculum to be decolonized, there are few resources available to think through, in granular detail, the difference that would be made to specific topics, themes, and perspectives as a consequence of such moves. This is what this book provides.

The book emerges from the Connected Sociologies Curriculum Project, a project of the Sociological Review Foundation, which was set up in 2020.[1] Over four years, it developed an innovative online curriculum with video lectures and resources for use by teachers, students, and educators. This book brings together some of the most important topics and issues covered in the online curriculum to provide an additional resource, with increased depth and range, to support critical thinking in the social sciences.

Specifically, it brings together a variety of social scientists who are cognizant of the broader challenges posed by arguments for decolonizing the curriculum and who bring those insights into a transformation of their research and teaching of core concepts and categories. The book is organized in terms of five sections: 'The Making of the Modern World'; 'The Politics of Inequality'; 'Migration, Diaspora, and Asylum'; 'Multiculturalism and Anti-Racism'; and 'The Environment'. The chapters in each section address a key issue within the broader theme and present an understanding of it in relation to the colonial histories that are often missed.

In this introductory chapter, we set out why the modern world is so important to the structuring of the social sciences and why it is important to acknowledge the absence of colonial histories from standard accounts of modernity. We then provide a brief overview of each section. While many of the cases and examples discussed across the chapters concern Britain, including the wider British Empire historically, they also seek to illustrate broader global processes. The intention is to enable the reader to make connections to similar events and developments in other parts of the world.

Modernity and the social sciences

The idea of the *modern* world is central to the social sciences and to sociology specifically. It is generally accepted that the discipline of sociology, for example, emerged out of the conditions of modern society and represented a distinctively modern form of explanation of that society. Whatever their other differences, the early sociologists believed themselves to be living through a – or perhaps *the* – great transformation in history. They were primarily concerned with understanding how this transformation had begun and influencing how it would be brought to the completion they believed to be inherent within it. That is, the modern world was understood both in terms of a new world that had come into being in Europe, as well as a project that would eventually encapsulate the whole world.

The modern world, or modernity, is theorized in terms of establishing a temporal rupture, that is, a break in time, that separated a traditional agrarian past from a modern industrial present. This temporal rupture was also seen to be geographically located in Europe, or the West more broadly, and marked a clear cultural difference between 'the West and the rest' (Hall 1992). The historical events that standardly support such understandings of rupture and difference as defining the modern world are: the political revolutions in the United States (1776) and France (1789) and the industrial revolution that took place in the 19th century in Britain.

The political revolutions are seen as bringing into being the institutions of the modern nation state and forms of democracy; the industrial revolution is regarded as central to changes in the economy from the previous predominance of agriculture to modes of industrial capitalism. This latter revolution is often presented as *the* modern discontinuity. Both revolutions are further underpinned by a cultural revolution, or revolution in the system of knowledge and beliefs, as embodied in the Renaissance and the accompanying Scientific Revolution and 'voyages of discovery'.

Each of these events, as Bhambra (2007) has set out, is understood to have its origins in Europe and to have developed endogenously, that is, internally to the society under discussion. Each is further posited as singular and world-historical and foundational to our understanding of the modern world. In this way, Europe (or the West more broadly) comes to be conflated with the very idea of modernity. The rest of the world is understood as external to these world-historical processes and colonial connections and processes are presented as insignificant to their development. Yet, each of these revolutions was embedded within wider colonial connections that have been written out of social scientific accounts of modernity.

The historical processes of colonialism, empire, and enslavement were central to the conditions that enabled the Renaissance, the US and French revolutions, and the industrial revolution. However, they rarely enter the standard narratives of modernity or mainstream explanations of how the modern world came into being. Further, the potential contribution of other events and the experiences of those beyond the West are rarely considered as significant to the making of the modern world or, relatedly, of the social sciences. This book addresses many key lacunae, both in the history of the modern world and in our understanding of the contemporary world. Before discussing those in more detail, it is important also to acknowledge the scholarship that has enabled such work.

The importance of colonial histories in understandings of modernity

Within the broader academic landscape, there have primarily been two traditions that have been most significant in reconceptualizing understandings of modernity. These have been the traditions associated with post-colonial theory and the coloniality/modernity school of thought which is often also known as decolonial theory. The work done by scholars associated with these traditions has been particularly important in demonstrating the parochial character of arguments about the endogenous European origins of modernity. These theorists, as Bhambra (2014) has set out, have long argued for the necessity of considering the emergence of the modern world in the context of broader histories of colonialism, empire, dispossession, extraction, and enslavement.

Homi Bhabha (1994), for example, has been a central figure seeking to disrupt standard discourses of modernity by shifting the frame through which we view its associated events, and questioning which events we consider as significant and why. Bhabha argues for the need to rethink the conceptual paradigm of modernity on the basis of the experiences of those 'others' beyond the West who are often relegated to the margins if they are included at all. The task, as Bhabha (1994) puts it, is to take responsibility for the unspoken, unrepresented pasts that make up our disciplinary understandings in the present and, through an engagement with them, reconfigure how we understand the modern world.

The issue of epistemology, that is, of the politics of knowledge production, has been taken up by various post-colonial and decolonial theorists. Gayatri Chakravorty Spivak (1988), perhaps most famously, has, in her work, addressed the implications of colonialism in discussions of power and epistemic violence more generally. Her classic essay, 'Can the Subaltern Speak?', questions the failure of European theory to speak about colonialism and, in the process, she suggests that it ignores the significance of colonialism to the very production of the West. Maria Lugones (2007) has further argued for the importance of taking seriously the disruption of the social patterns, gender relations, and cosmological understandings of the communities and societies that were subject to European colonialism. As our ways of living in the world are shared, she argues, so our knowledge of the world is shared, and our focus must be on learning from and about each other.

In a similar vein, Anibal Quijano (2007) has argued that modernity is more appropriately understood in terms of a coloniality of knowledge that expresses its domination through political and economic spheres. Modernity, for him, has to be understood in terms of the colonial histories that were the context for its very emergence. He argues that it was with the 16th-century European conquest of the lands that we now call the Americas that a new world order emerged which ended up encapsulating the whole planet. This world order was known by Europeans in terms of modernity or rationality. However, Quijano argues that the structures of European colonial domination were so deeply imbricated in modernity that it is impossible to separate them: hence, his preferred formulation is 'modernity/coloniality' to acknowledge their co-constitution.

As Bhambra (2007, 2014) has argued, building on the work of post-colonial and decolonial scholars, acknowledging different histories should make a difference to how we then think about the social sciences. It is not sufficient to add new topics or histories or thinkers to our standard understandings without also considering why they had been absent in the first place. Further, it is important to ask what difference would be made to those standard understandings by taking into account these new topics, histories, and thinkers. This is something that is taken up in the chapters in this book. Before going on to outline those chapters, we briefly set out the importance of colonial histories for understanding the present.

Colonialism and presentism

Much research in the social sciences is presentist. Presentism entails exploring contemporary sociological and political issues only within the present moment. For example, through a survey, focus groups, or interviews which create a snapshot of the present. Aspects such as recent policy or social, economic, or political events are then brought in to offer context to this data. Where history is mentioned, this is often in a brief contextual introduction. History is rarely itself a significant part of the research or analysis in social science research. Against this backdrop of generalized presentism, colonial history is even further marginalized in the social sciences, and (until recently) not often considered. But when we take seriously not only history in general, but colonial histories specifically, we can start to understand a range of contemporary phenomena on a much deeper level. Across the chapters the authors ask: what difference does knowing colonial history make to how we understand this topic?

Taking colonial history seriously entails two moves. First, overcoming presentism, and recognizing that the world that we inhabit today has been forged over time. This does not mean that to think with colonialism is to say that everything is exactly the same as previously (the present is colonial – literally continuous of the past), or that it is completely different (colonialism has ended and everything has changed), but to be alive to the complexity of continuities and discontinuities. We may find empirical continuities, such as the existence of settler colonialism around the world (for example, in the Americas, Australia, and New Zealand), as well as discontinuities (for example, the formal end of the British Empire through the gradual ceding of territories and claims of political sovereignty overseas) with continuities nested within them (for example, trading and financial systems, language, currency, religion, and other relationships persisting). This also means that when we consider sociological topics such as racism, we need to understand how ideas of racial hierarchy and difference emerged in and through colonial projects, in order to serve elite interests, and how these persisted following the formal end of empires.

The second move is to overcome methodological nationalism. This means that we need to recognize that today's nation states have historically had shifting territorial jurisdictions which have expanded and contracted as empires have waxed and waned. Once we realize this, we do not only need to understand the present in the context of colonial history, we also then need to realize that historically people and places were deeply interconnected. As Radhika Mongia argues, methodological nationalism entails a misunderstanding of 'how definitions of the "national" are necessarily implicated in, and emerge from, non-national, cross-statal, trans-colonial, and inter- and intra-imperial forces' (2018: 3). You will notice, then, that in the various chapters the authors explain both how incorporating colonial histories into our understanding of (for example) the UK's non-doms, modern slavery, or pollution greatly enriches our understanding of them. But also, how doing so entails appreciating the connected (transnational) histories of different people, places, and ideas over time and into the present. Next, we offer an overview of the different sections of the book.

The making of the modern world

As set out earlier, most accounts of the modern world, or modernity, define it in relation to the processes of industrialization and democratization that were seen to occur in the West across the long 19th century. These processes, having been initiated in Europe, were then believed to have spread around the rest of the world. This section addresses the limitations of such narratives by offering six chapters that each address a key aspect of colonial history that is missing from the standard narratives of the making of the modern world.

Chapter 1, by Gurminder K. Bhambra, begins by asking why the Haitian Revolution, which occurred around the same time as the French and US revolutions, is missing from standard accounts of the political revolutions that define modernity. It sets out the ways in which this revolution brought about a modern state that both contested the colonial order responsible for their previous subjugation and set out radically new understandings for a world in which colonialism and slavery were abolished and equality was a defining characteristic. It also discusses how typical understandings of politics – for example, ideas about citizenship – are transformed in the process of taking the Haitian Revolution seriously.

Chapter 2 by Paul Robert Gilbert asks what difference is made to our understandings of the global economy when we take colonial histories seriously. He focuses, in particular, on processes of enslavement and extraction in the Atlantic and Indian ocean worlds and examines their entanglement in the emergence of processes of capitalism which otherwise tend to be understood separately. The chapter demonstrates how processes of colonial drain and deindustrialization can be seen to continue through to the present with the manifest ongoing inequalities between the Global South and the Global North.

The centrality of unequal exchange to the making of the modern world, particularly in terms of resource extraction and dispossession, is picked up and developed by Su-ming Khoo in Chapter 3. Here, she sets out the ways in which colonial plantations replaced pre-colonial nature–culture relationships and, in the process, established monocultures which depleted the land and its significance for us. Khoo brings a critical perspective to material ecological processes in a global historical context that sees colonialism as central to the development of ongoing global inequalities.

In Chapter 4, Maria del Pilar Kaladeen argues for the importance of understanding both enslavement and indenture as systems of unfree labour which existed across the British Empire. Indentured labour from India, and from across Asia, came to replace the earlier transatlantic trade in human beings and continued through into the early 20th century before it was eventually abolished (although there are echoes of such practices in contemporary global labour relations). Both systems were resisted by those who were subject to them and Kaladeen argues that it is important also to acknowledge the difference made to the configuration of the modern world by these acts of resistance.

In Chapter 5, Imogen Tyler draws together understandings of the plantation system, modes of unfree labour, and the emergence of an industrialized agricultural system. She focuses on the British, largely English, enclosure movement and examines the ways in which it was connected to broader movements of colonial enclosure globally. Tyler argues for acknowledgement of these connections to better understand the development of agricultural and industrial revolutions that tend to be seen as being solely of the West. Doing so, she suggests, would enable us to make sense of the ongoing global inequalities that are consequent to such systems and their connections.

This section is brought to a close with Chapter 6 by Deanndre Chen and Meera Sabaratnam. While the earlier chapters primarily looked at the significance of colonialism, this chapter examines the importance of decolonization to how the modern world came to be configured. Through their address of the history of decolonization in the 19th and 20th centuries, Chen and Sabaratnam also look at questions of resistance, agency, and the struggles of the colonized. They focus on the long decolonization process in Vietnam and end the chapter by drawing attention to the way in which our understanding of the modern world is enhanced by thinking about it in the context also of decolonization.

The politics of inequality

The chapters in Part II, 'The Politics of Inequality', highlight the centrality of colonialism to contemporary patterns of labour exploitation, global and local inequalities, and wealth accumulation. Sociological approaches to class or inequality that take nation states as their methodological and analytical 'container' will always come unstuck. This is precisely because they render invisible the role that colonial labour exploitation, enslavement, mobility, and settler colonialism played in shaping the politics of class inequality within former colonial centres like Britain. From the hostility that trade unions have shown to South Asian women working in Britain, to the tax abuse perpetrated by wealthy 'non-doms' taking advantage of laws designed to reduce tax burdens for those who profited from enslavement in the Caribbean and wider global processes of colonization, inequality in Britain is indelibly marked by histories of colonial connection.

As John Holmwood shows in Chapter 7, class relations in contemporary Britain have become something other than the antagonism between working classes and capitalists that Marx might have envisioned. The way in which they have been shaped is not merely a national story of enclosure, industrialization, and class struggle, but is also a story of working conditions 'at home' being improved by settlement and exploitation in the colonies, as the chapters in Part I also attest. Holmwood highlights the error in assuming that class relations constitute 'objective' social conditions whereas ethnicity and gender make up 'subjective' identities overlain atop class structures.

This point is taken up by Sundari Anitha in Chapter 8 on the Grunwick strike. Nowhere could it be clearer that rooting a sociological analysis in the idea of an 'objective' class position determined by workers' relationship to exploitative capitalists is entirely inadequate. Anitha reminds the reader that trade unions in the 1960s and 1970s were overtly hostile to 'foreign' workers (many in fact colonial subjects, as discussed in Part III) whom they viewed as undercutting wages. The Grunwick strike is frequently overlooked in British public (or sociological) memory, perhaps because it troubles methodologically nationalist understandings of class struggle. The Grunwick strike, and the women workers' face-off with new paramilitary policing units, can only be properly grasped from a position that appreciates the politics of inequality in light of histories of colonial connection.

In Daniel Renwick's chapter on the Grenfell Tower fire (Chapter 9), histories of hostility to migration from the Commonwealth – and contemporary 'hostile environment' policies – once again take centre stage. Housing politics in London are shaped by the hostility of councillors and rock-star architects to the racialized poor who often occupy housing estates in 'prime real estate'. It was the desire of the wealthiest municipality in London to remove the 'eyesore' of a tower block inhabited by Black[2] and Asian citizens and migrants that led to a decision to camouflage it in flammable cladding and ignore residents' complaints about fire safety.

As much as the chapters in Part II highlight the role of colonial exploitation, settlement, and extraction in bolstering the incomes of residents of the UK, this does not mean that there is no poverty to be found here. Kayleigh Garthwaite's chapter on the institutionalization of 'emergency' food aid in the UK (Chapter 10) highlights the systematic failure of governments over the last decade and a half to ensure adequate incomes – or access to welfare for vulnerable migrants with 'No Recourse to Public Funds'. As Kelbert (2022) shows, even domestic policy discourse on poverty within the UK cannot be understood outside histories of colonial connection. News outlets and politicians have been routinely hostile to the notion that there might be a *political failure* which could explain long-term food poverty in the UK, preferring to locate such poverty in discourses of moral failing.

From this perspective, poverty only 'belongs' in the Global South – an understanding that fails to acknowledge the histories of colonialism through which such inequality is produced. Genevieve LeBaron and Ali Bhagat, in Chapter 11, take up the weakness of 'new slavery' studies that likewise locate modern slavery in the individual practices of criminals, refusing to acknowledge the histories of colonial incorporation which have rendered people in some geographical and social locations more vulnerable to exploitation and forced labour. The notion that modern slavery in the Global South is a product of cultural 'backwardness', and that long-term food poverty in the UK is a product of moral failings, are the flip sides of a broader failure in the social sciences to take colonialism and its histories seriously in developing concepts and frameworks for understanding the politics of inequality.

Part II closes with Chapter 12, by Katie Higgins, in which she turns her gaze 'upwards' to the wealthy elites who have occupied the upper echelons of British society for the last 200 years. From merchants and plantation owners, to industrialists profiting from cotton mills fed by enslaved people (and the smashing of Indian cotton production), to financial elites who emerged to recycle capital into the formal and informal empire, colonialism made the British elite. Today, Black and Asian individuals have entered lists of the country's richest, but this capacity for individual mobility through wealth and status groups, as Holmwood shows in Chapter 7, should not allow us to collapse back into a methodologically nationalist study of class. The diversification of the *Sunday Times* Rich List does not negate the existence of a broader structure of inequality that was forged by ongoing colonial histories.

Migration, diaspora, and asylum

Part III explores the ways in which colonial histories continue to shape contemporary immigration policies, particularly in the Global North. It aims to explain how colonial logics of racial hierarchy and civilizational difference underpin immigration policies today. This results in racially stratified policies of mobility (who can move freely and under what conditions), immobility (who is immobilized and under what conditions), inclusion, and exclusion.

In Chapter 13, James Hampshire examines the significance of colonialism and racism to the development of citizenship and immigration policies in Britain. The chapter also addresses how the legacies of colonial citizenship affect the lives of people today. This is done through case studies of the Windrush scandal and the Hong Kong British Nationals visa scheme. This is followed by Chapter 14 by Lucy Mayblin, 'Asylum in Britain and the Legacies of Colonialism'. It focuses on one particular immigration category, people seeking asylum, and examines the British response. The chapter explains why we need to know the colonial dynamics around the drafting of the 1951 Refugee Convention and the 1967 Protocol (which globalized this beyond Europe) in order to fully understand the politics of asylum today.

The next chapter, Chapter 15 by Ipek Demir, shifts the focus to diasporas. Diasporas are communities who have been scattered across regions and places, often away from where their forebears are thought to have lived. The chapter explains why we should recognize such communities as makers of modernity and our contemporary globalized world, instead of merely an outcome of modernity and globalization. The chapter also locates understandings of diaspora in the wider context of decolonial/anti-colonial resistance. It illustrates that diasporas have their roots in empire and colonialism, but that they also transform life in their new homes as they seek to undo the racialized hierarchies associated with the earlier formations. This is followed by a focus on questions of the family and intimate relations in Chapter 16 by Joe Turner. The chapter examines how ideas of family emerged out of, and were globalized by, colonialism. This, then, has significant implications for people who wish to migrate as a family or a couple today, as some kinds of kinship relations are valued more than others.

The final two chapters in Part III focus on politics. Chapter 17, by Karim Murji, explores the connections between these themes in two periods of British history, the 1970s and the 2020s. It contextualizes the present by looking back to a time when race and racism were critical in the articulation of populist politics, especially because of the way they were connected to a particular crime – mugging. Since 2016, populism and authoritarianism have again come to the surface, often mixed with anti-immigrant nationalism. Finding the connections between the two can help the reader to reflect on how the past and present are connected – is there a direct line from one to the other, or are there more changes than continuities?

The final chapter in the section, Chapter 18 by Michaela Benson, asks how recognizing connected sociologies and histories transforms how we understand who can move, where, and on what terms. It sets out the connections between the formation of national citizenships and the colonial governance of populations, including their access to mobility. The shifting status of the people of Hong Kong is used as a case study to demonstrate the significance of the coloniality of British citizenship for making sense of the post-Brexit migration regime. It reveals that the provisionality and contingency of legal statuses are an integral mechanism of migration governance.

Multiculturalism and anti-racism

Part IV examines anti-racism and multiculturalism and the ways in which minoritized communities in the Global North have been racialized and othered, and how they have resisted and demanded equality and inclusion. The chapters situate these debates not just on the standard axis of nationalism and the history of the nation state, but by exploring their relationship to colonialism. They show lineages, linkages, and continuities between colonialism and contemporary ways in which certain populations have been excluded, othered, managed and policed, including the struggles that *previously-colonized-and-now-minoritized* populations in the Global North have developed against those exclusions.

In particular, the chapters outline how Britain's colonial history frames contemporary debates around rights, equality, integration, and racism. They examine how migrant populations have been 'managed' within Britain, the ways in which these communities have resisted racism (both at a state and interpersonal level), led anti-colonial movements, and struggled for equality. This section also shows the relevance of multiculturalist integration for the inclusion of religious and other minorities in post-colonial states. The contributions examine integration, anti-racist resistance and organization, and multiculturalism both conceptually and by looking at particular case studies. These include attacks on multiculturalism, the Birmingham Trojan Horse affair, the Prevent Duty, 'fundamental British values', the British Black Power movement, Black feminist organizing, and the policing of people of colour.

In Chapter 19 on British Black Power (BBP), John Narayan examines its history through a transnational perspective, showing how BBP's anti-racism went beyond the island story and was closely tied to anti-imperialist movements in the Third World. His chapter focuses on the three main tenets of BBP, namely political Blackness, anti-imperialism, and the relationship between race and class. Questioning the rise of instrumentalist and neoliberal approaches to racial equality, Narayan underlines the radical critique BBP offered through rethinking class and race when reframing class struggle, and in connecting anti-racism in Britain to anti-imperialist movements in the Third World. The chapter also calls for a recovery of such transnational perspectives in order to expand the global coordinates of anti-racist struggle today, and for us to go beyond neoliberal approaches to racial equality.

In Chapter 20, Alexandra Wanjiku Kelbert continues the examination of anti-racism, this time through a focus on the history of Black feminist organizing in Britain. She highlights how this organizing has been typically marginalized by both British feminism and anti-racist histories. Her chapter makes a case for how certain archival methods can help fight against erasures by identifying archival materials hidden in footnotes, in pictures, and the margins of archives. These investigations enable us to rethink not just given histories of feminist history and anti-racist organizing, but also rethink the process of history-making itself. This includes the gaps between what we are told happened and what happened, who was included and who was left out, and thus highlight the centrality of the politics of knowledge production about the past and our need to research and include those who have been erased from history.

Chapter 21, by Tariq Modood, shifts the focus to another case of inclusion, this time to the multiculturalist integration of minoritized groups. By differentiating multiculturalist integration from other modes of integration (assimilationist, individualist-integration and cosmopolitanism) and by arguing against the simple and reductivist view that multiculturalism is about 'separate communities', Modood offers a view of multiculturalism which is based on solidarity and dialogical interaction between national majorities and minorities. It is also one which is against the domination by hegemonic nationals or a single set of norms. Modood's chapter argues how anti-racist movements did not always include religious minorities in discussions of anti-discrimination and anti-racism. His framework offers religious groups, including Muslims, the same positive recognition as other groups.

The chapters that follow also emphasize the inclusion of Muslims in the Global North as central to questions of equality, anti-racism, and citizenship today. John Holmwood (Chapter 22) and Shereen Fernandez (Chapter 23) separately focus on historical and contemporary examples of the surveillance and policing Muslims have faced in the Global North. Holmwood's chapter discusses the claim of a plot to 'Islamicize' schools in British cities with significant Muslim populations, namely in Birmingham, Bradford, and Oldham. The affair not only became a major news story in 2014, but also led to the development of the UK government's counter-extremism policy, Prevent, in 2015, and the duty to promote 'fundamental British values in schools' in England and Wales. Holmwood discusses the Trojan Horse affair as a moral panic in Britain and situates it within the context of government and media attacks on multiculturalism. He argues that the affair is an example of the failure of 'muscular liberalism' rather than a failure of multiculturalism.

Fernandez's chapter focuses on how counterterrorism policies developed from the 'War on Terror' to another war; namely a 'war *of* terror' for Muslims. She examines how this combined Islamophobia, Orientalism, surveillance, and pre-emptive policing in the creation of racialized and securitized populations. Even though 9/11 shifted the trajectory of nation states in terms of security initiatives globally, Fernandez highlights how many of these policies are rooted in a colonial imagination which typically views people of colour as external and outside of the nation state. This is why the final chapter, Chapter 24, by Vanessa E. Thompson is timely in delving into the history of policing in Europe, its function and logic, showing continuities and discontinuities between policing under colonialism and today. The chapter provides a foundational critique of policing, discusses policing as a method of racial capitalism, and reveals the potential that abolitionist resistance presents.

The environment

Part V grounds topics like pollution, climate change, the Green New Deal, and commodities in a global material, historical, and political ecology framework that acknowledges the colonial origins of environmental crises. In the opening chapter, Chapter 25, Su-ming Khoo shows how the 'economic logic of pollution' drives racialized inequalities in globalized markets. The quest for economic growth, industrial production, and economic efficiency results in unequal harms; allowing some bodies and places to be more readily polluted than others. Looking to Latin America, Andrea Sempértegui, in Chapter 26, explains how it offers an obvious starting point for understanding extractivism as the basis of global development, capitalist accumulation, and environmental spoilage. Latin America also contains examples of Indigenous, environmental, and feminist resistance to extractivism and alternatives to environmental devastation.

Harpreet Kaur-Spannos highlights the Global North's disproportionate responsibilities for climate change and the 'green' economy's extractive foundations. Chapter 27 shows how 'green' resource grabs, unfair labour practices, and greenwashing replicate colonial patterns of exploitation in the present. In turn, Mitul Baruah offers wider reflections on political ecology using the case of catastrophic flooding in Assam, India, to understand its ongoing importance. His chapter, Chapter 28, demonstrates how colonialism transformed nature and nature–society relations globally and sets out the ongoing legacies of such processes in the present.

While the Global South is the focus of many of the chapters in this section, this is not to suggest that environmental destruction consequent to climate change does not also have an impact in the Global North. In Chapter 29, Max Haiven explores how palm oil permeates just about everybody's everyday lives. Its history compels us to acknowledge the legacies of racist imperialism, but its ubiquity shows how everyone is interconnected, bearing responsibilities for ecological, economic, and social justice. Finally, the section closes with Andrew Baldwin's chapter, Chapter 30. This sets out how the 'climate refugee' has become a racial category that enables capitalism to adapt to climate challenges. He argues that a different ethics and politics is needed to resist the injustices of capitalism in light of climate change.

Conclusion

In standard accounts of the social sciences, modernity is seen to come into being as a consequence of the 'twin' revolutions – the French and the industrial. In more critical work, it has also long been associated with the processes of dispossession, enslavement, colonialism, extraction, and imperialism. This understanding of the co-constitution of coloniality-modernity is central to any proper appreciation of the modern world. While the privileging of Europe, and the West, in the context of a history of colonialism and slavery that covered almost the entirety of the globe, would be understandable, what is less so, is the failure of most social scientists who privilege Europe and the West then also to consider the histories of colonialism and slavery that enabled Europe, and the West, to achieve this dominance.

Addressing the construction of modernity requires a more adequate engagement with the history, and present, of the world. It is only by understanding how Europe came to represent the world at large, and offering a more adequate explanation of the interconnections that came to constitute it as such, that it is possible to think a social science beyond its parochial limitations. Put more simply, as Bhambra (2014) has argued, any transformation of understandings would require a reconstruction 'backwards' of our historical accounts of modernity, as well as 'forwards' in terms of constructing a social science adequate for our age. The chapters collected here seek to do just this and our arguments for remaking the social sciences are set out further in the Conclusion to the volume.

Notes

[1] The Connected Sociologies Curriculum Project was funded by the Sociological Review Foundation and the initial project team was made up by Gurminder K. Bhambra, Amit Singh, and Ishan Khurana. Over the four years of the project, the following also joined the project team: Lukas Kikuchi, Jackson Harms, Alexandra Wanjiku Kelbert, Jennifer Doveton, and Isabel Sykes. You can see details of the project here: https://www.connectedsociologies.org/

[2] In this book we have capitalized all ethnicities – e.g. Black, Indigenous, South Asian, White – as is now the norm in the sociology of race and ethnicity. This treats all ethnicities as formally equal and avoids representing Whiteness as invisible and standard, with other ethnicities marked as visible and other. Where there is a quotation from another text we have kept the original usage.

References

Bhabha, H.K. 1994. *The Location of Culture*. Routledge.

Bhambra, G.K. 2007. *Rethinking Modernity: Postcolonialism and the Sociological Imagination*. Palgrave Macmillan.

Bhambra, G.K. 2014. *Connected Sociologies*. Bloomsbury.

Hall, S. 1992. 'The West and the Rest: Discourse and Power', in S. Hall and B. Gieben (eds) *Formations of Modernity*. Polity Press and Open University, pp 275–331.

Lugones, M. 2007. 'Heterosexualism and the Colonial / Modern Gender System', *Hypatia* 22(1): 186–209.

Kelbert, A.W. 2022. 'It Shouldn't Happen Here: Colonial and Racial Discourses of Deservingness in UK Anti-poverty Campaign', *Critical Social Policy* 42(4): 565–585.

Quijano, A. 2007. 'Coloniality and Modernity/ Rationality', *Cultural Studies* 21(2): 168–178.

Mongia, R. 2018. Indian Migration and Empire: A Colonial Genealogy of the Modern State, Duke University Press.

Spivak, G.C. 1988. 'Can the Subaltern Speak?', in C. Nelson and L. Grossberg (eds), *Marxism and the Interpretation of Culture*. University of Illinois Press, pp 271–313.

PART I

The Making of the Modern World

Edited by Gurminder K. Bhambra

1

The Haitian Revolution in the Making of the Modern World

Gurminder K. Bhambra

Objectives

- This chapter asks why the Haitian Revolution has been missing from standard social scientific accounts of modernity.

- It sets out a brief account of the Haitian Revolution and why it should be understood as bringing about a *modern* state.

- It discusses what difference taking the Haitian Revolution seriously makes to our understandings of social science concepts, in particular of citizenship.

- It locates the Haitian Revolution in the wider context of anti-colonial resistance in the making of the modern world.

Introduction

The Haitian Revolution is one of the most far-reaching revolutions of the modern period. After over a decade of revolutionary unrest, the independent state of Haiti was established in 1804. Central to its new constitution was its status as a fully sovereign state, the abolition of slavery, and equality in the eyes of the law. At a time when no other political movement in the Atlantic was explicitly calling for the end of slavery and colonization, the Haitian Revolution had these commitments as its bedrock. Yet very few social scientific accounts of modernity even mention Haiti, let alone afford it the significance it deserves (see Bhambra 2016).

Most accounts of the making of the modern world present its history in terms of the 19th-century industrial revolution in Britain and the earlier political revolutions associated with the United States (1776) and France (1789). These political revolutions are widely regarded as foundational events of world history as a consequence of them being understood to be democratic revolutions organized around new understandings of equality and the redress of older forms of social and political hierarchies. This is so despite the franchise – the right to vote – being restricted to propertied White men; although the idea was that once established in these terms the franchise could be extended as a matter of its own internal logic. However, what was omitted was that the dispossession of Indigenous peoples and the enslavement of them and transported Africans were central to the social arrangements of each indicating their colonial and racialized character.

In contrast, the Haitian Revolution, which took place within 30 years of the US and French revolutions, acknowledged Indigenous peoples, abolished slavery, and established a written constitution in which colour was no bar to political participation. However, the Haitian Revolution is rarely regarded as a world historical revolution. The historian, Eric Hobsbawm, for example, scarcely mentions it in his classic book, *Age of Revolution*. Even 'global' histories, such as Christopher Bayly's *Birth of the Modern World*, or Jürgen Osterhammel's *Transformation of the World*, devote considerably more attention to the United States and France than to Haiti.

One key exception is the book, *The Black Jacobins*, by C.L.R. James, which was published in 1938. It first brought to international attention the events in Saint-Domingue (as Haiti then was) that went on to become known as the Haitian Revolution. In this book, James sets out why the revolution came to be and the manner of its accomplishment. His concern in *The Black Jacobins* was, at least, twofold: to recover Black agency in history and to make more widely known the events that brought the modern republic of Haiti into being. Until then, if the Haitian revolution had been mentioned, it was usually explained as the French Revolution spreading to the colonies. This would suggest that there was no Haitian Revolution in its own terms, just a Saint-Domingue episode of the French Revolution (Sala-Molins 2006).

However, the Haitian revolutionaries not only transcended the language of the European Enlightenment – of which the French Revolution was seen to be the embodiment – but they also gave it a meaning that would subsequently be rescinded by the French, supposed initiators of Enlightenment. As Anna Julia Cooper (2006 [1925]) wrote in her book, *Slavery and the French and Haitian Revolutionists*, if the White French revolutionaries had taken the issue of slavery seriously and both abolished slavery and renounced empire, they could have shaped the revolution more favourably to address their own stated universal concerns of equality and liberty. Instead, dominant French understandings of equality and citizenship, Cooper argued, remained bound by a racial particularism which prevailed over universal considerations (see May 2008).

So, what might we learn about the birth of the modern world and its transformation if we were to take the Haitian Revolution seriously? In this chapter, I suggest that the Haitian Revolution does not simply deserve to sit alongside the US and French revolutions; it far exceeds their scope and vision and should provide the basis for rethinking the claims associated with the other revolutions and our ideas of the nature of modernity itself. The chapter first sets out the history of the Haitian Revolution and then examines why it has been missing from standard accounts of the making of the modern world. It ends by asking what difference taking the Haitian Revolution seriously would make to our understanding of the concepts and categories of the social sciences, especially those of citizenship.

The Haitian Revolution

Saint-Domingue, as Haiti was known prior to the revolution, was a French colony in the western part of Hispaniola – an island in the Caribbean. It had earlier been colonized by the Spanish before being taken over by the French in 1626. During this early period of colonization, the Indigenous population on the island was largely eliminated. The plantation system set up by the Spanish was also taken over by the French who continued the practice of bringing over enslaved Africans to undertake coerced labour. At the time of the French Revolution, Saint-Domingue was the most profitable part of the French Empire.

Raw materials, primarily sugar, coffee, and cotton, were grown on plantations worked by enslaved Africans and then shipped to towns in France to be turned into commodities. A third of these commodities were consumed within France, with the rest being exported, including back to Saint-Domingue, which was the largest export market for metropolitan France (James 1989 [1938]). Colonialism and slavery were not simply profitable in their own right, but the expansion of available markets that was involved also contributed to the dynamism of what tends to be presented as an endogenous feature of the metropole.

Towards the end of the 18th century, there were estimated to be well over half a million enslaved African people living in Saint-Domingue together with a sizeable population of free and freed peoples of colour. Conditions in Saint-Domingue were harsh and have been understood to be among the harshest across the Americas. Even before the 1789 revolution in France there had been uprisings and unrest on the island. Within two years of the events in Paris, revolutionary unrest intensified in the colony and continued until the state of Haiti was eventually established in 1804.

In the early 1790s, revolts by enslaved people in Saint-Domingue had gained such impetus that the French government sent two commissioners, Léger-Félicité Sonthonax and Étienne Polverel, to the colony to quell the rebellions. Instead, upon surveying the situation, they decreed the abolition of slavery in 1793. This decree was ratified in the metropole, in Paris, at the National Convention in February 1794 and extended to all French overseas colonies. As C.L.R. James (1989 [1938]) sets out, in January 1794, three deputies from Saint-Domingue arrived in Paris to participate in the Constituent Assembly – Jean-Baptiste Bellay, a formerly enslaved person who had bought his own liberty through labour in his own time, Jean-Baptiste Mills, a mixed-race person, and Louis-Pierre Dufay, a White man. Their entrance, James states, aroused much excitement from the other assembled deputies as indicative of the last gasp of the 'aristocracy of the skin' and the move towards the consecration of full equality.

The three deputies were welcomed as representing the free citizens of Saint-Domingue. Bellay addressed the Assembly pledging support to the cause of the revolution in France and asking the Convention to declare slavery abolished. The Assembly, James notes, rose in acclamation and a decree was drafted and dispatched immediately to the French colonies stating: 'The National Convention declares slavery abolished in all the colonies, In consequence it declares that all men, without distinction of colour, domiciled in the colonies, are French citizens, and enjoying all the rights assured under the Constitution' (James 1989 [1938]: 140–141). Bellay's speech, according to James, 'introduced one of the most important legislative acts ever passed by any political assembly' (1989 [1938]: 140). Yet it is rarely mentioned in the literature on the 'age of revolutions' or of modernity that the most radical political statement of the French Revolution – that is, *the one with the greatest universal potential* – came from the colonial hinterland.

These tremendous achievements – of full racial equality and the abolition of slavery – were not long-lasting, however, as both were overturned within a few years. Slavery was re-established within the French Empire by Napoleon in 1802 and citizenship reconfirmed as the preserve of White men. It should be clear that Napoleon's mission to restore slavery in the French colonies was now *an active attempt to enslave fellow citizens*. This led to understandable outrage in Saint-Domingue. James reports Toussaint L'Ouverture, one of the leading figures within the Haitian Revolution, stating: 'I took up arms for the freedom of my colour, which France alone proclaimed, but which she has no right to nullify. Our liberty is no longer in her hands: it is in our own. We will defend it or perish' (James 1989 [1938]: 281). Defend it they did, as the war instigated by France, and aided by British and Spanish troops, led to the defeat of the French and a declaration of independence from France.

James credits Toussaint L'Ouverture, who had been born into slavery, for the Herculean task of fashioning an army from untrained individuals. His recruits, who often did not know how to use a gun, were turned into a force capable of defeating European troops (Hazareesingh 2020). Toussaint, himself, had no military background or training, but as James states, 'he incarnated the determination of his people never, never to be slaves again' (1989 [1938]: 198). Even after his arrest and subsequent deportation to France, Toussaint L'Ouverture had sufficiently laid the ground for the most extraordinary of political victories. He died in captivity in 1803, but by the end of the year, the revolutionary army had completely defeated the French. Toussaint's lieutenant, Dessalines, proclaimed Haiti's independence on 1 January 1804. The proclamation restated its commitment to the abolition of slavery and, in its constitution of 1805, its complete independence from France was asserted.

The modern state of Haiti and its immediate aftermath

One of the first acts by the revolutionaries after the proclamation of independence was to rename Saint-Domingue as Haiti (Ayiti). In doing so, they explicitly honoured the name that had been given to the island by the Taino Arawak people who had preceded them on the land and who had been largely wiped out by Spanish and French colonization (Geggus 2002: 207–220). An understanding of colonization as dispossession – and not simply the repudiation of enslavement – was central to their rejection of the preceding settler colonial regime. This was apparent in the working out of the Haitian constitution which, while not 'perfect', was nonetheless predicated on an understanding of citizenship that had greater universal applicability than similar notions developed in the US or French Revolutions (as discussed in the next section).

Haiti was the first republic to be based on the freedom of all its population and to be organized around a notion of Blackness that represented the political commitment of a population opposed to colonization and enslavement. While the United States and France maintained a racialized understanding of the political sphere in which only propertied White men were allowed to vote, Haiti made neither colour nor ownership of property a condition of political participation. Everybody who is Black is a citizen, the constitution declared. 'Blackness' was not, however, defined epidermally, that is, in terms of skin colour. It was not a category of exclusion based on an ascribed characteristic, but rather, it pointed to a political commitment of the population in terms of its opposition, or not, to colonization (see Narayan, Chapter 19, this volume).

'White' men – specifically those wishing to claim the title of master or proprietor – were forbidden to own property on the island. Clause 12 states: 'No whiteman of whatever nation he may be, shall put his foot on this territory with the title of master or proprietor, neither shall he in future acquire any property therein.' However, those indentured German and Polish workers, who had been brought to Haiti by the French, were regarded as Black, as were children born to White women on the island. Clause 13 states:

> The preceding article cannot in the smallest degree affect white women who have been naturalized Haytians by Government, nor does it extend to children already born, or that may be born of the said women. The Germans and Polanders naturalized by government are also comprized [sic] in the dispositions of the present article. (1805 Constitution of Haiti)

It is important to acknowledge that at a time when revolutionary leaders within Haiti were calling for the immediate and universal abolition of slavery and enacting the call for political equality through their revolution, there was no similar such call or act elsewhere across the Atlantic world. The American Revolution in the United States maintained slavery and the dispossession of Indigenous populations as central to the constitution of its own society; and the French maintained forms of domination and exclusion within their colonies and over their colonized populations. The revolution which established the modern state of Haiti was not an episode of the French Revolution but far exceeded its revolutionary potential in its own terms.

By making freedom from enslavement and from racial discrimination the bedrock of political understandings and unlinking citizenship from race, Sibylle Fischer (2004: 266) argues that the Haitian constitution radicalized and universalized the idea of equality far in advance of the other revolutions of the time. Despite this, or perhaps because of it, the French state refused to recognize Haiti and enforced a global economic blockade of the island, together with the British and the Americans, forcing it, within 20 years, to the point of bankruptcy.

The economic blockade was not only a punitive act to sanction Haiti for emancipating itself, but it sought also to manage the 'contagion' of revolution and self-emancipation from spreading to other societies organized on the basis of the enslavement of African populations across the Caribbean and the Americas. Knowledge of the Haitian Revolution circulated extensively among communities in struggle, both contemporaneously and in its aftermath. It was said to have influenced planned revolts against slavery in the United States, such as that by Denmark Vesey in 1822 in

South Carolina, and Nat Turner's rebellion in Virginia in 1831. It was also important in the development of independence movements across Latin America, via Simon Bolívar, and further afield such as with the Māori in New Zealand (Shilliam 2012).

Returning to the issue of the economic blockade, it was not until 1825 that the French monarch, Charles X, agreed to concede Haitian independence in exchange for reparations of 150 million francs. The claim was that the abolition of slavery, followed by the declaration of independence, had deprived French owners of their property and thus compensation ought to be paid. This property was understood in terms of land, estates, *and other people*; that is, those who had been enslaved and who were, as a consequence, considered as property.

Henri Christophe, who ruled the north of Haiti in the early period of independence, had fiercely opposed any compensation to be paid to the French, arguing:

> What rights, what arguments can the ex-colonists then allege to justify their claim for an indemnity? Is it possible that they wish to be recompensed for the loss of our persons? Is it conceivable that Haitians who have escaped torture and massacre at the hands of these men, Haitians who have conquered their own country by the force of their arms and at the cost of their blood, that these same free Haitians should now purchase their property and persons once again with money paid to their former oppressors? (cited in Beauvois 2017: 27)

It was not until after Christophe's death that any transaction was made possible between Haiti and France.

France demanded compensation of 150 million francs. To put this amount into context, in 1803 France had sold the entire territory of Louisiana (which at the time constituted over 800,000 square miles) to the fledgling United States, doubling its size, for 80 million francs. The coerced indemnity proved impossible to pay and the Haitian government had to take out loans from French banks 'entering a cycle of debt that would last into the twentieth century' (Dubois 2005: 304). This coerced debt determined Haiti's future poverty and was significant to the consolidation of France's ongoing prosperity. But perhaps the real significance of the indemnity was to punish a formerly enslaved colony that had the temerity to liberate itself from colonization and enslavement and become a sovereign state (Beauvois 2017).

The significance of Haiti for understandings of citizenship

While the Haitian constitution explicitly delinked race from citizenship and established equality in the eyes of the law, scholars still tend to regard the *idea* of universal citizenship as emerging from the French Revolution. Debates on modern conceptions of citizenship, for example, have tended to be framed in terms of modes of political inclusion within, and exclusion from, nation states. France is understood as the originary modern nation state, where conceptions of nationhood and citizenship cohere to create political unity. Its colonial context is elided because of the apparent universalism of the republican *claim* undergirding conceptions of citizenship. As such, the idea of universal citizenship emerging from the French Revolution comes to be seen as a process of extension and inclusion integral to democracy and the modern nation state more generally (see Hampshire, Chapter 13, and Benson, Chapter 18, this volume).

The standard argument is that the idea of universal citizenship emerged in France and, even if it did not initially include everyone, it did over time acknowledge those exclusions and engage in a process of extending citizenship to those others who had not been included. The struggles of unpropertied European men and European women, for example, against their exclusion from the political process, was based on an understanding that they had always been a part of modern societies and were unjustly excluded from being understood as full members of it. Hence, over time, modern citizenship was extended to them as it was acknowledged that they had always been a part of modern societies. The place of colonized others is more difficult to resolve, in part, because they are not recognized as part of the societies in which such debates were taking place.

There tends to be an insistence that 'colonial others' – usually abbreviated to understandings of race – only entered Europe and European debates in the post-Second World War period. This fails to recognize their inclusion, albeit hierarchically structured, within the empires that many European countries had long established. Scholars, for example, often present the history of the French state in terms of the predominantly White population that largely inhabited the 'hexagon' of the metropole. Within such understandings, colonial subjects of the French Empire are not regarded as members of the same political entity despite living in lands alongside White French subjects who governed over them and had established legal codes which regulated their lives.

In the late 17th century, for example, the French state established the *Code Noir* which was a set of rules and laws to regulate the lives of the enslaved in the French Caribbean. In subsequent years, its reach was extended to cover the conditions governing the lives of those within French colonies and those who had migrated from the colonies to the French national state. As Tyler Stovall (2006) argues, it was one of the first major examples of the conflict between political and legal equality, on the one hand, and racial discrimination and domination, on the other, within the French state; with the French state here now being understood to include its colonial territories. The *Code Noir* constructed full citizens as White and others as outside of citizenship despite being (coerced) members of the same political community.

During the revolutionary period in France, as David Geggus (1989) has argued, there were many debates over whether Black men could be citizens or whether colour, itself, was a radical obstacle to civic and political equality. Many of these debates turned on the group identity, that is, race, ascribed to individuals. In 1791, for example, it was proposed that only 'non-whites born of free parents, not freedmen' should be accorded political equality (Geggus 1989: 1303). This limited decree was passed in May of that year and overturned a couple of months later. Events in Saint-Domingue intensified over the summer as a consequence of this rollback, leading to further unrest and upheaval. This put increased pressure on French legislators to concede full racial equality, which they did in 1792, and then eventually to abolish slavery, as set out earlier, in 1794 (Geggus 1989).

This tumultuous period offers up a moment of history in which arguments for universal (male) equality transcended, however fleetingly, the racial divisions that were otherwise being maintained. These extraordinary achievements, however, did not last, with slavery being re-established within the French Empire by Napoleon in 1802 and citizenship reconfirmed as the preserve of White men (with property). Nonetheless, the fact that the contestations happened is significant and points to more complex histories of citizenship and equality than those presented within the mainstream of the social sciences. The failure to locate the French nation within the broader colonial processes of the French state is what enables scholars to regard some subjects as external to the nation and therefore outside of its understanding of those who were entitled to claim citizenship.

Ultimately, the failure to transcend racial categories had White French citizens deny the claim for participation and representation being made by Black appellants. This suggests that ideas of equality, political participation and membership, in their dominant French articulation, were, and are, limited by race. That is, they were shaped through an explicit refusal to accept the equality of races and a commitment to processes of colonization, slavery, and indenture. The concept of citizenship that emerged from the French Revolution, then, was not a universal concept. It was structured on the refusal to countenance racial equality as central to it.

This chapter has argued that it is not sufficient to understand the *event* of the Haitian Revolution in its own terms. It is also important to think about the fact that the revolutionaries' demands for freedom and equality were being made against the country which is otherwise seen as the fount of such demands. The Haitian Revolution does not simply stand alongside the French, it calls into question the very claims associated with it. As such, it is necessary to take the Haitian Revolution seriously in terms of its contribution to the making of the modern world and examine how it enables us to rethink the standard conceptual understandings of the social sciences.

Haiti as an exemplar of anti-colonial resistance

While the Haitian Revolution is one of the clearest examples of anti-colonial resistance, it has not been the only one. In the early 17th century – 200 years before the establishment of the modern state of Haiti – a group of people, both Indigenous and Africans who had escaped from slavery after the Dutch invasion of the Portuguese colony of Brazil, created the state of Palmares. Palmares was a self-governing territory, in what is now the state of Alagoas in north-eastern Brazil, which was in existence across the 17th century (1605–1694). According to Siba Grovogui, it exemplified a different type of modern state than any other in existence at the time given that it was predicated on 'the self-governing authority of its people' (2024: 535). In freeing themselves, the formerly enslaved did not become fugitives, but rather participated, in situ, in the creation of modern institutions 'based on the consent of the governed' (Grovogui 2024: 536). Palmares was destroyed in 1694 after a series of wars that brought the territory and its populations back under Portuguese colonial authority.

Like the Haitian Revolution that was to follow, the Quilombo dos Palmares calls into question the idea that the modern world and its concepts and categories were simply generated by Europeans to then be diffused around the rest of the world. Rather than starting with the European Enlightenment in terms of developing theoretical understandings of freedom and equality, it is salutary to begin with the enactment and expression of collective emancipation in both Palmares and Haiti.

To this, we could also add the legal case for the abolition of slavery that was brought before the Pope in 1684 by Lourenço da Silva Mendonça, a descendant of the Kings of Kongo in Africa. In contrast to most debates on abolition, which tend to focus on activities and practices across North America and Western Europe, Jose Lingna Nafafé (2022) argues that the legal and moral arguments against slavery were first initiated from Africa. The international legal case that Mendonça brought began with a statement of how Africans were captured, transported, and enslaved at the behest of the Portuguese who had established colonial enclaves in West Africa. It further drew on Mendonça's experience of the suffering faced by enslaved Africans in Brazil and their claims to freedom as instantiated in the Quilombo dos Palmares. The legal case was significant, then, not only in terms of being an earlier argument for abolition than is usually recognized, but in also providing a resource for more extensive understandings of freedom and emancipation than are to be found in discourses of European Enlightenment.

Fifty years after the Haitian Revolution, in 1857, we also see a significant rebellion against British colonial rule in India. It was the largest anti-colonial revolt of the 19th century and was brutally suppressed with hundreds of thousands of people killed in the process. It would be a further century before political independence was accomplished in India to be followed by a wave of similar such movements across Asia and Africa (see Chen and Sabaratnam, Chapter 6, this volume). The systematic dismantling of the old colonial order across the world only finally occurred in the mid-20th century.

Conclusion

The Haitian Revolution is significant in its own terms. It can be understood as the first state to abolish slavery, insist on equality before the law, and make colour no bar to political participation. However, it is not sufficient just to include Haiti in our discussions of the making of the modern world. Rather, we need also to understand how its omission structures and distorts dominant accounts of modernity such that what is then called for *is a reconsideration of what we had believed we had known about the modern world.*

The problem with simply 'adding' the Haitian Revolution, or any other event that had previously been excluded, to standard accounts – without rethinking the fundamental premises of those accounts – is that we are not then required to rethink the concepts that emerged from the understandings that were structured around particular exclusions. We are able to understand citizenship, for example, differently once we take the Haitian Revolution seriously.

The Haitian Revolution explicitly challenged colonization and enslavement, and, like other such events, it has been routinely silenced within social scientific accounts of modernity, of the making of the modern world. Michel-Rolph Trouillot (1995) suggests that it was the most radical revolution of its age and perhaps silenced, precisely, because of its radical nature. Reclaiming the significance of the Haitian Revolution to the making of the modern world is one step in also enabling us to remake the social sciences.

References

1805 Constitution of Haiti. http://faculty.webster.edu/corbetre/haiti/history/earlyhaiti/1805-const.htm

Beauvois, F. 2017. *Between Blood and Gold: The Debates over Compensation for Slavery in the Americas.* Translated by A. Everson. Berghahn Books.

Bhambra, G.K. 2016. 'Undoing the Epistemic Disavowal of the Haitian Revolution: A Contribution to Global Social Thought', *Journal of Intercultural Studies* 37(1): 1–16.

Cooper, A.J. 2006 [1925]. *Slavery and the French and Haitian Revolutionists.* Edited and translated by F. Richardson Keller. Rowman & Littlefield.

Dubois, L. 2005. *Avengers of the New World: The Story of the Haitian Revolution.* Harvard University Press.

Fischer, S. 2004. *Modernity Disavowed: Haiti and the Cultures of Slavery in the Age of Revolution.* Duke University Press.

Geggus, D.P. 2002. *Haitian Revolutionary Studies.* Indiana University Press.

Geggus, D.P. 1989. 'Racial equality, slavery, and colonial secession during the constituent assembly,' *American Historical Review,* 94 (5): 1290–1308.

Grovogui, S.N. 2024. 'The Myth of Westphalian Common Sense: Abjuration and Republicanism in Quilombos's Palmares', *South Atlantic Quarterly* 123(3): 529–548.

Hazareesingh, S. 2020. *Black Spartacus: The Epic Life of Toussaint Louverture.* Allen Lane.

James, C.L.R. 1989 [1938]. *The Black Jacobins: Toussaint L'Ouverture and the San Domingo Revolution.* Second Edition. Vintage Books.

May, V.M. 2008. '"It is Never a Question of the Slaves": Anna Julia Cooper's Challenge to History's Silences in Her 1925 Sorbonne Thesis', *Callaloo* 31(3): 903–918.

Nafafé, J.L. 2022. *Lourenço da Silva Mendonça and the Black Atlantic Abolitionist Movement in the Seventeenth Century.* Cambridge University Press.

Sala-Molins, L. 2006. *Dark Side of the Light: Slavery and the French Enlightenment.* Translated and with an introduction by J. Conteh-Morgan. University of Minnesota Press.

Shilliam, R. 2012. 'Civilization and the Poetics of Slavery', *Thesis Eleven: Critical Theory and Historical Sociology* 108(1): 97–116.

Stovall, T. 2006. "Race and the making of the nation: Blacks in modern France," in M.A. Gomez (ed) *Diasporic Africa: A Reader,* New York: New York University Press, pp 200–18.

Trouillot, M.-R. 1995. *Silencing the Past: Power and the Production of History.* Beacon Press.

Video lecture

Bhambra, G.K. 2020. *The Haitian Revolution,* Connected Sociologies Curriculum Project. https://thesociologicalreview.org/projects/connected-sociologies/curriculum/mmw/haitian-revolution/

Additional resources

Bhambra, G.K. and Shilliam, R. 2020. *Haiti and the Making of the Modern World*, Connected Sociologies Curriculum Project. https://thesociologicalreview.org/projects/connected-sociologies/events/haiti_mmw/

QUESTIONS

1. What is the significance of the Haitian Revolution to our understandings of modernity?

2. How do the Haitian Revolution and the idea of Black citizenship extend our understandings of citizenship?

3. What explains the silence around the events of the Haitian Revolution in standard social science understandings of modernity and citizenship?

Worksheet 1. The Haitian Revolution in the Making of the Modern World

This worksheet is designed to support AS and A-level teaching on global development and social differentiation, power and stratification. It may also be useful for students studying AS and A-level History, particularly topics related to colonialism. In the online talk, Gurminder K. Bhambra compares the Haitian Revolution to the French and American revolutions, asking us to challenge contemporary understandings of abolition, democracy, and equality in the making of the modern world. These worksheet activities encourage students to think critically about dominant sociological and historical narratives of these topics, considering not only what they might reveal about contemporary society, but what may be concealed and/or omitted. Students are asked to think about why it is important to recover these 'silences of history', and how sociology can contribute to these efforts.

Time	Activity	Explanation
00.00–00.05	To warm up, answer these questions: *What is democracy? What are the features of a democratic society?*	This introductory activity gets students thinking about the significance of democracy to the modern world and acts as an entry point to the central themes of the lecture.
00.05–00.10	Recap of understandings of globalization.	It may be useful to remind students of the definition(s) of globalization.
00.10–00.15	At 4:37 in the talk, Bhambra points out that the abolition of slavery in Haiti happened as a result of events *in* the island, rather than in the metropole. *Why is this fact important to contemporary understandings of abolition?*	This activity asks students to start questioning dominant understandings of democracy and the making of the modern world, turning a critical lens to the core theme of global development and connecting to ideas of power and stratification in a global sense.
00.15–00.20	Watch the talk from 8:18 to 9:10. *In your own words, briefly summarize the significance of the renaming of Saint-Domingue as Haiti.*	Bhambra points out that Haiti was chosen as a name for the island to honour the people who had lived there prior to French colonization, and that this can be read as a fundamental rejection of settler colonialism. This activity prompts students to synthesize the key points of this section of the lecture in their own words, and encourages them to think about the significance of this decision within the wider contexts of colonialism, abolition, and democracy.
00.20–00.30	Watch the talk from 9:10 to 11:45. *How is citizenship understood in the Haitian constitution? What are the differences and similarities between this form of citizenship and citizenship in contemporary Britain?*	This activity pushes students to make comparisons between conceptualizations of citizenship in the Haitian constitution and contemporary understandings of citizenship in our own society. Students may draw links from other talks within the Connected Sociologies course, such as the critical engagement with ideas of citizenship within the 'Global Britain' lecture, as well as other sessions within the 'Migration, Borders, Diaspora' module.

Time	Activity	Explanation
00.30– 00.40	Thinking back to the first activity you completed on this worksheet, answer the following question: *Has learning about the Haitian revolution changed your initial answer about the features of a democratic society? If so, how?*	This activity encourages students to reflect on their earlier thinking, employing a critical lens to their own work and challenging themselves to develop their understanding of democracy further. This activity may work well as a group discussion.
00.40– 00.50	At 15:14 Bhambra uses the phrase 'the silences of history'. *What does this phrase mean? What can sociologists learn from 'the silences of history'?*	This activity encourages students to exercise their critical thinking about dominant narratives of society and what they may conceal/omit. This is helpful in developing students' ability to critically analyse sociological and historical arguments and develop more sophisticated academic skills.
00.50– 01.00	At the end of the talk, Bhambra leaves us with this question: 'What do we need to do, today, to reclaim the significance of the Haitian revolution to the making of the modern world?' *How can sociologists contribute to 'reclaiming the significance of the Haitian Revolution'? What might some potential outcomes be?*	This activity asks students to draw together what they have learned throughout the session and apply these lessons to a broader sociological query. The activity encourages students to think critically about different sociological research methods and approaches, which is a core topic in the A-level Sociology curriculum. It also encourages students to think about some of the impacts of sociological and historical research. In terms of potential outcomes, students might suggest that reclaiming the significance of the Haitian Revolution could help to address some of the 'silences of history', challenge dominant historical narratives of abolition, and/or develop our understandings of democracy.

This worksheet was developed by Isabel Sykes.

2

Understanding the Colonial Global Economy

Paul Robert Gilbert

Objectives

- This chapter challenges the tendency for social scientists to approach 'the economy' as a nationally bounded object operating according to its own rules.

- It argues instead for thinking in terms of the 'colonial global economy' and for understanding capitalist modernity as enabled and fundamentally arising from colonial processes of extraction and enslavement.

- It shows how processes of colonial drain and deindustrialization created a vast pool of underpaid labourers in the Global South whose cheap wages 'subsidize' consumption and ease economic policy making in the Global North.

- Finally, it cautions against recent high-profile approaches in the social sciences which purport to centre colonialism in their analyses, but reproduce Eurocentrism and methodological nationalism, doing little more than paying lip service to colonialism.

Introduction

Taking a colonial global economy perspective means rejecting the notion that capitalism and colonialism are separate processes, logics or historical trajectories that sometimes intersect. Instead, it means understanding the development of capitalism – from the establishment of private property rights to the management of modern European welfare states – as irreducibly entwined with colonialism and colonial histories (Bhambra 2020). This chapter proceeds by first examining how we ended up with an image of 'the economy' that is tied to individual nations and divorced from historical and structural dimensions of the colonial global economy. It then examines how colonial processes of dispossession and deindustrialization shaped global inequalities today, which is essential for understanding both the challenges of post-colonial economies and the economic policies which work (or do not work) in European former colonies. Finally, it cautions against recent approaches that appear to centre colonialism in the study of capitalism and economics, but which on closer inspection simply reproduce Eurocentric and methodological nationalist approaches that disguise and disavow the operations of a colonial global economy.

Disconnecting the economy from colonialism

Most of us will hear – or talk – about 'the economy' so frequently that it hardly seems worthy of special attention. From news reports about whether it is growing or in decline, to more informal discussions about how it impacts on job prospects or election outcomes, 'the economy' often appears to us as a natural object: something that has always been there and is governed by its own internal laws and principles. Yet the economy as we think of it today – as something attached to a nation state such that we can talk about 'the Brazilian economy' or 'the Sri Lankan economy', and as something which can be neatly summarized by measures like gross domestic product (GDP) – is a 20th-century invention.

Sociologists and political scientists have traced this idea of the economy as the measurable sum of all production, consumption and distribution of goods and services in a country to the 1930s and 1940s. On one side of the Atlantic, economists in the United States were developing huge data collection systems and infrastructures, which enabled price and production levels in all sectors of the economy to be analysed at once. Prior to this, economic booms and busts were seen as arising in particular industries or regions. With the new statistical infrastructure built up around the National Bureau of Economic Research, a picture of how the entire economy was functioning and moving could be generated for the first time. It is hard not to overstate the significance of this shift: viewing 'the economy' as an independent domain operating according to its own rules, and mapping neatly on to the nation state, was a revolutionary and highly consequential change.

These American innovations in measuring and visualizing the national economy made it possible for policy makers to monitor the effect of reduced bank lending or rising debt levels on the economy as a whole for the first time. On the other side of the Atlantic, John Maynard Keynes was developing what would become modern macroeconomics. His work encouraged government to think not only of individuals and their behaviour, but of how the aggregate level of consumption, production, unemployment, or saving impacted on the economy and society at the national level. Keynes showed that in times of recession, 'the economy' could not be left to individuals. If everyone tightened their belts simultaneously, the knock-on effect would be less consumption, less production, and therefore less work and income for everyone – a kind of death spiral that only government spending could reverse.

The marriage of US statistical innovations and Keynes' macroeconomics helped to concretize the notion of 'the economy' that we are left with today. At the same time, a division of labour emerged between economists (responsible for studying 'the economy' with its special laws of markets and prices) and sociologists (more properly concerned with institutions like social class; see Holmwood, Chapter 7, this volume).

The methodological nationalism of mainstream economists who study economic processes as if they only take place within individual nations has rarely been questioned within that profession. But the idea of 'the economy' as discussed here emerged in a context in which European colonial powers were starting to think about the loss of their imperial possessions.

The invention of the 'national economy' in Britain occurred in parallel to the invention of Britain as an island nation decoupled from its empire (see Hampshire, Chapter 13, this volume). Prior to this, economies were not managed at the national scale because access to cheap labour, land, and resources could be facilitated by colonial expansion. Anti-colonial economists in India articulated the idea of a 'national economy' as an alternative to the extractive form that British imperialism took, and there is evidence that Keynes' ideas about national economic management may have been shaped by his encounter with these economists' ideas (Goswami 2018).

Eurocentrism in economic sociology

Mainstream economists tend to take for granted the idea that the national economy exists and operates according to its own laws and principles without much reflection on the colonial context in which national economic management emerged as an innovation. But influential sociologists have been equally guilty of understanding the relationship between social institutions and the economy through a methodologically nationalist, and Eurocentric, lens. In an attempt to understand the relationship between classes, economic crises and political crises in European states, Frankfurt School sociologists like Jurgen Habermas (1973) introduced the notion of 'legitimation crises'. Crises of legitimation emerge, Habermas argued, when the state cannot guarantee or enable the demands for wages (and time, and security) that unions seek from the capitalist classes they work for. Following the 2008 Global Financial Crisis and Eurozone Crisis, Wolfgang Streeck (2014) returned to Habermas' idea of legitimation crises, to argue that European governments had been 'buying time', or postponing crises via sticking-plaster solutions since the 1970s. He argues that attempts were made to solve destabilizing social conflicts around access to wages first via wage inflation, then by government borrowing and spending, and then by the expansion of cheap credit (which precipitated the 2008 crisis). Streeck leaves a great deal out of his argument, but crucial for our purposes, he and others working in this tradition write as if there are only national economies, and no *colonial global economy*.

Habermas and Streeck both use the example of European wage disputes in the 1970s, and the apparent need for governments to resolve those disputes in a manner that avoids runaway inflation – but also prevents revolt by underpaid wage workers. From a colonial global economy perspective, the very idea that domestic policies and union–employer negotiations could be able to patch over these European tensions and prevent full-fledged legitimation crises is wrong-headed. A perennial puzzle for macroeconomists is: when productivity in industrial economies rises, and profits rise too, how can workers' demands for a higher share of those profits be met in a way that does not lead to a 'wage-price inflation' spiral? That is, how can workers gain the wage increases they are owed without capitalists then putting prices up to claw back their profit share, so making goods more expensive and triggering runaway inflation as other workers demand higher wages in response?

The answer, as Prabhat Patnaik (1997: 9) has argued, is that capitalist economies are able to stabilize themselves, permit real wages to rise with productivity, and avoid accelerating inflation because one section of the labour force employed 'indirectly' has their wage demands compressed. That is, primary commodity producers in 'peripheral' countries of the Global South are unable to enforce their own wage demands due to the vast 'reserve army of labour' in the primary commodity production sector who must act as 'price takers' for the industrialized North (Patnaik and Patnaik 2017: 52). These price takers in the periphery play a fundamental role in stabilizing capitalist economies around non-accelerating rates of inflation.

In other words, it is because workers producing primary commodities – from cocoa to t-shirts to lithium used in batteries – are not able to successfully demand higher wages that the goods they produce stay cheap. As a result, workers in the Global North are able to achieve a level of consumption that puts a halt on runaway demands for wage increases. This is not to argue that there is no poverty in the Global North: wage suppression, benefit cuts, and austerity policies have ensured that there is in fact *rising* child poverty and food poverty in the UK (see Garthwaite, Chapter 10, this volume). Yet the fact remains that even the capacity that mid-range earners in the UK have to meet their needs and donate food to food banks is enabled by treating workers in the Global South as 'shock absorbers' whose cheap wages subsidize the export of low-cost commodities to the Global North.

Mainstream economics has no interest in the *systemic* relations which lock countries in the Global South into relations of dependency and unequal terms of trade whereby they export cheap agricultural and mined goods in exchange for high-cost industrial goods. A considerable amount of industrial manufacturing now takes place across the Global South following a relocation of factories in search of cheap labour in the 1970s. But the same principle of unequal terms of trade applies. Because the intellectual property of manufactured goods – from iPhones to H&M or Primark t-shirts – is owned by Global North firms, the final profit from the sale of these goods is realized in the Global North, while countries like China and Bangladesh who export goods made in low-waged factories receive a fraction of the final selling price (see Muhammad 2011). Economic sociology has often avoided these systemic relations too, studying in ever greater detail the complexity of modern economic and financial systems, without considering the entanglement of those systems in global systems and colonial economic relations (Gilbert 2020).

Perhaps it is not surprising that sociologists like Habermas and Streeck adopt a methodologically nationalist and Eurocentric approach to their study of 'the economy' and legitimation crises. As Bhambra (2016: 188) has shown, this denial of long-standing histories of colonial connection in the study of European economic integration is not new for these scholars. What remains to be made sense of is how the 'vast pauperized mass' of a reserve army of labour came to exist in the Global South. For Utsa and Prabhat Patnaik (2017: 50), the large pools of unemployed workers in the Global South, which allow employers to push wages down since there are always many more out of work willing to work for subsistence pay, exist because of colonial processes of drain and deindustrialization.

In the next section, I examine in more detail these processes of drain and deindustrialization, and how they force us to rethink Eurocentric understandings of modernity as a process by which capitalism developed in Europe, to be emulated by the naturally 'undeveloped' nations of the South. Thinking in terms of the global colonial economy is vital if social scientists are to avoid falling into the trap of analysing 'the economy' and its relationship to social institutions on a methodologically nationalist basis, and with no regard to the historical colonial connections which gave rise to economies in Europe and elsewhere in the Global North.

'A vast pauperized mass': the drain and deindustrialization

Formal colonialism involved extraction of resources from colonized territories on a vast scale. Underpaid, forced, and indentured labour was commonplace (see Kaladeen, Chapter 4, this volume). The British administered their imperial territories to ensure the well-being of the predominantly White subjects 'at home' in the British Isles. In some cases, this involved benefiting from a 'triangular trade' whereby profits on sales of rubber from Malaya to the United States were transferred to Britain, allowing the UK to maintain its currency and trade balances at Malaya's expense (Sioh 2007). Following the Second World War, the British Treasury misled its colonies about the degree to which earnings from the sale of raw materials (such as Malaya's rubber exports) were used to prop up British government spending and domestic welfare spending, while colonies were often forced to adopt austerity policies or raise taxes on (non-White) colonial subjects (Narsey 2016).

Perhaps the most egregious version of this extraction of wealth is 'the drain' of wealth from British India. First discussed by Indian economists Dadabhai Naoroji and R.C. Dutt in the late 19th and early 20th centuries, the theory of the 'drain' has been revitalized by the more recent work of Utsa Patnaik (2017). Patnaik has shown repeatedly that British India was set up in a manner that caused Indian producers to pay for their own exports. The normal expectation is that when a country exports more industrial or agricultural goods, its earnings increase. Earning foreign currency like this is important, since it allows individuals and firms in those countries to import the goods they need in turn. In today's world, countries often need to export to one trading partner to earn dollars so that they can buy other goods that are priced and sold in dollars from a different trading partner. In the period that Patnaik wrote about (1765–1938), India had the world's second largest export surplus. This should have meant it was earning a huge amount of foreign currency from all the countries purchasing goods from India. This would have positioned India well to import the goods it required without incurring debt.

This is not what happened. Instead, Britain kept India perpetually indebted, by forcing traders who wanted to buy from India to deposit gold or currency in London, in exchange for rupee denominated bills which had to be used to pay for exports. The foreign exchange that Indian producers 'earned' never made it to India. Except, it gets worse: the few rupees which Indian producers earned (instead of the gold or currency deposited in London) had to be used to pay high taxation rates – and a huge proportion of those taxes were transferred again to London as 'Home Charges'. In effect, these were fees paid by colonized Indians for being colonized (Patnaik 1984). For the final twist, this wealth 'drained' from India was used to finance further colonial expansion and investment in Southern Africa and Latin America, enabling the further exploitation of colonies and accumulation of wealth in Britain.

Patnaik's (2017) conservative estimate for the amount drained between 1765 and 1938 is around £9 trillion, or ten times 'the economy' of the UK as measured by GDP in 2015. In addition to this process of extraction, India's thriving export sector was 'deindustrialized', discriminated against by policies which gave preference to manufactured goods made in Britain. This too contributed to the reserve army of labour, pushing industrial workers into the agricultural sector and forming what the Patnaiks refer to as a 'vast pauperized mass'. Unable to force their employers to increase wages, these labourers command low wages and so keep the cost of agricultural exports to the Global North down. As a result, workers in the Global North can be appeased with smaller wage increases and lower cost food, and runaway wage-price inflation is kept at bay through the operations of the colonial global economy.

The manufactured goods that were dumped on India at preferential prices, forcing Indian producers out of industrial work and swelling the ranks of the underpaid agricultural poor, included the cotton goods produced in the north-west of England, the cradle of Britain's industrial revolution. Of course, the cotton spun into cloth by advanced machinery in Britain was not grown on the British Isles. Like the sugar that fuelled the underpaid and underfed workers in the cotton mills, the cotton that they spun had been grown using enslaved labour in the plantations of the Caribbean. Much as the 'drain' of wealth from India enriched Britain, enabled further imperial expansion, and impoverished and deindustrialized India, enslavement and the plantation economy in the Caribbean result in huge transfers of wealth to Britain.

There have been numerous efforts in recent years to trace the destination of wealth extracted from enslaved people in the Caribbean. Some of the simplest records to use, however, relate to the compensation payment that was paid to *owners* of enslaved people, not freed former slaves themselves. This compensation was paid to those who had enslaved people in 1837, shortly after the abolition of slavery. Recipients of these vast sums can be traced to the founders of some of the UK's dominant banking, legal, and accountancy firms, and to civic institutions like railways and universities (Draper 2014). A colonial global economy lens reminds us that there are intimate connections between the draining of wealth from former colonies now considered in need of 'development', and public and private investment that shaped 'developed' countries like the UK. Colonial economic relations cannot simply be consigned to the past, and nor can we understand the fate of individual national 'economies' in isolation from global historical economic structures.

Caribbean nations have made repeated calls for reparations for the losses and injustices arising from the transatlantic trade in enslaved people, but the UK has long resisted these calls. In 2005, the figure calculated for the assets lost, wages withheld, and trauma inflicted on the descendants of enslaved people in the Caribbean was £7.5 trillion, three times the GDP of the UK in 2005 (Beckles 2007). A more recent calculation commissioned by the University of the West Indies puts the compensation owed by the UK to Barbados alone at US$4.9 trillion (around £3.8 trillion), with a total owed to Caribbean states of US$24 trillion (£19 trillion) (Bazelon et al 2023). It is important to note that the CARICOM Reparations Commission does not simply ask for a transfer of funds, but recognition (through apologies), repair (through the right of return, Indigenous rehabilitation, and African-Caribbean knowledge exchange) as well as resources (including investment in public health, literacy, and technology transfer). A crucial component of this would also be debt cancellation.

Caribbean countries are among the most indebted in the world, paying out millions every year to creditors that include Global North governments, international financial institutions, and private financiers. Exposure to extreme weather events intensified by climate change exposes countries including Grenada, Dominica, Barbados, and Jamaica to further indebtedness, as they are often obliged to borrow to pay for reconstruction after the hurricanes that have increased in intensity over recent decades. This provides the basis for further reparations claims. The enslavement and exploitation of people in the Caribbean who produced inputs for the industrial revolution, and the carbon emissions that accompanied the coal-driven industrial revolution and increase Caribbean vulnerability to hurricanes, should put Britain in debt to the Caribbean (Perry 2021). In reality though, the reverse is true, and debt repayments continue to flow from the Caribbean to the Global North.

One of the reasons that there has been so much resistance to calls for reparations in the UK is the failure to acknowledge that Britain profited from extracting wealth from the Caribbean. The production of national memory around the idea that Britain *ended* the trade in enslaved peoples, rather than established and benefited from it in a way that has shaped global economic inequalities to this day, has also acted as a brake on calls for reparation. This is despite the Trinidadian historian turned politician Eric Williams (1944) showing that Britain was built via the slave trade, and only ended the slave trade for commercial reasons, over 80 years ago.

Williams showed that the industrial revolution would not have been affordable without inputs derived from enslaved labour (and even the markets for enslavement, such as ironworks that produced manacles, were enabled by chattel slavery and plantation economies). Crucially, he also showed that Britain ended the slave trade only when an emerging industrial class wanted to break the stranglehold that the sugar and cotton plantation monopolies had on British trade: abolitionists may well have existed, but the enabling condition for abolition was the desire for a competing class of capitalists to undo the dominance of those who had made their fortunes in the Caribbean. Bizarrely, as Neptune (2019) shows, a new generation of scholarship on capitalism and slavery in the United States has refused to acknowledge Williams' contribution, either misrepresenting or sidelining his findings and 'reinventing' them anew. For Neptune (2019: 326), this is because crediting Williams with understanding the colonial global economy – of understanding that slavery was fundamental to the birth of industrial capitalism – would embarrass Global North academics and paint them as 'neither novel nor original, but fundamentally backward'.

How to talk about colonialism without talking about colonialism

This chapter has examined how we ended up with a concept of 'the economy' divorced from the realities of the colonial global economy, and which informs Eurocentric forms of analysis that do not take histories of colonial connection seriously. Over the last two decades, however, some branches of the social sciences have taken a curious turn, explicitly engaging with colonialism – yet, somehow, avoiding any analyses of a colonial global economy. The first of these approaches seems to centre colonialism in the exploration of economic issues by asking how the 'legal origins' of various institutions – whether they arose from UK-style common law, or Napoleonic civil law, traditions – impacts the way economies around the world function today (Djankov et al 2003). There is something straightforwardly Eurocentric about an approach that only considers historic developments within different European countries as the primary determinant of how different European powers' former colonies operate today. Indeed this 'legal origins' approach underpinned the World Bank's much criticized Doing Business Indicators (Djankov 2016). These indicators sought to rank countries around the world in terms of how easy foreign investors would find it to do business there, with strict labour protections and high social security protections causing countries to be ranked poorly. In other words, the legal origins approach provides a Eurocentric framework for talking about colonialism only insofar as European history has shaped former colonies and their legal institutions, and only where those legal institutions are of interest for Global North investors seeking a return.

A second, slightly more sophisticated approach, is the 'new institutionalism' of Daron Acemoglu, Simon Johnson, and James Robinson. These three economists were awarded the 2024 Nobel Prize in Economic Sciences for their work analysing how colonization shaped institutions that in turn determines whether former colonies are rich or poor today. Their fundamental argument is that there were two kinds of colonization: an extractive form in colonies where European mortality rates discouraged settlement, and a settler form in more favourable climates where more inclusive institutions were built. They argue for a link between extractive colonial institutions and poor growth and development today on the one hand, and between the institutions and infrastructures established in settler colonies and the seemingly better growth and development in those countries today (Acemoglu et al 2001). While providing the basis for bestselling books and a Nobel Prize, this approach is truly a lesson in how to talk about colonialism without confronting colonialism.

One of the most glaring omissions in this work is the treatment of settler colonies as the basis of inclusive institutions. Australia, Canada, New Zealand and the United States may have built institutions amenable to private property protection and capitalist growth. But these settler colonies were founded on violent, genocidal campaigns of oppression and extermination which persisted as structures, rather than evaporating after initial founding moments. As Ince (2024) has shown, Acemoglu, Johnson, and Robinson try very hard to maintain a separation between extractive colonial institutions and inclusive capitalist institutions. But this only works if you deny the role that extractive institutions and extractive forms of colonization played in the establishment of colonialism within Europe and at the global scale. This unsustainable tension is most apparent in Acemoglu and colleagues' confused approach to the transatlantic trade in enslaved people and the development of plantation economies.

While recognizing for brief moments that colonialism (and enslavement) fuelled European growth, they are not allowed to be 'part' of capitalism in these economists' narrative. If they allowed for the recognition of a colonial global economy, and gave up on treating capitalism and colonialism as two distinct logics, it would not be possible to attribute capitalist 'success' in the form of GDP growth merely to strong, inclusive institutions. The reality is, as Williams (1944) showed so long ago, that growth and economic success in capitalism's European heartlands was inseparable from brutal and extractive forms of enslavement and colonialism. In their insistence on methodological nationalism, and refusal to accept the inequalities in the colonial global economy are shaped by relations *between nations* within a global structure of dependency and exploitation, Acemoglu and colleagues never actually face up to the role of colonialism in shaping capitalist modernity.

Conclusion

This chapter began by historicizing the notion of 'the economy' as something that is nationally bounded and subject to its own laws and measurements. Instead, we can see that this notion of 'the economy' emerged as a product of British and American innovations in economics and economic policy management. But it was also a product of the historical moment during which fading colonial powers like Britain began to think of themselves as nations, where previously they had managed their economies as empires. Part of Britain's management of its colonial economy involved the draining of resources, the transportation and enslavement of Africans in Caribbean plantations, and the deindustrialization of India by giving preference to British manufactured goods. The result across many parts of the empire was the accumulation of capital in Britain (to be reinvested in further imperial expansion, or in public and civic infrastructure), alongside the impoverishment of an underpaid reserve army of labour. The low wages paid to this reserve army of labour in the Global South continues to subsidize consumption for those in the Global North – and crucially, this is not merely felt at the individual level. It is vital to the management of inflation, wage disputes, and poverty within the Global North. There is no economy outside historic and contemporary colonial connections, and the structural nature of relations between nations within the colonial global economy must be kept in sight if we are to avoid the deracinated analyses of colonialism and capitalism which have recently found favour with Nobel Prize committees.

References

Acemoglu, D., Johnson, S. and Robinson, J.A. 2001. 'The Colonial Origins of Comparative Development: An Empirical Investigation', *American Economic Review* 91(5): 1369–1401.

Bazelon, C., Vargas, A., Janakiraman, R. and Olson, M.M. 2023. *Quantification of Reparations for Transatlantic Chattel Slavery*. The Brattel Group.

Beckles, H.M. 2007. '"Slavery was a Long, Long Time Ago": Remembrance, Reconciliation & the Reparations Discourse in the Caribbean', *Ariel* 38(1): 9–25.

Bhambra, G.K. 2016. 'Whither Europe? Postcolonial versus Neocolonial Cosmopolitanism', *Interventions* 18(2): 187–202.

Bhambra, G.K. 2020. 'Colonial Global Economy: Towards a Theoretical Reorientation of Political Economy', *Review of International Political Economy* 28(2): 307–322.

Djankov, S. 2016. 'The Doing Business Project: How It Started: Correspondence', *Journal of Economic Perspectives* 30(1): 247–248.

Djankov, S., La Porta, R., Lopez-de-Silanes, F. and Shleifer, A. 2003. 'Courts', *Quarterly Journal of Economics* 118(2): 453–517.

Draper, N. 2014. 'Helping to Make Britain Great: The Commercial Legacies of Slave-ownership in Britain', in C. Hall, N. Draper, K. McClelland, K. Donington and R. Lang (eds) *Legacies of British Slave-Ownership: Colonial Slavery and the Formation of Victorian Britain*. Cambridge University Press, pp 78–126.

Gilbert, P.R. 2020. 'Expropriating the Future: Turning Ore Deposits and Legitimate Expectations into Assets', in K. Birch and F. Muniesa (eds) *Assetization: Turning Things into Assets in Technoscientific Capitalism*. MIT Press, pp 173–201.

Goswami, M. 2018. 'Crisis Economics: Keynes and the End of Empire', *Constellations* 25(1): 18–34.

Habermas, J. 1973. 'What Does a Crisis Mean Today? Legitimation Problems in Late Capitalism', *Social Research*, 40(4): 643–667.

Ince, O.U. 2024. 'Saving Capitalism from Empire: Uses of Colonial History in New Institutional Economics', *International Relations* 38(4): 589–614.

Muhammad, A. 2011. 'Wealth and Deprivation: Ready-made Garments Industry in Bangladesh', *Economic and Political Weekly*, 46(34): 23–27.

Narsey, W. 2016. *British Imperialism and the Making of Colonial Currency Systems*. Palgrave Macmillan.

Neptune, H.R. 2019. 'Throwin' Scholarly Shade', *Journal of the Early Republic* 39(2): 299–326.

Patnaik, U. 1984. 'Transfer of Tribute and the Balance of Payments in the CEHI', *Social Scientist* 12(12): 43–55.

Patnaik, P. 1997. *Accumulation and Stability under Capitalism*. Oxford University Press.

Patnaik, U. 2017. 'Revisiting the "Drain", or Transfers from India to Britain in the Context of Global Diffusion of Capitalism', in S. Chakrabarti and U. Patnaik (eds) *Agrarian and Other Histories: Essays for Binay Bhushan Chaudhuri*. Tulika Books, pp 277–317.

Patnaik, U. and Patnaik, P. 2017. *A Theory of Imperialism*. Columbia University Press.

Perry, K.K. 2021. 'The New "Bond-age", Climate Crisis and the Case for Climate Reparations: Unpicking Old/New Colonialities of Finance for Development within the SDGs', *Geoforum* 126: 361–371.

Sioh, M. 2007. 'Pricing Race, Circulating Anxieties, and the Fate of Malaya's Currency Reserves at Independence', *Cultural Critique*, 65: 115–139.

Streeck, W. 2014. *Buying Time: The Delayed Crisis of Democratic Capitalism*. Verso.

Williams, E. 1944. *Capitalism and Slavery*. The William Byrd Press, Inc.

Video lecture

Gilbert, P. 2020. *What is the Colonial Global Economy?*, Connected Sociologies Curriculum Project. https://thesociologicalreview.org/projects/connected-sociologies/curriculum/colonial-global-economy/what-colonial-global-economy/

> **QUESTIONS**
>
> 1. Where did the contemporary notion of 'the economy' come from and what does it disguise?
>
> 2. How do the Patnaiks argue that surplus labour in the Global South impacts Global North countries' abilities to fight inflation and deal with class conflict?
>
> 3. How did the transatlantic trade in enslaved people and plantation economies in the Caribbean shape modern Britain, as well as the Caribbean?
>
> 4. What does it mean to say that Acemoglu, Johnson, and Robinson talk about colonialism without ever talking about colonialism?

Worksheet 2. Understanding the Colonial Global Economy

This worksheet is designed to support AS and A-level teaching on the topics of globalization and global development, and social differentiation, power and stratification. The online talk by Paul Robert Gilbert provides students with an introduction to the colonial global economy. Gilbert explains how the global economy is built on enduring colonial relations, institutions, and arrangements. He explains, using contemporary examples such as the COVID-19 pandemic, how the colonial global economy operates through racialized forms of exploitation and extraction on multiple levels, from international economic law to global supply chains. The activities ask students challenging questions about the relationships between narratives of capitalist 'progress' and historical institutions of slavery, as well as the relationships between globalization, international trade, labour relations, and dimensions of global inequality.

Time	Activity	Explanation
00.00–00.05	To warm up, answer the following question: *What does it mean to say that our global economy is colonial?*	This warm-up activity gets students thinking about the key question underpinning this lecture, with the view that the session will enable students to develop more detailed answers to this query. The activity may work well as a group discussion.
00.05–00.10	Recap of understandings of globalization	It may be useful to remind students of key theories related to globalization and global development.
00.10–00.15	Watch the talk from 2:00 to 2:40. *Why do you think Gilbert starts his lecture with this quote from Utsa Patnaik's 'Revisiting the "Drain"'?*	Gilbert explains that Patnaik's work sets out how wealth was 'drained' from India under British rule using underhand fiscal tactics. He is setting up the background for this talk, which connects historical systems of colonial extraction to the organization of the contemporary global economy. This activity gets students thinking about how Britain's colonial past is integral to understanding its economic present. It also encourages students to think about the role of academic scholarship in revealing different perspectives on globalization.
00.15–00.25	Watch the talk from 4:06 to 5:53. *What did the COVID-19 pandemic reveal about the colonial global economy?*	Gilbert explains that the COVID-19 pandemic brought in a period of unprecedented government intervention into global economies, including the initiation of 'arbitration'. This process, he explains, saw the UK providing contracts to produce ventilators and personal protective equipment to some companies and not others, and commandeering healthcare facilities. This activity helps students to understand the ways in which the colonial global economy operates within the context of a contemporary crisis. It asks them to think about the consequences of events such as the COVID-19 pandemic for global political and economic relations, global development, and inequalities, which are key themes within the A-level Sociology curriculum.

Time	Activity	Explanation
00.25–00.35	At 8:19 Dr Gilbert draws on the work of Antony Anghie to explain that the global economy is based on 'a long-standing commitment to the idea that non-European or postcolonial sovereignty is and always will be contingent on the foreigners' "right to trade"'. *Using your own interpretation of the above concept, explain why international trade is a sociological issue.*	This activity asks students to consider a central theme within the A-level Sociology curriculum, which is the role played by international trade in processes of globalization and global development. It also encourages students to think about the relationships between the colonial global economy and social inequality, which is another key topic within the curriculum. Furthermore, the question helps students to interpret academic theories and put complex concepts into their own words.
00.35–00.40	Watch the talk from 11:10 to 12:44. *How is contemporary labour exploitation shaped by colonial relationships?*	In this section Gilbert explains how, when the COVID-19 pandemic hit, apparel companies began cancelling their orders from garment factories in Bangladesh, resulting in wages going unpaid, workers struggling to afford food and basic supplies, and being made to return to work earlier than would have been safe. This activity asks students to consider the connections between colonial histories and contemporary labour relations, and has some important crossovers with 'The Grunwick strike' topic. Students may draw on their learning from this session to go beyond the question in thinking about how gender plays into these global labour relations.
00.40–00.50	Watch the talk from 13:30 to 15:14. *What is the role of academia in understanding and interpreting the colonial global economy?*	Gilbert suggests many accounts have purposefully misread scholarship that makes connections between capitalism and the institution of slavery. This activity encourages students to recognize how bodies of scholarship can be overlooked or silenced by dominant narratives of modernity. Students may draw on their learning from 'The Making of the Modern World' talk in answering this question.
00.50–01.00	Drawing on what you have learned throughout this talk, answer the following question: *Why is it important for us to understand that capitalist 'progress' and the institution of slavery are intertwined?*	This concluding activity asks students to bring together what they have learned in this session by setting out, in their own words, the connection between capitalism and slavery that underpins the colonial global economy. Students may take Gilbert's cue in drawing upon the work of Eric Williams. They are also encouraged to use their learning from other topics in thinking about the enduring significance of historical processes of colonial extraction and exploitation. In doing so, they are drawing on a key theme within the A-level Sociology curriculum, which requires students to consider different concepts of modernity and post-modernity.

This worksheet was developed by Isabel Sykes.

3

Colonial Extraction and Dispossession

Su-ming Khoo

> **Objectives**
>
> - This chapter suggests that material ecological processes of colonial extraction and dispossession are insufficiently addressed in standard social scientific accounts of modernity which treat them as 'externalities'.
>
> - It develops a critical explanation of unequal exchange by discussing material processes of dispossession and extraction, focusing on key historical examples of global exchange of biota (living organisms), silver, sugar, timber, and fertilizer.
>
> - The examples highlight the extent of violence, extirpation (death), and injustice involved in the material processes that form the basis of lasting global inequalities.
>
> - The chapter introduces a critical perspective on global commodities, law, and conservation, linking 'environmental' resource conflicts, broader struggles against historical global injustices, and demands for *material* decolonial justice.

Introduction

This chapter introduces colonial resource extraction and dispossession as central processes in the systematic making of the modern world. The formation of the modern-colonial, capitalist world economy was a lengthy, complex historical process occurring over more than five centuries, shaping contemporary globalization through diverse, complex, and overlapping processes. This chapter takes a materialist approach to global systems, centring ecological flows of matter, energy, and life. It counters a tendency within modern social theory to ignore and downplay material factors, treating them as abstract 'externalities' that can be omitted from systematic consideration.

The modern world economy can be imagined as a system that harnesses flows of resources and energy towards a concerted aim: the generation and accumulation of profit, or capital. Two questions arise: how did these processes begin in the first place, and how did these processes of accumulation result in inequalities across different regions and for different groups of people? This chapter examines some historical processes that created the global system centred on capital accumulation, while extirpating and displacing colonized peoples and transforming landscapes. Matter and life are converted into 'resources' for capital when capitalism and colonialism work together to appropriate them as fruits of unequal exchange. This combined process means that a 'colony' is never simply a formal political entity, it is also a systematic machine for unequal material exchange, creating capital that some accumulate at others' expense. Capitalist value is created when resources are enclosed and 'cheapened' (see Gilbert, Chapter 2, this volume). Critical world-ecologists, Raj Patel and Jason Moore (2018: 3), argue that 'cheapening' lies at the heart of unequal exchange. Their work points to the cheapening of seven central resources – nature, money, work, care, food, energy, and lives – as central to the creation and maintenance of global inequalities.

Standard theories of the modern world explain capitalism's historical development as a universal, general process originating in Europe, in the late 18th and early 19th centuries. Technological, economic, political, and social changes are presented as evolutionary developments in standard 'Eurocentric' accounts. The rest of the world benefited from a diffusion process, going through progressive stages of 'development' and 'modernization', by following in the footsteps of Europe's earlier achievement. Colonialism, conquest, displacement, extraction, and extirpation are downplayed in standard accounts of global modernity. Systemic change is explained in terms of Europe's superior knowledge and technological innovations, especially focusing on the 'industrial revolution'. European innovations were later diffused to less socially and technologically advanced and economically 'less developed' regions of the world. The global development of markets, technologies, private property, laws, and regulations are all portrayed as European innovations that are superior, beneficial, universal, progressive, and largely inevitable in their global spread.

Critical and anti-colonial perspectives offer alternative social scientific accounts of modern capitalist development. These alternatives focus on the fundamentally unequal characteristics of Eurocentric capitalism. Against universality and inevitability, these critical alternatives point to a specific system of relationships and flows that historically achieved domination over the world's economy and society through conquest, coercion, and colonialism. Current global inequalities are therefore rooted in such processes which persist in new, 'neocolonial' forms after the end of direct, formal political control by European powers.

Systematic inequalities of money and debt have been extensively discussed by critical, decolonial social scientists. However, their material aspects are often separately treated as 'environmental problems' and accorded less systematic attention. Some of these environmental aspects are examined in more detail in the final section of this book. Ecologically unequal exchange and ecological debt are less frequently discussed problems, mainly because conventional economic thinking considers material, environmental factors to be 'externalities' that can be excluded from economic accounting, models, and systematic theories.

Unequal material exchange and the beginnings of dispossession

A materialist focus on unequal exchange helps us to think through the ways in which inequalities are not accidental, but historically structured and systematic. Unequal exchange is explained by decisively asymmetrical processes of dispossession and extraction. The extraction of resources disproportionately benefits powerful, formerly and currently imperial, colonial, and metropolitan powers, places, and social groups; while 'cheapening', 'wasting', 'externalizing', dispossessing, and peripheralizing less powerful, currently or formerly colonized people and places. Unequal ecological exchange represents doubled injustice because less powerful, more disadvantaged people (and places) suffer disproportionately from physical, material, and environmental harms. This happens while they are also entitled to less than their fair share of resources such as land, water, minerals, plants, and animals. The past and current global system thus unjustly allocates two functions to the less politically and economically powerful countries, regions, and peoples – as 'taps' for valuable resources to flow away from them, and as 'sinks' for disposing of unwanted and harmful effects which flow into them. This 'taps' and 'sinks' idea is explored in more detail in Chapter 25 of this volume.

Many of today's 'environmental' inequalities and conflicts have roots in long histories of colonial dispossession and extraction. Material realities are central to understanding what we mean by 'colonization' itself, linking political processes of conquest and domination to physical lands, substances, life-forms, and labour. Colonialism occupied land and turned people and nature into human and natural resources for a singular aim – the accumulation of capital. Historical processes of extraction, dispossession, replacement, and extinction drove *colonization* and *ecological imperialism* over a long period of 500 years and more, connecting land-grabbing, resource wars, slavery, the extensive spread of commodity plantations, and the exploitation of extractive sites like mines. Much of the world's human, biological, and cultural life was displaced, enclosed, and threatened with extinction. While law and conservation are conventionally expected to regulate and ameliorate environmental problems, they frequently collude with colonizing processes, enabling lands to be 'emptied' by expelling, dispossessing, and displacing Indigenous people, animals, and plants. Following dispossession, ecosystems could be reshaped, reorganizing lands, waters, plants, and animals to single-mindedly work to generate capital.

As Imogen Tyler's chapter in this section (Chapter 5) sets out, the transition towards modern capitalism within Britain involved processes of 'enclosure', dispossessing common people and preventing them from using common lands for grazing, growing food, or collecting wild food and medicine. Common lands were presumed to be 'waste' needing 'improvement', enabling their redefinition as exclusive private property. Less powerful people were shut out from resources that they had previously been allowed to use according to tradition. Law and official regulations enabled these resources to be reserved for the more powerful, concentrating landowners' and institutional power. The landless were left with little choice but to work for wages, in order to survive and pay rent and taxes. Enclosure increased land values for owners, who controlled land and labour to produce food and materials for sale and profit, not direct use. As profits were extracted and accumulated, resource and power gaps widened, hardening patterns of dispossession and inequalities. This pattern expanded across the oceans as monarchies and adventurers engaged in exploration and conquest, increasing European control over other parts of the world.

'Columbian exchange': ecological imperialism or colonial syndemic?

Voyages of exploration during the early modern period (the late 1400s to the early 1600s) were sponsored by European powers in search of gold, spices, and new lands to conquer. Exploratory sailings by Cristoforo Colombo (Christopher Columbus) in 1492–1502, Amerigo Vespucci in 1497–1502, Vasco da Gama in 1497–1499, and Ferdinand Magellan and Juan Sebastian Elcano in 1519–1522 enabled European powers to map and organize expeditions to conquer, emigrate to, colonize, and trade (Arnold 2006). Between the 1500s to the 1900s, separate land and sea routes that were previously controlled by different powers in different regions became interconnected into a single global system, dominated by competing and collaborating European powers: Spain, Portugal, the Netherlands, France, and Britain.

European conquest and colonization vastly altered distributions of people, goods, and biota, that is, living things like plants, animals, and microbes. As Europe's 'Old World' and the 'New Worlds' of the Americas and Australasia became connected by conquest and trade, people, crops, animals, materials, and microbes moved between them. This phenomenon is described as the 'Columbian exchange', after Columbus (Crosby 1986). However, the exchange was so unbalanced that it might alternatively be called a 'syndemic', the combined impact of colonial violence, extirpation, and replacement. The flows of organisms, people, materials, and profits primarily benefited Europe and people of European descent, while disproportionately harming, displacing, and in some cases eliminating non-European people and biota. European conquerors and colonists, enslaved people and labourers brought 'Old World' diseases like measles, influenza, smallpox, cholera, typhus, plague, and yellow fever to the 'New World' together with livestock, crops, pests, and weeds. The conquerors and colonists were better able to survive diseases which had co-evolved with livestock such as cattle and pigs across Europe, Asia, and Africa. 'New World' people, lacking prior exposure, were far more likely to die from transferred diseases, while only one disease, syphilis, is known to have transferred from the Americas to Europe. European conquerors and colonists were given permission by their governments to appropriate lands, loot, profits, and scientific 'discoveries', for example, crops like maize, potatoes, tomatoes, tobacco, peppers, and rubber; while African and Indigenous people were enslaved and forced to produce while deriving few benefits.

The word 'colonialism' derives from the Latin, '*colonia*'. This word originated in the Roman Empire, describing lands given by the imperial government (27 BCE–476 CE) to citizens, oftentimes veteran soldiers. Colonies encouraged Roman citizens to settle, farm, occupy, maintain, and expand the Roman Empire's presence in newly conquered areas. The earliest use of the word in English recorded by the *Oxford English Dictionary* occurs in 1550, first describing the 'colonization' of Scottish lands by England, and then the Spanish colonization of the Americas (Oxford English Dictionary 2025). Magellan's voyages (1519–1522) finally proved that Columbus had not 'discovered' a new sea route to Asia, but a 'new' continent previously unknown to Europeans. Renaming the land known to Indigenous inhabitants as 'Awya Yala' or Ixachitlān as 'America', after the Italian cartographer Amerigo Vespucci, enabled its colonial appropriation and the dispossession of Indigenous people (*Decolonial Atlas* 2015).

Since many Indigenous people died from disease, and survivors resisted enslavement, colonizers turned to transported enslaved people and foreign labourers to make colonies feasible and profitable. People were violently extracted from Africa and enslaved, and their unpaid labour and progeny taken, and forced to work alongside 'cheapened' labour of Indigenous and imported workers. Colonists, enslaved people, and migrants carried diseases and pests (such as lice and rats), which spread among the Indigenous populations. The 1500s were described as an era of 'megadeaths and megadroughts' in the Americas (Acuna-Soto et al 2002). The strains of colonial conquest and war combined with deforestation. A period of climate change known as 'the little ice age' combined with prolonged droughts worsened the impacts of hunger and disease. When the Spanish conqueror Hernan Cortés first encountered the Aztec Empire in 1519, its capital city, Tenochtitlan (modern Mexico City), was possibly the largest in the world, at least double that of London or Lisbon, containing 22 million people. In 1521, Cortés defeated the Aztec Empire, claimed its lands for the Spanish Crown and renamed it the Viceroyalty of Spain. By the end of the 1500s, Tenochtitlan's population had collapsed, with only two million remaining (Acuna-Soto et al 2002).

The Spanish conquerors destroyed Indigenous livelihoods and cultural artefacts, bent on looting, annihilating Indigenous people, and replacing Indigenous culture with European Christian religion and culture. Aztec treasuries and libraries were destroyed, with only a few original Aztec books surviving. The 'Florentine Codex' is a rare example, compiled by the Spanish Franciscan missionary, Bernadino de Sahagún, and Indigenous Nahua people, to document the existing culture, religion, economy, and society. The numerous aspects of Indigenous life at the time of Conquest include accounts and illustrations of the smallpox epidemic brought by the invaders (León 2006: e75–e76), with catastrophically unequal consequences. Far greater numbers of Indigenous people died from diseases like smallpox, in addition to the ravages of colonial war and slaughter. Extirpation, the mass deaths of Indigenous people, allowed their societies and lands to be conquered and any survivors to be dispossessed of wealth, culture, knowledge, and resources.

The lands that were eventually called the 'Americas' became dominated by people of European origin and their descendants; their landscapes transformed by European-modelled colonial plantations, livestock, and grasses (Crosby 1986). The 'Columbian exchange' involved a combination of intentional and inadvertent processes of unequal exchange. The connected evolution of 'Old World' disease microbes, weeds, crops, and animals across Europe, Asia, and Africa made this collection of biota into effective companions and tools for dispossessing and displacing Indigenous people, leading to the complete transformation of landscapes and ways of life. Crosby (1986) coined the term '*ecological imperialism*' to describe unequal processes of extirpation and replacement, enabling European empires to control and successfully colonize newly conquered lands.

'S*yndemic*' is an epidemiological term describing a bio-social complex in which several biological and social interactions come together to increase susceptibility and worsen health outcomes for a population (Singer et al 2017). The colonial syndemic describes the combined direct impacts of war, forced labour, enslavement and slave importation, and changes in crops and livestock, hunting to extinction, and deforestation, and indirect effects of unintentional factors like disease epidemics, accidentally introduced pests, and the unpredicted vigour, invasiveness, and destructiveness of European grasses, livestock, and other accidentally introduced species.

Existing Indigenous powers, like the Aztec and Inca empires, were also responsible for material pressures on their Indigenous subjects, extracting resources and labour. These internal pressures interacted with colonial war and conquest, disease and ecological imperialism. The multiple and combined effects made the Columbian 'exchange' into a catastrophic, multifaceted *syndemic* attacking the lives and health of Indigenous societies. Greatly weakened, Indigenous societies were unable to resist the impositions of conquerors and settler-colonial social, cultural, and economic systems. European conquest and expanding colonization set in place unequal flows of people, disease, materials, labour, and biota, leading to long-distance extraction of resources, lands, and profits benefiting Europeans, European powers, and settlers of European origin while eliminating, dispossessing, and taking labour, resources, and biota from Indigenous people and lands.

A materialist approach to extraction

Material flows make up the stuff of extraction, which accompanied and followed invasion and disease. A good example that links material extraction and the world economic system is money. This mostly consisted of stable, scarce 'precious' metals like gold and silver until paper money became the global standard. Europeans needed money to wage war and pay for trade goods, especially tea, silk, and ceramics from China. The Chinese empire had little demand for European-made goods to directly exchange for Chinese products, so payment was demanded in silver. Spanish conquerors initially increased their money supply by looting, melting down precious metal objects, and transporting looted gold and silver to Europe. By the 1540s, Spanish forces established control over important silver mines in Zacatecas and Guanajuato (now Northern Mexico), and Potosi in the Viceroyalty of Peru (now Bolivia). These former Aztec and Inca mines produced an estimated 150,000 tons of silver between 1500 and 1800, some 80 per cent of the entire world's production. Sixty per cent of the world's silver in the 1500s was extracted from the Potosi mine alone. Spanish processes made silver extraction more efficient, increasing the yield and profitability of the silver mines (Moore 2007).

The gigantic increase in silver from Latin America funded the expansion of European war and global trade. New World silver made the Spanish silver coin, the *real de a ocho* (peso) the main international trading currency between 1500 and 1800, enabling

Europeans to pay for Chinese goods, while satisfying China's need for silver. Paper banknotes had been used by the Chinese almost a thousand years before Europe, however the instability of paper money led Chinese authorities to revert to silver, the reason for their insistence that Europeans pay in silver for trade goods. From around 1800, European money began to take the form of paper notes, promissory notes that an issuing bank or authority promised to redeem in gold or silver. The increasing power of the British Empire meant that British pound sterling in the form of notes began to replace coins, mainly Spanish silver coins as the leading global trade currency. From the 1800s on, European money began to de-materialize into the paper form of promissory notes and banknotes (Kampmann nd). This increased convenience, but also increased risk as more currency could be issued than the actual amount of precious metal available to redeem the total amount stated on the notes. Global money supply expanded beyond the material limitations posed by the scarcity of precious metals.

Sugar: plantation, deforestation, slavery, and fertilizer

'New World discoveries' were not only important sources of imperial loot and money, but also lands that could be colonized for plantations producing new trade commodities. Sugarcane was one such valuable trade crop, highly prized since medieval times. Initially a rare, expensive luxury only accessible to royalty and aristocrats, sugar became more widespread and affordable to lower and aspiring classes as sugar plantations spread, increasing production and trade (Mintz 1986: 96). Originating from Southeast Asia and Papua New Guinea, sugar was cultivated and traded throughout the Arab world since the 8th century CE. Portuguese and Spanish colonists developed plantations in the Southern Mediterranean, Madeira, and the Canary Islands in the late 1400s. These became unsustainable after a relatively short time due to deforestation, drought, and climate change. Madeira (the 'Isle of Wood') became almost entirely deforested within a few decades, making continued cultivation unsustainable (Moore 2009).

The 'discovery' of Brazil and the Caribbean islands offered alternative locations for sugar production. The plantation model of capitalist production is a model of *cultigen* monoculture, devoting extensive areas to a single, standardized, and usually foreign crop. Plantation sugar is an intensive crop, requiring not only warm climates, but also profligate amounts of wood, water, soil fertility, and labour in several forms. Enslaved people from Africa, indentured labour from Asia, and forced native labour were used to clear land, plant and harvest crops, and process the sugar. The 'cheapening' of nature, money, work, care, food, energy, and lives in the plantations and factories made large-scale, labour-intensive sugarcane farming and processing into an efficient and profitable enterprise (Patel and Moore 2018).

The capitalist quest to continuously expand the production of agricultural commodities is inherently linked to dispossession, 'cheapening', unequal exchange, and widening metabolic rifts. Every imported commodity that led to the development of modern world capitalism in the 1500s required wood. One pound of sugar required approximately 60 pounds of fuelwood to produce it (Moore 2009: 350, 376). Capitalist production for export thus required great amounts of unequal material exchange, causing 'metabolic rifts' as industrial amounts of materials were extracted from one place, depleted, or removed to another place. Fast-growing cane plants remove nutrients from the soil, and use up wood, metal, enslaved and cheapened labour to produce sugar in colonial plantations for profitable trade, and the accumulation of profit and capital in distant colonial metropoles.

The development of capitalism, agriculture, and industry, increased circulation of money, and metabolic rifts had already begun to result in a series of ecological crises within Europe itself. As capitalism, empires, and colonialism spread, these crises extended geographically. When urbanization and commercial crop production intensified across Europe, soil fertility declined, creating demand for imported fertilizer to remedy soil decline. Fertilizer demand drove the War of the Pacific (1879–1884), over guano and Chile saltpetre supplies. Chile invaded Bolivia and Peru, seizing Bolivia's coastline and Peru's guano islands. These locations were the world's richest fertilizer resources, until the invention of chemical fertilizer in the 20th century replaced guano and mineral saltpetre (Cushman 2013).

Doctrines of dispossession: questioning law and conservation

Settlement and colonization did not only involve dispossession by violent seizure. Legal doctrines and administrative regulations were also key to defining dispossession as a legal process, granting rights to settlers and colonizers to take materials, and own and use lands. Law defined colonization as just and proper, through the legal doctrines of discovery and *terra nullius* (declaring a place to be 'empty land', or 'nobody's land'), which justified the dispossession of prior inhabitants and the taking of lands and resources into colonizers' ownership (Watson 2011). Discriminatory racial ideology justified European people and activities as superior, while 'cheapening' Indigenous people, whose presumed inferiority justified their dispossession. Unequal laws and regulations continue to maintain unjust dispossession, extraction, and accumulation, as long as the discriminatory reasoning underlying colonial assumptions, laws, and regulations remains.

In ancient Roman law, the term *res nullius* ('non-things') was applied to things without owners, wild animals, 'lost slaves', and abandoned buildings. *Res nullius* could be lawfully taken. British authorities declared Australian lands to be *'terra nullius'*, justifying colonial seizure. Aboriginal Australians were not seen as capable of legally owning the lands they inhabited, while colonizers were granted ownership following the colonial legal 'doctrine of discovery' (Watson 2011). Dispossession of Aboriginal Australians was justified by arguing that they were either simply absent, or that their claim to their own lands was inferior because they were not using land for a form of agriculture recognized by Europeans. Dispossession and colonization were equated with the 'improvement' of 'waste lands' (Pateman 2007). In other words, colonizers' ignorance of Aboriginal livelihoods and their assumption of superiority depended on the debasement or 'cheapening' of Aboriginal humanity, law, livelihoods, and culture. This 'cheapening' justified dispossession and the reallocation of land to European settlers for colonial ranching, plantations, and mines.

Despite the British Crown's claim of sovereignty over its colonies, the legal doctrine of continuity acknowledged that Indigenous people had certain rights over lands that they had been continuously inhabiting. These are rights of use, not ownership, and are called native, Indigenous or Aboriginal rights (Watson 2011). An important test case taken at the end of the 20th century by Indigenous Torres Strait Islanders challenged Australian law justifying the exclusion of Indigenous people from their own lands. Following a decade in the courts, the 1992 *Mabo* v *Queensland* judgment rejected the *terra nullius* claim, restoring native title to land wrongfully seized by British settlers (Pateman 2007).

Despite the outcome of the Mabo judgment, it remains clear today that there are difficult to resolve limits on what today's sovereign states, which were historically based on colonial dispossession, will be willing to concede and offer to historically dispossessed Indigenous peoples. Conflicts are bound to continue between sovereign powers over colonially 'discovered', appropriated, and developed resources. This is obvious when we examine attempts to 'conserve' resources in order to sustain continued extraction. Such 'conservation' for extractive purposes is bound to clash with Indigenous and local claims to access and use resources on lands that were originally inhabited, before their exclusion was legalized. The overall problems of material colonial extraction and dispossession have not diminished. Metabolic rifts and ecological exhaustion continue to increase to serve the demands for resource extraction and the continued generation and accumulation of capital in the name of economic growth.

As colonial demands for resources increased, colonial administrators developed regulations and practices of 'scientific conservation' to ensure continued access to important resources like wood. Local communities were excluded and blamed by colonial administrators for resource depletion, while large-scale extractive activities were enabled to continue. In colonial India, local communities were blamed for harvesting wood for small-scale subsistence activities, like firewood for cooking, or for the construction of shelter and hand tools, while large-scale colonial industrial timber extraction was sustained. Peasants and tribal people were prevented from using the forests for fuel, fodder, food, and medicine, while forests became reserved for colonial uses like railways, construction, or even the conservation of valued wildlife like tigers. Formal independence did not change this situation, as the post-colonial Indian government continued to practise colonial patterns of exclusion and dispossession (Guha et al 2012). Commercial and industrial interests continue to enjoy legal and regulatory precedence today, while the needs of local peasants, pastoralists, and artisans are ignored. The poor and less powerful are dispossessed, their use of resources to meet everyday needs are treated as crimes, causing ongoing tensions and conflicts. At the same time, richer and more powerful authorities extract resources to accumulate capital, a process Benjaminsen and Bryceson (2012) call 'green and blue grabbing'.

Conclusion

This chapter has set out the importance of a materialist approach to understand the detailed material realities behind unequal exchange and metabolic rifts. Capital is produced through dispossession, replacement, and extinction; processes with colonial roots. Unequal exchange acts as the material and economic mechanism for producing and perpetuating global inequalities. The discussion in this chapter began with the so-called 'Columbian exchange' of people and biota, suggesting that it can be understood as a catastrophically unequal syndemic of extinction and replacement. Colonial plantations replaced pre-colonial nature–culture relationships with monocultures that continuously require deforestation, slavery, drought, soil exhaustion, and the need for new lands. The legal 'discovery' and definition of 'empty lands' serves to dispossess original inhabitants so that resources can be appropriated and extracted. Conservation arose as a movement to maintain access to resources for extraction, while expelling and dispossessing local inhabitants. Material flows and metabolic rifts continue unabated under current conditions of economic growth and globalization, which intensify demands for resources, resulting in neo-colonial land and resource grabbing.

A materialist approach critically understands unequal exchange as material processes of dispossession and extraction. These processes can have inadvertent as well as intentional drivers. The chapter has discussed key historical examples of global biota exchange, silver, sugar, timber, and fertilizer. The fascinating global history of these and many other colonial trade and plantation commodities – and Patel and Moore's arguments that capitalism depends on the cheapening of nature, money, work, care, food, energy, and lives – can be further explored to gain material understanding of dispossession and unequal exchange and their globally and ecologically unjust origins and consequences. Some of these aspects are further explored in this book's final section.

By critically questioning the 'cheapening' assumptions that are inscribed in colonial law and conservation, we can attend to their continuing unequal and unjust implications for Indigenous and subsistence resource users long after formal political 'decolonization'. We can make important linkages between historical dispossession, material unequal exchange, law and conservation, and the 'cheapening' of nature, money, work, care, food, energy, and lives. Understanding the historical imperial, colonial origins of struggles against unjust 'cheapening' helps us to better appreciate broader demands for decolonial social, economic, political, and ecological justice in the present, and to look towards different futures.

References

Acuna-Soto, R., Stahle, D.W., Cleaveland, M.K., and Therrell, M.D. 2002. 'Megadrought and Megadeath in 16th Century Mexico', *Emerging Infectious Disease* 8(4): 360–362. https://www.ncbi.nlm.nih.gov/pmc/articles/PMC2730237/

Arnold, D. 2006. *The Age of Discovery, 1400–1600*. Routledge.

Benjaminsen, T.A. and Bryceson, I. 2012. 'Conservation, Green/Blue Grabbing and Accumulation by Dispossession in Tanzania', *The Journal of Peasant Studies* 39(2): 335–355. https://doi.org/10.1080/03066150.2012.667405

Crosby, A.W. 1986. *Ecological Imperialism: The Biological Expansion of Europe, 900–1900*. Cambridge University Press

Cushman, G.T. 2013. *Guano and the Opening of the Pacific World: A Global Ecological History*. Cambridge University Press.

Decolonial Atlas. 2015. 'Endonyms of the World's Landmasses', 23 February. https://decolonialatlas.wordpress.com/2015/02/23/endonyms-of-the-worlds-landmasses/

Guha, R., Sundar, N., Baviskar, A., Kothari, A., Pathak, N., Saxena, N.C., et al. 2012. *Deeper Roots of Historical Injustice: Trends and Challenges in the Forests of India.* Rights and Resources Initiative. https://rightsandresources.org/wp-content/uploads/2014/01/doc_5589.pdf

Kampmann, U. nd. 'The Impact of Silver from the New World', *Money Museum.* https://www.moneymuseum.com/en/archive/the-impact-of-silver-from-the-new-world-32?slbox=true

León, P.M. 2006. *The Broken Spears: The Aztec Account of the Conquest of Mexico.* Beacon.

Mintz, S.W. 1986. *Sweetness and Power: The Place of Sugar in Modern History.* Penguin.

Moore, J.W. 2007. 'Silver, Ecology, and the Origins of the Modern World, 1450–1640', in J.R. McNeill, J. Martinez-Alier, and A. Hornborg (eds), *Rethinking Environmental History: World System History and Global Environmental Change.* AltaMira Press, pp 123–142.

Moore, J.W. 2009. 'Madeira, Sugar, and the Conquest of Nature in the "First" Sixteenth Century: Part I: From "Island of Timber" to Sugar Revolution, 1420–1506', *Review (Fernand Braudel Center)* 32(4): 345–390.

Patel, R. and Moore, J.W. 2018. *A History of the World in Seven Cheap Things: A Guide to Capitalism, Nature, and the Future of the Planet.* University of California Press.

Oxford English Dictionary. 2025. Colony (n.), Etymology https://doi.org/10.1093/OED/9523112047

Pateman, C. 2007. 'The Settler Contract', in C. Pateman and C. Mills, *Contract and Domination.* Wiley, pp 35–78.

Singer, M., Bulled, N., Ostrach, B., and Mendenhall, E. 2017. 'Syndemics and the Biosocial Conception of Health', *Lancet* 389(10072): 941–995. https://www.thelancet.com/journals/lancet/article/PIIS0140-6736(17)30003-X

Watson, B.A. 2011. 'The Impact of the American Doctrine of Discovery on Native Land Rights in Australia, Canada, and New Zealand', *Seattle University Law Review* 34: 507–551.

Video lecture

Khoo, S. 2020. *Colonial Dispossession and Extraction,* Connected Sociologies Curriculum Project. https://thesociologicalreview.org/projects/connected-sociologies/curriculum/mmw/colonial-extraction-and-dispossession/

Additional resources

'Materialism', *Global Social Theory.* https://globalsocialtheory.org/topics/materialism/

'Settler Colonialism', *Global Social Theory.* https://globalsocialtheory.org/concepts/settler-colonialism/

QUESTIONS

1. How does unequal exchange work through material processes? Can you think of another example of a material substance or commodity that involves unequal exchange?

2. Have historical incidents of material dispossession or extraction resulted in current inequalities or injustices? Can you think of an example?

3. Do you think historical injustices committed by people and governments in the past require people and governments in the present to find solutions?

Worksheet 3. Colonial Extraction and Dispossession

This worksheet is designed to support AS and A-level teaching on social differentiation, power and stratification, and globalization and global development. It focuses on the relationships between globalization and the environment, and globalization and global inequality, through the lens of colonialism. This worksheet may also support teaching in relevant modules across AS and A-level History and/or Geography. In this session, Su-ming Khoo explains how the historical development of the capitalist economy is built on the extraction, colonization, and dispossession of Indigenous nature and peoples. Using the colonization of the Americas in the 16th century as her starting point, Khoo explains processes and consequences of colonizing materials, life, nature, and labour. The worksheet encourages students to explore the connection between global capitalism, colonialism, and the climate crisis further, asking them to make contemporary connections to the themes.

Time	Activity	Explanation
00.00–00.05	To warm up, answer this question: *How do you think globalization impacts the environment?*	This activity introduces students to a central topic – globalization – in the A-Level Sociology curriculum. The broad question is designed to encourage students to draw on their existing knowledge, with the view that they will reflect and expand on this knowledge later in the session.
00.05–00.10	Recap of understandings of globalization.	It may be useful to remind students of the definition(s) of globalization.
00.10–00.15	Watch the talk from 2:36 to 3:30. *What does it mean to take a material approach to understanding colonialism?*	Khoo explains that a material approach brings 'flows of matter, energy and life' into consideration in the examination of imperialism, understanding how these are harnessed for capital accumulation. This introduces students to a new perspective on studying colonialism, helping them to understand the different angles from which this topic can be explored and, in turn, allowing them to begin comparing and evaluating these different approaches for themselves.
00.15–00.25	Watch the talk from 4:54 to 7:16. *In your own words, why is the Columbian exchange an example of ecological imperialism?*	Khoo explains that the destruction of the Aztec capital by Cortes happened through a combination of environmental and disease crises, or 'megadroughts' and 'megadeaths'. This question is designed to get students thinking about the connections between imperialism and ecological crisis, which will help them to complete the more advanced activities further on in the session. It will also help to ensure that students are familiar with the key terminology of 'ecological imperialism' before going ahead to complete these activities.

Time	Activity	Explanation
00.25–00.35	At 7:19 Khoo explains that 'a syndemic describes several biological and social interactions that come together to increase susceptibility and worsen health outcomes'. *What are the different interactions that happened during the colonization of the Americas to make it a syndemic?* It may be helpful to visually illustrate the relationships between these interactions and their consequences.	By exploring the connection between the biological and social interactions during the colonization of the Americas, this activity enables students to gain a greater understanding of how sociology relates to ecology, history, and biology.
00.35–00.40	Watch the talk from 16:03 to 17:27. *In your own words, summarize how the legal emptying of Australian lands demonstrates the connection between racialized ideology and ecology.*	Khoo describes how the dispossession of Indigenous people in Australia was made legal because the Indigenous populations were considered 'not human' and more akin to wild animals. Understanding the racial ideologies that underpin imperialist power is a key theme throughout this course, and in thinking about this example students might draw connections to other topics, for example 'Colonial Global Economy'.
00.40–00.50	At 20:51, Khoo states that the 'worst effects' of ecological imperialism are 'felt by those who have contributed least to the problem and who have suffered the most dispossession'. *Why is the climate crisis a sociological issue?*	This question encourages students to think beyond the topic material and draw connections to their wider learning. They are being asked to make links between globalization and the environment, and globalization and global inequality, which are core themes in the A-level Sociology curriculum. This activity may work well in the form of a group discussion or pair work.
00.50–01.00	Thinking back to the first task you did in this session, and given what you have learned from this topic, answer the following question: *How would you describe the relationship between globalization and the climate crisis?* You may wish to create a visual illustration or diagram to demonstrate your thought process.	This activity asks students to reflect on their learning throughout the topic and build on their existing knowledge. Students may now be able to engage more critically with the relationship between globalization, colonialism, and climate crisis. It may be useful to provide students with an example from the topic, such as the growing of sugarcane, to provide an anchor for their thinking. Students may wish to create a flowchart or spider diagram to illustrate the connections they are identifying.

This worksheet was developed by Isabel Sykes.

4

Enslavement, Indenture, and Resistance in the British Empire

Maria del Pilar Kaladeen

> **Objectives**
>
> - This chapter sets out to consider the ways in which systems of unfree labour in the British Empire were interconnected and successive.
>
> - It seeks to understand the legacies of enslavement and indenture across the Atlantic and Indian Ocean worlds.
>
> - It explores how the global colonial plantation operated as an extractive labour force and consumer of unfree labour.

Introduction

Enslavement and indenture are both systems of unfree labour. Such systems, including serfdom and bonded labour, have been common across the world and throughout history. In this chapter, I look specifically at enslavement and indenture in the context of European colonialism. It was during this period that such structures were systematized through national and international law. Understanding such systems requires us also to understand the history of empire, the forced or coerced movement of peoples and the diasporas this created, the economics of empire, and the ongoing impact on societies of the large-scale moral and religious justifications employed in the furtherance of such endeavours on plantations largely centred in what we now call the Global South. In relation to economics, as Caribbean historians like Eric Williams (2005) have pointed out, it is impossible to separate the wealth generated from the use of unfree labour in the British Empire to large scale events that benefited Britain, like the industrial revolution (see Gilbert, Chapter 2, this volume). Moreover, as the work of Walter Rodney (1972) has reflected, the economic development of European colonial powers was dependent upon the strategic underdevelopment, through the extraction of human and material resources, of the Global South.

Despite the extent to which unfree labour was a feature of the British Empire, narratives about its history during the period of British colonialism centre primarily on the enslavement of Africans and the subsequent abolition of both the trade in enslaved people (1807) and the use of enslaved labour (1833). Until relatively recently, Indian indenture (1834–1917), a system of unfree labour that followed slavery, has been absent from educational syllabuses, unrepresented in cultural institutions and unacknowledged in any formal way in British society.[1] This is remarkable given the amount of people, approximately 1.25 million in total, who were part of this coerced migration, which also included the transportation of people from China.

It could be argued that the obvious omission of indenture in national histories of empire was caused by the uncomfortable place that the system occupies in the British colonial project. The type of imperial triumphalism that was indulged in following the abolition of slavery, which in part continues today (see LeBaron and Bhagat, Chapter 11, this volume), would have been disrupted by any acknowledgement that following abolition, the British transported thousands of people from India and China to countries across its empire and, in the case of the Caribbean and Mauritius, did so specifically to mitigate the economic consequences of their loss of an enslaved labour source.[2] So successful was Indian indentured labour considered to be, that it was later implemented in South Africa in 1860, formalized in Malaysia in 1872, and in Fiji in 1879.

When historical narratives that centre on enslavement and indenture in the British Empire do materialize, they frequently present the two systems as consecutive. They represent indenture as a modified version of slavery in which Indian bonded labourers came to replace enslaved Africans in the Caribbean following the abolition of slavery in the 19th century. Looking at the history of enforced and coerced labour in the British Empire through this lens prevents a consideration of how widespread and consistent forms of unfree labour were in British colonial territories and how in contrast to the narrative that indenture was something that replaced slavery, we will see that it was a system that had been used before in British colonial history pre-dating the enslavement of Africans in British colonies in North America and in Barbados in the Caribbean, where White indentured labourers worked on tobacco and sugar plantations (Galenson 1981; Beckles 1989).

Decentring the Caribbean in relation to the history of enslavement and indenture fosters awareness of how far other forms of unfree labour, simultaneous with and consequent to abolition, took place in other parts of the British Empire. Moving beyond the enslavement of Africans and indenturing of Indians, Australia operated a system called 'blackbirding', which targeted the Indigenous people of the South Sea Islands in the 19th century, kidnapping them from their islands and forcing them to work on sugar plantations in Queensland (Sparrow 2022). In South Africa, Chinese indentured labourers were used as miners, working in perilous conditions in Witwatersrand between 1904 and 1910. Importantly, the use of Indian indentured labourers, across the British Empire between 1834 and 1917, did not originate in the Caribbean but in Mauritius, where successive European empires (Dutch, French, and then British) had created a plantation economy which like the Caribbean, was dependent upon unfree labour.

I have outlined how we might conceive of ideas around the 'start' and 'end' of systems of unfree labour as open to problematization. The notion that 'abolition' is a static and complete event is important when we consider the work of academics, in particular scholars of law, who have gone some way to showing how far the legal forms of enslavement and indenture feature in contemporary contracts pertaining to precarious workers. Diamond Ashiagbor (2021) has highlighted how these types of contract disproportionately affect racialized workers, making a direct link between the legal framework that controlled unfree labour and contemporary labour inequalities. Moving beyond the legal forms, sociologist Kamala Kempadoo (2017) has convincingly written about how we might usefully make connections between indentured labour as it operated in the British Empire, and some modern forms of human trafficking (see LeBaron and Bhagat, Chapter 11, this volume). Academic work like this has value in terms of demonstrating a troubling counter to notions of abolition, suggesting instead that systems of unfree labour and their legacies function on a continuum of reform and reinvention.

Making the distinction: bonded and enslaved labour

While discussing the histories of enslavement and indenture together, it is important, at the outset, to state that enslavement and the subsequent trade in African men, women, and children represented the most extreme manifestation of any system of unfree labour in the British Empire. What defined slavery as different from indenture was the presumption of the possession of another person, and any children they may have, as property. Where indenture involved an agreement to work for a specified time, usually in return for an outward voyage and lodging, and *could* feature coercion; enslavement was involuntary, interminable, and would tie generations to the same plantations without hope or expectation of freedom. It is indisputable that in the years of the British trade in enslaved persons, thousands of Africans died on the voyages from the coast of West Africa to British colonies in North America and the Caribbean. While we go on to examine the injustices inherent in the system of indenture, it must be stressed that the 'middle passage' and the extreme brutality of plantation life, as experienced by African enslaved people, was extraordinary in its size and its horror.

What is achieved by discussing both systems together, however, is that we can understand how expressly the dual forces of colonialism and capitalism depended on unfree labour that dehumanized successive racialized groups, to produce maximum profit with minimal labour costs. In addition, we can appreciate how far the notion of 'abolition' can continually be brought into question. While acknowledging the atrocity and duration of the British trade in enslaved people, as it relates to West Africa and the Caribbean, looking at the global history of the British in relation to unfree labour allows us to reject ideas that the African slave trade was an anomaly in the history of an otherwise benign colonial project. By taking an overview of the role that the British played in the development of systems of unfree labour, we can see that the extraction of labour in relation to the colonial project was analogous to its existence. The 'post' abolition enslavement of Pacific Islanders in the latter half of the 19th century and the carceral conditions experienced by Chinese indentured labourers in South Africa in the early 20th century are two examples of this (Huynh 2024).

Colonialism, land, and labour

It is impossible to separate European colonial projects from the plantation and, in the case of many former colonies, the sugar plantation in particular. In reference to the spread of Spanish colonialism across the Caribbean and the Americas, alongside the pursuit and theft of valuable metals such as gold and silver, existed an awareness of the value of the land and its agricultural potential (see Khoo, Chapter 3, this volume). The presumption of ownership over land extended, in the case of the Spanish Empire, to the presumption of the ownership of the labour of the people who inhabited that land. The question of how the labour of Indigenous people might be demanded 'legally' was manifested in the Spanish colonial system of '*encomienda*', a grant given by the Spanish Crown, to Spaniards in the Americas and the Philippines, permitting them the legal 'right' to demand the labour of the Indigenous communities of these regions (Higman 2011).

Returning to the rejection of the idea of abolition as a finalized act, the case of unfree labour in the Spanish Empire is an important example of how we might understand the idea of abolition as problematic. It is commonly understood that when the work of Bartolomé de las Casas (1484–1566) exposed the exploitative and oppressive treatment of Indigenous people under *encomiendas*, the perturbation this caused in Spain put an end to the system. In reality, each Spanish territory operated differently and *encomiendas* continued until the late 18th century. In addition, while the Spanish were debating the ills of enslaving a population that was already decimated by its encounter with European labour demands and diseases, they had already begun to use African enslaved labour in their colonies (Walvin 2022).

From the point that the British gained a foothold in North America and the Caribbean, there was an understanding that the riches of the Americas lay in the potential they offered for the growth of valuable plantation crops such as tobacco and sugar. Britain's relationship with the Americas, as with its other colonies, was one framed by the extraction of resources. From the quests for gold in the Guianas in the 16th century, to the 17th-century forging of plantations in North America and the Caribbean, British colonialism would forever change the lives and landscapes of the Indigenous communities who lived in these regions.

The labour that these British plantations would demand resulted in the enslavement and transportation of almost three and a half million men, women, and children, from Africa, in a trade in human lives that lasted from 1662 until 1807. When the use of enslaved labour was abolished in 1833, a powerful Caribbean plantocracy, desperate to maintain the profits it made from sugar and determined not to pay the emancipated fairly, tried African and Portuguese indentured labourers as replacements (Schuler 1980; Menezes 1992). In colonies like Trinidad and Guyana, where a liberated population were less reliant on sugar plantations for work and planters were more desperate to attract their labour, the colonists sought to copy existing systems in Mauritius and Réunion by bringing Indian indentured labourers to the region in 1838 (Guyana) and 1845 (Trinidad). Labouring on the same plantations, occupying meagre lodgings that had housed the enslaved before them, they inherited a plantation world shaped entirely by over 100 years of bondage.

European indentured labourers

In the introduction of indentured labourers into the Caribbean in the 19th century, Britain was revisiting a system that it had used almost 200 years earlier in its North American colonies and the Caribbean. The roots of unfree labour in the British Empire lie with the importation of White indentured servants to these places in the 17th century and pre-date the introduction of enslaved Africans. This early system of indenture is inseparable from the development of the plantation economy, specifically as it referred to tobacco (Virginia) and sugar (Barbados). Similarly, we cannot disconnect the arrival of indentured Europeans to the Americas from the development of later laws and contracts that were designed to extract the maximum labour from indentured individuals.

There is no doubt that the development of colonization and the growth of empire relied heavily on an increased acceptance of the concept of a racialized 'other' whose dehumanization justified his bondage or unfree state. It is also clear, however, as scholars such as Eric Williams and Hilary Beckles have shown, that European encounters in the colonies were informed by existing structures of serfdom. These involved wealthy landowners leasing hereditary plots of land to tenants, who in turn relied on that land and its cultivation for their existence. Systems of unfree labour were not born in the Americas, either in the case of Britain or other European colonists. However, that they became influenced by developing ideas about racial and religious hierarches is seen in the origins of the *encomienda* system, which, although operated by the Spanish in the Americas, had its origins in Spain during the period of the *Reconquista*, when Muslim and Jewish landowners were compelled to pay tributes to those 'gifted' their land as thanks from the Spanish Crown, for their part in the reconquering project.

What is clear in relation to the entrance of European indentured labourers to Barbados is that there was never a distinct plan to operate a system of White indentured servitude in the island. Historian Hilary Beckles, however, stresses how crucial to the early life of the colony this community were, emphasizing that following a period where private individuals recruited for their own interests, in later years the state became heavily involved with the indenture system, providing the legal and administrative network necessary for its operation (1989: 39). As with Indian indenture, the interests of the planters became intertwined with the interests of the colonial state, preparing the way for legislation and governance that was dominated by the control of unfree labour. Crucially, in line with later forms of unfree labour, and in particular indenture, we are also able to understand the significant part that coercion and force played in this early system of servitude. In response to demands for more labour, convicts were shipped to Barbados following legislation that allowed transportation as a sentence of the court (Beckles 1989: 56).

There is no doubt that White servitude in the Caribbean featured the worst elements of indenture systems. The indentured, although locked into time-bound agreements of three to five years, which limited their obligation to their employer, were treated as the property of their master passing from owner to owner and being appraised as part of an estate after a master's death. As with enslavement and the later Indian indenture system, White indentured servants were involved in resistance movements, and their discarding in favour of a workforce that the White plantocracy found it easier to dehumanize configures them as part of a chain of disposable plantation labour consumed by 'King Sugar'.

Resistance to African enslavement in the British Empire: the Demerara Uprising

Consistently, every form of unfree labour in the British Empire was subject to the resistance of those from whom it tried to extract that labour. Whether it was the White indentured labourers of Barbados plotting armed revolts (Beckles 1989: 172), or blackbirded South Sea Islanders organizing collectively against their deportation as a result of the 1901 Immigration Restriction Act (Australian National Maritime Museum 2025).[3] In the UK, comparatively little is known about the considerable challenges to colonial rule that unfree labourers presented in various European colonies. The recent bicentenary of the Demerara Uprising (1823) brought more attention to the role of resistance in the period of slavery in the Anglophone Caribbean.[4] Yet a significant event like the Berbice Slave Rebellion of 1763, which also took place in Guyana, then under Dutch rule, came close to ending slavery almost three decades before the Haitian Revolution and is largely unknown beyond Guyana where a statue of the uprising's leader, 'Cuffy' (Kofi), commemorates this crucial moment in national history (Kars 2020).

The Demerara Uprising of 1823 offers a window through which we might consider how dramatically the professed objectives of empire differed from its actions. During the 1823 uprising, thousands of enslaved workers across plantations on the east coast of Demerara took control of the area demanding their freedom. In response to an uprising that involved minimal violence on the part of the enslaved, who were more concerned with gaining strategic control of their enslavers rather than bloody revenge, the colonists, once they had quelled the uprising, tortured and hung hundreds of those involved. In addition, an English missionary, John Smith, was sentenced to death by court martial despite his very tenuous links to events.[5] Ultimately saved by a reprieve following pressure in England, Smith died in jail before this news reached Guyana.

The Demerara Uprising reveals the extreme contradictions inherent in empire, which on the one hand professed a mission of enlightenment and Christianity, constructing its subjects as barbarous 'others' in need of both elements, and, on the other, consistently demonstrated practices that revealed itself to be operating solely in advancement of its mercantile interests, employing unspeakable violence when control of these interests was challenged. Like many non-conformist missionaries, Smith's presence in the Caribbean was a source of tension because this group were connected to the abolitionist movement. Upon meeting the governor for the first time, Smith was told that if he taught any of the enslaved to read, which was his stated intention, he would be thrown out of the colony.

We have considered here the significance of two major uprisings in the history of the former British sugar colony of Guyana, albeit one of which occurred under Dutch rule. There is a wider point to be made here concerning the extent of such uprisings and their frequency across the Anglophone Caribbean, in relation to how these events challenge public perceptions of the period of enslavement. A leader in the international campaign for reparations for Caribbean enslavement, Hilary Beckles has usefully contested the idea of the period of African enslavement in the Caribbean as a site dependent upon White abolitionist action by referring to this period as a '200 Years' War' (Beckles 1991: 363). As James Walvin has said of this period, it is as much a history of resistance as it is of enslavement (1996: 117).

Resistance: the rule of law

While there is no sense in which the level of resistance offered by anti-slavery activists ever met those of the enslaved, it is important to recognize the role White abolitionists and other colonial figures played at crucial points within both systems of indenture and enslavement. Their use of the legal system to agitate for rights for the enslaved or the indentured showed the rule of law had limited application in the case of colonial, racialized subjects. In *Black Ivory*, James Walvin refers to early abolitionist Granville Sharp's (1736–1813) attempt to try the crew of the ship *Zong* in a criminal court for the murder of the enslaved Africans, who were thrown overboard to secure an insurance payment for 'lost cargo'. Walvin cites this case as an important moment in the British anti-slavery movement, emphasizing that the entire system rested on the acceptance of the enslaved person as 'property'. This public questioning of the status of the enslaved as 'chattel', as proposed by Sharp, Walvin interprets as 'the first tug which would unravel the entire garment of the slave system' (2001: 17).

The conflict between the rule of law and the management of unfree labour was a preoccupation during the period of indenture also. For it to be able to continue to the satisfaction of the planters, the system of indenture demanded that labour offences, civil in nature, be treated as criminal. As legal scholar Tayyab Mahmud (2013: 234) points out, this was a contradiction in the legal form itself and its end result was that vulnerable labourers, those that were sick or pregnant, were frequently sent to prison for 'absenteeism'.

It is unsurprising then that one of the most powerful criticisms of this aspect of indenture came from a stipendiary magistrate named George Des Voeux (1834–1909), who triggered the first inquiry into indenture in the Caribbean and reawakened the interest (albeit temporarily) of the Anti-Slavery Society, who had all but accepted the indenture system after an early intervention in its first years (Scoble 1840). Des Voeux wrote a letter to the Colonial Secretary State in 1869 listing the faults within what he deemed to be a justice system entrenched in bias, that failed to protect the Indian indentured labourer. One of his concerns was the lack of impartiality in the colonial justice system, as magistrates trying cases against planters would typically be accommodated in the home of the same plantation owner (Parliamentary Papers

1871). Legal scholar, John McLaren, has written extensively about the conflicted lives of colonial judges. Recounting the experience of Joseph Beaumont (1829–1885), who was Chief Justice of Guyana during Des Voeux's time in the colony, and John Gorrie (1829–1892), who was a judge in Mauritius and a Chief Justice in both Fiji and Trinidad, he reflects on how both men had limited power to affect the mistreatment of Indian indentured labourers, stressing that 'the deployment of the rule of law' would always be compromised in 'multiracial colonial possessions' for 'the governor's vision of what was good for the colony' (McLaren 2011: 272).

Indian indentured labour in the British Empire

From the slow march of the abolition of the slave trade in 1807 to the abolition of the use of enslaved labour in 1833, Caribbean plantocracies began to entertain the idea of reviving an indenture-like system that would provide an uninterrupted source of cheap labour. Once legitimized it was an incredible force that, though hampered by resistance, thundered successfully on for decades and was arguably only stopped in its tracks by the growth in the production of beet sugar.

Beyond the Caribbean and Mauritius, Indians were also taken as indentured labourers to East Africa to build the Kenya–Uganda railway and a system similar to indenture, the *Kangani* system, was responsible for the transportation of Indians from the south of India to Sri Lanka. The main plantation crop produced by Indian indentured labourers was sugar, however they were also involved in the manufacture of cocoa (Trinidad), rubber (Malaysia), and tea and coffee (Sri Lanka). While the British used indentured labour in their own colonies, they also facilitated the use of indentured labourers in other European colonies by permitting the Dutch and French to operate depots in India that allowed them to transport Indian indentured labourers to places like Guadeloupe and Martinique (France) and Surinam (the Netherlands).

Indian indentured labourers were largely recruited from Uttar Pradesh and Bihar. Some colonies favoured labour from the south of India and others only recruited from there intermittently. In the Caribbean, stereotypes about South Indian labourers charged that they were less easy to control and only a minority were ever indentured there. Overwhelmingly, Indian indentured labourers were agricultural workers recruited for their capacity to perform this labour, but this was never the only case. In Guyana, a Bengali man named Bechu, the only Indian indentured labourer to testify in front of the Royal Commission into the sugar industry in 1898, described his working life in service to colonial figures, prior to recruitment through the indenture system (Seecharan 1999). Usually bound to work for a period of three to five years, workers would then be given the option to re-indenture or perform a period of industrial residence, after which they would qualify for a return voyage to India. Most Indian indentured labourers chose not to return and remained in the colonies to which they had been sent, largely remaining in employment that was tied to the plantation.

When looking for archival evidence that would show what was 'wrong' with the system of Indian indenture, it is the moments of resistance, when indentured labourers or colonial authorities pushed back against the system, that point us to the flaws. From the very beginning of the system of indenture, stories of kidnapping, sexual assault, and the physical abuse of indentured labourers abounded. Inquiries in India about the treatment of indentured labourers in Mauritius temporarily halted the system (Parliamentary Papers 1841). The additional intervention of the Anti-Slavery Society provided a powerful challenge to the system (Scoble 1840). Moreover, in the opening decade of the 20th century, this resistance was reinforced by the efforts of the Indian nationalist movement who argued that the treatment of Indian labourers overseas was indicative of the disdain that the British held for the country and its people. Campaigns discouraging potential indentured labourers were carried out in typical recruitment areas.

Like enslavement, indenture was the subject of sustained resistance from indentured labourers. It is crucial that indenture be examined in its own context and its own particular set of circumstances. This would enable us to understand that indenture was neither a 'new' system of slavery nor a modified version of slavery. Such interpretations occlude the fact that indenture was a system in motion, continually changing and developing in response to resistance from the indentured and reforms demanded by the colonial Indian government.

Conclusion

In this chapter, we have considered how enslavement and indenture were key features of British colonialism. We have additionally explored some of the reasons why the system of Indian indenture is not more widely known, emphasizing its reach beyond the Caribbean and the extent to which it troubles the idea of 'abolition'. We have also considered how contemporary scholarship in the fields of law and sociology have shown us how we live with the legacies of unfree labour. We have seen, for example, that scholars of law are seeking to draw attention to the ways in which the legal forms of slavery and indenture persist in contracts governing labour, disproportionately affecting racialized workers.

Notes

[1] The BBC Bitesize website, a resource designed to help secondary school students with private study, now features a short section on indenture. This suggests that teachers are introducing the topic as a non-statutory part of teaching on the British Empire. In addition, cultural institutions and archives such as the British Library, Victoria and Albert Museum, National Archives, and Museum of London have recently featured website articles, displays, and events that engage with the literary or artistic output of descendants of indenture. It must be stressed, however, that these are minor in nature and no permanent exhibition acknowledging the system of Indian indenture exists in the UK.
[2] Around 18,000 Chinese indentured labourers were taken to British Caribbean colonies in the 19th century.
[3] This act is also referred to as the White Australia Policy.
[4] Writer Thomas Harding (2022) attempted to bring this story to popular view with his account of the uprising, *White Debt: The Demerara Uprising and Britain's Legacy of Slavery*.
[5] One of the leaders of the action was a deacon in Smith's chapel.

References

Ashiagbor, D. 2021. 'Race and Colonialism in the Construction of Labour Markets and Precarity', *Industrial Law Journal* 50(4): 506–531.

Australian National Maritime Museum. 2025. *Blackbirding: Australia's Slave Trade?* https://www.sea.museum/en/first-nations/blackbirding-australias-slave-trade

Beckles, H.M. 1989. *White Servitude and Black Slavery in Barbados, 1627–1715.* University of Tennessee Press.

Beckles, H.M. 1991. 'Caribbean Anti-Slavery: The Self-Liberation Ethos of Enslaved Blacks', in H. Beckles and V. Shepherd, *Caribbean Slave Society and Economy: A Student Reader.* Ian Randle Publishers, pp 363–372.

Galenson, D.W. 1981. *White Servitude in Colonial America: An Economic Analysis.* Cambridge University Press.

Harding, T. 2022. *White Debt: The Demerara Uprising and Britain's Legacy of Slavery.* Weidenfeld and Nicolson

Higman, B.W. 2011. *A Concise History of the Caribbean.* Cambridge University Press.

Huynh, T. 2024. 'From South Africa to the World: The Political and Legal Legacies of Chinese Indenture in the Transvaal', *Slavery & Abolition* 45(3): 461–480.

Kars, M. 2020. *Blood on the River: A Chronicle of Mutiny and Freedom on the Wild Coast.* Profile Books.

Kempadoo, K. 2017. '"Bound Coolies" and Other Indentured Workers in the Caribbean: Implications for Debates about Human Trafficking and Modern Slavery', *Anti-Trafficking Review* 9: 48–63.

Mahmud, T. 2013. 'Cheaper Than a Slave: Indentured Labour, Colonialism and Capitalism', *Whittier Law Review* 34: 215–243.

McLaren, J. 2011. *Dewigged, Bothered and Bewildered: British Colonial Judges on Trial, 1800–1900.* University of Toronto Press.

Menezes, M.N. 1992. *The Portuguese of Guyana: A Study in Culture and Conflict.* William Goodenough House.

Parliamentary Papers. 1841. Vol. XVI, Report of the Committee Appointed to Inquire Respecting the Exportation of Hill Coolies.

Parliamentary Papers. 1871. Vol. XX, William Des Voeux to Earl Granville, 25 December 1869, pp 1–14.

Rodney, W. 1972. *How Europe Underdeveloped Africa.* Bogle L'Ouverture Press.

Schuler, M. 1980. *'Alas, Alas, Kongo': A Social History of Indentured African Immigration into Jamaica, 1841–1865.* Johns Hopkins University Press.

Scoble, J. 1840. *Hill Coolies: A Brief Exposure of the Hill Coolies in Mauritius and British Guiana and of the Nefarious Means by Which They Were Induced to Resort to These Colonies.* Harvey and Darton.

Seecharan, C. 1999. *Bechu: 'Bound Coolie' Radical in British Guiana, 1894–1901.* UWI.

Sparrow, J. 2022. 'A Slave State: How Blackbirding in Colonial Australia Created a Legacy of Racism', *The Conversation.* https://theconversation.com/friday-essay-a-slave-state-how-blackbirding-in-colonial-australia-created-a-legacy-of-racism-187782

Walvin, J. 1996. *Questioning Slavery.* Routledge.

Walvin, J. 2001. *Black Ivory: Slavery in the British Empire.* Blackwell Publishing.

Walvin, J. 2022. *A World Transformed: Slavery in the Americas and the Origins of Global Power.* Robinson.

Williams, E. 2005. *Capitalism and Slavery.* Ian Randle Publishers.

Video lecture

Kaladeen, M. 2021. *Indian Indenture in the British Empire*, Connected Sociologies Curriculum Project. https://thesociologicalreview.org/projects/connected-sociologies/curriculum/mmw/indenture-and-indian-ocean-world/

QUESTIONS

1. How do systems of unfree labour like indenture problematize our understanding of the abolition of the use of enslaved labour?

2. How does the resistance of the indentured shape our understanding of this system?

3. In what ways do we live with the legacies of unfree labour in our contemporary world?

Worksheet 4. Enslavement, Indenture, and Resistance in the British Empire

This worksheet is designed to support AS and A-level teaching on social differentiation, power and stratification, globalization and global development, and sociological theory and methods. In this talk, Maria del Pilar Kaladeen outlines the system of indenture, whereby two million men, women and children were taken from India to labour on sugar colonies across the British Empire between 1834 to 1920, the majority never returning to India. This talk connects with other topics in detailing the 'hidden histories' underlying the making of the modern world, and expressing the importance of recovering these silenced perspectives. By exploring the history of indenture and its contemporary legacies, this worksheet aids students' critical thinking around ideas of sociological consensus and conflict, concepts of modernity, and debates surrounding subjectivity and objectivity. In its focus on British colonial history and its legacies, this worksheet may also be helpful to students studying relevant modules in A-level History.

Time	Activity	Explanation
00.00–00.05	To warm up, answer this question: *What do you think are the characteristics of unfree labour?*	This activity introduces students to a central theme of the talk and may work well as a group discussion or a partner activity.
00.05–00.10	Recap of understandings of globalization and global development.	It may be useful to remind students of some of the key concepts and terms related to globalization and global development.
00.10–00.15	Watch the talk from 0:00 to 1:37. *What is indenture?*	Kaladeen explains that the system of indenture, which lasted from 1834 to 1920, brought over two million men, women, and children from India to other parts of the British empire to work on sugar, rubber, tea, and cocoa plantations. Indentured labourers, she explains, would typically agree to work for periods of 3–5 years and terms would usually include provision for a return passage, though most did not return. By ensuring that students understand the definition and context of indentured labour, this activity sets them up well for understanding and completing subsequent activities.
00.15–00.25	Watch the talk from 1:37 to 2:11. *What is the concept of Jahaji Bhai? What is the significance of this collective?*	Kaladeen explains that Jahaji Bhai is a term meaning 'the brotherhood of the boat', which describes familial connections between immigrants who made the crossing from India to the countries in which they would become indentured labourers. This activity encourages students to start thinking about the legacies of indentured labour, within the context of what Kaladeen calls 'the Indian indentured labour diaspora'. Students may make connections between this concept and the ideas expressed in the talk on 'Diaspora'.

Time	Activity	Explanation
00.25–00.35	Watch the talk from 2:12 to 3:18. *What makes the history of indenture a 'hidden history'? What might be the reason for this silence?*	Kaladeen argues that the history of indenture sits uncomfortably alongside preferred representations of the history of abolition. Asking students to think about how narratives of modernity are constructed and what may be omitted from these histories relates to central topics within A-level Sociology theories and methods: debates about subjectivity and objectivity, and ideas of consensus and conflict over social theories. In contemplating these ideas, students may draw connections between the 'hidden history' of indenture and the 'silences of history' spoken about in the talk on 'The Haitian Revolution'.
00.35–00.45	Watch the talk from 4:53 to 5:52. *Why is it important to pay attention to the difference between how historians write about indenture and how people experienced it?*	Leading on from the questions above, this activity asks students to delve further into debates over sociological subjectivity and objectivity, and the nature of 'social facts'. These are core topics within the A-level Sociology curriculum. To help with answering these questions, a brief recap of the use of oral histories and lived experience in sociological and historical research might be useful.
00.45–00.55	At 7:50 Kaladeen says that 'the indentured did not passively experience the system and its injustices, and the ways in which they chose to fight back ranged from individual to community acts of resistance'. *What is the significance of efforts to organize against and resist the system of indenture?*	This activity prompts students to grapple with ideas of consensus and conflict in relation to sociological and historical issues, which are key themes within the A-level Sociology curriculum. Leading on from previous activities, students are asked to develop their critical thinking skills in considering the constructed nature of narratives of modernity, and the problematic nature of these representations. This section has strong links to 'The Haitian Revolution' talk, which could provide a useful point of comparison.
00.55–01.00	Watch the talk from 10:17 to 12:17. *How can literature contribute to the recovery of 'hidden histories'?*	Kaladeen argues that literature written by descendants of indentured labourers can constitute a form of resistance to indenture by challenging the dehumanizing language and narratives in colonial representations of this period. This activity encourages students to apply what they have learned in this talk to think about how interdisciplinary connections between sociology and arts and humanities subjects could contribute to the recovery of 'hidden histories', drawing on a central theme across many of the talks of hidden and silenced historical perspectives.

This worksheet was developed by Isabel Sykes.

5

Enclosures and the Making of Modern Britain

Imogen Tyler

Objectives

- This chapter asks why the English enclosure movement has been considered in isolation from colonial enclosures.

- It offers a brief history of land enclosures in England and outlines the standard account of their role in the making of modern Britain.

- It troubles this account by examining the entangled relationship between domestic and colonial enclosures.

- It considers how resituating domestic enclosures in a wider context enriches our understandings of the making of Britain.

- It asks how this more expansive account might deepen social scientific understandings of ongoing forms of global capitalist enclosure.

Introduction

The English enclosure movement involved the privatization of common land which rural peasants had previously had the right to use and access. Land enclosures began in the 13th century but were at their most intensive between 1750 and 1850, when enclosures by Act of Parliament (Inclosure Acts) saw a quarter of common land transformed into exclusive property of wealthy landowners. Standard social scientific accounts of the English enclosure movement posit that this systemic transfer of land into private ownership fatally eroded rural subsistence economies, and in so doing facilitated the industrial revolution that transformed Britain into (the world's first) modern capitalist state. As Karl Marx famously argued in *Capital*, 'agricultural people [were] first forcibly expropriated from the soil, driven from their homes, turned into vagabonds, and then whipped, branded, tortured by laws grotesquely terrible, into the discipline necessary for the wage system' (1887: 117).

What is omitted from this standard account is that when land enclosures were at their height, Britain became the world's largest colonial power. While the English enclosures involved what Marx described as 'the systematic robbery' of land from rural peasants, British colonial conquest involved land theft and the dispossession of Indigenous peoples on a staggering global scale. This chapter challenges the artificial separation of domestic and colonial land enclosures. It begins by detailing the history of land enclosures in England and then outlines E.P. Thompson's account of how enclosures facilitated the industrial revolution. It argues that this account fails to consider how practices and policies of domestic land enclosure were inspired, justified, and funded by British colonial expansion (and vice versa). Finally, it illustrates some of these connections through the case of British slave-trading dynasty, the Hindes, who invested their profits from colonial slavery in land, farms, country estates, and textile mills in north-west England.

The central argument of this chapter is that modern Britain was forged through *a colonial enclosure movement* that involved the theft of land, the installation of monoculture agricultural systems, and the exploitation of enslaved people on plantations and waged workers in connected factory systems across the British imperial world. The chapter ends by asking how reframing the English enclosure story within the context of British colonialism might sharpen our comprehension of ongoing state and corporate practices of capitalist enclosure in the contemporary world.

Additional note: Wales, Scotland, and Ireland

As this chapter is concerned with troubling the standard account, it focuses on the English enclosures, however the same privatization of common land took place in Wales, which was fully incorporated into English legal systems by the 16th century. The unification of England and Scotland in 1707 saw the formation of *the Kingdom of Great Britain*, and while Scotland continued to operate under a different legal system, there are significant parallels between land enclosures in England and Scotland. For example, Scottish peasants experienced a similar loss of common land (notably grazing rights) and the Scottish clearances (1750–1860) saw the mass eviction of tenants (crofters), primarily so that landowners (clan chiefs and/or British aristocrats) could introduce large-scale sheep farming.

During the period that is the primary focus of this chapter, Ireland (Eire) was under English (later British) colonial rule. From the 16th century onwards, land was confiscated from the Indigenous Irish population by British settlers. This land theft was a contributory factor in the Irish Famine (1846–1852) that killed over one million people and led to the mass emigration of Irish peasants to England and North America. While the significance of this history is beyond the scope of this chapter, it is important to highlight that by 1850 around 25 per cent of the population of Lancashire, the heartland of British industrial revolution, were Irish-born, and that many of these migrants lived and worked in often appalling conditions in Lancashire mill towns.

In short, connected forms of *British* elite-led land enclosures, dispossession, forced and coerced migration, and labour exploitation can be traced within the different regions and land masses that today comprise the United Kingdom of Great Britain and Northern Ireland, as well as within the colonized territories that formerly constituted the British Empire.

The standard account of the English enclosures

In medieval England most rural communities were governed by manorial lords. While lords and manorial courts ruled over the land, rural peasants held customary rights to use and to access cultivated common land and uncultivated 'waste land' (such as marsh land or upland moors). What these rights entailed differed from place to place, but often included rights to farm strips of land in designated open fields and/or rights to use the waste land to graze animals. These land-use rights were not evenly distributed. For example, a tenant smallholder (a small-scale farmer who paid rent to the manor) would have different land-use rights from a village-based family of weavers, who might have access to a plot of land to grow vegetables and access to uncultivated land to graze animals, gather wood, and dig turf for fuel. In return for their 'common rights', peasants often undertook seasonal work for the manor and/or paid tithes (local taxation, often paid as a percentage of the crops or other goods produced).

Enclosure usually involved parcelling together smaller plots of land, a practice known as engrossing, to create larger holdings. The enclosed land was marked out and secured with ditches, fences, hedges, or stone walls. The engrossing of land into large farms and estates enabled landowners to introduce new methods of agricultural production (such as crop rotation) so they could produce greater yields of cash crops (such as grains), and/or it enabled them to turn land into large grazing pastures for sheep (wool was a profitable commodity). In some cases, landed elites simply wanted to stop peasants using, accessing, or living on the land so they could create private parks and hunting estates.

Enclosures always involved the revocation of the rights of commoners. In short, by enclosing land, elites obtained exclusive land-use rights. This marked a fundamental shift in the meaning of land, from a 'commonwealth' whose bounty belonged, if only in a limited sense, to the whole community, to land as property (a private asset). The motivation behind enclosures was economic, landed elites could hoard the profits from agricultural production for themselves, increase rents, and sell land on at inflated prices – a process of privatization and extraction which contemporary economists call '*assetization*'.

Numerous methods (legal and illegal) were employed to get people off the land. For example, landowners evicted tenants from cottages and smallholdings (which might have been in families for generations) or they employed nefarious practices such as introducing deer onto land to destroy commoners' crops. Once land was enclosed, farmers and gamekeepers policed the new boundaries and prosecuted people caught trespassing. Enclosures were enforced through social and political oppression. Landowners controlled local government and administrated systems of crime and punishment. Only landowners could elect members of parliament, who duly passed laws that enforced and protected these new property rights. For example, in 1723, parliament passed the 'Black Act' that made trespassing on private land, poaching for fish, cattle, deer, hares, and rabbits, and even cutting down trees or damaging orchards, crimes punishable by death.

Enclosures made rural peasants vulnerable to the whims of the landowners. In periods when there was no paid agricultural work available, they faced homelessness and hunger. As poet Robert Crowley reflected after the 1549 Kett's Rebellion, a peasant uprising against land enclosures in Norfolk:

> If I should demand of the poor man of the country what thing he thinks to be the cause of Sedition, I know his answer. He would tell me that the great farmers, the graziers, the rich butchers, the men of law, the merchants, the gentlemen, the knights, the lords. ... Men without conscience. Men utterly devoid of God's fear. ... Men that would have all in their own hands; men that would leave nothing for others; men ... that be never satisfied. Cormorants, greedy gulls; yea, men that would eat up men, women, & children, are the causes of Sedition! They take our houses over our heads, they buy our lands out of our hands, they raise our rents, they levy great (yea unreasonable) fines, they enclose our commons! (Crowley 1872 [1550]: 132–133)

Because peasants' land-use rights were often customary – based in tradition and established through practice as opposed to legally codified – they had few ways of contesting enclosures. Despite this, resistance was often fierce. For example, in the 17th century, groups called Diggers and Levellers (so named because their protests included digging up the new hedges/fences and levelling ditches) organized protests and riots, printed anti-enclosure tracts, and petitioned King and parliament.

The Midland Revolts (1607) were a series of uprisings in Northamptonshire, Leicestershire, and Warwickshire, against the enclosure of common land for sheep pastures. The Diggers of Warwickshire described the landowners as '[e]ncroaching tyrants who grind the poor on the whetstone of poverty so they may dwell themselves in their herds of fatt weathers [sheep] ... only for their own private gain ... they have depopulated and overthrown whole towns and made thereof sheep pastures, nothing profitable for our commonwealth' (1607). These uprisings culminated in the Newton Rebellion, which saw a thousand displaced peasants squatting on newly enclosed land. King James I tasked an aristocratic landowner (Sir Edward Montagu) with quashing the rebellion. Around 50 people were killed, and the ringleaders tortured and executed, their dismembered bodies paraded around towns and villages to deter others. The Midland Revolts were a highly significant moment in English history, when common people engaged in armed conflict over land rights. They are also a reminder of the violence that the ruling classes were willing to employ to appropriate common land.

The English enclosures and the making of the working class

The impact of enclosures has been vigorously debated by historians. Some argue that they led to an increase in agricultural productivity that helped feed Britain's growing population, others that they brought few if any benefits, except to rapacious landowners, who were greatly enriched. The socialist historian E.P. Thompson concluded that the English enclosures were 'a plain enough case of class robbery, played according to … rules of property and law laid down by a Parliament of property-owners and lawyers' (1963: 218). Thompson's book, *The Making of the Working Class in England* (1963), formed the basis of many subsequent accounts of the role of enclosures in facilitating the industrial revolution and transforming Britain into a modern capitalist state.

In 1773, parliament streamlined the process through which landowners could apply to enclose land, and Thompson focuses on the period 1780–1832 when parliamentary enclosures were at their height. Thompson examines how arguments for agricultural efficiency and productivity were used by the elites to justify the privatization of common land. Advocates for enclosure claimed that common land was badly managed, and that uncultivated waste lands were unutilized 'empty spaces'. The economic case for enclosures was supported by moral arguments that painted rural peasants as lazy, uncivilized, and unruly. For example, the influential agricultural writer, Arthur Young, described the commons as a 'breeding-ground "for barbarians … nursing up a mischievous race of people"' (cited in Thompson 1963: 219). In short, 'enclosure propagandists' argued that revoking commoners' rights would not only improve the land but would 'improve' rural people, forcing them to become more industrious, disciplined, and law-abiding (Thompson 1963: 217).

Thompson argues that the theft of common land fatally undermined the capacity of rural peasants to maintain an independent means of subsistence. Landless labourers became caught in cycles of precarious work and poverty, and many became dependent on parish relief (local welfare paid for by taxes levied on property owners). Laws were also passed (for example, the Combination Acts) that made it a criminal offence for labourers to organize for higher wages and/or better working conditions.

The question of what to do about the rising cost of supporting 'paupers' (a stigmatizing term meaning people without the means to sustain themselves) became central to national political debate. A 'long war of attrition … on the right of poor-relief' began (Thompson 1963: 222) with new laws introduced (for example, the Poor Relief Act 1722) that deterred people from applying to the parish for assistance, by, for example, forcing people into workhouses and/or making them undertake hard labour. Rules of settlement meant pauperized rural labourers risked losing their rights to poor relief if they left one area to seek work elsewhere. Despite this, Thompson concludes that the combined effects of enclosures, the erosion of rights to poor relief, and punitive laws, led to waves of migration 'from village to town, and county to county' (1963: 224), as English agricultural labourers and cottage-based weavers joined the stream of Irish migrants into manufacturing towns. In this way, land enclosures were formative in the industrial revolution.

The Making of the English Working Class documents how working people resisted both land enclosures and their exploitation in the new industries, such as mines and textile factories. Diggers and Levellers were succeeded by Luddites who set about destroying the new industrial machines that threatened their livelihoods, such as threshing machines (for example, the Swing Riots of 1830) and steam-powered factory looms (for example, the Power Loom Riots of 1828). Thompson argues that working people became increasingly conscious of the ways in which their interests were opposed to those of the propertied classes, and the grievances of distinct groups shaped a new working-class consciousness. Working-class political organizing – for example, unionization and struggles for voting rights – led to democratic reforms offering some protections against the extractive practices of the ruling elites.

However, Thompson's account of the formative role of the English enclosure movement in the making of modern Britain excludes vital connections between domestic enclosures and British colonial conquest that saw huge tracts of land in the Caribbean and Americas, the Indian subcontinent, Australasia, and Africa stolen from Indigenous peoples, surveyed, parcelled up, fenced in, and sold into British hands. By the end of the 19th century the British 'owned' over one-quarter of the planet's land mass and exercised control over 400 million people. In short, the standard English enclosure story is a provincial story that obscures *colonial enclosures*.

Making connections between domestic and colonial enclosures

There are multiple ways to make connections between domestic and colonial enclosures. For example, Carl Griffin (2023) highlights the 'bi-directional flow' of colonial thinking, policies, and practices in the language used by advocates for English enclosures. While colonialism is ordinarily understood as *external* to the colonizing state, Griffin demonstrates that the English enclosures were conceived as a form of *internal colonization*. We can also consider how domestic enclosures led to the emigrations from the British Isles to colonized lands. For example, the dispossessed English, Welsh, and Scottish peasants who emigrated (sometimes voluntarily, sometimes under force), to work as indentured servants, labourers and/or became settler colonialists in British colonies. Clare Anderson (2022) has examined the role of 'punitive mobility' in settler colonial expansion, a history that includes 50,000 convicts transported as indentured labour to Britain's North American colonies (across the 18th century) and the 160,000 convicts transported to Australia between 1787 and 1868 (see Kaladeen, Chapter 4, this volume).

Another way to reveal these connections is by 'following the money'. For example, we can track the sources of the wealth that the elites used to privatize land in England (see Higgins, Chapter 12, this volume). In *The Book of Trespass*, Nick Hayes (2020) offers examples of East India Company men made rich through the colonial plunder of the Indian subcontinent, and British Caribbean plantation owners made wealthy through the forced labour of enslaved Africans who on their return 'stormed the English countryside like lottery winners', enclosing land and developing vast country estates (2020: 105). This brings us to perhaps the gravest omission from the standard account, the relationship between the English enclosures, British colonial slavery, and the expansion of the British-Caribbean plantation system.

Britain's Caribbean plantations were developed on land stolen by British (and other European) colonizers from Indigenous populations, who were either killed, captured as slave labour, and/or killed by imported diseases. This land was surveyed, parcelled up, and sold to British settlers. New systems of labour-intensive, monocultural agricultural production met European consumer demands for tropical produce (for example, sugar), provided raw materials for textile and manufacturing industries (for example, cotton), and created profitable new markets for British exports.

One of England's first Caribbean colonies was Barbados. Settled in 1627, it would remain a British colony until 1966. A 1657 map of Barbados (Figure 5.1) reveals the names of the English men who have enclosed land for plantations. At the top of the map, two escaped Africans are being hunted down by an armed English colonist on horseback. England (later Britain) rapidly expanded its Caribbean colonial possessions, and it was the 3.4 million Africans trafficked across the Atlantic on British slave-ships (1640–1807) that provided the labour force that enabled British settlers to clear and cultivate the land.

Historians such as Catherine Hall (2024) have detailed how British plantation societies were grounded in the violent, racist subjugation of Africans. As Trevor Burnard states, enslaved Africans 'worked in the killing fields of … plantations where they worked harder than any other group of people in the eighteenth century and for less rewards … starved, brutalized, and traumatized … [while] their owners became some of the richest people in the British Empire' (2023: 396).

The British slave trade and the British-Caribbean plantation system peaked between 1740 and 1807, and as Eric Williams argued in *Capitalism and Slavery* (1944), by 1750 every trading and manufacturing town in England had connections to the slavery business (see Berg and Hudson 2023). The profits amassed by slave-traders, merchants,

Figure 5.1: 'A topographicall Description and Admeasurement of the Yland of Barbados in the West Indyaes', Richard Ligon, 1657

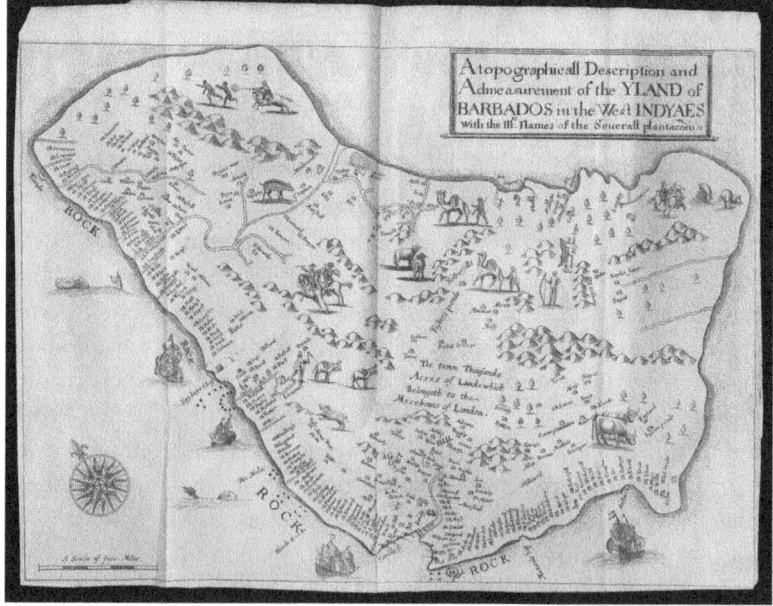

Source: Newberry Library, Edward E. Ayer Collection, Ayer 1000.5 .B22 L7 1657 https://collections.newberry.org/asset-management/2KXJ8ZWQKT_W

planters, and financial speculators flowed back into Britain and was an important source of the wealth that financed land enclosures and the physical infrastructure of the industrial revolution: for example, the mills, factories, mines, canals, and roads (see Gilbert, Chapter 2, this volume).

In short, both domestic and colonial land enclosures were underpinned, at least in part, by *the enslavement* of African men, women, and children, and their violent transformation into the object-assets of British slave-owners. And the technological advancements, and the systems of management and finance (banking, mortgages, loans, insurance) innovated through 'the slavery business' (Hall 2020), were the blueprint for the development of capitalist systems of agriculture and industrial development domestically and across the modern world.

Case study: the Lancaster Hinde family

In the 18th century the colonial port town of Lancaster in north-west England was the fourth-largest slave-trading port in Britain. While it would soon rapidly be eclipsed by Liverpool (60 miles further south), for over a hundred years Lancaster families were enriched through the slavery business. No family better illustrates this than the Hindes, whose careers as slave-traders and colonial merchants from the mid-1700s until abolition in 1807, and as mill-owners (from 1796), local politicians, and members of the Lancashire judiciary, saw them rise from middling farmers into the ranks of landed gentry.

At the head of this family was Thomas Hinde (1720–1798), fourth child of a farmer who (likely) served an apprenticeship on Lancaster ships before becoming one of the town's first slave-ship captains. Thomas Hinde's career as a slave-trader would span 40 years, during which time he invested in at least 34 slaving voyages to West-Africa. One of his early business partners was fellow Lancastrian Miles Barber (1733–1786+), who developed a large complex of slave barracoons and slave factories, headquartered at 'Factory Island' on the Iles de Los off the coast of Guinea, which supplied captured Africans to British slave ships.

Thomas Hinde's sons, Thomas (1757–1829), John (1762–1810), William (1773–1834), and Samuel (1778–1840) and his nephew, Joshua (1761–1825), all joined the family slavery business. Thomas, William, and Samuel became major slave-ship owners and investors (operating out of Liverpool), while John was sent to Jamaica where he was a Kingston-based slave factor (selling cargoes of enslaved Africans) and served as an elected member of the Jamaican colonial government. John died in Kingston in 1810 bequeathing property (a plantation, urban property, and enslaved people) to his family in Liverpool and Lancaster. Cousin Joshua also made his fortune as a Caribbean slave factor.

Between 1740 and 1807, Hinde family slave ships transported upwards of 8,000 African children, women, and men into plantation slavery. In 1806, William and Samuel, keen to capitalize on a boom in the prices paid for enslaved people in Caribbean markets in the years immediately prior to the abolition of the trade, commissioned the building of a new slave-ship, the *Trafalgar*. This was the last slave-ship built in Lancaster and in 1807 made one of the last 'legal' British slave voyages from West Africa to the Caribbean (Tyler 2023).

Figure 5.2: *St. James's Chronicle* or the *British Evening Post*, 6 December 1764, 'Runaway Slaves in Britain' database

> RUN away from Lancaster, on Friday the 23d Day of November last, a Negro Man named Harry, about twenty Years old, five Feet four Inches high, strong made, and one of his Ears bored; the Colour of his Clothes is unknown, as he absconded in the Night without his Clothes, and is supposed to be gone for London. Whoever secures the said Negro shall be well rewarded, and all Expences paid, upon applying to Mr. James Hinde, Merchant, in Lancaster, or Mr. Smith, Book-keeper, at the Swan-with-two-Necks, Lad-Lane, London.

Source: British Library: Burney Collection (Online)

The Hinde families' return cargoes to England included the slave-produced plantation goods of mahogany, sugar, and cotton, and they were a significant importer of raw cotton into Liverpool. This return cargo occasionally included enslaved people. For example, a 1764 advertisement offers a reward for the capture of a runaway 'Negro man' named Harry, escaped from the Hinde family in Lancaster (Figure 5.2). James Hinde, the merchant named in the advert, is Thomas Hinde's brother. A 1761 baptismal record for 'an adult negroe' called Henry Hinde suggests Harry may have arrived in Lancaster that same year, perhaps on Thomas Hinde's slave-ship the Lancaster which trafficked 250 enslaved people from West Africa to Jamaica in 1760, arriving back in the town in 1761.

The Hinde men invested their slave-derived wealth into property and land in and around Lancaster. In 1806, Joshua Hinde applied for an Inclosure Act to bring Scotforth common into private ownership and proceeded to turn the 86 acres he was awarded into a private country estate; the estate on which Lancaster University is sited today. His wealthier cousins, William and Samuel, would acquire over 1,000 acres between them. Until 1815, the Hindes continued to operate and own ships that traded directly with the Caribbean (primarily Jamaica) but increasingly speculated in the local textile industry.

In 1795, Thomas Hinde and his sons took over the lease of a textile mill in Dolphinholme near Lancaster. Installing new machinery, they turned it into the largest mill in north Lancashire and the first mechanically operated worsted mill (spinning woollen cloth) in the world. At its height it employed an estimated 1,000 workers (a combination of factory operatives and outworkers who combed the wool prior to its weaving). Surviving accounts suggest working conditions at the mill were exploitative and living conditions in the tied-cottages overcrowded and insanitary. Diary entries written in 1796 by farmer Timothy Cragg note that 'the wages of the persons employed in the factory are not sufficient for their subsistence', a situation that led to an exodus of workers, and periodic outbursts of industrial action (2006 [1796]: 88). Cragg describes how a group of 50–60 mill workers:

went all in company to Lancaster to Captain Hinde (Thomas Hinde Sr) to beg for more wages, but he [said] had no hand with the Factory, it was his son and he was at Liverpool so they came back as they went. A rough ragged company like as of some poor house had been broken loose. (2006 [1796]: 88–89)

A substantial proportion of the Hinde's workforce would have been children. An account written by Benjamin Shaw (1772–1841), an apprenticed child labourer at Dolphinholme Mill (in the years immediately preceding the Hinde's ownership), describes how several families of poor cottage-based knitters and weavers from remote Dentdale (some 40 miles away), were persuaded to leave their village and take up employment at the mill. As Shaw writes 'we were 7 childrer & they like large families the Best, for the Chidrers sake' (1991: 26). Shaw recalls how his 'little Brother Joseph, got catched in the wheels in the factory, and got his hand ill crushed, & cut, one finger taken off, & the other Broken & Sadly mangled … after which he sickend & died aged 11 or 12 years' (1991: 6, 26).

Thomas, William, Samuel, and Joshua Hinde all served as Justices of the Peace in Lancaster, presiding as judges at petty sessions (criminal hearings for non-capital offences) where they passed sentences of hard labour on the poor for offences such as pilfering food from orchards, poaching, and trespassing; crimes of hunger often prompted by loss of rights of access to common land.

William and Samuel also served on Grand Juries at the Lancaster Assizes (regional trials for capital offences) during a period when Lancaster was at the vanguard of a repressive state crack-down on Luddite uprisings and unrest in the northern manufacturing districts. Indeed, after a strike by wool-combers in Dophinholme Mill in 1832, William Hinde successfully sued his own striking workers at the Assizes for occupying his factory cottages while they refused to work; they lost their homes and jobs.

The history of the Hinde family offers a glimpse into how slave-derived wealth facilitated land enclosures and industrial revolution in England, and the ways in which the propertied classes used the British judicial system to ruthlessly police, defend, and prioritize property rights. It also reveals how slave-derived wealth enabled formerly 'middling classes' to rise into the upper echelons of British society, and gain positions of significant social and political power. Indeed, two of William Hinde's daughters married cousins of William Gladstone, the prime minister of Britain and the son of the powerful and immensely wealthy Liverpool-based Guyanese slave and plantation owner John Gladstone.

Conclusion

Histories of the transformation of Britain into a modern nation state are often presented as progress stories. They relate how land enclosures, agricultural improvements, and technological innovations facilitated the new industries of textiles, coal, and steel that ushered in the modern age, even while emphasizing some of the human costs of these changes for those displaced from the land, or those who laboured in the new factories and dwelt in industrial slums. What is obscured in national historiography is the wider context of slavery and British colonialism that enabled this great transformation. This chapter has sought to demonstrate that the English enclosure movement was part and parcel of a much vaster *colonial enclosure movement*, the blueprint for which was the plantation system, an industrial monoculture agricultural system.

Troubling the artificial separation of domestic and colonial enclosures allows us to untangle the knotted webs of relations between different but connected forms of exploitation and dispossession. For example, the unpaid labour of the enslaved was a primary source of the surplus value that underpinned the free but exploited waged labour of the British working class (see Holmwood, Chapter 7, this volume). In short, we cannot disentangle land enclosures and industrialization in Britain from British slave factories on the West African coast, British-owned slave-ships, and British-owned Caribbean plantations; they are part and parcel of what Walter Johnson describes as 'concretely intertwined elements of a larger unified though internally diversified structure of exploitation' (2004: 306). This colonial factory-system was driven by British elites and justified by supremacist ideologies and the manufacture of racist and classed hierarchies of human life-value.

The racism, poverty, and inequalities that characterize the global capitalist world economy today are legacies of this history. As is the global ecological crisis precipitated by monoculture plantation systems, and the climate crisis ushered in by the coal-powered, carbon-hungry industrial age. And capitalist enclosures continue apace (see Linebaugh 2014). European empires were supplanted by multinational corporations, and these new empires continue to extract (what remains) of the Earth's natural resources: land is enclosed, forests swallowed up, air and oceans poisoned, while the planet warms uncontrollably. The vast wealth and power of these corporations dwarfs that of most nation states, and the political influence of the new global billionaire class (whose interests they serve) facilitates the ongoing systematic privatization (enclosure and assetization) of public/common goods (public land, education, housing, and health services) across the world.

> They take our houses over our heads, they buy our lands out of our hands, they raise our rents, they … enclose our commons! … Men without conscience. … Men that would have all in their own hands; men that would leave nothing for others; men … that be never satisfied. (Crowley 1872 [1550]: 132–133)

References

Anderson, C. 2022. *Convicts: A Global History*. Cambridge University Press.
Berg, M. and Hudson, P. 2023. *Slavery, Capitalism and the Industrial Revolution*. Polity.
Burnard, T. 2023. 'Plantation Slavery in the British Caribbean', in Pargas, D.A. and Schiel, J. (eds), *The Palgrave Handbook of Global Slavery throughout History*. Palgrave Macmillan, pp 395–412.
Cragg, T. 2006 [1796]. *The Writings of the Cragg Family of Wyesdale*. Edited by K. Navickas. Record Society of Lancashire & Cheshire. Volume 142, pp 35–53. http://rslc.org.uk/api/file/Vol_142.pdf
Crowley, R. 1872 [1550]. *The Select Works of Robert Crowley*. Edited by J.M. Cowper. Early English Text Society.
Diggers of Warwickshire. 1607. 'Declaration of the Diggers of Warwickshire (1607)'. https://mpese.ac.uk/t/DeclarationDiggersWarwickshire1607.html

Griffin, C. 2023. 'Enclosure as Internal Colonization: The Subaltern Commoner, *Terra Nullius* and the Settling of England's "Wastes"', *Transactions of the Royal Historical Society* 1: 95–120.

Hall, C. 2020. 'The Slavery Business and the Making of "Race" in Britain and the Caribbean', *Current Anthropology*, 61(S22): S172–S182.

Hall, C. 2024. *Lucky Valley: Edward Long and the History of Racial Capitalism*. Cambridge University Press.

Hayes, N. 2020. *The Book of Trespass: Crossing the Lines that Divide Us*. Bloomsbury.

Johnson, W. 2004. 'The Pedestal and the Veil: Rethinking the Capitalism/Slavery Question', *Journal of the Early Republic* 24(2): 299–308.

Linebaugh, P. 2014. *Stop, Thief! The Commons, Enclosures, and Resistance*. PM Press.

Marx, K. 1887. *Capital: A Critique of Political Economy*. 1st English edn. Progress Publishers.

Shaw, B. 1991. *The Family Records of Benjamin Shaw, Mechanic of Dent, Dolphinholme and Preston, 1772–1841*. Edited by A. Crosby. Record Society of Lancashire and Cheshire.

Thompson, E.P. 1963. *The Making of the English Working Class*. Vintage.

Tyler, I. 2023. 'The Last Slave Ship Built in Lancaster', Centre for the Legacies of British Slave-ownership. https://lbsatucl.wordpress.com/2022/08/15/the-last-slave-ship-built-in-lancaster/

Williams, E. 1944. *Capitalism and Slavery*. University North Carolina Press.

Video lecture

Tyler, I. 2020. *Enclosures and the Making of the Modern World*, Connected Sociologies Curriculum Project. https://thesociologicalreview.org/projects/connected-sociologies/curriculum/mmw/enclosures-and-state-formation/

Additional resources

Enclosure Maps Data Archive. http://www.enclosuremaps.data-archive.ac.uk

Legacies of British Slavery Database. https://www.ucl.ac.uk/lbs/

QUESTIONS

1. What are enclosures?

2. What is the relationship between enclosures of land and people within England and within English colonies, that are taking place at the same time?

3. Why is a more connected global-colonial history of enclosures important for understanding the making of the modern Britain?

4. In what ways might the history of enclosures (and people's resistance to them) help us understand contemporary forms of 'capitalist enclosure' (of land, nature, and other shared and common/public goods) in the contemporary world?

Worksheet 5. Enclosures and the Making of Modern Britain

This worksheet is designed to support AS and A-level teaching on social differentiation, power and stratification, globalization and global development, and culture and identity. Due to its focus on the history and contemporary legacies of British colonialism, it may also be useful for supporting students' learning in relevant AS and A-level History and/or Geography modules. The online talk takes a critical approach to dominant narratives of Britain's transformation into a modern capitalist state. By examining the formation of different enclosures, both on land in England and in overseas English colonial territories, Imogen Tyler traces the history of the formation of a new, multiracial class society born out of British imperialism. The topics covered in this session connect ideas of globalization to ideas of social class and identity, which are two key topics on the A-level Sociology curriculum. The worksheet builds on other talks within the Making of the Modern World section in developing students' ability to think critically about dominant sociological and historical narratives of global development and progress.

Time	Activity	Explanation
00.00–00.05	To warm up, answer this question: *What are enclosures?*	This activity introduces students to the key concept of the session. Establishing what students already know about the definition(s) of enclosure will enable them to monitor and reflect on how their knowledge expands throughout the session.
00.05–00.10	Recap of understandings of social class and identity.	It may be useful to remind students of the definition(s) of social class.
00.10–00.15	Watch the talk from 6:48 to 8:55. *What are the three functions of enclosures?*	Tyler explains that the enclosure of land can mean: (1) the gathering of scattered strips of land into large new, closed-off fields; (2) the elimination of common rights that people had to access and use common land; and (3) the eviction (sometimes violently) of people from their homes and/or the refusal to renew tenancies on this land. This activity allows students to build on their initial definitions of enclosures and starts them thinking about the social and economic processes involved in the formation of enclosures, which is key to the subsequent activities in the session.
00.15–00.20	At 10:48 it is stated that 'as land was commodified as property, social and economic relationships between people were transformed'. *How does the enclosure of land contribute to social inequality and stratification?*	This activity asks students to draw connections between the enclosure of land and the structure of society, in terms of how power and status is established and transferred, which is a core theme on the A-level Sociology curriculum. For visual learners, it may be helpful to draw a mind map showing the relationships between the enclosure of land, the people possessing the land, and those being dispossessed of it.

Time	Activity	Explanation
00.20–00.30	Watch the talk from 13:46 to 15:24. *What is the relationship between the enclosures happening 'at home' in England, and the enclosures in overseas colonial territories? What can this teach us about globalization?* You might choose to draw a visual illustration of enclosures 'at home' and enclosures overseas and the relationship between them, for example a Venn diagram.	By asking students to think about the relationships between enclosures in England and enclosures in overseas colonies, this activity helps students to understand the vital role played by British colonialism in the formation of social class. In doing so, it draws an important connection between two core topics on the A-level Sociology curriculum: social identity and globalization.
00.30–00.40	Watch the talk from 19:42 to 22:10. *Why is it important to challenge dominant national narratives that focus on British progress and innovation? How can sociology contribute to these efforts?*	This activity asks students to pull together what they have learned throughout the session in thinking critically about dominant narratives of the making of the modern world, critically evaluating the information and perspectives included in these narratives and identifying where perspectives have been left out. This is a key theme across the module. Students might identify efforts to recover lost/ignored/repressed historical perspectives, and/or centre marginalized voices, as a way in which sociologists aim to challenge dominant narratives of British history.
00.40–00.50	At 22:23 it is explained that social and cultural historians such as Catherine Hall are seeking to challenge dominant narratives of national history by 'bringing race and slavery home'. *What does it mean to 'bring race and slavery home'? Can you think of other examples of this from your wider learning across this section?*	Tyler explains that 'bringing race and slavery home' describes how, according to Catherine Hall, the history of Britain has been transformed over the last decade by new histories of slavery and British colonialism, aided by new digital databases and research tools. This approach challenges and expands dominant narratives of the formation of the English working class, which focus mainly on the industrial revolution. This activity encourages students to think about how race, slavery, and colonialism vitally underpin the making of British society, and the modern world more broadly. Students might identify other sessions on this module such as the Haitian Revolution and Colonial Dispossession and Extraction as sharing these themes and contributing to challenging dominant narratives of global development and British identity.

Time	Activity	Explanation
00.50–01.00	Considering what you have learned throughout this session, answer the following question: *How can the global colonial history of enclosures help us to understand how corporate capitalism works in the contemporary moment?*	This activity asks students to reflect on their learning throughout the session and think about how the history of enclosures as narrated by Tyler is important in a contemporary context. The connection between contemporary capitalism and British colonial history is a core theme of this section and encourages students to apply a critical lens to dominant narratives of globalization and global development.

This worksheet was developed by Isabel Sykes.

6

Decolonization in the Making of the Modern World

Deanndre Chen and Meera Sabaratnam

Objectives

- This chapter looks at the processes through which a world of empires became a world of independent states.
- It looks at the interlocking historical drivers of these global changes.
- It examines the question of whether decolonization represented a deeper or more superficial transformation of the global order.
- It asks how and why the question of decolonization continues to resonate today.

Introduction

Much of the world, across recorded human history, has been governed by 'empires' – that is, expansionary, internally differentiated political structures with a centre and peripheries. This would include the Roman Empire, the Aztec Empire, and the British Empire even though there are significant differences between these types of empire. Yet today, most of the world is governed by 'nation states' – clearly bordered political formations with mostly universal citizenship practices. Underpinning these states is the principle of 'national self-determination', that is, the idea that a people should choose their own government. Just a century ago, it was thought impossible that the whole world could be self-governing, and yet only 40 years after that practically all of the world was made up of independent states. We call the process of dismantling empires and establishing self-rule 'decolonization'.

For a long period of time, social scientists and historians did not devote a lot of attention to understanding or explaining decolonization. A common assumption was that the Western powers, weakened by the devastating Second World War and with the steer of the United States, agreed to withdraw peacefully from their empires.

While the number of sovereign states in the system increased, then, the system itself was not seen to have fundamentally changed – only expanded. Yet, the fuller story is more complex and significant; and poses some fundamental questions about how the world works today.

This chapter begins by setting out a historical account of decolonization, before discussing the significance of these processes and asking why the idea of decolonization continues to resonate today.

Decolonization as a historical process: what the world was like under empires

Although common in history, empires had particular importance as a political form in the *modern* world, and in particular the phenomenon now understood as 'the Rise of the West'. Until the 16th century or so, Europe was not home to the world's largest or richest political units – these could be found in imperial China, India, or Persia. In particular, the Ottoman Empire, centred around modern-day Turkey, had significant control over key trade routes from Asia into Europe.

Western European colonial expansion outside Europe is usually dated to the voyage of Columbus to the New World in 1492, which was the beginning of the Spanish conquest of the Americas. Vasco de Gama's navigation around the Cape of Good Hope in 1498 began Portugal's imperial projects in Asia. From this period onwards, European monarchs and their subjects competed to secure territory, trade, commodities, and power in all corners of the world, and quickly became wealthier and more powerful.

In many cases, these newer European colonial projects had a distinctively extractive form which supported the development of capitalism as an economic system (see Gilbert, Chapter 2, this volume). Unlike many of the previous land empires, such as the Mughal Empire and the Chinese empires, these colonial empires had distinct legal codes and rules which governed people and property differently to the metropolitan centre. These rules were increasingly organized according to the principles of civilizational difference between the metropole and the colonies, and racial hierarchies within the colonies (Bhambra 2024).

Colonial powers had different methods of enforcing their rule. Force and violence were important underpinnings, via the military defeat of local rulers, the policing of trade routes, or the suppression of resistance (often using locally hired forces). They also collaborated, both with local rulers for access to people, goods, or territory, or with each other to recognize the boundaries of each other's rule and principles of colonial entitlement. In some instances, colonial projects were not conducted by the states themselves but by companies with a royal warrant for trading monopolies, such as the British East India Company, the French Compagnie des Indes (incorporating all the colonial companies), and the Portuguese Companhia de Moçambique. At their most powerful, these trading companies could raise armies and even taxes among the local population. However, when resistance became sufficiently threatening to arrangements such as these, direct rule by the nation state was often imposed, as the British did in India, and the Portuguese and French did in Africa and south-east Asia.

However, colonial empires were not able to rule distant territories indefinitely. In the Western hemisphere, the United States and Haiti (see Bhambra, Chapter 1, this volume) underwent different kinds of revolutions which resulted in declarations of independence in 1776 and 1804, respectively. In the following two decades, all but two of the Spanish colonies in South America declared and made war for their own independence. That said, apart from in Haiti, where slavery was abolished and racial equality proclaimed, the independent states of the Western hemisphere maintained their settler colonial character, use of enslaved labour, and formal racial hierarchies. All the former colonies also maintained high levels of economic integration into the European-centred colonial economies.

Elsewhere, European colonial projects in Asia, Africa, and Oceania, particularly led by the British and French, continued to grow in influence and power through the 19th century, culminating in the Berlin Conference of 1884–1885 in which the whole of continental Africa was divided up into agreed spheres of territorial influence between them.

20th-century waves of 'decolonization': resistance over the long term

Even though many people may have lived under empire, and it remained a durable form of rule, particularly in its colonial forms it was often unpopular. Resistance to this kind of rule persisted and grew in more and less spectacular ways that made it more difficult, dangerous, or expensive for imperial powers to govern colonies over time (Chatterji 2018). Political protests and formal demonstrations, such as strikes and sit-ins, were increasingly common in the early 20th century. This included non-cooperation, such as not paying taxes, not volunteering for the military, and not growing crops the colonial powers prescribed.

A notable example is the Aba Women's War. In 1929, in what is present-day Nigeria, thousands of women organized against an attempt to impose colonial taxes on women and exclude their role in political governance. In protest against the impending taxes and continued exclusion from governance, women from villages in eastern Nigeria gathered at government offices to sing their grievances to the British colonial administration's courts and chiefs. The demonstrations escalated to riots that resulted in the destruction of government offices and courts (Uchendu and Okonkwo 2021). Although taxes were eventually imposed on women, the Aba Women's War resulted in some women being admitted to government in the native courts.

Armed rebellions and armed insurrections were also a long-term driver of decolonization. These rebellions challenged colonial assumptions about consent for colonial rule and the cost of maintaining it. This was the case in the 1857 Uprising in India, which involved mass armed resistance. Indian soldiers mutinied against British authorities and seized control of Delhi. The British eventually suppressed the rebellion after violent conflict that saw the destruction of entire villages and cruel executions by British forces, and the massacre of British soldiers and civilians by Indian militants. The uprising sent shockwaves through the European powers, who assumed that people in their colonies would be loyal to them under their rule (Bender 2016).

Finally, the intellectual basis of empire was being increasingly challenged. The 'civilizing mission' that was being used to justify empire was critiqued for the violent ways in which it was carried out. This was seen in the case of the Belgian Congo. King Leopold claimed he was going to take control of the Congo to bring civilization and suppress the slave trade. Instead, King Leopold's rule in the Congo consisted of a hugely exploitative and murderous regime. The reporting of the atrocities in the Belgian Congo brought to light the violence that underpinned Europe's 'civilizing mission' and spurred a more critical discussion about it (Hochschild 1999).

Accelerating decolonization

Decolonization accelerated in the early 20th century, fuelled by anti-colonial sentiment. International political movements began to emerge, such as the Pan-African Congress, which saw scholars and leaders such as W.E.B. Du Bois and Kwame Nkrumah come together to discuss their common situation. These connections facilitated global support to end discriminatory regimes and provided an avenue to challenge empire if colonized populations could not do so militarily (Thomas and Thompson 2018). Nationalist mass movements formed, as is the case in India where Indian intellectuals and political activists formed mass organizations to make demands of the British Empire such as greater political representation and eventually for independence.

The First World War required empires to mobilize their entire colonial structures into a war, which included bringing soldiers to fight in Europe and reorganizing colonial economies to produce goods to support the war. The whole world was engaged in this process, and this allowed the colonies and colonial subjects to increase their demands on empires. The Russian Revolution of 1917 was also a key event that inspired and catalysed nationalist movements. The Russian Revolution saw the overthrow of a massive empire and its takeover by a movement of the so-called 'common people' which was destabilizing for the ways in which subjects thought about their relationship with their empires, and this continued to be the case during the 20th century.

The principle that peoples should be able to choose their own governments – 'self-determination' – was explicitly discussed and gained some legal standing at the international level, most notably in Wilson's Fourteen Points adopted as part of the Treaty of Versailles after the First World War. While it was only intended to apply to parts of Europe formerly under the rule of the Austro-Hungarian, German, and Ottoman Empires, many others living under colonial rule argued it should be applied more universally. Successful rebellions against colonial rule in the early 20th century, such as the Irish War of Independence in 1919–1921, added to the buildup of pressure for decolonization, which increased during the 1930s and 1940s.

It is also the case that the Second World War presented a material opportunity to accelerate the decolonization process. During the war, even victorious colonial powers in Europe such as Britain and France were significantly weakened and had depended strongly on recruiting troops and resources from the colonies for the war effort, while also attempting to quash the nationalist sentiment. Colonial subjects in the colonies took advantage of this weakness and general disarray to assert their demands for self-rule forcefully. This can be seen in the case of India, where attempts to reassert colonial discipline over the Indian National Army in the wake of their collaboration with Axis powers during the war resulted in massive unrest (Bose 2011). It became clear to Britain that it would be unable to continue to rule, leading to the independence and partition of India in 1947.

Perhaps more broadly, the war had challenged the ideological underpinnings of colonialism. Martinican intellectual Aimé Césaire famously argued in 1954 that colonialism and fascism were built on the same dehumanizing principles, and that fascism simply produced in Europe what Europe had been doing to the colonies for a long time (Césaire 2000). This kind of argument became more widely circulated as resistance to empire accelerated. As more independent states were added to the United Nations, they were able to organize together and press for decolonization as a universal principle (Mazower 2009). By 1960, the United Nations had declared in favour of decolonization, and this triggered a rapid turnover of territories gaining their independence.

Reactions from empire

Colonial powers were nonetheless convinced for a long time in the 20th century that they would be able to maintain their power and made use of a range of tactics to combat the demands being made for decolonization. They would initially try to defer such demands by claiming that colonies were not ready and that a transfer of power would only take place when they had been trained in the arts of government and civilization. Such thinking was at the heart of the Mandate System set up in the wake of the First World War as former Ottoman colonies were experiencing waves of nationalism and demands for self-rule. There were also accommodations on the part of colonial powers, such as implementing reforms that gave colonial subjects more political power, for example, political representation. When these attempts did not work, colonial powers would respond more aggressively by repressing independence movements using force or miliary campaigns. Some empires, such as the French and Portuguese, tried to get around the legal demand for self-determination by claiming that the colonies were overseas territories that were no different from the metropole.

We could argue that there was some kind of acceptance after the Second World War that empires could no longer hold onto their colonies for much longer. In this case, colonial powers would accept independence and facilitate a transition of power. The independence granted to colonies was sometimes more in name and there was still intervention in the affairs of countries post-independence. The Belgian Congo is a key example. The leader who was chosen after independence, Patrice Lumumba, was assassinated by a combination of a secessionist movement and the Belgian secret service because Belgium wanted a leader that would allow them ongoing preferential access to Congolese mineral resources.

Case study: a 'long' decolonization process: Vietnam, 1900s–1975

The case of Vietnam demonstrates that independence and decolonization is not a moment, but an ongoing struggle. Vietnam was colonized by France in the mid-19th century and formed part of French Indochina that also included Laos and Cambodia. Vietnam was a source of raw materials for the French Empire, providing rice, rubber, and coal to the metropole. The Vietnamese had attempted to oppose French rule through an armed rebellion (Singh 2015), tax protests, notably the mass demonstrations that took place in 1908, and government reforms (Marr 1980). The Vietnamese Revolutionary Youth League was formed overseas in 1925 which advocated for communist revolution.

During the Second World War, Japan occupied Vietnam. At the end of the Second World War, France looked to re-establish its control of Vietnam with the help of Britain. However, Vietnamese communist leader Ho Chi Minh declared independence in 1945 and was supported by Vietnamese nationalists, known as the Viet Minh. Ho Chi Minh held a presence in North Vietnam, while France maintained control of South Vietnam, resulting in contestations over who was the legitimate government of Vietnam.

Following a series of conflicts, the Viet Minh defeated France in 1954, which led to negotiations and eventually an agreement in the Geneva Accords that dealt a blow to the French Empire. France was to withdraw from Vietnam, and the country would be temporarily partitioned along the seventeenth parallel into North and South Vietnam. The United States, fearing the spread of communism in Asia, provided military and economic assistance to South Vietnam and its autocratic leader, Ngo Dinh Diem.

By the early 1960s, communist forces in the south (known as the Viet Cong), supported by the north, led a movement to gain power and unify Vietnam. This prompted more aggressive US involvement in Vietnam consisting of bombings in the north and sending troops to fight in the south. It was only after years of bombing and fighting in the region in the 1960s, and a successful show of force by the Viet Cong and north Vietnamese in 1968, known as the Tet Offensive, that the United States began to withdraw from Vietnam. Although the United States had withdrawn by 1973, fighting persisted in Vietnam between communist and non-communist forces until 1975 when communist forces took control of Saigon, the capital of South Vietnam, reunifying the country.

Decolonization: imitation or revolution?

Today, we have a world that looks in principle very different to the world controlled by empires in the early 20th century, in which people were ruled by distant metropoles and their representatives, and a hierarchy between people existed through the construction of different rules and racial identities. We now live mostly in a world of nation states that are in principle separated by borders and politically independent from each other. Each state has its own leader and form of government. National states and their leaders have, in principle, control over their economic policies. International law recognizes the inviolability of sovereign states, which means that armed territorial conquest or colonial occupation of other states is illegal. The political status of individuals has changed from that of colonial subjects loyal to a European crown to that of full and equal citizens, entitled to a range of human rights and universal provisions such as health and education.

But how should we interpret the meaning of these shifts? There have been changing interpretations of the significance of decolonization in the scholarship over time.

An earlier school of thought understood decolonization as the transplanting of a European-originated modern political form worldwide, while later scholarship sees decolonization as a potentially more revolutionary change in the modern world itself.

The first school of thought sees decolonization processes as representing the transplanting of the European form of statehood – national sovereignty and self-determination – into the colonies (Jackson 1990; Clapham 2002). However, for scholars such as Jackson, this was seen as ultimately unfortunate, as they were seen to lack the requisite socio-historic elements to make the state itself 'work'. Being only states in legal name (*de jure*) but not reality (*de facto*), such states were often destined to remain weak and subject to predatory forms of elite nationalism, ultimately 'failing' in the tasks of sovereignty and governance. Understood in this way, decolonization was an improvised and imperfect importation of political models that were not fitted to their new environments.

In contrast, the second school of thought argued that decolonization presaged a radical shift and a transformation in the nature of modernity itself. It changed people's expectations of what was possible both politically and economically (for example, Duara 2003; Thomas 2024). Decolonization rejected the colonial right to conquer and rule. What had once been a dominant principle in the world was now deemed illegal by international law. Decolonization also rejected the discourse of 'backwardness' used to justify governing people and territories. It was no longer acceptable to argue that some people were less civilized or inadequately rational for self-rule, which had been a norm for several hundred years.

There were significant changes in the economic planning in the colonies as they attempted to take ownership of their commodities from private actors and colonial powers. The economic objectives of post-colonial states shifted to prioritize explicitly the well-being of their own people over the colonial metropole. With an awareness of continuing colonial influence, and control over key resources and trades, post-colonial states attempted to carve out a New International Economic Order to form a basis for their own resource exploitation and development. This would have nationalized key resources and enacted other kinds of economic sovereignty. While these attempts were not ultimately successful, they represented a different vision for what the global economy should look like.

Decolonization also fostered the development of transnational or trans-racial bonds between newly independent states. This was nurtured by political projects such as the development of the idea of the 'Third World', and events like the Bandung Conference. Transnational bonds were also evident in coalitions like the Non-Aligned Movement, which was an attempt to distance the formerly colonized areas from the West. There was also the emergence of newer international instruments, such as the international aid system. This generated a new set of relationships and dynamics between states, some of which were seen to continue a paternalistic approach with others seen as a more solidaristic and reparative act.

For empires themselves, colonial powers like Britain and France no longer held the same kind of dominance in the world. While they still held positions of relative power, influence, or prestige in terms of leadership of the Commonwealth in Britain's case, or backer of the CFA franc in France's case, they were no longer rulers of significant parts of the world. Moreover, as they sought workers from across their ongoing or recent colonial territories to support public services and post-war industrialization activities, they experienced significant levels of migration to the metropole, which in turn changed metropolitan societies. The end of empire also impacted the levels of wealth available for colonial economies, meaning that the dividends of empire increasingly could not subsidize public services as they once had (Bhambra 2022).

The extent of decolonization's impact on the making of the modern world remains an open question, and one which will continue to be relevant as former subjects of empire gain in size and strength in the 21st century.

The end of colonial relations?

While the formal status of empire might be over, there is continued debate about whether the relations between former empires and their former colonies remain colonial in their nature.

In economic terms, for example, there are a number of similarities between the colonial period and the present. Countries which were colonized for access to commodities such as gold, copper, and rubber continue to have economies designed to export those products to support manufacturing and the profitability of companies located elsewhere. This limits how much money they can make via trade. These countries continue to have to generate foreign exchange in order to repay debts to Western creditors, meaning that they have fewer resources to spend on public services and infrastructure for their people, which in turn limits human capital and resource use in the country. Many are also economically dependent on sending skilled and unskilled labour abroad to work at lower wages in formerly colonial countries in order to send back financial remittances to their countries of origin (see LeBaron and Bhagat, Chapter 11, this volume).

In social terms, certain hierarchies still also prevail. These include the benchmarking of educational content against those available in former colonial powers, leading many to seek degrees from universities in those countries. By implication, this requires fluency in the languages, academic norms, and social customs of those countries. In cultural terms, the worlds of art, literature, fashion, and travel continue to be dominated by the institutions of Western countries. Politically, it also seems that countries are not on an equal footing in terms of voting power in international institutions such as the United Nations Security Council or International Monetary Fund, or in terms of prosecution under international law.

These hierarchical patterns lead many to understand the current world order as still 'colonial', and, therefore, as unjust. This therefore means that the idea of 'decolonization' continues to have relevance and resonance in the present, as people seek to further transform these structures.

For example, students in post-apartheid South Africa launched a protest movement in 2015 which became known as #RhodesMustFall and then #FeesMustFall, which initially drew attention to the ongoing presence of a statue of the colonial mining magnate Cecil Rhodes on the campus of the University of Cape Town. However, it sparked a wider conversation about the persistence of colonial hierarchies in educational practices and content in South Africa, as well as the barriers to education posed by the university fee regime. Many understood this as a call to 'decolonize' and 'Africanize' education in the country. In recent years, calls have been made to 'decolonize' diverse fields such as art, sport, beauty, and so on. In general, these calls have looked to make these fields more global, racially inclusive, and geographically representative.

Is decolonization still the right answer?

Others have, however, challenged this more contemporary way of thinking about decolonization and its desirability. As observed by the scholars Tuck and Yang (2012), decolonization in its territorial sense still represents an ongoing political horizon for Indigenous peoples living in settler colonial states, such as the United States, Canada, Australia, and New Zealand. In these spaces, fundamental relations of sovereignty and the return of land are what decolonization means to Indigenous peoples. By rendering decolonization as a metaphor for racial inclusion in settler societies, they argue there is a risk of overlooking these Indigenous political claims.

Others have argued that even in formerly colonized spaces, decolonization may be the wrong framing through which to approach problems. Nigerian philosopher Olúfẹ́mi Táíwò (not to be confused with Olúfẹ́mi O. Táíwò discussed below), for example, argues that if decolonization is taken to mean the complete rejection of every aspect of the colonial past, from culture, politics, institutions, and ideas, then it extends to almost every aspect of life in former colonies. This generates the question of whether it is possible to ever fully reject and disconnect from the legacies of colonial rule, or whether it is even desirable to do so (Táíwò O. 2022). This might undermine the agency of people in post-colonial societies to pursue their own political, economic, or social projects in the modern world. More critically, it overlooks the moments in which oppressed people did successfully adopt and adapt ideas, processes, and institutions from colonialism to further their own purposes and liberation. The consequence is to erase the contributions of colonial societies to making the modern world as post-colonial *and* colonial people.

Others have argued for a more forward-looking approach to decolonization that focuses on the spirit of repair. Olúfẹ́mi O. Táíwò, for example, agrees with the claim that there are significant ongoing legacies of colonial harm, most notably through the ecological catastrophe induced by colonial capitalism (see Khoo, Chapter 3, this volume). However, he is concerned with the amount of effort that is put towards criticizing all the legacies of colonial rule, and how it may come at the expense of positively constructing the more just world that would-be decolonizers claim to advocate. In Táíwò's view, decolonization should not just be about fighting what we stand against – in this case, colonial structures – but also a worldmaking practice where we construct what we stand for (Táíwò O.O. 2022).

Conclusion

Decolonization is a major force that is still shaping the modern world and has ongoing relevance to this day. It is a force that has produced the world that we know and live in today, and how we understand it. As a set of historical processes, it fundamentally shifted how we understand the organization of political rule within and between societies, how we understand human rights, and how we think about the achievement of freedom. This was achieved both slowly, over centuries of resistance to empire, and quickly, in the collapse of empires in the middle of the 20th century which remade the political map.

As a political ethos, decolonization continues to ask questions about how it is that the modern world functions – how resources are distributed, what social and political values are promoted, and whose voices are heard. In short, it currently frames a lot of questions to do with global justice, democracy, and what it means to be human. These questions are perennial questions in human history and will continue to resonate in the future.

References

Bender, J.C. 2016. *The 1857 Indian Uprising and the British Empire*. Cambridge University Press.

Bhambra, G.K. 2022. 'Relations of Extraction, Relations of Redistribution: Empire, Nation, and the Construction of the British Welfare State', *British Journal of Sociology* 73(1): 4–15.

Bhambra, G.K. 2024. 'Empires and Colonialism: An Essay in Historiographic Reconstruction', *Tidsskrift for samfunnsforskning* 65(3): 192–205.

Bose, S. 2011. *His Majesty's Opponent: Subhas Chandra Bose and India's Struggle against Empire*. Belknap Press of Harvard University Press.

Césaire, A. 2000. *Discourse on Colonialism*. Edited by R.D.G. Kelley. Monthly Review Press.

Chatterji, J. 2018. 'Decolonization in South Asia: The Long View', in M. Thomas and A.S. Thompson (eds), *The Oxford Handbook of the Ends of Empire*. Oxford University Press, pp 251–275.

Clapham, C. 2002. 'The Challenge to the State in a Globalized World.' *Development and Change* 33 (5): 775–95. https://doi.org/10.1111/1467-7660.t01-1-00248.

Duara, P. 2003. 'Introduction: The Decolonization of Asia and Africa in the Twentieth Century', P. Duara (ed), *Decolonization: Perspectives from Now and Then*, 19–36. Routledge.

Hochschild, A. 1999. *King Leopold's Ghost: A Story of Greed, Terror, and Heroism in Colonial Africa*. First Mariner Books Edition. Houghton Mifflin.

Jackson, R. H. 1990. *Quasi-States: Sovereignty, International Relations and the Third World*. Vol. 12. Cambridge University Press.

Marr, D.G. 1980. *Vietnamese Anticolonialism, 1885–1925*. Vol 33. University of California Press.

Mazower, M. 2009. *No Enchanted Palace: The End of Empire and the Ideological Origins of the United Nations*. Princeton University Press.

Singh, S.K. 2015. 'Colonialisms, Nationalism and Vietnam's Struggle for Freedom', *Proceedings of the Indian History Congress* 76: 620–630.

Táíwò, O. 2022. *Against Decolonization: Taking African Agency Seriously*. C. Hurst and Company (Publishers) Limited.

Táíwò, O.O. 2022. *Reconsidering Reparations*. Oxford University Press.

Thomas, M. 2024. *The End of Empires and a World Remade: A Global History of Decolonization*. Princeton University Press.

Thomas, M. and Thompson, A.S. 2018. 'Rethinking Decolonization: A New Research Agenda for the Twenty-First Century', in M. Thomas and A.S. Thompson (eds), *The Oxford Handbook of the Ends of Empire*. Oxford University Press, pp 1–26.

Tuck, E. and Wayne Yang, K. 2012. 'Decolonization Is Not a Metaphor', *Decolonization: Indigeneity, Education & Society* 1(1): 1–40.

Uchendu, E. and Okonkwo, U. 2021. 'The Aba Women's War of 1929 in Eastern Nigeria as Anti-Colonial Protest', in J. Hobson (ed), *The Routledge Companion to Black Women's Cultural Histories*. Routledge, pp 245–254.

Video lecture

Sabaratnam, M. 2020. *Decolonization*, Connected Sociologies Curriculum Project. https://thesociologicalreview.org/projects/connected-sociologies/curriculum/mmw/decolonisation/

QUESTIONS

1. How did empires maintain their rule?

2. What were the primary drivers of decolonization?

3. Did decolonization transform the world?

4. Can you change a political system without changing an economic one?

5. Why is there debate about the contemporary relevance of decolonization?

Worksheet 6. Decolonization in the Making of the Modern World

This worksheet is designed to support AS and A-level teaching on social differentiation, power and stratification, globalization and global development, and sociological theory and methods. In this online talk, Meera Sabaratnam maps out the global transition from empires to nation states as decolonization unfolded in the 20th century, and the ongoing implications of these shifts. She outlines different narratives describing the causes of decolonization, the extent of its global transformative consequences, and prompts students to ponder the question: why do people still talk about decolonization today? The worksheet stretches students' critical thinking skills, asking them to consider how the themes in this session relate to the wider contexts of modernity explored in this section. This session and the accompanying worksheet provide a comprehensive and stimulating introduction to decolonization for students who are already familiar with the history of British colonialism. As such, it may also be helpful for students studying A-level History.

Time	Activity	Explanation
00.00–00.05	To warm up, answer this question: What is decolonization?	This talk is suited to students who already have a good understanding of colonialism. Therefore, this activity is designed to refresh students' knowledge about a term with which they are hopefully already aware. For a reminder, students can watch the talk 0:45 to 1:19 for Sabaratnam's definition.
00.05–00.10	Recap of understandings of globalization and global development.	It may be useful to remind students of some of the key concepts and terms related to globalization and global development.
00.10–00.15	Watch the talk from 2:25 to 4:10. Summarize the key shifts Sabaratnam names as being part of the global transformation from transnational empires to nation states.	Sabaratnam talks about: (1) the changed political status for individuals: from colonial subjects to post-colonial citizens; (2) a transitional move away from racial hierarchy and towards equality; (3) a shift from colonial to national economic control; (4) the emergence of international laws around human rights; and (5) the illegality of armed territorial conquest. This activity asks students to summarize the key arguments in this section using their own words and gets them thinking analytically about the transformational shifts instigated by decolonization. This connects with a core theme within the A-level Sociology curriculum: changes in structures of inequality.
00.15–00.20	At 4:13 Sabaratnam poses the question: 'why don't we hear more about decolonization?' Write a short paragraph answering this question, drawing on your wider learning from this module.	This question prompts students to place decolonization within the wider context of what they have learned regarding the making of the modern world. Students may draw on ideas about how narratives of modernity have been constructed and by whom, which perspectives are platformed in these narratives and which are elided, and debates surrounding subjectivity and objectivity. These are all key questions within the sociological theory and methods topic on the A-level Sociology curriculum.

Time	Activity	Explanation
00.20–00.30	At 10:38 Sabaratnam explains that there are two different reasons why the Second World War is often viewed as the 'breaking point' for decolonization: one linking the defeat of Hitler to the delegitimization of colonialism, and another emphasizing the role of the colonies themselves in opposing colonial rule more assertively. Drawing on your wider learning across this module, answer the following question: *What has been the role of anti-colonial resistance in the making of the modern world?*	This activity gives students the opportunity to make connections between the role of resistance within decolonization, and other narratives of resistance that have emerged elsewhere. For example, students may compare this opposition of colonies to colonial rule with the role that resistance played within the Haitian Revolution. By asking students to consider how changes in structures of inequality come about, and the consequences of these events, this activity draws on a key theme throughout the A-level Sociology curriculum.
00.30–00.45	At 17:37 Sabaratnam introduces two opposing views regarding the significance of decolonization to the making of the modern world. Thinking about her arguments, create a mini essay plan showing how you would answer the following question: *To what extent did decolonization constitute a transformation in the nature of modernity?*	Sabaratnam explains that in one school of thought, which dominated most of the 20th century, decolonization is viewed as a global imitation of European 'modernity', where the rest of the world caught up to and adopted the European model of capitalism. An opposing narrative views decolonization as a radical transformation in the nature of modernity itself, and a shift in global understandings of politics and economics. In this activity, students are asked to critically evaluate the two sides of an argument and plan an essay explaining their decision-making, providing a useful opportunity to practice an exam-style question.
00.45–00.55	Watch the talk from 22:50 to 25:20. *Can you think of some recent examples of decolonial discourses in the media?*	The role of the media within sociological discourse is an important running theme through the A-level Sociology curriculum. This activity encourages students to consider the media as a lens through which the ongoing processes and implications of decolonization play out. In answering this question students may draw on examples of recent protests against statues of colonial figures (such as the toppling of Edward Colston's statue by Black Lives Matter activists in Bristol in June 2020).

Time	Activity	Explanation
00.55–01.00	Drawing on what you have learned throughout this session, answer the following question: *Can decolonization ever be finished?*	This question prompts students to apply what they have learned in this session to a wider sociological question that will stretch their critical thinking skills. They are being prompted to think about the significance of ongoing discourses of decolonization to contemporary understandings of modernity. This acts as a summarizing activity and may work well as a group discussion.

This worksheet was developed by Isabel Sykes.

PART II

The Politics of Inequality

Edited by Paul Robert Gilbert

7

Class, Capitalism, and Colonialism

John Holmwood

Objectives

- This chapter sets out the sociological distinction between traditional and modern societies and the representation of the latter as capitalist modernity.

- It discusses Marx's understanding of the capital and labour relation, and class polarization, as central to the social dynamics of capitalist modernity.

- It sets out how capitalism led instead to a more differentiated class structure, involving multiple class positions, and how sociology shifted from using class as a major explanatory category to class as a descriptive category.

- It argues that a dynamic analysis can be recovered by correcting the discipline's neglect of colonialism in the development of modern society.

- It concludes by suggesting that sociology needs to incorporate a colonial political economy in contrast to capitalist political economy to better understand modernity and its global inequalities.

Introduction

Sociology is widely understood as a discipline that emerged alongside modern society and takes for itself the special task of interpreting the nature of modern society and its distinctiveness from other societies that had preceded it (Bhambra 2007). This involves identifying distinctive social structures of economic inequality occurring alongside new democratic forms of political representation which are contrasted with those of pre-modern societies. To be sure, the development from the traditional to the modern takes place over several centuries – from the 16th and 17th centuries onwards in Europe – so the development of the 'new' within the 'old' takes time to be discerned. As it does, however, so the social changes are understood to have a world historical significance; that is, the transformations taking place within Europe are held to define a new world order and to create an imperative of development and a common future for humanity.

The new social, economic, and political structures are not given detailed sociological expression until the mid-19th century onwards by Karl Marx and Max Weber (among others) when the contours of modern sociology begin to be set. They have remained relatively unchanged since then, with class analysis a central focus of the discipline and class taken as a defining feature of modern society. In this chapter, I will consider how modern capitalism and the class relations held to define it are understood within sociology and the broader social sciences. These class relations are argued by many in the social sciences to provide the dynamic for wider social developments. However, we will see that the expected social developments, including the manner in which other populations outside Europe are brought into their processes, are different to what was initially expected. The chapter will trace these problems to an initial failure, that of the neglect of colonialism as central to modernity. I will begin by setting out the key features of the sociological understanding of modern capitalist economy and the class relations central to it.

The emergence of class

Capitalism is an economic system based upon private property, where those who own property have an unrestricted right to dispose of their property as they wish. They are free to dispose of it, use their capital to acquire other property, and direct its productive capacities. This involves an entrepreneurial orientation to profit that Max Weber famously described as the 'spirit of capitalism'. Capitalism is initially associated with a range of commercial and trading activities involving the arbitrage or trade of goods produced under different kinds of economic arrangements. Over time capitalism develops as an economic system of manufacture in its own right, directed at the production of goods through the organization of labour within factories, and involving investment in machinery to increase production.

At its core, capitalism involves an economic order of market and exchange relationships. Here, commodities – or goods and services – are produced for sale on a market. The production and sale of commodities involves the bringing together of the means of production (raw materials, tools, and so on) and labour, usually by a party with the financial means to make the necessary outlays. Here, labour – or more properly, as Marx would put it, *labour power* (the capacities embodied in labour) – itself becomes a commodity, sold and purchased on the labour market (Carver 2018). The difference between the returns accruing to the owners of the means of production and those accruing to labour are understood to be a surplus that is appropriated by the former.

The capitalist system is essentially 'individualistic' in the sense that the capitalist claims ownership as an individual right and the worker is identified as having rights in his or her body and its disposition on a labour market, where returns (wages) are based on individual contributions to the process as determined by the labour market. This can be contrasted with earlier forms of economy where labour was bound in relations of reciprocal obligation to a master (as in medieval artisanal guilds) or through work on the land of a lord (as in feudalism) in exchange for the right to use some of that land for subsistence and access to common land for foraging and the keeping of livestock.

Traditional, or feudal, society, then, is understood as a social order in which economic relations are embedded in communal relations. These involve *estates* or *status* groups that were organized both vertically and horizontally, as argued, especially, by Weber (see Cox 1945). For example, an 'estate' was made up of those associated with a specific activity or function, such as agriculture, commerce, or the military and church. In the case of the former, this involved hereditary owners of landed estates, as well as those involved in work on their land tied in relations of dependence and reciprocal obligations – typically, that status was registered by their description as agricultural *servants*.

Status groups represented those in privileged positions and were maintained by endogamy (marriage among the members of the group). Thus, the families associated with landed estates may also provide officers and officials within the military and church, especially those of highest rank. The commercial estate associated with the guild organization of production (also organized in terms of master and servant relations) may involve wealthy individuals, but they were less likely to be incorporated into the highest status group, thereby making them an ideal vehicle to carry aspirations for a different economic order (as set out by Weber, for example, in his *Protestant Ethic and the Spirit of Capitalism*).

During the long transition to capitalist modernity, these relationships and the normative order that sustained them – the 'moral economy' – was transformed by the expansion of private property in land and the conversion of obligations of service into wages (see Tyler, Chapter 5, this volume). The private enclosure of the land for purposes of 'improvement' involved the displacement of agricultural labourers who swelled the population in towns. This accelerated the process of the breakdown of the guild system and facilitated the development of workshops that would expand to become the factories of early capitalism.

In its Marxist version, class analysis proposed that class inequalities should be understood through the primary relationship of capital (owners of the means of production) and labour (the sellers of labour power). This formed an exploitative relationship where the capitalist appropriated profit from the production and sale of commodities, at the same time as a competitive labour market determined that the price of labour (wages) would be pegged to the minimum necessary for subsistence (see LeBaron and Bhagat, Chapter 11, this volume).

Marx further thought that the labour process of capitalism would involve the reduction of skilled labour to unskilled labour, reinforcing a downward pressure on wages. Since, for Marx, the capital–labour relation as a relation of domination and exploitation was intrinsic to capitalism as a mode of production, he argued that class conflict and opposition were inescapable. The sociological conditions of capitalist production also produced circumstances in which workers would become increasingly aware of their collective interest in pressing not just for higher wages, but for the overthrow of the wages system itself and the transformation of capitalism. In this way, an economic division would be transformed into new forms of solidarity and social and political divisions within a society that would become increasingly class-divided.

Marx's account contained two key assumptions. The first was that the expansion of capitalism would have continued transformative effects, bringing an ever-larger proportion of the population into working-class employment. The second was that

that there would be a reduction of skilled to unskilled labour as a consequence of mechanized industrial production. In this context, the likely response by workers would be to organize to mitigate the effects of competition on wages, which would otherwise tend to fall to subsistence (since the wage was paid to the worker as an individual, this was also something that increased the pressure on wages as erstwhile dependants – wives and children – were forced into the labour market in order to meet basic needs).

For Marx, the struggle to maintain wages was part of the process by which a proletariat would come to understand that the problem of their poverty was systemic and lay with the wages system and the nature of capitalism itself. In this way, class division was central to understanding the dynamics of change within capitalism and its future development including towards the revolutionary transformation of society and the overcoming of private property. If few sociologists accepted that as a necessary development, it was widely assumed that class politics would at least produce major changes in terms of the amelioration of inequality through state-directed social reforms under the influence of class-based political parties.

From polarization to differentiation

While powerful, the analysis provided by Marx depended on sociological conditions that were not met. Marx (and other sociologists) neglected the fact that the level of wages also depended on the supply of labour and labour itself needed to be *reproduced*. Amelioration became possible within capitalism and not in direct opposition to its core relationships. High working-class fertility was an issue of early capitalism contributing to the supply of labour. But families could also seek to control family size – as part of what became known as the 'demographic transition' from high to low birth and death rates in late 19th-century Europe (Levine 1987). Lower death rates also indicated an improvement in the conditions of life, which further indicated a shift away from the general impoverishment outlined in Marxian theory.

The emigration of a 'surplus population' in Europe to participate in colonial settlement in European colonies also affected the domestic labour supply. Impoverishment was one of the drivers of emigration, but by reducing the oversupply of labour at home, it contributed to the improvement of domestic conditions. At the same time, emigration provided an overseas labour force (alongside forced labour in the colonies) that contributed to improvement of domestic living conditions due to the import of cheaper foodstuffs from overseas plantations and other revenues for domestic use.

Similarly, whereas high birth rates contributed to a traditionally gendered division of labour, their fall also provided opportunities for women to have longer spells in the formal labour market without direct responsibilities for children. Equally, the development of capitalism seemed not to be associated with a general reduction of skilled labour to unskilled labour. New forms of skill and new occupations – for example, in white-collar work and retail associated with the rise of mass consumption (especially in the 20th century) – followed from the rise in living standards. In this context, the sociological analysis of class shifted away from the historical trajectory of capitalism and its internal dynamics of change towards class understood as a differentiated system of socio-economic positions within a supposed 'national' economy.

Under the influence of Weber's understanding of class as position within a market, class analysis shifted away from the two-class model proposed by Marx to one of multiple classes presented hierarchically, rather than in oppositional terms (Savage 2016). For example, John Goldthorpe and his colleagues initially proposed a four-class scheme of petty bourgeoisie (small employers and self-employed), the service class, or salariat (professional and managerial groups), the routine non-manual class (typically lower grade clerical 'white-collar workers'), and the working class (foremen and technicians, skilled, semi-, and unskilled manual workers). The scheme is based on employment (the capitalist class of property owners is not included) and can also be broken down into further categories (Goldthorpe 2000).

Of course, there is no reason why there cannot be further distinctions and in the full scheme, the service class is divided into two further upper and lower groups (Class I and Class II), as is the routine non-manual class which is divided into higher (Class IIIa and Class IIIb) and lower grades, where the former involves a mixed form of regulation and the latter a modified labour contract. A separate group of farmers and small-holders can be posited within the petty bourgeoisie (Class IVabc) and agricultural labourers are identified as a separate group within the working class (Class VIIb). The four-class scheme became a seven-class and then a nine-class scheme.

As the scheme is expanded, so, too, the numbers in each category changes, with the 'working class' becoming a smaller proportion of the population in advanced capitalist economies. Unlike with a polarized understanding of class, 'social mobility' becomes a pertinent issue produced, at least in part, by the 'pull' effect following from the increase over time in the proportion of higher-level occupations. In other words, if the class structure changes, such that, over time, there is a greater proportion of higher class positions compared with lower class positions, then that, in itself, creates opportunities for mobility.

A differentiated class structure has other consequences. Marx had anticipated that differentiated occupations would come to be resolved into two great classes. If that had occurred, the opportunity for employees to exert control over specific labour markets would have been substantially reduced. This is why Marx argued that differences associated with age, gender, and ethnicity would be reduced. In contrast, with a much more differentiated set of occupations it becomes easier for specific groups of workers, in conjunction with employers, to maintain control of access to employment. In consequence, women are much more likely to be concentrated in the routine non-manual category and men more widely distributed. Similarly, ethnic minorities are disproportionately concentrated in lower positions (see Anitha, Chapter 8, this volume).

In this way, 'ethnicity' and 'gender' intersect with 'class', but that becomes possible only because what was expected of class does not occur. Class polarization is no longer understood to be the central dynamic of capitalism, but, by the same token, class is no longer the primary determinant of struggles over reform and amelioration. In this context, it would be problematic to argue that ethnicity and gender represent 'subjective identities' and that class is the underlying 'objective' condition, despite this frequently being the language that is used by sociologists. There is nothing natural – or historically grounded – about the 9 (or more) classes to which individuals are now assigned by sociologists that would lead to their incumbents adopting that identity rather than any other. Rather class position is a label attached by sociologists, not something that arises in the lived experiences of those to whom the label is attached.

'Class' remains significant in the sociological imagination, at the same time as it is declining in the public imagination. Of course, opinion surveys can be conducted to show that a significant proportion of the population identifies themselves as 'working class', but it is not clear what that means. On the one hand, it is simply a recognition that employment – working – is, for a large part of the population, the basis of their primary claim upon resources as a wage or salary. Or, in the context of the experience of social mobility produced, in part, by changes in the occupational structure, it describes the fact that many people in what sociologists describe as non-manual class positions have a family history where parents or grandparents had manual occupations. Here, self-identification as being 'working class' describes where an individual is from and a family trajectory.

Whereas for Marx and earlier generations of sociologists, class analysis was a means of understanding the future trajectory of capitalist modernity, class has become part of the sociological repertoire for describing economic inequality and its relation to other outcomes, such as health morbidity, educational achievement, and so forth. However, economic inequality – especially, class identification – has become detached from political identifications such as those associated with a right–left spectrum of political parties in Western democracies. Inequality remains significant in claims that right-wing populism – as evident in the election of President Trump in the United States and the Brexit referendum in the UK – derives support from a 'left behind' White working class (see Dodd et al 2017; Murji, Chapter 17, this volume). Here the problem is that it is 'Whiteness' that is significant, rather than 'class'. The 'left behind', in class terms, are made up of ethnic minority as well as White voters, yet it is race and ethnicity that trumps class. The following section sets out the flaw in sociological accounts of class and suggests a way to address this.

Modern colonialism

Although the rise of right-wing populism disrupting political identifications in Europe and the United States is apparent over the last decade – say from Trump's first presidential victory, and after Brexit – it has been evident as a latent issue for a much longer period. In 1948, the Trinidadian-born US sociologist, Oliver Cromwell Cox, first set out that the flaw in sociological approaches to class and social stratification was that they separated sociological definitions of class position from processes of class formation associated with the lived experience of class (Cox 1948).

According to Cox, the standard sociological practice was to define 'objective class' according to some set of criteria, assign populations to these classes (or aggregates), and then consider their 'subjective' responses to membership in these common aggregate groups. As Cox suggested, variation within supposedly discrete aggregates is potentially as considerable as that which divides groups, since the indicators that are used to construct the aggregates are distributed continuously (more or less income, more or less authority in the workplace, and so on). The real substance of class, for Cox, lay in solidarities constructed through action. 'Class', he argued, is constructed in action and association, not from the *a priori* definitions of sociologists. For him, 'race' was a disrupter of those solidarities, and it was necessary to understand its role in modern societies in the United States and elsewhere.

It might appear that Cox is making an argument for an understanding of capitalism as 'racial capitalism', that capitalism is grounded in racialized differences that pre-exist capitalism and are not undermined by the logic of capitalist markets as Marx has supposed (Robinson 2021 [1983]). However, this is not straightforwardly the case. Here, I will draw attention to the way in which Cox understands racial stratification to derive its origins from colonialism. In what follows, I will not be arguing for an idea of 'colonial capitalism' (as if the two bear a contingent relation and colonial capitalism is one of the possible forms that capitalism can take). It is to argue for a political economy of colonialism within which the structures and processes that are otherwise attributed to capitalism are located and reconceptualized. In this way, we will be able to understand that the regime of private property attributed to capitalism was inaugurated by colonialism and that its expansion does not follow a model of the export of capitalism and its markets (Bhambra and Holmwood 2023).

The period during which the structures of the modern state were being formed – structures associated with political sovereignty and the rule of law – was also the period of colonial expansion by force and the consolidation of overseas territories into their political systems. There was also colonization by European powers considered as 'less than modern', such as Portugal and Spain, as well as later colonial ventures by the new 'nation states' of Italy and Germany after 1862 and 1864 respectively, and by Belgium after 1909. European overseas colonialism was continuous with modernity.

Colonialism is not simply a companion condition of the emergence of capitalism, which is otherwise understood through its immanent logic (an impulsion outwards – whether of markets or production). In many discussions of the history of capitalism, typically four stages are presented. As Fraser and Jaeggi, for example, have recently put it: 'first, mercantile or commercial capitalism, followed by so-called "liberal" (competitive) capitalism, then state-managed (or social-democratic) capitalism, and finally, financialized capitalism' (2018: 64).

Mercantile capitalism is defined by the increasingly global trade in luxury commodities conducted by private European corporations operating under royal charters. The activities of these companies were not simply profit-seeking through turning the terms of trade to their advantage, but also involved claims for jurisdiction and sovereignty in the name of European monarchs. As such, their activities occur in the context of the appropriation of lands, via the elimination and dispossession of Indigenous peoples, and the beginnings of the systematic trade in human beings that would enslave millions of Africans and transport them, as commodities, to the New World (see Kaladeen, Chapter 4, this volume). Rather than understanding this stage as 'mercantile capitalism', it is better understood, as Bhambra (2021) sets out, as 'colonialism through private property' and its extended imposition and reproduction.

In other words, enclosure and dispossession of common rights in the name of private property is a process integral to colonialism, of which capitalism is a part (see Tyler, Chapter 5, this volume). Whereas enclosure in Europe is seen to create a nascent class of free labour, the incorporation of lands elsewhere does not. With the availability of unfree labour elsewhere, free labour becomes a category of social distinction (status) within an extended 'commonwealth' – a status of populations at its centre, not its peripheries – rather than simply a primary economic category of an emergent modern capitalism.

Colonialism through commercial corporations is succeeded, according to Bhambra (2021), by 'colonialism as a national project' whereby European states began the process of restricting the external activities of private companies through the establishment of direct colonial rule and incorporating colonies and imperial possessions within a nationally organized political economy. This includes the utilization of labour – both enslaved and indentured – but also extends to direct appropriation through taxes and other forms of extraction upon colonial populations. The monies derived from empire are used both in the metropole and in the furthering of elite economic interests in the dominions and settler colonies (including those not under direct political control, such as the United States and Argentina).

State-managed colonialism facilitated the development of what is otherwise seen as global industrial capitalism emanating from activities in the metropole. As Patnaik and Patnaik argue, even countries without colonies benefited from the colonial drain from India, for example, as more than 'four-fifths of export of capital from Britain went to developing continental Europe, North America, and regions of recent White settlement such as Argentina, South Africa, and Australia' (2017: 184). These processes necessarily impinge upon what is otherwise seen as the domestic class formation of *national* societies in Europe and North America. This class formation is typically presented in terms of an organized working class and its struggles for a welfare state and the partial decommodification of labour. The colonial context is rarely acknowledged within such constructions.

What are frequently presented within sociology as separate national societies – Britain, France, the United States, and so on – are interconnected by colonial processes that run through them. This does not mean that those processes produce common effects. For example, the United States did not develop a common and public welfare state as became typical across Europe. Instead, it had segregated 'Fordist' welfare arrangements which provided benefits through private corporations that were themselves racially segregated (see Bhambra and Holmwood, 2018). For the most part, Europe's racial divide lay outside national borders in transfers of wealth from the colonies to the metropoles and in the restricted movement of people from the colonies (see Hampshire, Chapter 13, this volume).

What I have set out here is a sketch of a political economy in which colonialism is central rather than contingent (see Gilbert, Chapter 2, this volume). There is no underlying logic of capitalism that can be separated from colonialism. Given that colonialism operates through forms of domination in which only national populations are considered to provide the legitimacy on which sovereignty rests, it is not possible for it to be anything other than a racialized system – as I have been arguing, that of colonial racialization. The amelioration of class division by the emergence of liberal welfare states in the West is made possible by the patrimony of empire, while the end of empire reduces that patrimony but – paradoxically – does not revivify class division. Instead, it invigorates a populist politics of resentment against former colonial subjects and citizens, now reframed as immigrants (see Benson, Chapter 18, this volume).

However, this does not mean that polarization is not a feature of modern social stratification. It is, once we look outside the sociological framing of 'national societies'. Moreover, polarization also inheres in the relations of private property – possession and dispossession – that colonialism produces; and the end of colonialism does nothing to dispel. Marx's analysis was that private property created a propertyless class which was, nonetheless, incorporated into the economic system, based as it was on free labour. There is no straightforward mechanism of reincorporation associated with colonialism and the capitalism that develops within it.

Colonialism provides a patrimony that allows amelioration of populations within the advanced (colonial) capitalist countries, but the end of colonialism puts that amelioration under pressure. The modern system of private property also creates a global system of accumulation that contributes to climate change with devastating consequences for populations dispossessed by colonialism (see Khoo, Chapter 3, this volume). Here we see the problem of the hold of 'class analysis' over the sociological imagination. A future that conforms with Marx's idea that global capitalism contains the seed of its own destruction through proletarian revolution is sociologically implausible to say the least. However, a national politics of the amelioration of inequality through economic growth exacerbates problems elsewhere.

Conclusion

This chapter has sought to show how sociology has been constructed around a distinction between traditional and modern society. In making this distinction, the central dynamic in the production and development of modernity has been attributed to a political economy of capitalism and the class relation central to it. The chapter has shown how 'class' has been transformed from explaining the development of modernity into a means of describing the structure of inequalities with only a contingent relation to political change. This has displaced sociology from addressing the central problems of global inequality and, in particular, the issues of race and ethnicity that are increasingly divisive issues within modern democracies.

It has been suggested that part of the problem has been the failure of sociology to understand how modern capitalism was, itself, a product of European colonialism and that a colonial political economy has been central to its social dynamics. Understanding class in the context of colonial political economy enables a different understanding of modernity, its trajectories and its discontents, especially those associated with climate change inaugurated by the system of private property itself inaugurated by capitalism.

References

Bhambra, G.K. 2007. *Rethinking Modernity: Postcolonialism and the Sociological Imagination*. Palgrave Macmillan.

Bhambra, G.K. 2021. 'Colonial Global Economy: Towards a Theoretical Reorientation of Political Economy', *Review of International Political Economy* 28(2): 307–322.

Bhambra, G.K. and Holmwood, J. 2018. 'Colonialism, Postcolonialism and the Liberal Welfare State', *New Political Economy* 23(5): 574–587.

Bhambra, G.K. and Holmwood, J. 2023. 'The Trap of "Capitalism", Racial or Otherwise', *European Journal of Sociology* 64(2): 163–172.

Carver, T. 2018. *Marx*. Polity.

Cox, O.C. 1945. 'Estates, Social Classes and Political Classes', *American Sociological Review* 10(4): 464–469.

Cox, O.C. 1948. *Caste, Class and Race: A Study in Social Dynamics*. Doubleday and Company Inc.

Dodd, N., Lamont, M. and Savage, M. (eds). 2017. 'Post-Brexit and Trump', special issue of *British Journal of Sociology* 68(S1).

Fraser, N. and Jaeggi, R. 2018. *Capitalism: A Conversation in Critical Theory*. Polity.

Goldthorpe, J.H. 2000. 'Social Class and the Differentiation of Labour Contracts', in J.H. Goldthorpe (ed), *On Sociology: Numbers, Narratives and the Integration of Research and Theory*. Oxford University Press, pp 206–229.

Levine, D. 1987. *Reproducing Families: The Political Economy of English Population History*. Cambridge University Press.

Patnaik, U. and Patnaik, P. 2017. *A Theory of Imperialism*. Columbia University Press.

Robinson, C. 2021 [1983]. *Black Marxism: The Making of the Black Radical Tradition*. Penguin.

Savage, M. 2016. 'End Class Wars', *Nature* 537(7621): 475–479.

Video lecture

Holmwood, J. 2024. *Class, Capitalism and Colonialism*, Connected Sociologies Curriculum Project. https://thesociologicalreview.org/projects/connected-sociologies/curriculum/politics-inequality/class-capitalism-and-colonialism/

Additional resources

Marx: Colonialism and Capitalism, Connected Sociologies. https://thesociologicalreview.org/projects/connected-sociologies/curriculum/modern-social-theory/marx-colonialism-class-capitalism/

Weber: Religion, Nation and Empire, Connected Sociologies. https://thesociologicalreview.org/projects/connected-sociologies/curriculum/modern-social-theory/weber-religion-nation-empire/

World Inequality Report. https://wir2018.wid.world/

QUESTIONS

1. In a Marxist view, how is labour under capitalism organized differently from feudalism?

2. What assumptions underpin Marx's view of class dynamics in capitalism?

3. What are the main features of a multi-class approach to modern social stratification?

4. Why does European colonialism continue to matter in understandings of class?

Worksheet 7. Class, Capitalism, and Colonialism

This worksheet is designed to support AS and A-level teaching on the topics of culture and identity, social differentiation and power, and globalization and global development. In this online talk, John Holmwood discusses the fundamental role played by colonialism in the classed stratification of modern society. He first sets out the standard Marxist understanding of the formation of class identities under capitalism. He then problematizes the key assumptions upon which this understanding is based. In doing so, he argues for a political economy of colonialism which reconceptualizes capitalism. The activities in this worksheet are intended to help students to both comprehend and challenge common understandings of social class and its formation within the context of capitalist modernity.

Time	Activity	Explanation
00.00–00.05	To warm up, answer the following question: *How do sociologists distinguish between 'traditional' and 'modern' society?*	This warm-up activity introduces students to a central topic of the session. Students are encouraged to draw on their learning from the Making of the Modern World section in thinking about dominant narratives of modernity.
00.05–00.10	Recap of understandings of culture and identity	It may be useful to remind students of key terms and concepts related to culture and identity, specifically regarding social class.
00.10–00.15	Watch the talk from 1:20 to 2:26. *In a Marxist view, how is labour under capitalism organized differently to labour under feudalism?*	Holmwood explains that, according to Marx, class is identified with an economic order of market and exchange relationships in which the production of commodities uses labour power, which itself becomes a form of commodity. Under the feudal system, in contrast, labour was understood as a form of obligation to a master. This section is designed to ensure that students have a confident grasp on a Marxist theory of labour and how this relates to class formation under modernity.
00.15–00.25	Watch the talk from 4:12 to 5:32. *What was the role of land and property in the shift from feudalism to capitalism? Can you draw on some examples from other sessions on this course?*	Holmwood explains that, during the long transition to capitalist modernity, feudal relationships were transformed by the expansion of strict private property rights, private enclosures of land, and the displacement of agricultural labourers. The shift from feudalism to capitalism also included the development of towns, new industrial workshops, and eventually factories. These questions encourage students to draw on their learning from across the module in considering the role of property, land possession, and dispossession in the making of the modern world. Students may draw links to the 'Colonial Extraction and Dispossession' (Chapter 3) and 'Enclosures and the Making of Modern Britain' (Chapter 5).

Time	Activity	Explanation
00.25–00.30	Watch the talk from 6:40 to 7:54. *What two assumptions underpin Marx's theory of the class system, according to Holmwood?*	Holmwood explains that Marx's account of the formation of social class rests on two key assumptions: (1) that the expansion of capitalism would have continued to have transformative effects, bringing an ever-larger proportion of the population into working-class employment; and (2) that there would be a shift from skilled to unskilled labour as a consequence of mechanized industrial production. As a result of continued struggles over wages, Holmwood explains, Marx believed that the working classes would grow to understand their impoverishment as a systemic issue within capitalism. This activity asks students to summarize and articulate the central assumptions upon which Marx's theory rests in their own words, ensuring that they have a confident grasp of the two main points.
00.30–00.40	Watch the talk from 10:35 to 12:51. *Why did Marx see social identities such as age, gender, and ethnicity as different to class identity? What is the problem with this viewpoint, according to Holmwood?*	Holmwood sets out that, in a traditional Marxist theory of polarized classes, social differences such as age, gender, and ethnicity are understood as superficial in comparison to class distinction. Holmwood argues, however, that the multi-class scheme allows us to see how these social identities all intersect with class in important ways. These questions prompt students to think about the importance of intersectionality when discussing social class. Students may be able to think of examples of the intersections between these social inequalities by drawing on their learning from other chapters, for example on 'The Grunwick Strike' (Chapter 8) or 'British Black Power' (Chapter 19).
00.40–00.50	At 18:04 Holmwood argues that 'there is no underlying logic of capitalism that produces class separate from colonialism'. *What does he mean by this? Write a short paragraph explaining his central argument in your own words.*	Holmwood argues that, while class formation is typically presented in terms of an organized working class and its domestic struggles, the colonial context is rarely acknowledged. He explains that, as state-managed colonialism developed, it facilitated the development of global industrial capitalism, and free and unfree labour were both integral to this shift. Narratives of class formation, he argues, must recognize the centrality of enslaved and indentured labour, as well as taxes and other forms of colonial extraction, in the establishment of the modern society and its system of distribution. This section invites students to draw together their learning from the previous activities in synthesizing the main argument Holmwood is putting forward in this session. Students are prompted to think critically about the intersections between capitalism and colonialism in the formation of class. In doing so, they are encouraged to examine the impact of modernity on global social inequalities, which is a key theme within the A-level Sociology curriculum.

Time	Activity	Explanation
00.50–01.00	Drawing on what you have learned throughout this session, answer the following question: *How and why should sociologists go beyond a Marxist understanding of class when discussing the making of the modern world?*	This activity builds on the previous section by asking students to go beyond a summary of Holmwood's argument and articulate their own understanding of why critiquing a Marxist understanding of class is useful. This activity may work well as a group discussion.

This worksheet was developed by Isabel Sykes.

8

The Grunwick Strike: Uncovering Migrant Women's Contributions to Struggles for Workers' Rights in the UK

Sundari Anitha

Objectives

- This chapter probes why the Grunwick strike has been missing from or misrepresented in standard accounts of sociology of work and contemporary British (labour) history.

- It sets out a brief account of the Grunwick strike and why it should be understood as a key moment in British labour history.

- It discusses what difference taking the Grunwick strike seriously makes to our understandings of intersectionality in relation to inequalities and resistance at work.

- It locates the Grunwick strike within the wider context of resistance to racism and labour exploitation in the UK, and to South Asian histories of migration.

Introduction

The Grunwick strike that took place in the late 1970s was the most prominent of the many occasions when South Asian women fought for their rights as workers, but this history of migrant workers' contribution to the struggle for workers' rights in the UK has been hidden from dominant accounts of British history. Academic and policy debates and popular constructions about migrants in Britain often focus on the cultural contribution of migrants and their communities – what has been criticized as the focus on 'saris and samosas' in Black History Month events. Such a focus commonly neglects migrants' contributions to achieving rights for workers. Studying about this important and often overlooked event can shed light on the intersection of gender and race in the shaping of British labour histories. In relation to dominant discourses about South Asian women in the UK, the story of resistance from a group of South Asian women workers also foregrounds a hidden history that dispels existing stereotypes and misconceptions about them.

The chequered history of trade union representation of migrant (women) workers in the UK

The story of the Grunwick strike remains largely unknown and is not studied within standard accounts of contemporary British history. While Grunwick is somewhat better known within labour history, it is (mis)remembered as story of trade unions' successful representation of migrant women workers (Anitha and Pearson 2018). These accounts elide the long history of trade union failures in representing migrant, racially minoritized, and women workers. Within these accounts, Grunwick is also constructed as a turning point in trade union representation of migrant workers in the UK, which presents a simplistic history of the change that is not borne out by the events of the Grunwick strike itself, nor by subsequent events in British labour history. To understand the significance of the Grunwick strike, we need to examine the history of trade unions in multicultural Britain.

Trade unions in the UK have a long history of outright discrimination and neglect towards the needs of minority and women workers (Sivanandan 1977). When post-war labour shortages led the British government to look towards the colonies as sources of labour, British trade unions articulated concerns that foreign workers would be used to undercut wages. They demanded that the numbers of immigrant workers should be limited and, in some cases, demanded that they should be the first to be made redundant if jobs were lost. Racism was an inherent feature of the British labour market in the post-war era, whereby exclusionary practices such as the 'colour bar' preserved the economic interests of the White working class through the exploitation of migrant labour (see Hampshire, Chapter 13, Benson, Chapter 18, this volume). Over the 1950s through to the 1970s, in the context of complicity by their trade unions, the everyday practices by management relegated women and racially minoritized workers to unskilled and low-paid work (Virdee 2014), thereby constructing a gendered and racialized division of labour.

This discrimination and disadvantage perpetrated by employers, fellow White workers, and their trade unions was challenged by racially minoritized workers through self-action as well as by mobilizing the support of their communities. One early instance of such resistance was in protest at the policy of the publicly owned Bristol Omnibus Company, which refused to employ Black and South Asian people as bus crew, which was supported by the White workforce and unchallenged by their trade union (Jones 2015). In 1963, a local community group, the West Indian Development Council, encouraged a Black man called Guy Bailey to apply for a job as a bus conductor and when the company refused to interview him despite his qualifications, mounted a community boycott of the bus service calling for an end to the colour bar. This action drew national attention to the issue of racial discrimination and resulted in victory after two months.

Over the 1960s and early 1970s, trade unions remained reluctant to support strike action which had its basis in discriminatory management practices. This included strikes by the South Asian workforce in the foundries in the Midlands and beyond, and strikes at the Mansfield Hosiery in Loughborough in 1972 and at Imperial Typewriters in Leicester in 1974. In May 1974, when over 500 South Asian workers went on strike at the Imperial Typewriters factory in protest at the lack of opportunities for promotion and unpaid bonuses for South Asian workers (Wilson 1978: 56–58), their union, the Transport and General Workers' Union, went on to actively oppose the strikers. The strike was sustained by widespread support by community organizations, but the strikers eventually had to return to work having won few concessions.

Despite the long involvement of Black and minority ethnic workers in working-class organizations in Britain, trade unions failed to adequately address the needs of women and minority ethnic workers in the decades leading to the Grunwick strike. This neglect has been attributed variously to the ambivalence or hostility of early trade unions towards tackling racism and discrimination at work, exclusion strategies against Black and women workers, a broader trade union reluctance to take on issues specifically affecting women members, and the unrepresentative nature of the union decision-making structures which were effectively dominated by White men: a charge that arguably holds to this day.

Telling the story of the Grunwick strike: challenging erasures and stereotypes of South Asian women in the UK

Previous historiographies of Grunwick did not centre the lives, struggles, and resistance of the South Asian women who led the strike at the Grunwick factory. In celebratory accounts of the Grunwick strike, the story that was told was from the perspective of the trade unions. The voices of the striking women themselves were absent from these extant accounts. This erasure of the women strikers was emblematic of the larger erasures and stereotypes of South Asian women in media, policy, academic, and public discourses in the UK.

Dominant representations of South Asian women in Britain locate them within their family and community lives; the women themselves are constructed as passive, confined to the domestic sphere and lacking agency. Their roles as citizens, as workers, and as active members of trade unions who have contributed to the struggles for workers' rights in the UK is elided in historical accounts and contemporary popular discourses. Remembering the Grunwick strike also challenges these stereotyped constructions of 'the South Asian woman'.

Much of the early scholarship on South Asian migration to and settlement in the UK relied on celebratory accounts of male pioneers and privileged male voices as representative of the experiences of the entire communities (Anitha and Pearson 2018: 18–26). The gendered processes of migration for men and women and the particular experiences of women outside the 'the family, community, and culture' were neglected. Where there was attention to women's experiences, the focus was on the family and community, which was seen as a repressive domain in accounts that stereotyped South Asian migrant women.

Such constructions about South Asian women's role in early academic scholarship and in broader public discourses can also be observed when policy makers and media 'expect' to find women confined in the 'problematic private sphere', which then shapes and constrains their representations of British Asian women. When minority ethnic women come to the attention of policy makers, it is often as vectors of the integration of their community rather than as active citizens and participants in the labour market in their own right.

Both the invisibility of women in some of the early anthropological accounts of the South Asian diaspora and the hypervisibility of women in recent policy and media discourses are premised on similar culturally essentialist representations of South Asian women – as predominantly passive, apolitical, limited to and by their domesticity, wholly determined by their (repressive) culture, and as forever victims (Mohanty 1988). Such representations are limited in scope, 'fixed' within a wider construct of homogeneous and unchanging religious beliefs, and offer little possibility of recognizing the struggles and processes of empowerment of South Asian women through social or political agency (Puwar and Raghuram 2003).

Wilson (1978) presented one of the earliest contributions to an alternative account of South Asian women's agency. She documented hitherto hidden aspects related to their migration and settlement, the challenges facing these women in the UK including experiences of loneliness and culture shock, their experiences of marginalization and oppression at work, as well as how women of South Asian origin exercised their agentic capacity despite the constraints placed upon them. Locating South Asian women within an intersection of gender, race, and colonialism, she emphasized the agency and political struggles of South Asian women in the UK, with a particular focus on their role in a gendered and racialized labour market. Brah (1996) also drew attention to the importance of challenging the homogeneous and simplistic migratory histories that are often ascribed to South Asian communities abroad.

A focus on the role of South Asian women in the Grunwick strike can help us understand how their working lives and struggles in Britain were shaped by the different economic and political situations in their places of settlement. It can contribute to the task of deconstructing the category of women of South Asian descent by utilizing an intersectional lens to understand their location and agency in the UK labour market with reference to their diverse histories of migration and settlement, (changing) class positions, different geographical origins, ethno-linguistic identity and castes (see Holmwood, Chapter 7, this volume). In doing so, it can help us move beyond simplistic constructions of agency and celebratory accounts of resistance that are uncoupled from the gendered, racialized, and classed contexts within and despite which they are articulated and enacted (see Murji, Chapter 17, this volume).

The nature of labour exploitation at the Grunwick factory: an intersectional perspective

The Grunwick strikers were English educated migrants of South Asian origin whose families had settled in countries in East Africa during British colonial rule and were the middling class between the British rulers and native Africans. Following independence and the Africanization policies of the new governments, many people of South Asian origin chose to leave, while others were forced to flee, for example, when the Ugandan dictator Idi Amin ordered the expulsion of Asian people from Uganda on 4 August 1972. They held British rather than Indian citizenship but faced a struggle to establish their families in London's unwelcoming society (see Benson, Chapter 18, this volume). Despite their middle-class background, many women, determined to contribute to their families' well-being and their children's futures, accepted low-paid factory and manual work.

In a period of expansion for the domestic photographic market which was flourishing in the wake of cheap package holidays abroad and the associated enthusiasm for family photos, the Grunwick photo processing plant expanded its capacity and began to rely more and more on the cheap labour supplied by South Asian women migrants, who were considered good workers. However, while these women were willing to accept low status employment, they were unwilling to accept the degrading treatment typically meted out to 'unskilled' immigrants in London's workplaces. The strategy of the Grunwick factory owners reflect how intersections of gender and race shaped employer constructions of migrant (women) workers in the UK labour market. They hired workers who exhibited all the classic characteristics of cheap labour – for example, labour that was readily available, that cost little or nothing to recruit, that was willing to accept low hourly and weekly wages, that offered flexibility in terms of hours, overtime, and seasonal demand, and that was assumed to be docile, and therefore unlikely to resist continuous efforts to increase their productivity (MacKenzie and Forde 2009).

Management controls played on the gender, race, and migrant status of the workers, escalating the demand for higher productivity, while seeking to reduce any control or autonomy of the workforce over the labour process. The pressure of work escalated as the company expanded, and productivity was increased through an authoritarian management style where workers were under constant surveillance and were humiliated through being 'told off' in full sight of their co-workers. Women workers were made to ask for permission from male managers before they could use the toilets. As Jayaben Desai, the leader of the Grunwick strike, remembered:

> They had made 'rules and regulations' that you had to get permission to go to the toilets. This woman said to me that she felt ashamed to ask to go to the toilet, so she held back and was in extreme discomfort and felt a burning sensation. I told her, 'Why do you feel ashamed, when he has no shame making you ask loudly, why should you feel ashamed. Learn how to say it in English – "I want to go to the ladies" and then just say so without any hesitation'. (Jayaben, cited in Anitha and Pearson 2018: 111–112)

The pay at Grunwick was at the lower end of the rates of pay found in the by no means highly paid industry of photo processing. Overtime sometimes extended until 10pm, and employees were sometimes told at the last minute that overtime would be required. This had a particularly adverse impact on women, as it interfered with their 'second shift' of childcare and domestic work in the evening. The 'second shift' was a term coined by Arlie Hochschild and Anne Machung (1989) to draw attention to the unpaid labour that women commonly undertake – cooking, cleaning, and caring for their children – after they return home from paid work. In the face of an unanticipated demand for overtime, the women workers at Grunwick were also scared of going home late in the evenings – this was a period of heightened racism against South Asian migrants among others (see Murji, Chapter 17, and Narayan, Chapter 19, this volume). While the nature of the labour exploitation played on the Grunwick workers' gendered and racialized disadvantages and constructions as 'cheap labour', the impact of these forms of managerial control can also be understood through an intersectional lens.

The Grunwick strikers were predominantly Gujarati Hindus of East-African origin who had arrived in the UK between the late 1960s and the early 1970s, largely from urban, English-language-educated and middle-class backgrounds (Wilson 1978: 55). At the time of the Grunwick strike they were mostly in their twenties and thirties. These workers have been described as 'twice-migrants' who prospered in Africa under colonial rule by occupying an intermediary class position between the colonial rulers and the native population. They came from households that previously had employed servants; they were used to the status and respect that accompanied their relatively privileged social status in East Africa (Bhachu 1985). This fuelled their resentment at what they perceived as degrading treatment relating to use of toilets, the arbitrary imposition of compulsory overtime as well as the low pay and poor working conditions common in many small businesses during the 1970s.

The Grunwick strike: resistance and solidarity

In the hot summer of 1976, a group of workers led by the now renowned Jayaben Desai, walked out of a photo processing laboratory, Grunwick, in protest against arbitrary and humiliating management. The stage was set for what was to become a long and historic battle. On the evening of 20 August, when Jayaben Desai began preparing to go home, her manager confronted her with a demand for overtime. Mindful of the complicated bus journey home and her 'second shift' of cooking and cleaning that awaited her, she protested. When her manager summoned her, heated words were exchanged, and Jayaben walked out with these now famous words: 'What you run here is not a factory, it is a zoo. There are monkeys here who dance to your tune, but there are also lions here who can bite your head off. And we are the lions, Mr Manager! I want my freedom!' (Jayaben, cited in Anitha and Pearson 2018: 113).

The workers who participated in the initial walkout subsequently joined the white-collar trade union APEX, and their demands came to be centred on the right to union recognition and collective bargaining. After several months of local picketing, the tactic of mass picketing – developed during the miners' strike in 1972 – was vigorously deployed at Grunwick. Growing support from rank-and-file trade unionists, students, workers, anti-racist and feminist groups, as well as political parties on the British left, swelled the ranks of the pickets week after week to an estimated 20,000 on a 'National Day of Action Against Grunwick' on 11 July 1977.

Coverage of this strike dominated the media between 1976 and 1978. This was perhaps the first strike in the UK in which images of South Asian women were dominant, and the imagery was met with surprise despite the history of industrial militancy of South Asian women in the previous two decades. The other prominent imagery in the front pages of the newspapers was that of massed ranks of predominantly male pickets, which fell straight into a conventional and long-established stereotype of the threatening urban crowd (McDowell et al 2014: 603). Media representations of the Grunwick strike focused on public disorder and represented the pickets as the aggressors and elided any violence by the police.

Documents released to the National Archives reveal that concerns for the policing of public order at Grunwick reached the highest echelons of British government. Notes from a meeting at Chequers (the prime minister's country home) on 26 June 1977 suggest that the prime minister, James Callaghan, encouraged the Home Secretary to put pressure on the Police Commissioner to adopt a more proactive response to the demonstrations and pickets, mindful of the 'danger of bringing the government down'. The Grunwick strike marked the first time that the Special Patrol Group, an elite paramilitary-style squad trained to deal with public disorder and acts of terrorism, was deployed in an industrial dispute, a precursor to its wide deployment in the 1984 miners' strike. There were more than 550 arrests during the strike, which was more than in any industrial dispute since the General Strike of 1926.

Concerned at the scale of the industrial dispute, the Labour government of the day appointed Lord Scarman to lead a Court of Inquiry on 30 June 1977. The political climate became more hostile as an increasing unpopular Labour government struggled for survival. The Union of Postal Workers acted to boycott mail from Grunwick – on which the firm depended to reach its client base. Meanwhile, the Scarman Inquiry (Scarman 1977) recommended union recognition and reinstatement of the workers. However, George Ward, the owner of Grunwick, refused to recognize the union or reinstate the sacked workers. In the face of effective mobilization by the far right to support the owner of the Grunwick factory and under pressure from the Labour government of the day, which had a wafer-thin majority, the Trades Union Congress (TUC) and APEX retreated from mass picketing and effectively withdrew their support from the Grunwick strikers.

With dwindling backing from the labour movement, the frustrated strikers held a hunger strike outside the TUC headquarters in November 1977. As Jayaben Desai put it, official support from TUC was 'like honey on the elbow – you can smell it, you can feel it, but you cannot taste it' (cited in Anitha and Pearson 2018: 129). In the end, the strike was abandoned on 14 July 1978, without any of the strikers' demands being met. The striking women were left feeling abandoned and disillusioned with the trade union movement.

The significance of the Grunwick dispute for an intersectional understanding of inequalities and resistance at work

What began as resistance to managerial control and a protest in defence of workers' dignity and respect became transformed into a dispute about pay and union recognition. Though it ended in a defeat, the Grunwick strike is widely celebrated as an example of labour solidarity in Britain in support of women and migrant workers, and is constructed in trade union accounts as a turning point in their representation of minority and women workers.

At Grunwick, changes in the labour process combined with different elements of the women workers' experience and identity and propelled them into collective action against their employees. The Grunwick strike was a spontaneous act of resistance to managerial control in the face of underlying grievances related to pay and poor working conditions. The workers resorted to collective action based in large part on the discordance between their perceptions of themselves in terms of their identities as women and as workers and formed as much by their experience of migration and their class dislocation, as by any overt racist or discriminatory practices. A useful framework for understanding their position is offered by the feminist framework of intersectionality, which stresses the significance of interlinking social relations of power (Crenshaw 1989). As the dispute indicates, resistance comes not just from the experience on the production line; it is also the result of the intersection of a range of factors embodied in the workers themselves – their class, ethnic and gendered identities, and their experiences of migration; all of which intersect and contribute to their perception of injustice and the need for collective action to restore their sense of worth and dignity that has been affronted by unjust treatment in the workplace.

Focusing on the Grunwick strike enables us to explore the agency of South Asian women workers and renders visible the experiences of women whose voices continue to be marginalized. These women's dissent continues to be represented through familiar Orientalist constructions – both in mainstream media and some trade union accounts – as exotic, impulsive, and somehow unusual compared to the norm of the White male industrial worker. Remembering the Grunwick strike also enables us to challenge the stereotyped constructions of South Asian women as docile and limited to the domestic sphere, and to restore to historiographies the stories of South Asian women workers' mobilizations in support of workers' rights in the UK.

These strikes led by migrant workers in the 1960s and 1970s, particularly the Grunwick strike, are commonly recognized as key factors that impelled the TUC to take measures aimed at recognizing and responding to gendered and racialized discrimination in the workplace (Sullivan 2012). In spite of the way in which the British trade union movement has constructed the now historic Grunwick strike as an emblematic turning point in its representation of Black and minority ethnic and women workers, trade unions' structures, procedures, and legal frameworks have remained slow to deliver any genuinely held aspirations to serve minority women effectively. Since Grunwick, the trade unions in the UK have adopted a variety of strategies and frameworks to address issues of diversity. However, the underlying assumption has been that minority ethnic and women workers lack a propensity to unionize, which has precluded any radical re-examination of trade union structures and practices that might serve to exclude particular interests.

The Grunwick strike took place at the beginning of an era characterized by the strengthening of the workers' legal rights. However, this was paralleled by the weakening of other rights which had facilitated collective bargaining, including rights of trade unions to organize. In 1979, a newly elected Conservative government introduced a set of measures that profoundly changed the regulatory framework in which unions operated. The decades since the Grunwick strike have also been characterized by a profound shift in the nature of the economy, from large factories employing relatively stable and full-time workforces to new models of precarious employment.

The historic struggles for workers' rights waged in the 1970s continue to have relevance in the current context of the 'gig economy' characterized by the quasi-self-employment status of those working for technology-enabled companies such as Uber (taxis) and Deliveroo (meal deliveries). In spite of some significant legal victories, these burgeoning service sectors, which employ large numbers of migrant workers, remain largely unorganized. Trade union approaches to gender have been more effective than to issues of race/racism. However, issues raised by multiple forms of inequalities experienced by intersectional location of racially minoritized women workers remain largely unrecognized as race and gender have tended to be examined in discrete ways and initiatives have remained piecemeal and fragmented (see Kelbert, Chapter 20, this volume). Unions have little influence on the working conditions of migrants who often work in low-paid and precarious jobs. The current context poses new challenges to securing the rights of the most vulnerable sections of the workforce in a context where trade unions remain constrained by both nature of labour market in an era of globalization and restructuring and by increasing restrictions on trade unions.

The Grunwick strike took place about nine years after Enoch Powell's 'Rivers of Blood' speech used violent imagery to oppose the immigration to the UK of British passport holders from the Commonwealth countries (see Hampshire, Chapter 13, this volume). In response to this speech, shop stewards of the dockworkers' union marched to parliament, calling for an end to migration. At this famous Grunwick picket in the summer of 1977, the banner of the very same dockworkers' union could be seen among the thousands of other banners, held by shop stewards and ordinary dockworkers who were now marching to demand union recognition and workers' rights for migrant women. In the aftermath of Brexit, when the rhetoric of the threat to British jobs posed by migrant workers was used to mobilize votes, the significance of the Grunwick strike lies in its reminder to us of a moment in British history when the White working class saw common cause with migrant women workers, and thereby constructed through their imagination and action a British working class that incorporated women and racially minoritized workers (Virdee 2014).

Conclusion

The Grunwick strike enables us to restore to British history the hitherto hidden accounts of the contribution of migrant women workers to the struggle against racism and labour exploitation and for workers' rights. The Grunwick strike can help us understand contemporary social and political issues such as the intersection of gender and race in relation to labour exploitation as well as resistance to racism and exploitation at work. It also challenges the erasures and stereotypes about South Asian women in the UK. The hidden history of Grunwick indicates that there might be other histories to uncover – in your families and your communities – which tell a different story of women's working lives, of the contribution of migrants to Britain and of workers' struggles against exploitation.

References

Anitha, S. and Pearson, R. 2018. *Striking Women: Struggles and Strategies of South Asian Women Workers from Grunwick to Gate Gourmet*. Lawrence & Wishart.

Bhachu, P. 1985. *Twice Migrants: East African Sikh Settlers in Britain*. Tavistock.

Brah, A. 1996. *Cartographies of Diaspora: Contesting Identities*. Routledge.

Crenshaw, K. 1989. 'Demarginalizing the Intersection of Race and Sex: A Black Feminist Critique of Antidiscrimination Doctrine, Feminist Theory and Antiracist Politics', *University of Chicago Legal Forum* 1(8): 139–167.

Hochschild, A. and Machung, A. 1989. *Working Parents and the Revolution at Home*. Viking.

Jones, E. 2015. 'The Bristol Bus Boycott of 1963', *Black History Month*, 365. https://www.blackhistorymonth.org.uk/article/section/civil-rights-movement/the-bristol-bus-boycott-of-1963/

MacKenzie, R. and Forde, C. 2009. 'The Rhetoric of the "Good Worker" versus the Realities of Employers' Use and the Experiences of Migrant Worker', *Work, Employment and Society* 23: 142–159.

McDowell, L., Anitha, S., and Pearson, R. 2014. 'Striking Narratives: Class, Gender and Ethnicity in the "Great Grunwick Strike", London, UK, 1976–1978', *Women's History Review* 23(4): 595–619.

Mohanty, C.T. 1988. 'Under Western Eyes: Feminist Scholarship and Colonial Discourses', *Feminist Review* 30: 61–88.

Puwar, N. and Raghuram, P. 2003. *South Asian Women in the Diaspora*. Berg.

Scarman, L.G. 1977. *Report of a Court of Inquiry into a Dispute between Grunwick Processing Laboratories Ltd and Members of the Association of Professional, Executive, Clerical and Computer Staff*, Cmnd 6922, Sessional Papers. HMSO.

Sivanandan, A. 1977. 'The Liberation of the Black Intellectual', *Race & Class* 18: 329–343.

Sullivan, W. 2012. 'Black Workers and Trade Unions 1945–2000', in *Britain at Work*. London Metropolitan University. http://www.unionhistory.info/britainatwork/narrativedisplay.php?type=raceandtradeunions

Virdee, S. 2014. *Racism, Class and the Racialized Outsider*. Palgrave Macmillan.

Wilson, A. 1978. *Finding a Voice: Asian Women in Britain*. Virago.

Video lecture

Anitha, S. 2021. *The Grunwick Strike*, Connected Sociologies Curriculum Project. https://thesociologicalreview.org/projects/connected-sociologies/curriculum/british-citizenship-race-and-rights/grunwick-gate-gourmet/

Additional resources

Anitha, S. and Parmar, M. 2015. 'On the Picket Line: Jayaben Desai from East Africa to Grunwick', *Our Migration Story*. https://www.ourmigrationstory.org.uk/oms/from-east-africa-to-grunwick-jayaben-desai

Anitha, S. and Pearson, R. 2021. 'The Grunwick Protests: Remembering the 1970s Strike for Migrant Workers' Rights', *BBC History Magazine*. https://www.historyextra.com/membership/the-grunwick-protests-remembering-the-1970s-strike-for-migrant-workers-rights/

Anitha, S., Pearson, R. and McDowell, L. 2018. 'From Grunwick to gate gourmet: South Asian women's Industrial Activism and the Role of Trade Unions'. Revue Française de Civilisation Britannique [Online], XXIII-1. https://journals.openedition.org/rfcb/1790

BBC Radio 4, *Great Lives*, 'Ayesha Hazarika on Jayaben Desai'. https://www.bbc.co.uk/programmes/b09yddxk

Educational resources on migration, history of women and work and on the Grunwick strike. www.striking-women.org

Striking Women. https://www.striking-women.org/sites/striking-women.org/files/striking_women_for_download_opt.pdf

> ### QUESTIONS
>
> 1. Why was there a need for organizing specifically by women?
>
> 2. Who were the women involved in the Grunwick strike? How did their location at the intersection of gender, race, and class shape their experience of oppression and exploitation at work?
>
> 3. Though the Grunwick strikers failed to meet their objectives, why do we consider their struggles an important moment in British labour history?
>
> 4. What challenges do workers face in the contemporary UK?

Worksheet 8. The Grunwick Strike: Uncovering Migrant Women's Contributions to Struggles for Workers' Rights in the UK

This worksheet is designed to support AS and A-level teaching on the topics of culture and identity, social differentiation and power, and globalization and global development. In this online talk, Sundari Anitha details the events of the Grunwick strike, which took place in the late 1970s, and which was led by South Asian women fighting for their rights as workers. She emphasizes the need to challenge dominant representations of South Asian women in Britain as passive and lacking in agency, emphasizing their roles as workers outside the domestic sphere and as active members of trade unions who have been key players in struggles for workers' rights. This worksheet draws on key themes from across the A-level Sociology curriculum in encouraging students to examine the resistance by these workers through the lens of intersectionality. Students are challenged to think about how work and labour rights play into racialized, gendered, and classed social identities, and connect the events of the Grunwick strike to contemporary issues surrounding workers' rights.

Time	Activity	Explanation
00.00–00.05	To warm up, answer the following questions: Why do workers go on strike? Can you think of any famous strikes?	This activity is designed to warm students up to the topic, and may work well as a group discussion. Some well-known strikes that students could identify may include the miners' strike (1984–1985) or the women's strike (2017).
00.05–00.15	Recap of ideas on culture and identity.	It may be useful to remind students of some of the definitions of different social identities and their interactions.
00.15–00.20	Watch the talk from 3:16 to 5:24. What relationships between work, migration, and gender does Anitha set out here?	Anitha explains that many of the South Asian women who migrated to the UK as citizens in the 1960s and 1970s had very little previous waged work experience outside the home. As well as experiencing racism in the UK, they were also dealing with new forms of work and labour relations as they joined factories and assembly lines. This activity helps students to make sense of the contexts within which the Grunwick workers found themselves as migrant women factory workers. It encourages students to start thinking about how the workers' gendered, classed, and racialized identities intersect, which is an important theme within this chapter and in the wider A-level Sociology curriculum.
00.20–00.25	At 6:47 Anitha explains that, under the factory working conditions, 'women had to raise their hands if they wanted to go to the loo and they had to ask loudly in front of all the other workers, and the managers were White men'.	This activity encourages students to think about how the employees' identities as South Asian women and migrant workers subjected them to oppressive conditions that played out along the lines of gender as well as race and class. The questions challenge students to apply an understanding of intersectionality to their thinking about these experiences, assisting them in advancing their academic vocabulary.

Time	Activity	Explanation
	How did intersectionality shape these women's experiences of workplace exploitation?	
00.25–00.35	Watch the talk from 9:45 to 11:25. *What was significant about the level of support for the Grunwick strike?*	Anitha explains that the support received for the strike was unprecedented because historically, when migrant workers and women workers had tried to organize strike action, they found very little support from their trade unions or from co-workers. Workers usually faced a fight against these groups in addition to their employers. This activity might prompt students to reflect on the warm-up task in considering why people strike, and what they know about the level of support received for any well-known strikes they had identified. They may think about whether the social positions and identities of the striking workers had an impact on what support was gained for those strikes, and how they were represented in the media.
00.35–00.40	Watch the talk from 11:26 to 12:41. *What role does the media have to play in migrant workers' struggles?*	Anitha details how the media downplayed the police violence used to break up the strike, and connects this to media portrayals of the miners' strike a few years later. This question builds on the previous task by asking students to think critically about the role of the media in portraying certain social inequalities and struggles. Considering the role of the media in sociological and historical narratives, particularly pertaining to globalization and migration, is a recurring theme within this module and a core topic within the A-level Sociology curriculum.
00.40–00.50	Watch the talk from 14:36 to 16:02. *In what ways do workers' challenges today reflect those faced by the workers of the Grunwick strike? Can you think of some examples?*	Anitha draws connections between the exploitation faced by the migrant workers of the dispute and the challenges faced by workers today within the contexts of globalization, austerity, the COVID-19 pandemic, Brexit, and the rise of White nationalism. This activity pushes students to place the sociological issues set out in this session within their own contemporary contexts. For examples of recent workers' struggles, students might recall the investigations into the dangerous working conditions of garment factories during the COVID-19 pandemic.
00.50–01.00	Drawing on what you have learned in this session, answer the following question: *What is the legacy of the Grunwick strike? What can we learn from the migrant women workers' efforts?*	This concluding activity asks students to collate their learning and synthesize the contemporary significance of the events described in the session. They may draw on Anitha's observation that the Grunwick strike was significant for the fact that the White working class saw common cause with the migrant women workers. They might also reflect on their thinking around intersectionality to consider how social identities and backgrounds shape working conditions.

This worksheet was developed by Isabel Sykes.

9

Staying Put in a Hostile Environment

Daniel Renwick

Objectives

- This chapter explains the 2017 Grenfell Tower fire in the context of race and class inequalities, gentrification, and regulatory failures by the state.

- It situates the fire in North Kensington's history as the site of racist murders, riots, and excessive policing of the Black community since the mid-20th century, and shows links between campaigns for justice from the Windrush scandal and Grenfell bereaved and survivors.

- It examines to what extent the 'hostile environment' had a bearing on the fire at Grenfell Tower.

- With a wider understanding of the politics of race, migration, and urban redevelopment, it shows that the racialized working class is disproportionately exposed to deadly fires.

Introduction

The fire at Grenfell Tower on 14 June 2017 came barely a week after Theresa May had lost the Conservatives' parliamentary majority and Labour's Jeremy Corbyn came far closer to state power than most had thought possible. It happened at the height of the 'hostile environment', a policy developed when May was Home Secretary, seeking to deter migrants from the UK. Despite years of border politics and immigration controls, fears and misapprehensions over the consequences of 'uncontrolled migration' had, in part, led to the vote on Brexit. As Home Secretary, May had paid for vans encouraging undocumented and irregular migrants to leave the country voluntarily (Travis 2013). As prime minister, she promised a 'red, white and blue Brexit', insinuating further shifts to the right, given that the plebiscite on the European Union was read strictly as a vote on migration. Supposedly reading the room, declaratives followed, like 'The time of free movement is over.'

This was not just the position of the Tories but was accepted as the 'will of the people' and called for by Labour in its most radical form; with Jeremy Corbyn himself making statements to the same effect. His Labour proposed new migrants paying upon entrance to the UK to mitigate their effects on the communities surrounding their hostels and other types of temporary accommodation (Brooks 2016). The public mood pulled from the plebiscite was reduced to a wish to make life intolerable for those enjoying the 'pull factors' of British life: unsatisfactory jobs, tax credits, dilapidated houses. And for those lucky and resilient enough, 'leave to remain' and a chance to join a waiting list for domicile on a housing estate, many of which were 'slum-like' after years of managed decline. Grenfell was no exception, despite the costs of a regeneration process which sought to modernize the block but was riddled with austere decisions and fatal cost-cutting.

Grenfell burned in Britain's most unequal borough, in its most unequal city. Such an event should have punctured the inflated moral crisis of Brexit, migration, and the 'left-behind' in post-industrial areas (see Murji, Chapter 17, this volume). Brexit had been explained as the outcome of the 'White working class' feeling abandoned by the state, due to their depleted existence in deindustrialized areas where no meaningful jobs had come in the wake of a shift to a globalized economy, where production was outsourced to the developing world (see Holmwood, Chapter 7, this volume). London was posed as an exception, a country unto itself, filled with a 'metropolitan elite' who served international capital and were, in the words of May, 'citizens of nowhere' because they had sympathies and solidarities that went beyond a myopic nationalism. The analytic frame meant the left-behind of London were invisibilized, the poverty suffered by racialized communities downplayed. But the simple reality of what happened at Grenfell could and should have popped the myth and shown how both small town and big city suffered as Britain globalized and financialized, and neoliberalism bedded in, replacing the welfare state with a market state.

Grenfell was a high-rise tower once touted for demolition as part of a sweeping local plan to shift the demography and social geography of the locality. When these plans were blighted, the local authority instead clad the building – primarily for aesthetic purposes – to match the new leisure centre and school built around the tower. Years of deregulation led to a shift from prescriptive to performance based regulatory structures, meaning materials that were outright banned came to be acceptable in building. In a context of pressure to reduce construction-related emissions, coating buildings in plastics was a cost-effective way of retrofitting insulation. The language in 'Approved Document B' was quietly tweaked – seemingly at the behest of the building industry – permitting combustible cladding and insulation on high rises, with a broken testing regime allowing products that failed catastrophically to be sold and marketed as safe (Apps 2018). Flammable cladding became the primary cause of the fire's spread, exacerbated by the flammable insulation, leading to the most destructive residential fire of post-war Britain.

Grenfell sits in the heart of the Notting Dale ward, where at least 70 per cent of the population live in social housing. Grenfell was deemed an 'eye-sore' by the designers commissioned by the council to reimagine the land. They did not like the high-rise tower being the highest point of the area. When demolition was no longer an option, a cheap plastic cladding was chosen instead. Such substandard materials were not used on the new leisure centre, nor the school, only where people lived. This was a state crime whose victims were the multiracial working class of London.

Building for, not with: muting community voice

The Grenfell Action Group (GAG) was formed to provide community voice and resistance to the redevelopments that were stripping tenants of their rights, communal and open spaces, and safety. They had called for oversight into the redevelopment, which they believed was presenting risks to their lives, and was being imposed in top-down ways; such concerns were dismissed as complaints from people getting redevelopment for free. Instead of being conceived of as a legitimate voice from below, the GAG and its members were dismissed as 'agitators' and 'rebel residents'. They were muted, blocked on the servers of the Kensington and Chelsea Tenant Management Organization (KCTMO), meaning staff could not access the website which became a mechanism of community voice and resistance.

The KCTMO imposed their top-down plans for redevelopment at the behest of the local authority, the Royal Borough of Kensington and Chelsea. As Grenfell resident and GAG author Edward Daffarn (2021) put it, 'they didn't do things with us, they do things to us'. The nature of the changes to the block angered many of its residents, including the movement of boilers within flats and the state of communal spaces while the works were ongoing. This led many tenants and leaseholders to demand as much information as possible to understand the threats posed to them. Had the right to know been respected, the residents could have stopped disaster. Instead, the cladding put a veneer over the risks, as well as covering the eyesore of the brutalist estate, while the KCTMO and the Royal Borough of Kensington and Chelsea 'marked their own homework', in the words of Edward Daffarn. Such methods shielded from view their lack of compliance with fire safety and a repairs list that continued to grow. This way of treating residents was part of a process of managed decline and organized abandonment.

The community of North Kensington have weathered many storms with waves of gentrification hitting the local community hard. The term gentrification was coined by Ruth Glass in work relating to the area and an analysis of the West Indian community on the contested ground of housing. While Glass' work derives from looking at an interplay between 'natural' classes and migrants, the term and Glass' work have often been confined to class. As Bockman (2025) has argued, there is always a racial element to gentrification, with social Darwinist and eugenic undertones, as Robbie Shilliam and I argued in *Squalor* (2022). The multiracial community forged through the struggles of yesteryear came together in community groups like the Westway23 and named the schemers behind the local plan, pointing at executives in the council like Deputy Leader Rock Feilding-Mellon and the CEO of the Westway Trust Angela McConville.

In opposition to social cleansing, the community proposed for common land to be declared and opened as reparations for a community blighted by what Sivanandan (1979) called 'disorganic development', where Britain's history of empire provided it with the necessary labour pools to recover from the damage of the Second

World War. The empire gave Britain settlers and not migrants, for when most were recruited to work, they were colonial subjects (see Hampshire, Chapter 13, and Benson, Chapter 18, this volume). Britain began a legislative and political process to restrict 'coloured' migrants, believing that controlling the non-White population, controlled racism.

London – and especially its most central zones – was worth too much to accommodate so many low-paid and unemployed residents on its most expensive land. Patrik Schumacher, the architect and director of Zaha Hadid Architects, had called in 2016 for London to be cleared of its social housing in central areas, with the supposedly unproductive displaced to make way for 'my people, who are working very hard and generating value'. The right-wing think tank, Policy Exchange, agreed, and were advising the government to designate housing estates as brownfield sites, essentially old industrial land that can be cleansed and built upon. For those in power, North Kensington had for too long been a zone of transition for migrant populations. Much of the area's housing, particularly around Notting Hill and Ladbroke Grove, had been built for a middle class who could no longer afford their homes as the effects of the Great Depression hit. The houses were bought up by landlords and subdivided. In the 1950s and 1960s, buyers like Peter Rachman became notorious for their preference for recently arrived migrants, whose precarious presence could be exploited.

The importance of Grenfell in Britain's social history goes beyond the disaster, for it represented a punctuation in the will to cleanse the city, particularly the borough. Following the fire, social housing estates have not only been maintained, but regenerated. If it were not for the fire, the fate of the South Kilburn estate, or South Acton, would have been shared. Towers once categorized as 'sink estates' have been rebuilt, turned from flats to apartments, catering to young professionals and international capital over and above the established residents. Mass death highlighted the plight of the area, and the locality received clemency from the state as a consequence. Grenfell made North Kensington exceptional.

Race, class, and North Kensington

The history of the area is a history of race and class. Known in Dickensian Britain as one of London's worst slums, Notting Dale was associated with pig farms and potteries. It was considered lawless, and was a black site on Charles Booth's map of London,[1] denoting that it was filled with what he called the criminal classes who would not easily be inducted into the world of work. Such classifications have persisted through the ages. The area was also known for accommodating large numbers of Irish and European migrants, with a sizeable Spanish and Portuguese population providing some context for the famous Portobello Road, and the stunning Spanish school at the Golborne end. A history of militant solidarity is also woven throughout the area, with a mural paying tribute to the volunteers in the international brigades who died fighting Franco's fascist forces in the Spanish Civil War. No such mural exists for the locals who died fighting in Chechnya, Afghanistan, and Syria, but the community bears these scars too. Fears of social unrest framed policing in the wake of the fire, where social order was prioritized above all else (see Fernandez, Chapter 23, and Thompson, Chapter 24, this volume).

Earlier, North Kensington was known for its Caribbean community who laid roots in the area after the Second World War. Pioneers like Baron Baker, who had served in the RAF during the war, settled in North Kensington and helped form the community organizations that would assist Caribbeans laying root in this alien and unwelcome place, where fascists organized openly on the street calling for repatriation and 'n****r-hunting' reached fever pitch in 1958, before Kelso Cochrane was killed in 1959. The history of race and class in North Kensington formed the basis of the Notting Hill Carnival, first with Trinidadian revolutionary Claudia Jones organizing the indoor carnival, before Rhaunne Laslett and Russ Henderson's community fete became the first carnival to move through the streets of the area.

Rock Against Racism had its second national gig in the area, where clashes with fascists took place outside the event. The association between the area and radical Black British history is fundamental to the area's sense of self (see Narayan, Chapter 19, and Kelbert, Chapter 20, this volume). But while this history is written in the stone of the area, the forces of gentrification and the passage of time have seen much of that population pass away or move away, priced out of the locality. Ladbroke Grove and Notting Hill, once a notable cultural hub equivalent in UK history to New York's Harlem, was being reduced to a playground for economically mobile elites.

The history of the Windrush generation is alive in the arts of the carnival. Mas bands have their costumes made locally, at long-standing hubs like Mahogany on the Harrow Road in Harlesden. The country's top two steel bands are based in the area, with Mangrove (a carnival community linked to Crichlow's restaurant) and Ebony globally recognized pan orchestras. National bands like Metronome and Pan Nectar also hail from the area. Alongside the carnival, on the Saturday evening Panorama takes place on Kensal Road, an event that brings steel bands from around the country and arrangers from around the world. Caribbean elders of the area perished in the fire, carnivalists survived the fire, and the wider community mourned, so it was natural for the Notting Hill Carnival to mark the fire.

There have been spaces created, and a minute's silence held, every year since the fire – to varying degrees of effectiveness – but the director of the Notting Hill Carnival, Matthew Phillip, said unequivocally that the Grenfell community and the carnival community are one and the same. The Mangrove mas band have made the Windrush a theme of their costumes, while going out of their way to pay the necessary respects to the bereaved and survivors from the fire. There are strong bonds between the Caribbean community and the Grenfell community. The Windrush scandal was viscerally felt, and the carnival itself became a way of expressing and venting the rage in creative waves, and the politics easily dove-tailed with the pursuit of justice for Grenfell.

The radical Black history of Ladbroke Grove and North Kensington has its roots in empire, in colonial education systems, in the Second World War and the employment drives in the colonies as Britain sought to rebuild itself from the ruin of war (see Anitha, Chapter 8, this volume). The history of racialized communities fighting state racism, the history of 'political Blackness' (see Narayan, Chapter 19, this volume) and the radical anti-imperialist politics of post-colonial liberation all have profound links to the area. Yet since the 1980s, the attritional battle of gentrification and neoliberalism has seen huge changes to the area, with the old front-line now unrecognizable, filled with boutiques and pastel houses.

Yet, more significantly, the population housed in the area's remaining social housing also shifted to populations outside of the recognized systems of British colonialism. Moroccan, Filipino, Sudanese, Eritrean, Iranian, Somali, and other communities settled in the area and took domicile in the social housing of the borough. And it was these communities that were most affected by the fire. The demographic breakdown shows that British-born citizens (many of whom were racialized) made up the majority of the deaths, with the Moroccan community suffering the worst losses of foreign-born citizens. Of those who perished in the fire, 85 per cent were'"of colour'.

Most were British citizens, which should not be surprising given that access to state provisions and support has become laden with conditionalities. Part of the hostile environment has been to deny people the right to access welfare if they are not British. Most of those who are undocumented languish in squalor with a policy of 'No Recourse to Public Funds', with no access to state support or subsidized provisions (see Mayblin, Chapter 14, this volume). It is therefore irksome that so many have fostered the assumption that hundreds of undocumented migrants live in the remaining council housing high-rises.

Grenfell Tower as a hostile environment

The hostile environment was created to deter migrants from Britain's shores and ended up stripping rights and entitlements away from the generation who were brought up British, as colonial subjects and then citizens who had the right to remain. The injustices of the Windrush scandal showed that the racial logic of controlling migration meant that, in the words of Sivanandan (1991), Britain's racialized communities 'wore their passports on their faces'.[2] The migrations of the latter 20th century were often associated with wars and economic pressures globally, but Britain didn't distinguish between Commonwealth and the rest of the world. What it was concerned with was 'non-White' immigration in total, believing that control of the flows of migration controlled the pitch of racism. The 'hostile environment' had brought 'no Blacks, no dogs, no Irish' into the 21st century. As Colin Prescod and I wrote, following the fire at Grenfell, the messaging from the structural racism of local and national politics 'still faintly echoing down the years from half a century ago, says, disturbingly, "Keep Britain White"' (Prescod and Renwick 2017).

When Grenfell happened, there were fears of the death toll being in the hundreds, given the sheer scale of the fire and the failure to evacuate the building. Residents were advised to 'stay put' by the fire service, despite the fire's spread being out of control. The KCTMO's residency list was out of date at the time of the fire. There were no evacuation plans for vulnerable residents and the fire service were not furnished with the details of who needed assistance to get out once the 'stay put' policy came to an end, two hours after the fire started, when the fire had already consumed most of the building and killed many due to the toxic fumes released.

With London concealing a population estimated to be the size of Sheffield in undocumented and irregular migrants, activists, including myself, called for amnesty so anyone who did not have the right to remain could still access services and support for what they had suffered. The government created a Residents' Policy and a Relatives' Policy, which led to 15 'survivors' of precarious migratory status receiving support and 219 relatives of those affected granted an extended stay in the UK while they sought justice for their loved ones. Yet, to many in the community – including many of the bereaved survivors – the attachment of irregular and undocumented migration to the tower was pernicious.

The instinct of many progressives was to speak for the potentially invisibilized of the moment, and to speak the names of the undocumented who perished in the fire. For the first few months, such assumptions were commonplace, but there were always local suspicions – particularly from Grenfell residents – who felt that the depiction of the block and its resident community as undocumented and illegal worked to undermine their rights. Grenfell United, the survivors and bereaved group representing the majority of the community, found that of those who accessed state support on the basis of their undocumented status, only one lived in the tower. A closer look at the 'survivors' policy' reveals that the numbers also include those from housing around the tower itself. Further, there was much speculation that Grenfell's death toll was much higher than official estimates and the final count of 71, due to the supposedly high number of undocumented people living in the tower, however, little data corroborates this claim. The number followed an extensive police search through the CCTV of the building going back months and the forensics within the tower, which were at best partial due to the fire reaching temperatures higher than a crematorium's furnace.

In the context of Brexit and a wide antipathy to undocumented people in Britain, there was an efficacy to portraying the block as populated by 'illegals'. Campaigners speculate that such stories proliferated to mitigate the scale of the crime and dilute the rage that something so ghastly could befall British subjects. Fires like Grenfell should not happen, but if these people were not here, accessing housing that should have been demolished, then they would not have died, the racist logic goes. Part of the community's response has therefore been to accentuate their Britishness and their rights as such.

The Grenfell community held silent walks on a monthly basis for almost three years after the fire, at none of these walks and actions were names said beyond the count. Moreover, a number of the individuals who the state granted support to have subsequently been charged with fraud, having falsely claimed to have lived in the tower. So while the press reported high numbers of people fearful to access state support in the immediacy of the fire due to their migratory status, actuality has shown something different. While there were individuals who accessed sites and spoke to media in the immediacy of the fire who claimed undocumented status, only one person can be confirmed to have lived in the tower when the fire happened.

For the most part, the survivors of Grenfell did not access state support in the wake of the fire, because the state had failed and was continuing to fail them. The distrust in the state was predicated on a litany of abuses, much of which remain unaccounted for. The community demanded that the local authority be put into special measures, but such demands were muted. Much of the discussion on Grenfell, however, has focused more on the fire as a 'heuristic', allowing the fire to function as a peg to hang broad understandings of race and class upon. This does a disservice to the community and cause. The theoretical frame of the fire takes precedence over the real, fuelling right-wing speculation that the government actively suppressed the undocumented death toll.

For all the declarative statements made by poets and professors in the immediate aftermath of the fire, Grenfell now functions as a line on the inventory of state racism. There are facts that simply cannot be denied, like the class and race make-up of who lived in the tower, and who died in it. In a country that prioritizes spectacles like the Bibby Stockholm prison barge to hold irregular migrants, it is not hard to see how Grenfell also functions to repel people from seeking safety and security on British shores, let alone seeking to live in its remaining social housing. Grenfell was in-and-of-itself a hostile environment. But was it so for reasons of race? It has been argued that were Grenfell in a more affluent area, it would have been evacuated. Also, barristers like Imran Khan have suggested that the 'stay put' policy enacted by the London Fire Brigade was itself racist. This is addressed in the next section.

Was Grenfell the outcome of class and racial discrimination?

The Grenfell Public Inquiry has said, after all their forensic work, that race is not the reason the fire happened, nor why it killed. The reason the London Fire Brigade failed to evacuate the block is that they had no training to do so, and no protocols to fall back on, despite having many warnings of the threat of cladding fires that simply were not disseminated to the rank and file. While the race and class make-up of the tower was salient in the public's eye, the inquiry has not found such discrimination causal in relation to the fire. In its first phase report, Martin Moore-Bick and his team were careful to signpost the arguments made about race and class and how such discussions exceed the bounds of their terms of reference. However, in their second phase report, the Public Inquiry team asserted that due to public and political pressures, they looked for race and class explanations of how the fire was able to happen and found none. The cladding scandal, which is national in scope, has seen all manner of buildings covered in plastics that are in essence solidified petrol. It was not just housing for the racialized that was adorned with combustibles, but hospitals, hotels, schools, military barracks, and fancy apartment complexes. A cavalier attitude towards safety in the pursuit of profit and the privatization of the means to regulate industry led to the structural conditions by which the fire was able to happen, and none of this – the inquiry held – pertains to race or class.

Instead, what the Grenfell inquiry saw was how supposedly regulatory bodies became servile to industry's interests. How civil servants had been seduced by the profit incentives of corporatism over and above the need to guard life. In short, Britain PLC prioritized profit before people, to devastating effect. The inquiry concluded that the fact the fire burned where it did and killed who it did was merely coincidental. It was happenstance and could have afflicted students living in death traps like The

Cube in Bolton, where many of the defects that were built into Grenfell were also apparent. It was only the fire at Grenfell that led fire services around the country subsequently to evacuate residents in the event of a cladding fire, breaking with the 'stay put' policy that had proved so deadly.

There is a cold logic to the inquiry's findings and the ubiquity, around the country, of the combustible materials that killed at Grenfell. The use of those materials was not restricted to social housing where racialized communities predominate, but, as Stuart Hall reminds us, 'race is the modality in which class is lived' and fires have not killed like they did at Grenfell Tower. There are buildings included in the cladding scandal where remediation is deemed necessary, but where cladding is merely a decorative strip. Grenfell, however, was so covered in combustibles that even its architectural crown had Arconic's combustible cassettes covering it. Apartment owners in buildings constructed under the lax regulation of recent decades have faced huge financial burdens to address the threats to life that are in the very materials used to construct their homes. Because they are leaseholders, they have been hit by exorbitant service charges, while finding their homes worthless on the market due to the need of remediation. Many have been financially crippled as a consequence and have pushed for significant changes in leasehold law.

But the threat that Grenfell revealed is not an abstraction. It is more than financial; it is existential and mortal. While fires could have killed young professional leaseholders in new builds, the deadly fires of Grenfell, and Lakanal House before it, were on estates where cladding was retrofitted to blocks being beautified in projects of 'redevelopment'. Both were originally planned for demolition. And while there is deadly cladding on blocks owned by millionaires, it remains the case that there is a far higher likelihood that Britain's racialized working classes – those who are able to access the welfare state – are housed on the higher floors of tower blocks. As Danny Dorling (2011) has shown, 'most children who live above the fourth floor of tower blocks in England are Black or Asian'. And it is they who have been over-represented in fatalities. Even the Grenfell Public Inquiry team have left a trail of breadcrumbs, signifying that race and class discrimination could be found in housing allocation. But that transcended their terms of reference. There is much work to be done to establish truth.

Conclusion

Grenfell got the world's attention and was a 'failure of state' admitted in real time by then Prime Minister Theresa May. The work of remediation and repair had to be campaigned for. Aftercare and suitable rehousing has had to be campaigned for. The failures of state have continued, and Grenfell's story told correctly can chart them from before the fire, to during the fire and after; with some failures going on until this very day. But at least there are responsibilities that the state has towards these victims. The hostile environment has made it such that those deemed to be illegal are rendered into a state of exception, where they can suffer disasters and have no recourse to state support of any kind.

On 5 March 2023, a fire broke out in a room in Shadwell, East London. The room was shared by 20 people. The battery of an e-bike of one of the tenants ignited a fire while being charged, while the residents were asleep. The fire killed one of the residents and rendered 19 homeless, revealing the appalling precarity suffered by those trying to get a foothold in the country. Of the 19 who survived, most were either undocumented or on student visas, meaning they had no recourse to public funds. Those classed as British have the right to access public funds and the job market, in theory at least, meaning they can rebuild lives in the wake of disaster. But those who never had those rights fall off the cliff-edge of life in modern Britain. The aftercare for such communities is based on charity, not legality. Where the class contempt of Grenfell worked on the basis that residents should be happy so long as they were getting it for free, the hostile environment means that mortal risks are par for the course should you choose to take domicile in a country without the necessary paperwork.

In the interplay between possibility and actuality and calculations of risk, there are threats against life that we can see through Grenfell – the threats go from leaseholders in new builds to undocumented renters in private accommodation. There are failures of state due to the effects of privatization and there are discriminations baked into the housing allocation and understandings of who lives in social housing and why. Grenfell Tower contained multitudes and its destruction through a politics riddled with contempt and malfeasance remains a state crime. Yet there are other disasters pregnant in Britain that should, like Grenfell, be addressed through their singularity and, where applicable, their generality.

There is a simple story of the tower's redevelopment and destruction, one in which the local authority, and those it contracted, saw the best course of action as demolition, as they sought to reimagine the area and shift its demography. When this course of action was out of their budget, they cut costs on the project, and it proved deadly. Would such contempt befall residents in a more affluent housing development? The cladding scandal seemingly affirms that Grenfell's fate was shared across a sector so poorly regulated that the profit incentive took precedence over guarding life. Grenfell, and the scandals that fall out of it, show that policies and practices burst from their bounds and afflict people from an array of communities and backgrounds. Left unaddressed, the working class, immigrants, and the undocumented will not be the only victims of state hostility. As the bereaved and survivors have warned, 'Grenfell Two is the in the post', and we don't know which address it is going to afflict next.

Notes

[1] See https://booth.lse.ac.uk/map
[2] https://www.statewatch.org/statewatch-database/our-passports-on-our-faces/

References

Apps, P. 2018. 'How Tweaked Guidance Led to Combustible Insulation on High Rises', *Inside Housing*, 13 September. https://www.insidehousing.co.uk/insight/how-tweaked-guidance-led-to-combustible-insulation-on-high-rises-57877

Bockman, J. 2025. 'The Origins of the Concept "Gentrification" within Empire and Decolonization: Ruth Glass and Claudia Jones in London', *Journal of Urban Affairs*, 1–17.

Brooks, T. 2016. 'This Is Personal: Why Corbyn was Right to Pledge to Revive the Migration Impact Fund', *Labour List*, 29 September. https://www.theguardian.com/uk-news/2013/oct/31/go-home-vans-11-leave-britain

Daffarn, E. 2021. *Witness Statements to Grenfell Tower Inquiry*, 21 April. https://www.grenfelltowerinquiry.org.uk/evidence/edward-daffarn

Dorling, D. 2011. 'Unique Britain', *Open Democracy*, 15 May. https://www.opendemocracy.net/en/shine-a-light/unique-britain/

Prescod, C. and Renwick, D. 2017. 'Fighting Fire', *Institute of Race Relations*, 3 August. https://irr.org.uk/article/fighting-fire/

Renwick, D. and Shilliam, R. 2022. *Squalor*. Agenda Publishing.

Sivanandan, A. 1979. 'Imperialism and Disorganic Development in the Silicon Age', *Race & Class* 21(2): 111–126.

Sivanandan, A. 1991. 'Our Passports on Our Faces'. Excerpts from a speech given to the Refugee Council's Annual Conference, November 1991. https://www.statewatch.org/statewatch-database/our-passports-on-our-faces/

Travis, A. 2013. '"Go Home" Vans Resulted in 11 People Leaving Britain, Says Report', *The Guardian*, 31 October. https://www.theguardian.com/uk-news/2013/oct/31/go-home-vans-11-leave-britain

Video lecture

de Noronha, L. 2020. *From Windrush to Grenfell*, Connected Sociologies Curriculum Project. https://thesociologicalreview.org/projects/connected-sociologies/curriculum/british-citizenship-race-and-rights/from-windrush-to-grenfell/

QUESTIONS

1. How have histories of migration and Caribbean community organizing in North Kensington shaped both council approaches to gentrification and community responses to the fire?

2. In the context of the hostile environment, why did Grenfell residents and survivors resist the depiction of the tower residents as undocumented and illegal?

3. What does Renwick mean that the Grenfell fire acted as a 'heuristic', a peg on which to hang understandings of race and class?

4. Does Renwick agree with the Grenfell Public Inquiry's conclusions that race is not the reason that the fire happened or caused mass death? Why?

Worksheet 9. Staying Put in a Hostile Environment

The online talk associated with Chapter 9 of the book is provided by Luke De Noronha. The worksheet is designed to support AS and A-level teaching on the topics of culture and identity, social inequality, power and stratification, and globalization and global development. In this online talk, de Noronha gives an overview of the Windrush scandal and the Grenfell fire, arguing that they raise urgent questions for sociologists. He draws important connections between the two events, explaining how they reveal the ways in which racism is built into the social, political, and institutional structures that organize UK society. In doing so, he invites students to consider who is allowed to be a political member of the nation and who is excluded. This theme connects to the broader topics covered in the book. The activities in this worksheet will help students to take up the sociological questions de Noronha sets out. They invite students to think critically about the roles played by race and racism in the establishment of British citizenship, immigration policies, and narratives of national identity and belonging.

Time	Activity	Explanation
00.00–00.05	To warm up, answer these questions: What do you already know about the Windrush scandal? What do you already know about the Grenfell fire?	This warm-up activity may work well as a group discussion and is designed to ascertain the level of knowledge students already have about these events. Students might start thinking about what sociological connections might be drawn between these two events.
00.05–00.10	Recap of understandings of globalization.	It may be useful to remind students of some key definitions related to globalization.
00.10–00.15	Watch the talk from 3:35 to 4:51. How does de Noronha describe the connection between the Windrush scandal and the Grenfell fire? Why is this connection important?	De Noronha describes how the Windrush scandal and the Grenfell fire serve as reminders of how racism isn't just about interpersonal intolerance but is built into social and political structures in the UK. Taking up the core A-level Sociology topic of social inequality, power, and stratification, this activity prompts students to consider how inequalities are built into the power structures of contemporary society. This may be a good opportunity to introduce the term 'institutional racism' to students if they are not already aware of it.
00.15–00.25	Watch the talk from 4:52 to 6:45. Who are migrants? What are the social and political implications of this label?	De Noronha explains that the term migrant is highly politicized and racialized, only being applied to specific groups of people who enter the UK for more than a short stay. Other people may be called ex-pats, or students, for example. This activity gets students thinking about how social identities are formed and the political implications of the labels attached to them. Students might draw connections between this topic and Chapter 21 ('Modes of Integration'), specifically the idea that identities can be imposed 'from the outside in' as well as formed 'from the inside out'.

Time	Activity	Explanation
00.25–00.35	Watch the talk from 8:42 to 12:26. *In what ways did the immigration policies introduced between 1948 and 1981 change British citizenship? What role did racism have to play in these shifts?*	De Noronha traces the introduction of policies which narrowed the parameters of UK citizenship, removing the rights of citizens from former colonies to settle in the UK and excluding racialized citizens in the country. The activity prompts students to develop their understanding of institutional racism in considering how race and racism have shaped UK immigration policies and definitions of citizenship. This section has strong connections to Chapter 13 ('The Making of British Citizenship'), which may help students to answer these questions.
00.35–00.40	Watch the talk from 18:18 to 19:50. *What can the Windrush scandal and the Grenfell fire teach us about the hostile environment immigrants are subjected to in the UK?*	De Noronha explains that both the Windrush scandal and the Grenfell fire reveal how the hostile environment created by UK immigration policies is justified by racism. While there is a political consensus that the victims of these events deserved better, he argues, they prompt us to think about how everyone deserves better than the hostile environment at all times. This activity asks students to think about the sociological implications of these contemporary events and articulate their significance to questions of social inequality, power and stratification. This is a core topic within the A-level Sociology curriculum.
00.40–00.50	Watch the talk from 20:46 to 22:23. *What are some issues associated with the argument for rights on the basis of 'contribution'?*	De Noronha states that some people argue that citizens from former colonies deserve rights because of their historical 'contribution' to the British empire, as if repaying a debt. However, he disagrees with this view because it implies that people only 'deserve' basic rights in certain contexts. This activity prompts students to weigh up a sociological argument and its counterargument, developing their critical thinking skills. It also challenges them to consider the moral dimensions of sociological questions. Students might take up de Noronha's cue in thinking about how debates surrounding human rights are really asking us to decide what kind of society we want to live in.
00.50–01.00	Drawing on what you have learned throughout this session, answer the following question: *How is the struggle against racism connected to the struggle for freedom of movement?*	This concluding activity pushes students to consider the relationships between social and political struggles, within the UK and also in a wider, global context. In the A-level Sociology curriculum, students are required to critically consider the relationships between globalization, global development, and social inequalities, and this activity prompts students to do so. Students might find it helpful to articulate these relationships in a visual way.

This worksheet was developed by Isabel Sykes.

10

Exploring the Growth of 'Emergency' Charitable Food Aid in the UK

Kayleigh Garthwaite

Objectives

- This chapter provides an appraisal of the notion of 'emergency' food provision in the UK, highlighting problems inherent within the continued expansion of charitable food aid.

- It highlights how institutionalizing the provision of charitable food absolves governments of their responsibility to ensure that people are receiving an adequate income.

- It shows that large corporations donating to food banks in exchange for tax incentives are often the real beneficiaries, as opposed to underpaid workers of those same corporations who rely on food bank provision.

- It argues for renewed focus on the structural causes of poverty to repurpose 'emergency' charitable food provision in the UK and in other 'rich but unequal' countries.

Introduction

Since 2019, there have been more food banks in the UK than there are branches of the fast-food chain McDonald's. Austerity measures, amplified by a continual erosion of the social security system, led to 'emergency' charitable food aid provision in the form of food banks, food pantries, and related forms of food provision becoming an increasingly expected and visible part of daily life (Beck and Gwilym 2022). This was exacerbated by the COVID-19 pandemic, with record levels of need, including the 'newly hungry' who were accessing charitable food for the first time.

It is important to note differences in terminology when discussing charitable food. In a UK context, a 'food bank' refers to a place where people experiencing poverty can receive parcels of 'emergency' food, the majority of which is donated by the general public. In North America, this model would be known as a 'food pantry'. In the US context, the term 'food bank' more closely aligns with the work of food distribution charity FareShare in the UK, which operates the warehousing of surplus food that is then diverted to charities for distribution to people. Power et al (2020) note that prior to the COVID-19 pandemic, there were three main ways that food banks received food: surplus food redistributed directly by supermarkets or indirectly by charities, such as FareShare; food donated by the public directly to the food bank, or through other charities/organizations (for example, a local church); and food purchased in bulk by the food bank from local supermarkets and shops.

In the UK, the most well-known charity operating food banks is Trussell, a large, national, Christian franchise which operates a voucher system for people seeking 'emergency' food provision. Their first food bank was opened in 2000 and was 'created in a garden shed and garage in Salisbury' (Trussell nd). There are currently over 1,300 food bank centres in the Trussell network. Over 90 per cent of the food given out via their network is donated by the public. The Independent Food Aid Network (IFAN), a network of independent, grassroots food aid providers working together to ensure food security for all, have found that there are at least 1,172 independent food banks operating across the UK in addition to Trussell food banks, run by schools, universities, hospitals, football clubs, and the Salvation Army. Overall, they estimate there to be more than 3,500 independent food aid providers distributing meals and other forms of food aid across the UK.

The COVID-19 pandemic and subsequent cost-of-living crisis, together with political instability and worsened global food insecurity due to the invasion of Ukraine, have resulted in the entrenchment and corporatization of food aid becoming ever more prominent in the UK and internationally. The COVID-19 pandemic exacerbated the acceleration of charitable food aid and led to dramatic increases in food insecurity in the Global North, particularly for people in marginalized communities (Cohen et al 2021), reflecting an intersectionality of experience shaped by race, disability, and gender. In response, governments and the private sector increased 'emergency' food aid initiatives but did not address the structural causes of food insecurity, further embedding them as a false solution (see LeBaron and Bhagat, Chapter 11, this volume). In part, this reluctance to address structural drivers of food poverty and insecurity arises from a tendency in UK political discourse to disavow poverty as a 'political' problem. Poverty *within* the UK is only rendered palatable for policy makers and media pundits once 'it is stripped of any political ramifications – where poverty is seen as exclusively elsewhere (the Global South), as the remit of philanthropy as opposed to democratic action, and/or is redirected [away] from any anti-capitalist or anti-austerity commitments' (Kelbert 2022: 567).

As a result, 'emergency' food aid is struggling to meet the demands of people living on a low income. The latest IFAN survey (August 2024) of independent food banks found that nearly 80 per cent of services had seen a drop in food donations while nearly half of the organizations contributing to the survey had seen a drop in financial donations. Nearly all of the contributing organizations had purchased food to make up for depleted food donations. If demand were to increase, more than half of contributing organizations said they would need to reduce the size of the food parcels they provided or might not be able to help everyone who asked for support.

The most recent Trussell statistics (2024) show that more than 3.1 million emergency food parcels were distributed in 2023–2024 – an increase of 94 per cent over the past five years. More than 1.1 million of these parcels were distributed to families with children. Between April 2023 and March 2024, the number of people that used a food bank for the first time was 655,000. More than half of households experiencing food insecurity and three-quarters of people referred to food banks in the Trussell network say that they or a member of their household are disabled (Bull et al 2023). Trussell also note that while White people make up the majority of people who use food banks, Black people are over-represented compared to the demographics of the UK working age population (9 per cent needed food banks versus 3 per cent in the population).

This chapter provides a timely and much-needed appraisal of the notion of 'emergency' food provision in the UK, highlighting the problems inherent with the continued expansion of charitable food aid, and the role of corporations in sustaining and maintaining food banking. The chapter draws attention to the politics of food insecurity in 'rich but unequal' countries, although this is not intended to flatten the differences between food insecurity in the Global North and Global South. Hunger across the developing world is often a function of countries being obliged by international financial institutions to reduce food grain production, in order to expand the production of tropical fruits and vegetables for export to the Global North (Patnaik 2024; see Gilbert, Chapter 2, this volume). Many tropical commodities (from tinned pineapple to coffee and rice) turn up frequently in 'emergency' charitable food provision, and the capacity of donors to afford these products is of course a product of low prices and low agricultural wages in the Global South. This does not, however, fully insulate food insecure families in the UK from hunger that is intensified by the impact of austerity on households' purchasing power. The following sections explore, first, the institutionalization of charitable food in the UK and, second, why it is important to challenge and problematize the growth of corporate involvement in charitable food aid provision.

Institutionalization

Since 2010, the UK has seen a continued growth in 'emergency' charitable food provision. Austerity, the inadequacy of the social security system, in particular benefits sanctions and the problems associated with the rollout and implementation of Universal Credit, resulted in growing numbers of people seeking 'emergency' food aid. The COVID-19 pandemic exacerbated the need for charitable food, and many people found themselves needing to use a food bank for the first time. Termed 'the newly hungry' (Butler 2020), there was a renewed spotlight on food bank use as a result of middle-income families who were seeking support as a result of the financial pressures of the pandemic. The cost-of-living crisis placed further demands on charitable food, with food banks reporting having to ration the food given out as a result of shortages in donations, and in some cases having to turn people away (Forrest 2022).

Charitable food aid has rapidly become a popular and well-supported 'solution' to poverty and food insecurity in the UK. The public are encouraged to donate to food banks in supermarkets, at football matches, in schools, and in their workplaces. Photographs of smiling cross-party MPs at newly opened food banks or food donation drives are regularly featured in the media. Feel-good stories of children raising money or donating their pocket money to food banks are met with warmth and gratitude. However, this support is often framed in tropes of deservingness (Price et al 2020), whereby moral judgements and an 'Othering' of those who access charitable food is ingrained in public opinion. This can be linked to wider media and political rhetoric surrounding food bank use, and indeed poverty, more generally (Garthwaite 2016a; Kuskoff et al 2023). This wider narrative of deservingness questions the motives and needs of those seeking assistance in the form of charitable food, which in turn can have a very real and tangible impact upon the experience of those seeking help in terms of stigma, shame, and embarrassment (Garthwaite 2016b).

There is a lack of evidence on the effectiveness of charitable food to relieve food insecurity (Tarasuk et al 2020). Not all people who experience poverty and insecurity will seek assistance in the form of charitable food. For those that do, the assistance received is temporary, time-limited, and partial. It can be unfit for purpose, with food being unsuitable for certain health conditions (Garthwaite et al 2015), inedible, or past its best. There may also be cultural and socio-economic barriers that prevent people from accessing and consuming the type of food donated (Jones et al 2022). As Berg and Gibson (2022: 3) explain, 'charitable food distribution has continued to grow, but it has done little to solve the problem'. They go on to argue that '[i]nternational food banks often share something else with their US counterparts: they give the misleading impression that they are fully solving the hunger problem' (Berg and Gibson 2022: 5).

Further institutionalizing the provision of charitable food absolves governments of their responsibility to ensure that people are receiving an income that allows them to fulfil their basic needs, such as accessing food. Beck and Gwilym (2022: 11) recognize this, and argue that 'the food bank exists as a safety-net for the failure of the welfare state to address the issue of "Want", one of the five giants to be tackled by Beveridge and the post-war [UK] government'. This failure then creates greater openings for the corporate capture of public policy and funding as part of what Andy Fisher calls the 'hunger industrial complex' (Fisher 2017). Together with this wider public support, increases in the provision of charitable food have been accompanied by growing corporate partnerships in the UK, as the following section will detail.

Corporatization

The role of corporate philanthropy in supporting and maintaining charitable food aid is an under-discussed topic in the UK, but one that deserves far greater attention. Writing in a North American context, Fisher (2017) describes how a self-perpetuating 'hunger industrial complex' is a central part of the charitable food system. Significant here are the ways in which the growing role of corporations in responses to food insecurity makes possible the further retreat of the state. With charitable food, we see responses that involve individuals, local authorities, voluntary sector organizations, and private sector companies in numerous ways, but often instead, and in place of, an active role for central government.

How corporations benefit from the very existence of 'emergency' food provision needs to be explored and critiqued. For instance, employees of Walmart, Sainsbury's, Asda, and Amazon have all been reported to use food banks, despite their employers being frequent donors to charitable food aid (Fisher 2017). Companies such as Sainsbury's and Asda have been criticized for not providing their workers with a Real Living Wage or adequate employment rights, yet ironically, they are some of the most vocal supporters of the 'emergency' food system. In 2022, Trussell partnered with gig economy firm Deliveroo, where some riders are only paid £2 an hour, and are unable to access holiday pay or pensions. It is not only within the UK that supermarkets fail to provide adequate wages to their workers. Oxfam has found that workers in supermarket supply chains frequently lack enough food to eat, and that just 10 per cent of shareholder returns from the biggest supermarkets (including Sainsbury's) would be sufficient to lift 30,000 South African agricultural workers in UK supply chains out of poverty (Wilshaw 2018). The capacity of firms like Sainsbury's and Asda to donate to food banks used by their UK employees is in part a function of the incorporation of extremely low-waged workers whose position in a colonial global economy hinders their ability to demand higher pay (see Gilbert, Chapter 2, and LeBaron and Bhagat, Chapter 11, this volume).

Caraher and Furey (2022) have raised awareness of the role of unhealthy food commodity industries, such as McDonald's, Cadbury, and Coca-Cola, and their relationships with the charities Trussell and FareShare. They point out that in forming such relationships, the charities benefit from a 'halo effect', allowing companies to benefit from a positive image, at the same time appearing to fulfil their corporate social responsibilities (Mendly-Zambo et al 2021). As Azadian et al (2023) have pointed out, company executives are often on the board of charitable food organizations, shaping decisions and benefiting from tax incentives to donate. Like Azadian et al (2023), Spring et al (2022) have argued that ultimately it is big businesses who are the greatest beneficiaries of charitable food aid, rather than people seeking 'emergency' food themselves.

Problematizing charitable food – and imagining alternatives

'Emergency' charitable solutions cannot address the ingrained poverty and insecurity that people are facing. Long-term solutions are needed that focus on providing people with an income that allows people to afford to buy, choose, and eat the food they want. While acknowledging that charitable food aid responds to an immediate and necessary need for people seeking assistance, the problems inherent in relying on charitable food aid are many and must be explored.

It is well documented that receiving food from a food bank is not a socially acceptable means of consumption. The shift from entitlement to charitable provision brings increased stigma and shame for people who are seeking food aid, which can be gendered and racialized (van der Horst et al 2014; de Souza 2019). Silvasti (2015: 478, 480) has commented that 'it should be underlined that charity food is never an entitlement, it is a gift' that does not 'offer legitimate access to all citizens, equally'. The often conditional nature of access to charitable food, together with a lack of choice and dignity, can result in stigma, shame, and embarrassment for people experiencing food insecurity (Douglas et al 2015; Purdam et al 2016).

The solution to 'food poverty' – a question of someone having inadequate food for themselves and their family – is to provide food in the form of charitable provision through food banks. In responding to food poverty with charitable food via 'emergency' food aid, there is a danger that the problem appears to be one that is being solved (Riches 2018), while at the same time the state is being relieved of responsibility to provide an effective social security system, alongside employment that provides a decent income for people and their families.

There are also inevitable power imbalances in people accessing charitable food, which are heightened by fixed ideals around gratitude and deservingness (van der Horst et al 2014; Caplan 2016; Garthwaite 2016b). Douglas et al (2015) use the term 'compulsory gratitude' to indicate the relationship between the food giver and receiver. Charity is not offered to social equals, thus recipients remain separate from volunteers in terms of both status and expectations, as 'social honour accrues to those who volunteer; stigma to those who are clients' (Poppendieck 1999: 254). In the following, alternatives to charitable food are considered, including the potential for solidarity movements to advocate for approaches based on rights and social justice, rather than charity-led provision.

IFAN in the UK has been a leading advocate for dignified, nutritionally adequate, and culturally appropriate charitable food provision. Through local-level partnerships, IFAN is pioneering a 'cash first' approach to food insecurity, where people are provided with money to make their own choices rather than vouchers to access 'emergency' food through a food bank, aligned to its broader call for a systemic approach to tackling poverty. 'Cash first' leaflets have been co-designed with local stakeholders and are being implemented in almost 100 local authorities in the UK.

Trussell have also been trialling a cash first approach. An evaluation of a cash first approach pilot with Leeds City Council found that the majority (86 per cent) of people who received a cash grant did not use a food bank in the period they were receiving grant instalments (Lipscomb and Walker 2022). Households provided with grants were texted a PIN code which they could type into an ATM to receive the cash, which was then spent on items such as food, gas, and electricity. While a cash first approach offers a more tailored and dignified approach, it still represents a short-term response rather than a long-term solution. There are also difficulties in resourcing a cash first response, including staff time and funding, especially given cuts to local authority budgets. Further, it is not legally possible for a Local Welfare Assistance Scheme to support people classified as having No Recourse to Public Funds (see Renwick, Chapter 9, and Mayblin, Chapter 14, this volume), so a cash first approach is currently not inclusive for all (Lipscomb and Walker 2022).

The Global Solidarity Alliance for Food, Health and Social Justice (GSA) are a group of non-governmental organizations, national networks, 'emergency' food providers, grassroots activists, and scholars concerned about hunger and poverty in rich but unequal countries who have flagged the inherent issues in corporate philanthropy in the charitable food aid space. They argue that:

Beginning to end hunger will involve re-imagining unjust hierarchies of power that corporate charity tends to reinforce. Our funding strategies, both public and private, must seek to reform the food production, distribution and labor practices and the punitive welfare policies that aggravate the inequities currently mapping onto our feeding lines. (The Global Solidarity Alliance for Food, Health and Social Justice np)

There are clear examples of charitable food spaces that are shifting towards models based on social justice. For example, some US and Canadian food banks within the GSA are transforming their provision away from redistributing surplus food and towards addressing the root causes of food insecurity and poverty. For example, the Community Food Bank of Southern Arizona refocused its funds and staff capacity to centre community development, economic justice, and the right to food, in solidarity with the movement for migrant justice. Its leadership worked to ensure that food donors provided fair conditions for their workers, and led a campaign to raise the local minimum wage in Tucson to US$15 an hour.

Other community food initiatives have also become more prevalent (Kneafsey et al 2017; Coulson and Milbourne 2021), and are often aimed at trying to ensure dignity, choice, and an alternative to the stigmatizing conditions and conditionality that can be associated with accessing 'emergency' food. Social pantries, pay as you feel cafes, food co-operatives, and community fridges have risen in popularity in recent years in the UK. These are often run by volunteers, and require a huge amount of time, effort, and coordination. However, tensions around deservingness and morality can still be present, as Andriessen et al (2022) found in their research in a social grocery in the Netherlands. They observed how '[t]o appear deserving and realize the cultural repertoire of "good" social grocery behaviours, food aid receivers negotiate multiple at times conflicting moralities' (Andriessen et al 2022: 305), resulting in shifting notions of deservingness which are defined by 'thrift, utility maximization, civility and honesty, loyalty and trust, freedom and fairness' (Andriessen et al 2022: 297). As with 'emergency' charitable food, community-level solutions cannot replace the systemic change in public policies needed to address the root causes of poverty and resultant food insecurity; this requires a guaranteed adequate income floor for all, through an adequate social security system and secure, well-paid employment.

The opportunities for realizing this type of approach have been threatened, first, by the pandemic, and second the cost-of-living crisis, as 'emergency' food providers are being required to meet an immediate and growing need, reducing the time and energy that is needed in being able to advocate for alternatives. However, all of these efforts should not be the responsibility and burden of community or charitable organizations; the government is the duty bearer and should be ensuring people's basic needs are met.

Conclusion

While 'emergency' charitable food may feed people for the moment, ultimately it does not address the structural inequalities that lead people to access food in this way to begin with (see Gilbert, Chapter 2, this volume). Responding to the immediate food needs of people living in poverty is undoubtedly critical and much needed, but at the same time there must be a greater emphasis and attention towards identifying longer term opportunities for structural change.

Questioning who is benefiting from the rise of 'emergency' food aid is a central part of this process. Are people accessing 'emergency' food the real beneficiaries? Seeking support from a food bank can be a deeply distressing, dehumanizing, and stigmatizing experience, despite the best efforts of volunteers and organizations to eradicate this. Notions of deservingness can inevitably creep into exchanges between volunteers and people seeking 'emergency' food provision; exchanges which can be bound by rules, regulations, and conditionality. Involving the perspectives and opinions of people seeking 'emergency' food, as well as those running and volunteering in charitable food spaces, is therefore essential in discussions of food bank exit strategies and ending charitable food, in order to understand what needs to change, and how this can be realized. Critiquing the role of corporations in propping up and sustaining the 'emergency' food system is a discussion that can cause discomfort and unease, yet it is necessary if we are to try to find an alternative to the current embeddedness of so-called 'emergency' food provision in the UK. It is also vital to understand the role that exploitation of agricultural labour in the Global South plays, placing profitable corporations in a position to bolster the 'emergency' food provision scheme while keeping even their direct employees on suppressed wages.

A vital element of this process is to build on solidarity movements and advocate for change. We need to challenge and resist the continued myth that the 'emergency' charitable food system is an adequate and acceptable 'solution' to poverty and food insecurity. Charity shifts attention away from structural issues and leads to temporary fixes which are neither dignified nor long-term. It can provide short-term relief but leaves underlying causes of chronic food insecurity and poverty unaddressed. This chapter has elevated the issues inherent within a continued entrenchment of 'emergency' food assistance, while simultaneously emphasizing the possibilities of solidarity in thinking through alternatives that are based on social justice and rights, rather than charity. A renewed focus and attention on the structural causes of poverty overall – not just on food poverty – and shifting policy and practice towards building more equitable and resilient food systems for all, needs to be at the forefront of discussions of how to rework and repurpose 'emergency' charitable food provision, in the UK and in other 'rich but unequal' countries.

References

Andriessen, T., Morrow, O., and van der Horst, H. 2022. 'Murky Moralities: Performing Markets in a Charitable Food Aid Organization', *Journal of Cultural Economy* 15(3): 293–309.

Azadian, A., Masciangelo, M.C., Mendly-Zambo, Z., Taman, A., and Raphael, D. 2023. 'Corporate and Business Domination of Food Banks and Food Diversion Schemes in Canada', *Capital & Class* 47(2): 291–317.

Beck, D.J. and Gwilym, H. 2022. 'The Food Bank: A Safety-net in Place of Welfare Security in Times of Austerity and the Covid-19 Crisis', *Social Policy and Society*, 1–17.

Berg, J. and Gibson, A. 2022. 'Why the World Should Not Follow the Failed United States Model of Fighting Domestic Hunger', *International Journal of Environmental Research and Public Health*, 19(2): Article 814.

Bull, R., Miles, C., Newbury, E., Nichols, A., Weekes, T. and Wyld, G. 2023. *Hunger in the UK*. The Trussell Trust. Available at: https://www.trussell.org.uk/publications/hunger-in-the-uk (Accessed 2/9/25)

Butler, P. 2020. 'Growing Numbers of "Newly Hungry" Forced to Use UK Food Banks', *The Guardian*, 1 November. https://www.theguardian.com/society/2020/nov/01/growing-numbers-newly-hungry-forced-use-uk-food-banks-covid

Caplan, P. 2016. 'Big Society or Broken Society? Food Banks in the UK', *Anthropology Today* 32(1): 5–9.

Caraher, M. and Furey, S. 2022. 'The Corporate Influence on Food Charity and Aid: The "Hunger Industrial Complex" and the Death of Welfare', *Frontiers in Public Health*. doi:10.3389/fpubh.2022.950955

Cohen, A., Garthwaite, K., Goodwin, S., Guthrie, J., and Heipt, W. 2021. 'Food Banks and Charity as a False Response to Hunger in Wealthy but Unequal Countries', in *Right to Food and Nutrition Watch: A Critique to Corporate Solutions to Food Crisis*, pp 20–25 Global Network for the Right to Food. FIAN International. https://www.righttofoodandnutrition.org/en/publication/food-banks-and-charity-false-response-hunger-wealthy-unequal-countries/

Coulson, H. and Milbourne, P. 2021. 'Food Justice for All? Searching for the "Justice Multiple" in UK Food Movements', *Agriculture and Human Values* 38(1): 43–58.

de Souza, R.T. 2019. *Feeding the Other: Whiteness, Privilege, and Neoliberal Stigma in Food Pantries*. MIT Press.

Douglas, F., Sapko, J., Kiezebrink, K., and Kyle, J. 2015. 'Resourcefulness, Desperation, Shame, Gratitude and Powerlessness: Common Themes Emerging from a Study of Food Bank Use in Northeast Scotland', *AIMS Public Health* 2(3): 297–317.

Fisher, A. 2017. *Big Hunger: The Unholy Alliance between Corporate America and Antihunger Groups*. MIT Press.

Forrest, A. 2022. '"Overwhelmed" Food Banks Forced to Turn People Away After Running Out of Food', *The Independent*, 14 August. https://www.independent.co.uk/independentpremium/uk-news/cost-of-living-food-banks-b2145417.html

Garthwaite, K. 2016a. *Hunger Pains: Life Inside Foodbank Britain*. Policy Press.

Garthwaite, K. 2016b. 'Stigma, Shame and "People Like Us": An Ethnographic Study of Foodbank Use in the UK', *Journal of Poverty and Social Justice* 24(3): 277–289.

Garthwaite, K.A., Collins, P.J., and Bambra, C. 2015. 'Food for Thought: An Ethnographic Study of Negotiating Ill Health and Food Insecurity in a UK Foodbank', *Social Science & Medicine* 132: 38–44.

Independent Food Aid Network (IFAN). 2024. *IFAN Survey August 2024*. https://www.foodaidnetwork.org.uk/_files/ugd/95a515_8bf00bfefae34840bf0c73e9a3d5b326.pdf

Jones, J.C., Christaldi, J., and Castellanos, D.C. 2022. 'The Acorn Squash Problem: A Digestible Conceptualization of Barriers to "Emergency" Food Assistance', *Public Health Nutrition* 25(4): 1045–1049.

Kelbert, A.W. 2022. 'It Shouldn't Happen Here: Colonial and Racial Discourses of Deservingness in UK Anti-poverty Campaign', *Critical Social Policy* 42(4): 565–585.

Kneafsey, M., Owen, L., Bos, E., Broughton, K., and Lennartsson, M. 2017. 'Capacity Building for Food Justice in England: The Contribution of Charity-led Community Food Initiatives', *Local Environment* 22(5): 621–634.

Kuskoff, E., Clarke, A., Perales, F., and Parsell, C. 2023. 'Recognition or Redistribution? How Mainstream Media Frames Charitable Responses to People Experiencing Poverty', *Sociology* 57(1): 157–174.

Lipscomb, K. and Walker, C. 2022. 'An Evaluation of the Leeds City Council Cash Grant Pilot Programme – Final Report'. Vantage Point Research. https://www.trusselltrust.org/wp-content/uploads/sites/2/2022/11/Vantage-Point-Research-Leeds-Cash-First-evaluation.pdf

Mendly-Zambo, Z., Raphael, D., and Taman, A. 2021. 'Take the Money and Run: How Food Banks became Complicit with Walmart Canada's Hunger Producing Employment Practices', *Critical Public Health*: 1–12.

Patnaik, U. 2024. 'The Many Republics of Hunger', *Agrarian South* 13(4): 489–505.

Poppendieck, J. 1999. *Sweet Charity? 'Emergency' Food and the End of Entitlement*. Penguin.

Power, M., Doherty, B., Pybus, K., and Pickett, K. 2020. 'How COVID-19 has Exposed Inequalities in the UK Food System: The Case of UK Food and Poverty', *Emerald Open Research* 2: 1–30

Price, C., Barons, M., Garthwaite, K., and Jolly, A. 2020. '"The Do-gooders and Scroungers": Examining Narratives of Foodbank Use in Online Local Press Coverage in the West Midlands, UK', *Journal of Poverty and Social Justice* 28(3): 279–298.

Purdam, K., Garratt, E.A., and Esmail, A. 2016. 'Hungry? Food Insecurity, Social Stigma and Embarrassment in the UK', *Sociology* 50(6): 1072–1088.

Riches, G. 2018. *Food Bank Nations: Poverty, Corporate Charity and the Right to Food*. Routledge.

Silvasti, T. 2015. 'Food Aid: Normalizing the Abnormal in Finland', *Social Policy and Society* 14(3): 471–482.

Spring, C., Garthwaite, K., and Fisher, A. 2022. 'Containing Hunger, Contesting Injustice? Exploring the Transnational Growth of Foodbanking-and Counter-responses-Before and During the COVID-19 Pandemic', *Food Ethics* 7(1): 1–27.

Tarasuk, V., Fafard St-Germain, A.A., and Loopstra, R. 2020. 'The Relationship between Food Banks and Food Insecurity: Insights from Canada', *VOLUNTAS: International Journal of Voluntary and Nonprofit Organizations* 31(5): 841–852.

The Global Solidarity Alliance for Food, Health and Social Justice (GSA) (np) https://rightsnotcharityorg.wordpress.com/ (Accessed 2/9/25)

Trussell. 2024. 'End of Year Stats 2023–24'. https://www.trussell.org.uk/news-and-research/latest-stats/end-of-year-stats

Trussell (nd) Our Story. Available at: https://www.trussell.org.uk/our-work/what-we-do/our-story (Accessed 2/9/25)

van der Horst, H., Pascucci, S., and Bol, W. 2014. 'The "Dark Side" of Food Banks? Exploring Emotional Responses of Food Bank Receivers in the Netherlands', *British Food Journal* 116(9): 1506–1520.

Wilshaw, R. 2018. *UK Supermarket Supply Chains: Ending the Human Suffering Behind Our Food*. Oxfam. http://hdl.handle.net/10546/620428

Video lecture

Garthwaite, K. 2022. *Exploring the Growth of Charitable Food Aid in the UK*, Connected Sociologies Curriculum Project. https://thesociologicalreview.org/projects/connected-sociologies/curriculum/politics-inequality/food-aid/

Additional resources

In addition, the following also deepen understanding of the sociopolitical dimensions of food aid, exploring themes such as stigma, emotional impacts, and the historical context of food banks.

Lambie-Mumford, H. 2019. 'The Growth of Food Banks in Britain and What They Mean for Social Policy', *Critical Social Policy* 39(1): 3–22.

Williams, A. and May, J. 2022. 'A Genealogy of the Food Bank: Historicizing the Rise of Food Charity in the UK', *Transactions of the Institute of British Geographers*. https://rgs-ibg.onlinelibrary.wiley.com/journal/14755661

QUESTIONS

1. What is charitable food aid and who uses it?

2. How does charitable food aid address immediate hunger needs, and what are the longer-term social implications of relying on such aid in communities?

3. Why might it be problematic for corporations to fund charitable food aid?

4. What are examples of alternatives to charitable food aid provision through food banks, and what can these look like?

Worksheet 10. Exploring the Growth of 'Emergency' Charitable Food Aid in the UK

This worksheet is designed to support AS and A-level teaching on the related topics of work, poverty and welfare, social inequalities, and the relationship between sociology and social policy. In this online talk, Kayleigh Garthwaite encourages students to think critically about how food insecurity is addressed by charities, corporations, and governments in the UK and the Global North. The session gets students thinking about how contemporary crises such as the COVID-19 pandemic and the cost-of-living crisis accelerate existing social inequalities. It also addresses important problems with charitable aid such as experiences of stigma, narratives of 'deservingness', and issues of dignity and choice. The worksheet is designed to stretch students to consider how dominant narratives of food insecurity relate to wider attitudes towards poverty. Building on the ethnographic study introduced in the chapter the worksheet also aids students in thinking about sociological research methods that are used to investigate structural inequalities, and the potential benefits and challenges of these.

Time	Activity	Explanation
00.00–00.05	To begin, answer these questions: *What are food banks and who uses them? Can you think of any recent examples of food banks being shown or spoken about, for example in the news?*	This short warm-up exercise is to get students thinking about the place of food banks in our society and what common perceptions of food bank use might be. This will feed into later discussions surrounding common narratives of poverty.
00.05–00.10	Recap of understandings of poverty and welfare.	It may be useful to remind students of the definition(s) of poverty and of its different forms and the relevance of food insecurity to this.
00.10–00.20	Watch the talk from 2:15 to 3:40. Garthwaite explains that there has been a rise in food bank use in recent years, to the point where there are now more food banks in the UK than branches of McDonald's. *What three factors does Garthwaite identify as contributing to the increasing number of food banks? How might each of these factors have contributed to the rise in food bank use?*	Garthwaite mentions that (1) a decade of austerity, (2) the COVID-19 pandemic and (3) the cost-of-living crisis have all contributed to the rise in food banks in the UK. This activity is designed to encourage students to think about how poverty intersects with contemporary events and crises. It also stretches them to think about the relationship between sociology and social policy in considering the real-life impacts of government policies such as austerity measures and COVID-19 rules.
00.20–00.25	At 3:45 Garthwaite states: 'We know that the pandemic has really exposed food injustices and food inequalities in the so-called Global North, in these rich but unequal countries such as the UK, and Europe, and North America, but this has been particularly a problem for people in marginalized communities.'	This question prompts students to draw connections between the topic of poverty and other social inequalities they have learned about in related modules, for example inequalities related to social class, gender, ethnicity, and age.

Time	Activity	Explanation
	In what ways might food insecurity and other socio-economic inequalities impact people in marginalized communities more than others?	
00.25–00.35	At 7:10 Garthwaite introduces her ethnographic research project in a food bank in Stockton-on-Tees. What is ethnographic research? What do you think of this approach as a method to study social inequalities?	Giving students an example of ethnographic research and encouraging them to think about its values as well as its potential challenges connects to the Sociology A-level requirement for students to analyse and evaluate research methods.
00.35–00.45	Watch the talk from 10:57 to 14:15. Based on her ethnographic work in a food bank, what does Garthwaite say are the main problems with charitable food aid? How do these issues relate to what you already know about poverty in contemporary society?	Garthwaite summarizes the following issues with charitable food aid in the UK: - Stigma: problems of lack of choice in charitable food aid, issues of gratitude, and popular narratives of 'deservingness'. - Conditionality: issues with meeting criteria for accessing food aid. - Ethics and morality: the power imbalance of charity workers and those seeking charity, as a 'gift relationship'. - Structural issues: charitable food aid depoliticizes food poverty and does not tackle the underlying structural inequalities that cause people to seek food aid.
00.45–00.50	Think back to the first activity where you considered examples of how food banks, and the people who use them, have been talked about in the media or in politics. How do the concepts 'choice', 'gratitude', and 'deservingness' relate to these examples?	This activity prompts students to reflect on their work so far in the session and apply what they have learned to think critically about the ways in which poverty is represented in contemporary society. They can also be stretched to think about how these narratives of poverty relate to the other social inequalities they are familiar with. For example, they could be encouraged to think about how different social groups dealing with poverty are presented by the media.
00.50–01.00	At 17:52 Garthwaite explains her work with the Global Solidarity Alliance (GSA) which she describes as 'an international network of practitioners, academics, and activists' which also includes 'people with lived experience of poverty and also lived experience of working in food banks'. In what ways could an organization like this help to address the problems with charitable food aid we have already discussed? What kind of challenges might they face?	Students are required to exercise critical thinking to analyse the approach to food aid being put forward by Garthwaite and think about both the promises and potential challenges of this approach. This activity rounds out the session by challenging students to think beyond the session material and apply what they have learned throughout the session to form their own evaluations of the ideas being presented to them.

This worksheet was developed by Isabel Sykes.

11

Race, Colonialism, and Modern Slavery

Genevieve LeBaron and Ali Bhagat

Objectives

- This chapter argues that it is important to understand how ongoing dynamics of racism and colonialism shape the patterns of forced labour, and must be addressed in solutions to it.

- It argues that the popular 'new slavery' framing of contemporary forced labour focuses excessively on stories of individual exploitation and abuse. By failing to challenge systemic injustice, such an approach allows politicians to perpetrate dangerous politics that can harm the people they claim to help under the banner of combating slavery.

- The chapter suggests that we must focus on lived experiences of those on the margins of the global economy who are vulnerable to forced labour and modern slavery.

- It argues that corporations must be held accountable for perpetuating the conditions and practices of modern slavery to which one in 150 people are currently subjected.

Introduction

While most people think of slavery as a historic problem, unfortunately, modern forms of slavery are on the rise. Globally, 50 million people – around one in every 150 – are estimated to be experiencing modern slavery by the International Labour Organization, Walk Free, and International Organization for Migration (2022: 4). Global prevalence estimates of modern slavery are still at an early stage and the numbers are unlikely to be precise. Nevertheless, the preliminary numbers show that slavery has not simply disappeared after being outlawed in most countries across the 19th century, but rather remains widespread today.

There are different types of modern slavery. Forced labour is the most common form that it takes today. The legal definition of forced labour, established by the

International Labour Organization in 1930, is 'all work or service which is exacted from any person under the threat of a penalty and for which the person has not offered himself or herself voluntarily' (ILO 1930). In other words, forced labour means that someone is being forced to work at a job involuntarily and cannot leave because they are experiencing coercion by their employer. Coercion might take the form of physical violence to the worker, threats of violence to them or their family, or withholding a worker's passport.

Most forced labour takes place at the hands of businesses producing goods that we use every day, like computers, meat, clothes and shoes, coffee and tea. It can take place along every stage of the supply chain. The term 'global supply chain' refers to the networks of production and distribution spread across multiple countries that ultimately produce goods. If we take the example of a laptop computer, that means there could be forced workers along various stages of the supply chain, including: extracting minerals like copper, gold, and cobalt; making the component parts like glass and batteries; assembling the computer; packaging the computer; and selling it in a store. However, there are also predictable patterns surrounding the workers who become vulnerable to forced labour and the businesses who use it (LeBaron 2021), as we explore in this chapter.

Awareness of the problem of forced labour has surged over recent decades. Rarely does a new week pass without an article about forced labour being published in *The Guardian*, *The New York Times*, *AP*, and other newspapers and online media sites read by millions of people around the world. Prominent athletes, musicians, and actors have joined the cause to end contemporary forms of slavery, including Cher, Colin Farrell, Jada Pinkett Smith, and Pharrell (International Labour Organization 2025). Governments have passed a slew of new laws trying to curb business use of forced labour and human trafficking in their supply chains. New multilateral efforts have been pledged, such as through the G7 (which is comprised of France, the United States, UK, Germany, Japan, Italy, and France). Businesses have formed taskforces to combat the problem, including the Global Business Coalition Against Human Trafficking led by Amazon, Google, Coca-Cola, Marriott, and other companies, and they hold sessions on modern slavery at music festivals like SXSW and the World Economic Forum. Religious and civil society initiatives like Operation Underground Railroad have launched crusades to 'rescue' people from jobs they consider to be slavery (though the workers themselves and their families sometimes see things differently).

A new body of academic scholarship, too, has arisen to deepen awareness and knowledge about the problem, which is often called the 'new slavery' literature. Authors like Kevin Bales and Benjamin Skinner have helped to popularize the idea that a modern form of slavery is thriving in the contemporary global economy, and that there are more slaves today than at any other time in human history (Bales 2004; Skinner 2008; Bales and Soodalter 2009). When they explain why slavery is so popular today, they often blame governments of less rich countries, corruption, cultural backwardness, population growth, or the moral shortcomings of individual perpetrators. As Kevin Bales put it, 'government corruption, plus the vast increase in the number of people and their ongoing impoverishment, has led to the new slavery' (2004: 14).

One problem with this explanation is that it is profoundly ahistorical. Not only does it attribute modern slavery to the backwardness of entire countries and cultures, but it also overlooks the role of colonial capitalism in creating the conditions where forced labour continues to thrive (see Gilbert, Chapter 2, and Kaladeen, Chapter 4, this volume). By colonial capitalism we mean the intertwined nature of colonial conquest and domination with the spread of markets, private property, and profit-driven production. These include: dispossession and expropriation (such as land theft and destruction of Indigenous ways of being); colonial histories of forced labour (which continue to shape the lives of workers and communities); the ongoing role of wealthy states and corporations in engineering trade systems that yield highly unequal wealth distribution which create pressure towards endemic exploitation, violence, and coercion; and racial dynamics in national economies and global trade (see Khoo, Chapter 3, this volume). It also overlooks the deep linkages between historic trade in enslaved people and contemporary forms of forced labour.

We argue in this chapter that there is a need to better understand how colonial and racial dynamics shape the context in which modern forms of forced labour occur and are made use of by businesses. Viewing contemporary forced labour through the lens of colonial and racial politics shifts common understandings of the root causes of these problems, as well as possible solutions to them.

The problems with dominant accounts of modern slavery

Newspapers and media sites depict modern slavery using attention-grabbing words like slaves and enslavers, chained, whipped, forced, coerced, illegal trade of human beings, starved, and sex trafficking. Story after story tells us that enslaved people are making the food we are eating, the clothes we are wearing, and the cars we drive – and describes their horrible conditions perpetrated by bad guys and criminals. No doubt, there is truth in these accounts. But the constant flow of sensationalist headlines by news organizations dependent on clicks and engagement can also create the skewed perception that if we just rescue the workers and lock up the bad guys, the forced labour will stop. But the reality is far more complicated.

The new body of academic research on modern slavery is quite diverse. But a very influential stream of that research – the 'new slavery' literature – bears much in common with dominant media accounts of forced labour. Authors in this tradition are seeking to raise attention about the problem by zeroing in on stories of individual abuse and exploitation, and the people – and only occasionally the businesses they are part of – that perpetrate these practices. Influential books in this tradition include *Disposable People: New Slavery in the Global Economy* (Bales 2004), *Modern Slavery: A Global Perspective* (Kara 2017), and *Nobodies: Modern American Slave Labor and the Dark Side of the New Global Economy* (Bowe 2007). Without question, analysis like this played an important part in putting modern slavery at the top of the policy priority list at the outset of the 21st century.

But as academics and researchers have learned more about the nature of forced labour in the contemporary global economy, such accounts have come under fire. The critiques of the 'new slavery' literature developed by scholars like Elena Shih, Janie Chuang, Sam Okyere, Julia O'Connell Davidson, Nandita Sharma, Kamala Kempadoo, Lyndsey Beutin, and others include that this perspective:

- distorts the true nature and causes of the problem and effective solutions to it;
- gives the impression that if you lock up individual perpetrators through criminal justice solutions, modern slavery could disappear;
- explains the causes of slavery and bondage as being rooted in the past, rather than contemporary economic dynamics;
- obscures and obfuscates worker agency;
- by failing to challenge systemic injustice, it allows politicians to perpetrate dangerous politics that can harm the people they claim to help under the banner of combating slavery;
- can crowd out support for labour and migrant rights (see Anitha, Chapter 8, and Murji, Chapter 17, this volume);
- can mask and naturalize the racial, colonial, gendered, and economically unequal fabric of the global economy; and
- attributes to cultural backwardness and 'traditional' societies what are in fact results of contemporary capitalism, including the ongoing role of wealthy states and corporations in engineering global supply chains that yield unequal wealth distribution and can result in endemic exploitation, violence, and coercion for people with less power.

At their core, these criticisms of the 'new slavery' framing of the problem are worried that in their quest to draw attention to the cause, scholars are over-simplifying the dynamics surrounding forced labour today. This is then leading to problems and weaknesses in the solutions and interventions created by government decision-makers, civil society and advocacy organizations, international organizations and others.

Given the theme of this volume, we focus on the blind spots of dominant framings in relation to racial and colonial capitalism. Before explaining more about what the new slavery approach misses, we will first define our key terms. Colonialism is a set of ideas, policies, and practices through which a country establishes control over a foreign territory. During the formal colonial era of world history (15th to mid-20th century), European powers asserted control – often through violence and force – over much of the rest of the world. This included exploiting Indigenous people, pillaging natural resources, and imposing European laws and ways of life through cultural superiority. During this same period, the global capitalist economic system – through which land, labour, and capital are privately owned and operated to maximize profit instead of providing for social need – was formed and expanded. The idea that we continue to live in a 'colonial global economy' seeks to 'recognize the significance of historical colonial relations to both the establishment and continued reproduction of global political economy' (Bhambra 2020: 307). In other words, it captures the ways in which legacies of colonialism and ongoing colonial practices continue to shape people's lives.

Race refers to the organization of people, cultures, and societies based on phenotypes or perceived physical differences and attributes. Race is a social construction which gives social significance to characteristics such as hair texture, skin colour, and facial features. Despite having no scientific basis, racial classification continues to be used to sustain privilege and social hierarchy. Importantly, the pseudoscience around race (also known as race-thinking) emerges in step with European colonization thereby justifying the conquest of non-European lands and people. Race-thinking allowed for immensely violent colonial policies such as the classification of Indigenous Australians as 'fauna and flora' and Africans as non-people.

These types of policies allowed Europeans to dispossess Indigenous peoples from their lands and abduct millions of Africans in the transatlantic trade in enslaved people. Race and colonialism are inextricably linked, and race-thinking emerges as a way to exploit the labour of racialized non-European people (Fields and Fields 2012). For example, in the context of the historic slave system in the United States, White people had the legal right to own and exploit Black African people who were denied basic human rights and bought and sold as property. The point of this system was to produce all sorts of commodities such as sugar, tobacco, and cotton very cheaply. White/European supremacy provided the ideological backbone to support this type of exploitation.

These examples of exploitation are perhaps best encapsulated by the term 'racial capitalism', which seeks to capture the ways in which capitalism and racism are co-constitutive, or, in other words, understand why racial inequality is so persistent in the capitalist global economy. Historian Cedric Robinson is often credited with first using the term racial capitalism (Robinson 2000), as he sought to understand how the rise of capitalism and the exploitation of non-European peoples (especially Africans), including through slavery, were mutually reinforcing processes in the context of colonialism. Using examples such as the transatlantic trade in enslaved people, the Irish famine, and apartheid South Africa, Cedric Robinson and scholars such as Jodi Melamed, Robin Kelley, and Saidiya Hartman argue that all capitalism is racial capitalism. By this they mean that historical and contemporary capitalist expansion rests on the exploitation of racialized people.

Some scholars have sought to combine the concepts of 'colonial capitalism' and 'racial capitalism' into one concept: 'colonial racial capitalism' (Koshy et al 2022). This concept seeks to capture how the exploitation of colonized people and their labour has been shaped by social construction of racial categories. There is a lot of debate around how precisely colonialism, racism, and capitalism fit together and exactly what force is causal of various outcomes. We sidestep some of those questions, as they are not critical for our purposes. The key point we wish to make is simply that although racism and colonialism are not commonly discussed in the 'new slavery' literature, it is important to understand how both ongoing dynamics of racism and colonialism shape the patterns of forced labour and must be addressed in solutions to it.

Understanding racial and colonial dynamics

Unfortunately, while historic systems of slavery were widely outlawed across most countries in the 19th century, and today forced labour is illegal in most countries in the world, people are not born into the global economy or labour market on fair and equal footing. Historical processes like colonialism, the trade in enslaved people, and expropriation have integrated some countries on less advantageous terms. Meanwhile, the countries that benefited from the wealth extraction and geopolitical control associated with colonialism and historic trade in enslaved people continue to command considerable power in the global economy. As such, there is persistent inequality in the value of people's work on the global labour market depending on whether they are born in a rich and powerful country or not. Many people try to improve the value of their labour by migrating to richer countries where wages are higher. Compounding this, within national economies, individual social differences – the intertwined identities of race, class, gender, ability, sexuality, and other embodied identities – can shape people's experiences, pay, and conditions in the labour market.

When we centre the dynamics of colonialism and race in analysing forced labour, some of the trends associated with contemporary forms of it make more sense. For instance, the International Labour Organization estimates that practices of modern slavery are most prevalent in Africa and Asia-Pacific, as well as among Europe and Central Asia, where migrants are disproportionately vulnerable (2022: 18). Across Africa, forced labour has been documented as particularly prevalent in countries that experienced slavery, or where those of slave descent continue to face ongoing discrimination (ILO 2005, 2009). It is not coincidental that the sites and spaces where there are high concentrations of forced labour occur in countries that were former sites of colonial extraction.

The colonial linkages persist – many countries in Africa, Asia, and Latin America remain poorly integrated, commodity dependent, and rife with low-value added processes in supply chains (Coke-Hamilton 2019); this means that the workers in such countries often have a very difficult time making enough money and experience higher rates of poverty. That poverty, in turn, shapes their vulnerability to forced labour because workers can scarcely refuse to work – even where they have real concerns about the pay and conditions. The patterns and ongoing dynamics of colonialism shape the contemporary global labour market in ways that help to explain why workers in some countries are persistently vulnerable to forced labour.

At the same time, the International Labour Organization's data has long made it clear that forced labour does not happen according to random patterns. Rather, social differences shape the patterns of forced labour and which individuals are most likely to experience it. Indigenous peoples, racialized populations, migrants, as well as women and girls, are disproportionately concentrated in contemporary forced labour. For instance, rates of forced labour have been documented as especially high among lower caste persons in India, Indigenous minorities in Nepal, and Indigenous people in Latin America (LeBaron et al 2019). In part, this relates to the legacies of historic enslavement and colonialism which created an association between certain identities and highly exploited labour, which are today reinforced as bias and discrimination in labour markets, as well as ongoing dynamics of prejudice and the unequal footing on which some groups of people enter the labour market compared to others. As well, it relates to employers' preferences. For instance, in a study of sugar production in Brazil, Nicola Phillips (2013) found that workers experiencing forced labour were disproportionately racialized men, since employers reported their gender and racial characteristics suited them best for what is extremely demanding physical labour (see also McGrath 2013).

Lacking availability of decent work means that large swathes of the global population have had little choice but to seek work in the bottom rungs of the supply chain, no matter how poorly paid, insecure, and exploitative that work might be. We live in a moment where global displacement has reached unprecedented heights due to conflict, violence, economic insecurity, and climate change. This means that more people than ever before are forced to move away from their traditional lands and livelihoods across international borders. The formerly colonized territories on the continents of Asia, Africa, and South America are in turn producing the largest numbers of migrants and refugees as their lands become uninhabitable due in part to the legacies of racial and colonial capitalism.

As various scholars have discussed (Mullings 2021; Rajaram 2021; Morris 2023), groups like migrants and refugees are in search of work and often face exploitation due to their race, gender, and foreigner status. For instance, even in a country like Canada which is known to champion human rights across the planet, the United Nations Special Rapporteur called Canada's use of migrant workers a 'breeding ground for slavery' (Cecco 2024). The findings of the Special Rapporteur indicate that migrant workers who were brought to Canada under the Temporary Foreign Worker Program faced debt bondage, emotional and psychological abuse, wage theft, hazardous workplace conditions, long work hours, sexual violence, and labour exploitation. These migrants come from poorer Global South countries such as Jamaica, Mexico, and Guatemala, indicating the ongoing devaluing of racialized labour in the colonial global economy.

Asylum seekers and refugees, unlike migrant workers, are not officially labourers but recent studies have shown that these groups are facing exploitation at various stages in their displacement journeys in places like detention centres, refugee camps, and in cities of relocation (see Mayblin, Chapter 14, this volume). For example, Ali Bhagat's study (2023) of queer refugees in South Africa, France, and Kenya identifies instances where refugees engage in unpaid work, unsafe sex work, and exploitative gig work in order to survive in contexts where they lack human rights and face xenophobic and homo/transphobic social violence. Similarly, Julia Morris' (2020) study in Jordan highlights the ways in which Syrian refugees (and non-Syrian migrant workers) end up in precarious and hazardous informal work that shores up profits for private sector actors while bolstering the reputation of international organizations and government. Despite growing evidence of poor working conditions, exploitation, and various forms of violence, refugees continue to engage in these forms of labour because the alternative is facing severe violence or death in their countries of origin. Many asylum seekers and refugees are undocumented or struggle to gain legal recognition, which further contributes to their precarity. Not all of these situations amount to forced labour; however, the key point is that more severe forms of exploitation like forced labour thrive where more minor forms of everyday exploitation are widespread.

The irony of forced labour in the current era of capitalism is that in spite of the violence and exploitation that it can carry, workers sometimes enter into such relations knowingly because the alternative is economically even more bleak. For instance, many people in economically disadvantaged countries even struggle to even sell their labour on the market at all and rely on piecemeal forms of assistance from non-governmental organizations, kinship ties, community networks, international aid, and state assistance in order to survive. Others rely on informal sector options like sex work or waste-picking. It is not unimaginable that those who struggle to access the means of their survival also get folded into the extremely insecure low-value-added end of the supply chain.

Just as acknowledging colonial and racial capitalism shifts our understanding of the problem, so too should it shift our understandings of solutions. Given the systemic dynamics that underpin vulnerability to forced labour, it is not enough to simply put forward individual-level solutions like incarcerating perpetrators. Rather, there is a need to deal with the underlying root causes of forced labour, which include racial and economic injustice and inequality, and inequality between nations.

Conclusion

Acknowledging colonial and racial capitalism demands innovative, radically inclusive strategies to combat the pervasive issue of modern slavery. Reimagining labour protections within contemporary capitalism is essential. These should be targeted at the populations most vulnerable to forced labour, including Indigenous peoples, women, and migrant and refugee workers. Migrants and refugee individuals – predominantly racialized, undocumented, and originating from formerly colonized countries in the Global South – remain at the forefront of global exploitation, and their lack of protection and opportunities for decent work in the global economy provide a clear example of how colonial and racialized capitalism connects to forced labour.

Scholars of racial capitalism emphasize that all capitalism is inherently racial, with historical patterns of enslavement, domination, and poverty perpetuating severe inequalities today. Compounding this are colonial borders that impose violence and deny fundamental human rights under the guise of protecting the nation state amidst rising xenophobia, anti-migrant sentiment, and White supremacy (Walia 2013; Cross 2020; see Murji, Chapter 17, Narayan, Chapter 19, and Kelbert, Chapter 20, this volume). Migrant workers need to be protected, particularly when they are brought to countries to produce cheap commodities, engage in piecemeal agricultural work, and conduct gig work – all areas where protections are glaringly insufficient.

Research on modern slavery must also pivot away from sensationalist narratives found in 'new slavery' literature, which often obscure the colonial legacies and geopolitical forces shaping exploitation. Centring the voices of marginalized groups through intersectional perspectives – attending to race, gender, sexuality, class, caste, and ability – offers a pathway to uncover hidden dynamics and amplify the lived experiences of those on the margins of the global economy. Moreover, corporations must be held accountable for perpetuating these conditions, as their failure to protect workers directly contributes to systemic exploitation. Scholars of racial capitalism such as Cedric Robinson remind us that, despite widespread racial and economic violence, solidarity movements have historically resisted these injustices. Situating modern slavery within the broader framework of global capitalism can strengthen transnational solidarity among workers, unions, and activists working towards equitable supply chains.

While not exhaustive, these approaches – coupled with environmental justice (see Baruah, Chapter 28, this volume), worker-driven social responsibility programmes, trade reform, and a challenge to capitalist profit ideologies – highlight the urgent need to address how racial and colonial capitalism continue to shape labour dynamics in both the Global North and South.

References

Bales, K. 2004. *Disposable People: New Slavery in the Global Economy*. University of California Press.

Bales, K. and Soodalter, R. 2009. *The Slave Next Door: Human Trafficking and Slavery in America Today*. University of California Press.

Bhagat, A. 2023. 'Queer Global Displacement: Social Reproduction, Refugee Survival, and Organized Abandonment in Nairobi, Cape Town, and Paris', *Antipode* 55(5): 1517–1537.

Bhambra, G. 2020. 'Colonial Global Economy: Towards a Theoretical Reorientation of Political Economy', *Review of International Political Economy* 28: 307–322.

Bowe, J. 2007. *Nobodies: Modern American Slave Labor and the Dark Side of the New Global Slavery*. Random House.

Cecco, L. 2024. 'UN Envoy Calls Canada's Use of Migrant Workers "Breeding Ground for Slavery"'. https://www.theguardian.com/world/article/2024/aug/13/canada-foreign-workers-un-report

Coke-Hamilton, P. 2019. 'We Must Help Developing Countries Escape Commodity Dependence'. *World Economic Forum*. https://www.weforum.org/stories/2019/05/why-commodity-dependence-is-bad-news-for-all-of-us/

Cross, H. 2020. *Migration beyond Capitalism*. John Wiley & Sons.

Fields, B.J. and Fields, K.E. 2012. *Racecraft: The Soul of Inequality in American Life*. Verso Books.

International Labour Organization. 1930. C029- Forced Labour Convention, 1930 (No. 29). ILO.

International Labour Organization. 2005. *A Global Alliance Against Forced Labour*. ILO.

International Labour Organization. 2009. *The Cost of Coercion*. ILO.

International Labour Organization. 2025. *End Slavery Now*. https://www.ilo.org/about-ilo/artworks/artworks-topics/take-stand-against-modern-slavery/end-slavery-now

International Labour Organization, Walk Free, and International Organization for Migration. 2022. *Global Estimates of Modern Slavery: Forced Labour and Forced Marriage*. https://www.ilo.org/sites/default/files/wcmsp5/groups/public/%40ed_norm/%40ipec/documents/publication/wcms_854733.pdf

Kara, S. 2017. *Modern Slavery: A Global Perspective*. Columbia University Press.

Koshy, S., Cacho, L., Byrd, J., & Jefferson, B (eds). 2022. *Colonial Racial Capitalism*. Duke University Press.

LeBaron, G. 2021. 'The Role of Supply Chains in the Global Business of Forced Labour', *Journal of Supply Chain Management* 57(2): 29–42.

LeBaron, G., Kyritsis, P., Thibos, C., and Howard, N. 2019. *Confronting Root Causes: Forced Labour in Global Supply Chains*. https://www.opendemocracy.net/en/beyond-trafficking-and-slavery/confronting-root-causes/

McGrath, S. 2013. 'Many Chains to Break: The Multi-Dimensional Concept of Slave Labour in Brazil.' *Antipode* 45(4): 1005–1028.

Morris, J. 2020. 'Extractive Landscapes: The Case of the Jordan Refugee Compact', *Refuge* 36(1): 87–96.

Morris, J.C. 2023. *Asylum and Extraction in the Republic of Nauru*. Cornell University Press.

Mullings, B. 2021. 'Caliban, Social Reproduction and Our Future Yet to Come', *Geoforum* 118 : 150–158.

Phillips, N. 2013. 'Unfree Labour and Adverse Incorporation in the Global Economy: Comparative Perspectives on Brazil and India.' *Economy and Society* 42(2), pp 171–196.

Rajaram, P.K. 2021. 'Refugees as Surplus Population: Race, Migration and Capitalist Value Regimes', in *Raced Markets*. Routledge, pp 97–109.

Robinson, C. 2000. *Black Marxism: The Making of the Black Radical Tradition*. University of North Carolina Press: Chapel Hill.

Skinner, B. 2008. *A Crime So Monstrous: Face-to-Face with Modern-Day Slavery*. Free Press.

Walia, H. 2013. *Undoing Border Imperialism*. Vol 6. Ak Press.

Video lecture

LeBaron, G. 2021. *Global Supply Chains and Unfree Labour*, Connected Sociologies Curriculum Project. https://thesociologicalreview.org/projects/connected-sociologies/curriculum/colonial-global-economy/global-supply-chains-and-unfree-labour/

Additional resources

Bhagat, A. 2024. *Governing the Displaced: Race and Ambivalence in Global Capitalism*. Cornell University Press.

Kamala, K. and Shih, E. (eds). 2023. *White Supremacy, Racism, and the Coloniality of Anti-Trafficking*. Routledge.

Kelley, R.D.G. 2017. 'What Did Cedric Robinson Mean by Racial Capitalism?', *Boston Review*, January. https://www.bostonreview.net/articles/robin-d-g-kelley-introduction-race-capitalism-justice/

US Department of Labor. 2024. *List of Goods Produced by Child Labor or Forced Labour.* https://www.dol.gov/agencies/ilab/reports/child-labor/list-of-goods. This list is produced annually by the United States Department of Labor and covers all of the goods known to be produced with child and forced labour. It is the most authoritative description of the goods produced with child and forced labour in the economy today, with the 2024 list encompassing 204 goods from 82 countries.

QUESTIONS

1. What do explanations of modern slavery overlook if they focus only on the individual victims and perpetrators rather than root causes?

2. How can we best understand the role of colonialism in shaping vulnerability to forced labour?

3. How should we understand the role of race and racism in shaping vulnerability to forced labour?

4. Why is forced labour more common in some parts of the world compared to others?

5. What are the linkages between historic and contemporary systems of forced labour?

Worksheet 11. Race, Colonialism, and Modern Slavery

This worksheet is designed to support AS and A-level teaching on the topics of globalization and global development, social differentiation, power and stratification, and research methods. In the online talk, LeBaron explains how global supply chains under contemporary capitalism depend on and reinforce relations of unfree labour. The themes in this talk are developed in this chapter on Race, Colonialism, and Modern Slavery. While dominant narratives of unfree labour define it as a modern issue, sometimes called 'new slavery', LeBaron articulates how forced labour relations are rooted in historic and ongoing processes of colonial capitalism. The worksheet activities build on LeBaron's analysis in encouraging students to consider how unfree labour operates within the context of globalization, and how sociologists can connect these labour relations to histories of colonialism within Britain and beyond. By exploring LeBaron's project, which investigates working conditions in the tea industry, students are also asked to explore some research methods which can help us to situate global supply chains within the legacies and ongoing processes of colonial global capitalism.

Time	Activity	Explanation
00.00–00.05	To warm up, answer the following question: What do you understand about the term 'unfree labour'?	This activity is designed to warm students up to the topic of the session, assessing their existing level of knowledge. This may work well as a group discussion.
00.05–00.10	Recap of understandings of globalization.	It may be useful to remind students of key theories related to globalization and global development.
00.10–00.15	Watch the talk from 1:44 to 3:02. What is the definition of forced labour? How does it relate to concepts such as modern slavery and human trafficking?	LeBaron explains that forced labour is labour that a worker is made to do against their will under some form of coercion. She also explains the interconnections between forced labour and related terms such as modern slavery and human trafficking, which students are encouraged to reflect on. This activity ensures that students have a good understanding of the central terms that underpin this session, and provides an entry point into LeBaron's subsequent critique of dominant narratives of unfree labour as 'new slavery'.
00.15–00.25	Watch the talk from 3:15 to 4:48. What does unfree labour look like in contemporary capitalist society? Can you give some examples?	LeBaron explains that unfree labour is an endemic part of the production of a wide variety of goods in our global economy, including gold, tea, coffee, and cocoa. It also thrives, she explains, in the service sector, in domestic labour relations, and in many other forms of work. This activity prompts students to acknowledge the enduring prevalence of unfree labour in the colonial global economy. It also relates to the interconnected themes of global development, trade, and global inequality, which are core topics within the A-level Sociology curriculum.

Time	Activity	Explanation
00.25–00.35	At 10:53 LeBaron states that 'contemporary unfree labour relations in supply chains need to be understood in the context of the legacies and ongoing dynamics of colonial global capitalism'. *How can this be done? What is the role of sociologists in this process?*	This activity takes up several core themes within the A-level Sociology curriculum, including the relationship of identity to production, consumption and globalization, concepts of modernity, and the sociological implications of globalization and the formation of the transnational capitalist class. Students are asked to go beyond the session material in applying their learning to wider questions surrounding the role of sociologists in situating social issues within historical contexts. Students may also draw on some wider themes from this book, including from chapters on the 'Colonial Global Economy,' 'Class, Capitalism and Colonialism', and 'The Grunwick Strike', in answering these questions.
00.35–00.45	Watch the talk from 11:15 to 12:42. *What research methods did LeBaron use to investigate forced labour in the global tea supply chain? What are the positives of these research methods? What are some potential challenges?*	LeBaron talks about her investigations into global business models of forced labour in tea supply chains, as part of which she interviews workers in the tea industry about their experiences. This question asks students to evaluate the qualitative research methods employed in this project and think about their positives as well as the potential challenges, which is a key requirement within the A-level Sociology curriculum. Students may identify the capacity of interviewing to help researchers hear from marginalized perspectives, and they may identify some ethical or practical challenges the researchers may have faced in carrying out this project.
00.45–00.50	Watch the talk from 16:00 to 17:05. *What role does indentured labour have to play in the global tea supply chain?*	LeBaron explains that many of the workers she spoke to as part of her research were descendants of indentured labourers, connecting the subject matter of this session to another chapter addressing 'Indian Indenture'. Students are encouraged to draw connections between these sessions and to think about the significance of indenture as part of a wider system of unfree labour within the colonial global economy.
00.50–01.00	Drawing on what you have learned throughout this session, answer the following question: *What can the global tea supply chain teach us about how colonial capitalism works today?*	This concluding activity asks students to consider how the case study of the global tea industry offers a lens through which to examine wider systems of colonial global labour exploitation. In doing so, it encourages students to bring together what they have learned from this session, as well as in their wider learning on this course, applying a critical lens to concepts of modernity and narratives of global development.

This worksheet was developed by Isabel Sykes.

12

The UK's Elite: Colonial and Transnational Dynamics

Katie Higgins

Objectives

- This chapter asks how the British Empire, and its demise, has shaped the UK's elite.

- It sets out who the UK's elite were in the 19th century, how they have changed over time, and their imperial and transnational dynamics.

- It argues that colonial histories help us to understand why national boundaries have only ever been a partial container of the UK's elite.

Introduction

Economists such as Thomas Piketty in *Capital in the Twenty-First Century* have played a key role in redirecting attention towards the disproportionate wealth of those in the top percentiles of society – such as the top 1 or 0.1 per cent. Rather than engage in intractable debates over the definition of a clear threshold of poverty, this novel approach to inequality shifts attention to the distribution of income and wealth – bringing those at the very top into focus (Savage 2022). While making important advances in how we understand the making, remaking, and loss of power, status, and wealth, the burgeoning field of scholarship on elites, with its tendency to focus on nationally bounded case studies, is open to a similar line of critique targeted at studies of inequality more broadly.

The sociologist Gurminder K. Bhambra (2020: 70) has criticized a tendency to organize long-term, comparative analysis of inequality *within* nations and thus erase colonial formations. Focusing on Piketty's newer work, *Capital and Ideology*, Bhambra argues that methodological nationalism risks separating colonial states, such as the UK, from enslavement and colonialism happening geographically elsewhere when, in fact, they were both integral to it. As Piketty himself points out, within colonial states, such as Britain, 'one-fifth to one-quarter of what people owned at the time was held abroad. ... The interest, dividends, profits, rents, and royalties earned in the rest of the world thus substantially boosted the standard of living in ... colonial powers' (cited in Bhambra 2020: 76). As with studies of inequalities, so with studies of their main beneficiaries – in this chapter, I argue that approaching elites through a lens attentive to colonialism brings important actors, processes, and relationships into view (see Gilbert, Chapter 2, this volume).

It is useful to clarify what I mean by elites, which has been described as 'probably one of the most misused words in the sociological lexicon' (Scott 2003: 155). Sociological definitions of this term range from the broad to the more exacting. On one end of the scale, 'elites are those with vastly disproportionate control over or access to a resource' with 'transferable value' – where 'resource' and 'transferability' are defined socially (Khan 2012: 362). On the other end of the scale, an 'elite in the fullest sense is a social grouping whose members occupy similarly advantaged command situations in the social distribution of authority and who are linked to one another through demographic processes of circulation and interaction' (Scott 2003: 157). In this chapter, my interest is in unpacking some of the imperial and transnational dynamics of the wealthy and high status in the UK over time, for which I use elite as an overarching term.

First, I address the changing dynamics of the propertied upper classes from the 19th century until the First World War. Second, I consider how far White and non-White high-status families were able to reproduce themselves over this period, and the strategies people of colour use today to respond to racial inequalities in their elite careers through examining people in the social registry, *Who's Who*. Third, I explore some of the transnational dynamics of today's rich in the UK – focusing in particular on people with a non-domiciled tax status and featured in *The Sunday Times Rich List*. Lastly, in the conclusion, I make the case that attention to colonial histories helps make sense of the fact that national boundaries have only ever been a partial container of the UK's elite.

Who were the UK's elites in the 19th century?

The UK's aristocracy have long sought out leisure, marriage, and careers beyond the island's borders. During the 19th century, the landed gentry visited and married other aristocrats across the European continent. Once the British Empire provided suitably secure, lucrative, and ornamental roles for the upper classes, they actively pursued careers in desirable imperial postings. This was in a context where they were otherwise experiencing a steady decline in status, influence, and wealth as the economy industrialized and the state democratized (Cannadine 1990). At the same time, in the UK, there were already concerns about the arrival of some international plutocrats during this period, with the historian David Cannadine (1990: 28) highlighting 'American multimillionaires, and Jewish adventurers, who brutally and brashly bought their way in'.

Aristocrats aside, the 19th century saw the rise of a manufacturing property-owning class with fortunes rooted in the industrial revolution. In *The Empire of Cotton*, the historian Sven Beckert argues that a single commodity – cotton – was the 'launching pad' of this industrial revolution. Beckert (2015) tells the story of the rise and fall of European dominance in cotton and argues that this commodity made and remade global capitalism. Adopting a global scale of analysis, he links the vast profits made possible by the transportation of slaves from Africa to plantations across the American South, to the intensification of the removal of Indigenous peoples and self-sufficient farmers from their land, to loans and investment from merchants and bankers in North America and Europe, and to the violent expansion of European trade networks into Asia and Africa (see Kaladeen, Chapter 4, this volume).

As the world's most industrialized city in the late 19th century, Manchester was at the centre of this 'global web of agriculture, commerce and industrial production' (Beckert 2015: 1). Rather than any particular religious beliefs, geographical conditions, or liberal institutions, Beckert argues that the city and its resident capitalists' fortunes are inseparable from the fact Britain was 'an imperial nation characterized by enormous military expenditures, a nearly constant state of war, a powerful and interventionist bureaucracy, high taxes, skyrocketing government debt, and protectionist tariffs' (2015: 9). In short, '[s]lavery, the expropriation of Indigenous peoples, imperial expansion, armed trade, and the assertion of sovereignty over people and land by entrepreneurs' were central to the transformations ushered in by this new age of capitalism – and to the expanding wealth of the UK's property-owning class (Beckert 2015: 10).

The transformative role of the industrial revolution for global capitalism, however, does not necessarily equate with a central role for the industrial capitalist in the upper classes during this period. Drawing on probate valuations of people who left £500,000 or more from 1809 to 1939, the historian Bill Rubinstein (1981) surveyed Britain's wealthy and their social and economic characteristics. He argues that Marxist ideas of the UK's capitalist elite in the 19th century were overly centred on industrialists and the industrial revolution. While the relationship of industrial capitalists with their employees was certainly the focal point of class struggle, he argues that it does not necessarily follow that industrial capitalism was centrally important for the bourgeoisie (see Holmwood, Chapter 7, this volume). In fact, he argues, this view has distorted our knowledge of the British elite. Instead, he found that a disproportionate number of fortunes in this period were earned in the City of London and in commerce and finance, by merchants, bankers, ship owners, and insurance brokers, for instance, rather than in manufacturing and industry.

Consequently, Cain and Hopkins' (1986) 'gentlemanly capitalism school' argued that more emphasis should be placed on how British imperialism was driven by the business interests of the City of London and the financial sector, rather than provincial manufacturers or geopolitical strategy. At this time, London already stood at the centre of a well-developed network of international services, and these expanded rapidly as world trade increased in the second half of the 19th century. Important though the manufacturing sector was, they argue that its representatives lacked prestige and direct access to the inner circles where policy was formulated.

In fact, Britain's post-war economic decline has been attributed to the failure of newer economic elites breaking away from the continued dominance of aristocratic and land-owning classes. The power of the landed aristocracy was initially rooted in agrarian capitalism. Despite the rise of the industrial revolution and its urban bourgeoisie, however, the landed gentry continued to dominate the ruling class. Excluded from the charmed circles of decision-making, industrialists were only incorporated as a subordinate class into the aristocratic ruling bloc. This continuity is evidenced, for instance, through the lack of challenge to traditional institutions of power in the UK – such as monarchy, peerage, the City, and the Church. In fact, in his analysis of the English upper class from 1945 to the present, the sociologist Daniel Smith (2023) argues that aristocratic idioms of kinship, inheritance, and the family house, along with the ruling institutions of the English upper class – such as schools and private members' clubs – still play a key role in assimilating newcomers and providing a route to legitimate belonging in British society (2023: 22).

While clarifying in some senses, the popular national view of Britain as shifting from an agrarian economy rooted in land ownership, to an industrial economy rooted in commercial and manufacturing ownership, tends to focus on domestic trends and to underplay the centrality of empire to the state and to the economy (see Tyler, Chapter 5, this volume). For instance, more than half of the money at the disposal of the British government at the close of the 19th century was derived not from subjects within the British Isles, but from the taxes and tribute of populations from across the empire (Temple 1884, cited in Bhambra 2020: 77).

Towards the end of the 19th century, the owners of substantial land, commercial, and manufacturing property began to merge into one unified property class (Scott 1982). Up to the First World War, this emerging property class saw their market situation, social status, and lifestyle increasingly assimilate to one another to the extent they became better described as 'a business class'. With the rise of joint stock companies, wealthy business families were no longer so often tied to particular enterprises, but more commonly diversified across various business interests, which alongside the continued role of shared schools, universities, and members' clubs, drove their gradual integration as a class. In the next section, we turn to the question of elite family reproduction over time in more detail and ask how far people of colour and their descendants were able to enter the elite.

Elite reproduction and difference over the last 125 years

How have the UK's elites changed over time? In *Born to Rule*, the sociologists Sam Friedman and Aaron Reeves (2024) analyse 125,000 people included in the elite social registry – *Who's Who* – over the last 125 years to answer this question. *Who's Who* is the leading biographical dictionary of 'noteworthy and influential' people in the UK. It makes selections based on a mix of positional and reputational grounds. Around 50 per cent of entrants are included automatically upon reaching a prominent occupational position. These positions span multiple professional fields. For example, Members of Parliament, peers, judges, ambassadors, FTSE100 CEOs, Poet Laureates, and Fellows of the British Academy are all included by virtue of their office. The other 50 per cent of entrants are selected each year by a board of long-standing advisors, who make reputational assessments based on a person's perceived impact on British society. *Who's Who* has been published in its current form every year since 1897.

Friedman and Reeves reveal that Britain's upper echelons are no longer as closed as they once were. Since the end of the 19th century, who gets to join the ranks of this high-status list has become more open in terms of schooling, gender, and (to a lesser extent) ethnicity. Nevertheless, their main argument is the persistent nature of recruitment from very privileged backgrounds. For instance, White people entered in *Who's Who* in the beginning of the 20th century were 120 times more likely to see their descendants also included in the social registry than the general population (Friedman and Reeves 2024: 109). Their findings provide another set of evidence for the importance of a historical perspective to understand elites today. Friedman and Reeves (2024) attribute this durability of families in *Who's Who* to their dynastic wealth, social connections, and access to elite channels of recruitment, such as private schools and prestigious universities.

Friedman and Reeves found that around 2 per cent of entrants in *Who's Who* have consistently been people of colour since it was established in 1849 (2024: 215).[1] Their findings show that this group has also been able to help their descendants enter the elite. However, their elite reproduction was much less certain than for their White counterparts. Around 20 per cent of people of colour listed in an elite social registry today have a descendent who was also in *Who's Who*. While this figure is much higher than for the general population, it is only one third of the rate of elite reproduction for White families. For White families, 57 per cent had a descendent who was also in *Who's Who* (Friedman and Reeves 2024: 111). Relations with the imperial establishment play a key role in these relatively high rates of elite reproduction among people of colour. As an example, the British Indian lawyer and statesmen, Satyendra Prasanna Sinha (1863–1928), was granted a hereditary peerage in 1919 to steer India-related legislation through the House of Lords, which his descendants continue to inherit up until today (Friedman and Reeves 2024: 111). In contrast, while anti-imperial activists were also sometimes included in *Who's Who*, their descendants very rarely appeared again in later years – in fact, there is only one known example.

Building on this research through a qualitative interview-based study with people of colour included in *Who's Who* today, Higgins et al (2024) interviewed 30 Asian, Black, and mixed heritage people entered in *Who's Who*. The vast majority of them, or their parents, were part of the migration of British 'overseas citizens' to the UK, moving to this context as British subjects from colonies or former colonies in Africa, the Caribbean, and South Asia (see Hampshire, Chapter 13, and Benson, Chapter 18, this volume). They mapped three strategies interviewees use to respond to racial inequalities in their elite careers – 'challenging', 'diversifying', and 'role modelling'. They also examined their understanding of the label 'elite', and explored how these were classed, gendered, and racialized.

Higgins et al found that both those 'challenging' and 'diversifying' elite organizations were oriented towards broader societal change, even if they drew on different political traditions to achieve that goal. For participants using the 'challenging' strategy, this societal change was rooted in structural approaches to anti-racism often based in community activism. They defined themselves in opposition to the already established elite. Participants using the 'diversifying' strategy took a more liberal approach to societal change, emphasizing reform. They were ambivalent about the label of elite, but more readily accepted recognition from established elites as a strategy to advance collective racialized interests. Finally, in a context where they were the first, the only, or one of very few minoritized elites, the individual career success of participants using the 'role modelling' strategy was itself imbued with meaning for other minoritized individuals. Participants using this strategy were the most likely to accept the label of elite, if it indicated meritocratic excellence, or to deny that they were elite at all, and instead to emphasize their ordinariness.

While not claiming that their study was representative, Higgins et al (2024) found, among their interviewees, 'challenging' and 'diversifying' were more typically used by individuals from a working-class background and/or who were part of hyper-racialized Muslim groups. The interviewees using 'diversifying' who did not fit this pattern were all women. In contrast, 'role modelling' was more typically used by individuals from a middle- or upper-middle-class background. Given that the interviewees as a whole, and the strategies 'challenging' and 'role modelling', were male-dominated it is striking that 'diversifying' was female-dominated. These distinctions point to the mutual constitution of class, gender, and religion in shaping how racial inequalities surface, and leave questions unanswered about the role of caste, for instance. Next, I focus specifically on the question of whether, and if so in what form, those at the top of the wealth and income distribution hold international ties.

How global are the UK's elite?

Just as for the landed gentry in the 1800s, the arrival of the wealthy from other countries continues to spark controversy among some of the resident elite. Peter York, who gained fame through a satirical account of a new breed of upper-class Londoners in *The Official Sloane Ranger Handbook* with Ann Barr in 1982, reflected decades later in 2015 that 'an extraordinary mixture of Russian oligarchs, Middle Easterners, new petrodollar types from Nigeria, Indians, Malaysians, and latterly Chinese [were] driving up the prices of London property and driving out all but the richest, most adaptable Sloanes' (York 2015). Aside from such anecdotal, and often stereotypical, accounts in the media, the economist Arun Advani and colleagues have made significant headway on more systematically analysing the international links of the UK's wealthy.

One way to study the international links of the UK's wealthy is through *The Sunday Times Rich List* – which ranks the 1,000 richest individuals and families with significant business ties to the UK. If you skim through the top ten in recent decades, you will find the majority of entries were born abroad, or if they were born in the UK, they have often moved elsewhere, at least for tax purposes. In 2024, this was true of nine of the richest ten individuals in the country, for example. Beyond the ten richest, Arun Advani and colleagues (2022a) worked out the international ties of the richest 1,000 individuals and families in the UK in 2022. These individuals – who make up 0.0005 per cent of the adult population – own roughly 4 per cent of total wealth in the UK. They found that international connections increase the further you travel up the wealth distribution – so 11–12 per cent of people with less than £100 million have some kind of international connection, but almost half of billionaires are foreign residents, foreign nationals, or both. For those with £100–500 million in wealth who are foreign nationals, the majority are from Europe and the White settler Anglosphere,[2] while billionaires echo these geographies but also include emerging economies such as China, India, and countries in the ex-USSR. Alongside these geographical clusters, it is also worth noting that they found one in seven billionaires reside in zero- or low-tax jurisdictions – such as the Bahamas, the Channel Islands, and Monaco.

Beyond the 1,000 richest individuals and families in the UK, Advani and colleagues (2022b) went on to look at the UK's non-dom population (a tax status that was abolished in April 2025 by the Labour Government). A 'non-dom' was resident but not domiciled in the UK, which had significant tax advantages. Essentially, non-dom status meant that you paid no income tax, capital gains tax, or inheritance tax on foreign wealth. This quirk of the tax system was a legacy of the British Empire. In 1799, when income tax was invented, a lot of the UK wealthy held assets abroad, such as a sugar plantation in Jamaica. At the time, you had to import sugar back into the UK before you could export it elsewhere. However, the domicile system meant you would only pay tax once your sugar had reached the UK – which effectively deferred the payment of tax to mitigate the risk that the ship might sink, for example, and thus the asset might never reach the UK.

More recently, as you now no longer need to bring assets held elsewhere back into the UK, non-dom status provided a route for people to avoid paying tax on money held abroad. Advani and colleagues (2022b) worked out that from 2001 to 2018, the number of UK residents who claimed non-dom status in any single year ranged between 70,000 and 90,000 people – representing only 0.1–0.2 per cent of UK adults. While small in number, the overwhelming majority of this population were positioned towards the top of the UK's income distribution, and the share of non-doms rose steeply with income – so while small in number, non-doms were among the highest earning residents in the UK.

Non-doms share the geographical origins of the Rich List - (1) Western and Northern Europe; (2) the White settler Anglosphere; (3) and emerging economies such as China, India, and Russia (the latter of which were also found to be the fastest-growing populations of non-doms in recent years). While the concept of a 'transnational capitalist class' explored the impact on the business class of the global spread of transnational corporations, empirical work has since emphasized the ongoing regional and national ties of such elites. Similarly, Advani et al's (2022a, 2022b) analysis of the UK's Rich List and non-doms shows that these groups are global, but their global links have a distinct geography – concentrated around clusters in Europe, the White settler Anglosphere, and emerging economies.

The UK's colonial past – and the channelling of wealth, objects, and decision-making to London for centuries – is essential to understand the city's position today as an economic and cultural hub for the world's wealthy. 'Golden citizenship' or 'golden visa' programmes, which secure citizenship or residence for international arrivals to foreign nation states, at a price, are vital tools to ease the mobility of the rich (Surak 2023). While data is patchy, it appears the consumers of these programmes are 'largely members of the nouveaux riches from countries outside the Global North', such as 'China and South-east Asia, Russia and the post-Soviet countries, and the Middle East' (Surak 2023: 17). The rights and benefits conferred by different citizenship are unequal, and these programmes are a route for the wealthy from otherwise low- and middle-income countries to acquire the rights and benefits of wealthier nation states. The UK does not offer citizenship by investment. In fact, the UK's so-called 'golden visa' programme was cancelled in 2022 in light of national security concerns around the possibility of corruption and money laundering following the Russia–Ukraine conflict. However, the government has enabled new schemes since then as alternatives for foreign investors interested in moving to the UK.

Conclusion

Engaging with colonial histories sheds light on the UK's wealthy and high status in both the past and today. The fortunes of the aristocratic landed gentry and industrial bourgeoisie were often tied to the UK's role as an imperial state, such as owning shares in plantations or importing cotton from plantations for their factories. The assets propertied elites were able to acquire during this period, alongside cohesion-building elite institutions such as schools, universities, and clubs, have played a central role in the reproduction of elite status over time. Research on the *Who's Who* reveals that people of colour have been a consistent if minor part of Britain's elite from the 19th century. Looking ahead, what kinds of leaders emerge from contemporary protest movements, whether the advances made in diversifying the leadership of influential organizations will gain traction or lose ground, and how far, if at all, more diverse representation will translate into a more equitable redistribution of power and resources remain urgent questions. The international ties of the UK's rich today are also tied to colonial histories, whether through the relic of non-domiciled tax status or the enduring attraction of the UK (and more specifically London) for affluent migrants from the Anglosphere, Europe, or emerging economies.

These imperial and transnational dynamics reveal the UK's national borders have only ever been a partial container of its elite. For future research on this theme, this chapter is another reminder of the importance of expanding beyond methodological nationalism in our research design and Western conceptual frameworks, even as regional and national ties continue to play a crucial role. A more global focus that is aware of our shared histories is needed to fully understand who the UK's elite are, and what this tells us about how power and inequality operate from above.

Notes

[1] Aside from this positional and reputational definition of an elite, Friedman and Reeves also identify a subgroup of people in *Who's Who* that are also among the top 1 per cent of the wealth distribution – which amounts to around 20 per cent of all the entries – and who have distinctive political preferences (2024: 208).

[2] The White settler Anglosphere is a racialized category and an informal grouping of English-speaking states with a core comprised of the United States, the UK, Canada, Australia, and New Zealand.

References

Advani, A., Summers, A., and Tarrant, H. 2022a. 'Who are the Super-rich? The Wealth and Connections of the Sunday Times Rich List', *CAGE Policy Brief* no 37.

Advani, A., Burgherr, D., Savage, M., and Summers, A. 2022b. 'The UK's "Non-doms": Who Are They, What Do They Do, and Where Do They Live?', *CAGE Policy Brief* no 36.

Beckert, S. 2015. *Empire of Cotton: A Global History*. Vintage.

Bhambra, G. 2020. 'Narrating Inequality, Eliding Empire', *The British Journal of Sociology* 72(1): 69–78.

Cain, P. and Hopkins, A. 1986. 'Gentlemanly Capitalism and British Expansion Overseas I. The Old Colonial System, 1688–1850', *Economic History Review* 39(4): 501–525.

Cannadine, D. 1990. *The Decline and Fall of the British Aristocracy*. Yale University Press.

Friedman, S. and Reeves, A. 2024. *Born to Rule: The Making and Remaking of the British Elite*. Harvard University Press.

Higgins, K., Friedman, S., and Reeves, A. 2024. '"Outsiders on the Inside": How Minoritized Elites Respond to Racial Inequality', *Ethnic & Racial Studies*, Online First, 1–21.

Khan, S. 2012. 'The Sociology of Elites', *Annual Review of Sociology* 38: 361–377.

Rubinstein, W. D. 1981. *Men of Property: The Very Wealthy in Britain since the Industrial Revolution*. Rutgers University Press.

Savage, M. 2022. *The Return of Inequality: Social Change and the Weight of the Past*. Harvard University Press.

Scott, J. 1982. *The Upper Classes: Property and Privilege in Britain*. Springer.

Scott, J. 2003. 'Transformations in the British Economic Elite', in M. Dogan (ed), *Elite Configurations at the Apex of Power*. Brill, pp 155–173.

Smith, D. 2023. *The Fall and Rise of the English Upper Class: House, Kinship and Capitalism since 1945*. Manchester University Press.

Surak, K. 2023. *The Golden Passport: Global Mobility for Millionaires*. Harvard University Press.

York, P. 2015. The fall of the Sloane Rangers, Prospect Magazine. Accessible at: https://www.prospectmagazine.co.uk/society/47259/the-fall-of-the-sloane-rangers (Accessed 10/9/2025).

Video lecture

Advani, A. 2022. *The UK's Global Economic Elite*, Connected Sociologies Curriculum Project. https://thesociologicalreview.org/projects/connected-sociologies/curriculum/politics-inequality/the-uks-global-economic-elite/

QUESTIONS

1. What actors, processes, and relationships come into view when we study the colonial histories of the UK's elites?

2. What can we learn about the economy and the state through studying how the UK's elites have changed over time?

3. How do colonial histories help us understand the contemporary transnational dynamics of the UK's elites?

Worksheet 12. The UK's Elite: Colonial and Transnational Dynamics

The online talk associated with Chapter 12 of the book is provided by Arun Advani. This worksheet is designed to support AS and A-level teaching on the related topics of globalization, global development, and social inequality, with a specific UK focus. The talk by Advani introduces students to the concept of a 'global economic elite' within the UK, with a specific focus on the international connections of this group. Students are encouraged to think about how this group of people fits into their understandings of globalization and global development, which are key themes within the A-level curriculum. This session and worksheet also connect with related areas of the curriculum such as social differentiation, power and stratification, and culture and identity. By focusing on the economic elites within UK society as opposed to disadvantaged groups, these activities encourage students to think about how issues of wealth and power play into the social inequalities they may have studied in other sessions. As a topic with a strong economic focus, this worksheet may be particularly useful for students who are interested in or are already studying economics alongside sociology.

Time	Activity	Explanation
00.00–00.05	To begin, answer this question: What people or images come to mind when you think of the UK's economic elite?	This short warm-up exercise is to get students thinking about what preconceptions they might have surrounding the wealthy elite members of UK society. For example, what genders and ethnicities are students picturing when they are imagining a member of the UK elite?
00.05–00.10	Recap of understandings of globalization and global development.	It may be useful to remind students of the definition(s) of globalization.
00.10–00.20	At 1:38 Advani explains that his approach to studying inequality as an economist is by using quantitative data, such as tax data, to learn more about the UK's economic elite. What is the difference between quantitative and qualitative data? Can you think of some potential advantages and disadvantages of this approach?	This question allows students to recap on what they already know about the different research methods used within sociology. Encouraging them to think about the potential advantages and disadvantages of a quantitative approach to studying inequality aligns with the Sociology A-level requirement for students to analyse and evaluate research methods.
00.20–00.25	Watch the talk from 6:37 to 8:12. What is the difference between someone's 'residence' and their 'domicile?' What is a 'non-dom'?	Advani explains that, while a person's 'residence' describes where they live, their 'domicile' describes where they feel that their 'permanent home' is. A 'non-dom', therefore, is someone who has a 'residence' in the UK, but who is not 'domiciled' here. This question ensures that students are familiar with the technical terms being used in the session and allows them to start thinking critically about the utility of these terms.

Time	Activity	Explanation
00.25–00.35	How might the terms 'residence' and 'domicile' be useful for studying the sociological impacts of globalization? What are some potential challenges of defining a person's 'home'?	Advani explains that a person's 'domicile', meaning their 'permanent home', is difficult to define because it is a personal feeling that is potentially changeable. This activity challenges students to apply the concepts in this session to the wider topic of globalization and to think critically about the utility of economic terms to studying sociological notions of 'home' and ideas of 'belonging'.
00.35–00.45	Watch the talk from 9:00 to 12:25. What role, according to Advani, has British colonialism played in the creation of the term 'domicile'? Why is understanding colonialism important in the study of globalization?	This activity pushes students to place the material being presented to them in the wider context of their learning around globalization, global development, and stratification. It also encourages interdisciplinary thinking, allowing students to make connections with other relevant subjects that they may be studying or are intending to study alongside Sociology, such as History, Geography, or Politics.
00.45–00.55	At 18:12 Advani talks through a map which shows the London geography of 'non-doms'. He explains that, using this quantitative data, it is possible to see the impact of these global elites' international connections on the local geography of London. Thinking back to the activity earlier in this session where you recapped the advantages and disadvantages of using quantitative data to study inequalities, answer the following questions: What can this map tell us about the global elite who live in London? What information would you like to know about this group that the map cannot tell us? Can you think of some potential methods of attaining this information?	This activity encourages students to develop the work they did earlier, pushing them to apply what they already know about the advantages and disadvantages of quantitative data collection to the session material. By asking the students to think about the potential limitations of this data set, and encouraging them to come up with additional research that could supplement the findings of this study, they are not only fulfilling the Sociology A-level requirement to analyse and evaluate research methods, but are being stretched to develop their own ideas for sociological research.
00.55–01.00	Reflecting on what you have learned from this talk, and the activities on this worksheet, answer the following question:	This recap activity asks students to draw together and reflect on what they have learned throughout the session.

Time	Activity	Explanation
	Why is studying the UK's global economic elite useful for learning about globalization and its relationship with social inequality?	In answering this question, it might be useful for students to reflect on other approaches to studying globalization and social inequality. For example, students may be familiar with studying social inequality with a focus on disadvantaged social groups, and it may be interesting for them to consider the value of studying the extreme elites at the other end of this spectrum. Furthermore, this question asks students to reflect on the relationship between globalization and social inequality, encouraging them to draw connections between topics in the Sociology A-level curriculum.

This worksheet was developed by Isabel Sykes.

PART III

Migration, Diaspora, and Asylum

Edited by Lucy Mayblin

13

Colonialism, Immigration, and the Making of British Citizenship

James Hampshire

Objectives

- This chapter examines how colonialism has shaped British citizenship and immigration.
- It outlines the history of immigration to Britain since 1948.
- It explores how racism influenced the development of citizenship and immigration policies.
- It analyses how the legacies of colonial citizenship affect the lives of people today, through case studies of the Windrush scandal and the Hong Kong British Nationals visa.

Introduction

Citizenship can be understood as membership of a nation state, a status that entitles its holder to rights, including the right to enter and reside in that state (Joppke 2010). The 20th-century philosopher Hannah Arendt (1973) famously described citizenship as 'the right to have rights'. Without citizenship a person is stateless and without rights. At the same time, the rights that attach to citizenship vary enormously depending on *which* state's citizenship a person holds. Most people born in a wealthy, secure country will enjoy more rights than people born in a poor, war-torn country.

The emergence of citizenship is closely associated with the development of the modern state. In standard accounts, citizenship replaced subjecthood as modern states emerged to govern distinct nations in Europe and America during the 18th and 19th centuries. Although citizenship is now widely understood as membership of a nation state, the citizenship laws of many European nations were forged through their colonial projects, as I discuss in what follows.

This chapter shows how *colonial* citizenship preceded *national* citizenship in the British case, and how national citizenship was carved out of colonial citizenship as the British government sought to control post-war immigration. The chapter has two main aims: first, it shows how the development of British citizenship can only be understood within the context of colonialism, decolonization, and the racialized politics of immigration; and, second, it shows why the colonial legacies of citizenship still matter today.

The first half of the chapter charts the complex history of citizenship and immigration in Britain. It shows how citizenship was first introduced into UK law in 1948 as Citizenship of the United Kingdom and Colonies, which granted all people born or naturalized in the British Empire the same set of rights. As colonial citizens migrated to Britain in the post-war decades, the British government passed legislation to limit their rights. A separate British national citizenship was only created in 1981. The second half of the chapter explores how the entanglement of citizenship, colonialism, and racialized immigration controls continues to affect people's lives today, by examining the Windrush scandal and the Hong Kong British Nationals (Overseas) visa scheme.

From subjects to colonial citizens

Before the Second World War, there was no such thing as citizenship in British law. People born in the UK, its Dominions, or one of its colonies were *subjects* of the British monarch. Citizenship was first introduced into law by the British Nationality Act of 1948 (BNA 1948), but the citizenship created by this law was in fact colonial, not national. The BNA 1948 created two main statuses: Citizenship of the United Kingdom and Colonies (CUKC), which covered people born in the UK and any of its colonies, and Citizenship of Independent Commonwealth Countries (CICC), for those born in independent countries of the Commonwealth such as Australia, Canada, India, and South Africa. Together, these statuses included nearly all people born or naturalized in the UK, Commonwealth, or one of the British colonies. All were granted the same set of rights, including the right to live and work in Britain.

Although it represented a constitutional revolution, the BNA 1948 was not the product of a radical upheaval in the style of the American or French Revolutions; or even the Haitian (see Bhambra, Chapter 1, this volume). There was no public debate or constitutional convention to discuss the proposed Bill. Rather, citizenship was introduced into UK law as a pragmatic response to legislation in Canada. The colonial citizenship that the BNA 1948 created was backward-looking, intended to maintain colonial ties that were perceived to be under threat.

In 1946, the Canadian government had legislated to create a separate Canadian citizenship. Concerned that this represented a breach of the indivisibility of subjecthood through the empire and Commonwealth, the British government passed the BNA 1948 to shore up a uniform status for all British subjects. The Canadian legislation, and the potential of it being emulated elsewhere, was seen by British politicians as a threat to Commonwealth unity.

The reactive and apparently technical nature of the BNA 1948 goes some way to explain why its profound implications were so little discussed at the time, but it is not a sufficient explanation. A more deep-seated set of beliefs about empire were involved. Most British politicians, Conservative and Labour, believed in the idea that

British subjects should be able to move freely within the empire and Commonwealth. In practice this meant the freedom of White citizens of what was known as the 'Old Commonwealth' – Australia, Canada, and New Zealand – to migrate. The Act was not intended to facilitate migration from the 'New Commonwealth' countries of Africa, Asia, and the Caribbean. At no point during the parliamentary debates or internal government discussions was the potential of New Commonwealth citizens to exercise their right to reside in the UK discussed. This seems like an incredible oversight today, but in the 1940s the British political elite considered such immigration unthinkable, so they did not discuss the implications of the BNA 1948 for immigration control.

In short, the introduction of citizenship into UK law was colonial through and through. The BNA 1948 was a response to the actions of a former dominion of the British Empire; its passage was motivated by imperial politics; and the citizenship categories it created were explicitly colonial. The colonial definition of citizenship would enable post-war immigration and limit the ability of the British government to impose immigration controls. As Hansen puts it, 'the story of post-war migration is the story of citizenship' (2000: 35).

'Citizens who do not belong': race and immigration in the post-war period

This story began just a few months after the BNA 1948 became law, when the *Empire Windrush* arrived at Tilbury Docks, just outside London, carrying 1,027 people from the West Indies. It was the first arrival of what was to become a migration of thousands of people from the Caribbean, then South Asia and Africa. The people who arrived on the *Windrush* were not strictly speaking immigrants. They held the same citizenship status – CUKC – as people born in Britain, so legally they were colonial citizens moving between different countries of the empire and Commonwealth. In British political debate, however, they were viewed – then and now – as immigrants, and moreover they were racialized as 'coloured immigrants'.

Something of a national myth has developed around the migration of the late 1940s and 1950s. According to this version of events, colonial immigrants were invited to work in Britain after the war and welcomed into a 'tolerant country'. In fact, most CUKCs funded their own passage and arrived to find a society characterized by widespread racism (see Murji, Chapter 17, this volume). There were some recruitment programmes for the National Health Service and London Transport, but they were relatively small schemes; most people who moved to Britain arrived without a prior job offer. They were legally entitled to do so because of their status as CUKCs.

Contrary to the myth of invitation, the British government's response was far from welcoming. During the 1940s and 1950s, both Labour and Conservative politicians were concerned about 'coloured' immigration and pursued a 'policy of obstruction' (Spencer 1997: 46). A range of administrative measures were used to obstruct migration from the Caribbean, Indian subcontinent, and West Africa, including measures to hinder the issue of travel documents, attempts to increase the cost of passage from the Caribbean, and a publicity campaign in Jamaica to deter would-be emigrants. As the Home Secretary, David Maxwell-Fyfe, stated in 1954: 'such administrative action as is possible to discourage immigration of coloured people into this country from the colonies has been taken over the last few years' (quoted in Hampshire 2005: 22).

As it became clear that measures to restrict immigration were having little effect, the government began to discuss new legislation. There were only two possibilities. Either the colonial citizenship regime created by the BNA 1948 would have to be abolished or immigration laws differentiating the rights of CUKCs would have to be introduced. The government was reluctant to abolish CUKC as it was trying to replace the formal control of empire with an informal sphere of influence through the British Commonwealth. It was believed that the abolition of colonial citizenship would hasten decolonization and antagonize newly independent governments. In addition, some politicians of the time were committed to the imperial rhetoric of *Civis Britannicus sum* (I am a British citizen) and the freedom of movement between the Commonwealth and 'Mother Country' that this implied.

Thus, the government chose not to abolish colonial citizenship but introduce distinctions between citizens based on their 'belonging'. The 1962 Commonwealth Immigrants Act applied immigration controls to all Commonwealth and colonial citizens except those born in the UK or those holding a passport issued under the authority of the UK government. The Home Secretary, Rab Butler, told parliament that the Act restricted the right to enter the UK to CUKCs 'who in common parlance belong to the United Kingdom' (quoted in Hampshire 2005: 30). A small quota for economic immigrants was created and, in one of the most controversial aspects of the legislation, Irish citizens were exempted from controls.

It is important to note that throughout this period, public debate about immigration was openly racialized. The 1962 Commonwealth Immigrants Act did not make explicit racial distinctions, but the government was motivated to act by concern over public opposition and politicians' own beliefs about the development of Britain into a multiracial society (Paul 1997; Hampshire 2005). Although it made no mention of race, the Act was designed to restrict 'coloured' immigration. As the minutes of the Cabinet meeting at which the legislation was discussed, put it: 'the Bill itself applies to all Commonwealth citizens, irrespective of colour; but it would be evident in its operation that the control was being applied in practice only to coloured people' (quoted in Hampshire 2005: 69).

Citizenship and immigration control in the 1960s and 1970s

Just six years after the 1962 Act, the 'Kenyan Asians Crisis' prompted the Labour government to pass new immigration legislation. After achieving independence from Britain in 1963, the government of Kenya had initiated an 'Africanization' campaign, under which South Asians living in the country were restricted to certain sectors of the economy and removed from the civil service. Facing economic exclusion, a growing number fled to the UK. In 1967, about 13,600 Kenyan Asians arrived in Britain.

Under the terms of the 1962 law, most CUKCs had been made subject to immigration controls. However, the mechanism used to impose controls meant that people from South Asia who had migrated to Kenya when it was part of the British Empire were exempt. Whereas most CUKCs living in the empire or Commonwealth had their passports issued by colonial authorities, the Kenyan Asians held passports that had been issued under the authority of the British government, largely because they applied before Kenyan independence (for details of the legal story see Hansen [2000: 165–176]). Since the 1962 legislation exempted anyone with a passport issued by Britain, the Kenyan Asians retained the right to enter the UK. The 1968 Act removed that right.

The 1968 Act was a deeply controversial piece of legislation. The Labour government was responding to anti-immigration hysteria in newspapers and what it believed to be growing public opposition to immigration. The proposed law left about 200,000 Kenyan Asian CUKCs effectively stateless. The Bill divided the Cabinet, with opposition led by the Commonwealth Secretary, and when it was debated in parliament it was fiercely criticized by both Labour and Conservatives MPs. The Labour Home Secretary, James Callaghan, defended the Bill by invoking the idea of 'belonging' first used in 1962: the aim, he said, was 'to deprive citizens of the United Kingdom and colonies who did not belong to this country … of their automatic right to enter this country' (quoted in Hampshire 2005: 36).

The Commonwealth Immigrants Act 1968 changed the basis for immigration controls from the authority that had issued a CUKC's passport to where they, or a recent relative, had been born: from now on, only people who were born or naturalized in the UK, or who had at least one parent or grandparent who was UK-born or naturalized, had an automatic right to enter the country. Thus, a descent-based differentiation was introduced: the rights of citizens now depended on where a person or their recent ancestors were born. The Home Office insisted that the 'test adopted is geographical not racial' (Hampshire 2005: 76) but the effect – and indeed the intention – was to deny most Black and Asian CUKCs a right of entry, while retaining that right for the descendants of Britons living in White-majority settler colonies.

The month after the 1968 Act was passed, Enoch Powell made his infamous 'Rivers of Blood' speech. The Conservative leader, Ted Heath, dismissed Powell from the Shadow Cabinet for his 'racialist' speech, but Powell's popularity with parts of the electorate helped the Conservatives win the general election in 1970 and shifted the party's position on immigration. The Conservative manifesto promised 'that there will be no further large-scale permanent immigration'. In 1971, the Conservatives introduced an Immigration Bill, which was intended to fully close the door.

Ted Heath's Conservative government still did not abolish CUKC. Instead, it extended the idea of descent-based citizenship rights by introducing the concept of 'patriality' into UK law. After the 1971 Immigration Act, only 'patrials' had the right to enter the UK. To qualify for patrial status a person had to be either a UK-born CUKC or have a parent or grandparent who was born in the UK. This meant that nearly all citizens of the New Commonwealth countries in Africa, Asia, and the Caribbean were subject to immigration control, while many citizens of the White-majority Old Commonwealth countries, such as Australia, Canada, and New Zealand, continued to enjoy the right to enter Britain.

From colonial to national citizenship

In 1981, the British government finally abolished the category of CUKC and replaced it with national citizenship. Most CUKCs living outside Britain had lost their right to enter the UK in the 1960s, making colonial citizenship a legal status with few concrete rights. In 1977, the Labour government had put forward proposals to reform nationality law and create a 'British citizenship', but it was the Thatcher government, elected in 1979, that legislated to decouple nationality and immigration law. From this point on, the right to live in Britain would be reserved for national citizens.

The British Nationality Act of 1981 (BNA 1981) repealed the BNA 1948 and created a new citizenship scheme with three main categories. British Citizenship – defined to the exclusion of the colonies for the first time – was granted to all persons with the 'right of abode', which in practice meant people born or settled in the UK. This replaced the concept of 'patriality', introduced in the 1971 Immigration Act to distinguish between colonial citizens. Two subsidiary categories were created for those not entitled to full British citizenship: British Dependent Territories Citizenship (BDTC) and British Overseas Citizenship (BOC). BDTC was granted to residents of the remaining colonial territories, most of whom lived in Hong Kong, as well as Bermuda, the British Virgin Islands, Gibraltar, and the Falkland Islands (though the latter were upgraded to full British citizenship after the Falklands War). BOC was a residual category for those entitled to neither of the first two categories: it included some East African Asians and Malaysians. Neither BDTC nor BOC carried a right to enter the UK. The term 'Commonwealth citizen' replaced 'British Subject', but this was not a status that could be directly acquired, rather it was an umbrella term for citizens of a country that is a member of the Commonwealth of Nations. Commonwealth citizenship does not confer a right to enter the UK, though it does generate voting rights for legal residents in the UK and some other member countries.

The other major reform of the BNA 1981 was its qualification of the principle of *jus soli* (literally right of soil, or place of birth). Previously, any person born in the UK or one of its colonies was entitled to CUKC status. After the Act came into force, citizenship was no longer automatically granted at birth: a child born in the UK must also have at least one parent who is a British citizen, a British Dependent Territories citizen, or a permanent resident of the UK.

The Act was partly a legal tidying-up exercise, partly a domestic political intervention, and partly an acknowledgement of the post-colonial international order. The Kenyan and Ugandan Asian crises had shown the need to clarify the rights of various categories of citizen, while the intermeshing of nationality and immigration legislation had created an increasingly complex legal situation. At the same time, the Conservative government wanted a restrictive approach to immigration: before her election Margaret Thatcher had famously said that British people were 'rather afraid that this country might be rather swamped by people with a different culture', a statement partly motivated by the electoral threat of the far-right National Front. As Stuart Hall (1979) argued in his prescient analysis of Thatcherism, although Enoch Powell had personally failed, Powellism was part of the conjunctural success of the right in the late 1970s.

Perhaps the most important driver of the creation of British citizenship was a belated recognition of Britain's place in a post-colonial world. The imperial logic that had held CUKC in place for three decades, despite its evisceration by immigration law, had evaporated. Earlier concerns about alienating recently independent Commonwealth countries had faded and the pro-imperial wing of the British establishment was dying out. Furthermore, Britain's entry into the European Economic Community in 1973 had reoriented its political and economic interests towards Europe. In a post-colonial world, colonial citizenship no longer served a political purpose.

Despite the abolition of colonial citizenship, Britain's colonial past continues to shape its citizenship and immigration policies today. In the remainder of this chapter, I discuss two contrasting cases – the Windrush scandal and the Hong Kong British Nationals (Overseas) visa – which show how the legacies of Britain's colonial citizenship regime extend to the present, impacting the lives of thousands, if not millions, of people.

Legacies of post-colonial citizenship: the Windrush scandal of 2018

The Windrush scandal was caused by the collision of policies intended to target irregular immigrants, known as the 'hostile environment', with a citizenship regime forged through colonialism. The 'hostile environment' was a set of administrative and legal measures launched by the Coalition government in 2012, during Theresa May's tenure as Home Secretary.[1] As May put it, the intention was 'to create, here in Britain, a really hostile environment for illegal immigrants'. By making everyday life difficult for those without authorization to be in the country, the government hoped to facilitate the removal of irregular immigrants, while also deterring future arrivals and visa overstaying.

The Immigration Acts of 2014 and 2016 provided the legislative basis of the hostile environment. These Acts required private businesses and public bodies to perform identity checks and refuse services if people were unable to demonstrate their right to be in the UK. Banks, landlords, the National Health Service, and other organizations were effectively co-opted into immigration control. The internalization of immigration control was not a new idea (the previous Labour government had floated similar proposals), and similar policies exist in other countries. But the hostile environment was imposed in a country that lacked a universal ID card system, and a society that included a significant number of people who had migrated under very different citizenship laws.

As various organizations began to implement the legally mandated checks, thousands of Black Britons of Caribbean descent who were going about their daily lives – opening bank accounts, visiting the doctor, applying for driver's licences, and interacting with public authorities – were wrongly identified as 'illegal immigrants' due to a lack of documents proving their right to live in the UK. The Windrush generation, who had migrated from Caribbean countries between 1948 and the early 1970s, often arrived in the UK without individual passports or visas (Slaven 2022). This was perfectly legal at the time. Individual documentation was not required – many people travelled on a shared passport – and on arrival immigration officers granted permanent settlement to nearly 60,000 people. CUKCs from the Caribbean, and many of their children, possessed citizenship rights, but they were not issued with documents to prove it, and the Home Office did not keep systematic records of their names.

Having lived in the UK for decades without needing identity papers, the Windrush generation found themselves having to prove their right to be in the country. Those who did not have the requisite documents were told that they were 'illegal immigrants'. They faced an institutional culture of suspicion, disbelief, and racism. Thousands of people were denied work, refused healthcare, and excluded from public services (Gentleman 2019); many experienced serious financial hardship and ill health; several lost their homes; and some were wrongfully detained in immigration removal centres and threatened with deportation. At least 83 people, and possibly twice that number, were deported: forcibly removed from a country they had every right to call home (Rawlinson 2018).[2]

An official investigation into the Windrush scandal, conducted by Wendy Williams, Inspectorate of Constabulary, was published in 2020. It found that 'members of the Windrush generation and their children have been poorly served by this country ... with jobs lost, lives uprooted, and untold damage done to so many individuals and families'. Williams was 'unable to make a definitive finding of institutional racism' within the Home Office but she concluded that there was an 'institutional ignorance and thoughtlessness towards the issue of race and the history of the Windrush generation within the department, which are consistent with some elements of the definition of institutional racism' (Williams 2020: 7). Richard Black, a Windrush man who was stranded in Trinidad for 38 years after the Home Office denied his British citizenship, was more direct: 'to me it's a racist situation' (Black 2023).

Post-colonial protection: the Hong Kong British Nationals (Overseas) visa

A very different legacy of post-colonial citizenship can be seen in the recent creation of a bespoke visa for the residents of Hong Kong (see Benson, Chapter 18, this volume). As discussed earlier, BNA 1981 abolished the colonial category of CUKC and created a British national citizenship for the first time. The Act dealt with the vestiges of empire by creating two subsidiary citizenships for those who did not qualify for British citizenship: BDTC and BOC. Neither came with the right to enter or reside in the UK; they were 'impoverished legal identities' (Hansen 2000: 214).

Most residents of Hong Kong, which was the largest remaining British colony, had been granted BDTC status. In bilateral negotiations with China about the future of Hong Kong during the 1980s, the British government agreed to replace BDTC with a new status of British National (Overseas). The Hong Kong (British Nationality) Order of 1986 granted this status to any Hong Kong BDTC who registered before 1 July 1997, when sovereignty would revert to China.

British National (Overseas) (BN(O)) came with a British passport and diplomatic protection, but its holders were not entitled to live or work in the UK. After the Tiananmen Square massacre in 1989, the British government offered full British citizenship to 50,000 holders of BN(O) status to enable them to move to the UK, but applications were more limited than expected and most BN(O)s remained in Hong Kong.

In 2020, following the introduction of a new National Security Law in Hong Kong, the British government decided that the 'one country, two systems' approach, which had been agreed with the Chinese government, had been breached. The Conservative government launched a Hong Kong British Nationals (Overseas) visa, which allowed holders of BN(O) status to migrate to the UK. Applicants were required to show that they could support themselves in the UK for six months, pay the visa fees (a comparatively low figure of £180 per applicant for a 30-month visa or £250 for a five-year visa), as well as the Immigration Health Surcharge of £1,560 for 30 months or £3,120 for five years. Visa holders could live, work, and study in the UK. The scheme was presented as humanitarian protection for British nationals threatened by repression.

The Hong Kong (HK) BN(O) visa stood out against the Conservative government's otherwise restrictive approach to refugees and asylum-seekers. The two existing humanitarian schemes, the Vulnerable Persons Resettlement scheme, introduced during the Syrian war, and the Afghan Resettlement schemes, admitted only small numbers of refugees. Moreover, in 2023 the Conservative government had passed legislation to make it practically impossible for people arriving in the UK to claim asylum (Yeo 2024). Given that an estimated 2.9 million British Nationals lived in Hong Kong, and no limits were placed on the number of people who could be granted visas, the HK BN(O) visa appeared anomalous.

Between its introduction in January 2021 and September 2024 a total of 174,307 visas were granted.[3] This makes the Hong Kong visa smaller than the Ukrainian schemes introduced following the Russian invasion in 2022 (265,150 visas issued up until September 2024), but much larger than the resettlement schemes for Syrian refugees (21,698 people between 2015 and 2020) and Afghans (30,412 people resettled until September 2024).

The British government's approach to Hong Kong reveals how colonial history shapes official ideas about who is deserving of protection by the British state. The Home Office stated that 'the visa reflects the UK's historic and moral commitment to the people of Hong Kong'.[4] Politicians in both major parties depicted the BN(O) visa as a matter of obligation arising from Britain's colonial history. The Chair of the House of Commons Foreign Affairs Committee, Tom Tugendhat, argued that the British government should have granted Hong Kongers full British citizenship back in 1997: 'the extension of overseas citizenship, which is in many ways a second-tier citizenship, was a mistake, and I think it's one that should be corrected'.[5] While official justifications emphasized historical obligations, there were also economic interests at work, with applicants viewed as a potential source of skilled workers after the UK's exit from the European Union. Whatever the motivations, the visa bucked a wider trend to restrict those seeking political asylum in the UK. As Benson, Sigona, and Zambelli argue, the government's approach 'reveal[ed] the coloniality of the post-Brexit migration regime, while also being informed by geopolitical tensions, namely the deterioration of the UK's relationship with China' (Benson et al 2024: 271).

Conclusion

This chapter has shown how British citizenship and immigration policy were shaped by colonialism. Immigration from the 1940s to the present, and thus the development of Britain as a multiracial society, cannot be understood outside the context of colonial and post-colonial history. Citizenship of the UK was colonial before it was national; colonial citizenship was steadily eroded by policies intended to restrict racialized immigrants from the New Commonwealth, while allowing continued access to the Old Commonwealth; and when national citizenship eventually emerged, it was shaped by racial logics and accompanied by residual post-colonial categories.

The entanglement of citizenship, immigration, and colonialism is far from a matter of narrow academic interest. The treatment of the Windrush generation in the hostile environment shows how colonialism, intermixed with racism and anti-immigrant attitudes, has profoundly affected people's lives. The creation of the HK BN(O) visa illustrates how post-colonial ties and obligations continue to influence who Britain admits as humanitarian migrants. The rights of British citizenship were forged through colonial history, and they continue to be shaped by the legacies of that history.

Notes

[1] This sentence uses the past tense only because the 'hostile environment' was rebranded as the 'compliant environment'. Many of the policies remain operational and substantively unchanged under this new term.

[2] Oral history interviews with some of those affected can be found at https://windrushscandal.org/project/windrush-scandal-survivor-interviews/

[3] https://www.gov.uk/government/statistics/immigration-system-statistics-year-ending-september-2024/how-many-people-come-to-the-uk-via-safe-and-legal-humanitarian-routes#british-national-overseas-bno-route

[4] https://www.gov.uk/government/news/hong-kong-bno-visa-uk-government-to-honour-historic-commitment

[5] https://www.theguardian.com/politics/2019/aug/13/uk-british-nationality-hong-kong-citizens-tom-tugendhat

References

Arendt, H. 1973. *The Origins of Totalitarianism*. Harcourt.

Benson, M., Sigona, N., and Zambelli, E. 2024. 'The UK's "Safe and Legal" Humanitarian Routes: From Colonial Ties to Privatizing Protection', *The Political Quarterly* 95(2): 263–271.

Black, R. 2023. *Oral History Project: The Windrush Scandal in a Transnational and Commonwealth Context*. Interviewed by Eve Hayes de Kalaf, 10 November. https://windrushscandal.org/files/2024/02/Richard-Black.pdf

Gentleman, A. 2019. *The Windrush Betrayal: Exposing the Hostile Environment*. Guardian Faber Publishing.

Hall, S. 1979. 'The Great Moving Right Show', *Marxism Today*, January.

Hampshire, J. 2005. *Citizenship and Belonging: Immigration and the Politics of Demographic Governance*. Palgrave Macmillan.

Hansen, R. 2000. *Citizenship and Immigration in Post-war Britain: The Institutional Origins of a Multicultural Nation*. Oxford University Press.

Joppke, C. 2010. *Citizenship and Immigration*. Polity.

Paul, K. 1997. *Whitewashing Britain: Race and Citizenship in the Postwar Era*. Cornell University Press.

Rawlinson, K. 2018. 'Windrush: 11 People Wrongly Deported from UK have Died – Javid', *The Guardian*, 12 November.

Slaven, M. 2022. 'The Windrush Scandal and the Individualization of Postcolonial Immigration Control in Britain', *Ethnic and Racial Studies* 45(16): 49–71.

Spencer, I.R.G. 1997. *British Immigration Policy since 1939: The Making of Multi-racial Britain*. Routledge.

Williams, W. 2020. *Windrush Lessons Learned Review*. Home Office.

Yeo, C. 2024. 'Repairing the United Kingdom's Asylum System', *The Political Quarterly* 95(2): 243–252.

Video lecture

Hampshire, J. 2021. *Colonialism, Immigration, and the Making of British Citizenship*, Connected Sociologies Curriculum Project. https://thesociologicalreview.org/projects/connected-sociologies/curriculum/british-citizenship-race-and-rights/postwar-citizenship-britain/

QUESTIONS

1. What is citizenship? Why does it matter?

2. How did colonialism shape citizenship and immigration policy in Britain?

3. What role has racism played in the politics of immigration from 1945 to the present?

4. How do colonial legacies continue to shape the lives of British citizens and immigrants?

Worksheet 13. Colonialism, Immigration, and the Making of British Citizenship

This worksheet is designed to support AS and A-level teaching on globalization and global development and social differentiation, power and stratification. In this online talk, James Hampshire examines how Britain's colonial and post-colonial history has shaped notions of national British citizenship, focusing on the post-war introduction of citizenship into UK law, the influence of post-colonial immigration, and contemporary legacies of this period. Connecting colonial and post-colonial narratives of citizenship to contemporary events such as the Windrush scandal and Brexit, this talk connects with other topics in developing student understandings of the ongoing ramifications of British colonial history and its impact on contemporary sociological issues. In prompting students to think critically about the dimensions of power and inequality at play in the intersections between colonialism, immigration, and citizenship, this worksheet connects to several core topics within the Sociology A-level curriculum. It may also be helpful to students studying relevant modules in A-level History.

Time	Activity	Explanation
00.00–00.05	To warm up, answer this question: *What makes someone a British citizen?*	This warm-up activity offers an open-ended introduction to the key theme of the session, and may be well suited to a group discussion.
00.05–00.10	Recap of understandings of globalization.	It may be useful to remind students of some of the key concepts and terms related to globalization.
00.10–00.15	At 2:35 Hampshire says that British citizenship in the post-war period was 'chiselled out of the ruins of empire'. *What do you think he means by this?*	Hampshire explains that British subjects became citizens only after the Second World War during Britain's retreat from empire, and that this citizenship was not national but explicitly colonial. The relationship between colonialism and British citizenship is the central theme running through this session, so this activity ensures that students understand the significance of this link in thinking about what it means to say that British citizenship was 'chiselled' from empire. Students might draw some thematic connections between this talk and the 'Decolonization' chapter in thinking about this relationship.
00.15–00.25	Watch the talk from 4:51 to 7:54. *What is the significance of former Home Secretary Jim Callaghan's stated intention to prevent the immigration of 'citizens who do not belong'? What does his intention reveal about the relationship between race, immigration, and citizenship in post-war Britain?*	This question encourages students to think about how issues of power and stratification play into the making of British citizenship, as well as ideas of social belonging and exclusion, and dimensions of inequality. These are key recurring themes within the A-level Sociology curriculum. Students may draw on learning from other chapters such as 'Global Britain' and 'Family, Intimacy and Migration' in thinking about the role of race and racism within British citizenship and immigration policies.

Time	Activity	Explanation
00.25–00.35	Watch the talk from 13:05 to 15:54. *What can the Windrush scandal teach us about the making of British citizenship?*	This activity encourages students to place the making of British citizenship in the post-war period within a contemporary context. Connecting with other sessions, such as the 'Making of the Modern World' topics, activities like this one ask students to think about the ongoing, contemporary ramifications of historical narratives of modernity. Students may find it beneficial to see some examples of media coverage of the Windrush scandal to help them with this activity.
00.35–00.45	Watch the talk from 16:27 to 19:26. *What are the similarities between the making of British citizenship in the post-war period and Britain's departure from the European Union under Brexit, according to Hampshire? Write a short paragraph summarizing the main points.*	Hampshire explains that immigration was a political motive in both of these instances. He also explains that these case studies demonstrate how ideas of citizenship and rights within Britain are shaped by political projects that extend beyond the nation. This activity asks students to synthesize the information they have heard into their own words, and in doing so strengthen their understanding of how Britain's colonial past continues to shape contemporary socio-political events.
00.45–00.55	At 20:30 Hampshire states that 'citizenship can be thought of as the formal definition of membership and of belonging'. *Why is the idea of belonging important to our understandings of British colonialism and British citizenship?*	Questions surrounding who 'belongs' in certain countries and/or societies are key to understanding the sociological implications of colonization, decolonization, globalization, and global development. Understanding how changing notions of 'belonging' in turn relate to social stratification and dimensions of inequality is also helpful in developing students' critical thinking skills with relation to these topics. Students may draw on similar material from the 'Global Britain' and 'Rethinking Diaspora' chapters in answering this question.
00.55–01.00	Drawing together what you have learned throughout this session, and in your wider learning, answer the following question: *What is the sociological significance of the post-war making of British citizenship to Britons today?*	This question prompts students to bring together what they have learned throughout the session, connect it with wider themes, and apply their knowledge to a challenging sociological question. It encourages students to consider the enduring significance of the events of the post-war period Hampshire has detailed, and they may draw on his examples of the Windrush Scandal and Brexit to evidence their arguments.

This worksheet was developed by Isabel Sykes.

14

Asylum in Britain and the Legacies of Colonialism

Lucy Mayblin

Objectives

- This chapter explains the response of successive British governments since the 1990s to people seeking asylum.

- It sets out a brief account of the drafting of the 1951 Refugee Convention and the 1967 Protocol on the Status of Refugees.

- It explains why we need to know the colonial dynamics at the time of drafting the convention and protocol in order to fully understand these agreements.

- It discusses the relevance of this founding colonial context in understanding the politics of asylum today.

Introduction

The cross-border movement of people seeking asylum has become one of the most contentious political issues of our time. This phenomenon is frequently described by politicians and media commentators as a 'crisis' whereby people are illegally and illegitimately entering countries for nefarious reasons. The crisis framing presents current events as historically unprecedented – a new emergency which necessitates exceptional responses outside of the normal workings of politics and law. Crossing borders to seek asylum has therefore been criminalized, both rhetorically (in terms of how asylum seekers are discussed in public discourse) and legally (with new laws). The UK, like other Western states, has also implemented a range of measures to make life difficult for people who have applied for asylum, and has curtailed the possibility of being successfully recognized as a refugee in the country.

Because of the political intensity of debate in this area in Western countries, research on the subject has also increased in Europe, North America, and Australasia over recent decades. A plethora of research has emerged across the social sciences since the 1990s, establishing a field of study called 'refugee and forced migration studies' with journals and research centres, university degrees, textbooks, and conferences. Often researchers are critical of the actions of governments to limit the movement and rights of people seeking asylum. However, scholars have also inadvertently tended to contribute to the narrative of crisis by framing the present as unprecedented.

In this chapter I explore what it means for our analyses of the present if we take a longer view. The chapter goes back to the 1951 Refugee Convention, which is the founding international legal basis for refugee rights and explains how colonial logics shaped it. Recognizing that this founding moment of refugee rights was not a pure articulation of human equality, as it is sometimes described, allows us to understand that the contemporary exclusions and dehumanization of people seeking asylum from host states such as Britain are continuous with the past rather than discontinuous. It also draws our attention to the racial politics of asylum over time, which helps us to understand the racism that we can see in this policy area today.

Asylum in Britain

An asylum seeker is someone who applies for asylum (or refuge), in a foreign country, because they are being persecuted in their country of origin or citizenship. The category 'asylum seeker' is therefore an administrative category, referring to someone who has submitted an application for asylum in a country which has signed up to international refugee law. In Britain the word 'refugee' tends to refer to someone who has made an application for asylum and their application has been granted, so they are allowed to stay and have refuge, though often for a limited period of time. This right, to apply for asylum and get a fair assessment of one's application, is enshrined in the 1951 Convention relating to the Status of Refugees, and the 1967 Protocol, discussed further in what follows.

Great Britain is an island situated in the north-west of Europe and is very far away from any major conflict zones. It's geographical location alone means that out of the 38 million refugees in the world in 2024, not that many people sought asylum in the country. Most refugees travel to countries close to the country which they fled. Thirty-nine per cent of all refugees in the world currently (as of 2024) reside in just five countries: Iran (3.8 million), Turkey (3.3 million), Colombia (2.9 million), Germany (2.6 million), and Pakistan (2 million). Of all the refugees in the world, around 0.5 per cent are in Britain (all data from UNHCR 2025). This is not only because of the geographical location of Great Britain. A range of laws have been introduced over the past 30 years which have made it very difficult for people to reach this country for refuge, and these are approaches which are also used by most other Western states, including across Europe.

Britain's borders with continental Europe are not actually located on British soil, they are located in France and Belgium precisely to prevent those without visas from entering Britain. In northern France, the vast architecture of control to prevent such migration includes (among other things) kilometres of fencing, secure lorry parks, giant X-ray machines for lorries to drive through, sniffer dogs trained to locate humans, infra-red scanners, CO_2 detection equipment, man-made lakes, and drones (Mayblin et al 2024). The impossibility of stowing away in a vehicle is the reason that, since 2018, people have begun to attempt crossing the English Channel in small boats.

For ports further afield, carrier sanctions – fines for airlines or ferry companies if someone boards without appropriate travel documents – are a key tool for border control. Although refugees are meant to have the right to travel without appropriate documents, they cannot actually apply for asylum without first setting foot in the country they want to apply for asylum in. Here, the airlines or ferry companies take the role of border guards, stopping people boarding a plane to claim asylum in a destination country. In this way, states do not break international law straightforwardly, but they certainly violate the spirit of it. If you have ever wondered why people pay 40 times the cost of a ferry ticket to cross the Channel in a small dinghy, carrier sanctions are the reason. David Fitzgerald (2019), a leading migration studies scholar, calls this 'the catch-22 of asylum policy' – we may give you asylum if you can get here, but we will do all we can to stop you from getting here.

Another tactic used by British governments to limit the rights of people seeking asylum has been to make the lives of those who do manage to make it to Britain and apply for asylum (illegally and often dangerously, by necessity) very difficult. For example, people are dispersed around the country on a no choice basis to very poor-quality housing in the poorest areas. Since 2020 they have been housed in cheap hotel accommodation for years on end in poor conditions, in disused army barracks, and on a prison barge docked in the sea. People who are awaiting a decision on their asylum application do not have the right to work and are instead made dependent on welfare support. This welfare support is well below the levels which are provided to unemployed citizens (who are understood to be living at the poverty line). Rates of asylum support are calculated on the basis of what the poorest 10 per cent of the British population spend on essential living items only. This is around one-third of the income of the poorest 10 per cent of Britons, who we know are struggling themselves. This puts people in the asylum system well below the poverty line. In my research I have found it to be common for people to limit their meals to one or two per day, to walk miles to hospital appointments because they cannot afford buses, and to be unable to afford appropriate clothes and shoes for the weather, or toiletries (Mayblin 2019). There have also been a range of measures introduced since the early 2000s to make it harder for people to be successful in their applications for asylum. For example, making the definition of what persecution is very narrow, the level of documentary evidence required to prove it very high, limiting rights to appeal an asylum decision, and dramatically shrinking the pool of legal aid lawyers so most people do not have legal advice or representation through the process.

For many years it was common for scholars explain these hostile measures in terms of the increase in asylum applications received since the 1990s. A standard narrative emerged by which scholars would explain that the 1951 Refugee Convention (discussed in the next section) opened up the right to asylum at a time when refugees were only European. When large numbers of people from outside Europe started becoming refugees and applying in Western states in the late 1990s, then they logically responded in a hostile way. In other words, the hostile measures are due to the unprecedentedness of the situation. However, when we look back at the reality of the situation during the late 1940s and early 1950s, we do not find a radically different number and type of refugee.

The 1951 Refugee Convention

In order to make sense of the state's responses to refugees today, we need to go back in time to the establishment of refugee rights on an international scale. The 1951 Refugee Convention is commonly understood to have established the rights of refugees internationally. It emerged in response to the displacements caused by the Second World War within Europe. In that context people who had been displaced had found that they had rights only as a consequence of being a citizen of a particular state. If that state persecuted them or cast them out, as had happened to Jewish and other people at the hands of the Nazi regime, they lost all rights to anything – food, shelter, work, survival. In this situation persecuted and displaced people were reliant solely on other people's and states' willingness to be kind to them. Nobody had any legal duty to take foreign nationals or stateless peoples in, and many people wanting to flee the Nazi regime were let down by Britain and other countries. The 1951 Convention relating to the Status of Refugees (commonly referred to as the Refugee Convention) was meant to be a solution to this terrible situation. The world's powerful states at the newly formed United Nations agreed a suite of rights that people fleeing persecution would now have, and duties that signatory states would also have. They did this in order to protect future refugees. The rights enshrined in the 1951 Refugee Convention include the right to cross a border without appropriate travel documents (for example, visas) and the right to apply for asylum in a host state and have a fair assessment of that application, among other protections. The convention of course had to include these things because someone fleeing Damascus in Syria or Kabul in Afghanistan cannot wait for a visa application to be processed when they are fleeing a regime that threatens their life. Often people do not have access to their passport in the turbulent circumstances of a warzone.

The rights and duties enshrined in the Refugee Convention only apply where a state has signed up. In 2024 there were 149 signatories, but many of the countries that host the largest number of refugees are not signatories, for example, Jordan, Lebanon, and Bangladesh. Britain was involved in the drafting of this convention and was a founding signatory. However, in the years since 1951, Britain has become very unwelcoming to people seeking asylum, as set out in the previous section. A reasonable question is *why*. Why is Britain so hostile to people seeking asylum, when it signed up to these commitments to protect persecuted people in need in 1951, and even when the numbers of people applying for asylum in the country now are so small compared to other places? One way of making sense of this is to go back to 1951.

Britain in 1951 was an empire, not the small country that we know today, and the world in 1951 was still very much a colonial world. A key feature of colonialism was the dominance of hierarchical conceptions of humanity. Put simply, human beings were not thought of by powerful people in Britain as all being equal. Instead, the idea of racial difference, and hierarchy within that difference, dominated. This was not just about people's skin colour or hair texture, by this time it combined both physical characteristics and cultural traits in a complex taxonomy of human hierarchy which always placed White people, and particularly Europeans, at the top. We should not be surprised, then, to discover that the colonial powers and the White settler colonies such as Australia, argued forcefully at the convention negotiations that colonized peoples and people of colour were not ready for human rights, and that they should not be included in the new laws around refugee rights.

The work of Jamaican philosopher Sylvia Wynter (2003) can help us to understand race not as an aberration of European modernity and the emergence of human rights, but instead as something that was integral to it. Wynter argues that the category 'human' was implicitly hierarchical, with the full rights-bearing human being the White man. The idea of 'man' within human rights therefore ultimately relied on a fundamental exclusion of colonized others who were cast as not only unable to bear rights but also as not quite or non-human. Indeed, it was unthinkable for the human rights of refugees to be applied to colonized peoples in 1951. If persecution by the governing state is grounds for applying for asylum, millions of people living under conditions of colonial oppression would have had claims to refugee status, and the colonial powers, who were central in the convention drafting process, would have found themselves designated major human rights violators (see Mayblin 2014, 2017).

The 1951 Refugee Convention, after much debate, was limited to European refugees displaced before 1951 only. Of course, there were objections to this. The representatives of recently independent countries such as Pakistan argued vocally and relentlessly, in anti-colonial terms, that excluding non-Europeans was implying a hierarchy of humanity. It also made no sense since there were millions of refugees outside of Europe who needed help at that time, not to mention states who needed help in supporting them. Note here that despite contemporary claims that refugees in the 20th century were mainly a European phenomenon, in fact there were millions of refugees outside of Europe at the time of drafting the Refugee Convention. For example, millions of people had been displaced in the partition of India to create the state of Pakistan.

After much debate about the problematic Eurocentric nature of the proposals, a 'territorial application clause' was nevertheless proposed and passed in the negotiations. Article 40, paragraph 1 of the final Refugee Convention document, stated: 'Any State may, at the time of signature, ratification or accession, declare that this Convention shall extend to all or any of the territories for the international relations of which it is responsible. Such a declaration shall take effect when the Convention enters into force for the State concerned.' Despite at this time holding significant overseas territories, the UK extended the convention only to the Channel Islands and the Isle of Man. We can see, then, how racist colonial logics meant that refugee rights were never imagined by the British government as something that should be available to all humans in the world. Those to be excluded were Black and Brown people living in the colonial and post-colonial world.

By the 1960s, more and more countries were gaining independence from colonial rulers (see Chen and Sabaratnam, Chapter 6, this volume). The fallout from decolonization meant that there were a lot of refugees, particularly in Africa.

The newly formed Organization for African Unity, which later became the African Union, was planning to draft its own convention on refugees since the 1951 Refugee Convention did not help them in dealing with these new displacements. Refugees were defined in the convention as people displaced *in Europe before* 1951. The United Nations body responsible for refugees, the United National High Commissioner for Refugees (UNHCR), was concerned that new regional conventions might damage the international scope and power of their organization. In response they led the drafting of a new protocol, signed in 1967, which amended the 1951 convention and lifted the geographical restriction as well as reference to people displaced before 1951 (see Davies 2007).

Not all signatories to the 1951 convention also signed the protocol, but Britain was one of the signatories. Yet little changed in Britain in relation to refugees for a few of decades. Most people applying for asylum here were fleeing the Soviet Union, and giving them refuge was highly convenient for Cold War politics. There was no question of whether they were able to integrate, and the fact that they might want to get a job in Britain did not seem to undermine their claim to have been persecuted. In other words, they were not attacked for being economic migrants in disguise. But expanding the right to asylum in international law does not erase the racist views that had dominated British colonialism.

Post-colonial asylum

In the early 1990s, a combination of events came together. There were ongoing and new conflicts around the world and, at the same time, the rise of cheaper international air travel meant that some people who had money were able to flee to places that were further afield like the UK. These people came to be thought of as 'new' refugees. There was actually nothing distinct about them in relation to the situations they were fleeing or the legitimacy of their claim for asylum. However, they were often Black and Brown, and in an increasing number of cases, they were fleeing formerly colonized countries – the countries whose nationals Britain had gone to such efforts to exclude from refugee rights, and human rights more broadly, in the 1940s and 1950s. The response to their arrival sparked the passing of now 12 rafts of primary legislation which steadily began to strip them of their rights under international law.

People seeking asylum came to be cast as exceptional, as not really refugees but actually economic migrants, as probably lying and trying to cheat the asylum system. In response, successive governments (Labour and Conservative alike) have systematically denied people seeking asylum their rights, they have excluded them (physically, economically, politically, and socially), impoverished them, and exposed them to harm and increased risk of death, whether from drowning or from poverty. We can understand these measures not as new and different, or inexplicable acts of inhumanity, nor as reasonable responses to an overwhelming tidal wave of arrivals. We can understand them as consistent with colonial logics; that is, with colonial ways of imagining the world and the various people in it, including hierarchical conceptions of human worth based on skin colour, culture, religion, and nationality.

B.S. Chimni, a key scholar of refugee studies, has argued that the pervasive idea that contemporary refugees are new – greater in number and different in character to mid-20th-century refugees – is a myth (Chimni 1998). He calls this the 'myth of difference'. Two phenomena – the increase in asylum applications, and the punitive response by Western states – have garnered a significant amount of academic attention and often they are seen as causally linked: restrictive measures were introduced because numbers of applications were 'at intolerably high levels' (Hansen 2003: 35). But Chimni's concern is not simply with the policy response. He is also concerned with the ways in which academic scholarship has reinforced the myth of difference. He observes that 'there is constant reference in the [academic] literature to the enormous magnitude and the unprecedented nature of the contemporary crisis' (Chimni 1998: 356). From looking at the convention negotiations we know that there were millions of refugees outside of Europe in the past, and that they were purposefully excluded from refugee rights because of the dominance of the colonial powers at the United Nations. For Chimni, then, academics have contributed to the legitimizing of the containment of refugees from what he refers to as the 'Third World', outside of the 'First World' (see also Achiume [2022] for an overview of these dynamics).

In fact, these new refugees are not different in terms of the legitimacy of their claim to asylum under international law. What is different is that they were from the 'Third World', usually from former European colonies. Migration expert Hein de Haas observes that many aspects of international migration are completely misconstrued by commentators, politicians, and publics alike. Since the 1950s refugee numbers have been between 0.1 and 0.35 per cent of the global population, and refugee numbers have fluctuated between nine and 21 million depending on international conflicts (de Haas 2024). As already noted, most refugees also stay in their region of origin, often in countries neighbouring their own. De Haas (2024) summarizes: 'the facts defy the idea that swelling masses of refugees are on their way to the Wealthy West' (2024: 50) and there is 'no evidence of a rise in "bogus asylum claims"' (2024: 51).

If we recognize that there is no fundamental difference between historic displacements and events today, we can then understand that states such as Britain still view Black and Brown refugees from outside of Europe as less deserving of asylum, as they did in 1951. What we find is a continuity with the past rather than discontinuity. We can thus recognize that some of the logics of colonialism – dominant understandings of the world and the various people in it – have not changed so much in the past 70 years. The hierarchy of humanity, where some human beings are understood to be more fully human and thus more deserving of access to human rights, continues to operate. For example, when millions of Ukrainians were displaced following the full-scale invasion of their country by Russia in 2022, the UK government arranged for them to be able to travel safely to Britain via planes, ferries, and Eurotunnel. No Ukrainians found themselves in the position of contemplating crossing the Channel in small boats. This is quite right and allowed them to access their human rights to refuge. Such rights are not, however, extended to Syrians, Afghans, or Eritreans who find themselves in northern France wishing to seek asylum in the UK.

Recognizing the continuities between colonial histories and logics and practices today is part of an approach that is often termed 'post-colonial'. Through taking this post-colonial perspective, we can see how the treatment of people seeking asylum is connected to other examples of people being denied access to rights and justice (see Renwick, Chapter 9, Fernandez, Chapter 23, and Thompson, Chapter 24, this volume). For example, we could make connections with racially based stop and search policing or the stripping of citizenship from racialized Britons. That is, where some people are treated in ways which would be unthinkable if they happened to other groups of people. Thus, in understanding this very particular topic of the response of the British state to people seeking asylum, we also need to understand how it is connected to other topics where we can see the legacies of colonialism at work in Britain today.

Conclusion

This chapter has discussed how successive British governments since the 1990s have responded to people seeking asylum with hostility. New laws have been introduced which have sought to prevent people from arriving in Britain to make an asylum application, have sought to limit their chance of success if they do manage to arrive and apply, and have sought to make their lives as difficult as possible while they do so. So grave is the situation of people who are awaiting a decision on their application for asylum that these are some of the most marginalized people in Britain today – economically, socially, and politically. The usual standards that apply to alleviating poverty, to housing standards, and to human rights, seem not to apply in the same way to people who are seeking asylum. Alongside this, there has been widespread media hostility to such people, framing them as 'bogus asylum seekers' and 'illegals breaking into Britain'. In other circumstances we might frame such treatment at a societal level as persecution.

This situation has led many scholars to research the situation of refugees and people who are seeking asylum, to interrogate the policy approach, laws, media representations, and political rhetoric. In general, academics are highly critical of the status quo. However, there has been a tendency to perpetuate the myth that refugees in the past were all European, were small in number, and that refugees today are therefore new and different. This idea that the contemporary situation is unprecedented is presentist, in that it ignores historical facts. It is also problematic in that it ignores the continuities between past colonial logics of exclusion from human rights, and frames contemporary exclusions as rational responses to an exceptional situation. When we look to the past, however, we find continuity, and this allows us to develop a deeper and fuller understanding of the current moment.

Research which seeks to develop an understanding of the present based on analyses of histories of colonialism, and which traces the continuities between past and present logics and practices, is often labelled 'post-colonial'. Taking a post-colonial perspective can help us to understand hostility to refugees today on a much deeper level. By identifying key continuities in dominant underpinning policy logics, such as ideas of differential and hierarchical humanity, we can also make connections between this issue and other issues. For example, torture, rendition, citizenship stripping, or racist policing. In this way, we need always to recognize that the politics of asylum is not exceptional nor outside of the normal workings of liberal politics. It is part of wider structures and systems of governance which are long-standing.

References

Achiume, T.E. 2022. 'Racial Borders', *The Georgetown Law Journal* 110: 445–510.

Chimni, B.S. 1998. 'The Geopolitics of Refugee Studies: A View from the South', *Journal of Refugee Studies* 11(4): 350–374.

Davies, S.E. 2007. 'Redundant or Essential? How Politics Shaped the Outcome of the 1967 Protocol', *International Journal of Refugee Law* 19(4): 703–728.

de Haas, H. 2024. *How Migration Research Works*. Penguin.

Fitzgerald, D. 2019. *Refuge beyond Reach: How Rich Democracies Repel Asylum Seekers*. Oxford University Press.

Hansen, R. 2003. 'Migration to Europe since 1945: Its History and its Lessons', *Political Quarterly* 74(1): 25–38.

Mayblin, L. 2014. 'Colonialism, Decolonization, and the Right to be Human: Britain and the 1951 Geneva Convention on the Status of Refugees', *Journal of Historical Sociology* 27(3): 423–441.

Mayblin, L. 2017. *Asylum After Empire: Colonial Histories in the Politics of Asylum Seeking*. Rowman & Littlefield.

Mayblin, L. 2019. *Impoverishment and Asylum: Social Policy as Slow Violence*. Routledge.

Mayblin, L., Davies, T., Isakjee, A., Turner, J., and Yemane, T. 2024. 'Small Boats, Big Contracts: Extracting Value from the UK's Post-Brexit Asylum "Crisis"', *The Political Quarterly*. https://doi.org/10.1111/1467-923X.13412

United Nations High Commissioner for Refugees (UNHCR). 2025. www.UNHCR.org

Wynter, S. 2003. 'Unsettling the Coloniality of Being/Power/Truth/Freedom: Towards the Human, after Man, its Overrepresentation - an Argument', *The New Centennial Review*, 3(3): 257–337.

Video lecture

Mayblin, L. 2020. *Asylum in Britain and the Legacies of Colonialism*, Connected Sociologies Curriculum Project. https://thesociologicalreview.org/projects/connected-sociologies/curriculum/migration-borders-diaspora/asylum-britain-and-legacies-colonialism/

Additional resources

Decolonial Approaches to Refugee Migration, Nof Nasser-Eddin and Nour Abu-Assab in Conversation. https://www.berghahnjournals.com/view/journals/migration-and-society/3/1/arms030115.xml

Detention Action. https://detentionaction.org.uk/

Joint Council for the Welfare of Immigrants. https://jcwi.org.uk/

Living Refugee Archive. https://www.livingrefugeearchive.org/

Migrants Organize. https://www.migrantsorganise.org/

The Refugee Council. https://www.refugeecouncil.org.uk/

Refugee History. http://refugeehistory.org/

UNHCR. https://www.unhcr.org/uk/

QUESTIONS

1. What do you think the dominant representations are of refugees in Britain?

2. What was the colonial context to the drafting of the 1951 Geneva Convention and the 1967 Protocol?

3. How can colonial histories help us to understand the response of the British state to people seeking asylum today?

4. In what ways is the treatment of people asylum connected to other injustices? Can you think of some examples and try to articulate the connections?

Worksheet 14. Asylum in Britain and the Legacies of Colonialism

This worksheet supplements existing teaching on the topics of global development as well as stratification and differentiation. It is specifically designed to help students make sociological connections between different topics and themes explored as part of the Sociology curriculum, as well as other relevant subjects (for example, History, Geography, and/or Politics). The online talk by Lucy Mayblin and this worksheet help stretch students who have already been introduced to demographic trends in the UK since 1990, especially related to migration and globalization ('Families and Households'), and the distribution of poverty ('Work, Poverty and Welfare'). By touching on a range of topics, and suggesting the ways in which they are interrelated, this worksheet aims to help students think critically around questions of migration, poverty, and how these relate to a broader historical context as legacies of colonialism.

Time	Activity	Explanation
00.00–00.05	Before we start, answer these questions: *In your own words, and based on what you might know from other session, or from the news, define the terms 'refugee' and 'asylum seekers'. Can you remember and summarize specific news stories where these terms have been used?*	This is a short warm-up exercise, for students to try and remember any content previously covered on the topic, and apply some of their own critical thinking skills. It also helps set up a broader context for the upcoming discussion.
00.05–00.10	Recap of previous relevant sessions on poverty.	The teacher may choose to reuse previous class material on migration or colonialism.
00.10–00.15	Watch 0:20–1:03 *What do you think are important parts of the context for the creation of the 1951 Refugee Convention? What had just happened around that time, and what other things were ongoing?*	This question connects the topic of migration in the UK, to broader topics covered in Sociology, including globalization, the Second World War, the Holocaust and persecution of Jewish people, Roma communities, communists and LGBT populations in Nazi Germany and Eastern Europe, ongoing colonialism, and the first wave of independence being won in countries like Syria and Jordan (1946), India and Pakistan (1947), and Egypt (1952).
00.15–00.25	Watch 1:04–4:20 Here Mayblin gives an outline of the context behind the passing of the 1951 Refugee Convention. Despite many sensationalist news stories which suggest that Britain is overflowing with refugees, only 0.5 per cent of the global refugee population lives in the UK. *What are some of the factors that explain such a low percentage?*	This question is designed to stretch students in thinking about how some of the topics covered in class have real-life impacts in the policy making arena. The majority of refugees live in neighbouring countries to where they have come from (for example, Turkey, Uganda, Colombia, Pakistan, Kenya). The UK is physically/geographically remote from the world's conflict areas. Extreme border control.

Time	Activity	Explanation
		Huge fines meted out against carriers (for example, airlines and ferry companies) means it is virtually impossible to enter the UK safely. Carrier fines are the reason why, for those of you who have ever boarded a flight, you have to show your passport to the aircrew before boarding, despite them not actually being border agents.
00.25–00.35	Watch 4:23–5:43 At 4:44 Mayblin explains that asylum seekers do not have the right to work and the welfare support that they receive is different to the welfare support received by other welfare recipients, with asylum seekers receiving on average less than 50 per cent of normal welfare benefits. As a result, asylum seekers often live well below the poverty line. *How does this connect to other lessons you may have had about social class, stratification, and poverty?*	This question prompts the students to make connections between this lesson and the AS/A-level curriculum on the topic of poverty and stratification, and pushes them to use their critical thinking skills and articulate their own view on the topic This suggests that the state can often play a role in creating poverty, and people's socio-economic status/experiences It adds some complexity to classical arguments around class and social stratification.
00.35–00.40	Watch 5:43–10:39 *Why do you think the 1951 Refugee Convention was limited to 'European refugees displaced before 1951 only', until amendments in 1967 following pressure from the now African Union?*	This question prompts the students to use their critical thinking skills and draw on what they may have learnt in other lessons. 1951 was still a time of empire, and so colonial ideas around racial difference and human hierarchies were dominant, therefore shaping international law.
00.40–00.50	Watch 10:39–13:35 *What are the measures listed by Mayblin which point to Britain being hostile to asylum seekers?*	Framing of 'economic migrants' to delegitimize the claims of some (usually Black and Brown asylum seekers from formerly colonized countries). Framing of 'economic migrants' as 'trying to cheat the system'. Successive rounds of legislation designed to strip asylum seekers of their rights under international law. Physical, economic, political and social exclusion (for example, no right to work, no right to vote, and so on). Putting people at risk of death from drowning (through carrier fines for example) or poverty (through 50 per cent of normal welfare benefits explored previously).

Time	Activity	Explanation
00.50–01.00	*Based on what you have learnt in this lesson, and things you might know from other lessons or following the news, in what ways are asylum policies consistent with colonial logics?*	This question prompts the students to use their critical thinking skills and articulate their own view on the topic. It also pushes the students to make connections between this lesson and other lessons (including from other subjects) as well as from the news. While this question is relatively open-ended, below is a prompt for discussion if needed: Differential treatment based on country of origins (for example, resettlement schemes put in place rapidly for Ukrainian refugees versus no resettlement schemes for people fleeing Sudan or Palestine).

This worksheet was developed by Alexandra Wanjiku Kelbert.

15

Diasporic Interventions: How Diasporas Have Shaped Modernity and Challenged the Global North

Ipek Demir

> **Objectives**
>
> - This chapter discusses why we should recognize diasporic communities as authors, as one of the makers of modernity and our contemporary globalized world instead of merely an *outcome* of modernity and globalization. It shows how diasporas have shaped the modern world, including the Global North.
>
> - It locates understandings of diaspora in the wider context of decolonial/anti-colonial resistance that has shaped the modern world rather than trapping this concept, as has often been the case, solely in discourses of homeland politics, nation states, hybridity, or the tyranny of in-betweenness.
>
> - It offers strategies for questioning the essentialism and primordialism associated with diaspora and offers a heterogeneous and temporal understanding of diaspora.
>
> - It illustrates that diasporas can not only have their roots in empire and colonialism, but that they also throw up issues in the metropole as they seek to undo the racialized hierarchies entrenched in empire and colonialism. It positions diasporas from the Global South as primary agents of decolonization of the Global North.

Introduction

Post-war history of the Global North, in general, has two simultaneously told stories on the race/migration nexus, and on modernity and progress. On the one side, we have anti-immigrant discourses and a history of immigration politics focused on restricting citizenship and violent policing of borders. On the other hand, in the post-war era, we have also seen an ever-increased push for valuing diversity, anti-racism, multicultural politics, and accommodation of difference. This includes things such as anti-discrimination laws being introduced, Equality, Diversity, and Inclusion policies being adopted in workplaces, as well as calls for decolonization in educational institutions and museums. Gains were achieved not only through legislation but there has also been increased public and political reckoning with racial inequalities and colonial legacies. These two developments, interestingly, have occurred alongside one another – there has been an intensification and proliferation of racist border regimes in the Global North, at same time as proliferation of progressive interventions, if not demands, for anti-racism and diversity.

At first sight these two stories provide us with an important social scientific puzzle of our time. How do we make sense of this puzzle? In my view, one central aspect of the answer needs to take account of diasporas. This is a puzzle we can begin to tackle if we take diasporas and their interventions into the Global North seriously; as 'the Global South in the Global North', expanding equalities, rights, and liberties. Even though my discussion in this chapter will focus on diasporas who have moved from the Global South to the Global North, much of what I offer, and the conceptual tools I provide, can also be used for understanding, for example, South to South diasporic migrations, allowing us to see diasporas as makers of modernity and our contemporary globalized world.

Diaspora theorizing and research

The term diaspora originates from Greek and is associated with spreading and scattering. Diasporas are communities who have been scattered across regions and places, often from where their forebears are thought to have lived. With an increase in international migration from the Global South to the Global North in the post-war period, research interest in diasporas has proliferated. Despite the use of the concept of diaspora having multiplied and migrated to many fields and disciplines, however, understandings of diaspora, especially empirical diaspora research, has remained limited to single case studies (Faist 2010) and often as a movement of peoples between nation states. This has trapped understandings of diaspora into the discourses of homeland politics. Here I will outline how we can amplify the impact of diaspora research and theorizing if we locate diasporas in the wider context of anti-colonial resistance in the making of the modern world.

Diaspora theorizing flourished in the 1990s. Two main trends which conceptualized diaspora emerged and were successful in refining understandings of diaspora. One was offered by Safran and Cohen who developed ideal-type characteristics of a typical diaspora and provided refined versions of the key characteristics of diaspora, focused on relations with homelands (for example, Safran 1991; Cohen 1996, 2023 [1997]). The second approach was less concerned with origins, roots, and homelands. This approach paid attention to diasporic identity and space, especially to the multiple, hybrid, and fluid nature of diasporas. Brah (1996), Bhabha (1994), Gilroy (1993), and Hall (1990), for example, successfully and effectively critiqued the privileging of the point of origin in diaspora theorizing and also examined the hybrid nature of diasporic identity focusing on, for example, how diasporas create new practices (for example, culinary, linguistic, cultural) which are hybrid in nature, merging the 'origin' and 'settlement' contexts. However, such a focus did not always allow us to understand what was special and different about diasporas, given the fluid, hybrid, and fuzzy aspects of many other identities we study in social sciences.

Importantly, however, the theorists of diaspora mentioned earlier, who established the field in the 1990s, made empires and colonialism central to diaspora research, unlike much diaspora research which followed them. In what follows, I will argue that we should return to understanding diaspora in the context of empire and colonialism and push against what I have called 'methodological amnesia' and 'methodological nationalism' in diaspora theorizing and research.

Why we need to understand diasporas beyond the framework of methodological nationalism and methodological amnesia

Methodological nationalism refers to the way in which the nation state is used as the sole unit of analysis in the social sciences. Understandings of social processes are reduced to the national-territorial, to its spatial boundaries and resources. Nation states are important and are a key context for social life, of course. However, researchers should not use explanatory categories, concepts, and understandings which are solely locked into the sources and vocabularies of the nation and the nation state, making the nation state the unique and exclusive container for social structures and processes, ignoring others.

Methodological nationalism and the spatial limitations it brought have been questioned in the social sciences, but especially in migration studies (Wimmer and Glick Schiller 2002). What I call methodological amnesia is thus a close sibling to methodological nationalism. It is the idea that in the social sciences we often overlook the temporal dimensions that go beyond the history of the nation state. In other words, it refers to how conceptualizations and the boundaries of social scientific research often ignore the colonial and imperial axis of social processes. This axis has not been made central by scholars who have questioned methodological nationalism; their focus has remained on spatial boundaries and transnationalism. We need to push against both the spatial and temporal limitations, and thus against methodological nationalism and methodological amnesia. This is because we recognize that many aspects of social life, economy, and politics are transnational in nature; and, second, that historically, states have had shifting territories and been part of large and interconnected empires which we need to include in our understandings of the present.

In diaspora and migration research, methodological amnesia refers to how this temporal dimension has steadily ignored the movements of peoples. This has also been questioned, for example by Mayblin and Turner (2020). However, diaspora research has come to be dominated by single-case nation-state studies which remain wedded to the idea and history of the nation state as the primary vehicle of diasporization. Yet many diasporic migrations were made in, through, or by empires, including the emergence and collapse of these empires and the nationalist projects that followed them. Empires and colonialism, and subsequent nationalist projects, are central to the creation of, for example, Slavic and Jewish diasporas (Austro-Hungarian Empire),

Jewish and Circassian diasporas (Russian Empire), Arab diasporas (French Empires), Afro-Caribbean and South Asian diasporas (British Empire), and Armenian diasporas (Ottoman Empire). Empires and colonialism, through settlements, wars, plantations, indenture, expansions, the movements of people through force or voluntarily or via population exchanges have often been instigators of diaspora (see Kaladeen, Chapter 4, this volume). The subordination and colonization of peoples, the expansion and retraction of empires have generated, churned out, and proliferated diasporas.

Diaspora research which ignores the colonial and empire axis of diasporas contributes to North-centric understandings of migration, diasporas, and ethnic diversity. Such understandings are problematic because they act as a justification for hard violent borders, reinforcing the idea that policing of borders of nation states (and especially borders of the Global North) are warranted and necessary. Here I have in mind, for example, recent examples of those refugees drowning in the Mediterranean and the English Channel, violence at the US/Mexico border, the Turkey/Europe border, and the Belarus/Polish border. There is also the symbolic violence people from the Global South face even if they do not have to cross barbed wire fences. The borders of the Global North are maintained, for example, through airline carrier sanctions or restrictive and humiliating visa policies. These have narrowed safe options for those from the Global South to move, even 'legally'. Violent borders within the Global North also continue once those from the Global South arrive there, for example, in the form of securitization, surveillance, offshoring, counterterrorism strategies against racialized migrants, punitive settlement and citizenship regimes, the hostile environment in housing and health services, and the harsh policing which sustain and reinforce bordering regimes (see Murji, Chapter 17, Holmwood, Chapter 22, Fernandez, Chapter 23, and Thompson, Chapter 24, this volume).

Diaspora research which ignores the colonial and empire axis of diasporas also reproduces the dominant but inaccurate view that diversity is something that happened to the Global North recently. Cultural plurality is part of the fabric of European history and society and is ignored in citizenship tests, in history books, in annual commemoration ceremonies, and also in cultural products such as films. The absence of diasporas in our explanations today overlooks that much of European history happened outside of Europe.

Confining discussions of diaspora to the politics of 'their' nation state can also place boundaries on diaspora's citizenship in the new home, leaving a question mark over the extent to which they can really belong. It misses the point that diasporas have made, namely the phrase that 'we are here because you were there'. It continues to reproduce the assumption that diasporas belong elsewhere, that is, their nation state, with the consequence that their citizenship in the new home is regarded as contingent and revokable, even when there are centuries of linkages and lineages that were created through empire.

We can think of the Windrush scandal which emerged in 2018 in the UK as an example. Legal and administrative systems introduced in 2012 were aimed at removing migrants from the UK. Members of what has come to be called 'the Windrush generation' were victims of these policies. Afro-Caribbeans from the Windrush generation, over time, came to be categorized as 'immigrants', though they had arrived rightfully, and as citizens. Some of them were forcibly removed from the UK from 2010 onwards when the government introduced the policy of creating a 'hostile environment for immigrants'. For them, this occurred despite the fact that they or their parents had come to the 'mother country' as Commonwealth citizens. Afro-Caribbeans had in fact been part of the British Empire for centuries. Through restrictive citizenship regimes over the decades (see Hampshire, Chapter 13, this volume), the Windrush generation were therefore turned into 'migrants' from 'citizens' by British authorities (Cowan 2021). Leaving the relationship between empire and diaspora unacknowledged and unexplored has consequences not just for diaspora research but can shape the reality of many diasporic people's lives in the Global North today. It can mean even those diasporas who have extremely close historical and cultural links with the metropole, including those who have only lived in the metropole, can continue to be construed as 'other' and their presence can require verification and authentication, or even expulsion.

Refugees from Syria in Turkey are another recent case in point. In this case, the historical and emotional connections, affinities, and lineages of Syrians with Turkey through centuries of Ottoman rule and domination are not sufficiently recognized. The incitement to deport Syrians from Turkey has been enabled by methodological amnesia, through the telling of a glorious yet highly sanitized and Turkified version of the Ottoman Empire. The racial othering of Syrians in Turkey is also connected to Islamophobic, anti-Arab, and Orientalizing discourses. Ottoman Orientalism and Kemalist Orientalism are often revived in modern Turkey, and especially in relation to refugees from Syria and 'the East', reproducing methodological nationalism and methodological amnesia.

How diasporas have intervened and shaped our world is missing from standard research on diaspora

Like much of migration studies, diaspora studies has often looked at push factors or pull factors to explain the movement of peoples. Push factors relate to what is happening within a nation state, forcing groups to leave; pull factors relate to factors in the receiving state, inviting people to choose it as a destination country. While such a focus has to some extent enabled us to examine the exclusion and inclusion of minoritized populations and diasporization in general, I argue that social scientists have not paid enough attention to how diasporas have intervened and shaped our globalized world in standard accounts of modernity and globalization, or in standard understandings of diaspora. We should make central how diasporas need to be understood as part of anti-colonial struggles which have transformed and effected modernity and globalization. Many diasporas have questioned inequalities and exclusions and forced changes, and expanded understandings of freedom and equality in the making and shaping of our modern world.

Not all who cross borders and migrate can be considered as part of an anti-colonial story; in fact some can be regarded as peoples who have reproduced and entrenched Northern ideologies. This is why my conceptualization sees diaspora as a special case of migration whereby politicized decolonial/anti-colonial subjectivity is associated with mobility. As such, this approach brings a temporal dimension to the concept of diaspora – that no particular group should be deemed as a diaspora eternally. Diaspora should not be seen as an everlasting feature of an entity or group. This in fact is what has led to the essentialism and primordialism associated with diaspora. While certain groups are couched as 'diaspora' easily and forever, others can be denied or not offered it easily. Diaspora as an analytical category is useful if we see and define diasporic groups through what they do and how they engage in the world through this anti-colonial subjectivity, for example even becoming a diaspora over time. Muslim diaspora is a case in point. The Muslim diaspora is re-emerging through this subjectivity, being mobilized in response to the historical spacio-cide (Hanafi 2013), the violence in Gaza and the West Bank, as well as Islamophobia globally. A politicized anti-colonial Muslim diasporic identity is being emboldened. Such an approach can also recognize heterogeneity within a diasporic group. Within an expatriated group, certain activities, peoples, or mobilizations can be seen as diasporic, rather than all members, and their actions hallmarked with the label. For example, rather than stamping all Muslims or all South Asians or all Chinese in the West as diasporic, we can conceive of those whose mobility is associated with a heightened politicized decolonial/anti-colonial subjectivity as part of that diaspora. Last but not least, such an approach takes us beyond ethnicity as being used interchangeably with diaspora. Rather than ethnic and/or national identity being seen the sole basis for qualifying for diaspora, we can recognize new subjectivities emerging, for example, the Muslim diaspora, Middle Eastern diaspora.

In the field of diaspora studies, we often start from the premise that diasporas are global and transnational, but how diasporas have been makers of modernity and globalization has not always been clear. I have therefore turned my attention and focus to this via offering a conceptualizing of diasporas of the Global South as 'the Global South in the Global North', and as one of the decolonizers of the Global North (see Demir 2017, 2022). This is important as standard North-centric understandings of political thought or modernity typically have not seen others, whether they be colonized, from the Global South, or racialized diasporas as sources of ideas and concepts, and especially of ideas and concepts bearing on the Global North. They have failed to recognize that racialized diasporas in the Global North, through their struggles, have conceptually and practically expanded ideas about equality and freedom in fundamental ways through their interventions in, and challenges to, the Global North, similar to anti-colonial struggles before. These struggles, even if recognized and cherished, are typically seen as 'their' struggle, not how they were sources and originators of ideas, concepts of freedom and dignity, as something the Global North also learned from, and thus contributing to the making and remaking of the modern world. Hence we need to ask, 'can the Global North rethink itself as having learnt from its racialized others and diasporas?'.

Diasporas in Europe have resisted and fought against discrimination, poor conditions, unequal treatment, challenged racist practices and laws, and have demanded equality, fairness, and dignity. The anti-slavery movements, rebellion, and emancipation demands in the colonies did this for centuries (see Bhambra, Chapter 1, this volume). This is also a struggle their children, as part of the Global South in the Global North, continue to have and are still carrying on, expanding our understanding of equality, rights, and freedom (see Anitha, Chapter 8, Narayan, Chapter 19, and Kelbert, Chapter 20, this volume). Such understandings should expand our understandings of diaspora. We should refuse attempts to reduce diasporic mobilization to homeland struggles or to the hybrid identities they develop. Next, I offer two brief examples to elaborate this point further.

The Bristol Bus Boycott of 1963, for example, was central to challenging racial discrimination by employers and unions in the UK. Afro-Caribbean diaspora had increased in Britain in the 1950s, following the 1948 British Nationality Act which allowed Commonwealth citizens to settle in the 'mother' country. The boycott came about following the Bristol Bus Company's refusal to employ Black or Asian bus crews, something which was legal at the time. The trade unions supported their bosses in their refusal to allow Afro-Caribbean workforce from being employed to work on the buses, but only to be hired to work in the garages. Afro-Caribbean diaspora had settled in the 'mother' country as Commonwealth citizens, not as migrants. Many had fought for Britain during the wars, or were the offspring of those who had. They were raised in line with the British educational system and had idealized visions of Britain. But they found a Britain with a colour bar, and one which refused to accept them as equals. They not only had to struggle with the management who refused them work due to the colour bar, but also with the unions and the local council who approved and endorsed the colour bar at the time.

The Afro-Caribbean diaspora mobilized and enrolled many others, including White and other Bristolians, the University of Bristol students, and other groups such as the Campaign Against Racial Discrimination. They led the organization of marches, protests, and blockades on the Bristol bus routes. They gained support from politicians such as Tony Benn and Fenner Brockway. They were also highly effective in drawing parallels transnationally, with apartheid in South Africa and segregation and racism in the United States. The campaign led the way for the passing of the 1965 Race Relations Act which outlawed discrimination in public places, for the first time in the UK. Later, the 1968 Race Relations Act outlawed it in employment, housing and service provision. Indirect discrimination was outlawed in 1976 and the Equality Act 2010 placed a duty on public authorities to actively promote race equality (as well as other protected characteristics). Until recently this watershed moment for British history in Bristol was hardly discussed or taught in the UK even though the bus boycott in Alabama, United States and the story of Rosa Parks are taught in UK schools and very well-known in the UK. Instead, racism and also anti-racism are typically seen or construed as an American issue. The mixed-Black mayor of Bristol, Marvin Rees (2016–2024), stated that even though he had grown up in Bristol, he had not heard of the boycott until much later in his life. However, the central point to take here is the fact that this struggle should not just be seen as 'their' struggle, but a struggle which expanded understandings and practices of liberty, equality, dignity, and freedoms. It is in that sense that diasporas need to be seen as intervening and expanding the Global North.

If we turn attention to another example, one of fighting fascism during the Second World War, we can also see diasporas demanding the recognition of their contributions, even if retrospectively. Soldiers from the colonies were central to the winning of the Second World War. For example, French colonial troops (soldiers of colour from the French colonies) constituted more than two-thirds of the free French forces in the Second World War. Their sacrifices are not often remembered, not due to naive forgetfulness or ignorance but also because they were deliberately excluded, for example, from the liberation of Paris at the end of the Second World War. The Allies explicitly sought to see Paris liberated by White soldiers. Soldiers from the colonies fought and died for the liberation of Europe but were denied visibility as liberators of a central capital in Europe. In a process of *Blanchiment*, the presence of White soldiers in the liberation of Paris was secured through purposeful deployment of volunteer soldiers from Spain to make up the numbers of White soldiers. The North African soldiers were not only refused visibility but were also denied war pensions for decades. This was only partially reversed in 2006 in France (with no back payments), thanks to the impact of the film *Indigènes* (Days of Glory) which told the story of North African soldiers who fought for the liberation of France. The film was directed by Rachid Bouchareb, a diasporic Algerian French film director and producer who intervened and challenged the White-washed story of the war in France and demanded recognition of their parents' contribution to fighting against fascism in Europe.

Backlash to diaspora in the Global North

Diaspora and their demands and interventions are also central to understanding the rise of nativism, populism, and authoritarianism in the Global North (see Murji, Chapter 17, this volume). It would be a mistake to narrowly conceive nativist movements in the Global North as being limited to the crisis of new migrations, often couched as 'unprecedented and extraordinary migrations', notwithstanding their importance. Recent migrations are 'unprecedented and extraordinary' only if we ignore the movements of people from Europe to other parts of the world, and if we forget that 'in the course of colonial history, European populations moved in greater numbers and with greater effect on the populations they encountered than is the case in the course of migration to Europe' (Bhambra and Holmwood 2021: ix).

We should consider nativist sentiments and gains in White identity politics as being closely linked to resentments towards settled diasporas of colour in the Global North, the decolonizations they bring and their demands for equality and justice – that is, as diasporas 'who do not know their place'. Hence anxieties about recent 'unprecedented and extraordinary' migrations are closely entangled with anxieties about existing diasporas of colour in the Global North and their continuing justice and equality demands as part of continuing the anti-colonial struggle.

Conclusion

This chapter has argued that understandings of diaspora should not be reduced to homeland politics or to hybridity. We should push back not only against methodologically nationalist discourses of diaspora which trap diasporas permanently in their 'homelands' but also challenge those discourses which trap them somewhere in between the homeland and the host country, purely in discourses of hybridity or the tyranny of in-betweenness. The chapter also offered strategies for questioning the essentialism and primordialism associated with diaspora, and offered a heterogeneous and temporal understanding of diaspora.

This chapter showed that diasporas are an antidote to methodological amnesia and methodological nationalism. Yet much of standard research on diaspora has reduced diasporas to the sources, histories, and understandings of the nation state; ignoring the colonial and empire axis in the formation and proliferation of diasporas. As the chapter has revealed, Eurocentric accounts of diaspora have not only omitted empires from discussions of diaspora, but they have also omitted diasporic agency and how diasporas have reshaped the modern world, including the Global North.

The chapter instead illustrated that diasporas not only often have their roots in empire and colonialism but that in the metropole they challenge the racialized hierarchies entrenched in those forms and processes. The chapter sees diasporas from the Global South as primary agents of the decolonization of the Global North, and provides some examples of these. The recent backlash to diaspora also needs to be part and parcel of our understanding of nativism and White identity politics which is on the rise.

In summary, the chapter set out a case as to why diaspora research can expand beyond a focus on homeland politics and begin to also make central how diasporas have intellectually and practically expanded ideas about equality and freedom for all, that is as instigators of ideas about freedom, equality, and dignity, and not purely of receivers of these. As such we can begin to appreciate how diasporas can be seen as makers and shapers of modernity and globalization, not just an outcome of our globalized world.

References

Bhabha, H.K. 1994. *The Location of Culture*. Routledge.
Bhambra, G.K. and Holmwood, J. 2021. *Colonialism and Modern Social Theory*. Polity.
Brah, A. 1996. *Cartographies of Diaspora: Contesting Identities*. Routledge.
Cohen, R. 1996. 'Diasporas and the Nation-State: From Victims to Challengers', *International Affairs* 72(3): 507–520.
Cohen, R. 2023 [1997]. *Global Diasporas: An Introduction*. Third Edition. Routledge.
Cowan, L. 2021. *Border Nation: A Story of Migration*. Pluto.
Demir, I. 2017. 'The Global South as Foreignization: The Case of the Kurdish Diaspora in Europe', *The Global South* 11(2): 54–70.
Demir, I. 2022. *Diaspora as Translation and Decolonization*. Manchester University Press.
Faist, T. 2010. 'Diaspora and Transnationalism: What Kind of Dance Partners?', in R. Bauböck and T. Faist (eds), *Diaspora and Transnationalism: Concepts, Theories and Methods*. Amsterdam University Press, pp 9–34.
Gilroy, P. 1993. *The Black Atlantic: Modernity and Double Consciousness*. Verso.
Hall, S. 1990. 'Cultural Identity and Diaspora', in J. Rutherford (ed), *Identity: Community, Culture, Difference*. Lawrence & Wishart, pp 222–237.
Hanafi, S. 2013. 'Explaining Spacio-cide in the Palestinian Territory: Colonization, Separation, and State of Exception', *Current Sociology* 61(2): 190–205.

Mayblin, L. and Turner, J. 2020. *Migration Studies and Colonialism*. Polity.

Safran, W. 1991. 'Diasporas in Modern Societies: Myths of Homeland and Return', *Diaspora* 1(1): 83–99.

Wimmer, A. and Glick Schiller, N. 2002. 'Methodological Nationalism and Beyond: Nation–state Building, Migration and the Social Sciences', *Global Networks* 2(4): 301–334.

Video lecture

Demir, I. 2022. *Rethinking Diaspora Lecture*, Connected Sociologies Curriculum Project. https://thesociologicalreview.org/projects/connected-sociologies/curriculum/migration-borders-diaspora/rethinking-diaspora/

QUESTIONS

1. How have diasporas shaped modernity and globalization?

2. What are the consequences of methodological nationalism and methodological amnesia driving our understanding of migration and diaspora?

3. Why is recognizing how diasporas of the Global South are central agents of the decolonization of the Global North important?

4. Why should we develop heterogeneous and temporal understandings of diaspora?

Worksheet 15. Diasporic Interventions: How Diasporas Have Shaped Modernity and Challenged the Global North

This worksheet is designed to support AS and A-level teaching on the topics of global culture and globalization, taking a focus on different conceptualizations of diaspora and how this term relates to ideas of empire and colonialism. In this online talk, Ipek Demir introduces the term diaspora and takes issue with the way in which the concept has been understood in sociological research. The session is a useful opportunity for students to engage with a term which is central to the core A-level Sociology topic of globalization. It also provides a clear example of how to critically assess a methodological approach, which is a key skill within the curriculum. The worksheet activities are targeted at students who already have a solid grounding in approaches to understanding globalization, and connects with central themes across this module, such as migration, citizenship, and colonialism.

Time	Activity	Explanation
00.00–00.05	To begin, answer this question: *Have you heard of the term diaspora? What is your understanding of this term?*	This activity introduces students to the key theme of the session and is an opportunity for them to test their existing understanding of this terminology. Pair work or group brainstorming might be a useful way for students to share their knowledge for this activity.
00.05–00.10	Recap of understandings of globalization.	It may be useful to remind students of some of the key concepts and terms related to globalization and migration.
00.10–00.15	Watch the talk from 0:32 to 1:50. *Summarize the key characteristics of diaspora in your own words.*	Demir emphasizes that there are many different characteristics of diaspora, and she identifies some in this first section. These questions build on the warm-up activity, encouraging students to expand on their initial understanding of diaspora.
00.15–00.20	Watch the talk from 2:05 to 3:21. *What does 'methodologically nationalist' mean? What are some problems with this approach, according to Demir?*	Demir explains that this approach has trapped discussions of diaspora in 'nation-centric' understandings of the term, describing diaspora as emerging out of struggles *within* nation states, rather than within the context of empire. This approach has brought temporal and spatial limitations to common understandings of diaspora. This activity encourages students to think about methodological approaches in sociology and how it is important to approach these through a critical lens. It also introduces the topics of empire and colonialism to this session, which are key to the concept of diaspora.

Time	Activity	Explanation
00.20–00.30	At 8:30 Demir references the retort 'we are here because you were there', emphasizing the spatial and temporal links between diaspora and empire. *How might rethinking diaspora influence our understandings of identity, home, and belonging, particularly in a British context? Draw a spider diagram showing how these terms might relate to one another.*	Asking students to visualize the connections between the terms 'diaspora', 'identity', 'home', and 'belonging' encourages students to think about ideas of national identity within a British context, connecting with other sessions on this module such as 'Global Britain'.
00.30–00.40	At 8:55 Demir says that diasporas have 'conceptually and practically expanded ideas about equality and freedom in fundamental ways, through their interventions and challenges to the Global North'. She gives the Black Lives Matter movement as an example. *Using examples from the media, describe some more instances in which diasporas have 'expanded ideas about equality and freedom' within and beyond the Global North.*	This activity encourages students to use their independent research skills to expand their knowledge beyond the material provided to them in the talk. The talk on British Black Power, the Grunwick Strike, and on Black British Feminism are also relevant and can be consulted. Teachers might encourage students to feed back their examples to the group in order to form a collective resource.
00.40–00.50	Watch the talk between 10:41 and 12:15, and reflect on what you have learned throughout this session. *Why is it important to move away from nationalist understandings of diaspora? Can you suggest some positive long-term consequences of understanding diasporas as 'instigators of ideas', not just 'receivers'?*	This activity enables students to draw together what they have learned throughout the session to articulate the importance of rethinking diaspora in their own words. It also pushes students to implement their new knowledge in suggesting some sociological consequences of rethinking diaspora.
00.50–01.00	Drawing on what you have learned in other sessions on globalization, answer this question: *Why is rethinking diaspora important to our expanding our understanding of globalization and its impacts?*	This activity acts as a summary and a gateway to connecting this session with other topics. It asks students to situate what they have learned in this session within the wider context of their learning around the topic of globalization, which is a compulsory module in the A-level Sociology curriculum.

This worksheet was developed by Isabel Sykes.

16

Making Love, Making Empire: Family, Colonial Racism, and Border Controls

Joe Turner

Objectives

- This chapter explores how ideals of 'family' are central to how racialization is structured in post-colonial states like Britain.
- It examines how dominant concepts of heteronormative 'family life' are used in the organization of immigration and border regimes in contemporary Britain.
- It demonstrates how contemporary ideals of 'family' (domesticity and socio-sexual intimacy) are born out of the history of colonial control and dispossession under formal empire.
- It shows how racialized appeals to 'family' were central to early 20th-century border controls and continue to justify restrictive immigration regimes today.

Introduction

It is an often-rehearsed cliché that 'love is without borders'. But in places like the UK and many other European states, there is no fundamental right to be together with someone that you love, or maintain social relations considered central to a 'family life', if these ties cross international borders. Instead, legal and state decisions are made over what constitutes a family which can be the basis of movement and settlement. This is despite the right to family life being enshrined in human rights legislation. This means that immigration controls often separate and exclude people based on not appearing to be the right kind of family, sometimes violently. This is one way that family and migration are connected. But, also, perhaps less intuitively, we can see in our current moment how state border regimes are equally justified by appearing to uphold and protect 'genuine' family and, even more abstractly, things like 'family values'. The state is presented as compelled to protect so-called *real* families against criminals, deviants, and other threats; through which the use of immigration regimes and state border violence is justified. In this chapter, I aim to make sense of how certain people get to be protected as a 'family', and how others are deemed as threatening, or un-familial, and how this is bound up with processes of colonial racialization.

One example of this relationship between family and borders in contemporary Britain is the state's deportation of 'foreign national offenders' (FNO). Here, the deportation of people with precarious immigration status, who have committed certain crimes (with sentences exceeding two years), is regularly justified on the basis of the need to protect 'hard-working' British families. People without a right to remain in the UK are detained and removed after serving a custodial sentence. They are removed to a country where they may hold citizenship, regardless of how long they have been in the UK, and often regardless of their family ties and social relationships here. Politicians and mainstream media outlets regularly present these deportations as 'protecting' the public (Sales 2021). This is despite the vast majority of FNO not being imprisoned for serious violent crimes or sexual assault, but instead often serving custodial sentences for repeated minor offences.

It is significant that people from former colonies have historically made up the majority of FNO forced removals from the UK, and that people racialized as Black (and Black Caribbean men specifically) within the criminal justice systems are more likely to be issued with deportation orders (De Noronha 2020). In the wake of these enforced removals, lives are destroyed, kinships torn apart, and children left parentless. Those subject to removal are left to rebuild their lives in countries they may have left when they were minors, and with minimal support networks and means of survival. What is significant is how certain intimacies are recognized by the state within its restrictive heteronormative and gendered claims to 'family' (such as hard-working 'British families') while others are deemed 'un-familial' and subjected to removals and the destruction of intimacies and family life.

Who gets to be a family, or more precisely, accorded the social and political status that comes from being recognized as a 'real' family, is, in states like Britain, always already shaped by colonial histories and post-colonial structures of race. This matters for how we understand the control over the movement of people today and who is subjected to state border violence. Family is often presented as natural and self-evident, often privileging White, cis-gendered, heterosexual, nuclear expressions. However, as feminists and queer scholars and campaigners have long argued, this is because these ideas of family have become dominant, not because there is anything natural about them. As dominant ideas of family are depoliticized, this means that appealing to ideals of heteronormative family can hide and obscure the historical prejudices and structural inequalities that have informed this dominance. For example, stereotypes of Black masculinity shape who is viewed as fulfilling the model of family upheld by the British state and these are informed by longer histories of colonial dispossession, exploitation, and enslavement (see Kaladeen, Chapter 4, this volume). Thus, the purpose of this chapter is to demonstrate the role that ideals of family played under European colonialism, so we can better understand how dominant ideals of family – often promoted and protected by the state – play an important role in racist border controls in contemporary Britain.

The chapter is organized in three parts: first, it explores the role of family and intimacy in European empires, and how certain forms of family became encoded as civilized or backwards; second, it explores the relationship between family and the control of mobility under the British Empire; and, third, it brings the discussion back to the present, by deepening and broadening the discussion of how ideals of family shape immigration regimes and border violence.

Making love, making empire

Dominant forms of family in Britain and Europe are deeply intertwined with not only patriarchy, enforced heterosexuality, and the demands of capitalism, but also the ideologies and practices of colonialism. Unpacking this involves recognizing that categories of race are also organized around sexualized and gendered forms of intimacy. To Roderick Ferguson (2003), this means understanding how non-European and negatively racialized peoples have been historically catalogued within what he calls 'taxonomies of perversion': where people are treated as more or less human depending on how their intimate lives and gender relations are judged to be organized.

Decolonial feminists such as Maria Lugones (2007) have demonstrated how patriarchal systems of gender were central to European colonial projects. Lugones shows how colonialism both interrupted and intervened in Indigenous and colonized people's sexual and gender relations. Evidence of socially accepted same-sex relationships, matriarchal social relations, or non-binary constructs of gender were taken as a sign of 'backwardness' by colonists and used as a justification of colonial conquest and violence (Lugones 2007). European invasion and settlement not only disrupted the social patterns and gender relations of non-European societies but cast alternative models of intimacy as sexual deviancies and abnormalities which evidenced colonized people's backwardness.

Alongside the hyper-sexualization of colonized peoples, Neville Hoad (2007), details how anthropologists and colonial administrators catalogued colonized peoples based on their imagined closeness to a European ideal of patriarchal, Christian marriage and domesticity. For example, 'Asiatic Muslim marriage' forms were viewed as too communal, while Brahmin marriages were cast as almost emulating European models of intimacy. At the same time, African marriage forms were frequently cast as too 'primitive' and closer to animal relationships (Turner 2020: 83). Thus, by the late 19th century, ideas of civilization were tied to an evolutionary model of marriage, where White bourgeois domesticity was viewed as the most evolved and civilized, with other forms presented as 'traditional' and stuck in various stages of pre-history.

In this way, communities subjected to colonization were frequently presented as failing the strict model of gender relations that emerged in bourgeois households in North Europe. Thus, colonial projects were presented as needed to 'civilize' or teach colonized people how to live, including what families should look like, and how men and women should behave. This provided the pretext for colonizers to not only dispossess people of their land and resources and to exploit them, but also to impose on communities what were viewed as proper rules of family life. So, colonizers imposed European laws of marriage, encouraged forms of wage labour that were deeply patriarchal, imposed laws on who was a family and how children could inherit wealth and property, and created systems of education to change social norms. In many examples, colonial and settler authorities removed children from their families in attempts to make them 'more European' – which obviously had deeply traumatic and violent consequences.

While the patriarchal family and household was viewed as desirable for the reproduction of social relations in imperial metropoles (at least from the mid-19th century) this was often underdeveloped in colonized states and opposed when it didn't fit with systems of extraction and exploitation that structured the colonial economy. The structure of colonial and imperial economies sought to create land for settlement, for plantations, for the extraction of resources and to create pools of mobile labour, and this often led to the active destruction of existing kinship patterns and family life (see Kaladeen, Chapter 4, and Tyler, Chapter 5, this volume). For example, when communities were dispossessed of access to land or forests for subsistence, or when migrant labour was needed for tea and coffee plantations in North India, or diamond mines in South Africa.

This was exemplified in the slave trade where kinship and communities were destroyed through enslavement and, equally, where plantation systems of property wrote enslaved people out of family law. Hortense Spillers (1987: 75) argues that slave-owning societies demonized Black intimacy but also that by the 19th century Black family had become rendered almost unthinkable within the 'dominant symbolic order' of what is considered 'family' in the United States. In southern states, enslaved children were the legal property of a slave master, and parental rights of guardianship did not apply to enslaved Black people. Thus, the dominant modes of intimacy (European and White) which Black labourers were expected to emulate, or at least desire, became based on denying the enslaved access to such rights. However, while the Black family was made unthinkable and right-less in slave societies, Patricia Hill Collins (2000) and bell hooks (1990) separately argue that Black kinships have historically emerged as sites of resistance and survival in the face of dispossession.

In this way, European and bourgeois formations of family were part of projects of White supremacy and bound up with racialization, dispossession, and exploitation. Ideals of the White bourgeois family were part of the spatial and temporal markers of empire: the imperial mapping of the world into spaces of civilization and spaces of savagery was in some cases premised on accounts and imaginaries of perversions from European ideals of 'family' and domesticity. This was used in colonies to justify and shore up colonial dispossession, violence, and subjugation. But it was also networked into metropoles with regard to who was identified as 'civilized' and how people were incorporated into capitalist political economy. In the next section, I set out the role this played in the control over mobility and the emergence of state borders.

Borders, family, empire

Migration studies scholars tend to focus on the internal histories of Europe, such as the control of vagrants, for a history of borders and immigration control. However, as

I have argued elsewhere (Turner 2020; Mayblin and Turner 2021), borders emerged as central tools of imperial and colonial rule. Empires were created and maintained through the control of movement. Systems of borders emerged to trap and immobilize racialized populations but also created patterns of forced movement. The modern system of state immigration control and citizenship that dominates the world order today was built out of these attempts at control. As Radhika Mongia (2018) has argued, the modern states' attempts to control international mobility through bordering began to be formalized in the push to regulate the movement of both indentured and non-indentured Asian labourers who were moved across European empires at the end of the 19th century. Whether in colonial Mauritius, Fiji, or in settler colonies of Australia, South Africa, North America, the first centralized state immigration and citizenship regimes emerged to dispel and filter the movement of labourers from India and China (see Kaladeen, Chapter 4, this volume).

There was no grand plan for the emergence of state border regimes; they emerged because they served a constellation of local elite, colonial, and imperial interests: from maintaining control over indentured men (Turner 2020), to providing cheap and expendable labour to new markets, to run plantations after the formal end of slavery, or to squash revolutionary and anti-colonial movements in port cities. Why intimacy becomes important to think with in this context is because the calculation around the introduction of border restrictions was in many settings tied up with normative framings around the promotion of White heteronormative family life. For example, in settler colonies indentured Asian men were frequently presented as a racialized-sexual threat to White women and to White settler social order, hinged as it was on the promotion of White domesticity and 'superiority'.

Local and imperial elites presented practices of encampment, deportation, and mobility restrictions on Asian labourers as tools to curb such 'dangers'. They also experimented with plans to encourage more Asian women to migrate so this would balance the racialized-sexualized order and create fewer opportunities for inter-racialized intimacy. At the same time, the emergence of state-controlled international border regimes and visa systems demanded that judgements be made about dependants (such as children, spouses, partners, parents, nannies, and so on) travelling with contracted labourers to work in settler states. This entailed making further judgements at state borders about what and who made up a normal/abnormal 'family' for the purpose of claiming entry and settlement.

In this way, racialized ideals of intimacy fed into broader imperial strategies to control movement and to categorize movement as valuable or without value across European empires. Immigration laws increasingly restricted the movement of Asian labourers to settler colonies, but once contracted and registered, indentured labourers still held the right to travel with their families. At the same time, vast numbers of indentured labours left India, because of existing forms of land grabbing and dispossession which, through changes to agriculture and land ownership, left many rural poor with no choice but to find work overseas. This meant that at various points across imperial space, whether in British, French, or Dutch colonies, border agents, medical inspectors, law makers, ship crews, and ticketing agencies made decisions about whether subjects could move, or settle, based upon the proof of 'family' ties to registered labourers and 'settled persons'. In doing so, this provided colonial and settler authorities with the opportunity to monitor and shape what cultural forms of kinship and intimacies were legally and culturally recognizable as 'marriage' or 'family'. Border controls created a powerful site which made certain intimate relationships possible as 'family' over others.

Bringing empire home

These practices of control across the British and other European empires did not remain confined to (settler) colonies but also 'boomeranged' back into how immigration and border regimes emerged in Britain from 1905. The role of intimacy in imperial border regimes equally structured early immigration regimes in European metropoles. For example, one of the earliest pieces of state deportation legislation in Britain was developed in the 1920s in response to a so-called 'race riot' in the northern English city of Liverpool in 1919, which resulted in the murder of Charles Wootton (from Trinidad) who was drowned in the river Mersey (May and Cohen 1974). Elites attempted to justify these violent attacks on Black sailors and the Black community through the racialized-sexualized narrative which was used across colonies. The *Times* newspaper, for example, argued that White men joining in the racist violence were merely defending their 'instinctive certainty that sexual relations between White women and coloured men revolts our very nature' (cited in May and Cohen 1974: 114).

The 1920 Aliens Order, and later the 1925 Coloured Alien Seamen Order, which followed this violence, allowed for the forced deportation of Black 'foreign' sailors. Many of whom were actually Crown subjects (that is, with colonial citizenship) but without formal documentation to prove their status. After the violence, Black sailors were excluded from parts of the labour market as companies in the docklands, often backed up by racist unions, began further prioritizing White workers. Such acts created a more exploitable workforce within Liverpool, just as at the time the British imperial state had heightened concerns about anti-colonial resistance emerging across the British Empire (May and Cohen 1974). The extra powers given to the police and port authorities in Liverpool docks and across English cities allowed for opportune suppression of collective activity that looked 'anti-colonial' in character.

In these brief examples, we can see how borders were energized by normative appeals to racialized intimacy and fears over 'inter-racial' sex both in colonies and in the imperial metropole. Borders could be used as a means of preserving and policing the limits of a racialized conception of family. Equally, borders worked to produce modes of dispossessive violence. Black sailors with a right to reside in Britain could be removed through de facto police and immigration powers just as those within the Black community who were not caught up in removals were made precarious within existing systems of racialized exploitation and had their families torn apart. While an idealized and elite fantasy of 'White family' was to be protected at all costs through state violence, the families of those racialized as Black 'foreign sailors' were not even recognizable. To return to Hortense Spillers' work on family touched upon earlier, despite protests by Black community members, the dominant social calculus of 'family' could not recognize Black families as intimacies worthy of protection, but instead problems to be removed.

This, of course, links up with how immigration rules developed in Britain over the course of the 20th century. As Nadine El-Enany (2020) has detailed, after immigration acts in the 1960s and 1970s cut off Commonwealth citizens' right to move and settle, family migration routes became a key means for people to access their previously held rights to the imperial state and the wealth and services hoarded there, and to connect with diasporas, communities, and extended kinship ties (see Hampshire, Chapter 13, and Demir, Chapter 15, this volume). Consequently, limiting the right to family migration in Britain has, since the 1960s, been a coded way of restricting the mobility of people from former colonies. This is sometimes subtle, sometimes deeply interventionist and violent. The most infamous example of this is probably the enforced 'virginity tests' which took place at Heathrow airport in the 1970s. This is where border officials assaulted dozens of Indian women in order to 'check' the supposed validity of Indian fiancés right to move to the UK by inspecting the women's hymens (for more on this see Smith and Marmo 2011).

What I want to focus on now is how these legacies shape contemporary immigration politics in Britain; and to explore how the role of family under colonialism, and the role of family in early immigration regimes, sets in place relationships that are reproduced today.

The (post)colonial present

In this next section I give some examples of the role family plays in contemporary immigration and border regimes and show the importance of needing to historicize these contemporary practices in the structures of colonialism.

Let's start with an example of how ideals of family are encoded into immigration practice today and the consequences these restrictive definitions have. The British state operates a highly restrictive family migration visa system (the visa that people need to move and settle on the basis of family life – as partner, spouse, dependant). Since 2012, there has been a salary threshold which residents in the UK have to earn before they can sponsor an international partner to live with them; in 2024, this was raised to £29,000 (and to £39,000 in 2025). This means that, as of 2024, 60 per cent of men and 70 per cent of women do not earn enough to sponsor a partner to live with them (or indeed sponsor other dependants such as children). At the same time, the couple have to prove they have what is deemed a 'sustaining' and 'genuine' relationship and can live together without state support. The visa is one of the most expensive routes to settlement in the world, costing between £11,164 and £35,090.

While not exceptional in Europe, the UK still ranks as the worst supporter of family unification in terms of rich Northern countries according to the Global Migration Index. These policies have created what activists call a 'crisis of separated families', with over 15,000 children thought to be affected by these policies (and many more in the asylum system). Through these practices, the Home Office is enabled to make judgements about what a supposed 'sustaining' and 'genuine' relationship and family is supposed to look like. Again, this relies on idealizing certain forms of intimacy over others which, as we have explored, are shaped by longer legacies of racialized colonial violence and dispossession.

In this context, it is worth noting that increasingly narrow definitions of family were brought into UK immigration law with the expressed purpose of policing so-called 'sham marriages' and actively weakening the rights of the movement of diasporas, specifically from former British colonies. The family visa was brought in after decades-long discussions about the so-called 'failures' of multiculturalism in Britain. Changes to the visa were said to be expressly about promoting integration, because these rights would only be extended to 'deserving' families who did not need support from the welfare state. As writers and activists like Amrit Wilson (2007) demonstrate, this was also wrapped up with a racist paternalism from the British state, where rare examples of 'forced marriage' and 'honour killings' were presented as endemic within South Asian communities in Britain. These racist stereotypes were weaponized to appear as if the state was protecting women and encouraging their 'integration' through immigration reforms.

This links up wider colonial representations regarding the hyper-patriarchal character of Muslim gender relations and politicized debates about a 'lack' of integration of Bangladeshi and Pakistani women into British society. Family migration routes were argued to lead communities into the living of 'parallel lives' in Britain. The racialized logics central to the justification of restrictive visas also shape how it operates and who it excludes. We know that refusal rates differ dramatically depending on where a partner applies from; for example, in 2015, the refusal rate for partners from Pakistan was 40.8 per cent, from Nigeria it was 49 per cent. This is compared to refusal rates of US and Canadian applications, which are about 10–16 per cent (Turner 2020: 113). So, there are significant racialized geographical and wealth disparities in terms of who can apply and who is granted rights to family life.

Such restrictions do not take place in a vacuum but are structured by and reproduce the broader patterns of racialization that shaped British colonialism. In contemporary Britain, family migration routes are targeted because while overall the number of people travelling for family unification is small, it often leads to a higher rate of settlement and access to citizenship. Within the British state's attempts to control family migration are manifest long-held anxieties about changing demographics – particularly with a focus on the biological reproduction of racialized and migrant communities and their 'inferior' and less civilized ways of organizing family life. Likewise, this connects to long-standing anxieties about maintaining the 'Whiteness' of Britain, born out of the ever vulnerable (if powerfully protected) racialized-sexualized order of empire. While explicit eugenics and biological ideas of race might not be explicitly vocalized in policy today, these ideas are replicated in elite fixations on things like reproduction and fertility. This is exemplified by far-right political movements but also replicated in concern for the proper cultural (rarely ever economic) integration of Muslim women in particular.

Restrictive ideals of family not only play a role in limiting and excluding routes to settlement in contemporary Britain, they also animate bordering practices and help structure the wider politics of anti-immigration. The British state is constructed as supposedly protecting genuine families and citizens, against variously racialized and sexualized threats; for example, from 'gangs', 'terrorists', or 'illegal migrants'. Gargi Bhattacharya et al (2020) have argued that in the diminishing social role of the British state, the state has to be increasingly depicted as the true masculine protector against threats, and to stand up for genuine 'hard-working' families and family values.

Let's take the example of the so-called 'crisis' of people moving across the English Channel to claim asylum to illustrate this in more detail. Asylum seekers and people on the move are regularly depicted in gendered and sexualized terms. Those making crossings in small boats across the English Channel to claim asylum are regularly presented as 'criminals' and potential terrorists or viewed as 'queue jumpers' and 'benefit scroungers'. People seeking asylum are also regularly depicted as 'single men' and presented as sexual and racialized threats to British society. This has allowed right-wing politicians to use the colonial logic of the 'failed' non-European family to attempt to destroy the rights of those claiming rightful sanctuary. In 2018, while defending his use of racialized propaganda during the Vote Leave (the European Union) campaign, Nigel Farage, then leader of the far-right Brexit Party, argued that those coming to the UK were not 'genuine refugees': 'where are all the women and children, the old people … these aren't refugees, not in the real sense of the word' (BBC 2018) he argued. This far-right rhetoric has become normalized in British politics with successive Conservative Party Home Secretaries using the higher proportion of so-called 'single men' crossing the Channel as evidence that they are economic migrants and are from cultures with 'values at odds with our country' (Suella Braverman cited in Adu and Syal 2023). Through the propagation of such arguments, asylum seekers are not only presented as 'bogus' but as a hyper-sexualized dangers and/or failed patriarchs, who have abandoned their country and family to war and ruin so they can prey on British society.

A prominent case of the way that ideals of family play a role in anti-immigration politics is the specific moral panic around child refugees. In 2016, a number of child refugees were given settlement in Britain through what became known as the 'Dubs Amendment' (after Lord Alfred Dubs, who campaigned on this issue). However, rather than being welcomed on arrival, they were turned into a national scandal when several MPs and national newspapers accused these children of being 'burly men' in disguise. The *Daily Mail* infamously argued that these 'youth' (also referred to as 'burly men' and 'lads', never as children) would pose a danger to English school girls if they were allowed into the country to settle, and to have access to education (Reid 2016). Several Conservative MPs argued that the Home Office and local authorities should use dental examinations, skull measurements, and X-rays to 'scientifically' assess the 'true' ages of child refugees 'in the future' (Weaver 2016).

This anxiety about child refugees not being 'real' children is directly linked to the need to symbolically defend White British families and so-called 'genuine' children. This was clearly evidenced in 2023 when the Immigration Minister, Robert Jenrick (Hansard 2023), argued that the 'evil' of 'young adults … posing as children, and ending up in our schools, in foster-care families and in unaccompanied-minor hotels, living cheek by jowl with genuine children', needed to be 'stamped out'. This 'stamping out' was enacted by the Nationality and Borders Act and the Illegal Migration Act which promoted interventionist practices to 'test' the ages of asylum seekers and the reintroduction of children and families with precarious immigration status being placed in detention. The manufactured scandal of child refugees also provided fuel for the Conservative and Reform politicians' push to rescind the Human Rights Act and leave the European Court of Human Rights in 2024. Part of this argument is about making it easier for judges to ignore the right to family life when making decisions about deporting people.

In depicting people on the move as racialized and sexualized threats, this normalizes and makes acceptable state border violence (such as detention, deportations, interventionist age tests, ignoring human rights law) just as family life only becomes a possibility for certain social groups. This again reproduces hierarchies around family and humanity, as I discussed earlier, which were first created under empire and still remain politically useful to differentiate people today. Dispossession and forms of violence are again levied on the bodies of people negatively racialized within colonial schemas of human worth and value. What is significant about thinking about this through the history of family as a normative social formation and ideal is how appeals to family can work to both animate forms of racialization and, at the same time, obscure and naturalize this process. After all, family (and, with this, childhood, gender relations, domesticity) is presented as common sense, de-political, private, and certainly nothing to do with colonialism and violence.

Conclusion

In this chapter I have explored how who gets to be a family, or more precisely, accorded the social and political status that comes from being recognized as a 'real' family in Britain today, is always already shaped by colonial histories and post-colonial structures of race. Colonialism relied on racialized-sexualized projects of control, which were orientated around the promotion and monitoring of intimacies. Models of White bourgeois family and domesticity were used to categorize colonized people as deviant, dangerous, and uncivilized, and this was used to justify forms of violent dispossession, exploitation, and oppression – including the promotion and restriction of international mobility. Imperial projects of border control involved categorizations of who could be a family for the basis of mobility and settlement.

At the same time, fears about inter-racialized sex and intimacies were also used to justify practices of mobility control in the name of protecting a colonial racialized and sexualized order. These practices and ways of thinking about family did not only govern the movement of people across the British Empire but became networked into immigration regimes in Britain throughout the 20th century. Understanding the historical relationship between dominants forms of 'family', mobility control, and colonial violence helps us better understand how restrictive immigration regimes and borders are naturalized and legitimated today. As we have seen, borders can limit who can be intimate with whom and restrict certain people's rights to settlement and mobility, at the same time borders can be legitimated by appeals to protect so-called 'genuine' family life. Thus, we need to consider how dominant formations of family have continued to be involved in the remaking of race and racism. This is one way in which the post-colonial present continues to be structured by colonial legacies.

References

Adu, A. and Syal, R. 2023. 'Suella Braverman Small Boat Arrivals Have Values at Odds with Our Country', *The Guardian*, 26 April. https://www.theguardian.com/uk-news/2023/apr/26/suella-braverman-small-boat-arrivals-have-values-at-odds-with-our-country

BBC. 2018. 'Interview with Nigel Farage', *The Today Programme*, BBC Radio 4, 19 October. www.bbc.co.uk/programmes/b07zx6k7

hooks, b. 1990. *Yearning: Race, Gender and Cultural Politics*. South End Press.

Collins, P.H. 2000. *Black Feminist Thought*. Routledge.

De Noronha, L. 2020. *Deporting Black Britain*. Manchester University Press.

El-Enany, N. 2020. *Bordering Britain*. Manchester University Press.

Ferguson, R. 2003. *Aberrations in Black*. Princeton University Press.

Hansard. 2023. 'Parliamentary Debate on Illegal Migration Bill', House of Commons. Volume 731 Column 152, 26 April.

Hoad, N. 2007. *African Intimacies*. University of Minnesota Press.

Lugones, M. 2007. 'Heterosexualism and the Colonial / Modern Gender System', *Hypatia* 22(1): 186–209.

Mayblin, L. and Turner, J. 2021. *Migration Studies and Colonialism*. Polity Press.

May, R. and Cohen, R. 1974. 'The Interaction Between Race and Colonialism: A Case Study of the Liverpool Race Riots of 1919', *Race* 16(2): 111–126.

Mongia, R. 2018. *Indian Migration and Empire*. Duke University Press.

Reid, S. 2016. 'Just How Old Do You Think These Migrant "Children" Are?' *Daily Mail Online*, 29 January. https://www.dailymail.co.uk/news/article-3422000/Just-old-think-migrant-children-Alarming-pictures-shed-light-growing-scandal-amid-asylum-crisis.html

Sales, D. 2021. 'Convicted Sex Offender from South Africa Wins Appeal against Deportation after Judge Ruled Home Office Did Not Give Him "Fair Opportunity" to Tell Court How HE Felt about His Crimes', *Daily Mail Online*, 6 October. https://www.dailymail.co.uk/news/article-10061141/Sex-offender-wins-appeal-against-deportation-wasnt-asked-felt-crimes.html

Smith, E. and Marmo, M. 2011. 'Uncovering the Virginity Testing Controversy in the National Archives: The Intersectionality of Discrimination in British Immigration History', *Gender and History* 23(1): 147–165.

Spillers, H. 1987. 'Mama's Baby, Papa's Maybe: An American Grammar Book', *Diacritics* 17(2): 64–81.

Turner, J. 2020. *Bordering Intimacy*. Manchester University Press.

Weaver, M. 2016. 'Give Child Refugees Dental Tests to Verify Age, says David Davies', *The Guardian*, 19 October. https://www.theguardian.com/world/2016/oct/19/child-refugees-dental-tests-verify-age-david-davies

Wilson, A. 2007. 'The Forced Marriage Debate and the British State', *Race & Class* 49(1): 25–38.

Video lecture

Turner, J. 2021. *Family, Intimacy, and Migration*, Connected Sociologies Curriculum Project. https://thesociologicalreview.org/projects/connected-sociologies/curriculum/migration-borders-diaspora/family-intimacy-migration/

QUESTIONS

1. What kind of relationships do you imagine when you hear the word 'family'?

2. How have restrictive concepts of family been used to exclude people from the UK?

3. Can you think of other areas of social control where appeals to family are used to justify authoritarian or violent state practices (for example, policing, welfare policy, and so on)?

4. How do we resist these practices? Do we also need to reimagine the connections and intimate relations of family and kinship?

Worksheet 16. Making Love, Making Empire: Family, Colonial Racism, and Border Controls

This worksheet is designed to support AS and A-level teaching on the topics of globalization, families and households, and demographic trends in the UK since 1900. It is suited to students who already have a broader understanding of British colonialism. The session encourages students to broaden their understanding of families and households, including the relationship of the family to social structure and social change, and the diversity of the contemporary family and household structures. Joe Turner's online talk and the worksheet activities encourage students to place these themes within the context of their existing learning around globalization, global culture, and migration.

Time	Activity	Explanation
00.00–00.05	To begin, answer this question: What is a family? Compare what you have written with the person next to you. Do your definitions match up? Are their differences?	This short warm-up exercise encourages students to start thinking about the nuance and diversity within cultural conceptions of family.
00.05–00.10	Recap of understandings of globalization.	It may be useful to remind students of the definition(s) of globalization.
00.10–00.15	Watch the talk from 4:08 to 5:15. What does Turner identify as the key restrictions on the notion of 'family' employed by UK immigration and asylum policy?	Turner explains that definitions of family according to the UK family immigration policy are restricted in the following ways: • Highly heteronormative, focusing on nuclear families and monogamous heterosexual marriages. • Highly classed, because the salary threshold is over the minimum wage. • Patriarchal and racialized because of inequalities within the labour market: women and racialized minorities are much less likely to earn enough to meet the criteria. This activity instructs students to digest the information in this section of the session and summarize Turner's arguments in their own words.
00.15–00.25	At 5:39 Turner explains that the introduction of the family visa in UK immigration policy is rooted in the 'hypervisibility' of Asian and Muslim communities, particularly stereotypical assumptions of the 'supposed hyper-patriarchal character of Muslim gender relations' and concerns surrounding the claimed lack of integration of Pakistani and Bangladeshi women into British society.	The first question pushes students to connect the themes of this session to their wider studies surrounding social inequalities in the UK, and particularly intersecting inequalities related to gender, ethnicity, and religion. The second question encourages students to start thinking about how narratives of British identity are culturally constructed, and how this relates to power and stratification. This activity provides an entry point into the discussions about British colonialism that follow in this worksheet.

Time	Activity	Explanation
	How do these narratives relate to what you already know about social inequalities and power in the UK? What is the significance of the idea of 'integration' in this context?	
00.25–00.35	Watch the talk from 11:10 to 12:35. *What was the relationship between work and British border controls in the late 19th and early 20th centuries?*	Turner explains that dominant concepts of family were central in the indentured labour relations of the British empire during this period. Centralized state border controls, he explains, can be traced back to the coercive movement of labour across the British empire. Controls were also rooted in concerns regarding the proximity of Asian labourers to White women in British settler states. Border controls were also justified as being needed to set boundaries on what social relations counted as a family in order to set rules around who could work and settle in British settler states. This activity enables students to apply their existing understandings of colonialism to ideas of family and migration that have already been covered in this session.
00.35–00.45	Watch the talk from 13:43 to 15:42 *Turner identifies two key ways in which colonial legacies impact immigration and border policies in Britain today. Can you summarize these two ways?*	Turner makes two key arguments for the impact of Britain's colonial history on contemporary border policies: 1. On the one hand 'examples of narrow restrictions of family in immigration policies work to actively control the movement of specific groups. These ideas reproduce colonial logics surrounding 'civilized' and 'uncivilized' family forms.' 2. 'The British state is constantly rationalized as the ultimate militarized patriarchal protector. Its constructed as supposedly protecting genuine families and citizens against various racialized and sexualized threats.' This activity works to draw together students' learning around British colonialism with contemporary ideas of migration and family. It encourages students to summarize the content of the session in their own words and pick out the key points they identify in the arguments.

Time	Activity	Explanation
00.45–00.55	At 15:43, Turner draws connections between the idea of the British state as 'protector' of families, and representations of asylum seekers and refugees as threatening. *Think of a recent example from the news or the media that supports this point. What are the perceived threats to the 'genuine' British family? How does this connect with what you have learned in this session about definitions of family in UK immigration policy?*	This activity encourages students to use their learning from the session to think critically about popular cultural representations of family and migration, developing their critical thinking skills and enabling students to think about the contemporary relevance of themes of colonialism. Relevant examples for this exercise might include posters from pro-Brexit campaigns or political discourse surrounding small boats.
00.55–01.00	Reflecting on what you have learned from this session, and the activities on this worksheet, answer the following question: *How have historical and contemporary patterns of migration in the UK informed dominant ideas of what family is?*	This recap activity rounds out the session by asking students to reflect on, summarize, and articulate what they have learned in their own words, drawing together the themes of family, globalization, and colonialism. The question links back to the first activity in the worksheet.

This worksheet was developed by Isabel Sykes.

17

Populism, Migration, and the Politics of Racism

Karim Murji

Objectives

- This chapter explores the connections between racism, populism, and politics in two periods or eras in Britain – the 1970s and the 2020s.

- It contextualizes the present by looking back to a time when race and racism were critical in the articulation of populist politics, especially because of the way they were connected to a particular crime, mugging.

- It shows that, in the past decade, populism – and authoritarianism – again came to the surface, often mixed with anti-immigrant nationalism.

- Locating this in the Brexit period and linking it to the present, the chapter asks the following key questions. How do we connect the past and present – is there a direct line from one to the other, or are there more changes than continuities? And, if racism is crucial to both periods, what is similar and different about it, then and now?

Introduction

This chapter explores the connections between racism, populism, and politics in two periods or eras in Britain – the 1970s and the 2020s. It contextualizes the present by looking back to a time when race and racism were critical in the articulation of populist politics, especially because of the way they were connected to a particular crime, mugging. This is the core argument of a classic text, *Policing the Crisis*, that linked race and nation to empire, the economy, and the role of the state as key components of the crisis of the 1970s. They gave rise to a form of politics that came to be called authoritarian populism. In the past decade populism – and authoritarianism – again came to surface, often with anti-immigrant nationalism. Locating this in the Brexit period and linking it to the present, the key questions in this chapter are: How do we connect the past and present – is there a direct line from one to the other, or are there more changes than continuities? And, if racism is crucial to both periods what is similar and different about it, then and now?

In December 2024, the historian and journalist Taj Ali drew a connection between past and present by asking what the 1964 election tells us about politics in 2024. Ali (2024) is not alone in calling the election in Smethwick, West Midlands, the most racist election in British political history, as the same comment was also made on its 50th anniversary (Jeffries 2014). The explicit racism used by the Conservative political candidate in that campaign makes it one of the most notorious moments in British politics. Ali's argument is that hostility against Black and Asian immigrants at that time is parallelled by the aggression to migrants in recent years, whether as in former Prime Minister Rishi Sunak's 'stop the boats' slogan, or the current Labour government's recourse to another three-word refrain – 'smash the gangs'. Whether from right or left, politicians across the divide like to rely on 'tough' language and measures to show how determined they are to stop or limit irregular migration and control the border. Thus, Ali (2024) as well as Younge (2024) see a clear thread linking past and present: the use of racism to make migrants into scapegoats, and irrespective of which party is in government, little has changed over time, whether it is 50 or 60 years.

I am also interested in how we connect past and present, but I want to explore whether drawing a flat or direct line across time is a useful way of understanding racism in politics. A sense that nothing changes is commonplace. While there clearly are continuities across decades there may also be changes and differences that require a closer look, rather than a flattening analysis. It is my view that race, or rather racism, underscores the political era we are living in but this amounts to more than just saying that race is important. Rather, what matters more is to understand how race *articulates* key elements and periods of British politics. To develop this perspective, I will focus on two periods in Britain, the 1970s and the past ten years. What did it mean to see the politics of race and racism as crucial then, and what does it mean to do so now? In what ways is it useful to connect these eras, and what is distinct about now?

Race, politics, and the state in the 1970s

The term 'crisis' can be overused in sociology, making it difficult to assess when (or if) one crisis ended and another begins. Britain in the 1970s is often regarded as a decade of crisis due to major events such as a prolonged strike by coal miners and many other industrial disputes, a three-day working week (where commercial consumption of electricity was limited to three consecutive days each week to save energy), various shocks to the economy, all topped by an infamous 'winter of discontent' in 1978. It was a period 'characterized by a melancholic apprehension of national decline and frozen inertia, and then a panicked disorder [as] inflation spiralled' (Seaton 2015: 2). All this foreshadowed the election of Margaret Thatcher as prime minister in 1979 and the onset of monetarism and neoliberalism, commonly known as Thatcherism.

This is the political and economic context in which the book, *Policing the Crisis* (Hall et al 1978), located 'the moment of mugging'. How did this crime – combining the separate legal offences of robbery and theft – become one of the defining words of the 1970s? Starting with media (newspaper) reports, Hall et al argue that mugging was treated in sensationalist ways in the media, often framing it as a new or unprecedented type of crime – a form of violent street criminality committed mainly by young Black men, on elderly (White) victims. The extent and misleading nature of the media coverage led Hall et al to call mugging a moral panic. This term, derived from a classic work, *Folk Devils and Moral Panics* (Cohen 1973), centres society's response to young people as an indicator of anxiety about social change. In the 1960s and 1970s, this meant changing moral standards around marriage, relationships, sex, and sexuality, with a revolution in gender roles and family life that came to be known as 'the permissive society', marking a major shift from the imagined moral standards of previous decades.

What then was the apprehension that the response to mugging expressed? Adopting a critical and Marxist framework, *Policing the Crisis* shared the view that a moral panic reflects or conveys society's deep worries about the nature and pace of social change. By calling this a crisis and centring the role of the state they saw the response to mugging as founded in three interrelated domains of change in Britain:

- The sense of British imperial decline, following the independence of former colonial nations in South Asia and Africa.
- The stagnation of the British economy through the 1970s, which right-wingers saw as due to powerful trade unions, taking strike action, while left-wingers attributed it to chronic underinvestment in skills and productivity.
- Immigration, especially from the colonial countries that had close ties to Britain, mainly people of African-Caribbean and South Asian descent.

So, the analysis of *Policing the Crisis* connects a type of crime to history, economics, and migration. Yet, critically, race is the key to each of these three domains. It provides the articulating 'hinge' between them. Post-war immigration was encouraged in Britain from the 1950s onwards. Around 300,000 people came from the West Indies, most famously from the 1948 Windrush moment onwards, while around 300,000 people came from the South Asian subcontinent. As citizens and subjects of British colonies the UK was the 'mother country' (see Hampshire, Chapter 13, and Benson, Chapter 18, this volume). Many of these people were recruited for and employed in public service jobs, or in low-skilled manufacturing work. Over time, there emerged a sense of competition between the migrants and White workers who saw their jobs under threat, particularly as the British economy hit harder times in the late 1960s (see Anitha, Chapter 8, this volume). The stagnation of the economy, combined with rising inflation – so-called 'stagflation' – set the scene for the economic crisis of the 1970s. Meanwhile, the era of independence of colonial countries becoming independent from the 1950s onwards conveyed the diminished status of Britain as no longer an empire nation.

The response to mugging condensed or symbolized the crisis of Britain and the British state. It was a symptom or a surface manifestation of deeper structural issues – historical, economic, and political. Depicted as a crime of Black on White, it articulated – it joined together – social anxieties about race and migration, combined with British economic and imperial decline. Starting from a series of local, and sometimes minor, criminal acts, *Policing the Crisis* put race and nation at the core of the analysis, intersecting it with class and colonialism, to produce an argument about how crime, or mugging especially, was treated as an alien and foreign occurrence in Britain, due to the supposedly different culture and standards of migrants. Black and Asian people were depicted as an 'alien wedge' who had changed the character of Britain, making areas unrecognizable.

The key expression of this was by the Conservative politician Enoch Powell, and his infamous 'Rivers of Blood' speech in which he predicted race wars. A less direct version conveying that ordinary British people (meaning White) were living in fear of Black and Asian people in their neighbourhoods was expressed by Mrs Thatcher, when she said in a 1978 TV interview that:

> [P]eople are really rather afraid that this country might be rather swamped by people with a different culture and, you know, the British character has done so much for democracy, for law and done so much throughout the world that if there is any fear that it might be swamped people are going to react and be rather hostile to those coming in. (cited in Smith 2022)

While there have been frequent denials that the mention of 'different cultures' was a coded form of racism, this 'swamping' statement is infamous as a moment in British politics. Its electoral payoff is evidenced by the sweeping Conservative victory, due partly to the switch of voters from the far-right National Front who felt that Mrs Thatcher was speaking for them.

This is a form of populism, where a politician appears to express the will of 'the people', often through resorting to a form of regressive nationalism with the use of symbols such as the flag, as well as claims about 'British character', insinuating that migrants from the former colonies somehow do not share those attributes. Combined with simplistic tropes of the national economy as akin to household budgeting, these were powerful popular and cultural elements of Thatcherism. As much as anything else, Hall et al were drawing attention to a momentous change in the culture of politics that the idea of authoritarian populism sought to capture, though populism is never defined in *Policing the Crisis*. The resources of the state, particularly in the form of harsh policing and law and order, were mobilized against 'the enemy within' – whether that was seen as Black people, street criminals, immigrants, or striking trade unionists – as expressions of the popular will, or national sentiment. For Hall (1988), this is the key to Thatcherism: it had a 'rigorously populist character' founded on an ideological project built on 'representations of "the people", of "the nation", of "our culture and way of life", of the "instincts of the ordinary British people", etc … [that it] can claim … simply to have "rediscovered", awakened from their deep national slumber'. Crucially, one of the main achievements of populism is to deny or suppress the ideological character of a particular sense of the people and the nation that it constructs by making it seem like 'just plain common sense' (Lawrence 1982).

Politics and populism now

The sketch of the 1970s/1980s centres race in British politics. To examine whether, or in what ways, the past is connected to the present, the immediate links are opposition to migration and populist politics. Understood as a style of and in politics, more than as a set of policies, the idea of populism has been around for well over a century, but it has become prominent again recently. For the Cambridge Dictionary, it was the word of the year in 2017, as their website notes: 'What sets populism apart… is that it represents a phenomenon that's both truly local and truly global, as populations and their leaders across the world wrestle with issues of immigration and trade, resurgent nationalism, and economic discontent.'[1] Populism has, arguably, become the dominant form and force in contemporary politics. But what does it actually mean? Bartle et al (2020: 67) say that:

> 'Populism' is often used imprecisely to describe anti-establishment political movements which propose simple solutions to complicated problems and which advocate popular policies that liberals find uncomfortable … we characterize [it as a] … sentiment among European mass publics as a mindset that combines a preference for strong national foreign policies with opposition to immigration, anti-Europeanism, an antipathy to the liberal human rights agenda and a right-wing political orientation.

Immigration and nationalism stand out here as clear echoes of the 1970s but the mention of human rights is a first sign that now is not the same as then.

The 2017 date for the word of the year is not unrelated to Donald Trump's first term as president of the United States. The wider local and global manifestations of populism are noticeable across the globe, for example, in India, the Philippines, Argentina, Hungary, Poland, Italy, France, Greece, Austria, and, as we will see, Britain. In many of these countries, elected politicians frequently appear as autocratic, even anti-democratic demagogues, creating fears of a new age of fascism (DiMaggio 2021). Across the board populist leaders claim to speak for 'the people', and against elites, while often calling for severe anti-migration and law and order policies. When this is called populist authoritarianism, it provides another link to the 1970s (Inglehart and Norris 2017).

What, though, of the place of race and racism in this? In Britain, Brexit was the main expression of a populist surge when the referendum took place in 2016. Anti-Europeanism and anti-immigration rhetoric drove the Vote Leave campaign. As Hall (1988) indicated, the skill of politics is to make it seem like they are merely expressions of popular opinion, rather than ideology. Consequently, politicians are not 'just' giving voice to the resentments that people have – they actively mobilize, or even create, the very antipathies they claim to be speaking for. Populists identify, name, and thrive on stigmatizing some groups as enemies, often this is the powerless (such as migrants), but sometimes it can include elites, like judges. The political nadir of this was a notorious 'Breaking point' poster used by United Kingdom Independence Party (UKIP) in the referendum campaign, showing a long line of Syrian refugees seeking to enter Britain

(Bradshaw and Haynes 2023). Not far behind was the claim that 70 million Turkish people could enter Britain if it remained in the European Union (EU).

The case for Brexit was often given in terms of the economic benefits to Britain from not being part of the EU, as it could then freely do business with the rest of the world. However, there is good evidence that what drove support for Brexit was not economic but the appeal of a sovereignty that the nation would reclaim when separated from the EU (Gordon 2016). This is the fantasy of 'Little England' and the 'island nation' that is underpinned by a wistfulness for empire (Bhambra 2017). Brexit, for Valluvan and Kalra (2019), is a symptom of 'postcolonial melancholia', an expression of a narrow nationalism founded in the politics of Thatcherism in the 1980s. The backwards-looking nature of nationalism is commonly noted; it is what Bauman (2018) called 'retrotopia', a search for a utopia to be found in the past. While the sense of being rooted in nostalgia sounds familiar, it is noteworthy that Melhuish (2024) found that support for Brexit contained both backward- and forward-looking points of view, so this is not the same as the 1970s.

Brexit and Britain do not exist in a self-contained bubble. An explicit hostility to migrants can be found across many countries. This has informed a reactionary populist politics of nationalism, securitization, and Islamophobia, founded on dehumanization and extreme cruelty. Multiple deaths – such as those of migrants in small boats in the English Channel – are causally discounted, for example. This is the authoritarianism that devalues human lives and in the case of the Trumpian border policies in the United States, even glories in how brutal it is towards migrants. De Genova (2018) argues that the migrant crisis is constitutive of the crisis of European borders and is rooted in an unresolved racial crisis founded in the post-colonial condition of Europe. Within the UK, Redclift and Rajina (2021) connect Brexit and the hostile environment (see Renwick, Chapter 9, this volume) to anti-migrant racism and Islamophobia.

One expression of this hostile climate was the riots that occurred across mainly English towns and cities in August 2024. They were a form of populist uprising, driven by a sense that politicians are out of touch and fail to represent common sentiment. The rioters were overwhelmingly White men, and the ostensible cause was that the killer of three young girls in Southport, Lancashire was a migrant or a refugee, which turned out to be a false rumour on social media. The rioters targeted hotels where people seeking asylum were temporarily housed, as well as Muslim places of worship. Some of them sang 'Rule Britannia', or chanted 'we want our country back', and, when interviewed, they said they wanted to 'stop the boats'. These vocabularies are not accidental or incidental. They echo the political rhetoric of the UK Conservative government (that was deposed in the election of July 2024). So, it is possible to see why Ali (2024) and Younge (2024) maintain that migrants are being made scapegoats for social problems. For both, this hostility displays clear connections to the past, where sentiments about empire and the nation resonate in recent street and official politics. This is the viewpoint that we need 'only connect' to see the thread linking past and present.

However, if we look more carefully there are differences between then and now. One is that while the anti-migration sentiment of Brexit was diffuse, there was a strong element of opposition to free movement, one of the central pillars of the EU.

Much of this was directed against 'Eastern European' (Poles and Romanians, mainly) migrants who had the freedom to settle in the UK. These predominantly 'White' migrants do experience hostility and this maybe even something akin to racism, but it is not the same migrant population from former British colonies who were subjected to violent racism when they arrived. In addition, not all White migrants are the same. While people of Indian, Nigerian, and Polish descent are among the most numerous migrants in London, also in the top ten are people from Ireland, France, the United States, and Germany.[2] Yet people from these latter communities are rarely spoken of as immigrants, thus sweeping statements about hostility to migrants, or even White migrants, lack nuance.

Whiteness matters in other ways too. In the 2010s, a specific racialized form – the 'White working class' – has become commonplace. Along with the idea of the 'left behind' people of 'red wall', usually Labour, constituencies in northern England, these terms are a form of 'racial grammar' (Pitcher 2019) in Britain. The political expression of this was the record Conservative victory in the 2019 UK general election, on the promise to 'get Brexit done', as well as to 'level up' the northern regions of England. This grammar conveys the idea that while White working-class people may display base ethno-nationalism, their concerns are nonetheless well-founded and need to be addressed. As is often the case in Britain, this focus on the lowest ranks of society commonly overlooks elite and state racisms. Giving voice to this sense of White grievance and disadvantage are politicians, usually from the right, but also some from the left, who speak about the limits of tolerance of the British people (Paterson and Karyotis 2022). In plainer terms, this is expressed as 'no one asked' the British people if they wanted to be a country of mass immigration – a claim that simply overlooks the long period of the British Empire, as well as the fact that only one in six people in the UK are classed as 'foreign born'.[3]

White resentment was evident in the 1970s, mainly taking the form of marches by the far-right National Front. Sociologists employ the idea of racial disavowal to capture the underlying opinions of people who express racist views with the qualifier 'I'm not racist but ...'. In the past decade, even this disclaimer is being missed out as crude racism is widespread on social media, as well as in the riots of 2024. Social media amplifies these voices, but they do not come from nowhere. Part of racism then and now is the way it is made semi-respectable or 'mainstreamed' (Mondon and Winter 2020); for instance in the form of the 'swamping' remarks, or through the common backlash against 'woke-ism' and culture wars in recent years. Through language and images, White resentment has been weaponized, as crude populism from the right or for 'muscular liberalism' (Jose 2015) against backward cultural practices.

Popular resentment about immigration is the singular issue most consistently disrupting electoral politics, Crewe (2020) argues. He believes that this resentment could be eroded or even vanish if only governments would deal with immigration properly. From this perspective, the problem is that irresponsible leaders 'exploit' the legitimate grievances of ordinary people. However, this underestimates the role of ideology and language – such as calling all people on boats 'illegal immigrants' – in creating the migration crisis. It is not a surprise that immigration is a key political concern, as polls showed that it was in the top four most important issues to voters in the 2024 UK general election. Once again, not all 'immigrants' are equal; the most hostile views are to immigrant groups perceived as culturally distant, usually due to following religions such as Islam. In other words, (perceived) cultural and race difference rather than mobility per se is what matters. Hence, another significant difference is that the role of religion is more central than it was five decades ago as race and religion are linked through Islamophobia (see Holmwood, Chapter 22, and Fernandez, Chapter 23, this volume). And again, this is not just about rioters in the street but comes from elites, such as when think tanks and politicians are part of events titled 'Is rising ethnic diversity a threat to the west?', in which 'ethnic diversity' is an unsubtle code for race, or Muslims.

Finally, populism now and then is not the same. While commonly seen as a form of politics that claims to speak for 'the people', and against elites, even this simple definition does not stand up to scrutiny. Populists of the Brexit era, notably former UK Prime Minister Boris Johnson, spent a lot of time attacking elites, such as UK supreme court judges, when they delayed the passage of Brexit legislation. This was populist because judges were cast as subverting the express wishes of the populace in the referendum. Yet, in this moment, figures such as Johnson, but also Nigel Farage, from clearly elitist backgrounds (private schools, Oxbridge), claimed to stand for the people against the elite. In the 1970s, Mrs Thatcher also claimed to speak for 'ordinary people'. While she was not herself from an elite background, most of her attacks were on people from or in the lowest social strata – immigrants, trade unionists, people on welfare. Unlike Johnson's attack on judges, this is 'punching down', while protecting the traditional elites (Knott 2020). This makes populism a paradoxical force – clearly it is effective, but it is also malleable and utilized in quite different forms (Clarke and Newman 2017).

Conclusion

Tracing the connections between politics, populism, and racism then (the 1970s/1980s) and now (2010s/2020s) reveals that there are continuities around nationalism, hostility to migrants, and anti-immigration populism. However, drawing a direct line across time is only partially useful as doing so flattens out substantial changes and differences. Racism in Britain is not quite the same, with a degree of shift from post-colonial subjects of the British Empire to migrants from diverse countries. Islamophobia is now much more significant. Likewise, populism is evident across the decades, always claiming to speak for 'the people' but the forms it takes are not identical. The internal enemies of the 1970s are not the same as the mixture of external and internal threats to the nation, as they are depicted now. Populism draws on race, but it does so selectively, and the links are not always the same. Nor are the key players, as 'liberal racism' has become mainstream rather than a fringe concern. Crucially, this means that racism is now more than the far right and it is being ideologically bolstered by think tanks and people declaring an intellectual rationale for it. Authoritarianism, arguably seen as exceptional in the 1970s, is in many ways the normalized response mode to crises in the 2020s. Both continuities and changes across time matter in analysing the present.

Notes

1. See: https://www.cam.ac.uk/news/populism-revealed-as-2017-word-of-the-year-by-cambridge-university-press
2. This is based on data from https://trustforlondon.org.uk/data/demographics/migrants/
3. This data is from https://migrationobservatory.ox.ac.uk/resources/briefings/migrants-in-the-uk-an-overview/

References

Ali, T. 2024. 'Labour or Tory, Both the Same. Both Play the Migrant Bashing Game', *The New Arab*, 18 December. https://www.newarab.com/opinion/labour-or-tory-both-same-both-play-anti-migrant-game

Bartle, J., Sanders, D., and Twyman, J. 2020. 'Authoritarian Populist Opinion in Europe', in I. Crewe and D. Sanders (eds), *Authoritarian Populism and Liberal Democracy*. Palgrave Macmillan, pp 49–71.

Bauman, Z. 2018. 'Retrotopia', *Revista Española de Investigaciones Sociológicas (REIS)* 163: 155–158.

Bhambra, G.K. 2017. 'Brexit, Trump, and "Methodological Whiteness": On the Misrecognition of Race and Class', *British Journal of Sociology* 68: S214–S232.

Bradshaw, A. and Haynes, P. 2023. 'The Assemblage of British Politics' Breaking Point', *Journal of Consumer Culture* 23(4): 971–989.

Clarke, J. and Newman, J. 2017. '"People in this Country Have Had Enough of Experts": Brexit and the Paradoxes of Populism', *Critical Policy Studies* 11(1): 101–116.

Cohen, S. 1973. *Folk Devils and Moral Panics*. Paladin.

Crewe, I. 2020. 'Authoritarian Populism and Brexit in the UK in Historical Perspective', in Crewe, I. and Sanders, D. (eds), *Authoritarian Populism and Liberal Democracy*. Palgrave Macmillan.

De Genova, N. 2018. 'The "Migrant Crisis" as Racial Crisis: Do Black Lives Matter in Europe?', *Ethnic & Racial Studies* 41(10): 1765–1782.

DiMaggio, A. 2021. *Rising Fascism in America: It Can Happen Here*. Routledge.

Gordon, M. 2016. 'The UK's Sovereignty Situation: Brexit, Bewilderment and Beyond …', *King's Law Journal* 27(3): 333–343.

Hall, S. 1988. *The Hard Road to Renewal: Thatcherism and the Crisis of the Left*. Verso.

Hall, S., Critcher, C., Jefferson, T., Clarke, J., and Roberts, B. 1978. *Policing the Crisis: Mugging, the State and Law and Order*. Macmillan (revised edition 2013).

Inglehart, R. and Norris, P. 2017. 'Trump and the Populist Authoritarian Parties: The Silent Revolution in Reverse', *Perspectives on Politics* 15(2): 443–454.

Jeffries, S. 2014. 'Britain's Most Racist Election: The Story of Smethwick, 50 Years On', *The Guardian*, 15 October. https://www.theguardian.com/world/2014/oct/15/britains-most-racist-election-smethwick-50-years-on

Jose, J. 2015. 'A Liberalism Gone Wrong? Muscular Liberalism and the Quest for Monocultural Difference', *Social Identities* 21(5): 444–458.

Knott, A. 2020. 'The New Moving Right Show', *Soundings* 75(75): 111–123.

Lawrence, E. 1982. 'Just Plain Common Sense: The "Roots" of Racism', in Centre for Contemporary Cultural Studies (ed), *The Empire Strikes Back*. Routledge, pp 45–92.

Melhuish, F. 2024. 'Powellite Nostalgia and Racialized Nationalist Narratives: Connecting Global Britain and Little England', *The British Journal of Politics and International Relations* 26(2): 466–486.

Mondon, A. and Winter, A. 2020. *Reactionary Democracy: How Racism and the Populist Far Right became Mainstream*. Verso.

Paterson, I. and Karyotis, G. 2022. '"We Are, by Nature, a Tolerant People": Securitization and Counter-securitization in UK Migration Politics', *International Relations* 36(1): 104–126.

Pitcher, B. 2019. 'Racism and Brexit: Notes towards an Antiracist Populism', *Ethnic & Racial Studies* 42(14): 2490–2509.

Redclift, V.M. and Rajina, F.B. 2021. 'The Hostile Environment, Brexit, and "reactive-" or "protective transnationalism"', *Global Networks* 21(1): 196–214.

Seaton, J. 2015. *Pinkoes and Traitors: The BBC and the Nation, 1974–1987*. Profile Books.

Smith, E. 2022. 'Rather Swamped: Thatcher, Moral Panics and Racist Rhetoric'. https://hatfulofhistory.wordpress.com/2022/11/01/rather-swamped-thatcher-moral-panics-and-racist-rhetoric/

Valluvan, S. and Kalra, V.S. 2019. 'Racial Nationalisms: Brexit, Borders and Little Englander Contradictions', *Ethnic and Racial Studies* 42(14): 2393–2412.

Younge, G. 2024. 'Scapegoating the Immigrant', *New York Review of Books*, 17 October.

Video lecture

Elliot-Cooper, A. 2021. *Colonial Policing Comes Home*, Connected Sociologies Curriculum Project. https://thesociologicalreview.org/projects/connected-sociologies/curriculum/policing/colonial-policing-comes-home/

QUESTIONS

1. Does evidence support or not the argument that the vote for Brexit was more about sovereignty and opposition to immigration than economics?

2. Were the 2024 riots in England race riots?

3. Is Islamophobia a form of racism?

4. To what extent is nostalgia for empire and the past generational, or do younger people also have this view?

Worksheet 17. Populism, Migration, and the Politics of Racism

The talk associated with Chapter 17 of the book is provided by Adam Elliott-Cooper. Crime and deviance is a core topic at AS and A-level. The worksheet supplements existing teaching on the topic of crime and deviance, and is designed to help stretch students' understanding of crime, policing, racism, and the role of the media. This talk and worksheet are aimed at students who have been introduced to some of the sociological perspectives on crime and deviance, as well as relevant concepts/definitions (ethnicity and social class in particular). It is useful if students have been introduced to ways of measuring crime (official statistics, self-report studies, victim studies, and so on) and understand something about the reliability and validity of these sources. Students need to have been introduced to the history of the Windrush generation, and migration of the 1940–1960s (if not, watch the brief summary in the video 2:30–4:07). The talk will complicate some of the explanations for the social distribution of crime in society, based around concepts of age, ethnicity, and class. It also gives the teacher the opportunity to introduce Hallsian sociology, and the concept of moral panics, thus stretching the students beyond traditional sociological perspectives on crime.

Time	Activity	Explanation
00.00–00.05	Before we start, answer these questions: What is crime? What is policing and how does it work?	This is a short warm-up exercise, for students to try and remember any content previously covered on the topic, and apply some of their own critical thinking skills.
00.05–00.10	Recap of understandings linked to crime: opportunities (for crime), socialization (primary, secondary), social control.	The teacher may choose to reuse previous class material, or use a summary.
00.10–00.15	Watch from 0:00 to 2:15 for a summary of the first part of Elliott-Cooper's talk on colonial policing. What tactics were employed in colonial policing? Which of these tactics appear to be similar to policing today?	The teacher may also encourage students to watch the talk in their own time.
00.15–00.25	At 5:22 Elliott-Cooper explains that 'What arose in the 1970s was the idea that there was an epidemic of mugging, a massive increase and a massive problem of mugging. And according to the British police, and the British government as well as the British media, this problem of mugging arose through Black people.'	This is partly a methodological question about the definition, labelling, and measuring of crime in itself, which then impacts the policing of crime. Mugging is a category of crime – so it encompasses a range of different crimes (for example, theft, robbery, assault). This creates the impression that there is a new/different problem. If there is a new problem, it can be attributed or blamed on new/different people. And the 'new' people which were blamed were young Black people in the inner cities. This then is said to require a different kind of policing.

Time	Activity	Explanation
	Watch 5:22–9:52. *If mugging has existed in Britain for hundreds of years, how did the press, the politicians, and the police create the impression that this was a new problem? And why?*	
00.25–00.30	What was the impact of the perceived 'mugging epidemic'?	Creation of suspect populations. Surveillance (for example, through suspicion 'sus' laws). Raids on Black businesses and Black homes.
00.30–00.40	How does this challenge or add a different perspective to the sociological perspectives on crime and deviance you are familiar with (for example, social control, right/left realism, feminist, Marxist)?	Instead of looking at the causes of crime, the case study of mugging shows that crime as a category can be flexible, and encourages us to think about the making of crime categories and criminalization as a process. If the students haven't been introduced to the concept of moral panics, they can refer to the chapter on the Trojan Horse Affair (Chapter 22). It is also an opportunity to explore Stuart Hall's theories on crime and deviance.
00.40–00.50	Watch video from 16:30–20:44 *Who else aside from Black communities is affected by 'colonial policing coming home'?*	Because Black people live alongside other working-class communities, working-class people of all ethnicities are affected by the techniques of racist/colonial policing (including increased militarization of the police, surveillance, use of tear gas, and so on) This question pushes the students to use their critical thinking skills and articulate their own view on the topic.
00.50–01.00	Watch video from 26:55 until 31:20 *Why do you think Elliott-Cooper makes a connection between colonial policing and policing in Britain? Go back to the question answered previously – 'What is crime?' and 'What is policing and how does it work?' Is there anything you want to add to your answers?*	These final questions prompt the students to make connections between this lesson and the AS/A-level curriculum on crime, as well as stretch their understanding of crime and policing through (1) using their critical thinking skills and (2) making broader historical connections.

This worksheet was developed by Isabel Sykes.

18

The British Migration–Citizenship Regime: From Decolonization to Brexit

Michaela Benson

> **Objectives**
>
> - This chapter asks how recognizing connected sociologies and histories transforms how we understand who can move, where, and on what terms.
> - It sets out the connections between the formation of national citizenships and the colonial governance of populations, including their access to mobility.
> - It examines the shifting status of the people of Hong Kong to demonstrate the significance of the coloniality of British citizenship for the post-Brexit migration regime.
> - It reveals that the provisionality and contingency of legal statuses are integral mechanisms of migration governance.

Introduction

Citizenship today denotes membership of a national community. Our passports and national identity cards attest to this status. Such documents may be used to demonstrate eligibility for the rights and social entitlements granted to members of a particular national community, but they also signal the terms on which their holders are able to cross international borders: how where you are from denotes which international borders you can cross, where you can move to and settle, and on what terms.

What emerges from this is a picture of a global migration regime characterized by vast inequalities, that map onto how different countries – whether those from which people originate, or are seeking to move to – are positioned in relation to one another within a global hierarchy. Such inequalities between different nations have their roots in colonialism. As such, inequalities in who can move where and on what terms are similarly shaped by colonial histories.

In the mid-20th century, as the world order shifted from one organized around empires, to one where the nation state was the predominant political unit, citizenship developed in ways that signalled membership of a particular national community. It identified who could enter (or leave) a particular country, making clear the sovereign power of states to control mobility across their borders. As such, where people are born (or where they have rights to nationality), and in consequence, which national citizenship(s) they are eligible for, has implications for their access to immigration and settlement in other countries around the world, as states pick and choose who they will allow across their borders and on what terms.

Recognizing the connections between citizenship and migration allows us to see not only the inclusive dimensions of citizenship but also how the process of making citizens that accompanied the shift towards an international world order was exclusionary. It led to the development of a hierarchy that is reproduced through the global migration regime today. As I discuss in this chapter, scholarship is increasingly recognizing the colonial origins of current governance practices that distinguish between nationals, migrants, and refugees (see Hampshire, Chapter 13, and Mayblin, Chapter 14, this volume).

This chapter examines how recognizing colonial histories of governing mobility changes understandings of development of the British migration–citizenship regime in the period from decolonization in the mid-20th century to Brexit in the early 21st century. In particular, it makes the case for recognizing the coloniality of British citizenship, a concept that communicates the enduring colonial legacies within the UK's migration and citizenship regime, past and present. It considers how understanding migration this way reframes understandings of the contemporary immigration provisions for the UK's former colonial citizens. It documents this through the consideration of Britain's treatment of the people of Hong Kong – a British crown colony until 1997, when its sovereignty was transferred to the People's Republic of China (PRC). Previous scholarship has traced the co-constitution of British immigration and nationality legislation, demonstrating how immigration legislation was used to deny Britain's Black and Brown citizens from the Commonwealth the rights of citizenship. Yet, the Hong Kongers – arguably Britain's last colonials – are notably absent from such accounts. Turning attention to the Hong Kongers, a group who have been repeatedly positioned within a grey zone between migrants and citizens, the chapter reveals the coloniality of the current migration regime.

The coloniality of migration and citizenship

While making citizens and their 'others' is a relatively new phenomenon tied to the making of the modern nation state, such practices sit within longer histories of controlling movement. In what follows, I draw on scholarship that puts to work decolonial theorist Anibal Quijano's (2000) 'coloniality of power' in making sense of the global migration regime. This is a concept that recognizes the enduring legacies of colonialism in the contemporary world order. Identifying the origins of migration governance in colonial practices, those working in this tradition signal their understanding of colonialism as deeply implicated in capitalism as a global economic structure (see Gilbert, Chapter 2, this volume). They might refer to this as colonial capitalism or racial capitalism, signalling the reach of colonialism around the world and its continuing significance in the inequalities evident in the global migration regime. For scholarship on migration and citizenship, this means recognizing the colonial origins of migration and citizenship regimes today, and how migration governance reproduces global social inequalities.

Such scholarship documents how inequalities wrought through colonialism are baked into the global migration regime. They are sustained through the governance practices by which states seek to control the movement of people across international borders, sorting and classifying people with consequences for their rights to move to a particular nation state, and with what rights and entitlements upon arrival (Mayblin and Turner 2021). Field-leading work in this area considers the coloniality of the global refugee and asylum regime (Gutiérrez Rodríguez 2018) and the coloniality of citizenship (Boatcă and Roth 2016).

Importantly, while immigration controls and national citizenship are relatively recent inventions, decolonial approaches encourage us to recognize the connections to longer histories of controlling mobility and sorting populations. In particular, they draw attention to hierarchies of labour that classified people in a range of positions from free to enslaved (and unfree) in the colonial world, and the significance of these for who could move on their own terms, whose movements were more closely controlled, or indeed, out of their own hands, as in the case of those enslaved (see Kaladeen, Chapter 4, this volume).

Around the world today, governments control movement through their border regimes; determining who can enter, on what terms, and the consequent stratification of rights and entitlements. At one end of the spectrum are those deemed eligible for free movement or other forms of enhanced rights to entry and settlement. While at the other, are those denied entry, who find themselves forced to seek alternative routes that leave them undocumented.

The coloniality of migration and citizenship signal how the global spread of capitalism through colonialism, the controls over the movement of people, and the racial hierarchies that were integral to the production of a colonial-capitalist world order, are important for understanding how nation states today police their borders, and the resultant inequalities. A central mechanism in institutionalizing colonial legacies within the global migration and citizenship regime was the formation of national citizenships. While the predominant approaches to understanding citizenship have focused on its inclusionary potential, these were also processes that entailed the exclusion and dispossession of colonial subjects (Bhambra 2015; Boatcă 2020). As Gurminder K. Bhambra (2015) argues, recognizing that these exclusions are integral to current nationality legislation calls for us to centre connected sociologies and histories in the pursuit of alternative conceptual understandings that situate the claims to equality upon which understandings of citizenship most often rest.

Governing migration and citizenship in 20th-century Britain

Colonial histories of controlling movement offer vital insights that can help us to understand migration governance practices around the world, and the inequalities reproduced through these. While research has considered what this means at a global or international scale, we can also see it at play in the formation and development of British citizenship. From the outset, its development was thoroughly intertwined with immigration controls. First introduced via the British Nationality Act 1948 (BNA 1948), citizenship was initially a status conferred on all those from the UK and its colonies which allowed free movement around the empire, replacing their common status as British subjects. Following the introduction of BNA 1948, those from the Caribbean colonies started to take up their rights to free movement, seeking passage to the UK for the purposes of finding work. The most well-known example of this is HMT *Empire Windrush*, which docked in London in 1948.

Yet, the historical record shows how the government of the time repeatedly sought ways to prevent the arrival of these colonial citizens from the Caribbean. Their efforts included attempts at re-routing boats to other British colonies. In the context of post-war reconstruction and significant labour shortages, when the UK was actively recruiting labour from Europe's refugee camps via the European voluntary workers scheme, seeking to turn away these citizens offers evidence of a racialized logic driving decisions about who could enter the UK. In time, the government would introduce legislation and policy designed to limit further migration from the colonies, starting with the introduction of the Commonwealth Immigration Act (CIA), 1962.

The 1960s was a period when many of Britain's colonies were completing the process of self-determination, gaining their independence, and establishing themselves as nation states. This was accompanied by the development of nationality legislation and defining who would be considered as a citizen. The working assumption of the British government was that these processes of independence would lead to a situation where citizenship in British legislation would only apply to those from the UK, as the nationality status of those from its colonies would align instead with that of the states within which they lived.

Ultimately, citizens from the colonies with no other link to the UK found themselves categorized as citizens while overseas, but migrants when seeking entry to the UK. It seems an oxymoron that it is possible to be named as a citizen of a particular country, while also being considered as a migrant at its borders. However, as I go on to discuss, this ambiguous positioning is not a thing of the past, nor is it accidental.

The British Nationality Act (BNA) 1981 brought about further changes to nationality legislation that reflected the restrictions previously introduced through immigration reform, enforcing these for the citizens of the small number of its remaining colonial territories. It limited the status of British citizenship to those born in or with a close connection to the UK. New nationality statuses were introduced that made clear that the people of these territories did not have the right to live in the UK. Their new status entitled them to passports that attested to their nationality status, but little more. This briefly stated history indicates the colonial entanglements in the development of British citizenship. Who was made a migrant and who became a citizen in the second half of the 20th century, and its consequences for the current migration and citizenship regime, reveal the enduring colonial entanglements that scaffold how Britain relates to its former colonial subjects (Prabhat 2020).

Whether people had moved or not was not the basis for these determinations. They were informed instead by racial logics, long at play in Britain's colonial forms of governance and, in particular, control over the movement of labour. Understanding that these processes of making migrants and citizens (and their others) were co-constitutive and significant to nation-building projects, calls into question any account that naturalizes these categories. Yet, these became institutionalized into British immigration and nationality legislation and related governance practices. Historian Kathleen Paul (1997) aptly identifies the process of making the British nation state one through which the imagined community was 'white-washed', with White Britons retaining the greatest rights and freedom from state controls over their movement.

Britain's last colonials

Up until now, my discussion has traced familiar territory for scholars working on the history of the British migration and citizenship regime. It has shown how immigration legislation was used to exclude Black and Brown citizens from the Commonwealth from the rights of citizenship in the UK. In this way, the British state exercised control over their mobility. In the remainder of the chapter, I turn to a population largely absent from these accounts: the people of Hong Kong. This absence is unsurprising in a context where Hong Kong is also absent from research on British imperialism. It is almost as though scholars simply did know what to make of Hong Kong, which seemed to contradict prevailing analyses of the British Empire.

Hong Kong remained a British colony until 1997, long after most Britain's former colonies had become independent. Indeed, unlike most of Britain's colonies, the distinctive circumstances of the British colonization of Hong Kong meant that it would not become a nation in its own right. In other words, the self-determination and independence that led to decolonization elsewhere was never on the table for Hong Kong. Instead, in 1997 the sovereignty of the territory was transferred into the hands of another world power: the PRC. From the changes introduced through the CIA 1962 to current provisions in British nationality and immigration legislation, what becomes clear is that the Hong Kongers have long been positioned in the grey zone between migrants and citizens.

At the time of BNA 1981, it was estimated that Hong Kong was home to an estimated 2.6 million strong population of British Chinese, which meant that they accounted for most of Britain's remaining colonial citizens. Indeed, those living in Britain's other remaining colonies are estimated to have numbered only half a million. As such, the Hong Kongers were by far the largest population to be impacted by the changes in nationality status brought in by the BNA 1981, granted the new status of British Dependent Territories Citizens (BDTC).

As I outlined earlier, the changes introduced through BNA 1981 were nominal. They were designed to address the mismatch between immigration legislation which determined that colonial citizens were subject to the UK's immigration controls, and their status as citizens. Despite this, many people in Hong Kong were concerned about what these changes signalled about the UK government's approach to the pending negotiations with the PRC about the future of the territory and its people (Dummett and Nicol 1990).

The exceptionality of Hong Kong as a British colony also translated into the treatment of the people of Hong Kong. On paper, the Commonwealth Immigration Acts were as significant for their migration to (and their deportation from) the UK as for other colonial citizens. Yet, there is also evidence that suggests that in this context they were considered as favoured migrants. For example, a preferential quota of work vouchers was issued to Hong Kongers in the late 1960s, which permitted them to live and work in the UK with Hong Kongers accounting for 1,500 of the 4,000 such vouchers issued to colonial citizens (Dummett and Nicol 1990: 206). At the same time, the UK was seeking ways to limit the arrival of British Asians from Kenya, this brief example making clear how hierarchies distinguishing between Britain's racialized colonial citizens were reproduced through the practices of migration governance.

When BNA 1981 was introduced, the people of Hong Kong found themselves reclassified as BDTC. While this was no more than a nominal change, it sparked concern among some Hong Kongers about what this signalled about how the UK would approach the pending negotiations between the UK and PRC. Others reclassified as BDTCs included the people of Gibraltar and the Falklands/Las Islas Malvinas; yet, in both cases provisions were introduced that allowed them to become British citizens despite not living in the UK. While there are clear geopolitical issues involved in both cases, it should not escape notice that these territories were home to majority White populations who through the changes regained the rights of citizens that were simultaneously being denied to the British Chinese of Hong Kong. Both the legislation and the decision-making relating to this further distinguished between Britain's colonial citizens on the grounds of race.

Further amendments to BNA 1981 were made to accommodate the agreements about citizenship made as part of the Sino–British negotiations (1982–1984). These were the negotiations that secured the 50-year transition period, the so-called 'One Country, Two Systems' solution, and with it, Hong Kong's constitution: Basic Law. Significantly, there was no opportunity for the people of Hong Kong to represent themselves within the negotiations – they were left to rely on their colonial administrators to secure the best possible outcome for their future. The resulting Sino-British Joint Declaration (JD) required that Britain replace the BDTC status of the British Chinese of Hong Kong with a new category that signalled the historical relationship to their former colonizers while making clear that they were not citizens in British law. It was in consequence of this that the new status of British Nationals (Overseas) (BN(O)) was introduced, an exclusive status that would take effect from 1 July 1997, the date that the PRC would assume sovereignty over Hong Kong.

This offered no more, no less than the previous status. It was heavily circumscribed, only available to those born and living in Hong Kong by the end of 1997, and not transmissible to the next generation. It gave its holders a passport, testified to their right to residence in Hong Kong, and offered consular support when travelling outside the UK and PRC. However, as a nationality status it was largely empty of meaning, a residual status that we might understand as an afterlife of empire signalling the historical relationship while offering very little in terms of rights and entitlements.

In 1989, the Tiananmen Square massacre and the subsequent uprisings in China and around the world saw the people of Hong Kong taking to the streets. In this way, they made audible their concerns about their future under Chinese rule. Taking to the streets was a route to political expression that Hong Kongers were otherwise denied. It led to their demands for British citizenship and right to live and work in the UK. Yet, as Ann Dummett and Andrew Nicol (1990) stress, the British government's response to Tiananmen showed up how the obligations implied by granting the Hong Kongers nationality were not sustained in practice.

In the wake of Tiananmen, there was significant emigration from Hong Kong, notably to Australia and Canada. The UK, however, made limited concessions, launching a scheme to allow up to 50,000 Hong Kongers to become British citizens. Rather than an offer that would allow them the right to live and work in the UK, there was a catch. These were passports to stay in Hong Kong. As Kathleen Paul (1997) makes clear, the rationale behind this was cynical. This status was available only to those who the British government felt were vital to maintaining the economic success of its colony in the final years under British administration, and which they feared was under threat due to widespread emigration (Jowett et al 1995).

From historical commitments to rediscovering colonial obligations

After 1997, Hong Kong and its people largely disappeared from the political agenda in the UK. Yet, from 2016 onwards what was happening in Hong Kong and to the Hong Kongers became once more of political interest to politicians in the UK. Briefly stated, from peaceful resistance, to protest and the development of large-scale social movements, from 2014 onwards Hong Kongers had been finding ways to express their discontent with changes being introduced by the Hong Kong government. The fear of those protesting was that the changes reneged on commitments outlined in the Sino-British JD, eroding Basic Law.

In 2020, the British government made their position clear. After several years of observations, the UK's Foreign, Commonwealth and Development Office made explicit their evaluation that the 'One Country, Two Systems' framework had been breached by the introduction of the National Security Law by the Hong Kong Executive. Condemning these actions, the British government introduced a range of measures including the provision of a bespoke visa opening a route to the UK for those from its 'last colony'.

Formally labelled the Hong Kong BN(O) (HK BN(O)) visa, from 31 January 2021, the UK government offered the people of Hong Kong a route to settlement after five years of lawful residence, and a year of indefinite leave to remain. This came through the offer of a humanitarian visa, justified on the grounds of the UK's historical obligations. The move seemed to reverse decades of policy, legislation, and practice that had successively eroded the rights of the Hong Kongers.

Initially, the visa was limited to those born in Hong Kong before the end of 1997 and their dependants – notably, making it out of reach to many of those who had joined the pro-democracy protests in Hong Kong. It was presented by the Conservative administration (2019–2024) as evidence of their 'fair and generous' approach to immigration, a flagship policy within their scheme of 'safe and legal (humanitarian) routes'. As a blanket provision to a named and circumscribed population, there were no quotas or caps placed on the visa. Between the introduction of the scheme and the end of September 2024, 215,612 HK BN(O) visas were granted. Understanding the visa in the context of this history, the visa seems more a small concession than evidence of the British government's generosity or its obligation to its former colonial citizens.

The various statuses bestowed by the UK government to the people of Hong Kong over the past century share in common incomplete access to the rights offered to citizens, while offering somewhat enhanced rights to entry and settlement to the Hong Kongers as migrants. The HK BN(O) visa is just the latest example. Indeed, this ambiguity is notable in the framing of the HK BN(O) visa, from its rhetorical positioning by Conservative politicians as evidence of their 'fair and generous' approach to migration to its location as a flagship policy within the suite of 'safe and legal (humanitarian) protections', a set of provisions which are neither located within the points-based immigration system nor the asylum system, but somewhere in between.

As I argue, the treatment of the Hong Kongers in British nationality and immigration legislation is notable for being *ambiguous by design* (see Benson 2023). In stating this, I build on Ann Laura Stoler's (2016) identification of the *exception by design* at the heart of citizenship legislation. As she argues, legal statuses that permit partial access to the basic rights of membership are best understood as a continuation of imperial forms of governance. While these are presented as anomalous in systems of classification that are assumed to produce clear-cut distinctions, the production and construction of exception or ambiguity – used here to signal the repeated repositioning of the Hong Kongers as between citizen and migrant – is integral to the mechanisms of control that sort and classify populations.

While my account has focused on the interstices of nationality and immigration legislation, it echoes work elsewhere that considers liminal legality (see, for example, Menjívar 2006), which recognizes those who occupy the grey zone between being documented and undocumented, and the impacts that this has on their lives. Acknowledging these ambiguous statuses also offers insights into the hierarchies of belonging and related stratification of rights and entitlements that are produced through migration and citizenship regimes. Indeed, what is also clear is how, as a form of humanitarian protection, the HK BN(O) visa occupies an ambiguous location between asylum and migration. As such, taking seriously colonial history both reframes understandings of this visa in ways that challenge the political rhetoric and discourse about this and offers pause for thought in thinking about the UK's post-Brexit migration regime.

The HK BN(O) visa was the first immigration provision to be introduced following Brexit, the UK's withdrawal from the European Union (EU), at the end of 2020. This is notable in a context where controlling migration and borders had been a consistent theme, from its significance to the original Brexit referendum campaign in 2016, through the negotiations between the UK and the EU, and into the UK government's ambitions for its future outside the EU. This had built on a wider context where, from the early 2010s, the Conservative government had embarked on a campaign which communicated that they were 'tough on immigration'. Branded as the 'hostile environment', immigration controls increasingly penetrated the everyday life of migrants and citizens alike (Yuval-Davis et al 2019; see Renwick, Chapter 9, this volume).

One notable example of this is the Windrush deportation scandal. This had seen Black Britons – long-term residents, many of whom had arrived in the UK as small children in the 1960s and 1970s – denied access to life-saving healthcare and benefits and being deported to former colonies in the Caribbean on the grounds that they could not provide the evidence required to demonstrate their lawful settlement. In contrast, prior to the launch of the HK BN(O) visa, border officers were advised that they could grant leave outside the immigration rules to Hong Kongers. The urgency this communicated was explained on the grounds of the UK's historical commitment to their former colonial citizens. As such, while the former colonial status of the Hong Kongers justified offering them safe haven and an immediate right to live and work in the UK, it took place in a context where the Windrush generation – similarly former colonial citizens – were recast as illegal immigrants, denied rights that they had been exercising for decades, and denied associated entitlements. This comparison further makes visible that the status of former colonial citizens is provisional, contingent, and, therefore, subject to change in the hands of the state, with potentially devastating consequences.

My final consideration here is the definition of the HK BN(O) visa as a form of humanitarian protection, one of the UK's 'safe and legal (humanitarian) routes'. This suite of humanitarian protections runs in parallel to refugee and asylum provisions as laid out by the UN Refugee Convention (see Mayblin, Chapter 14, this volume). In a broader context where the Conservative administration was seeking to introduce new restrictions to deem those entering the UK via irregular means (or unsafe routes) ineligible to claim asylum via the Illegal Immigration Act 2022 and operations that included 'stop the boats' and the Rwanda Deportation Plan, such 'safe and legal routes' were upheld as evidence of the UK government meeting international obligations. The provision of 'safe and legal routes' offering bespoke humanitarian protections was therefore part of wider shifts in the UK's migration and citizenship regime, where the government was seeking greater control over who comes to the UK and on what terms.

Prior to the launch of the HK BN(O) visa in 2021, the UK's safe and legal routes – the Afghani and Syrian resettlement schemes – had quotas in the tens of thousands. These schemes had taken a long time to pass through parliamentary processes, and implementation was slow. In contrast, applications to the HK BN(O) visa scheme were uncapped; applicants had only to demonstrate that they met the criteria, which was that they held BN(O) status or would have been eligible for this in 1997. Introduced remarkably quickly, visas were granted through this scheme on an unprecedented scale. In political debates, policy papers, and government rhetoric, the HK BN(O) visa was used to justify claims that the UK was meeting its international obligations to provide humanitarian protections, of offering safe and legal routes for people to come to the

UK. Yet the terms on which this was being offered were far removed from those outlined by the UN Refugee Convention (Benson et al 2024). The ambiguous legal positioning of the Hong Kongers was the latest in the British government exercising control over their mobility, but it also had an additional function within a political agenda that aimed at restricting asylum and brokering greater national control over who was granted humanitarian protection.

Within the suite of 'safe and legal routes', the HK BN(O) visa seems to offer favourable treatment. However, there is one further twist that bears consideration. Applicants are required to pay for their visas and the immigration health surcharge. Paying for protection and access to the public health service was not required for any other humanitarian routes established at that time, or for those seeking asylum. Defined as a form of humanitarian protection in practice, how the visa was set up more closely approximated those offered via the managed migration system. This last point offers a further indication of how the Hong Kongers are caught between migration and asylum.

Conclusion

Today, Hong Kong is home to the largest population of British nationals living outside the UK. Yet, within scholarship that examines migration and citizenship, the Hong Kongers and others like them – with a nominal status as British nationals, without the right to abode in the UK – are a significant blind spot. Considering their treatment strengthens arguments that the UK's migration and citizenship regime is structured by colonial logics, that sorting and classifying populations today reproduces the coloniality of the global migration–citizenship–asylum nexus.

Specifically, tracing connected sociologies and histories reveals that the HK BN(O) visa should not be taken at face value. While its architects promoted it as evidence of the UK's 'fair and generous' approach to migration, this is called into question by understanding that such provisions were a small concession for a colonial population whose rights had been markedly eroded, even while they remained under British administration.

But it also reveals another aspect of the migration and citizenship regime that deserves attention, the significance of ambiguity not only for the lives of those in the grey zone between migrants and citizens, migrants and refugees, but for what this reveals about hierarchies of belonging. Recognizing this makes clear the contingency of legal statuses, highlighting that who the British state considers to be migrants, citizens, and anything in between is anything but natural or self-evident. As such ambiguity is by design, and has consequences for lives and livelihoods.

However, as I have demonstrated in this chapter, such ambiguity is notable also in a global context where securing greater control over who can move, where, and on what terms has taken on increasing significance for states. The ambiguous positioning of certain populations between legal categories, or the introduction of new legal categories, is one that contests the international world order in the pursuit of greater sovereign power. In conclusion, the bespoke framing of the HK BN(O) visa continues the relative favouring of the Hong Kongers in contrast to other racialized colonial citizens, while its status as a form of humanitarian protection signals broader transformations into the UK's border regime after Brexit as it seeks greater control over its borders.

References

Benson, M. 2023. 'Hong Kongers and the Coloniality of British Citizenship from Decolonization to "Global Britain"', *Current Sociology* 71(5): 743–761.

Benson, M., Sigona, N., and Zambelli, E. 2024. 'The UK's "Safe and Legal" Humanitarian Routes: From Colonial Ties to Privatizing Protection', *The Political Quarterly* 95(2): 263–271.

Bhambra, G.K. 2015. 'Citizens and Others: The Constitution of Citizenship through Exclusion', *Alternatives* 40: 102–114.

Boatcă, M. 2020. 'More Equal than Others: Citizenship through the Lens of Coloniality', *Rassena Italiana di Sociologia* 61(4): 711–739.

Boatcă, M. and Roth, J. 2016. 'Unequal and Gendered: Notes on the Coloniality of Citizenship', *Current Sociology* 64(2): 191–212.

Dummett, A. and Nicol, A. 1990. *Subjects, Citizens, Aliens and Others*. Weidenfeld & Nicolson.

Gutiérrez Rodríguez, E. 2018. 'The Coloniality of Migration and the "Refugee Crisis": On the Asylum-migration Nexus, the Transatlantic White European Settler Colonialism-migration and Racial Capitalism', *Refuge* 34(1).

Jowett, A.J., Findlay, A.M., Li, F.L.N., and Skeldon, R. 1995. 'The British Who Are Not British and the Immigration Policies That Are Not', *Applied Geography* 15(3): 245–265.

Mayblin, L. and Turner, J. 2021. *Migration Studies and Colonialism*. Polity.

Menjívar, C. 2006. 'Liminal Legality: Salvadoran and Guatemalan Immigrants' Lives in the United States', *American Journal of Sociology* 111(4): 999–1037.

Paul, K. 1997. *Whitewashing Britain: Race and Citizenship in the Postwar Era*. Cornell University Press.

Prabhat, D. 2020. 'Unequal Citizenship and Subjecthood: A Rose by Any Other Name …?', *Northern Ireland Legal Quarterly* 71: 175–191.

Quijano, A. 2000. 'Coloniality of Power and Eurocentrism in Latin America', *International Sociology* 15(2): 215–232.

Stoler, A.L. 2016. *Duress: Imperial Durabilities in Our Times*. Duke University Press.

Yuval-Davis, N., Wemyss, G., and Cassidy, K. 2019. *Bordering*. John Wiley & Sons.

Video lecture

Benson, M. 2022. *'Global Britain' and the Coloniality of British Citizenship*, Connected Sociological Curriculum Project. https://thesociologicalreview.org/projects/connected-sociologies/curriculum/migration-borders-diaspora/coloniality-of-british-citizenship/

Additional resources

Benson, M. 2024. 'Britain's "Bespoke" Borders', *History Workshop*, 29 August. https://www.historyworkshop.org.uk/migration/britains-bespoke-borders/

Qureshi, F., Benson, M., Sigona, N., and Zambelli, E. 2024. 'S3 E9 (Not so) Safe Routes', *Who Do We Think We Are?* https://whodowethinkweare.org/podcasts/who-do-we-think-we-are/s3e9-not-so-safe-routes/

Vassiliou, J., Benson, M., and Kalivis, G. 2021. 'S1 E6 What Can the Hong Kong BN(O) Visa Tell Us about Borders and Belonging in Britain Today', *Who Do We Think We Are?* https://whodowethinkweare.org/podcasts/who-do-we-think-we-are/what-can-the-hong-kong-bn-o-visa-tell-us-about-borders-and-belonging-in-britain-today/

QUESTIONS

1. What is the significance of the formation of national citizenships for understanding global inequalities in who can move where and on what terms in the world today?

2. What is the coloniality of migration and citizenship?

3. How does the account of the shifting legal status and treatment of the Hong Kongers change understandings of Britain's current approach to immigration?

Worksheet 18. The British Migration–Citizenship Regime: From Decolonization to Brexit

This worksheet is designed to support AS and A-level teaching on the topics of global culture, globalization and global development, and demographic trends in the UK since 1900, with a particular focus on migration. Michaela Benson's chapter and talk are suitable for students who already have some understanding of globalization and British colonial history. The talk and related worksheet activities encourage students to think critically about historical and contemporary political contexts of British citizenship and connect these ideas to their existing understandings of globalization, global culture, and migration.

Time	Activity	Explanation
00.00–00.05	To begin, answer this question: Who are British citizens?	This starter exercise is designed to get students thinking about the boundaries and implications of the term 'citizen' in order to introduce them to the themes of the session.
00.05–00.10	Recap of understandings of globalization.	It may be useful to remind students of the definition(s) of globalization.
00.10–00.20	Watch the talk from 3:05 to 5:15. How did the British Nationality Act of 1981 change the definition of British citizenship? What were the different motivations behind this change, according to Benson?	Benson explains that the British Nationality Act of 1981 legally defined British citizenship as exclusively linked to the UK. Citizens of Britain's colonies were reclassified as British Dependent Territories Citizens (BDTC) and British Overseas Citizens (BOC). Benson describes how this Act 'closed a loophole' which had prevented people from Britain's overseas territories being able to migrate and settle in the UK. She argues that we can also see it as part of the political curation of British citizenship. This activity introduces students to a key moment within British immigration history which will aid their understanding of British demographic trends since 1900 and globalization. Asking students to think about the motivations behind this change encourages them to start thinking about citizenship as a political project as well as a social one.
00.20–00.30	Watch the talk from 8:30 to 15:29. Write a short paragraph summarizing how the citizenship status of Hong Kongers changed from 1948 to 1997. You may want to use Benson's timeline of key dates, or draw out your own, to help you. How does this timeline relate to what else you know about Britain's colonial history?	Benson explains that in 1948 the first Nationality Act in Britain was introduced which transformed Hong Kongers from British subjects to citizens of the UK and colonies. Immigration acts in the 1960s and 1970s made Hong Kongers deportable from the UK. They are citizens but are also made potential migrants in this period. In 1981 Hong Kongers become BDTC with no right of abode in the UK. In 1984 Hong Kongers become nationals instead of citizens ahead of the transfer from sovereignty from Britain to the People's Republic of China in 1997.

Time	Activity	Explanation
		In 1997 Hong Kongers are given some notional citizenship and a passport but no right of abode in the UK and become subject to immigration control. This activity is an opportunity for students to develop their skills at digesting information and summarizing the key points in their own words. The students are then stretched to connect beyond the given material to other topics in their studies.
00.30–00.35	At 16:50, Benson explains that the new bespoke opportunities for settlement being offered to Hong Kongers since 2021 are caught up within 'the political project of defining post-Brexit Britain and post-Brexit Britishness'. *Why do you think Benson draws a connection to Brexit here?*	This activity asks students to draw connections between what they are learning in the talk and relevant current political affairs, encouraging them to contextualize contemporary events such as Brexit within the broader themes of globalization, global development, and migration. Thinking about Britain's relationship with other countries in this way also fits in with the core curriculum theme of considering the cultural, political, and economic relationships between societies.
00.35–00.45	At 18:41 Benson points out that the new provisions for Hong Kongers 'have been promoted as evidence of the Home Office's fair and generous approach to immigration'. *How does this perspective compare to what you have learned about UK immigration practices in other topics? Can you think of some examples from the media to illustrate your points?*	This activity provides students with the opportunity to exercise their critical thinking skills, which will help them with the course aim to critically evaluate evidence. It is also a good opportunity for students to think about how the themes of power and stratification and social inequalities relate to immigration in a UK context.
00.45–00.55	At 20:52 Benson explains that she is 'sceptical' about the motivations behind the Hong Kong BN(O) visa, partly because 'a bespoke scheme such as this demonstrates that the government is now in a position to choose which particular migrants will be beneficial to "Global Britain"'. *Why does Benson highlight this as a concern? What might the potential long-term impacts of this visa be on British society?*	This activity connects students' learning around globalization and migration with other core themes, namely: power and stratification, and social inequalities. It stretches students to develop their analytical skills and think beyond the material presented to them, considering the potential sociological impacts of the issues they have been introduced to in the talk.

Time	Activity	Explanation
00.55–01.00	Reflecting on what you have learned from this talk, and the first activity you completed for this worksheet, answer the following question: *What are the main factors that inform the formation and boundaries of British citizenship?*	This recap activity rounds out the session by asking students to reflect on, summarize, and articulate what they have learned in their own words, drawing together the themes of migration, globalization, and UK demographic trends. By asking students to draw out the points they deem the most important from the talk, this activity also enables students to build their skills in assessing and evaluating evidence.

This worksheet was developed by Isabel Sykes.

PART IV

Multiculturalism and Anti-Racism

Edited by Ipek Demir

19

British Black Power

John Narayan

> **Objectives**
>
> - This chapter examines how the history of British Black Power transnationalizes the history of British anti-racism.
> - It sets out how British Black Power was based on an expansive sense of Blackness.
> - It discusses how British Black Power linked its anti-racism in Britain with anti-imperialism in the Third World.
> - It demonstrates how British Black Power's idea of anti-racism and anti-imperialism reframes class struggle in Britain, and the lessons such histories have for anti-racism today.

Introduction

Up until recently, the history of British Black Power (BBP) groups had been relatively neglected. However, the history of BBP has garnered renewed scholarly interest. These studies highlight how throughout the late 1960s and early 1970s the British state's approach to what was dubbed 'New Commonwealth immigration' – from Britain's colonies, and former colonies, in Asia, Africa, and the Caribbean – and the racial discrimination and racial violence endured by such 'coloured' immigrants brought forth the UK's own Black Power movement. Adapting the ideas and practice of its more famous US counterpart, with anti-colonial ideas and praxis from Africa, Asia, and the Caribbean, BBP was at the forefront of British anti-racism during the 1960s and early 1970s. Seeking to unite Commonwealth citizens, BBP operated through a diverse set of activists and groups, who created a 'Black' political identity and formed community-based responses to racial inequality, state racism, and police brutality, and forged international links with movements and states in the Third World or what we today call the Global South (see Bunce and Field 2013; Wild 2016; Angelo 2018; Waters 2018; Narayan 2019).

What might we learn about the history of anti-racism in Britain and also our contemporary moment by re-examining Britain's history of Black Power? The narrative of the downfall of British anti-racism and its politically 'Black' subject as a tragic state-induced phenomenon is well known. This timeline sees the vibrant and independent anti-racist movement, which created an unparalleled sense of unity between Britain's New Commonwealth communities, come apart at the seams as different ethnic groups were splintered through government-induced funding and essentialized into ethnic identities under an umbrella of 'multiculturalism' and 'ethnicity' that was defined and instrumentalized by the state and local government from the 1980s onwards (see Modood, Chapter 21, this volume).

In this chapter, I do not question this narrative but show how the history of BBP turns the island story of British anti-racism into a transnational story that linked anti-racism in Britain with anti-imperialism in the Third World. In doing so, BBP transformed British anti-racism, and the loss of its global coordinates is something we would do well to recover in the 21st century. The chapter first sets out the three main tenets of BBP – political Blackness, anti-imperialism, and reframing the relationship between race and class in Britain – and moves onto the fall of BBP and the rise of neoliberal approaches to racism. The chapter concludes by showing how the legacy of BBP holds important lessons for contemporary anti-racism today as the model of instrumentalized multiculturalism has been jettisoned by British governments who have mainstreamed anti-immigrant policies.

Political Blackness

US Black Power pioneer Stokely Carmichael's visit to London in July 1967 is often credited as being foundational to the formation of BBP. Britain had its dawn of Black Power with Michael X's formation of the Racial Adjustment Action Society in the wake of Malcolm X's visit to Britain in 1965, and the establishment of the United Coloured People's Association in June 1967 (UCPA). However, Carmichael's visit created an explosion of discussion around the idea of Black Power in Britain. This saw the emergence of the Black Panther Movement (BPM) in 1968, the Black Unity and Freedom Party (BUFP) in 1970, the Black Liberation Front (BLF) in 1971, and other Black Power groups in urban centres such as London, Manchester, and Birmingham.

The US Black Power movement heavily influenced BBP, with groups such as the BPM taking their name from their US counterpart. BBP groups also took on board their US counterparts' ideas of community control, cultural identity, and self-defence against racial violence. However, although BBP groups differed on ideological prerogatives, with some groups emerging out of one another due to ideological disagreements on issues such as cultural nationalism or the role of Marxism-Leninism in Black Power, most of the prominent BBP groups embraced 'political Blackness'. This marks a distinction between BBP and its US counterpart.

Political Blackness centred on the idea that that the common experience of colonial rule and subsequent fight against state racism in the UK united the members of the African, Caribbean, and Asian communities as 'Black' peoples. The British state had been confronted with the faces and lives of its former, and then still existing, empire when it had drawn on labour from the Commonwealth during post-war reconstruction. The post-war economy had seen the establishment of a racialized division of labour on the UK mainland. New Commonwealth citizens often occupied the bottom rung of the labour market, regardless of their previous class trajectory, as White male workers moved into higher paying skilled manual roles that informally discriminated to keep non-White labour out of such jobs. British society's insidious racism against its racialized citizens had also resulted in informal colour bars in workplaces and unions, and racial discrimination in housing and policing (see Anitha, Chapter 8, this volume). This economic discrimination was accompanied with violence against migrant communities with flashpoints such as White-on-Black rioting in Nottingham and Notting Hill in the 1950s leading to widespread racial violence in the 1960s (see Renwick, Chapter 9, and Murji, Chapter 17, this volume). This spectre of racial violence would become even more concrete with the amalgamation of racist groups under the banner of the National Front in 1967.

Worried by the effects of 'coloured immigration' on British society, with race riots and debates about cultural essentialism, and a slowdown in economic growth, the state pursued a series of racist Immigration Acts (1962, 1968, 1971) designed to limit New Commonwealth immigration (see Hampshire, Chapter 13, and Benson, Chapter 18, this volume). This state racism peaked with the 1971 Immigration Act and its move towards partiality, which effectively linked immigration to the ability to trace Anglo-Saxon heritage. 'Patrials' were defined as British subjects and UK Commonwealth citizens who, either themselves or through a parent or grandparent, had been born, adopted, naturalized, or registered in the UK. Those who lacked this close familial connection or had not legally lived in the UK for five years – including all non-citizens – were classified as 'non-patrials'. While non-patrial British subjects living in the UK at the time the Act was passed retained their right to remain in the country, non-patrials living abroad could only enter with a work permit, which did not grant the right to permanent settlement. Since many patrials were descendants of UK colonists, the group was predominantly White. In contrast, non-patrials generally came from colonized or formerly colonized nations and were often people of colour.

Through immigration control or racial discrimination New Commonwealth citizens were excluded from gaining access to the socio-economic and political safeguards of British democracy. For example, the 1965 Race Relations Act failed to secure protection against discrimination, or to provide a remedy for the unfairness of mainland Britain's racial division of labour. At the same time, the two main political parties – Labour and the Conservatives – both sought to legislate against coloured immigration. This forced New Commonwealth communities into pursuing a more radical political response to racial oppression (Wild 2016). Under the signifier of a collective Black political subject, which did not override ethnic, religious, or national identities, activists attempted to create a common political identity that could facilitate cooperation between New Commonwealth communities in the pursuit of racial justice. As the legendary director of the Institute for Race Relations, Ambalavaner Sivanandan, recalled, this was a time when 'Black was the colour of our politics not the colour of our skin' (Sivanandan 2008: 2).

BBP outwardly projected 'political Blackness', with groups such as UCPA offering early definitions of the concept. The UCPA referred to its members as 'Black Brothers and Sisters from Asia, Africa, the Caribbean and the Americas' and argued that history was now being driven by the formation of two 'irreconcilable camps' between those from 'Asia, Africa, the Caribbean and the Americas' and 'Western imperialist' nations. Political Blackness was also central to the Marxist-Leninist BUFP, which emerged out of the UCPA, and the anti-vanguardist BPM. Even the more Afrocentric-focused BLF defined 'Black people as all non-White peoples of African, Asian, Caribbean and Latin American origin who share the common enemy, and common oppressor' in a manifesto called 'Revolutionary Black Nationalism' (Narayan 2019: 5).

BBP groups created grassroots community campaigns against racist immigration controls, police brutality, racist discrimination in the workplace, housing, and education, and the threat of racial violence on behalf of all of Britain's non-White communities. Although the logic of BBP's political Blackness was the narration of the common experience of Black subjects, this did not stop such groups attending to specific forms of racism suffered by certain communities. BBP groups regularly reported on the politics of the African diaspora, with the BPM publishing Kwame Nkrumah's 'Message to the Black People of Britain' and groups such as the BLF promoted Pan-Africanism. BBP groups also campaigned against police brutality faced by those within the African diaspora. However, groups such as the UCPA and BPM also created links with London's Pakistani Progressive Party and the Pakistani Workers' Union. This allowed them to focus on the prevalence of attacks against South Asians that arose in the late 1960s.

The murder of Tosir Ali in 1970 would see BPM members helping to form street patrols in South Asian communities in London's East End (Ashe et al 2016). Although small numerically, with groups such as the BPM made up of the tens rather than hundreds, BBP groups were often able to mobilize hundreds and thousands from wider local and national communities for rallies and demonstrations. As Angelo (2018) notes, the rate of activism by groups such as the BPM was high with the staging of over 100 protests between 1969 and 1973 and over 70 cultural events during this period. This activism highlights how BBP's idea of political Blackness and its sense of solidarity was key to mobilizing people in different New Commonwealth communities and across different forms of racist discrimination and violence.

Anti-imperialism

BBP's idea of political Blackness was not simply a reflection of the divisions of UK race relations but was also informed by what W.E.B. Du Bois had famously called the problem of the 20th century: 'the colour-line'. During the process of decolonization after the Second World War – where European nations lost their colonies – and driven by mass movements and the failures of capitalist development, the 'darker nations' of the Third World – Europe's former colonies – were drawn loosely together through a shared history of being the victims of Western imperialism (see Chen and Sabaratnam, Chapter 6, this volume). They were also drawn together as they were the target of Western neo-imperialism – the continued attempts by former colonial powers to economically, politically, and militarily control their former colonies. Through organizations such as the Non-Aligned Movement, the Group of 77, and UN Conference on Trade and Development, the Third World nations embarked upon a 'Project' to remodel geo-economic and geopolitical structures to reflect the interests of all of humanity and not just those in the West (Prashad 2007).

BBP's idea of political Blackness linked the struggle for minority rights at home with the struggles of the global majority abroad. Black people 'over here' were literally taken to be Third World people from 'over there'. The interlinking of the domestic anti-racist struggles in Britain and anti-imperialism can be found in the various BBP groups' publications. The newspapers and news bulletins of BBP groups reported on racism and anti-racism in the UK and juxtaposed such stories with international news on Ethiopia, Jamaica, the Black Power movements in the United States and Trinidad, Dalit activism in India, apartheid South Africa, the independence struggles of Bangladesh, Sri Lanka, Zimbabwe, Guinea Bissau, Angola, Mozambique, Aboriginal rights in Australia, and the US withdrawal from Vietnam, among others. Part of the rationale behind these stories was educative, providing readers with a cognitive map of the anti-imperial struggles across the Third World. Via these stories, readers were introduced to revolutionary actors such as the US Black Panther Party, Amilcar Cabral, Australian Aboriginal activist Bobbi Sykes, Mozambique's FRELIMO, the Black Panthers of Israel, the Dalit Panthers of India, and the Palestine Liberation Organization (Angelo 2018).

These stories also highlighted how racial oppression in Britain was directly linked with imperial oppression in the Third World. For example, in 1973 the BUFP ran a story in its newspaper on the exploitation of Filipino immigrant sewing workers in the UK, labelling them 'Bonded Slaves'. At the bottom of the article, readers were instructed to turn a few pages to read about how such migrant workers were engendered by Filipino Dictator Ferdinand Marcos and US neo-imperial intervention in the Philippines. This interlinking of contexts also informed BBP activism, with groups such as the BPM holding solidarity demonstrations that highlighted the struggles against racism in Britain and the repression of Black Power groups in the United States and Trinidad. This anti-imperialism also allowed anti-racists to move beyond simply embracing binary definitions between First (White) versus Third (Black) World forms of oppression. Anti-racists in the 1960s and 1970s regularly indicted non-White dictators in Third World states and formed solidarity with Irish republicans – who had been kicked out, or rather not yet allowed into, the category of Whiteness. The BPM joined anti-internment demonstrations in London in 1972, parading a banner that read 'The Black Panther Movement Stands in Total Solidarity with the Irish Liberation Struggle' (see Narayan 2019). What this shows us is that BBP's focus on anti-imperialism, when combined with its idea of political Blackness, was an attempt to place anti-racist activism in the UK in a global context.

Race and class in Britain

BBP groups also reconceptualized how class struggle should be approached in Britain. Although critical of Britain's socialist movements, which often saw issues of race and anti-racism as diversions from class struggle, BBP groups were anti-capitalist and firm believers in the idea of revolutionary socialism. BBP groups thus took on board Marxist ideas of class struggle and re-theorized such ideas to account for the relationship between imperialism, racism, and revolution.

BBP approached the interrelationship of race and class through two contradictions. On the one hand, there was the contradiction between 'the oppressed and oppressors, i.e. the ruling class'. On the other hand, although Black people largely belonged to the 'proletariat', there was, at this historical conjuncture, a contradiction between Black people and 'the proletariat of imperialist countries'. In effect, the BBP argued that most of the White working class had 'joined forces' with the ruling class. Black people would thus be on the side of the proletariat when and if their White counterparts abandoned their racist nationalism (Narayan 2019: 12–13; see Holmwood, Chapter 7, this volume).

BBP's recognition of the problem of neo-imperialism allowed such groups to view the interrelationship between Britain's class and anti-racist struggles through a global rather than national lens. Groups such as the UCPA and the BLF used this global context to dismiss White society's potential to wake up and rise above the West's racism and imperialism. For these groups, the cause of BBP was solely rooted in the cause of Third World-ism or Pan-Africanism. This was a direct response to how the White working class and its institutions were indifferent to anti-racist struggle in Britain during the late 1960s and early 1970s. The Trades Union Congress, for instance, while fighting the Industrial Relations Bill (1971) – which sought to regulate trade union activity – made no link or common cause with campaigns against the 1971 Immigration Act. Those further on the left, such as the Communist Party of Great Britain, while understanding the plight of Britain's Black population, also saw BBP as counterproductive to class struggle.

Yet, groups such as BPM and BUFP did not give up on Britain's White population. The BPM, for example, reported on the causes of White-led working-class struggles such as the miners' strike and the Upper Clyde shipbuilders' 'work-in' in 1972. In theory groups such as the BPM and BUFP advocated for cross-racial solidarity. However, this was made on the grounds of radically altering the tenets of class struggle in Britain. The BUFP, for example, ran editorials in its newspapers that labelled the Trades Union Congress and the Labour Party as 'reactionary organizations' or 'state' organizations that failed to understand the global nature of class oppression. This position framed the 'role of Black workers' in the UK around an idea of decolonizing Britain's trade unions. This hinged on imploring Black workers to join unions, 'despite the contempt we hold for these capitalist-controlled institutions', and for Black workers to form 'Black caucuses within trade unions' and in partnership with 'progressive White workers' to seize the initiative to 'spearhead the defence of workers' against capitalist exploitation. Crucially, this could only be achieved through Black workers pushing workers in Britain to establish 'strong links with the exploited workers of the Third World'. The overriding messages of BBP here was the need to link struggles in the UK with a wider assault against global capitalism in the 'Third World' rather than just focusing on the internal class politics of Britain.

Fade to Black

Even as BBP groups disbanded throughout the early 1970s – through internal disagreements and external pressure from the state – the impact of BBP's ideas filtered through British anti-racist activism. Groups such as the Asian Youth Movement would take ideas of political Blackness and the need to link anti-racism to anti-imperialism into their anti-racist activism. While former BBP members would help form groups such as the Race Today Collective, the Brixton Black Women's group, and the Organization for Women of African and Asian Descent – who continued to generate links between race, gender, anti-racism, and anti-imperialism (see Ramamurthy 2013; BBWG 2023; Kelbert, Chapter 20, this volume). Yet, as the neoliberal revolution enacted by Margaret Thatcher's government took hold of Britain's economy in the 1980s it was accompanied by a neoliberal approach to racism, which was embraced by the state and successive governments as a response to militant forms of British anti-racism.

As Shafi and Nagdee (2021) outline, the state's reaction to British anti-racism and the legacy of BBP from the early 1980s onwards was to usher in a form of 'anti-racism from above' that looked to contain the radical demands of British anti-racism through state funding and state defined ideas of multiculturalism that destabilized inter-ethnic solidarity. The British state also offered cultural explanations for the effects of institutional racism – poverty, poor housing, educational disadvantage – on Britain's minority communities. Minority communities were taken to be culturally maladjusted or unable to assimilate into and succeed in the British way of life. For example, on the back of the 1981 urban rebellions by Black communities across Britain against institutional racism and police brutality – most famously in Brixton – the Scarman report centred the definition of racism away from structural and institutional explanations to cultural and individualist explanations such as Caribbean family values and second-generation minority identities.

The link between state racism, exploitation, and global inequality that had been central to BBP was declared unimportant to understanding racism and replaced with static ideas of cultural disadvantage and the need to expand entrepreneurism among racially disadvantaged groups. This saw minority communities, movements, and groups encouraged by the state to disarticulate racisms (anti-Blackness, Islamophobia, xeno-racism) around distinct and separate ethnic communities and categories (for example, Black, Asian, Muslim). At the same time, tensions over the use of the politically Black signifier – where some communities could feel homogenized or at odds with another – and the lure of state funding pulled inter-community solidarity apart (Sivanandan 2008).

Communities who suffered from structural and institutional racism were now encouraged to compete with one another as market actors to obtain economic resources and policy attention from the state – even when their goal was to obtain less attention from the state. These processes also saw the state domesticate issues of racism as matters of the nation state. The idea of anti-racism was now infused with ideas of national market correctives and representational equality: Black and Brown faces in state and business offices, across screens, and on sports pitches. This neoliberal form of anti-racism was about inclusion into the system – for an emergent minority middle class who could theoretically now ascend into the academy, politics, and the media – rather than the national and global institutional and economic transformation demanded by BBP a decade earlier.

Recovering British Black Power's idea of anti-racism

What, then, is the contemporary relevance of the history of BBP for British anti-racism today? As suggested at the start of the chapter, there is a tendency to read the development of British anti-racism as an island story – where racialized subjects have only sought their rightful inclusion into British society on the UK mainland. What this story has tried to show is how the history of BBP internationalizes this story and transforms how we could perceive anti-racism. Here I want to draw out three lessons we can learn from the history of BBP for the contemporary moment: the link between anti-racism and anti-imperialism; the practical ideas of anti-racist struggle in Britain; and how we need radical forms of solidarity to achieve a more just world. These lessons are even more needed as more recent British governments have seemingly critiqued even state-led instrumentalist multiculturalism in the name of 'integration' and readily mainstream anti-immigrant views on migration and asylum.

In the first instance, the history of BBP shows how confronting the violence of state racism at home should also mean confronting the racialized imperialist system that underpins and, in many instances, engenders such state racism. The link between state racism and the contour of the current global economy makes it clear that in tandem with confronting racist borders, police forces, and prisons, we must also confront the racism of global governance institutions such as the International Monetary Fund, World Bank and World Trade Organization, trade and arms agreements, patents and intellectual property rights that facilitate imperialist exploitation and expropriation in the Global South.

Globally, the most entrenched institutional racism is rooted in the global economic system and its governance, which perpetuate crises in health, food, energy, debt, and climate change mitigation.

BBP demanded a form of anti-racist internationalism that sees issues such as labour, land and resource exploitation in the Global South, sovereign debt, patent rights, institutions of global governance, and global capital itself as anti-racist concerns; and causes and peoples' movements in the Global South as potential anti-racist issues (see Narayan 2023).

What such a conception of the relationship between anti-racism and anti-imperialism does is to expand the idea of the class struggle in Britain both horizontally and vertically. On the horizonal scale, current anti-racism, much like the old one located in BBP, should not seek merely to put Brown and Black faces in high places in dealing with the problem of ethnic inequality in Britain. Here, the link between anti-racism and class struggle in the UK should see the former expand the idea of class struggle.

Therefore, a class movement expanded through its experience as race must fight for more than higher wages, better conditions, and state services. It must also demand an end to the super-exploitation of racialized and gendered labour, stop the imprisonment of working-class people abandoned by the state, and dismantle border regimes that target the victims of imperialism and climate change.

Added to these horizontal forms, anti-racism should be a practical anti-racism that attempts to challenge the vertical domination of the most oppressed: the racialized majority outside of Britain. Anti-racist struggles in Britain thus should conjoin and find praxis with the struggles of dismantling the oppressive structures of the global economy that subjugate vast swathes of the Global South. It should in turn advocate for solidarities and policy changes around issues, such as illegal occupation of land by nation states, the dismantling of the UK and global arms industry, the eradication of odious sovereign debt in the Global South, and the reform or abolition of global governance and international financial institutions.

Finally, to achieve this, such an anti-racism must be able to form solidarities and interconnections between those under racial oppression both within and outside Britain. In the Brexit referendum of 2016, for example, multiple racisms were evoked by the Leave campaign to secure Britain's exit from the European Union. Political elites evoked a racialized nationalism of a 'White England' whose state and resources were threatened by White Eastern and Central Europeans and Black and Brown migrants who may or may not be Muslims. This set of events also saw a surge in racist hate crime against the New Commonwealth communities who had become established. Such a situation is not fully explainable through positions solely rooted in xeno-racism, Islamophobia, or anti-Blackness. Rather, what is needed is a form of analysis that can map how the politics of Whiteness intersects with anti-Blackness, Islamophobia, and xenophobia, and how this is linked to the wider coordinates of British, European, and global capitalism. This, ironically, is the politics of political Blackness that we have all too easily dismissed or forgotten.

Indeed, such a conception of solidarity is needed more than ever: Western domination of the global economy and global governance institutions are increasingly contested by rising powers such as the BRICS bloc, rising inequality, and forms of authoritarianism within nations; automation and outsourcing have seen the working classes of Western nations lose elements of their privileged role in the global economy; a plethora of non-White ethnic minorities within Britain continue to find themselves at the bottom of indicators such as wages and labour exploitation and others are seen as model minorities; and flows of migration induced by either war, inequality, or climate change crash against racist Western border regimes. While we may wish to jettison the BBP's idea of political Blackness and its 'Black' subject, due to the fears of ethnic homogenization or the erasure of the different forms and processes of racism suffered by different ethnic minority groups, or quite simply because it seems outdated, we would do well to recover BBP's interlinking of anti-racism with international forms of solidarity against exploitation in the wider world.

Conclusion

This chapter has examined the history of Black Power in Britain and highlighted the transnational nature of BBP. The formation of BBP through migration to the UK mainland from Asia, Africa, and the Caribbean gave Black Power in Britain a distinct transnational accent. This saw BBP groups adapt the US call for Black Power around a form of political Blackness that sought to create solidarity and collaboration between those from the New Commonwealth. As we have seen, this form of political solidarity was tied to an anti-imperialism that located anti-racism in the UK with anti-colonial struggles in the Third World. BBP thus redefined the nature of class struggle in Britain, showing how anti-racism and the struggles of colonized people abroad were key to understanding class in the UK. It is this legacy of reading racism and anti-racism in the UK through a global lens that BBP provides us with today.

References

Angelo, A.-M. 2018. ' "Black Oppressed People All Over the World Are One": The British Black Panthers' Grassroots Internationalism, 1969–73', *Journal of Civil and Human Rights* 4: 64–97.

Ashe, S., Virdee, S., and Brown, L. 2016. 'Striking Back Against Racist Violence in East London: 1968–70', *Race and Class* 58: 34–54.

BBWG. 2023. *Speak Out: The Brixton Black Women's Group*. Verso Books.

Bunce, R. and Field, P. 2013. *Darcus Howe: A Political Biography*. Bloomsbury Academic.

Narayan, J. 2019. 'British Black Power: The Anti-imperialism of Political Blackness and the Problem of Nativist Socialism', *The Sociological Review* 65(5): 945–947.

Narayan, J. 2023. 'New Times or New Circuits: Recovering Sivanandan's Political Economy', *Race & Class* 65(1): 14–33.

Prashad, V. 2007. *The Darker Nations: A People's History of the Third World*. The New Press.

Ramamurthy, A. 2013. *Black Star: Britain's Asian Youth Movements*. Pluto Press.

Shafi, A. and Nagdee, L. 2021. *Race to the Bottom: Reclaiming Anti-racism*. Pluto Press.

Sivanandan, A. 2008. *Catching History on the Wing: Race, Culture and Globalization*. Pluto Press.

Waters, R. 2018. *Thinking Black: Britain, 1964–1985*. University of California Press.

Wild, R. 2016. 'Black was the Colour of Our Fight: The Transnational Roots of British Black Power', in S. Tuck and G. Kelley (eds), *The Other Special Relationship: Race, Rights and Riots in Britain and the United States*. Palgrave Macmillan, pp 25–46.

Video lecture

Narayan, J. 2020. *British Black Power*, Connected Sociologies Curriculum Project. https://thesociologicalreview.org/projects/connected-sociologies/curriculum/british-citizenship-race-and-rights/british-black-power/

QUESTIONS

1. How did political Blackness attempt to unite New Commonwealth migrants? What were its limitations?

2. How and why did British Black Power link anti-racism to anti-imperialism?

3. How did British Black Power attempt to reframe the idea of class politics in Britain?

4. What do you think we can learn from the history of British Black Power for anti-racism movements today?

Worksheet 19. British Black Power

This worksheet is designed to support AS and A-level teaching on globalization and global development, culture and identity, and social differentiation, power, and stratification.

In his online talk, Narayan examines the distinctive form of the Black Power Movement that took place in Britain in the late 1960s and early 1970s. Narayan explains that Black Power was rooted in anti-colonial politics, New Commonwealth immigration, and decolonization. As such, the themes covered in this talk have strong connections to other sessions on this course. This worksheet encourages students to critically reflect on these themes and explore the legacies of British Black Power for contemporary anti-racist movements.

Time	Activity	Explanation
00.00–00.05	To warm up, answer this question: *What do you already know about the Black Power movement?*	This warm-up activity offers students the opportunity to share their existing knowledge about the Black Power movement, with the aim of developing this throughout the talk. Students may have heard about the movement as it existed in the United States, but be less familiar with its establishment in the UK.
00.05–00.10	Recap of understandings of culture and identity.	It may be useful to remind students of some of the relationships between different identities, particularly ethnicity and social class.
00.10–00.20	Watch the talk from 1:01 to 3:31. *What are the three main factors contributing to the establishment of Black Power in the UK, according to Narayan? Can you identify any historical crossovers with other talks on this course?*	Narayan explains that (1) New Commonwealth immigration and settlement, (2) pervasive racial discrimination in mainland Britain (partly as a result of Britain being brought face to face with its colonial British subjects) and (3) influence from Marxism, US Black Power and anti-colonial activism and discourse in the Third World were the main factors contributing to the rise of Black Power. In this activity, students are encouraged to identify crossovers between these important historical factors and other contexts. For example, New Commonwealth immigration and settlement was a key context in the 'Making of British Citizenship' session. Anti-colonial activism and discourse in the Third World also features prominently in a number of other talks, including 'Decolonization'.
00.20–00.25	At 5:36 Narayan states that 'Black Power in Britain is really about the failure [of the state] to secure economic and social justice for non-White citizens'. *What is the relationship between racial and socio-economic inequality?*	Narayan draws connections throughout his talk between racism and capitalist, class exploitation. This question encourages students to reflect on this, exploring the interconnections between different dimensions of inequality, which is a key theme within the Sociology A-level curriculum.

Time	Activity	Explanation
00.25–00.35	At 10:25 Narayan states that one of the goals of British Black Power was to challenge the idea that 'people of colour both in the UK and outside of the UK were often not seen as the main agents of history'. *What does it mean to be an 'agent of history'? Where else in your wider learning have you heard of this concept?*	This activity encourages students to use their critical thinking skills in examining the nature of social and historical 'facts', the perspectives of social history that are prioritized and those that are elided. This is a key topic of enquiry within the 'theory and methods' module of the Sociology A-level core curriculum. Students might draw connections between this concept and the 'silences of history' that are spoken about in 'The Haitian Revolution' talk, or the 'hidden histories' that are mentioned in the 'Indian Indenture' talk, or the chapter on diasporas of the Global South.
00.35–00.45	Watch the talk from 15:03 to 18:30. *What do you think is the relationship between social activism and academia?*	Narayan explains that part of the legacy of the British Black Power movement has been to influence subsequent anti-racist groups and some academic literature, such as Stuart Hall et al's *Policing the Crisis*. This activity encourages students to think about the connections between social activism and social history, and the role played by academia in this relationship. This in turn challenges students to think about the contexts within which academic knowledge is produced and be reflexive about their own learning.
00.45–00.55	At 18:34 Narayan explains that British Black Power and its legacy are part of a 'global revolt against anti-racism'. *What is the relationship between the aims of the British Black Power movement and global exploitation?*	This activity asks students to think about the connections between the British Black Power movement and global anti-racist struggles. Students might bring in their learning about global anticolonial activism and discourse from other talks, such as the 'Decolonization' section.
00.55–01.00	Drawing on what you have learned throughout this session, answer the following question: *What can anti-racist movements today learn from the British Black Power movements of the 1960s and 1970s?*	This question acts as a summary activity, prompting students to draw together their learning from this talk and apply it to a contemporary context. Students might reflect on Narayan's arguments that British Black Power reveals the importance of connecting struggles against domestic racism with struggles against international capitalist exploitation. This activity may work well as a group discussion.

This worksheet was developed by Isabel Sykes.

20

(Un)archiving Black British Feminisms

Alexandra Wanjiku Kelbert

Objectives

- This chapter introduces the history of Black feminist organizing in Britain as having been marginalized within two movements, namely British feminism and anti-racist history.

- It offers a frame through which to critically think about what we do not know, and why, about the history of feminist organizing in Britain by connecting the process of history-making to structural power.

- It discusses how Black feminist thought enriches feminist practice.

- It highlights some of the archival methods by which we may bring to the surface marginalized histories and it uses these to rethink both feminist history and feminist practice today.

Introduction

HMT *Empire Windrush* docked in the Tilbury docks in Essex on 22 June 1948, marking the beginning of a wave of migration often referred to as the 'Windrush era' and with it the dawn of modern British race relations. The ship's records, now kept in the National Archives, account for 1,027 passengers, 684 men, 257 women, and 86 children under 12. By the 1950s, equal numbers of women and men from all over the empire were entering Britain. Yet, the contribution of racially minoritized women to British feminist and anti-racist history has often been overlooked.

As Britain sought to recruit cheap labour from its colonies, the political drive for migration, often framed through the lens of economic necessity, ignored the gendered and racialized nature of the labour market into which these Commonwealth citizens entered. In the 1950s and 1960s, racially minoritized women, primarily from the Caribbean and the Indian subcontinent, found themselves situated in a complex, multilayered web of social, political, and economic inequalities, in a society structured by racism and sexism (see Anitha, Chapter 8, this volume).

Immigration law and welfare policy reinforced the assumption that migrant workers were always men. Migrant women were usually thought to come as either wives or children, rather than as workers in their own right (Mirza 1997: 7). Upon arrival, many women found that doors were closed to them due to racism and sexism. Although skilled, many had to find work where they could, often for lower wages. Thus, Asian women worked primarily in the private sector, in factories and production lines, while Caribbean and African women found work in public services and care industries, including the newly created National Health Service, but often in nursing roles below their skill level (Bryan et al 1985).

In the 1960s and 1970s, British race relations were characterized by a two-part consensus. On the one hand, from the late 1960s there was an increased commitment to reduce racism and promote 'tolerance' through the Race Relations Acts of 1965 and 1968 which aimed to eradicate racial discrimination. On the other hand, successive governments embraced a politics of immigration control premised on racism, most notably with the Immigration Act of 1971. It was in this paradox that the Black[1] feminists organizing in the 1970s to 1990s found themselves.

By the 1970s, resistance to both racism and sexism was coalescing into organized movements. The Women's Liberation Movement, which sought to address the oppression of women in the home, workplace, and broader society, became a prominent force in Britain. However, the movement often struggled to integrate the specific concerns of racially minoritized women, ignoring racism internally and rejecting it as an agenda for political action (Amos et al 1984). Similarly, Black women's significant contribution to anti-racist and Black Power groups was often undermined by men who both 'set the agenda and stole the show' (Bryan et al 1985: 144). These barriers and exclusions did not deter many Black women from throwing themselves into community activism both in the women's movement and in anti-racist struggles.

Still, in stark contrast with other progressive struggles from the 1970 to 1990s, such as the miners' strike or the Greenham Common occupation, very few books and official records came out of the heyday of Black feminist organizing in Britain. For Terese Jonsson (2020), dominant historical narratives of feminism continue to construct British feminism as 'a story that belongs to white women' in a way which still shapes feminist theory and practice today.

How does the history of Black women's feminist activism in the 1970s through to the 1990s challenge this claim that British feminism belongs to White women? How might we move this history from the margins to the centre? This chapter seeks to answer these questions and explore the development of Black British feminism and the often-overlooked histories and achievements of its key movements. The chapter also examines how Black feminism challenges dominant feminist narratives, and how it forges distinct modes of resistance and solidarity. Crucially, by pushing back on the notion that history and history-making are neutral processes, and by placing archives within a broader structure of power, this chapter offers a framework through which to account for Black women's organizing in Britain. In so doing, it also remedies the gaps in social sciences and historical research.

Black British feminist organizing

The 1970s in Britain marked a vibrant period of anti-racist and feminist organizing, as both movements gained momentum and became more visible. Collective action, grassroots campaigns, and significant protests brought issues of race and gender into the national consciousness, reshaping the social and political landscape of Britain. Yet, both anti-racist and feminist groups in Britain, while advocating for justice and equality, often ended up marginalizing racialized women.

Within feminist movements, the focus was predominantly on the issues facing White, middle-class women. The feminist movement of the time sidelined the unique struggles of racially minoritized women who were facing both gender and racial discrimination. Similarly, within mixed-gender anti-racist and Black Power groups, the concerns of racially minoritized women were often overshadowed by those of men. Issues of gender-based violence, reproductive rights, and sexual exploitation were frequently ignored or dismissed. Some were suspicious of women's liberation objectives, seeing feminism as White women's issue, in conflict with the aims of Black liberation. In this way, racialized women found themselves at the intersection of two oppressive systems – racism and sexism.

Many racially minoritized women chose to keep organizing alongside men, finding ways to push back on the expectations that they should always make the teas and take the minutes. Some specifically carved out women's spaces within mixed-gender organizations, with members of the Black Liberation Front setting up the group's Black Women's Action Committee in 1970. Study groups and women-only caucuses enabled Black women to explore their gendered experiences in relation to the wider struggle for liberation within the Black Power movement. Others, like Southall Black Sisters, decided to create their own groups to provide women with safe spaces in which to address often taboo issues within their communities.

In this context, throughout the 1970s and 1980s, racialized women in Britain began to forge their own political organizations, autonomous from both White feminist and Black Power groups. The formation of groups such as the Organization of Women of African and Asian Descent (OWAAD), which was founded in 1978 by African women active in the African Students' Union, marked a pivotal moment in Black British feminism. As an umbrella group, OWAAD united women from across the African, Caribbean, Asian, and South American diasporas, aiming to challenge both racism and sexism simultaneously.

OWAAD and the organizations that it comprised showed that women were not merely 'mothers of sons and carers of husbands' (Mirza 1997: 8) but political agents capable of engagement and subversion. OWAAD also demonstrated the importance of 'political Blackness' as an organic political consciousness for Black feminist activists. Indeed, 'Black' was embraced by many in the wider anti-racist movement as a political and anti-colonial alliance uniting people from across the diaspora in their struggle against racism, imperialism, and capitalism.

The emergence of a Black women's movement forced White feminists[2] to take note of the fact that the Women's Liberation Movement was set against the backdrop of not only anti-racist struggles in Britain, but the remaking of the British nation in the wake of African, Caribbean, and Asian decolonization. Thus, many of the key texts written by Black feminists at the time called for White feminists to engage with the complexity of this context. Some specifically called attention to White women's entanglement with Britain's history of imperialism both as settlers or colonial oppressors, and as beneficiaries of colonial wealth (Carby 1982; Amos et al 1984).

White British feminists advocated for a vision of 'universal sisterhood' suggesting that all women shared the same experiences. This overlooked the intersectional realities of race, class, and colonialism. Hazel Carby's (1982) influential essay, 'White Woman Listen!', pointed out the limitations of this narrow feminist framework and called out the invisibility of Black women in White women's theories. In this sense, Black feminist thought's greatest contribution was to draw attention to the ways in which racialized, gendered, and classed structures interact to position women differently in relation to racial and patriarchal systems of oppression.

This pushback on the notion of White womanhood as the universal experience informed Black British feminist campaigning. Recognizing that women's experiences were varied, Black and Asian feminists addressed different forms of oppression from those highlighted by White feminists. For example, where White feminists were campaigning for greater access to contraception or abortion, Black women were fighting against forced sterilization through the Depo-Provera drug, and Asian women were calling attention to state-sanctioned sexual assault in the form of mandatory 'virginity testings' conducted by immigration officials in Heathrow airport. Black women's organizations took up the issues of race, class, and gender together, with groups tackling sickle cell anaemia, the experiences of racialized children in a racist education system, prisoners' rights, immigration law, deportations as well as supporting decolonization struggles.

As an umbrella organization OWAAD published a newsletter, FOWAAD, to ensure 'that women from OWAAD knew what other women were doing and could be called upon to give practical support' (Brixton Black Women's Group 1984: 84). Being made up of different kinds of groups, with a range of interests and priorities, was both a strength and a weakness. Eventually, some contradictions started to surface, notably around the relative importance of decolonizing struggles versus local anti-racist struggles, sexuality, the role of men in the movement, the political principles of Afro-Asian unity, and the notion of 'feminism' in itself.

Reflecting on the demise of OWAAD after its five years of activity, members of the Brixton Black Women's Group argued that the organization struggled to deal with the differences that existed between groups and members in the pursuit of unity (1984: 86). Indeed, these internal conflicts revealed the diversity of thought within the Black British feminist movement, but also the ways in which organizing could be obstructed by ideological disagreements. While some of the history of Black British feminism is captured in historical narratives of British feminism, many of its smaller more localized groups and organizations remain invisible. In order to make sense of this gap, it is important to understand how historical narratives are produced and reproduced. This is why I next turn my attention to the issue of archives.

Archives as agents

Since at least the 1960s and 1970s, social scientists have been questioning whether it is truly possible to conduct research that is completely objective and free from bias (Ladner 1973; Hill Collins 1990). This questioning arose in the context of the increased influence of marginalized voices and the understanding that knowledge itself is shaped by power. Post-colonial scholars in particular have highlighted how dominant ideas in the social sciences and humanities are rooted in Eurocentric histories (Bhambra 2007). A key area of focus became understanding how histories, historical narratives, and memories are created, recognizing history-making as a political process where meaning is constructed.

Haitian anthropologist Michel-Rolph Trouillot (1995) explored how power influences the way history is written and known. He argued that access to the tools and platforms necessary to creating historical narratives is uneven. This unevenness leads to a gap between 'what happened' and 'what is said to have happened'. This gap forces us to interrogate the role of power in shaping our understanding of the past. Trouillot pushed back on the idea that historians simply 'reveal the past' (1995: 5), suggesting that their work is also influenced by power. Similarly, we can ask whether social scientists can truly document events without being affected by relations of power.

Archives and archival materials are some of the tools available to researchers to document and understand the past. Reflecting on Trouillot's work, Hazel Carby emphasizes the entanglement of historical narratives with power. She argues this entanglement is visible not just in the archives, but in the very processes through which we decide what counts as 'authentic' history (Carby 2015: xii). Carby goes further and suggests that archives often present a simplified and consensual version of history, obscuring the conflicts and complexity that existed (2015: xiii). This is echoed in the work of Ann Laura Stoler on Dutch colonial archives.

For Stoler, colonial archives are not just biased or inaccurate, but sites where the tensions and anxieties of colonial rule were concentrated (2008: 20). In that sense, it is important to interrogate who creates, controls, and maintains archives, and how they do so. Stoler's work shows us that by carefully and critically examining the archives it becomes possible to find hidden stories, even the ones colonial powers tried to hide. Stoler found hidden stories in unexpected places, which she calls 'archival asides': in the small details, casual sentences, photographs, and in the footnotes of official documents.

The historical and sociological research on the heyday of Black women's activism in Britain between the early 1970s and early 1990s provides a case in point to analyse how historical narratives are produced and how archival materials are entangled with power.

Hidden histories and marginalized voices

British sociologists and historians have largely ignored Black women's organizations (Sudbury 1998: 13). One way to look at this is to look at archives and examine in detail what has been documented, and what has *not*, all the while remembering that Black women's activism occupies a marginalized strand of both feminist (Jonsson

2020) and anti-racist history (Amos et al 1984; Bryan et al 1985; Grewal et al 1998). In her doctoral research, Julia Sudbury sought to explain the absence of Black women's organization from mainstream sociological and historical research (1998: 13). Specifically, she argued that Black women's activism had been overlooked and neglected by the existing methodologies of most social scientific research.

Indeed, while other progressive struggles from the same era are more widely documented, very few books came out of the heyday of Black feminism in Britain. In addition to Sudbury's 'other kinds of dreams' (1998), only a very small number of publications have come to form the bulk of accounts of racially minoritized women's experiences in Britain. The most well-known and widely distributed monographs in this regard are Heidi Mirza's *Black British Feminism* (1997), the recently republished *Heart of the Race* by former members of the Brixton Black Women's Group, Beverley Bryan, Stella Dadzie, and Suzanne Scafe (1985), and, more recently, Lawrence & Wishart's new *Radical Black Women* series spotlighting the contributions of Gerlin Bean and Amy Ashwood Garvey.

Unsurprisingly, most accounts of Black women's historical activism in Britain tend to be London-centric and primarily focused on larger organizations. The questions raised previously around who creates archives and what is seen authentic or worthy of being archived mean that the records of many Black women's organizations, which folded during the 1970s or early 1980s, were too often lost, scattered among activists' personal belongings, and discarded. For this reason, we are more likely to be familiar with the histories of the groups who kept meticulous records of their activities, including OWAAD's conscientious documentation through its newsletter and the published writings of members of the Brixton Black Women's Group or Southall Black Sisters. This explains the tendency to reduce Black women's activism to a handful of groups. Further, in London, the most well-known groups tend to be groups which received funding from the Greater London Council, including the three aforementioned organizations.

In this sense, we see an unevenness in the production of historical narratives around Black women's organizing akin to the gap Trouillot highlighted between 'what happened' and 'what is said to have happened'. This gap reproduces existing power differentials and unevenness with White feminist organizations and with male-led anti-racist organizations. These groups are more likely to be known and remembered, and in turn more likely to inform present-day activist thought and practice. With this in mind, what can sociological research do to challenge this unevenness? The following section aims to provide elements of answers by focusing respectively on, first, Julia Sudbury's unique methods to research women of colour's organizations in her book *Other Kinds of Dreams*, and, second, an oral history project, conducted by Mumbi Nkonde and I, thereby putting forward further tools to remedy, if only ever in part, some of the epistemic gaps in the histories of women of colour organizing.

'Other Kinds of Dreams'

In her doctoral research, Julia Sudbury (1998) sought to explain and remedy the absence of Black women's organizations from mainstream sociological and historical research. She highlighted not just the existence but also the diversity of Black women's organizations. Sudbury carefully crafted a research method to study Black women's organizations. Her interest in Black women's specific experiences and views about their identities as well as organizational debates meant that she prioritized face to face contact over other methods. She relied on collecting written material, conducting in-depth interviews, and participant observations.

Drawing on personal knowledge and written sources such as directories of community organizations and community newspapers (for example, the *Caribbean Times*), Sudbury identified 60 Black women's organizations in the UK. As she did not want to reproduce some of the biases prevalent in social scientific research, Sudbury developed a grid which incorporated the key variables she wanted to study. Sudbury used the grid to identify a range of organizations in terms of geographical location, funding, group membership, sexual orientation, key activity, and date established.

In this way, she selected 12 organizations to focus on, reflecting the diversity of Black women's organizations: Akina Mama Wa Afrika (London), Black Lesbian Group (London), Black Women for Wages for Housework (London), Black Women's Resource Centre (Sheffield), Cambridge Black Women's Support Group, Liverpool Black Sisters, Muslim Women's Helpline (London), Onyx (New Addington), Osaba Women's Centre (Coventry), Panahghar (Coventry), Shakti Women's Aid (Edinburgh), and Wai Yin Chinese Women's Society (Manchester).

While we should not position her work as exhaustive, Sudbury's research is useful in articulating an alternative to the dominant ways of seeing and doing research which have typically erased the experiences and contributions of Black women activists. Her work has allowed the surfacing of the diversity of Black women's organizations in the UK.

'Unarchiving British Black Feminisms' oral history project

In June 2018, Mumbi Nkonde and I started a research project aimed at uncovering some of the hidden histories of women of colour organizing in the 1970s–1990s, with some funding from the Feminist Review Trust. We were privileged to be part of a wider network of Black women radical archivists who helped to refine some of our thinking and hypotheses from the onset. Our starting point was informed by some of the work that had been done to archive the histories of radical Black activists such as the Remembering Olive Morris Collective and the 'Heart of the Race' oral history project at the Black Cultural Archives. In the course of the project, we identified and resorted to four tools which helped us bring new histories to light.

First, through conversations with people in our community, we discovered the work of the Abasindi Women's Co-operative (previously known as the Manchester Black Women's Cooperative). This group was instrumental in local anti-deportation campaigns as well as providing cultural and educational services in Moss Side (Jones and Watt 2015). It was a significant part of Manchester's Black feminist history, yet it had been largely missing from dominant feminist histories as well as anti-racist histories. Second, a conversation with an archivist helped us to generate new insights into the decision-making processes behind the curation of some of the archives of the Black women's movement. This revealed to us why some stories had come to light while others had remained hidden from the public eye.

Third, Ann Laura's Stoler's work on colonial archives gave us a frame through which to think about ways to find stories hidden in the archives. In the same way that Stoler seeks out 'archival asides', we were also able to look for these asides in existing archives of Black feminist organizing. For example, a deeper engagement with the Black Cultural Archives 'Heart of the Race: Oral Histories of the Black Women's Movement' revealed a group we had not come across in previous research. In one of the oral history interviews, Judith Lockhart, a former member of OWAAD, makes a passing mention of a woman named 'Mia', saying: 'Mia was involved in East London Black Women's Organization.'

This casual sentence shed light on the existence of another group, the East London Black Women's Association (ELBWO). From there, word searches in the oral history database for 'East', 'East London' and 'ELBWO' revealed more passing mentions of the group. Further engagement with the testimonies, and a conversation with Stella Dadzie, former member of OWAAD confirmed that a woman named Ama Gueye was a co-founder of ELBWO. A few weeks later, we were sitting in Ama's living room, listening to her stories, and sifting through her personal archives of ELBWO, the few fragments remaining after a fire engulfed the organization's building in 2004.

Lastly, in another almost accidental encounter, a close read of the footnotes of Nyhagen Predelli et al's book *Majority-Minority Relations in Contemporary Women's Movement* revealed the existence of another group. The footnote simply stated: 'In 1986, Afro-Caribbean members of Southall Black Sisters left to form the Southall Black Women's Centre' (Nyhagen Predelli et al 2012: 276). This easily missed footnote, just like the brief asides and passing mentions of ELBWO, reveal a pattern where Black women's organizations and achievements are in the margins rather than at the centre of dominant feminist and anti-racist histories and methodologies. Such engagements with 'archival asides' are examples of how we have begun to remedy Black women's organizations history and status in the feminist movement from being an afterthought.

Through oral histories and the meticulous combing of existing archives and grassroots records, we were able to piece together fragments of the stories of Black women's movements which were missing from the historical record. While surfacing the vital work done by groups such as Abasindi, ELBWO, and the Southall Black Women's Centre around immigration, reproductive rights, and local community organizing goes some way towards remedying the gaps in the narrative production of Black women's political history in Britain, it is also a reminder of what is missing from dominant historical accounts of British feminist and anti-racist histories.

Conclusion

From the 1970s, Black British feminist groups organized autonomously to challenge Black women's experiences of sexism and racism. Black feminists fought two battles simultaneously: one against male oppression, and the other for the liberation of all Black people. They campaigned against the issues affecting their communities, from racist policing to domestic violence, from deportations to the exclusion of their children from schools. Crucially, from this movement came a pushback against dominant feminist narratives centred around a White experience of womanhood which failed to account for the intersectional realities of race, class, and colonialism. The Black feminist movement also pushed back against the perception that Black feminist politics constituted a threat to Black liberation, showing that it was possible to challenge racism, sexism, and capitalism simultaneously.

Still, even today, the histories and achievements of Black women's organizations are critically missing from the retelling of British feminist history, and – albeit to a lesser extent – from British anti-racist history. Even within what is already a marginal history, organizations like Abasindi and the Southall Black Women's Centre remain hidden in the footnotes, in the margins of history. These gaps or silences in our archives and our movement histories teach us two things. First, a reminder that simply because we do not know about these struggles does not mean they did not happen; this should also lead us to consider that perhaps the gaps are in themselves a cause for enquiry. Second, knowing that there are marginal histories is an encouragement to do our own research outside of established academic and historical silos.

By pushing back on the notion that history and history-making is a neutral process, and by placing archives within a broader structure of power, this chapter offered a framework through which to account for and perhaps remedy the gaps in sociological and historical research around Black women's organizing in Britain. Importantly, in our attempts to fill those gaps it is crucial to remain attentive to the fact that the legacy of Black British feminism is complex, not only in terms of its theoretical contributions but also in how it has shaped the political landscape. As we continue to uncover and engage with these histories, we can draw valuable lessons about the complexities of solidarity, coalition-building, and the role of conflict in building robust and inclusive movements.

As we seek out Black feminist histories in our communities and our archives, we must remain vigilant, questioning whose histories are remembered, whose voices are centred, and how these histories might help us to reconstruct dominant paradigms around race, class, gender, and nation in Britain today. In September 2024, 20 years after a fire destroyed their building, ELBWO reopened its doors to the community in Newham, showing that Black women's organizations and many of the women who built and sustained them have carried on providing vital community work. It is a reminder that Black feminist history is still being written.

Notes

[1] In this chapter, I use 'Black' to refer to people of African, Asian, Latin American, and Middle Eastern descent in Britain. While the term 'people of colour' is widely used today, it fails to capture the fact that 'Blackness' as a political identity was an anti-colonial and anti-imperial rather than a racial one. Political Blackness was always fraught, many disagreeing with the framing already then, and so when appropriate I will refer specifically to 'African and Caribbean women' (see Narayan, Chapter 19, this volume).

2   It is important to note that there is a difference between 'White feminists' and 'feminists who are White'. The term 'White feminism' is a critique of a form of feminism centred around the experiences and struggles of White women, which often overlooks the experiences of racialized women. For more, see Hazel Carby's 'White Woman Listen!' (1982) and bell hooks' *Ain't I A Woman: Black Women and Feminism* (1981).

References

Amos, V., Lewis, G., Mama, A., and Parmar, P. 1984. 'Many Voices, One Chant: Black Feminist Perspectives', *Feminist Review,* 17: 1–2.

Bhambra, G. 2007. *Rethinking Modernity: Postcolonialism and the Sociological Imagination.* Palgrave Macmillan.

Brixton Black Women's Group 1984. 'Black Women Organizing', *Feminist Review,* 17: 84–89.

Bryan, B., Dadzie, S., and Scafe, S. 1985. *Heart of the Race: Black Women's Lives in Britain.* Virago.

Carby, H. 1982. 'White Woman Listen! Black Feminism and the Boundaries of Sisterhood', in Centre for Critical Cultural Studies (ed), *The Empire Strikes Back: Race and Racism in 70s Britain,* Hutchingson, pp 211–234.

Carby, H. 2015. 'Foreword', in M.-R. Trouillot, *Silencing the Past: Power and the Production of History,* pp xi–xiii. Beacon Press.

Grewal, S., Kay, J., Landor, L., Lewis, G., and Parmar, P. 1998. *Charting the Journey: Writings by Black and Third World Women.* Sheba Press.

Hill Collins, P. 1990. *Black Feminist Thought: Knowledge, Consciousness, and Politics of Empowerment.* Unwin Hyman.

hooks, b. 1981. *Ain't I A Woman: Black Women and Feminism.* Pluto Press.

Jones, A. and Watt, D. 2015. *Catching Hell and Doing Well: Black Women in the UK – the Abasindi Cooperative.* Trentham Books.

Jonsson, T. 2020. *Innocent Subjects: Feminism and Whiteness.* Pluto Books.

Ladner, J. 1973. *The Death of White Sociology.* Random House.

Mirza, H.S. 1997. *Black British Feminism: A Reader.* Routledge.

Nyhagen Predelli, L., Halsaa, B., Thun, C., and Sandu, A. 2012. *Majority-Minority Relations in Contemporary Women's Movements: Strategic Sisterhood.* Palgrave Macmillan.

Stoler, A.L. 2008. *Along the Archival Grain: Thinking through Colonial Ontologies.* Princeton University Press.

Sudbury, J. 1998. *'Other Kinds of Dreams': Black Women's Organizations and the Politics of Transformation.* Routledge.

Trouillot, M.-R. 1995. *Silencing the Past: Power and the Production of History.* Beacon Press.

Video lecture

Kelbert, A.W. 2021. *(Un)archiving Black British Feminisms,* Connected Sociologies Curriculum Project. https://thesociologicalreview.org/projects/connected-sociologies/curriculum/british-citizenship-race-and-rights/unarchiving-black-british-feminisms/

QUESTIONS

1. How does Black British feminist history challenge dominant narratives of post-war Britain?

2. In what ways does Black British feminist thought and activism challenge White feminist theoretical claims to universal womanhood?

3. If history-making is a political process of meaning-making, how might we surface marginalized histories?

4. Why is it important to examine and make explicit the conditions of knowledge production?

Worksheet 20. (Un)archiving Black British Feminisms

This worksheet is designed to support AS and A-level teaching on the topics of culture and identity, globalization and global development, social differentiation, power and stratification, and research methods. In her online talk, Alexandra Kelbert details how Black British feminism has highlighted the ways in which racialized, gendered and classed inequalities intersect, in Britain and internationally. She explains how Black British feminist groups emerging in the 1970s challenged narratives of universal White womanhood purported by the Women's Liberation Movement, asking questions about the scope of feminist thought and the formation of feminist knowledge. The activities explore some contemporary legacies of Black British feminism, as well as its significance for sociological aims to uncover hidden histories and centre marginalized perspectives. This worksheet is designed for students with a good existing understanding of feminism and has links to Chapter 19 (Narayan on 'British Black Power').

Time	Activity	Explanation
00.00–00.05	To warm up, answer these questions: Who are feminists? What are their aims?	This warm-up activity may work well as a partner activity or open group discussion. The questions are broad to encourage students to think critically about some preconceptions and assumptions around feminism and its aims. Students may identify some well-known historical feminist movements and figures, and discuss aims related to gender equality. The subsequent activities are designed to broaden students' understandings of feminism, in terms of how gender inequalities relate to class and race, and to challenge dominant narratives of feminism's history.
00.05–00.10	Recap of understandings of culture and identity.	It may be useful to remind students of some of the relationships between different identities, particularly ethnicity and gender.
00.10–00.15	At 6:10 Kelbert explains that the Women's Liberation Movement in the 1970s put forward an idea of 'universal sisterhood'. How and why do Black British feminisms in this period problematize the idea of 'universal sisterhood?'	Kelbert explains that Black British feminism exposed the fact that the Women's Liberation Movement had very little engagement with racial power and turned a critical lens to the feminist production of knowledge, challenging the notion of White womanhood as the universal feminist experience. This activity encourages students to think critically about dominant narratives of feminism and its history. It also gets students thinking about the concept of intersectionality in considering the relationship between different dimensions of inequality. This is a core theme within the 'social differentiation, power and stratification' topic of the A-level curriculum.

Time	Activity	Explanation
00.15–00.25	Watch the talk from 7:17 to 9:52. Then, reflect on your notes from the warm-up activity. *In what ways do the aims of Black British feminism reflect your understanding of feminism? What are the differences?*	These questions ask students to reflect on the significance of Black British feminism's aims of drawing together racialized, gendered, and classed structures. Students may identify that well-known aims of feminism focus on gender, and they are encouraged to reflect on whether they had considered intersectional inequalities and oppressions within their initial definition. These questions facilitate the broadening of students' critical thinking skills around these topics as the session progresses.
00.25–00.30	At 18:30 Kelbert talks about the importance of asking 'how we know what we know'. *What does this mean? Why is it important for sociologists, and other academics, to ask this question?*	By asking students to think about *how* knowledge is produced, this activity draws on key themes within the A-level Sociology curriculum, including thinking about sources of data, ethical considerations within research design and conduct, the relationship between theory and methods, and questions surrounding the establishment of 'social facts'. Students are asked to consider the significance of how history is constructed, how social narratives are formed, and by whom. Students might make connections to other sessions on this course which draw attention to hidden and elided perspectives.
00.30–00.40	Watch the talk from 18:44 to 22:18. *What are the methods Kelbert uses in the 'Unarchiving Black British Feminisms' project? How do these contribute to the recovery of hidden histories?*	Kelbert discusses her oral histories work in which she draws on personal connections and engagements with existing projects to uncover marginal histories. In this activity, students are expected to draw on their existing knowledge of different research methods to critically evaluate the methods used in this project. In considering how oral history work might contribute to the uncovering of histories, students might draw connections to other talks on this course concerned with the recovery of marginalized perspectives.
00.40–00.50	Watch the talk from 25:15 to 26:48. *What is the legacy of the Black British feminist organizations of the 1970s? What can we learn from these groups today?*	This activity asks students to apply what they have learned about the historical development of Black British feminisms to a contemporary context. Students might draw on Black British feminisms' aims of bringing together intersectional forms of inequality. They might draw links between these aims and the legacies of the British Black Power movement discussed in Chapter 19.
00.50–01.00	Drawing on what you have learned throughout this session, answer the following question: *How might sociologists continue the work of recovering or accessing Black British feminist knowledge and stories? What methods might we use?*	This concluding activity challenges students to go beyond the material in thinking independently about different sociological research methods and practical, theoretical and ethical considerations that might be relevant to this topic. Students might draw inspiration from Kelbert's oral history work, or other qualitative methods. As a starting point, it may be useful to direct them to Kelbert's encouragement (in the final two minutes of her talk) to allow research to be guided by methods, think about whose voices are heard in academic material and whose are missing, and to be attentive to the methodologies employed by sociologists.

This worksheet was developed by Isabel Sykes.

21

Modes of Integration, Multiculturalism, and National Identities

Tariq Modood

Objectives

- This chapter shows that integration requires a macro-level discussion of citizenship and national identity as well as 'difference'; there are different takes on national citizenship and each leads to a different understanding of integration.

- It counters the view that a free-floating cosmopolitanism is better than a politics based on rooted communities and their identities and argues that multiculturalism is a form of inclusive belonging to the national.

- It also shows that while earlier multiculturalists and anti-racists had a narrow understanding of religion, specifically Muslims (and their relationship to racism), the inclusion of Muslims is central to questions about integration in Western Europe today.

- Through a focus on migration and multiculturalism, it raises questions about what equal citizenship means in this post-colonial, ethno-racial, and ethno-religious context.

Introduction

The topic of multiculturalism, and its relation to integration and national identity, has become very important in many countries, such as the United States, Canada, Australia, and in Western Europe, including Britain; namely, in countries that experienced significant migration from former colonies and the Global South more generally after the Second World War such that those migrants and their children and grandchildren are now citizens of these countries. This significant, historic phenomenon that is deeply changing these countries, certainly their ethnic composition, raises the question of what equal citizenship means in this post-colonial, ethno-racial, and ethno-religious context.

While the integration of post-immigration minority groups is a much-discussed topic within the social sciences, especially in policy studies, and is sometimes even discussed in relation to multiculturalism, the two – integration and multiculturalism – are too often taken to be antithetical to each other. It is therefore important to relate the two to each other and discuss the two within a single theoretical framework of understanding and evaluation. The same point could be made about multiculturalism and the national, where the latter includes phenomena such as national identity and its adaptation to include newly settled minorities or new ethno-racial, ethno-cultural, and ethno-religious formations. This means that we need to refuse to define nationalism understood in terms – as is all too common – of cultural homogeneity and majoritarian populism and the like.

Political and academic discourses are divided between those that emphasize and value 'difference' and those which do the same with integration. This is usually based on narrow conceptions of integration as something that minority individuals must do or extending that to a focus on overcoming discrimination in, for example, the labour market, healthcare, criminal justice, electoral politics, and so on. It thereby misses that, on the one hand, integration cannot simply be discussed at an individual or even sectoral level, and on the other hand, that full integration requires some degree of subjective identification with the society or country as a whole. This chapter goes beyond such limited approaches by working at a macro-level and outlining four modes of integration – assimilation, individualist integration, cosmopolitanism, and multiculturalism – as four different political-conceptual understandings of citizenship. This is done in an explicitly normative-sociological way and shows how multiculturalism is an 'ism' that unites a respect for difference and a sense of national identity and belonging as a form of citizenship. In this way, the chapter counters a misconception that multiculturalism is about separate communities, is anti-national and anti-integration, relativistic, and not based on universal values. It also challenges the view that somehow a free-floating cosmopolitanism is better than a politics based on rooted communities and their identities.

Multiculturalist integration

Let's begin with integration. What I have to say about integration connects with but is not identical to how this rather rhetorical and political term is used by some others, including those who reject the term. Integration presupposes 'difference', that is to say some groups of citizens are identified as being different in some relation or other because integration or multiculturalism is about relations between citizens and citizens, and citizens and their polity or state or country (Kymlicka 1995; Modood 2013 [2007]). The difference in question is to do with race, ethnicity, and religion, broadly speaking what is referred to as 'culture' to distinguish it from socio-economic characteristics like class, which for a long time tended to dominate social analysis and political organization in most of the countries mentioned previously (see Narayan, Chapter 19, this volume). To talk about integration is then to focus on the non-economic identity of some citizens and on the relations between different identities in a citizenship context or in a polity.

Identity here has two aspects: what might be called 'from the outside in' and 'from the inside out'. By the former I mean how people from outside that group, especially minority groups, are perceived and treated. Typically, in the case of minorities, the outsiders are the majority or the dominant group or the long-settled group and see the minority in terms of negative or demeaning images, stereotypes, and generalization; minorities can thus in a real sense have certain identities imposed upon them by the majority or by dominant groups. It could be a colour identity, like Black or Brown or Red (as in 'Red Indians'). Or it could be some kind of distorted religious identity, based not on how that group understands its religion but how an outsider perceives it, compares it to their own and deems it inferior or heretical. Whatever it might be, a minority will be aware of that external 'packaging', indeed it cannot ignore that it is in a way part of their social location and their social identity.

Identity, however, has another aspect too, what I referred to as 'from the inside out': that is to say that all people, all groups have a sense of who they are as a group, have some sense about themselves, their own understanding of their own identity. To say that it comes from the inside is to say it comes from the group itself and they project that, insofar as they have the power to do so, in their relationships with others, including the shared social and public space in which they may be a minority. They may try to change that public space so that it better reflects their own identity rather than the imposed identity which could be quite distorting or inferiorizing.

Multiculturalism is a politics about these relationships and efforts to resist and change outsider identities, and the social relations based on them, in favour of insider identities; in the language of multiculturalism, the political project is to seek 'recognition', inclusion, and accommodation of the insider identity while opposing the identity that is imposed upon the minority. 'Recognition', adapted from Hegel, was made into a multiculturalist concept by Charles Taylor (1994), who characterized minorities as often suffering 'misrecognition' and in the contemporary period as 'struggling for recognition', seeking dignity and equality. This may be linked to economic relations but was distinct from them, consisting as it does in wanting to be accepted as a group that you understand yourself to be. Recognition here then means not just equality between individuals or non-discrimination, uniformity of treatment, but recognition of groups, of group difference, of equality across cultural difference within an equal citizenship.

Multiculturalism or multiculturalist integration, then, is about recognizing the identity of a group, the group as it is or aspires to be, not as it is created by an outside force, and including that identity and accommodating it into the shared public space. The recognition of a group, then, has an identarian or symbolic aspect, including symbolic inclusion with the national community, adapted as necessary (Chin and Levey 2023). It also entails institutional and legal aspects, including institutional and legal changes, to include the recognized group with practical effects entailed in the realization of meaningful recognition and new majority–minority relations. Because multicultural integration is two-way, it means that citizens cannot be divided into givers of recognition only or takers of recognition only. So multiculturalism is not just about majority recognition of minorities but the mutual recognition of all sub-groups of citizens and their right to belong to the body of citizens.

We can further understand the idea of multiculturalist integration by thinking of integration as having three levels. From the bottom up, there is what we might call everyday cultural encounters; meetings in public places including the workplace but also parks and theatres and shopping malls and so on (Wise and Velayutham 2009). The second level is what I will call the sectoral or legal. It is the legal status that a person or group of people have, their rights, their position in the labour market, how they are treated in the labour market, issues around residential concentration, and so on. This second level is very broad and encompasses many different sectors of society but nevertheless integration is incomplete without a third level, which I call 'macro symbolic'.

By 'macro' I mean that it is at a higher or more general level than the first two levels and it is symbolic because it is to do with our ideas, with certain meanings and historical or societal narratives; basically, the kinds of things that hang on identities, with a sense or senses that a society or a country has of itself. For just as groups can have a sense of their identity, their distinctiveness, so similarly can a country. In a report on integration by a commission in Quebec, it was stated that 'the symbolic framework of integration (identity, religion, perception of the other, collective memory, and so on) is no less important than its functional or material framework' (Bouchard and Taylor 2008). It is at this level, this macro symbolic level, that the political theory of multiculturalism operates and makes its distinctive contribution to how to understand and achieve integration. To appreciate this, let us think of how integration at this level is differently conceptualized and politically argued about.

Four modes of integration

There are at least four modes of integration: assimilation, individualist integration, cosmopolitanism,[1] and multiculturalism. I have tried to capture their key characteristics in Table 21.1. The first column on the left-hand side describes the different things that the table tries to capture; the top row is called 'objects of policy', what you might call the targets of policy, what is it that the policy is aimed at or who is it aimed at? The rest of the table consists of the three concepts, instantly recognizable as the famous triad of the French revolution: liberty, equality, and fraternity, or, if you like, solidarity, which perhaps is a more common way of expressing it today. I am trying to show in this table that each of these four modes of integration are about citizenship and citizenship integration; this being a key argument of this chapter. Yet, they each work with these three concepts – liberty, equality, and fraternity – in different ways because they have quite different understandings of what these concepts mean and therefore of citizenship.

For assimilation the objects of policy are individuals, who need to be detached from groups marked by difference, so that they cease to be particularly different; indeed, over time, such groups cease to exist or at least stand out as different. For individualist integration, the focus is on individuals – marked by difference but also how they are treated by society, especially discriminatory practices of state and civil society. That is a significant addition but on the other hand because it is an individualist perspective it loses sight of the groups that were an object of assimilation. The next row of the

Table 21.1: Four modes of integration*

	Assimilation	Individualist-integration	Cosmopolitanism	Multiculturalism
Objects of policy	Individuals and groups marked by 'difference'.	Individuals marked by 'difference', especially their treatment by discriminatory practices of state and civil society.	Individuals marked by 'difference', especially their treatment by discriminatory practices of state and civil society, and societal ideas, especially of 'us' and 'them'.	Individuals and groups marked by 'difference', especially their treatment by discriminatory practices of state and civil society, and societal ideas, especially of 'us' and 'them'.
Liberty	Minorities must be encouraged to conform to the dominant cultural pattern.	Minorities are free to assimilate or cultivate their identities in private but are discouraged from thinking of themselves as minority, but rather as individuals.	Neither minority nor majority individuals should think of themselves as belonging to a single identity but be free to mix and match.	Members of minorities should be free to assimilate, to mix and match, or to cultivate group membership in proportions of their own choice.
Equality	Presence of difference provokes discrimination and so is to be avoided.	Discriminatory treatment must be actively eliminated so everyone is treated as an individual and not on the basis of difference.	Anti-discrimination must be accompanied by the dethroning of the dominant culture.	In addition to anti-discrimination the public sphere must accommodate the presence of new group identities and norms.
Fraternity	A strong, homogeneous national identity.	Absence of discrimination and nurturing of individual autonomy within a national, liberal democratic citizenship.	People should be free to unite across communal and national boundaries and should think of themselves as global citizens.	Citizenship and national identity must be remade to include group identities that are important to minorities as well as majorities; the relationship between groups should be dialogical rather than one of domination or uniformity.

Note: * In all cases it is assumed that a backdrop of liberal democratic rights and values operate. The features highlighted here are in addition to or interaction with them.
Source: Modood (2012b: 33)

table shows that the policy for cosmopolitanism is the same as individualist integration but to which it adds societal ideas, especially of 'us and them'. While individualist integration is much more focused on discrimination, on practices and institutions, cosmopolitanism here, in my understanding of this 'ism', adds the level of ideas, the macro-symbolic; an object of policy shared by multiculturalism.

Turning to the first of the three citizenship concepts, assimilation's take on liberty is that minorities must be encouraged to conform to the dominant cultural pattern. The individualist integration take on liberty is that minorities are free to assimilate or cultivate their identities in private – in private being an important qualification – but are to be discouraged from thinking of themselves as a minority. Rather they should think of themselves as individuals. Cosmopolitanism's take on liberty is that neither minority nor majority individuals should think of themselves as belonging to a single identity but be free to mix and match. In contrast, multiculturalism's take is that members of minorities should be free to assimilate, to mix and match, or, and this is where it is different from cosmopolitanism, to cultivate group membership. Group membership here does not mean a singular thing. Not only will people be members of a variety of groups (an ethnic group, a gender, a nationality, and so on) but they should be able to be members in their own way. For example, there is no one way of being Black or a woman.

Turning to the concept of equality, assimilation tends to the view that the presence of difference provokes discrimination and so is to be avoided and uniformity of treatment is the goal. The individualist integration take on equality is that discriminatory treatment must be actively eliminated so everyone is treated as an individual and not on the basis of difference. Cosmopolitanism insists that anti-discrimination must be accompanied by the dethroning of the dominant culture; multiculturalism here differs from it as taking the view that in addition to anti-discrimination, the public sphere must accommodate the presence of new group identities and norms. So, notice here that unlike cosmopolitanism, which of course multiculturalism in some ways is close to, multiculturalism is not just about cultural symbols and nor is it focused just on the majority culture as domination. Rather, it is focused on accommodation of group identities and norms rather than on doing something to the dominant culture per se; there is no underlying hostility to majority or dominant culture, only to its exclusionary character. Which means that some aspects of the majority culture will need to be reformed to make it properly accommodative and respectful of difference, so that it can be a shared culture.

Finally, turning to fraternity or solidarity, for assimilation the target is the goal of a strong homogeneous national identity, that is what solidarity is taken to consist of. That is, as it were, too much solidarity in the view of individualist integration, for which absence of discrimination and nurturing individual autonomy within a national liberal democratic citizenship is quite enough. Cosmopolitanism says people should be free to unite across communal and national boundaries and should think of themselves as global citizens so there is no particular sense that the national citizenship is to be privileged, it is just one among a number of identities, possible forms of citizenship, possible statuses and senses of belonging. For multiculturalism, fraternity or solidarity means citizenship and national identity must include group identities that are important to minorities as well as majorities, and if this is not the case with an existing citizenship or national identity, they must be remade to be so and the relationship between groups should be dialogical rather than one of domination or conformity to a single set of norms.

Religion and multiculturalism

These, then, are four modes of integration, and multiculturalism is one of them; not some kind of antithesis to integration per se. I hope I have adequately brought out the overlaps and the contrasts, in particular between liberal individualist integration and multiculturalism, on the one hand, and between cosmopolitanism and multiculturalism on the other. Given my interest in multiculturalism, I now proceed to consider in this section the relationship between multiculturalism and religion, and in the next section, the relationship between multiculturalism and the national.

The reason for discussing the integration of religious diversity here is that it was initially overlooked by theorists and policy makers alike, an omission thought natural across the political spectrum. One can see that liberal individualist integration supports anti-discrimination and toleration but does not recognize religious groups. Yet secular multiculturalism or anti-racism, which by its nature is group-centred, tends to regard religion as exceptional (Modood 2013 [2007]). While favouring the public recognition of racial, ethnic, gender, and sexual identities, it shares the liberal assumption that religion is uniquely to be kept a private matter and kept out of the public space or at least the political space. Hence in a major book by Iris Marion Young, a pioneer of the political theory of difference, the word, 'religion', does not even feature in the index (Young 1990). Similarly, the first country to promote multiculturalism as a policy, Canada, left religion peripheral. Yet post-immigration multiculturalism has come to be majorly challenged by religion, specifically the presence of Muslims and Islam.

This is not just to do with scale, Muslims being the largest non-White grouping in Western Europe and possibly being an absolute majority of all such groups in this region. Rather, there has been a series of high-profile controversies in relation to free speech, religious dress, and security. The question of free speech erupted with the anger against Salman Rushdie's novel, *The Satanic Verses*, in 1988 and other high-profile cases have included offence taken by some Muslims at the satirical cartoon portrayals of the Prophet Muhammad in a Danish newspaper and the French magazine, *Charlie Hebdo*. The year 1988 was also the year in which three French schoolgirls were banned from school because they refused to take off a Muslim headscarf (the 'hijab'), which initiated national and international debates that have led to restrictive legislation and workplace rules against such dress and the wearing of a Muslim face mask (the 'niqab') in a number of Western European countries (Modood 2012a). Security emerged as an issue in relation to concerns about the integration of Muslims in the 1990s but became dominant with the terrorist attack on the United States in 2001, known as '9/11' (because it occurred on 11 September) and a number of other such attacks or plots in Western Europe (see Holmwood, Chapter 22, and Fernandez, Chapter 23, this volume).

The multiculturalist integration, shared by liberals, cosmopolitans, and anti-racists, is to resist group blame and fight back against the tarring and stereotyping of all Muslims by a panicky and prejudicial reaction. A multiculturalist feature of this is to see that the ways that Muslims are othered or misrecognized is a form of racism, to recognize that there are different forms of racism, not just those that have a White–Black form or even are necessarily to do with biology but involve the othering of communities or the cultural attribute of communities, what might be called cultural racism (Modood 2020). This can certainly involve religion, as the historic persecution of Jews attests. Today, it is most prominent in the targeting of Muslims, anti-Muslim racism, which is commonly called Islamophobia. Regrettably, this multiculturalist understanding of racisms was absent among anti-racists until the 21st century and so, for example, Muslims in Britain were left without legal protection against racial or ethnic or religious discrimination (in contrast to Jews and Sikhs who were understood to be simultaneously religious and ethnic groups in UK law).

Going beyond other modes of integration, multiculturalists offer religious groups the same positive recognition as other groups. This means that Muslims should be able to present themselves as Muslims (according to their own understanding of what it means to be a Muslim) in schools, universities, workplaces, media, politics, and so on. Just as Gay Pride or Black History Month are aspects of positive recognition, so similarly Muslims and Islam (and for that matter, people of all faiths) should be part of British education, civil society, arts and culture, institutions, and the remaking of national identity. Such recognition requires political and institutional leadership, but it is not about endorsing (the truth of) a religion. It is about the endorsement of Muslims as co-citizens and of their religion as part of their group identity (if they so choose) and so a part of the country we are becoming or aspire to be. If, for example, a prime minister joins Muslims for a meal marking the end of a day of fasting (iftar) in Ramadan, she is not signalling the superiority of Islam over other religions any more than her attendance at a Black cultural event is an expression of the superiority of Black culture over any other culture. Yet, just as a multicultural nationalism must embrace Black identity within what it is to be British today, so it must embrace all religious minorities and not just the Church of England or Christianity, as has been recognized by the UK head of state, King Charles III.[2]

Multiculturalism and the national

This nicely brings us to the idea of the national and the national citizenship in relation to multiculturalism. Here, we have to begin with the important point that multiculturalism does not accept the possibility of a culturally neutral state in the way that, say, individualist integration does.[3] The multiculturalist says no state can be culturally neutral because each state, for instance, has to operate in a language or at least a limited number of languages, say, in English or Chinese, and people who do not know that language will obviously have their citizenship severely curtailed, they will not be able to participate in the life of the civil society or in the life of the polity in anything like the same way. It is not just language; for instance, each state enforces a public calendar which specifies the days that employers may require employees to work and days which they may not insist on or have to pay some recompense for employees willing to work on those days. In Britain, Monday to Friday constitutes the working week, which employers must treat differently from the weekend; moreover, we have 'bank holidays' which are national holidays and includes holidays at Christmas and Easter. Why Christmas, one might ask, and why not Eid or Diwali? These are parts of the way that a state is not culturally neutral but reflects a particular history and cultural heritage; reflected in Britain in one way and, say, in India in another, and in Saudi Arabia in another.

This does not necessarily imply a tight, monistic, centralized state. Multi-level governance or rights, which emphasize the importance of the local or the supranational, like the European Union or international conventions like the United Nations Declaration of Human Rights, are consistent with the point about no such thing as a culturally neutral state as well as the focus on the national state (Fossum et al 2024). Multi-level governance or rights are consistent with multiculturalism, indeed might further it, as long as it does not require the devaluing of national citizenship, which remains the primary source of liberty, equality, and solidarity because that is the level at which the most important laws are made, the most important protections for minorities and for citizens in general are debated, thrashed out, and passed in law, or overturned by a future government, and it is where decisions are made in terms of funding, whether that be to do with schools or healthcare or defence. Similarly, with the distribution of money across the regions, across cities versus rural areas, and so on. The national, then, is a core part of citizenship. While it is not the only level at which our citizenship is manifested and so multiculturalism must work with all levels at which our citizenship is manifested, we have to acknowledge that these levels are not of the same importance or of the same value to individuals.

Moreover, as we have seen, we have to recognize that citizenship, besides being about rights and obligations, like obligations to pay tax and so on, involves fraternity or solidarity, or if you like, community, a sense of belonging. All of which entails valuing of and a sense of concern for their citizenship and therefore also for other citizens that they do not have in the same way for people who are not their citizens. It explains why so many citizens have so much emotional, imaginative, and identity investment in their national citizenship and national identity. Indeed, it is the latter that carries much of this weight and which supports citizenship because for a lot of people citizenship just by itself is quite a sort of dry, legalistic matter to do with passports and for most people only getting activated around politics at very limited times, primarily elections or crises. Hence, this is why citizenship tends to coalesce around a sense of nationality.

A robust legal and political structure is essential to citizenship, as the skeleton is to a body, but most citizens feel they need something more emotional and imaginative, typically, the idea of a country, a national story, a national history. Whether it is kings and queens or the rise and fall of certain kinds of cultures or projects or political movements, people identify much more and more easily, and more people identify with a national sense of belonging than just a belonging to citizenship. So, while citizenship is the core of multiculturalism, especially as a normative idea, it nevertheless works with the idea of the national because the national gives citizenship an emotional and imaginative character and resonance that it does not have by itself. That then leads to what I might call the greatest challenge that multiculturalism presents to citizens and that is not just simply anti-discrimination, not even simply the inclusion and accommodation of cultural difference but of rethinking what it means to be a citizen and what it means to be a member of this country, of what it means to be British or French, Canadian or Indian, and so on.

Conclusion

Too often, integration is thought to be something that only exists at the level of the everyday or about individuals. While this is true of some modes of integration, we do not fully understand what is at stake without thinking about the macro-symbolic and group identities. Thus, multiculturalism as a mode of integration includes retelling the national story, remaking the national story so it explains how the current composition of citizens became part of the national story. In the case of Britain that would involve thinking about the British Empire and everything that goes with it because that explains how the ethnic minorities became British; they did not become so, or at least many of them, like my father coming from Pakistan, become British by arriving at Heathrow airport or entering the island of Britain. He was made British, as were our ancestors, through the British Empire – hence the slogan, 'we are here because you were there!'

We have to tell a story about Britain which explains that we have been part of the British story and we therefore explain the importance of multiculturalism today and of reshaping British identity to include us in a fully multiculturalist way. That has been the key idea of the chapter, recognizing that integration is a contested, multi-level idea, that multiculturalism is one mode of integration and how it differs from other modes of integration, such as assimilation, individualist integration, and cosmopolitanism. Yet, like them, it can be understood in terms of liberty, equality, and solidarity but, importantly, group identities are to be included in multiculturalist integration. Citizenship cannot be understood as just being about individuals. It has to be understood also as an inclusive and multiculturalist form of national belonging. Religious identity no less than other identities should be part of this; multicultural nationalism should include the identities of citizens that are important to their bearers.

Notes

[1] What I characterize here as cosmopolitanism, an identarian cosmopolitanism (cf Waldron 1991) is in ordinary discourse often thought to be multiculturalism or part of multiculturalism, but it should become apparent why I think it is important to distinguish them. For an alternative understanding of cosmopolitanism and an attempt to create a diversity framework that holds together interculturalism, multiculturalism, transnationalism, and cosmopolitanism, see Fossum et al (2024).
[2] https://www.royal.uk/kings-remarks-faith-leaders
[3] This is one of the key differences between standard liberalism and Will Kymlicka's liberal multiculturalism (Kymlicka 1995). For a discussion of the commonalities and differences between Kymlicka's liberal multiculturalism and my multicultural nationalism see Levey (2019, 2024).

References

Bouchard, G. and Taylor, C. 2008. *Building the Future: A Time for Reconciliation*. Consultation Commission on Accommodation Practices Related to Cultural Differences, Quebec.

Chin, C. and Levey, G.B. 2023. 'Recognition as Acknowledgement: Symbolic Politics in Multicultural Democracies', *Ethnic and Racial Studies* 46(3): 451–474.

Fossum, J.E., Kastoryano, R., Modood, T., and Zapata-Barrero, R. 2024. 'Governing Diversity in the Multilevel European Public Space', *Ethnicities* 24(1): 3–30.

Kymlicka, W. 1995. *Multicultural Citizenship: A Liberal Theory of Minority Rights*. Clarendon Press.

Levey, G.B. 2019. 'The Bristol School of Multiculturalism', *Ethnicities* 19(1): 200–226.

Levey, G.B. 2024. 'Integrating Modood and Kymlicka on National Inclusion', in T. Sealy, V. Uberoi, and N. Meer (eds), *The Resilience of Multiculturalism: Ideas, Politics and Practice*. Edinburgh University Press, pp 166–187.

Modood, T. 2012a. '2011 Paul Hanly Furfey Lecture "Is There a Crisis of Secularism in Western Europe?"', *Sociology of Religion* 73(2): 130–149.

Modood, T. 2012b. *Post-Immigration 'Difference' and Integration: The Case of Muslims in Western Europe*. The British Academy.

Modood, T. 2013 [2007]. *Multiculturalism: A Civic Idea*. Polity Press.

Modood, T. 2020. 'Islamophobia and Normative Sociology', *Journal of the British Academy* 8(1): 29–49.

Taylor, C. 1994. *Multiculturalism: Examining the Politics of Recognition*. Princeton University Press.

Waldron, J. 1991. 'Minority Cultures and the Cosmopolitan Alternative', *University of Michigan Journal of Law Reform* 25: 751–794.

Wise, A. and Velayutham, S. (eds). 2009. *Everyday Multiculturalism*. Springer.

Young, I.M. 1990. *Justice and the Politics of Difference*. Princeton University Press.

Video lecture

Modood, T. 2021. *Modes of Integration, Multiculturalism and National Identities*, Connected Sociologies Curriculum Project. https://thesociologicalreview.org/projects/connected-sociologies/curriculum/british-citizenship-race-and-rights/modes-integration-multiculturalism-and-national-identities/

Additional resources

http://www.tariqmodood.com/
https://www.youtube.com/channel/UCeDQPzPEf1Kz73SMsRgVPQA

QUESTIONS

1. Does it make sense to think of multiculturalism in terms of liberty, equality, and solidarity among national citizens?

2. What is the difference between multiculturalism and other modes of integration?

3. Is the main thrust of multiculturalism to create separate cultures or to remake the country so that all can belong to it?

Worksheet 21. Modes of Integration, Multiculturalism, and National Identities

This worksheet is designed to support AS and A-level teaching on the topics of culture and identity, and globalization and global development. In his online talk, Tariq Modood draws out the key distinctions between multiculturalism and other forms of integration. Explaining how multiculturalism relates to concepts of liberty, equality, and solidarity, Modood explores the meaning of citizenship and its relation to nationality, identity, and belonging. This worksheet draws on key themes from the A-level Sociology curriculum and AQA A-level Politics paper, Political Ideas, encouraging students to explore questions of social identity within the context of globalization, and start to address challenging sociological questions about the making and potential remaking of citizenship. Modood's chapter has close thematic links to Chapter 13's topic of 'Colonialism, Immigration, and the Making of British Citizenship'., which may provide additional useful context to this session.

Time	Activity	Explanation
00.00–00.05	To warm up, answer the following questions: *What is identity? How is it formed?*	These warm-up questions may be suited to a group discussion. They get students thinking about the meaning and formation of identity, which is a core topic within the A-level Sociology curriculum, and they will be asked to reflect on these initial thoughts later in the session.
00.05–00.10	Recap of understandings of culture and identity.	It may be useful to remind students of some of the definitions related to culture, self, and identity.
00.10–00.15	Watch the talk from 1:40 to 2:50. *What does Modood mean by the phrase 'integration presupposes difference?'*	Modood explains that the concept of integration means that some groups of citizens are necessarily identified as different in some way, and that integration is about relations between citizens, as well as relations between citizens and their state. This question ensures that students understand the theoretical grounding of this topic, pushing them to show their understanding by putting the concept of integration into their own words.
00.15–00.25	Watch the talk from 2:50 to 5:35. *What is the difference between identity 'from the outside in' and identity 'from the inside out'? Which of these describe your definition of identity in the warm-up exercise?*	Modood explains that identity 'from the outside in' relates to the ways in which people are described, labelled, and stereotyped by others, having an identity imposed upon them. Identity 'from the inside out', he explains, pertains to a person's sense of self, which is then projected into their relationships and contexts. This activity asks students to reflect on the warm-up questions using their learned knowledge so far in the session, delving more deeply into theories surrounding identity and identity formation. Students might reflect on the extent to which they had considered external influences on the formation of identity at the start of this session, and where these influences might come from within their own social circles and communities.

Time	Activity	Explanation
00.25–00.30	Watch the talk from 15:25 to 17:09. *How do the concepts of cosmopolitanism and multiculturalism differ in their interpretation of fraternity? Why is this difference important?*	Modood explains that, where cosmopolitanism is the view that 'people should be free to unite across communal and national boundaries, and should think of themselves as global citizens', multiculturalism holds the view that, in order for solidarity to be achieved, 'citizenship and national identity must be remade to include group identities that are important to minorities as well as majorities'. This puts forward a 'dialogical' rather than 'uniform' view of integration, which is a key concept underpinning Modood's argument. This activity pushes students to examine the concept that citizenship must be 'remade' to create a multiculturalist society, and to think about the consequences of this for ideas of nationalism and national identity. Students may draw connections between these themes and the 'Colonialism, Immigration and the Making of British Citizenship' topic.
00.30–00.40	At 22:14 Modood explains that citizenship can inspire 'a sense of belonging' among people. *What do you think is the relationship between citizenship, national identity and 'belonging' for contemporary Britons?*	This question asks students to draw together some key concepts from this topic and consider how they interconnect within the contemporary moment. To illustrate their thinking, students may wish to draw a mind map or diagram to visualize the links between these concepts. Students may also draw on their learning from other topics on this course which have encouraged students to think about the concept of 'belonging' with relation to different nations and identities, for example the talk on diaspora.
00.40–00.50	Watch the talk from 23:52 to 25:07. *What is the relationship between citizenship and nationality? How do emotion and imagination factor into this relationship?*	Modood talks about how citizenship tends to 'coalesce' around ideas of nationality, and that collective notions of national history offer an emotional, imaginative connection to this feeling of citizenship. This activity asks students to consider the emotional dimensions of culture, identity, and selfhood. It also connects with the wider themes of historical and national narratives, and the constructed nature of these, which is central to 'The Making of the Modern World' chapters.
00.50–01.00	Drawing on what you have learned throughout this session, answer the following question:	This activity brings together Modood's arguments, asking students to consider the theoretical and practical challenges associated with the multiculturalist task of 'remaking' citizenship.

Time	Activity	Explanation
	What processes should be involved in the 'remaking' of citizenship as an 'inclusive and multiculturalist form of national belonging'? What challenges can you foresee?	Students may take Modood's cue that a vital part of this task involves 're-telling the national story'. They may also identify that concepts from other topics share in this goal, for example notions of recovering 'hidden histories' and marginalized perspectives, and challenging dominant national narratives. Challenges in the 'remaking' of citizenship might include methodological difficulties or ethical dilemmas, for example: who will be included in the task 'remaking' of citizenship? How can it be ensured that different voices are heard? What kinds of resistance might there be to this vision of multiculturalism?

This worksheet was developed by Isabel Sykes.

22

Anxieties of Multiculturalism: The Birmingham Trojan Horse Affair

John Holmwood

Objectives

- This chapter discusses the Birmingham Trojan Horse affair and its role in the development of the UK government's counter-extremism policy, Prevent.

- It shows how the affair arose in the context of debates over multiculturalism and a 'moral panic' over British Muslims and their perceived self-segregation.

- The chapter sets out the trajectory of the affair; how it began with a letter alleging a plot to take over schools, which was later deemed a fake, but still prompted extensive investigations.

- It concludes that the affair represents a failure of 'muscular' liberalism rather than of multiculturalism, as the government allowed false allegations to undermine successful schools, teachers, and what it means to be British after colonialism.

Introduction

The claim of a plot to 'Islamicize' schools across Birmingham, Bradford, and Oldham – the Birmingham Trojan Horse affair – became a major news story in the UK early in 2014. This supposed plot prompted a slew of school inspections and special inquiries, culminating in professional misconduct cases brought against teachers at a number of schools, most notably at Park View Educational Trust (PVET). It led to the introduction, in 2015, of 'the Prevent Duty' which required all public authorities to have 'due regard to the need to prevent people from being drawn into terrorism'. At the same time, a duty to 'promote fundamental British values' was also introduced into schools in England and Wales.

This chapter identifies the Trojan Horse affair as a 'moral panic', associated with perceived problems with the migration to Britain of former colonial subjects and their demands for equal treatment (see Hampshire, Chapter 13, Benson, Chapter 18, and Narayan, Chapter 19, this volume). The term 'moral panic' was coined by the sociologist Stan Cohen (1972) to describe the construction in the mass media of public anxieties about a supposedly 'deviant' group that is then subjected to sanction by the authorities.[1] The Trojan Horse affair was a moral panic with a special twist. It was manufactured at the centre of government which orchestrated media reporting through the leaking of sensational stories to the press. This framed the public narrative and legitimated the government interventions described earlier, which took place before the evidence was tested in misconduct cases brought against those alleged to be involved. These stories were featured uncritically in both the conservative press, such as the *Telegraph* and *Times*, to which they were leaked, and in the liberal media like the *Guardian* and BBC.

The misconduct cases against the teachers did not come to court until September 2015 and, when they did, many of the incidents that had figured in the media stories were not part of the charges against the teachers. More importantly, a general accusation of 'extremism' had been reduced to a lesser claim that senior leaders had allowed 'undue religious influence' over the curriculum. Even this charge was difficult to sustain, as we shall see. The cases collapsed in April 2017 following serious misconduct on the part of the lawyers acting for the government. However, the original narrative was hard to shake, reinforced, as it was, by the policy changes to which it had given rise.

Multiculturalism and the 'Big Society'

To understand the background to the affair, it is necessary to go back to a report published in 2000 by the Commission on the Future of Multi-Ethnic Britain (under the auspices of the Runnymede Trust). The report – popularly known as the Parekh report after the Commission's chairperson, Lord Bhikhu Parekh – set out measures to secure equal participation for all citizens, including those with historical links to Britain deriving from colonialism. The argument was subtle and inclusive. It set out the idea of Britain as a single political community with shared values, as well as made up of distinct communities with different histories and beliefs. It proposed that the identities of groups were important, but it also detailed the important commonalities (rights and responsibilities) of individual citizenship (see Modood, Chapter 21, this volume). It recognized that inequalities were experienced by individuals through direct and indirect discrimination but were also associated with the ascribed characteristics of groups and were, therefore, also systemic or structural.[2] This was evident across a range of areas, including policing, employment, and access to services, especially for our purposes, those of education, where ethnic minority children had educational outcomes well below the national average.

The advocacy of multiculturalism was immediately derided in the mainstream media, especially the conservative press. The recommendations were also rejected by the then Labour government. Notwithstanding, there were concerted actions by some local authorities to counter educational inequalities, including in Birmingham which was England's largest local authority and one of its poorest with a high proportion of ethnic minority children. Birmingham City Council (BCC) had initiated a school improvement programme in the early 1990s which was already showing positive results by 2003 when the local authority was awarded an 'outstanding' rating by Ofsted. The latter reported that attainment by pupils had risen at a rate faster than the national average and that it stood as 'an example to all others of what can be done, even in the most demanding urban environments'.

A later report, the Kerslake report, on BCC's wider failings, was published in December 2014. It identified serious concerns across a number of areas, with schooling a rare area of success. Using data from Ofsted it showed that Birmingham's local authority schools had outcomes above the national average and significantly outperformed other metropolitan areas such as Manchester, Liverpool, Newcastle, Leeds, and Sheffield (Kerslake 2014, Supporting Analysis 16). This contrasts with the comments of the Chief Inspector of Schools Sir Michael Wilshaw who, in an interview in December 2016 with *Times* journalist Sian Griffiths, said that the 'awful schools' in Birmingham had been his greatest cause of concern during his five-year term (Griffiths 2016).

Over time, what the Parekh report had presented as a failure of recognition across community differences came to be understood as a problem of the self-segregation of ethnic minority communities, especially Muslim communities. A new national government in 2010 – the Conservative and Liberal Democrat coalition – marked a shift in national policy *and* local implementation. In 2011, Prime Minister David Cameron attended the annual Munich security conference and announced that 'state multiculturalism' had failed (notwithstanding that the state had never promoted it). The speech indicated the need to advance a strong national identity to which ethnic minorities should assimilate, and a requirement to check organizations robustly before extending public support, whether nationally or locally: 'Do they believe in universal human rights – including for women and people of other faiths? Do they believe in equality of all before the law? Do they believe in democracy and the right of people to elect their own government? Do they encourage integration or separatism?' (Cameron 2011a). He described this as *muscular* liberalism.

The new government also challenged local authorities over what it saw as their failures to improve schools and instead to argue that social inequality was at the root of poor educational outcomes. 'Good schools' could make a difference despite local socio-economic disadvantage. Indeed, although the government did not point to Birmingham, it was an example of what was possible. The government's proposal, however, was to confront local authorities directly through the active promotion of the academy schools programme, first introduced by the previous Labour government on a targeted basis. The programme was now extended by then Secretary of State for Education, Michael Gove, with measures (new freedoms, plus extra funding) to encourage schools to decide to become academies. Schools judged to be unsatisfactory (by Ofsted) were also required to become academies under the guidance of a successful school as part of a Multi-Academy Trust.

A new regime of Ofsted inspections aligned with this agenda was introduced in 2012, with the Chief Inspector Michael Wilshaw stating that there was a need to 'challenge those who have power invested in them to make the difference, but too often make excuses for poor performance – it's just too hard, the children are too difficult, the families are too unsupportive, this job is far too stressful' (Richardson 2012). Governing bodies, Wilshaw stated, should be challenging head teachers to improve their schools, and good practice should be communicated across the education system. Significantly, Park View Academy was one of the first schools to be judged 'outstanding' under the new Ofsted inspection regime. 'Every school should be like Park View', Wilshaw said (Coughlan 2014).

The academy schools policy was part of a set of measures by the prime minister to promote the 'Big Society' which he set out in a speech delivered a week after his Munich speech. Britain needed, he argued, a 'social recovery to mend a broken society' and he went on to describe how it would be achieved:

> [F]irst of all, we have got to devolve more power to local government, and beyond local government, so people can actually do more and take more power. Secondly, we have got to open up public services, make them less monolithic, say to people: if you want to start up new schools, you can. (Cameron 2011b)

The stage was set. The academies programme devolved powers to local schools and their governing bodies and encouraged community engagement, but did so in a context where British Muslims were increasingly represented as potentially having values at odds with those of mainstream Britain. PVET was in the eye of the storm in what came to be known as the Trojan Horse affair.

The so-called 'plot'

The moral panic associated with the Trojan Horse affair began with a letter sent to BCC together with a document purporting to be from someone in Birmingham to a colleague in Bradford. The document outlined how senior teachers in schools could be undermined by concerted action by some governors and parents to allow the school to be 'taken over'. It described five stages involved in the plot and illustrated them with examples from Birmingham. The document described the writer as working closely with the Chair of Governors at PVET and stated that 'we have caused a great amount of organized disruption in Birmingham and as a result now have our own Academies and are on the way to getting rid of more Head teachers and taking over their schools'. The document called the process a 'Jihad'.

BCC investigated the letter together with the police and decided it was faked. However, it was leaked to the press in February 2014, with dramatic consequences. Michael Gove initiated a number of investigations through the Department for Education (DfE). These involved special Ofsted investigations of 21 schools and two Education Funding Agency (EFA) reports involving four of the schools (the EFA was responsible for academy schools), three of which were part of PVET (Park View, Golden Hillock, and Nansen), and a separate primary school, Oldknow Academy, which had also been judged to be outstanding. BCC commissioned a report, the Kershaw report, while Michael Gove commissioned a separate report to parliament under former head of counterterrorism at the Metropolitan Police, Peter Clarke, the Clarke report (Clarke 2014; Kershaw 2014). The two inquiries shared material and

Kershaw devolved issues of extremism to Clarke. The various inspections and inquiries took place sequentially from March to July 2014. The Due Diligence and Counter Extremism Unit of the DfE was involved at the outset in the Ofsted inspections and EFA reviews, and one of the inspectors from those reviews went on to act as education adviser to the Clarke review. In that sense, they were 'recycling' material rather than subjecting it to proper analysis; nor were the inspections and inquiries really separate from each other.

The official inquiries accepted that the original letter was fake, but they adopted its framing in their terms of reference. Media reports indicated that hundreds of teachers and governors were involved in the plot, but as the investigations unfolded, so the scale of the plot began to reduce. Evidence of behaviour aligned with one or another aspect of the 'plot', it was claimed, was found in most, but not all, of the 21 schools. However, only in the four academy schools mentioned earlier were all of the supposed five stages found. Initially, it was not clear how PVET and Oldknow were connected, but it would emerge that the DfE had sought a Memorandum of Agreement between them involving the possible incorporation of an Islamic faith school, Al-Furqan primary, into PVET with the support of Oldknow.

There was extensive leaking to the press from the inquiries which established a dominant narrative, one that was reinforced by the 'findings' of the Clarke inquiry. This involved the idea that 'successful headteachers' had been undermined by aggressive Muslim governors and teachers (some acting as governors in other schools) and that the latter were extremist. Thus, the Clarke report stated: 'I found clear evidence that there are a number of people, associated with each other and in positions of influence in schools and governing bodies, who espouse, endorse or fail to challenge extremist views' (Clarke 2014: 12). The report stated that the 'clear conclusion is that the Park View Educational Trust has, in effect, become the incubator for much of what has happened and the attitudes and behaviours that have driven it' (Clarke 2014: 13) and that

> there has been co-ordinated, deliberate and sustained action, carried out by a number of associated individuals, to introduce an intolerant and aggressive Islamic ethos into a few schools in Birmingham. … Whether their motivation reflects a political agenda, a deeply held religious conviction, personal gain or a desire to influence communities, the effect has been to limit the life chances of the young people in their care and to render them more vulnerable to pernicious influences in the future. (Clarke 2014: 14)

Those who were accused within the report had no opportunity to respond, or to have their responses weighed by the inquiries. Instead, Clarke set out 20 matters of concern, introducing them with the comment that '[i]t has been alleged that Park View School exhibits many of the most concerning features reported to this investigation. *It is only fair to point out the Trust disputed most, if not all, of the following allegations*' (Clarke 2014: 52; emphasis added). Clarke recommended that these allegations should be the basis of professional misconduct cases brought against those involved. In the meantime, the Clarke report had, it seemed, established the truth about the Trojan

Horse affair. All that remained was to learn the lessons and take appropriate action against the perpetrators. It would be over a year before those cases would go to court, and another 18 months before they were concluded.

The role of the government in the takeover of schools

The most obvious question for the media (and Clarke) to have asked was: how could a school be 'taken over'? It could happen only within and through the DfE's academies programme. The process involved school improvement officials at the DfE with meetings between the parties (presumably involving minutes) and agreements signed off by the Secretary of State for Education. Park View became an academy in April 2012, when it was invited by officials at the DfE to become a Multi-Academy Trust and sponsor two schools, Nansen primary in October 2012 and Golden Hillock secondary in October 2013. Much is made of the idea that 'successful' head teachers were undermined, but the only successful head teacher in the affair was the head teacher of Park View, Lindsey Clark, who would herself come to be accused of being part of the plot. Park View was asked to take over other schools because *they* were failing, and it was encouraged by the DfE to introduce its successful practices into them.

Park View did have extraordinary success. It had been a failing school, identified in the early 1990s in an infamous *Panorama* TV programme, 'The underclass in Purdah', as one of the worst schools in England.[3] Tahir Alam, a former pupil, had seen the programme and was moved to try to do something about it. He joined the school as governor in 1994 and became Chair in 1997, when Lindsey Clark was appointed head teacher. The school's results steadily improved. By 2006 it was judged by Ofsted to be one of the most improved schools in England and by January 2012, was judged to be 'outstanding'. Its examination results (against the standard of the proportion of pupils achieving five GCSEs at grades A–C, including Maths and English) put it into the top 14 per cent of schools nationwide.

At the same time, 98.8 per cent of Park View's pupils were from a Muslim background. While 15 per cent of pupils in schools nationally received free school meals (28 per cent in Birmingham), over 70 per cent of pupils received them in Park View, which indicates the socio-economic disadvantage experienced by many of the children. Over 80 per cent of pupils at schools nationwide spoke English as a first language (64 per cent in Birmingham), while in Park View that figure was only 7.5 per cent. This shows the immense challenges that the school managed to overcome. Oldknow primary school, not a part of PVET, had a similar record of success and was also judged by Ofsted in January 2013 to be 'outstanding'.

In the circumstances, it is not surprising that the DfE would seek Park View's expertise in helping to turn around other schools and that it would also see value in having them cooperate with Oldknow. In other words, 'co-ordinated, deliberate and sustained action, carried out by a number of associated individuals' is precisely the means of improving schools under the tutelage of a 'sponsoring' academy. But it wouldn't be a 'plot', it would be the government's schools improvement programme in action.

It was not until the professional misconduct cases were brought to court in September 2015 that the official narrative began to crack. This is because the 'findings' of the Clarke report had to be formulated as specific allegations and 'particularized', that is, provided with instances that would be the evidence for the allegations. This also meant that the National College of Teaching and Learning (NCTL), the regulatory agency for teachers based within the DfE, had to provide witness statements and supporting evidence. Many of the incidents that had been part of media reporting did not make it through the process because of a lack of evidence. Equally important, the charges were no longer framed as 'extremism', but as 'undue religious influence'. Indeed, the 'plot' had also become considerably reduced in scale, with just 12 teachers at four schools facing any kind of charge.[4]

Religion and schooling

The schools undoubtedly had an Islamic ethos, consistent with the very high proportion of Muslim pupils. Although the reports identified 'Islamic extremism', as we have seen, they also indicated that one of the problems was that these were 'secular' state schools that had practices more consistent with those of 'faith' schools. Here the inquiries failed to consider the religious requirements on all publicly funded schools in England. These are the object of criticism and lobbying by groups like Humanists UK and the Secular Society, but pending a change in the law, it is unlawful for schools not to abide by them.

All schools in England must provide compulsory religious education and daily acts of collective worship, primarily of a Christian nature. For local authority schools, the curriculum is provided by a local Standing Advisory Committee on Religious Education (SACRE), which also monitors the arrangements for collective worship. However, the arrangements for an academy are different and represented in their Memorandum of Agreement. They can follow their own curriculum, or they can choose to follow that provided by the local SACRE. The DfE set up no arrangement for managing collective worship.

Does this provide a 'glimmer' of what may have happened? Might Park View have misused the new freedoms afforded by its academy status?[5] Guided by the Clarke report, the NCTL proceeded unaware of this nuance. Nonetheless, if the allegation was 'undue' religious influence, what would constitute 'due' religious influence? The NCTL suggested that something like that provided by a SACRE would be appropriate (albeit that they did not have to adopt a SACRE curriculum), implying that Park View provided something very much different. However, Park View had continued with the SACRE curriculum.

What about collective worship? The NCTL accepted that many schools in England – perhaps a majority – do not comply with the requirement. Moreover, there is a provision for schools to have what is called a 'determination' for worship other than Christian if the background of pupils warrants it (otherwise parents can request their children not attend). Park View had applied to the Birmingham SACRE for approval for a determination for 'Islamic collective worship' which had been in place since 1997. Determinations last for five years when they are subject to renewal. Renewal of Park

View's determination fell due again in mid-2013, when, as we have seen, the DfE had no mechanism in place. It was the view of the EFA inspector who subsequently went on to advise Clarke that the school should have reverted to Christian worship and that failure to do so put it into breach of its 'Master Funding Agreement' (a generic statement of meeting the legislative requirements for religious education and collective worship). For the inspector, this represented undue religious influence.

It would transpire during the court proceedings that these details were known to Clarke but not discussed by him despite the fact that some of the supposedly problematic incidents he described had occurred when the determination was active. The Secretary of the Birmingham SACRE had provided documents to Clarke that collective worship had been approved, including its format and a schedule for assemblies. They had also written in 2013 to the DfE alerting them of the need for a process for the renewal of determinations and the schools in Birmingham that would soon need renewals and that had become academies.

The DfE was fully aware of the 'Islamic ethos' of Park View. It had approached the school to ask them to incorporate Al-Furqan, a failing Islamic faith primary school, into PVET on precisely this basis. Apparently, the DfE thought it appropriate that a school that Clarke said should have been 'secular' should incorporate a 'faith school'.[6] A Memorandum of Agreement was drawn up with Oldknow primary school for its acting head teacher to be seconded. The Secretary of State had already signed the document agreeing the 'takeover' of Al-Furqan (just as he had signed the other 'takeovers') when the Trojan Horse story broke.

Whose misconduct?

Ultimately, then, the misconduct case devolved to a series of allegations about individual incidents which were countered one by one at the senior leaders' hearing: that mentions of Islam were found in workbooks for subjects other than religious education; that there were no musical instruments (the inspector didn't look in the cupboard); that there was gender segregation of PE (allowed and quite common across schools); that there was an Islamic prayer displayed on the wall in the maths classroom (the assembly hall was undergoing renovation so the maths room doubled for collective worship).

These allegations were a subset of those that had appeared in the various reports (themselves not the same as those that appeared in the media). They were supported by witness statements from those that had spoken to Clarke. However, the prosecution was adamant that the statements were fully independent, and that lawyers had no access to the testimony provided to Clarke when the statements for the NCTL cases were drawn up. This is important. Were this not to have been the case then the Clarke testimony would have to be disclosed to the defence, when other discrepancies would be evident.

Since September 2015, the NCTL had affirmed that it had maintained a strict structural division from the DfE and had repeatedly confirmed that the solicitors preparing the NCTL case had no access to the Clarke witness transcripts or other evidence submitted to Clarke. The Panel in the senior leaders' case was convened again after a delay on 3 May 2017 when the NCTL passed a note to the Panel saying that there was substantially more material that should have been disclosed. It seemed that there had been a 'departmental misunderstanding' and that the Clarke transcripts and other evidence had been in the possession of the NCTL lawyers.

It transpired that the Clarke witness statements had been edited and redrafted to create witness statements in the NCTL hearing that were offered as wholly separate from the Clarke statements (any similarity had been said to be testament to the veracity of the witness). Neither the prosecuting counsel, nor the senior partner at the solicitors, made themselves available to explain what had transpired. The panel declared that 'there has been an abuse of the process which is of such seriousness that it offends the Panel's sense of justice and propriety. What has happened has brought the integrity of the process into disrepute' (NCTL 2017: paragraph 174). The hearing collapsed and the NCTL elected to take no further action.

Conclusion

The Trojan Horse affair began with allegations of egregious misconduct on the part of teachers and ended with misconduct by government lawyers, albeit that no actions were taken against those lawyers. We have seen that the Trojan Horse affair involved claims of the failure of 'state multiculturalism'. We can now see that local 'multiculturalism' had in fact succeeded. What failed was the 'muscular liberalism' that the government had asserted to be the foundation of fundamental British values. The British empire had been multicultural involving asymmetrical power relations; what proved difficult was for public authorities to accept multicultural equality. The government allowed false allegations of extremism to gain momentum and undermine schools, teachers, and governors that had contributed to a dramatic improvement in the education of ethnic minority pupils in Birmingham; outcomes would decline dramatically after 2014.

It is not difficult to understand that the government had a vested interest in the promotion of a Trojan Horse plot. Once they had fanned the media flames through leaking to sympathetic journalists, the truth of what happened called into question their own involvement through the academy schools programme and they managed the inquiries to limit scrutiny of the role of the DfE. What is less clear is why liberal commentators aligned themselves with it. Here the problem was an unwillingness to defend schools that adhered to the religious requirements on schools and did so enthusiastically because they believed in their value. In the case of PVET, this was because they believed that recognizing the significance of religion in the lives of their pupils, allowing them to express their 'whole selves' in school, would help academic performance.

The right-wing think tank Policy Exchange had earlier expressed their worries about the possible extremism of minority religions and encouraged political control over schools (they were also advocates of the academy schools). Liberal theorists of education were concerned about religion as such. Clayton et al, for example, believed that religious schools valued religious expression over educational outcomes, arguing, 'parents' freedom to educate their children as they prefer should be constrained by

(i) children's interest in receiving their fair share of educational goods, and (ii) the wider society's interest in the cultivation of educational goods such as democratic competence, tolerance and mutual respect' (2018: 5). And, further, that 'current legislation is too permissive to parents and insufficiently attentive to children's interests, in particular their interest in autonomy' (Clayton et al 2018: 9).

On this understanding, it is appropriate that schools should usurp parental rights in order to inculcate liberal values and secure educational outcomes. Despite publishing after the collapse of the misconduct cases, they do not discuss the Trojan Horse affair. What should be clear is that the pupils at Park View achieved autonomy through educational outcomes that secured their participation in society. There was no evidence that the pupils at the school lacked tolerance and mutual respect for societal values, only that commentators – liberal and conservative, alike – lacked respect for them and their parents.

I will leave the last word with a pupil from the school as spoken in a play by Lung theatre company. It was based on interviews with teachers, pupils, and parents, and used the transcripts from the misconduct hearings and testimony given to the Clarke inquiry, as recalled by the witnesses. Farah, a pupil at Park View during the most intense period of the affair, was one of those who had her fair share of educational goods disrupted. She failed to get the grades expected of her and was unable to go on to college:

> British Values are Islamic values. They're not something that's new to us because there's a label or a policy. To suddenly name it 'British values' as though Britishness is something I have to learn, something I have to become, rather than something I already am. I was born in Alum Rock, I've lived in Birmingham all my life. What about me is not British?

Notes

[1] Cohen's focus was on youth sub-cultures – 'Mods and Rockers' – and he argued that youth are a frequent source of adult anxiety. The Trojan Horse affair is a variation on that theme, young people supposedly at risk of 'radicalization'.

[2] As had been set out in 1999 by the Macpherson Report into the killing of Stephen Lawrence and its finding of 'institutional racism' in the police.

[3] This followed a major *cause célèbre* in 1984 when a headmaster in Bradford, Ray Honeyford, attacked ideas of multiculturalism, arguing that ethnic minority children should assimilate. At the height of the Trojan Horse scandal, liberal and conservative commentators alike promoted the idea that he had been castigated for racism, but seemed to have been proven right (see Jack 2014; Scruton 2014).

[4] When the Prevent Duty was introduced, it had been justified with the claim that Clarke's 'detailed report found evidence of "co-ordinated, deliberate and sustained action … to introduce an intolerant and aggressive Islamic ethos". His report described extremists gaining positions on governing bodies and joining the staff, unequal treatment and segregation of boys and girls, extremist speakers making presentations to pupils, and bullying and intimidation of staff who refused to support extremist views. In total around 5,000 children were in institutions affected' (HM Government, 2015: paragraph 22).

[5] In fact, none of the inquiries suggest that the policies and practices at Park View had recently changed and Clarke reached back into the period of its dramatic improvement.

[6] Clarke did not include Al-Furqan among the schools he considered. Kershaw did, but considered that the fact that the Chair of Governors and senior leaders at PVET turned up at Al-Furqan governing body meetings was inexplicable and an indication of the problem. He was not informed of the DfE's involvement.

References

Cameron, D. 2011a. 'Speech at Munich Security Conference', 5 February. https://www.gov.uk/government/speeches/pms-speech-at-munich-security-conference

Cameron, D. 2011b. 'Speech on Big Society', 14 February. https://www.gov.uk/government/speeches/pms-speech-on-big-society

Clarke, P. 2014 *Report into Allegations Concerning Birmingham Schools Arising from the 'Trojan Horse' Letter*. https://assets.publishing.service.gov.uk/government/uploads/system/uploads/attachment_data/file/340526/HC_576_accessible_-.pdf

Clayton, M., Mason, A., Swift, A., and Wareham, R. 2018. 'How to Regulate Faith Schools', *Impact* 25: 1–49.

Cohen, S. 1972. *Folk Devils and Moral Panics*. MacGibbon and Kee Ltd.

Commission on the Future of Multi-Ethnic Britain. 2018. *The Parekh Report: The Future of Multi-Ethnic Britain*. Runnymede Trust.

Coughlan, S. 2014. 'Trojan Horse: Ofsted Says Schools were Targeted', *BBC News*, 9 June. https://www.bbc.co.uk/news/education-27763113

Griffiths, S. 2016. 'Children at Risk in "Rotten Borough" Birmingham', *The Times*, 11 December. https://www.thetimes.com/uk/article/children-at-risk-in-rotten-borough-birmingham-fl5f00pkb

HM Government, 2015, *Counter-Extremism Strategy*. Available at: https://assets.publishing.service.gov.uk/media/5a80cddfed915d74e623089e/51859_Cm9148_Accessible.pdf.

Jack, I. 2014. 'Was the 1980s Bradford Headteacher Who Criticised Multiculturalism Right?', *The Guardian*, 13 June. https://www.theguardian.com/commentisfree/2014/jun/13/was-1980s-headteacher-who-criticised-multiculturism-right.

Kerslake, B. 2014. *Report on Birmingham City Council's Governance and Organizational Capabilities*. Available at: https://www.gov.uk/government/publications/birmingham-city-councils-governance-and-organisational-capabilities-an-independent-review.

Kershaw, I. 2014. *Investigation Report: Trojan Horse Letter* (Kershaw report). https://www.birmingham.gov.uk/downloads/download/6673/ian_kershaw_report

NCTL. 2017. Mr Monzoor Hussain, Mr Hardeep Saini, Mr Arshad Hussain, Mr Razwan Faraz, Ms Lindsey Clark: Professional conduct panel outcome. Available at: https://assets.publishing.service.gov.uk/media/5a81d56bed915d74e62345ce/PVL_Panel_decision_and_reasons_for_web.pdf

Richardson, H. 2012. 'Ofsted Chief Sir Michael Wilshaw: Teachers Not Stressed', *BBC News*, 10 May. https://www.bbc.co.uk/news/education-18025202

Scruton, R. 2014. 'Let's Face It – Ray Honeyford Got It Right on Islam and Education', *The Spectator*, 5 July. https://www.spectator.co.uk/article/let-s-face-it-ray-honeyford-got-it-right-on-islam-and-education/

Video lecture

Holmwood, J. 2020. *The Birmingham Trojan Horse Affair*, Connected Sociologies Curriculum Project. https://thesociologicalreview.org/projects/connected-sociologies/curriculum/british-citizenship-race-and-rights/birmingham-trojan-horse-affair/

Further reading

Cannizzaro, S. and Gholami, R. 2018. 'The Devil Is Not in the Detail: Representational Absence and Stereotyping in the "Trojan Horse" News Story', *Race Ethnicity and Education* 21(1): 15–29.

Holmwood, J. 2020. 'A Postcolonial Conservative Defence of Multicultural Equality', *Reset Dialogues on Civilizations*.

Holmwood, J. and O'Toole, T. 2018. *Countering Extremism in British Schools? The Truth about the Birmingham Trojan Horse Affair.* Policy Press.

Qurashi, F. 2018. 'The Prevent Strategy and the UK "War on Terror": Embedding Infrastructures of Surveillance in Muslim Communities', *Palgrave Communications* 4: 17.

Additional resources

Professor John Holmwood was an expert witness, for the defence, in the NCTL case brought against the senior leaders at PVET and an academic adviser to Lung theatre company. See his web page for resources – Ofsted reports, EFA reports, newspaper items, and other materials – related to the Trojan Horse affair: https://johnholmwood.net/birmingham-trojan-horse-affair-resources/.

QUESTIONS

1. How and why is multiculturalism seen as a failure?

2. Is there a problem of democratic governance in schools in England?

3. Should schools be secular spaces?

4. How does the Trojan Horse affair expose the limits of liberal modernity?

Worksheet 22. Anxieties of Multiculturalism: The Birmingham Trojan Horse Affair

This worksheet is designed to support AS and A-level teaching on the topics of educational policies, the role and function of the education system, and beliefs in society, including the significance of religion and religiosity in the contemporary world. In his online talk, John Holmwood sets out the contexts and controversies surrounding a 'plot to Islamicize schools' in Birmingham, Bradford, and Oldham, where misconduct cases were brought against teachers in 2015. Holmwood explains that, despite the collapse of the cases in 2017, the Birmingham Trojan Horse affair led to significant shifts in government anti-extremism policies. With links to the 'War on Terror' and 'Modes of Integration', this talk covers key themes within the A-level Sociology curriculum, including the significance of the relationship between religion, secularization, and globalization. The activities encourage students to critically evaluate arguments for and against secular education and tackle challenging sociological questions about the role and function of the British education system.

Time	Activity	Explanation
00.00–00.05	To warm up, answer the following question: *Should schools be secular spaces? Why/why not?*	This warm-up activity may work well as a group discussion and is designed to encourage students to discuss the issue at the centre of this topic, with the view that their arguments may develop and become more nuanced and/or sophisticated as the session progresses.
00.05–00.10	Recap of understandings of education.	It may be useful to remind students of theories related to the role and function of education.
00.10–00.15	Watch the talk from 2:29 to 4:00. *What was the significance of the 'Big Society' agenda to the Trojan Horse affair?*	Holmwood explains that the Conservative government's 'Big Society' agenda focused on 'opening up' public services, which included control of schools being taken away from local authorities. This led to the acceleration of the academy schools programme, which is a key context for explaining the Trojan Horse affair. This activity ensures that students understand the key contexts at the heart of this topic, and gets students thinking about the significance of educational policies to the role and function of the school system. This is a central theme within the A-level Sociology curriculum.
00.15–00.25	Watch the talk from 8:38 to 10:14. *Why was there very little public interest in the collapse of the so-called plot? What role did the media have to play in the Trojan Horse affair?*	Holmwood explains that the investigation comes to its resolution in May 2017 following the misconduct of lawyers acting for the Department for Education, who failed to provide documents in their possession which would have helped the teachers' defence. The mainstream media at the time dismissed this as a 'technicality', downplaying the collapse of the case. The relationship between the media and government policy is a key theme in various chapters and talks and this activity encourages students to think critically about this relationship.

Time	Activity	Explanation
00.25–00.35	Watch the talk from 15:35 to 18:13. *What is the relationship between the Trojan Horse affair and the 2015 Prevent Strategy? Summarize the key ideas in 3–5 bullet points.*	Holmwood articulates how the Trojan Horse affair influenced the 2015 Prevent Strategy, directing its focus towards non-violent extremism and leading the government to bring in new requirements to safeguard school children from radicalization. One consequence was that religious conservatism among students was now seen as a possible indication of vulnerability. This section has strong ties to Chapter 23 ('Security and the War on Terror: Predict, Prevent, Police), which may be useful in providing students with more context. Students may draw on their learning from this session in synthesizing the key aspects of the Prevent Strategy that relate to religion in schools. This connects to a key theme on the A-level Sociology curriculum, which requires students to consider the significance of religion and religiosity in the contemporary world, particularly within the context of globalization.
00.35–00.40	At 18:13 Holmwood explains that, as a consequence of the Trojan Horse affair, a requirement was introduced in 2014 to teach 'fundamental British values' in schools. *What is the significance of this requirement within the context of British multiculturalism?*	This question prompts students to reflect on their wider learning around integration and multiculturalism in a contemporary British context. They may take the cue from Holmwood's lecture in identifying that 'British values' within the context of the Prevent Strategy are defined in contrast to some beliefs that may be held independently by ethnic minorities, particularly regarding religion. Students may draw on their learning from Chapter 21 ('Modes of Integration Multiculturalism, and National Identities') to think about the sociological consequences of this.
00.40–00.50	Watch the talk from 19:00 to 21:42 and then reflect on your responses to the warm-up activity. *What do you think of Clayton et al's arguments for secular education? Explain to what extent you agree or disagree.*	Holmwood explains that Clayton et al's arguments for secular schooling suggest an opposition between the educational attainment of school children and the religious orientation of their parents. Furthermore, they imply that religious beliefs are possibly in conflict with democratic values. Students are encouraged to take up Holmwood's cue in critiquing these claims, to assess the merits of their argument, the evidence, and to articulate their own response. This aids in the development of students' critical analysis skills.
00.50–01.00	Drawing on what you have learned throughout this talk, answer the following questions: *How do you think schools in Britain should be governed? Who should have a say in what students learn, and who should not?*	This activity asks students to take their learning beyond the material provided, applying their critical thinking skills to a wider sociological question. Students should reflect on their answers to the warm-up activity in considering to what extent they agree or disagree with the principle of secular education.

This worksheet was developed by Isabel Sykes.

23

Security and the War on Terror: Predict, Prevent, Police

Shereen Fernandez

Objectives

- This chapter begins with an understanding of how the War on Terror has a longer history, which begins before 11 September 2001, and that it overlaps with types of surveillance and policing from earlier periods, such as the Troubles in Northern Ireland.

- Drawing on the use of the Prevent Duty in the UK, the chapter sets out how contemporary states are adopting a model of pre-emption as a counterterrorism measure and including them in public institutions such as schools and healthcare services.

- It considers how those racialized as Muslims are susceptible to such measures and explores what this tells us about the securitization of minorities.

Introduction

What happened on 11 September 2001 – what came to be known as 9/11 – shifted how governments thought and acted on security. On that day, several commercial planes were hijacked by members of the group known as Al Qaeda and were flown into buildings across the United States, with the most significant attack taking place at the World Trade Center in New York. Although violent attacks had occurred previously on US soil, this was arguably the first externally orchestrated assault on the United States that was considered 'successful', given the scale of the government's response, including President George W. Bush's actions, and the nearly 3,000 civilian fatalities. Furthermore, the attacks were seen as an attempt to destabilize US hegemony, meaning its global power and reach.

The televised nature of 9/11 added to its 'spectacular' nature, thus showing the power of the media in reproducing images of horror and tragedy to capture the hearts and minds of the public. Films made in Hollywood further cemented this 'spectacularism', bolstering support for the wars to come. In the immediate aftermath of 9/11, laws were created and strengthened in the United States, such as the US PATRIOT Act (2001) which curbed the civil liberties of US residents through the use of expansive and invasive surveillance. Most notably, however, was the creation of a Global War on Terror, undertaken by the United States and its allies, including the UK, to root out terrorism. This was initially associated with claims that there were 'weapons of mass destruction' in Iraq.

In his speech announcing the commencement of a War on Terror, President Bush made the claim that those who stand against terrorism will stand with the United States in this war: 'Either you are with us, or you are with the terrorists.' In the immediate aftermath of 9/11, the UK's response by then Prime Minister Tony Blair indicated unwavering support for the United States and led to British involvement in the War on Terror, primarily through its military support. The hardening of UK counterterrorism policy became normalized in the aftermath of the London 7/7 bombings in July 2005, which this chapter will examine in the context of the government's counter-extremism strategy, Prevent. Unlike war in the 'traditional' sense, the War on Terror was also about prevention and risk management, although it was packaged by US officials as a defence need in the name of global security. However, as this chapter will show, the War on Terror led to the *insecurity* of individuals racialized as Muslim in key sites such as the border, schools, and even their homes, leading to the War *on* Terror being better described as a 'war *of* terror'.

In naming the war as a war *of* terror, scholars such as Younis and Jadhav (2019) have shown how the practice of security was not only excessive, but was targeted on a select group of people, namely those who were perceived to be Muslim. Security in this chapter refers to the mechanisms deployed by the nation state to keep its citizens and borders safe, using public sector resources, private contractors and consultants to do so. This can be through the physical measures, such as barriers and the presence of police/military officers, or indirectly, through the existence of policies to constrain behaviour. This chapter will expand on the idea that as a result of the War on Terror, Muslims became viewed as a potential enemy within, despite political assertions that counterterrorism policies and practices were aimed at all forms of potentially violent extremism. The UK's flagship counterterrorism programme, known as CONTEST, has demonstrated this further, especially the use of the counter-extremism strand of the policy, the Prevent Duty, in civil society. The final part of this chapter will explore how the Prevent Duty operates in civil spaces such as schools, health bodies, and universities, first to show how counter-extremism is used by professionals who are now given the responsibility to assess what constitutes extremism and, also, how terms such as 'extremism', 'radicalization', and 'terrorism' have become embedded in our everyday language of security.

This chapter will argue for the importance of studying 9/11 in the present, particularly given continuing geopolitical tensions in the Middle East. The aim is to show that security initiatives implemented by states globally under the rubric of counterterrorism are based largely on the threat of terrorism deriving from 9/11, although in many cases, many security initiatives pre-dated 9/11 but came to be renewed as a result of it. It is important to remember that practices of securitization, which emerged during the War on Terror, have a long history and were also present during the period of European colonial expansion when they were directed at resistance on the part of dominated populations.

Security and the racial 'other': Muslims as the global 'enemy' from colonialism until the present day

The attacks on 9/11 prompted Muslims globally to be viewed through a lens of suspicion. Despite reassurances by politicians, such as US President George Bush, that the War on Terror was not a war on Islam or Muslims, Muslim communities globally did come to be viewed as a security threat. Prior to 9/11 in the UK, Muslims were seen primarily through an ethnic lens, rather than their religion, but, as argued by Humayun Ansari, '[b]eing born, bred and raised in Britain has not guaranteed automatic membership of the British nation … a performative belonging has been demanded through articulations and practices of "proper" political and cultural behaviour' (2018: xvii; see Modood, Chapter 21, this volume). The riots of 2001, in northern English towns (such as Bradford, Leeds, and Oldham), between White and ethnic minority youth further cemented this antagonism which viewed South Asians in particular as being unable to belong to a (White) British nation. Racialized communities in Britain often face the brunt of state policing measures, as seen more broadly with policies associated with the Windrush scandal and hostile environment (see Renwick, Chapter 9, this volume), to the heavy policing of the 2011 riots which were sparked by the fatal shooting of a young Black man, Mark Duggan, by police in London. Moving forward to the summer of 2024, race riots captured Britain in a more expansive way, but this time, the rioters were fuelled by the idea that Muslims should be considered external to the nation.

The construction of Arabs and Muslims as an 'Other' can be understood through the work of post-colonial literature theorist, Edward W. Said (1978), in his seminal book *Orientalism*, which has been used extensively by scholars to understand the virulent anti-Muslim discourse and practices of the War on Terror. Said argues that European nations during the period of imperialism in the 18th century designated Arab and Muslim majority nations as the 'Orient', denoting an inferiority to Europe. The framework of Orientalism has been instrumental in developing understandings of Islamophobia, which as Naved Bakali and Farid Hafez state, is 'a form of racism that is constructed through Western discourse, actions, and perceptions about imagined "Muslims" and "Islam"' (2022: 7).

The imaginative geographies produced through Orientalism have been used by other social scientists to consider how Muslims have been positioned as external to the nation. Arabs and Muslims are often seen through a homogenizing lens which views them as inherently violent, misogynistic, and in need of intervention by Western powers. The depiction of Muslims as 'Other', then, pre-dates the War on Terror, with European expansion through colonialism relying on Orientalist depictions of countries and peoples in the 'East' as irrational and in need of development. Many of these arguments were rehearsed in the lead up to the War on Terror, for example, with Afghan women portrayed in public discourse as without agency and in need of being saved.

Many of these arguments, using feminism as a developmental tool to help Afghan women, helped legitimize the invasion of Afghanistan by the United States and are also part of a longer history depicting Muslim women as inferior. The veiling practices of Muslim women have long been associated with feelings of anxiety by others and a preoccupation with the idea that Muslims are a 'contagion' in society; with Muslim communities seen as foreign bodies, potentially posing a risk to the health of the nation state.

One of the more recent ways in which Muslims have been flagged for suspicion and 'Othered' is through travel. The phenomenon known as 'Flying While Muslim' or 'Flying While Brown' denotes how the War on Terror created conditions in which those racialized as Muslims are stopped for security purposes on grounds that they are potential national security threats. There have been instances in the United States where faith clerics, known as imams, have been taken off flights as well as Muslim women wearing the hijab, thus showing that the visibility of Muslimness is construed as threatening behaviour and their bodies criminalized as a result.

In the UK, a similar preventative measure known as Schedule 7 of the Terrorism Act 2000 operates at borders to stop those considered to be suspicious, many of whom are Muslim. Under Schedule 7, examining officers are allowed to search belongings and ask for electronic devices to be surrendered, along with passwords. Unlike other legal measures, those stopped under this law have no right to legal counsel or right of refusal. Schedule 7 has been likened to a surveillance tool which has undermined the relationship between Muslims and the state, thus fostering feelings of discontent and anxiety. In the next section, I turn to how policing security threats has become pre-emptive in its stance before turning to the Prevent Duty as an example of how this has occurred in Britain.

Pre-emption as counterterrorism

Sociology and criminology have long discussed what policing is and its value to society. Criminologist Lucia Zedner, for example, argues that the 'police is synonymous with the modern state and public policing is one of the defining characteristics of state power' (2006: 78). In response to 9/11, policing has undergone several changes in relation to counterterrorism, mainly adopting a prediction model, known widely as pre-emption, as part of its strategies. Pre-emption relies on the idea that risk is one of the primary security factors which societies must consider and can identify in advance of offences being committed.

In the UK, the idea of countering terrorism pre-emptively did not emerge from the London bombings in 2005, but had been central to the policing of Irish communities in the wake of the 'Troubles' in the mid-1960s. This led to the creation of the Prevention of Terrorism Act in 1974, initially on a temporary basis. This Act permitted the use of stopping individuals based on suspicion and, as set out by Paddy Hillyard (1993), it granted police officers the ability to stop those they suspected to be Irish. Hillyard (1993) coined the term 'suspect community' to describe how the

Irish were viewed in society. Following the War on Terror, Muslim communities are considered as the 'new' suspect community. This is evident in the arbitrary detention and torture of Muslims in places like Guantanamo Bay prison and 'black site' prisons as well as the frequent stops at borders in Schedule 7 stops and harassment by the police.

The Irish Troubles and the War on Terror have exposed the limits and brutality of policing, although it could be argued that this has a wider context. As outlined by Adam Elliot-Cooper in *Black Resistance to British Policing*, the police are increasingly relied upon to 'incarcerate away' (2021: 15) societal issues that could perhaps be more appropriately considered to be a consequence of neoliberal policies that have reduced public welfare arrangements. The increasing presence of police in social spaces, such as schools, has a disproportionate impact on communities of colour and, as argued by Elliot-Cooper (2021), resistance to the police is very much a struggle also rooted in anti-racism (see Thompson, Chapter 24, this volume).

It should be noted that the context of policing as outlined by Elliot-Cooper (2021) is different to Prevent, in that stop and search is directed at uncovering evidence of a potential offence, namely a weapon. Prevent differs in that the behaviour and ideas being surveilled are all lawful and do not indicate an intention to commit an offence (as will be discussed further later in this chapter). However, what unites the two perspectives is the way in which policing more broadly targets racialized communities.

In relation to the War on Terror specifically, Elliot-Cooper argues that 'perceptions of criminality are used to legitimize the authority of government, with racial folk devils such as the gangster, the terrorist or the immigrant' allowing for the increased use of pre-emptive security on marginalized communities (2021: 14). It has been well documented how Babar Ahmad, who was arrested and charged on terrorism offences by the US and UK governments, had his London home raided by British police in 2003 and was inflicted with 73 injuries (Poynting 2016). During the raid and his arrest, police taunted him about his religion, shouting 'Where is your God now? … Pray to Him' (Poynting 2016: 206).

Given the move to a pre-emptive form of policing and understanding of crime which privileges 'risk' in society, security is much less physical and has taken the form of public policy and the creation of new laws. The now-repealed and replaced Prevention of Terrorism Act 2005 is an example of how pre-emptive policing became enshrined in law in response to the London bombings. The government further strengthened its counterterror laws and outlined its CONTEST strategy, encompassing the UK's primary counterterrorism measures. As noted by Charlotte Heath-Kelly (2012), although 'prevention' has undergone several iterations in relation to counterterrorism in the UK, we are seeing a more permanent form of prevention. While Heath-Kelly acknowledges how pre-emptive measures were utilized as a response to the Irish Republican Army (IRA), she states that 'this previous era of British policy utilized the term "prevention" but was not explicitly framed around the pre-emption of events or the interruption of pre-terrorism processes (like radicalization) which are understood to produce terrorism' (2012: 70). Notably, the Pursue strand of the UK's counterterrorism framework, which focuses on preventing terrorist attacks, applies to Northern Ireland, whereas the Prevent Duty, aimed at stopping individuals from becoming or supporting terrorists, does not. In the next section, I consider how one of the core security policies in the UK known as Prevent has utilized pre-emptive mechanisms on Muslim populations to counter the threat of terrorism.

The Prevent Duty in the UK

The Prevent Duty is a counterterrorism policy which was established in England, Scotland, and Wales on a statutory basis in 2015. This means that public authorities such as those responsible for schools, universities, and many healthcare settings are required to have 'due regard to the need to prevent people from being drawn into terrorism'. What this means is that those working in such institutions must refer those they believe to be at risk of radicalization to counterterrorism authorities. In schools and health services, the Prevent Duty is considered to be a safeguarding provision, emphasizing that those referred to Prevent have not committed an offence but there is a risk they may do so in relation to terrorism specifically. In schools, for example, teaching staff may be concerned that an individual is susceptible to 'extremism' because of something they have said or done, or some critical change in their circumstances, and are referred to Prevent through designated safeguarding leads (see Holmwood, Chapter 22, this volume).

Prior to 2015, the Prevent Duty existed on a non-statutory basis as part of a Prevent Strategy, meaning that it was not enforced in public institutions. The Prevent Strategy was introduced by the Labour government in 2003 and, as outlined by Fahid Qurashi (2018), it played a minor role in counterterrorism policing. Initially, the Prevent Strategy was heavily involved in community affairs primarily with Muslim communities, such as providing funding to organizations for community cohesion projects through the Building a Strong Britain Together initiative (see Holmwood and Aitlhadj 2023). The funding of community cohesion projects through Prevent was largely known in policy and academic circles as a 'hearts and minds' strategy; that is a strategy which aims to promote engagement, rather than disenfranchisement by targeting individuals through cultural and social means using consent as a mechanism. This sentiment, however, has been debunked, with academics such as Sabir (2017: 213) arguing that the Prevent Strategy was not necessarily about consent, but promoted coercive strategies such as surveillance. Nevertheless, Prevent gained significant political support following the 7/7 London bombings in 2005 to manage 'homegrown' terrorism.

The various UK governments to date state that the subsequent Prevent Duty is about early intervention and is likened to other safeguarding requirements. In the guidance document produced by the government, it states that support is offered to those who are considered susceptible to extremism and terrorism; and this support involves multiagency partnerships, including local authorities, members of the police, educational professions, healthcare workers, and social services. If a Prevent Duty concern is considered to be confirmed, cases may then be referred to a Channel programme, which is described as a 'voluntary process' where tailored support is offered. As no offences have been committed, the government states that Prevent Duty referrals 'will not show up on any criminal record checks', thus denoting that there will be no repercussions.

However, as Tarek Younis (2021) shows, a referral under the Prevent Duty, despite assurances that it is a 'safeguarding' check, is formulated upon Islamophobic and racist understandings which suggest that Muslims are a national security threat. Claims that there are no repercussions therefore are not entirely correct, given that they contribute to a mounting framework which sees those racialized as Muslim as prone to violence and criminal acts. Furthermore, as argued by Holmwood and Aitlhadj, the data obtained through Prevent referrals can be held on up to ten databases and can also be shared among other multiagency teams beyond Prevent, which demonstrates that 'the harms [of a Prevent referral] begin from the moment an individual is under consideration' (2023: 18).

Workers in public sector institutions receive training for the Prevent Duty, usually as part of safeguarding courses. This training is often conducted by safeguarding officials who work in these spaces, such as the designated safeguarding lead in a school, or by members of local authority Prevent Duty teams, or organizations cleared by the Home Office. In these training sessions, staff members are provided with examples of what constitutes 'extremism' and what would constitute alarming behaviour. When it comes to training public sector practitioners on the Prevent Duty, Fernandez (2024) shows that Prevent Duty training overwhelmingly encourages those racialized as Muslim to self-censor, meaning that it stops individuals from questioning trainers or their content for fears that they may be labelled as 'extremist' themselves.

The types of 'extremism' that the Prevent Duty deals with include Islamist terrorism, considered to be the primary threat to the UK, along with far-right ideologies and other 'smaller' concerns such as 'left-wing terrorism'. It should be noted however that a majority of referrals are considered to be from the 'mixed, unstable or unclear ideology' category, which is an indication of the eclectic and often confusing nature of the indicators (Holmwood and Aitlhadj 2023: 42). As Nadya Ali (2020) shows, the Prevent policy is underpinned by a logic which racializes Muslims as outsiders. This argument shows how violence, or non-violence in the remit of Prevent, carried out by those aligned with the 'far right' is often treated less severely than that which is considered to hail from 'Islamist' extremism.

This is, first, due to the idea that the nation is being defended by the 'far right' and, second, because many of their arguments mirror those made by the state itself. This is especially the case in the realm of immigration. As shown in the People's Review of Prevent, the Shawcross report, which sought to examine the Prevent Duty, failed to recognize the violence of those considered to be 'far right', and Shawcross instead argued that 'the address of right-wing extremism within Prevent is disproportionate' (Holmwood and Aitlhadj 2023: 25). We also cannot ignore the move of the Conservative government to the right and the adoption of right-wing policies by the Labour government, especially in response to the rising membership levels of electoral parties such as Reform UK and the growing anti-immigration seeds sown as a result of the Brexit campaign.

Many of these arguments looking at the disproportionate response to terrorism and extremism is underpinned by subjective understandings of what constitutes terrorism. As detailed in the Terror Trap report, Islamophobia has now become an industry in which actors are empowering one another to fuel and strengthen anti-Muslim rhetoric (Tazamal and Esposito 2021: 43). To suggest that the term 'terrorism' has only been used to describe Muslim groups is incorrect. As Stampnitzky sets out in the report, the term '"terrorism" must be understood as a socially constructed category', arguing that the term's meaning will likely change over time (2021: 30–31). Before the 1960s, for example, Stampnitzky argues that the term 'terrorism' was 'almost exclusively used to describe the violence of states' (2021: 31), as well as non-state groups such as the Italian Red Brigades, the Red Army Faction, and the IRA. It is clear, then, that what and who is defined as a terrorist is very much dependent on notions of power and racialized understandings of violence.

What this means for policies like the Prevent Duty is that there will always be a disproportionate response to violence because the definition of what constitutes terrorism and extremism fluctuates. We see this reflected in the political and social amnesia of current affairs, such as the 2024 summer riots in England and Northern Ireland directed against Muslim and immigrant communities. We must consider how years of Islamophobic rhetoric, which is ingrained in the fabric of counterterrorism and policies like Prevent, contribute to a heightened distrust and hostility towards Muslim communities globally.

Conclusion

In this chapter, I have examined how the events on 9/11 and the subsequent War on Terror have shaped how securitization and policing have become pre-emptive, with a specific focus on the targeting of Muslim communities globally. In doing so, I show how, although 9/11 changed the trajectory of nation states in terms of security initiatives, many of these practices can also be associated with long-standing colonial imaginaries which view non-White populations, in particular, as external and 'Other' to the nation state. Stampnitzky's work on the construction of terrorism further sets out how moral panics and anxieties about certain communities can become associated with 'terrorism' or 'extremism'. Recently, this can be demonstrated in the ways in which even peaceful pro-Palestinian supporters have been designated as supporters of hate and terror. As stated in the introduction, the War on Terror is increasingly understood as a war *of* terror, especially for those racialized as Muslim.

The section on the Prevent Duty in Britain demonstrates how these arguments are applied in practice and further supports the argument that we are seeing 'policing' move into our social spheres, such as schools. We see here how invasive these strategies are, despite suggestions that they operate in a pre-crime space and lead to no criminalization. As shown by Fernandez (2024), one does not need to be referred onto Prevent to feel its chilling presence. The surveillance and censorship experienced by those racialized as Muslims contributes to feelings of fear and anxiety, thus contributing to arguments which suggest that the War on Terror is in fact as a war *of* terror. Although the War on Terror may have 'formally' ended with a declaration by President Barack Obama in 2013, the existence of policies like Prevent are a reminder of the war's persistent nature.

References

Ali, N. 2020. 'Seeing and Unseeing Prevent's Racialized Borders', *Security Dialogue* 51(6): 579–596.

Ansari, H. 2018. *The Infidel Within: Muslims in Britain Since 1800*. Oxford University Press.

Bakali, N. and Hafez, F. 2022. *The Rise of Global Islamophobia in the War on Terror: Coloniality, Race and Islam*. Manchester University Press.

Elliot-Cooper, A. 2021. *Black Resistance to British Policing*. Manchester University Press.

Fernandez, S. 2024. 'When Counter-extremism "Sticks": The Circulation of the Prevent Duty in the School Space', *Identities* 31(5): 665–683.

Heath-Kelly, C. 2012. 'Reinventing Prevention or Exposing the Gap? False Positives in UK Terrorism Governance and the Quest for Pre-emption', *Critical Studies on Terrorism* 5(1): 69–87.

Hillyard, P. 1993. *Suspect Community: People's Experience of the Prevention of Terrorism Acts in Britain*. Pluto Press.

Holmwood, J. and Aitlhadj, L. 2023. 'The People's Review of Prevent: A Response to the Shawcross Report'. https://peoplesreviewofprevent.org/wp-content/uploads/2023/06/response-to-shawcross-1.pdf

Poynting, S. 2016. 'Entitled to be a Radical? Counterterrorism and Travesty of Human Rights in the Case of Babar Ahmad', *State Crime Journal* 5(2): 204–209.

Qurashi, F. 2018. 'The Prevent Strategy and the UK "War on Terror": Embedding Infrastructures of Surveillance in Muslim Communities', *Palgrave Communications* 4(17): 1–13.

Sabir, R. 2017. 'Blurred Lines and False Dichotomies: Integrating Counterinsurgency into the UK's Domestic "War on Terror"', *Critical Social Policy* 3(2): 202–224.

Said, E. 1978. *Orientalism*. Vintage Books

Stampnitzky, L. 2021. 'Terrorism: The Self-verifying Discourse', in S.A. Al-Arian, A. Qureshi, and L. Al-Arian (eds), *The Terror Trap: The Impact of the War on Terror on Muslim Communities Since 9/11*. Bridge Initiative and Georgetown University, pp 30–36.

Tazamal, M. and Esposito, J.L. 2021. 'The Islamophobia Industry: How the Post-9/11 Environment Cultivated a Network of Forces that Feed, Sustain, and Capitalize Off Anti-Muslim Bigotry', in S.A. Al-Arian, A. Qureshi, and L. Al-Arian (eds), *The Terror Trap: The Impact of the War on Terror on Muslim Communities Since 9/11*. Bridge Initiative and Georgetown University, pp 37–48.

Younis, T. 2021. 'The Psychologization of Counter-extremism: Unpacking PREVENT', *Race and Class* 62(3): 37–60.

Younis, T. and Jadhav, S. 2019. 'Keeping Our Mouths Shut: The Fear and Racialized Self-censorship of British Healthcare', *Culture, Medicine, and Psychiatry: An International Journal of Cross-Cultural Health Research* 43(3): 404–424.

Zedner, L. 2006. 'Policing Before and After the Police', *British Journal of Criminology* 46: 78–96.

Video lecture

Fernandez, S. 2021. *Security in the War on Terror: Predict, Prevent, Police*, Connected Sociologies Curriculum Project. https://thesociologicalreview.org/projects/connected-sociologies/curriculum/policing/security-war-terror-predict-prevent-police/

QUESTIONS

1. How is the War on Terror a symptom of broader anxieties related to racialized communities?

2. In what ways has securitization changed and why have nation states adopted a pre-emptive strategy in relation to counterterrorism such as the Prevent Duty?

3. How is gender used to strengthen arguments for the War on Terror and what relationship does this have to colonialism?

Worksheet 23. Security and the War on Terror: Predict, Prevent, Police

This worksheet is designed to support AS and A-level teaching on the key topics of crime and deviance, and socialization, culture, and identity. In this online talk, Shereen Fernandez details the securitization and anti-terrorism measures introduced during the Global War on Terror, following the attacks in the United States on 11 September 2001. Focusing on the introduction of the Prevent Duty in the UK, Fernandez explains how the War on Terror has been experienced by communities racialized as Muslim in their everyday lives and in public settings such as schools and healthcare institutions. This worksheet encourages students to think critically about topics related to crime and deviance, including crime prevention, crime and the media, social control, and surveillance, within the contemporary contexts of globalization and the War on Terror. Students are also encouraged to critically assess how the effects of crime prevention measures intersect with British cultures and identities.

Time	Activity	Explanation
00.00–00.05	To warm up, answer this question: *What does it mean to 'prevent' crime? What strategies might be used?*	This activity introduces students to the topic of crime prevention and asks them to start applying a critical lens to methods of preventing and controlling crime. Students might come up with examples of education and surveillance as forms of crime prevention.
00.05–00.10	Recap of understandings of crime and deviance.	It may be useful to remind students of some of the key sociological perspectives on crime prevention, crime control, and surveillance.
00.10–00.20	Watch the talk from 2:45 to 6:03. *How does Fernandez define a 'state of emergency'? Why is this significant to understanding US responses to 9/11?*	Fernandez defines a 'state of emergency' as a measure that 'suspends laws and grants permissions for governments to use extraordinary measures to manage situations'. The use of these 'extraordinary measures' in response to 9/11 have 'spiralled globally', leading to the invasion of Iraq and Afghanistan and the widely documented use of torture and abuse in Guantanamo Bay, among other consequences. This activity requires students to be able to identify and summarize a definition of an important concept in their own words and to identify the significance of this concept within the wider context of crime prevention and the War on Terror. In thinking about the extreme consequences of this 'state of emergency', students are encouraged to think about how ideas of political power and governmental control are important to the topic of crime and deviance.
00.20–00.30	Watch the talk from 8:03 to 9:40. *How does drone warfare affect the way in which crime is punished?*	Fernandez explains that, without the requirement for soldiers to be physically present to operate them, drones 'contravene the rule of law' because they 'do not allow an individual to be tried for their crimes'. This activity asks students to think about the ways in which the event of drone warfare significantly changes what it means for states to punish crime, and the role of the criminal justice system.

Time	Activity	Explanation
00.30–00.35	At 12:59, Fernandez explains that the Prevent Duty was introduced by the UK government in 2015 to tackle 'extremism', which was defined as 'active or vocal opposition to British values'. *What do you think of this definition of 'extremism'?*	Fernandez explains that the definition of 'extremism' offered by the Prevent Duty was vague, and appears to suggest that the promotion of 'British values' makes people less likely to engage in 'extremist' activities. This activity asks students to critically assess this definition and identify the ways in which it is potentially problematic. In unpacking the term 'British values', students are encouraged to refer to their learning around the topic of socialization, culture, and identity, and how this connects with the talk on the Trojan Horse affair.
00.35–00.45	At 21:28, Fernandez states that 'one of the most prominent effects of counter-extremism measures is the rise of Islamophobia in society' and shows some examples of this within mainstream media coverage of the War on Terror. *What role does the media play in societal understandings of crime and criminals? Can you think of some current examples from the media?*	This activity encourages students to apply their learning to new contexts, drawing on the key curriculum topic of crime and the media. Students might draw comparisons between the representation of Muslims in the media during the War on Terror and the representation of immigrants during the 2016 Brexit campaigns, and recent media coverage of the 'small boats' issue.
00.45–00.55	Watch the talk from 23:09 to 25:28. *What is the role of surveillance in crime prevention? Who does the watching, and who is being watched?*	Fernandez explains that campaigns such as British Transport Police's 'See it. Say it. Sorted.' initiative encourage the British public to become the 'eyes and ears' of counterterrorism and counter-extremism, and how this leads to certain groups, particularly those racialized as Muslim, to be subject to intense scrutiny in public settings such as airports. This activity pushes students to reflect on their understandings of crime prevention and surveillance and implement what they have learned from the session to critically assess how crime has been conceptualized within the Global War on Terror and the ongoing impact of this.
00.55–01.00	Thinking about what you have learned throughout this session, answer this question: *What does it mean to say that the War on Terror has 'come home' to the UK?*	This summary activity asks students to recap on what they have learned throughout the session, drawing together their learning around the prevention and punishment of crime during the War on Terror and how this intersects with themes of socialization, culture and identity, and power and control within a UK context. Drawing on Fernandez's arguments, students may identify the day-to-day experiences of those racialized as Muslim being subject to surveillance and scrutiny as one of the key ways in which the War on Terror has 'come home'.

This worksheet was developed by Isabel Sykes.

24

Policing, Racial Capitalism, and Abolition

Vanessa E. Thompson

> **Objectives**
>
> - This chapter discusses the relationship between policing and racial capitalism.
> - It sets out a brief account of the development of policing in Europe and traces its function and logic.
> - It discusses why we need a more foundational critique of policing in struggles for justice and democracy.
> - It introduces abolitionist politics in the struggle against policing.

Introduction

In the last decades, policing has become a major focal point of political activism and organizing, not only in the United States but also in various European countries. Against the background of the 2020 Black rebellions, after the murder of George Floyd in the United States, various anti-racist and anti-colonial collectives in Europe have also increasingly mobilized against state violence. These mobilizations presented the largest anti-racist mobilizations within Europe thus far. The protests also demonstrated that racist policing is not limited to the United States. Names of Black working-class people and migrants who lost their lives at the hands of police in the United States were called out and remembered in concert with names of Black people who lost their lives at the hands of the police in European countries, such as Oury Jalloh, Adama Traoré, Babacar Gueye, Christy Schwundeck, or Mike Ben Peter. The protests therefore revealed the transnational dimensions of struggles for Black lives and challenged the myth of a 'race-less' Europe.

Drawing on the work of various organizations and initiatives, which have been formed in the last few years and organized around the issue of racist policing in various European countries, the protests could lean on the work that has already been done in these contexts. On the one hand, this is a continuation of struggles that have a much longer history in the European context and within European colonies as well (Elliott-Cooper 2021). On the other hand, specific abolitionist claims and politics have gained crucial momentum in this political conjuncture as well.

This chapter discusses the relation between policing and racial capitalism within European contexts and engages with abolitionist forms of resistance. Delving into the history of policing in Europe, I discuss the (shifting) function and role of policing as a method of racial capitalism. This contributes to an anti-colonial critique of policing that is often not addressed in social theory or criminology. Employing anti-colonial frameworks such as Frantz Fanon's notion of combat breathing and bringing them into conversation with current modalities of policing, continuities as well as discontinuities of policing are fleshed out. Finally, this chapter engages with the potentials of abolitionist resistances and worldmaking. I mainly discuss the contexts of Germany and France, though transnational connections are highlighted as well.[1]

The development of policing within Europe

Policing in Europe developed closely alongside the development of the capitalist mode of production. It emerged in a specific time and place, and had a specific function. Historically, policing occurred to activate, protect, and ensure the sovereignty of (imperial) state authority through violence and coercive force. It furthermore played a crucial role in the creation of racial capitalist relations and the control and management of the mobility of labour power. Policing was first exercised in the form of laws and police science at the withering of feudalism in continental Europe (see Tyler, Chapter 5, this volume). Through these, and related violent measures, the masses were separated from the means of production and then criminalized for their practices of survival. They were also recruited into the capitalist wage relation as well as relations of less free and unfree labour (Neocleous 2000) – often structured through the technology of racism (Thompson 2024).

Michel Foucault (2004) famously describes, in his *History of Governmentality*, that the early notion of the police in Europe, the police before the 19th century, was rather a form of governance. It was concerned with a broad range of affairs, like regulating market prices, disease control, and educational issues, and was concerned with maintaining social order rather than with individualized criminalization. This included various practices, knowledge formations, and institutionalized articulations of political order, including recruitment into wage labour. Policing discourses and practices criminalized those who tried to survive outside of the wage labour relation as well as mobile subjects such as vagabonds (Loick 2018). This affected especially Roma people who have been criminalized and brutalized in Europe for centuries (Picker 2017; Jain 2021). Differential forms of labour exploitation and dehumanization throughout the history of racial capitalism (Robinson 1983; Alexander 2023; Virdee 2019) were thus also operationalized through police power.

This further includes the coercive incorporation of racialized labour on ships transporting enslaved people, the plantation, and the colonies (see Khoo, Chapter 3, and Kaladeen, Chapter 4, this volume). As European nation states were empires and not restricted to the geographies of Europe (Bhambra 2017), policing must also be analysed with regard to the coercive and controlling discourses and practices in the colonies (Hönke and Müller 2012). Merely discussing the development of the modern police within European and national framings, as is often done in critical criminological scholarship and critical social theory, obfuscates that police surveillance regimes are geographically as well as historically far more interlaced with each other. Surveillance and punishment techniques were developed in tandem with practices in the 'colonial laboratories'. This includes practices of surveillance, capture, and control on ships transporting enslaved people (Browne 2015) and the shores of Africa; spaces that were characterized through a legally sanctioned vulnerability to 'premature deaths' (Gilmore 2007) and often served as predecessors for and in relation to the modes of policing of especially Roma and White poor to become workers in the colonial metropoles.

This colonial relation of policing was especially reflected in the presence of the police in many European colonies. As Frantz Fanon writes:

> The colonial world is a world cut in two. The dividing line, the frontiers are shown by barracks and police stations. In the colonies it is the policeman and the soldier who are the official, instituted go-betweens, the spokesmen of the settler and his rule of oppression. In capitalist societies the educational system, whether lay or clerical, the structure of moral reflexes handed down from father to son, the exemplary honesty of workers who are given a medal after 50 years of good and loyal service, and the affection which springs from harmonious relations and good behaviour – all these aesthetic expressions of respect for the established order serve to create around the exploited person an atmosphere of submission and of inhibition which lightens the task of policing considerably. … In the colonial countries, on the contrary, the policeman and the soldier, by their immediate presence and their frequent and direct action maintain contact with the native and advise him by means of rifle butts and napalm not to budge. (Fanon 1963: 38)

Fanon points out the daily and violent presence of the police within the lives of colonized workers and further describes the differential mode of the policing of exploited workers in the so-called metropoles as part of the colonial divide. Furthermore, he refers to the interplay between the police and the military. A historicization of this is also relevant for contemporary police studies. For example, the current militarization of police forces in many working-class neighbourhoods of the Global North has to be read as a continuation of the militarizing force of policing as it was previously reserved for the colonies (Elliott-Cooper 2021). The connection between the inclusion of colonized subjects into colonial police forces and neoliberal diversification strategies within police institutions serves as another example. Further, as critical racism scholars have argued, with regard to contemporary policing in Europe, colonial methods were also brought 'home' in the context of labour migration from former colonies and European peripheries (see Anitha, Chapter 8, and Hampshire, Chapter 13, this volume).

The specific articulations of policing and its function are contingent to time and space, especially in relation to racial capitalist dynamics that also change through collectivized struggles waged against them (Loick 2018; Gilmore 2022). However, policing processes continue to play an indispensable, albeit differentializing, role (Browne 2015; Loick 2018; Thompson 2022) in the re-production of the racial capitalist order.

Policing the crisis

The contemporary conjuncture of policing is embedded in the dynamics and crisis-driven relations since the 1970s, though technologies and practices of containment and violence have of course much longer histories. We are currently witnessing a complex convergence in which racist nationalism, migration regimes, and carcerality (or systems based on imprisonment and confinement) are reconstructed and expand against the background of the poly-crisis of capitalism. This poly-crisis encompasses overaccumulation and labour, climate catastrophe, neo-imperialism and warfare, a crisis of mass displacement, care and social reproduction (Hall et al 1978; Gilmore 2007; Robinson 2020; Georgi 2019). As the abolitionist and Marxist geographer Ruth Wilson Gilmore argues in her analysis of the enormous expansion of the prison system in the United States, the mass expansion of the prison system is a congealing logical (but not inevitable) result of and 'response' to the crisis of the surplus of labour, land, finance capital, and state capacity.

Gilmore shows that major shifts in the political economy during the 1970s related to deindustrialization, capital mobility, and 'natural' disasters, produced a variety of surplus (people, land, finance capital, and state capacity) that were dealt with in certain ways. The crisis of Fordism in industrialized economies in the 1970s also enhanced various articulations of carceral/security 'fixes' in Europe. This crisis and its neoliberal response of austerity, privatization, and outsourcing cannot be understood without attending to the adjustments of securitization and militarization, as Stuart Hall and his colleagues also argued in their profound UK-based analysis of the moral panic around mugging and the criminalization of Black under-employed and jobless youth as an articulation of the 'policing of the crisis' (Hall et al 1978; Wacquant 2009; see Murji, Chapter 17, this volume).

Thus, the poly-crisis of racial capitalism has not only produced mass unemployment, precarity, and increasing poverty but also strategies of a carceral and militarized management of the crisis on local and global scales. With regard to policing in Europe, we can observe an expansion of urban policing (and moral panics that accompany the carceral expansion), especially in impoverished, often racialized working-class and working poor districts: from Berlin's Kreuzberg to the *banlieues* of Paris or Marseille, from London's Tottenham to the Bijlmer in Amsterdam, to Molenbeek and Schaerbeek in Brussels, and various other post-colonial European urban areas. This expansion unfolds as a state 'response' to the crisis produced by racial capitalism as well as to the resistances of the late 1960s and 1970s, wherein migrant workers organized mass resistance to state racism, regimes of super-exploitation, colonialism, and imperialism (see Anitha, Chapter 8, Narayan, Chapter 19, and Kelbert, Chapter 20, this volume).

The cycles of urban rebellions that are often a response to police killings of (post-)migrant working-class and working poor youth, like after the murder of Mark Duggan in Tottenham or after the murder of Nahel Merzouk in Paris in 2023, illuminate how the policing of the crisis is articulated in various urban European contexts. The function of policing in this conjuncture, besides protecting and ensuring the racial capitalist order and property relations, is the management and control of the under- and unemployed sections of the working class, often racialized and migrant, so-called refugee, and the criminalization of their means of survival, including breaking rules or trying to make ends meet in informal and criminalized economies.

Accounts of policing as forms of un-breathing

Various community organizations and networks, 'copwatch' collectives, human rights organizations, and legal networks in many parts of the world emphasize that everyday policing as a form of organized (silent, slow but also fast and loud) violence is part of the normal everyday experience for many vulnerable and racialized working-class groups especially experienced along the relations of gender, sexuality, migrant status, and mental health. These experiences are normalized as they are often not seen or registered by dominant parts of the society and rather represent the norm than an exception. Thus, what are often perceived as 'exceptions' or as 'individual cases' with regard to policing, such as incidents of police violence, represent an everyday experience for many marginalized people, especially members of multi-marginalized groups. Women and LGBTQI+/refugees/impoverished Black people, people of colour with disabilities, or illegalized migrant sex workers are particularly vulnerable, as intersectional and abolitionist feminists remind us, to racist police controls, abuse, and their various, also deadly, consequences.

Thus, policing draws on and shapes interdependent forms of violence, which means that subjects who experience interlocking forms of violence simultaneously, such as racism, migration regimes, hetero-patriarchy, ableism, and economic deprivation are particularly vulnerable to policing *and* experience policing alongside these dimensions of violence – such as the criminalization of poor and racialized communities, sexualized and gendered violence against women and gender non-conforming folks, and the pathologization of folks with disabilities. Further, policing, as an institutionalized practice of control and punishment, interacts with related coercive institutions in an intersectional way (not only with the prison or the detention centre, but also with the foster care regime, the social welfare and housing system, and psychiatric institutions).

In the German context, one can think of Christy Schwundeck, who was fatally shot in a job centre in Frankfurt am Main on 19 May 2011 while enquiring about her unemployment benefits. The case of N'deye Mariame Sarr, who was shot by police on 14 July 2001 in the house of her White ex-partner, is a further crucial manifestation of how racism, gender relations, migrant status, and dis/ability intersect in policing in late capitalism (Bruce-Jones 2014). In both cases, two or more police or security officers as well as one more person were present, and

Christy Schwundeck and N'deye Mariame Sarr were the only Black women in these respective situations. Both were in a situation of crisis. Christy Schwundeck was without money since 1 May as her unemployment benefits had not arrived. N'deye Mariame Sarr wanted to pick up her two-year-old child from her White ex-partner, from whom she had separated. He had brought the child to his parents and applied for sole child custody without letting her know. Both shots were fired shortly after police arrived. Mariame Sarr was one of the first persons who was shot by the new PEP (Polizei-Einsatz-Patrone), a special bullet with a mushroom effect, created to gun down 'very violent attackers', a category which is often already inscribed and tattooed on the skin of racialized poor folks. In both instances, public prosecutors closed the case on the grounds of 'self-defence'.

Multi-marginalized groups experience policing as a condition of *un-breathing* in various but interrelated ways. I conceptualize un-breathing as a material, social, and physical condition and experience. 'I can't breathe' were the last words of George Floyd. They were also the last words of Eric Garner, while being choked to death on 7 July 2014 in New York. Samuel Dolphyne in Finland remembers the last words of his friend Ofori as following: 'He was shouting and calling my name; Ofori, Ofori they are killing me. I can't breathe.' Wilson A. from Zurich, Switzerland was stopped and searched by police after a ticket control on 10 October 2009 on a tram after he came from a meeting with a friend. He was aggressively pushed out of the tram and then brutally beaten after he asked why police only controlled him and his friend.

Wilson A. told the police that he just had heart surgery, but the police continued and even insulted him with racist slurs. As stated in the many reports of support groups and his own testimony, Wilson A. could barely breathe. Since 2009, he and his supporters have been fighting for justice. The fierce refugee activist Sista Mimi, who was engaged in the refugee protests at the Oranienplatz and the Gerhart-Hauptmann School in Berlin, died on 11 December 2014. During her long-term self-organized refugee and migrant activism, she continuously argued that the repression by police absorbed her breath. The Black construction worker Adama Traoré, who died in police custody on 19 July 2016 in the northern suburbs of Paris, could also not breathe as a result of him being detained by police.

Escaping stop and search controls, being on the move and on the run, means to be out of breath. Breathing refers both to physical as well as social breathing. I approach these experiences through the framework of Frantz Fanon, who described that the colonial condition is characterized by 'combat breathing' (Fanon 1965). Combat breathing is embodied in and through the pant for breath, the gasp of air, the compression of air supply, the chokehold, the panic attack. It refers to the loss of breath when you find out that you have lost a loved one through police violence, and while you struggle for justice which is rarely achieved in a criminal justice system (which is a class system), as well as to the fear of being policed when going outside, in the grocery store, and so on. Policing as the condition of un-breathing endangers and renders impossible *life* for vulnerable working-class and working poor folks all over the world. Policing as the historical and constant condition of un-breathing is the stuff out of which modern security and subjectivity is made.

Resistances

The resistances against policing are multifaceted. Policed groups and communities have been reporting their experiences in various ways for decades, hence challenging the banalization of racist police practices within the contexts of Europe. The documentation of these racist practices that are rendered socially invisible plays a major role. In Germany, the Campaign for Victims of Racist Police Violence (KOP) has been documenting racist police operations since 2000 and established a legal aid fund. Various cop watch groups like the group Copwatch Frankfurt based in Frankfurt have also been documenting cases of racial profiling since 2013 and have established a telephone support line to report incidents of racial profiling.

In France, the Collective Against Stop and Search/Frisk Controls (*Le collectif contre le contrôle au faciès*), which was founded as an alliance of different anti-racist initiatives and civil society organizations in spring 2011, has established a phone line to report incidents of racial profiling and regularly hands out cards and further information on their documentation procedures in places that are heavily affected by racist policing (Keaton 2013). In doing so, the collective stays in contact with those affected by racial profiling and encourages them to act against it. This is not just about statistical recording in the sense of having a legal onus of proof, as many of these collectives know about the institutional injustice of the system. Rather, documentation initiatives show people affected by racial profiling that they are not alone and hence contribute to the denormalization of the problem.

Besides documentation, other forms of collective support are an integral part of the critical work against policing. For instance, creating spaces in which those affected by racist policing can share their experiences, identifying how they can combat this phenomenon, and making space to listen and be heard is foundational for the work against racial profiling. The initiatives mentioned earlier, as well as many others, have built support structures in which those affected by racial profiling are at the centre. Raising awareness among the majority of society also plays an essential role here. Such initiatives contribute substantially to the scandalization and denormalization of racist policing, whether through their own research, reports and interviews, or statements and campaigns.

The claims of the different organizations and collectives span from the abolition of preventive policing methods to the inclusion of racial profiling in anti-discrimination law. Especially the establishment of independent reporting and investigations complaints commissions is part of the claims of anti-racist organizations. But there are also approaches that seek more foundational societal transformations beyond this, consider the relation between policing and the capitalist order, and reject police 'solutions' or 'reforms' on the basis of an alternative understanding of safety and the transformation of social relations towards structures that aren't based on violence and exploitation.

Abolitionist approaches and politics aim towards broader social transformations and ask what people really need to be safe, instead of simply calling for more control by the police. Social solutions for problems that are created by a capitalist order, such as housing crises, lack of perspective of youth, and the pushing into illegalized economies are thus at the centre for abolitionist politics that do not seek simply to transform or reform policing, but to understand that policing itself is a method of a system of exploitation and dehumanization. Abolitionist collectives thus call for the decriminalization of poverty, migration as well as substance use, and aim to offer societal support for people that are criminalized and policed. They therefore look at the root causes of social problems instead of merely addressing symptoms of these problems. Many of the groups and collectives against policing and state violence formulate abolitionist demands and connect policing to broader questions of securing conditions for capital accumulation and urban development as well as the management of the crisis through regulation of surplus populations (Gilmore 2007; Johnson 2023).

Linking struggles around the social question with migrant justice and radical anti-racism, these collectives rally around the reallocation of resources for public housing, non-punitive welfare, education, self-determined healthcare as well as decriminalization, regardless of immigration status. The call to abolish the police, while at the same time reinvesting in community support structures, housing, social support, health and public infrastructure on local as well as global scales, is one example of abolitionist organizing. At the same time, abolitionist groups do not simply focus on policing, borders, or prisons, but also foster coalitions with wider anti-capitalist networks and unions, to push back against the system that is dependent on processes of criminalization such as policing, and exploits the vast majority of people on this planet.

Note

[1] This chapter summarizes arguments I have made in previous articles (Thompson 2021, 2022).

References

Alexander, N. 2023. *Against Racial Capitalism: Selected Writings*. Edited by S. Vally and E. Motala. Pluto Press.

Bhambra, G. 2017. 'The Current Crisis of Europe: Refugees, Colonialism, and the Limits of Cosmopolitanism', *European Law Journal* 23(5): 395–405.

Browne, S. 2015. *Dark Matters: On the Surveillance of Blackness*. Duke University Press.

Bruce-Jones, E. 2014. 'German Policing at the Intersection: Race, Gender, Migrant Status and Mental Health', *Race and Class* 56(3): 36–49.

Elliott-Cooper, A. 2021. *Black Resistance to British Policing*. Manchester University Press.

Fanon, F. 1963. *The Wretched of the Earth*. Grove Press.

Fanon, F. 1965. *A Dying Colonialism*. Grove Press.

Foucault, M. 2004. *Sicherheit, Territorium, Bevölkerung, Geschichte der Gouvernementalität I*. Suhrkamp.

Georgi, F. 2019. 'Toward Fortress Capitalism: The Restrictive Transformation of Migration and Border Regimes as a Reaction to the Capitalist Multicrisis', *The Canadian Review of Sociology* 56(4): 556–579.

Gilmore, R.W. 2007. *Golden Gulag: Prisons, Surplus, Crisis, and Opposition in Globalizing California*. University of California Press.

Gilmore, R.W. 2022. *Abolition Geography: Essays on Liberation*. Verso.

Hall, S., Critcher, C., Jefferson, T., Clarke, J., and Roberts, B. 1978. *Policing the Crisis: Mugging, the State and Law and Order*. Macmillan.

Hönke, J. and Müller, M.-M. 2021. 'Governing (In)security in a Postcolonial World: Transnational Entanglements and the Worldliness of "Local" Practice', *Security Dialogue* 43(5): 383–401.

Jain, R. 2021. 'Von der "Zigeunerkartei" zu den "Schweizermachern" bis Racial Profiling', in M. Wa Baile, S.O. Dankwa, T. Naguib, P. Purtschert and S. Schilliger (eds) *Racial Profiling. Struktureller Rassismus und antirassistischer Widerstand*. Transcript, pp 43–65.

Johnson, C. 2023. *After Black Lives Matter: Policing and Anti-Capitalist Struggle*. Verso.

Keaton, T.D. 2013. 'Racial Profiling and the "French Exception"', *French Cultural Studies* 24(2): 231–242.

Loick, D. 2018. *Kritik der Polizei*. Campus Verlag.

Neocleous, M. 2000. *The Fabrication of Social Order: A Critical Theory of Police Power*. Pluto.

Picker, G. 2017. *Racial Cities: Governance and the Segregation of Romani People in Urban Europe*. Routledge.

Robinson, C. 1983. *Black Marxism. The Making of the Black Radical Tradition*. Zed Press.

Robinson, W.I. 2020. *The Global Police State*. Pluto Press.

Thompson, V.E. 2021. 'Beyond Policing. For a Politics of Breathing', in K. Duff (ed), *Abolishing the Police*. Dog Section Press, pp 179–193.

Thompson, V.E. 2022. 'Policing Blackness in Europe. Colonial Entanglements and Contemporary Articulations of Struggle', in L. Djordjević, S. Constantin, T. Kiss, M. Payet, F. prina, M. Riekkinen, A. Tomaselli and B. Vizi (eds), *European Yearbook of Minority Issues*. Nijhoff, pp 27–48.

Thompson, V.E. 2024. 'Surplus People of the World Unite! On Borders, Policing, and Abolition', in S. Riva, S. Campbell, B. Whitener, and K. Medien (eds), *Border Abolition Now*. Pluto Press, pp 36–53.

Virdee, S. 2019. 'Racialized Capitalism: An Account of Its Contested Origins and Consolidation', *The Sociological Review* 67(1): 3–27.

Wacquant, L. 2009. *Punishing the Poor: The Neoliberal Government of Social Insecurity*. Duke University Press.

Video lecture

Thompson, V.E. 2021. *Policing in Postcolonial Continental Europe*, Connected Sociologies Curriculum Project. https://thesociologicalreview.org/projects/connected-sociologies/curriculum/policing/policing-postcolonial-continental-europe/

QUESTIONS

1. What is the role of policing in the development of capitalism?

2. Discuss how policing impacts the lives of marginalized groups in your context.

3. Discuss the potential of resistance collectives for broader struggles for justice and democracy.

Worksheet 24. Policing, Racial Capitalism, and Abolition

This worksheet is designed to support AS and A-level teaching on the key topics of crime and deviance, social order, and social control. It also draws on themes of social differentiation, power, and stratification. This online talk and worksheet are aimed at students who already have a good understanding of the relationship between colonialism and policing. Students may benefit from watching the talks on 'Colonial Policing', 'Colonial Policing Comes Home', and 'Policing in Schools' before starting this session. In this lecture, Vanessa E. Thompson gives an overview of some key anti-colonial, post-colonial, and Black critiques of policing and introduces some abolitionist initiatives and movements. It covers important sociological concepts such as intersectionality and provides a useful entry point for students to learn about the role of lived experience within sociological research.

Time	Activity	Explanation
00.00–00.05	To warm up, write three bullet points about the relationship between colonialism and policing, using your existing knowledge.	This question encourages students to recap on what they already know about colonialism and policing before engaging with this session, ensuring they have a grounding in the important themes of the lecture.
00.05–00.10	Recap of understandings of crime and deviance.	It may be useful to remind students of some of the key sociological perspectives on crime and deviance.
00.10–00.20	At 2:52 Thompson says that critical social theories of policing understand the police as 'a societal relation of power which reproduces discourses, practices and ideologies of criminalization that go beyond the mere institution of the police'. *In what ways does police power 'go beyond' the institution itself?*	This activity asks students to start thinking about the police within the wider contexts of social control and social order, which is a key theme throughout this talk.
00.20–00.25	Watch the talk from 8:27 to 10:22. *In addition to race, what other factors might influence the way a person experiences being policed?*	This activity encourages students to apply their knowledge of social inequalities to the topic of policing and asks them to begin thinking about intersectionality, which will be explored in more detail in subsequent activities. Students might identify factors such as class, gender, disability, and sexuality as impacting the way in which people experience being policed differently.

Time	Activity	Explanation
00.25–00.35	Watch the talk from 14:25 to 17:09. Why is listening to lived experience an important sociological method? What might be some challenges of using people's lived experiences in sociological research?	These questions ask students to critically assess methods used in sociological research, which is a core requirement in the curriculum. Students might talk about the necessity of foregrounding the experiences of marginalized groups in sociological research, and challenges might include issues around safeguarding and power imbalances in the research process.
00.35–00.40	Watch the talk from 17:10 to 18:04. What is intersectionality? Why is it important to this topic?	At 17:19 Thompson talks about how 'subjects who experience interlocking forms of exploitation and domination simultaneously ... are particularly vulnerable to policing'. By asking students to identify and summarize in their own words what intersectionality means, the activity allows them to build upon their earlier thinking around the ways in which different social inequalities interact and gives them the academic vocabulary for articulating this.
00.40–00.50	Watch the talk from 21:10 to 22:24. How might the concept of intersectionality help us to understand the injustices faced by Rita Awour Ojunge and her family?	This activity builds on the previous question, pushing students to apply their knowledge of intersectionality to the case study Thompson presents in the lecture. This activity stretches their critical thinking skills, and may provide a good basis for a group discussion or paired activity.
00.50–01.00	Drawing together what you have learned in this session, write a paragraph summarizing your understanding of the relationship between colonialism and policing, outlining the main points from the session.	This summary activity asks students to draw together what they have learned across the talks associated with this section of the book, to create connections across the different themes within crime and deviance, punishment, social order and control, and understand how the thread of colonialism underpins these.

This worksheet was developed by Isabel Sykes.

PART V

The Environment

Edited by Su-ming Khoo

25

Connected Sociologies of Pollution

Su-ming Khoo

Objectives

- This chapter argues that social science should pay systematic attention to pollution, helping to explain socially unjust distributions of pollution harm and their implications for global justice and solidarity.

- It shows that environmental injustice is driven by the 'economic logic of pollution' in globalized markets where the drive for industrial production and economic efficiency results in unequal patterns of environmental harm and pollution dumping, allowing some bodies and places to be more readily polluted than others.

- It explains how knowledge about pollution's extent and harm tends to be minimized or suppressed by industrial, military, and state interests, while civil society campaigns try to bring such problems to light, pressuring governments to control pollution out of concerns for health, safety, and environmental injustice.

Introduction

Pollution is an under-emphasized, but essential, topic for the social sciences. Pollution is not easily defined as there are many different types of pollution, with each type posing particular environmental, health, and social problems. 'Pollution' refers to adverse contamination of air, land, water, living beings, or ecosystems, posing hazards and harming health. The harmful nature of pollution means that governments must regulate it. However, governments are pulled in competing directions because citizens and industries tend to have different concerns about pollution: citizens usually want to minimize harm, while industries want to minimize costs.

Pollution increased as industrialization gained pace, intensifying during the later 19th century, when coal-based synthetic chemical industries developed. Since then, industrial societies have fostered close connections between industry and science, and accustomed people to the ubiquitous presence of harmful chemicals. The 20th century brought a new era of total war, involving massive use of chemical weapons that not only inflicted immediate casualties, but also caused widespread environmental contamination affecting people, fauna, flora, soil, and water over longer periods (Jarrige and Le Roux 2020: 182).

Pollution challenges conventional social scientific assumptions that social problems stem from ignorance, while knowledge enables solutions. Modern social science assumes that systematic studies should begin with clear definitions, quantify the defined problem, and understand it within clear timeframes. Today's pollution problems involve many novel substances that exist in huge quantities but are complex and difficult to identify or quantify. Many pollutants are more threatening in large quantities, but others may pose toxic threats in tiny concentrations. 'Forever chemicals' persist over timeframes that challenge human imagination, potentially accumulating over tens of thousands, or even hundreds of thousands, of years (Boyd 2022: 8).

Conventional modern thinking accepts that desirable economic developments inevitably involve undesirable consequences, or byproducts. Yet most systematic thinking, like mainstream economic theory, allows these consequences to be treated as 'external' to the economic activity that produced them, in effect externalizing the consequences, largely onto more vulnerable and marginalized communities (Boyd 2022: 66). Pollution is often seen in ahistorical, future-oriented, and wishful terms, hoping that better technologies will be invented to solve problems in the future. Yet pollution harms are historical, bio-accumulating in bodies of land, water, people, fauna, and flora as economic growth continuously demands industrial production 'taps' to produce and pollute. The principle of economic efficiency drives polluters to minimize the costs of dealing with pollution. In a competitive globalized world economy, cost efficiency drives pollution exports from high-cost to low-cost locations. 'Efficient' global trade results in pollution being dumped in 'sinks', creating toxic 'sacrifice zones', extremely contaminated areas where vulnerable and marginalized groups bear a disproportionate burden from pollution and hazardous substances (Boyd 2022: Summary).

Conventional approaches have failed to prevent the 'planetary boundaries' that represent the safe global operating space for humanity from being overstepped, while global injustice continues. This chapter proposes an alternative perspective based on pollution prevention (precaution) and remedies or reparations, following the principle of 'common but differentiated responsibility' (CBDR). Pollution should be prevented or treated at source (abated) and highly resourced parties must work harder to remedy accumulated harm to polluted people and places (reparations) and clean up pollution (remediation), prioritizing the most hazardous, historically most severe forms of pollution.

The planetary boundaries approach

The planetary boundaries approach is widely used to understand environmental problems. Nine 'planetary boundaries' indicate thresholds for potential global catastrophe: climate change, ocean acidification, stratospheric ozone depletion, nitrogen and phosphorous cycles, freshwater use, land use change, biodiversity loss, atmospheric, and chemical pollution. All nine thresholds concern pollution, including the three most urgent problems where the threshold has already been exceeded, putting the planet in the red 'danger' zone. These are: biodiversity loss, nitrogen and phosphorus cycles, and climate change (Rockström et al 2009).

The planetary boundaries approach aids an understanding of the scale and urgency of global environmental problems; however, its treatment of pollution is worryingly limited. Climate warming greenhouse gases (including carbon dioxide and methane) and ozone-depleting chemicals (chlorofluorocarbons, or CFCs) are represented as these have received considerable policy attention in recent decades. However, other pollutants have been relatively ignored, especially toxic chemicals affecting the survival, health, and functioning of humans, flora, fauna, and ecosystems.

Many pollutants derive from fossil fuels and fossil-fuel derived synthetic 'organic' chemicals, including agricultural pesticides, herbicides, fertilizers, and plastics. Until recently, the planetary boundaries model assumed that chemical and air pollution remained in the 'safe' green zone (for example, Rockström et al 2009), however this assumption was based on an absence of common measurements, not an absence of real and dangerous threats. These assumptions of safety have been overturned by recent research pointing to the dangers posed by the huge volume, variety, and complexity of polluting chemicals, plastics, and other substances that continue to be generated by modern industrial production, consumption, and disposal processes, even if exact identification and quantification of the threats remain largely unknown (Persson et al 2022).

While pollution poses clear threats to everyone and the whole planet, it is important to notice that all pollution is characterized by uneven distributions of harm from dumping, poisoning, and nuisance. The patterns of harm do not match the benefits of profits and convenience that come from polluting. Benefits and costs of pollution tend to follow radically different historical patterns. These are shaped by imperial and colonial legacies of dispossession, extraction, imperialism, and colonization that effectively defined some places and people as resource 'taps' and others as waste disposal 'sinks'. While Chapter 3 in this volume, 'Colonial Extraction and Dispossession', mainly discussed extraction via 'taps', this chapter is more concerned with what goes into 'sinks' and their effects. Pollution can be said to result in 'slow' violence, a type of violence that occurs gradually, out of sight, and is less noticeable because it is dispersed across time and space. Slow violence is violence perpetrated by some people, often unintentionally, but nevertheless unjustly at others' expense.

Pollution is often treated as a separate, less important topic to climate change, but climate change should arguably be seen as part of the larger pollution problem. Treating climate change as a pollution problem helps us to understand that it is not simply a problem of substituting 'clean', 'sustainable' for 'dirty', 'unsustainable' fuels, or consumer products or individual 'lifestyles'. Pollution is an important matter of global environmental health, and everyone's rights to enjoy a clean, healthy, non-toxic, and sustainable environment. This requires collective protection and global solidarity actions to combat environmental injustice.

Types of pollution

There are numerous types of pollution. Air pollution comes from burning fuels, industry, transport, and wildfires. Radiation pollution comes from nuclear energy generation and military weapons. Soil, freshwater, and marine pollution come from agricultural chemicals, sewage, mining, and industrial processes. Heat pollution, light pollution, and noise pollution also result from industrial processes, transportation, and urbanization. 'Persistent' pollutants do not break down easily, accumulating in the bodies of people, plants, animals, water, air, and soil, and increasing in toxicity over time. This chapter focuses on some different types of pollution, including intentionally and unintentionally manufactured chemicals, engineered materials like plastics, and chemical substances associated with war, but also with health protection, such as pest control.

Low- and middle-income countries bear the brunt of pollution-related illnesses, accounting for nearly 92 per cent of pollution-related deaths (Naidu et al 2021). Greenhouse gases impacting climate change are not usually classed as 'pollution', however nearly half of the world's population are highly susceptible to climate change, with climate crisis creating a new category of sacrifice zones arising from unabated greenhouse gas emissions. Some communities have become, and are becoming, uninhabitable because of extreme weather events or slow-onset disasters, including drought and rising sea levels (Boyd 2022: 5, 27).

Chemical pollution includes pesticides and fertilizers routinely used to produce food and other crops. Mining, industries, and cleaning products also produce chemical pollution. Plastics are chemically derived materials which are found everywhere on the planet, with toxic effects on ecology and human health. Plastic pollution ranges from the vastness of the 'Great Pacific Garbage Patch' of marine debris, spanning over 1.5 million square kilometres, large items like 'ghost' fishing nets, smaller items like plastic bags and shoes, and tiny 'microplastics' which are small enough to be inhaled, enter the bloodstream or breast milk, and bio-accumulate in bodily organs. Plastic is ubiquitous to consumer and industrial products, processes, and transportation because it is cheap, malleable, and durable. Plastics' durability means that they break into smaller pieces while remaining as 'forever' pollutants. As plastics break down, they leach out and absorb other toxic pollutants, which may be toxic in very low concentrations (Parker 2024).

Today, microplastics and traces of hundreds of industrial chemical pollutants can be detected in people's bodies. These chemicals may interact 'additively, multiplicatively, or antagonistically', producing 'cocktail effects' in mixtures which are difficult or impossible to measure. Many of the most toxic and hazardous polluting chemicals are hormone or endocrine disruptors, which affect the health and functioning of humans, other living beings, and ecology in complex ways (Liboiron 2021).

The BBC *Blue Planet II* documentary series raised global awareness about plastic waste and its effects on the marine environment after the programmes were broadcast in 2017–2018. Plastic use continues to expand regardless, running to hundreds of millions of tons annually. For several decades up to 2018, the world's main destination for plastic waste was China, where plastics were destined for recycling. However, only a small proportion of plastic waste is actually recycled. Eighty per cent of the world's plastic is landfilled, polluting land, water, and oceans. Increased concern over dumping and pollution led China to ban imports of many types of waste plastic in 2018 (Brooks et al 2018). However, increased environmental awareness and even strict government bans have not significantly reduced plastic production or pollution since 2018 (Dunn et al 2020).

Common but differentiated responsibilities

The environmental principle of CBDR establishes that everyone is affected by global environmental problems, however wealthier, more powerful sections of global society have benefited more from polluting to date, while accumulating greater resources that could be directed to remedy the problems. Wealthier and more powerful countries and social groups thus bear more responsibility for pollution, having benefited more from polluting activities. 'Polluter pays' and CBDR are environmental principles directing polluters to take responsibility for reducing pollution (abatement) and cleaning it up (remediation). People who have benefited less from producing pollution, and who suffer more from pollution harms, are entitled to assistance and remediation, according to principles of justice and social solidarity. For example, alternative economists like Jason Hickel attempt to quantify differentiated responsibilities for greenhouse gas emissions, arguing that historical emissions are a form of 'atmospheric colonialism' that require just reparations (Hickel 2020).

The problem of pollution illustrates that the Global South is a nuanced concept that connects disadvantaged geographies. The Global South includes locations in the geographical North, such as the location described by the geographer Thom Davies as 'Cancer Alley', a highly polluted region in Southern Louisiana, United States. Cancer Alley, a small community surrounded by concentrated petrochemical infrastructure, is a 'a postcolonial region' because the location of polluting infrastructure is rooted in historical legacies of racism and plantations (Davies 2022: 411). David Boyd, the United Nations Independent Expert on the Right to a Safe, Clean, Healthy and Sustainable Environment, names Louisiana's 'Cancer Alley', alongside another notorious pollution hotspot in Canada – 'Chemical Valley', in Sarnia, Ontario, which has disturbing health effects for the Aamjiwnaang First Nation (Boyd 2022: 43, 44). Davies and Boyd counter assumptions that pollution can be 'externalized' onto remote or obscure people, whose experiences somehow do not count, and who can be left to suffer in sacrifice zones.

From toxic awareness to transnational pollution and ecocide

In 1962, a US biologist, Rachel Carson, published *Silent Spring*, raising popular awareness about the harmful effects of DDT (Dichlorodiphenyltrichloroethane) and related chemical pesticides. DDT was used to control insect pests that spread diseases like malaria and typhus. Pesticides were initially promoted by governments and manufacturers in a context of Second World War government propaganda and quickly became very widely used in homes and agriculture. An environmentalist counter-movement began to question the spread of toxic industrial chemicals and counter-cultural sections of the public allied with concerned public health and environmental health scientists (Conis 2017). *Silent Spring* offered a dramatic account of long-term pesticide over-use, threatening extinction to wildlife like birds, through the bioaccumulation of toxins in the food chain and causing cancer in humans. *Silent Spring* gave a voice to growing public concerns about toxic chemicals, and campaigns to ban the indiscriminate use of pesticides eventually led to DDT and other Persistent Organic Pollutants (POPs, pollutants that do not break down easily, accumulating toxicity in the environment and biological tissues) being more strictly controlled; with DDT being banned in the United States in 1972.

In response to growing environmental awareness, the first United Nations Conference on the Human Environment was held in Stockholm in 1972, enabling the international community of governments to discuss and connect environmental issues in a cooperative way. The meeting was hosted by Sweden and its prime minister, Olof Palme's bold opening speech used a new word, 'ecocide', to criticize the international community's failure to control wartime uses of chemical, biological, and nuclear weapons, while raising awareness about peacetime environmental pollution and dumping. Palme presented environmental problems as threats to global peace and cooperation, not only to the environment and health. The environment cannot be defended by defending borders: 'the air we breathe is not the property of any one nation'.

The Stockholm conference set a precedent for regulating acid rain, a problem originating principally from power plants burning sulphurous coal and oil, and from vehicles. Polluting gases in the atmosphere travel across boundaries, to produce acid rain affecting ecosystems distant from the polluting origin point. Pollution's global nature requires global monitoring, assessment, and regulation. Palme criticized the international community for being unready to act on pollution control: 'We are not yet prepared to accept the full consequences of international solidarity' (Palme 1972). It was 1989 before the Basel Convention was in place to regulate the transnational spread of DDT and similar chemicals, though this only regulated the transportation and dumping of hazardous 'waste', not the production or use of the toxic chemicals as such.

The US imperial war to control Indochina (Vietnam, Laos, and Cambodia) began in 1955, and was ongoing in 1972, until the US defeat in 1975. Palme used the new term 'ecocide' to call out the US military's use of huge amounts of toxic chemicals, known by the code name 'Agent Orange' to destroy vast areas of forest and crops in South Vietnam, Laos, and Cambodia, between 1961 and 1971. Although pesticide chemicals became more nationally regulated in industrial nations from around 1970, international responsibilities for chemicals dumped during warfare and their long-term toxic effects continue to be disputed half a century later. The pollution of three million hectares of acres of forest and exposure of millions of Vietnamese, Laotians, Cambodians, and US military personnel, causing hundreds of thousands of deaths, have yet to be fully remediated or compensated (Jarrige and Le Roux 2020: 184).

The economic logic of pollution

Twenty years after the Stockholm Conference, the 1992 UN Environmental Programme's Rio Conference consolidated a set of global environmental principles, including the precautionary principle to prevent harmful pollution, the polluter pays principle, and the CBDR principle discussed earlier. Polluters have a vested interest in ignoring and minimizing pollution, accounting for as little harm and damage as possible, to reduce costs and maximize profits. Pollution is regulated by government authorities, who issue permits to the largest polluters, allowing a certain 'acceptable' level of pollution and imposing fines or sanctions if the permitted levels are overstepped. Potential or actual victims of pollution are not usually considered by pollution regulations. The costs of pollution can be lowered by ignoring harm and damage, and by moving the pollution to places where damage has the lowest economic valuation. This economic logic moves problematic or dangerous pollution like waste plastic or toxic chemicals from high-wage, high-cost Global North regions to low-wage, low-cost Global South regions. Profits and capital that result from polluting economic activities move in the reverse direction, to be accumulated by Global North industries and shareholders.

Pollution's unequal benefits and harms are transmitted by markets, using the apparently neutral theory of comparative advantage and mechanisms of global trade and finance. Low costs and wages and high rates of poverty-related disease, infant mortality, and low life expectancy confer competitive market 'advantages' on poorer, less industrialized regions. Lower costs make it economically efficient to move dangerous industrial 'taps' and pollution 'sinks' to less industrialized areas, while lower levels of historical industrialization and regulation make regions like Africa seem 'vastly' and 'inefficiently' 'under-polluted' (Vallette 1999), affording greater 'sink' capacity.

It is economically rational and efficient for less industrialized, less polluted, and lower wage regions to keep regulations lax, and encourage polluting industries to locate in the Global South, bringing polluting industries and jobs. Higher wage, more industrialized, and more historically polluted areas of the Global North find it cost-effective and easy to shift polluting activities to cheaper, less regulated 'pollution havens' in the Global South. The toxic and hazardous nature of pollution deepens the attraction towards low-wage 'sinks', since lower wages and lower life expectancies translate into lower insurance and compensation costs. A kind of vicious circle operates, where environmental health harms reduce life expectancy, cheapening life and further incentivizing the transfer of health-harming pollution as a cost-effective measure.

Socially constructed ignorance and colonial relations of dominance

In planetary boundaries thinking, pollution is justified as a less important issue on the ground of insufficient knowledge or scientific uncertainty about its extent and impact. Yet recent studies show how states and industries collude to reinforce non-knowledge, prevent stricter regulation, and excuse delay and inaction (Jarrige and Le Roux 2020). The active creation of ignorance and uncertainty concerning pollution, and its deleterious effects on human health, climate, and ecosystems, are not accidental omissions, they result from wilful ignorance and pursuit of systematic inaction.

Liboiron (2021) explains how the scientific theory of pollution reflects the underlying form of colonialism as dominating 'bad relations'. The colonial way of thinking defines unidirectional, extractive, managerial, and non-reciprocal colonial logics and relationships. Pollution theory is based on allowing a certain amount of pollution to occur, up to a defined threshold. It is premised on an assumed entitlement to somewhere, something, or someone to absorb the pollution and its harms. Colonialism defines the environment in an extractive manner, existing solely for value to be extracted, maximizing profit. Poorer, less polluted places and people are defined as failures at completely and efficiently polluting themselves for profit, and are presented as the potential beneficiaries, not victims, of colonial extraction and pollution. Pollution theory re-imagines disadvantaged people as competitors providing pollution sinks, while 'nature' merely stands as a reserve that guarantees extractive futures (Liboiron 2021: 65).

Pollution requires critical and decolonial thinking that connects pollution problems across the globe. Decolonial thinking exposes the colonial foundations of the 'economic logic of pollution' and resists its extractive and discriminatory logic of dispossession and extraction via 'taps' and toxic accumulation via 'sinks', producing toxic sacrifice zones. Conventional pollution regulations are based upon 'assimilation theory', which assumes land, waters, and people as 'sinks' to absorb the externalities of pollution. Pollution is the result of industrial production that requires both the resources that provide 'raw materials' and the assimilative capacity to dispose of the 'costs' of industrial production at the most 'efficient' (read lowest) cost.

Cost efficiency allows some people and places to accumulate income and wealth, while others accumulate contamination and toxins. Harmful pollution causes disease, harm, and trauma which are disproportionately suffered by disadvantaged and discriminated socio-economic classes, Indigenous people, and poor people in 'sacrifice zones'. The technical definition of pollution defines pollution as a certain concentration of pollutants that requires a 'carrying capacity' or assimilative capacity, critical load or permissible dose from certain bodies (of water, land or people) (Liboiron 2021: 40). Concepts of 'carrying capacity' work for some pollutants which have a 'safe dose', but they do not work for chemicals that are toxic in very small doses.

While economic efficiency and comparative advantage are logical principles, they also foster material forms of social and environmental discrimination which are extremely unjust. Pointing out the colonial origins of pollution, the overwhelming power of industrialism, and the prevalence of socially constructed ignorance may cause some discomfort, but this is necessary to overcome the worrying inaction on pollution, especially chemical pollution and plastics.

Norms, laws, and regulations holding back pollution have been slow to emerge and become quickly outstripped as many different pollutants are produced and combined. Modern, fossil-fuel driven industrial economies have accustomed their host societies to continuous, massive production of wastes and pollution, including many toxic and hazardous substances. These wastes pollute land, water, air, and living beings through a set of economic and regulatory relations that distribute benefits and harms unevenly.

Establishing regulatory responsibility is a complicated and difficult task as many different authorities are involved in regulating different types of pollution, while the corporations that constitute the most powerful and polluting entities have outstripped countries in terms of their sheer economic power and political and social influence.

The Intergovernmental Panel on Climate Change is a global scientific panel tasked with monitoring greenhouse gases, helping the global climate change treaty body to coordinate and bring about action. Despite the growing realization that pollution by chemical pollutants, plastics, and their byproducts may be a global environmental problem that is as severe as climate change, or even worse, the global monitoring of chemicals is comparatively weak (Persson et al 2022). The United Nations Environment Programme's chemicals monitoring programme, the Strategic International Approach to International Chemicals Management, has a very small budget, has held rather few meetings, has experienced many delays, and is only voluntary, rather than mandatory.

The ongoing scale of pollution, the hazardous, health-harming, and long-term problems it causes require not only major changes in awareness, but also urgent action to replace inaction. It may not be possible to eliminate pollution, but it is urgently necessary to abate or reduce the volumes of pollution being continuously produced and remediate some of its most toxic, discriminatory, and harmful effects. Contention and friction between industries and affected people cause conflict, but such conflicts also represent opportunities to do things differently, reduce harm, precautionarily avoid future harm, and redistribute the harms and benefits of pollution more fairly.

Conclusion

Pollution brings to light the critical intersection between political, social, economic, and scientific issues (Jarrige and Le Roux 2020: 6). It connects local environmental problems with global power, inequalities, and the effects of socially constructed ignorance. A critical approach to pollution goes beyond obvious statements about the need to control it, to consider unequal experiences and perspectives. Acknowledging the concerning lack of global action to prevent, control, and remedy pollution, a global perspective connects the beneficiaries of polluting activities with responsibilities for harms inflicted on polluted people and places.

Critical social science takes the understanding of pollution beyond strictly scientific and technical perspectives, connecting pollution problems to questions about social inequalities, and drawing attention to differentiated social, political, and economic responsibilities to limit and remedy pollution harms. Pollution occurs within a global economic system that has roots in colonial-modern transformations. Colonial histories designated land, air, water, flora, fauna, and people as resource 'taps' and pollution 'sinks', directing profits and benefits to the Global North, and harmful pollution to the Global South, thought of as 'vastly under polluted' and inefficiently exploited markets. Max Liboiron's (2021) book title expresses the colonial underpinnings of the global system of pollution bluntly: *Pollution is Colonialism*.

Unjust histories of dispossession, colonization, extraction, and related discriminatory structures of racism, classism, and sexism underpin more recent and current forms of pollution, experienced as environmental discrimination and injustice in the Global South. Pollution also helps us to understand the 'Global North' or 'Global South' as nuanced terms for describing advantaged and disadvantaged geographies, not literal geographical hemispheres. Global pollution connects Global Norths and Global Souths within and across geographical borders. The scope for country-based pollution controls is limited, necessitating global coordination and solidarity. However, countries are not necessarily the most influential actors in regulating or failing to control pollution today, since the majority of the world's wealthiest, most powerful entities are not countries, but corporations.

The eminent ecologist Robert May (2007) observes that there are many lamentable uncertainties and knowledge gaps in global environmental and ecological knowledge. We are aware that human and planetary health face major threats, yet large degrees of ignorance remain concerning the exact nature and scale of the threats. The questions that matter the most to ecology, according to May, are not ecological; they are ethical, economic, and political. The structural and historical legacies of imperialism and colonialism underlie these ethical, economic, and political questions to a great extent. Narrowly utilitarian considerations require nature to be conserved because it may be useful – providing resources, food, and medicines that we have not yet fully identified. Broader utilitarians accept that the extent of scientific non-knowledge about ecological systems may mean that we do not really know how the decline or disappearance of some elements might lead to catastrophic disruptions or complete collapse of the 'ecosystem services' that all humanity depends upon.

Most compelling of all are the ethical responsibilities of the present generation to ensure that future generations will have a habitable planet. This responsibility is not easily resolved due to inequality and differentiated responsibilities for abating and reducing pollution and remediating affected places and people. Thinking about pollution requires us to bring in the social, political, and economic structures of colonization, discrimination, and racism, and to critically appraise markets as historical social structures. These determine how much pollution is allowed, where it is allowed or encouraged to go, and the distributions of harm and benefit that follow the distributions of wastes and toxins and the harms they entail.

References

Boyd, D.R. 2022. 'The Right to a Clean, Healthy and Sustainable Environment: Non-toxic Environment', A/HRC/49/53. https://docs.un.org/en/A/HRC/49/53

Brooks, A.L., Wang, S.L., and Jambeck, J.R. 2018. 'The Chinese Import Ban and its Impact on Global Plastic Waste Trade', *Science Advances* 4(6): eaat0131. doi: 10.1126/sciadv.aat0131

Carson, R. 1962. *Silent Spring*. Penguin Books.

Conis, E. 2017. 'Beyond Silent Spring: An Alternate History of DDT', *Science History Institute: Environment*, 14 February. https://www.sciencehistory.org/stories/magazine/beyond-silent-spring-an-alternate-history-of-ddt/

Davies, T. 2022. 'Slow Violence and Toxic Geographies: "Out of Sight" to Whom?', *EPC: Politics and Space* 40(2): 409–427.

Dunn, M.E., Mills, M., and Veríssimo, D. 2020. 'Evaluating the Impact of the Documentary Series *Blue Planet II* on Viewers' Plastic Consumption Behaviors', *Conservation Science & Practice* 2(10): e280.

Hickel, J. 2020. 'Quantifying National Responsibility for Climate Breakdown: An Equality-based Attribution Approach for Carbon Dioxide Emissions in Excess of the Planetary Boundary', *The Lancet Planetary Health* 4(9): e399–e404. https://doi.org/10.1016/S2542-5196(20)30196-0

Jarrige, R. and Le Roux, T. 2020. *The Contamination of the Earth: A History of Pollutions in the Industrial Age*. Translated by J. Egan and M. Egan. MIT Press.

Liboiron, M. 2021. *Pollution is Colonialism*. Duke University Press.

May, R. 2007. 'Unanswered Questions and Why They Matter', in R. May and A. McLean (eds), *Theoretical Ecology: Principles and Applications*. Oxford University Press, pp 205–215.

Naidu, R., Biswas, B., Willett, I., Cribb, J., Singh, B.K., Nathanail, C.P., et al. 2021. 'Chemical Pollution: A Growing Peril and Potential Catastrophic Risk to Humanity', *Environment International* 156: 106616. https://doi.org/10.1016/j.envint.2021.106616

Palme, O. 1972. Opening Address to the UN Stockholm Conference on the Human Environment by Prime Minister Olof Palme, June 6, https://youtu.be/y0-kONrKS78

Parker, L. 2024. 'The World's Plastic Pollution Crisis, Explained', *National Geographic: Environment*, 23 September. https://www.nationalgeographic.com/environment/article/plastic-pollution

Persson, L., Almroth, B.M.B., Collins, C.D., Cornell, S., de Wit, C.A., Diamond, M.L., et al. 2022. 'Outside the Safe Operating Space of the Planetary Boundary for Novel Entities', *Environmental Science and Technology* 56(3): 1510–1521. https://doi.org/10.1021/acs.est.1c04158

Rockström, J., Steffen, W., Noone, K., Persson, Å., Chapin III, S., Lambin, E.F., et al. 2009. 'A Safe Operating Space for Humanity', *Nature* 461: 472–475. https://doi.org/10.1038/461472a

Vallette, J. 1999. 'Larry Summers' War Against the Earth', *CounterPunch*, Global Policy Forum. https://archive.globalpolicy.org/socecon/envronmt/summers.htm

Video lecture

Khoo, S. 2022. *Connected Sociologies of Pollution*, Connected Sociologies Curriculum Project. https://thesociologicalreview.org/projects/connected-sociologies/curriculum/environment-and-climate-change/connected-sociologies-pollution-/

Additional resources

BBC *Blue Planet* documentary series. https://www.bbc.co.uk/programmes/p04tjbtx

Mah, A. 2022. *Plastics and Toxic Colonialism*, Connected Sociologies Curriculum Project. https://thesociologicalreview.org/projects/connected-sociologies/curriculum/environment-and-climate-change/plastics/

Liboiron, M. and Murphy, M. 2021. 'Why Pollution is as Much About Colonialism as Chemicals', *Don't Call Me Resilient* podcast episode 11, 3 November. https://theconversation.com/why-pollution-is-as-much-about-colonialism-as-chemicals-dont-call-me-resilient-ep-11-170696

Olof Palme's opening speech at the 1972 Stockholm Conference on the Human Environment. https://www.youtube.com/watch?v=0dGIsMEQYgI

QUESTIONS

1. Which sections of global society are more likely to be affected by pollution and why?

2. What is the connection between the problem of pollution and the problem of discrimination? You might choose to focus on racial or any other type of social discrimination, economic or class discrimination, or geographical discrimination.

3. What problems arise when commercial markets are used to solve pollution problems? What principles can be used to respond to these problems?

4. Further investigate one example of air, water, or soil pollution or 'sacrifice zone'. What aspects of health are affected? What or who are more likely to be harmed and what or who are less likely to be harmed?

Worksheet 25. Connected Sociologies of Pollution

This worksheet is designed to support AS and A-level teaching on the topics of globalization and global development. Specifically, this session focuses on the relationships between globalization and the environment, war and conflict, and global inequalities. In this chapter and online talk, Su-ming Khoo explores the relationship between the climate crisis and colonialism, focusing on the topic of pollution. Using the 1972 United Nations Conference on the Human Environment as her starting point, Khoo examines the significance of chemical pollution within the context of the Vietnam War, and its enduring impacts. The activities in this worksheet prompt students to critically examine the colonial dimensions of pollution, understanding it not just as a term to describe environmental harm but as an infrastructural, economic, and political logic. Students are invited to draw connections between environmental violence and the other structural inequalities and injustices they have learned about, applying a decolonial lens to the topic of the climate crisis.

Time	Activity	Explanation
00.00–00.05	To warm up, answer the following question: *What do you think the term 'ecocide' means?*	This warm-up activity introduces students to a key term within this talk and gauges their existing knowledge about the topic, which will be built on throughout the session.
00.05–00.10	Recap of understandings of globalization and global development	It may be useful to remind students of key concepts related to globalization, particularly regarding the relationship between the environment and development.
00.10–00.20	Watch the talk from 0:39 to 3:00. *Within what context did Swedish Prime Minister Olof Palme use the term 'ecocide'? What was he asking of world leaders?*	Palme used the word 'ecocide' at the 1972 United Nations Conference on the Human Environment to refer to chemical warfare carried out by the United States in the war on Vietnam. His address to the conference expressed the need for world leaders to acknowledge the harm done by chemical, biological, and nuclear pollutants in the context of war and to view ecocide as a fundamental threat to world peace. This activity allows students to develop their understanding of ecocide following the warm-up activity, helping to set the context for this chapter and talk. The questions get students thinking about how environmental harm unfolds within the context of war, and how violence continues into peace time, a key theme within this talk.
00.20–00.25	At 4:00 Khoo says: 'We live in a social and economic climate of absences, silences, denied knowledge, and unaccounted harm and costs.' *How does the silence around environmental violence relate to the other silences you have learned about on this course?*	In this activity, students are challenged to extend their thinking beyond the chapter and talk, connecting the silences surrounding environmental violence to other silences, hidden histories, and marginalized voices that underpin this book. This also encourages students to start thinking about the connections between environmental harm and colonialism.

Time	Activity	Explanation
00.25–00.35	Watch the talk from 6:55 to 9:32. *How did the wartime thinking around pollution 'pollute' our peacetime following the Vietnam War?*	Khoo explains that certain levels of pollution were permitted to achieve military advantage during the Vietnam War. This idea bled into peacetime, continuing into the present day, whereby a certain amount of pollution is considered an acceptable 'trade-off' in exchange for economic or strategic benefit. This activity asks students to think critically about the relationship between environmental harm and capitalism. In doing so, it connects to a core A-level Sociology curriculum theme: the relationship between global development and the environment.
00.35–00.45	Watch the talk from 10:42 to 12:19. *What are the 'bad relations' described by Max Liboiron? How does this theory help us to understand the relationship between colonialism and pollution?*	'Bad relations', according to Liboiron, describe the relationship whereby a colonizing power sees land, labour, plants, animals, and finances as resources that should flow to the Global North, while waste, toxic effects, and ill health are encouraged to flow to the Global South. This activity introduces students to a concept that can help them to describe the relationship between environmental harm and colonialism. In thinking about how colonizing powers extract resources from other nations and populations to detrimental environmental effect, students may draw connections between this topic and the 'Colonial Dispossession and Extraction' topic.
00.45–00.55	Watch the talk from 12:20 to 14:47. *How does Khoo describe the relationship between pollution and racial inequality between the 1960s and 1980s?*	Khoo explains that, within the Global North, social movements for civil rights started to grow in tandem with environmental consciousness. As White, affluent people began moving out of cities to rural, cleaner environments, minoritized communities were more exposed to the hazards of pollution in city centres, while toxic waste disposal facilities tended to be located in poorer Black and minority ethnic neighbourhoods. This activity encourages students to think about how the environmental crisis relates to other social inequalities and injustices. Students are encouraged to begin viewing environmental harm not just as an ecological problem but one with fundamentally political and socio-economic consequences. In doing so, students are asked to consider the impacts of global development on both the environment and on social inequalities, which is a core theme within the A-level Sociology curriculum.

Time	Activity	Explanation
00.55–01.00	Drawing on what you have learned throughout this chapter and talk, answer the following question: *Why is it inaccurate to say that the climate crisis affects all humans equally?*	This concluding activity prompts students to bring together what they have learned using this chapter and talk in addressing a broader sociological question. Students are asked to delve into the sociological dimensions of the climate crisis, building on previous activities in thinking about how environmental violence intersects with social injustice. Students may notice parallels in the example of compensation given to US Vietnam War veterans for illnesses caused by herbicide release, but not to the Vietnamese victims who also suffered similar effects, as an example of the unjust consequences of environmental harm.

This worksheet was developed by Isabel Sykes.

26

Extractivism, Anti-Extractivism, and Post-Extractivism in Latin America

Andrea Sempértegui

> **Objectives**
>
> - This chapter explains the concept of 'extractivism' by centring on different approaches coming from Latin America.
>
> - While extractivism refers to the removal of great quantities of natural resources (hydrocarbons, minerals, or agricultural products) that are exported and processed abroad, this chapter expands this definition by tracing the work of critical scholars and social movements on extractivism as a colonial and patriarchal project of capitalist accumulation.
>
> - It shows how Latin America, a region characterized by the looting of its natural resources since colonial times, is an important place to understand extractivism as a situated and global phenomenon linked to different forms of development, capitalist accumulation, spoilage, and resistance.
>
> - By focusing on Latin America, this chapter shows how Indigenous, environmental, and feminist movements have contributed to the intellectual elaborations of this term and generated post-extractive alternatives amidst environmental devastation.

Introduction

The concepts 'extraction' or 'to extract' come from the Latin word 'extrahere', which means 'to pull out', 'withdraw', or 'remove'.[1] Many elements can be extracted from bodies, nature, and systems of human and non-human relations: from human blood to raw materials like copper, from chemical compounds like vitamins to automated data like personal bank information. In this chapter, I focus on a particular variation of this concept, namely on 'extractivism', which goes beyond the act of extraction itself even as it contains it. More specifically, I will focus on extractivism as a system that encompasses all of those 'activities which remove great quantities of natural resources that are not then processed (or are done so in a limited fashion) and that leave a country as exports' (Gudynas 2010: 1). Even though this definition might seem very descriptive, with the help of critical scholars and activists from Latin America, I will show how extractivism is a very expansive and malleable concept that points to a political, economic, and historical model of forced removal of raw materials, relations, and life, which can be traced back to the colonization of Abya Yala[2] (today known as the Americas) by European powers more than 500 years ago (Vela Almeida 2020).

When talking about natural resources, mining, in particular, dominates imaginaries surrounding extraction (Mezzadra and Neilson 2017). However, extractivism is not limited to the minerals or hydrocarbons we use for mass transportation, heating systems, and the production of batteries for computers and electric vehicles. Extractivism is also present in certain forms of capitalist intensive farming, forestry, and livestock (Acosta 2013). Recent scholarship has focused on other forms of extractivism, which include the 'extractive' operations of digital platforms, financial markets, and renewable energy sources (such as solar panels and wind turbines that involve direct and indirect extractive practices and different processes of dispossession) (Riofrancos 2020a). This ever-expanding set of extractive frontiers shows us that the concept is linked to how global forms of capitalist accumulation have mutated in the previous decades, where literal forms of land dispossession related to fossil fuels and green extractivism and apparently 'abstract' forms of capitalist accumulation related to financial and data extractivism share a common logic and are connected.

I start by focusing on Latin America as a generative place from which to think about extractivism as a political, economic, and historical system inaugurated with European colonial expansion. I then introduce the work of critical scholar-activists researching on and from Latin America, who have introduced, expanded, and infused the concept of extractivism with new and broader meanings. I organize these varied and plural approaches to extractivism in three parts. The first offers an overview of extractivism as a form of capitalist accumulation related to theories and critiques of development. The second centres on feminist, decolonial, and Indigenous approaches that have reconceptualized extractivism as a colonial and capitalist mode of dispossession that cannot be separated from patriarchal forms of occupying bodies, communities, and territories. The third focuses on extractivism as an expanded concept related to finance, the green energy transition, and the digital economy. I conclude with a brief summary and mention some examples of post-extractive proposals coming from Indigenous, environmental, and feminist movements in the region.

Latin America's colonial dependency on extractivism

Since the 1970s, dominant studies on oil or mineral-dependent states, coming mainly from academic research centres located in the Global North and funded by organizations like the World Bank, have focused on the almost causal relationship between resource dependency and authoritarianism and poverty. While some conclude that resources like oil represent a 'curse' for countries across the world because the state's dependence on oil rents increases these countries' ability to suppress democratic politics, impose authoritarian forms of governing, and gain people's political support in client fashion (this is in exchange of goods and services), others suggest that 'rentier' states are prone to increasing levels of corruption, economic underdevelopment, low taxation of the population, and resource-related armed conflicts (Karl 1997; Collier 2007; Kaldor et al 2007; Ross 2012).

Contrasting these approaches, which look at resource-producing states as almost 'destined' to poverty and underdevelopment and view impacted communities by extractive projects as passive actors, critical scholar-activists researching on and from Latin America have expanded, complexified, and multiplied the study of resource extraction. The reason why Latin America has become a centre for intellectual production on extractivism is twofold.

First, given the historical role of Latin American economies as exporters of raw materials since colonial times, several scholars argue that it is not possible to conceptualize contemporary forms of extractivism without understanding how former colonies, which then became independent nation states, have been relegated to the role of peripheral economies and exporters of raw materials to nourish the demands from political and economic powers.

Contrasting the 'resource curse' approaches that understand underdevelopment as a causal product of some countries' resource dependence, Latin American critical scholars have inverted these analyses and shown how the region's underdevelopment is a historical product of how the colonial and imperial looting of its minerals, metals, and other primary resources have nourished the development of Europe and countries like the United States (see Galeano 1997). Furthermore, and as I explain in what follows, many authors argue that the sustained economic and political dominance of metropolitan centres in the North is direct product of a capitalist world economy where some peripheral regions have specialized in the continuous extraction and export of their natural resources (see Coronil 1997). In other words, while capitalism has been mostly experienced as an expansion of the industrial economy, technological innovation, or financial dominance in the Global North, Global South regions like Latin America have been integrated in the capitalist world economy through the continuous expansion of their extractive frontiers (see Gilbert, Chapter 2, this volume).

Second, since the global energy boom in the 2000s – a period during which the high prices of commodities like oil, copper, and soy, due to the growing international demand for these raw materials, increased Latin American states' dependency on extractive activities – extractivism has widely circulated among different movements resisting the expansion of extractive projects. In fact, different Indigenous, Black, and peasant communities across the Americas have not been mere victims of the negative socio-ecological consequences of extractive projects or passive apolitical actors in resource-dependent states. Rather, they have played a crucial role in shaping recent approaches to extractivism and in offering alternatives towards post-extractive societies, as the political scientist Thea Riofrancos has analysed. For Riofrancos, extractivism or *extractivismo* (in Spanish) is a discourse shaped by social movements and grassroots activists who, 'through their intertwined activities of critique and mobilization', shape the lines of political confrontation around resource extraction and thus influence intellectual elaborations on this term (2020b: 16). Furthermore, and as I show in the following sections, social movements have transformed extractivism into a politically malleable concept that is being constantly rearticulated as communities organize against renewed forms of territorial occupation and dispossession.

In what follows, I offer a detailed overview of the different Latin American approaches that have broadened the concept of extractivism. This regional focus does not mean that this concept is not useful or does not apply to other regions like Africa, Asia, North America, or even Europe. On the contrary, the study of extractivism has been widely adopted, adapted, and further developed by scholars around the world. However, this regional focus will allow us to gain a situated perspective on how extractivism concretely shapes post-colonial societies and the global economy as a whole.

What are different approaches to extractivism coming from Latin America?

For simplicity, I have organized the different approaches to extractivism in three parts. Nevertheless, it is important to mention that these approaches are not separated from each other. On the contrary, they are interconnected and the people who have developed them are often in dialogue and critical engagement with each other.

Extractivism as a mode of capitalist accumulation and development

Scholars like Eduardo Gudynas (2010), Maristella Svampa (2015a), and Alberto Acosta (2013), among many others, differentiate different types of extractivism according to the different modes of capitalist accumulation that have characterized them. Even though Latin American history has been marked by the extraction of natural resources since colonial times, extractivism has mutated along with capitalism's different phases. In fact, these scholars argue that, with each phase of capitalism, resource extraction has changed and translated into new modes of accumulation – moving, for example, from colonial plunder to independence-era 'enclave economies'. These scholars also argue that the global demand for natural resources has also taken new shapes – with new economic powers like China driving the demand for raw materials since the 2000s. When we talk about modes of accumulation, we are talking about the ways in which resources are owned, administrated, and invested. Are resources owned and administrated by the state or by foreign companies? Is the money coming from extractive projects going to be invested in education or health? Or is it going to benefit private actors or be used to pay foreign debt?

This approach to extractivism as a mode of accumulation derives from the long-standing tradition of Latin American dependency theory in the 1960s and 1970s (Gonzalez Casanova 1965; Coronil 1997; Galeano 1997; Quijano 2000). In fact, the authors mentioned earlier have been influenced by theories and critiques of development, which contrast 'modernization theories' that argue that underdeveloped countries are in a similar situation to that of developed countries in the past and, therefore, their way to get out of poverty is to accelerate their integration into the capitalist world market. Dependency theory rejected this view, arguing that the so-called 'underdevelopment' of Latin America is a product of how colonialism and colonial structures have shaped the fate of independent nation states in the region. Furthermore, these scholars rejected the idea that underdeveloped countries are merely 'backward' versions of developed countries, evincing instead how the wealth of developed states (the 'core') depends on the continuous exploitation of natural resources in poor countries and in their position as periphery economies in the capitalist world system.

In the 2000s, with the 're-primarization' of Latin American economies characterized by the massive export of primary goods and the high price of commodities like minerals and metals due to their rising global demand (Burchardt and Dietz 2014), dependency theories were readopted and rearticulated by Latin American authors to make sense of the way in which self-declared progressive governments in countries like Argentina, Venezuela, Brazil, Bolivia and Ecuador were administrating resource extraction. According to authors like Eduardo Gudynas (2010) or Maristella Svampa (2015a), the dominant form of extractivism that characterized Latin America in the 1980s and 1990s was 'neoliberal extractivism', with institutions like the International Monetary Fund, the World Bank, and United States Department of the Treasury (the so-called 'Washington Consensus') dictating the terms of natural resource extraction.

This neoliberal mode of accumulation – characterized by the limited role of the state in extractive projects and the transfer of extractive licences to participants in the open market, the expansion of extractive projects as means to access international loans or to pay foreign debt, and the pastoral role of extractive companies who compensated for the state's absence in terms of social services and infrastructure projects in communities impacted by extractive projects – shifts at the turn of the century. With the electoral success of progressive governments, we see the implementation of a different type of extractivism, also called 'neo-extractivism'. This new extractivism is characterized by the massive territorial expansion of the extractive frontier to areas previously considered nonproductive, the increasing role of the state in extractive projects, and the state's investment of extractive revenues in infrastructural projects like highways and in developmental programmes aimed to reduce poverty.

While there were some improvements during the neo-extractive period, especially in terms of the reduction of poverty, scholars analysing neo-extractivism were mostly critical towards this mode of accumulation. For Alberto Acosta (2013), neo-extractivism did not only continue Latin America's peripheral role as exporter of primary commodities, but intensified the region's dependency in the global energy market by massively expanding extractive activities in territories where they did not exist before – through, for example, the implementation of 'mega-mines' or hydraulic fracturing (fracking), a technique used to extract natural gas or oil from shale and other rock formations. Furthermore, neo-extractivism became a developmental model, which prioritized the massive expansion of extractive projects to fund social programmes to reduce poverty and generate social legitimacy at the expense of several communities experiencing the negative socio-ecological impacts of extractive activities. In other words, entire communities and their territories were deemed as 'sacrifice zones' to enable social spending and public investment coming from extractive industries.

Extractivism as a colonial, capitalist, and patriarchal mode of dispossession

Even though different communities and social movements have resisted extractive projects earlier, the territorial expansion of the extractive frontier in the 2000s intensified dynamics of occupation and dispossession that have continued today. It is no coincidence that since the neo-extractive period there has been an explosion of conflicts over natural resource extraction in the region (Svampa 2015a). Despite the fact progressive governments enjoyed popular support and invested in developmental projects, many communities mobilized against the socio-ecological impacts of mining, oil, and fracking projects, among others. Furthermore, local communities mobilized against the kind of development they were offered by the neo-extractive state, which did not respect their ways of living, diminished alternative economic activities, and disrupted existing community networks of human and non-human relations (Vela Almeida 2020). Many of these communities have criticized the imposition of this model as a continuation of a colonial, racist, capitalist, and patriarchal vision of progress and modernization internalized by Latin American elites (Gago 2020), which threatens communities' relationship with their territories and life in its multiple forms (Cabnal 2015).

This explosion of anti-extractive struggles in Latin America has been led, primarily, by Indigenous, peasant, and Black communities. Many of them have featured significant participation and leadership by women (Svampa and Viale 2014). Important and visible examples include: Berta Cáceres who led the Lenca struggle against the Agua Zarca Dam in Honduras until her brutal assassination by hired hitmen linked to the hydroelectric company in 2016; Francia Márquez who led the Afro-Colombian resistance against illegal gold mining on their ancestral land in La Toma; and Máxima Acuña who has headed the peasant resistance against the Conga Mine in the northern highlands of Peru. The visibility of such anti-extractive leadership has prompted Latin American authors like Maristella Svampa (2015b) and Astrid Ulloa (2016) to coin terms such as 'feminization of struggles' and 'eco-territorial feminisms' to emphasize the leading role of these women in resisting the expansion of extractivism in the region.

These women leaders and their movements have not merely 'resisted' extractive projects. They have also shaped the contentious politics of natural resource extraction and infused extractivism with new and broader meanings. Different feminist, decolonial, and Indigenous scholar-activists, who have either been part or in dialogue with these movements, have specifically contributed to highlight the patriarchal dimensions of extractivism (see Cielo et al 2016; Rivera Cusicanqui 2017; Colectivo Miradas Críticas del Territorio desde el Feminismo 2018; see Kelbert, Chapter 20, this volume).

These dimensions include: the exclusion of women from decision-making processes, a product of how the state and extractive companies primarily engage with men in local communities; the introduction of hierarchical and monetarized relations by extractive companies, in which it is mostly men who are offered short-term jobs underpinning the figure of the 'male provider' and the 'dependent woman'; the disproportionate sexual and gendered violence Indigenous, Black peasant women experience as result of how the greater presence of male workers restructure community spaces and daily life in extractive circuits; and the several death threats against women leaders who resist or speak up against the negative impacts of extractive projects.

The patriarchal dimensions of extractivism have not implied that women leaders and activists have assumed a victimized position limiting themselves to speak up against the extractive violence they have experienced in their bodies and territories. On the contrary, they have also presented their own political proposals, thus positioning themselves as political and epistemic subjects in the broader Latin American resistance against extractivism. This is the case of the political proposal of the body-land territory, developed by the Maya-Xinka communitarian feminist and anti-mining activist Lorena Cabnal (2010), which, on the one hand, connects the exploitation and dispossession of land to the exploitation and dispossession of feminized and racialized bodies in contexts of extractive occupation and, on the other, enables a political understanding of the body as a 'territory' that has a vital relation to the places we inhabit and records our situated memories of oppression, resistance, and empowerment.

This is also the case of the Mujeres Amazónicas, a network of Indigenous women leaders from Ecuador's Amazon rainforest who have organized against the massive expansion of oil and mining projects in their territories. In their public speeches, manifestos, and declarations, this Indigenous women-led collective has presented the Living Forest Declaration, a proposal that declares the Amazon as a living entity, rather than an abstract idealization of nature, and seeks to establish a new relation to nature and the more-than-human entities that inhabit the rainforest (Colectivo Miradas Críticas del Territorio desde el Feminismo 2014).

Expanded notions of extraction: financial, green, and data extractivism(s)

Going beyond these approaches that analyse extractivism as a mode of accumulation that continues Latin America's peripheral role as exporter of primary commodities, scholars like Verónica Gago have further developed the notions of 'extraction' and 'extractivism' to illuminate contemporary forms of capitalist accumulation and exploitation in the region. For Gago, it is important to expand the concept of extractivism as going beyond the literal extraction of raw materials and to illuminate how 'the extractive logic' is present in other forms of accumulation, in which 'finance plays a key role' (2020: 91). When Gago talks about finance,[3] she is not talking about an extremely abstract form of speculation, rather, she is talking about concrete forms of capital accumulation like indebtedness, where financial entities like banks benefit from poor and de-waged populations who are forced to enter into debt in order to cover basic needs. Extractive operations in cases of indebtedness are characterized by, for example, how financial entities accept state subsidies or other forms of social cooperation as guarantee for impoverished populations to access credit lines in countries like Argentina. In these cases, financial entities 'extract' value from social relations that they did not contribute to organizing and exploit national and local legislation to overcome limits in interest rates (Gago and Mezzadra 2017: 584).

Forms of financial extractivism are, nevertheless, not disconnected from the literal extraction of natural resources. As Gago and other scholars have shown, there is a constitutive relation between finance and the funding of megaprojects (like open-pit mines), the production of new extractive frontiers to supply for green technologies and confront climate change (like lithium mines, large-scale solar and wind farms, and other forms of 'green extractivism'), and the manipulation of commodity prices in the global market (like oil). Furthermore, authors like Martín Arboleda examine how the explosion of mega-mines around the world is not only a product of the rising demand for mined materials crucial for the energy transition or the rise of countries like China as a new global power. In his book *Planetary Mine: Territories of Extraction under Late Capitalism* (2020), Arboleda explains how the mining industry's recent expansion is also a product of innovations in artificial intelligence, big data, robotics, and the computerization of labour processes. All of these geopolitical, technological, and organizational transformations have turned previously inaccessible territories into profitable investments for financial capitalism – namely, for financial institutions like J.P. Morgan, large shareholders like BlackRock, and venture capitalist investors like BHP Ventures.

This expansion of the concept of extractivism has not only been applied to green technologies and finance. Latin American decolonial authors like Paola Ricaurte (2019), Sebastián Lehuedé (2022), and Márcia Tait, Alcides Eduardo dos Reis Peron and Marcela Suárez (2022), have also applied this concept to contemporary processes of data production, circulation, and infrastructure. 'Data extractivism' refers to global processes where large volumes of data are cumulatively extracted from people and transformed into economic gains for Big-Tech companies like Meta, Google, or Amazon. The extractive qualities of data capitalism, or data 'colonialism', can be better grasped when one looks at how these international technology companies rely on their capacity to unlimitedly access and extract people's interpersonal relations and intimate expressions in 'virtual territories' like the internet, as data to be commodified and exchanged in the capitalist market (Ricaurte 2019).

In fact, many of these companies capture people's data without our informed consent at the expense of our security, freedom, and autonomy. Like financial extractivism, data extractivism is tidily connected to the extraction and massive use of natural resources like electricity, water, and land. The massive digital infrastructure data extractivism necessitates is ultimately connected to physical infrastructure that relies on private capital's ability to transform diverse territories into 'assets' – see, for example, projects like 'Datagonia' that aims to build a farm of data centres in the Patagonian region, thus transforming this place into a 'natural home' of data (Lehuedé 2022: 10).

Conclusion

In this chapter, we learnt how extractivism is a mode of capitalist accumulation that dates back to the colonization of the Americas. This mode of accumulation is characterized by how former colonies, which then became independent nation states, were relegated to the role of exporters of raw materials and colonial powers built political and economic dominance as importers and manufacturers of those raw materials (see Chen and Sabaratnam, Chapter 6, this volume). With the help of scholar-activists working on and from Latin America, we then learnt how this unequal relationship continued Latin America's peripheral role as exporter of natural resources in the world market, a historical and structural condition that has contributed to the region's 'underdevelopment'.

Even though extractivism as mode of accumulation has changed during capitalism's different phases – moving from neoliberal extractivism to neo-extractivism in recent decades – this structural condition has made it very difficult for many Latin American countries to generate other sources of income that are not dependent on extractive projects. Furthermore, since the global energy boom in the 2000s, there has been a massive expansion of the extractive frontier that has shaped the politics of Latin American governments up to the present, with negative socio-ecological impacts for the communities and population living adjacent or close to extractive locations and circuits.

We also learnt how impacted communities are not mere victims of extractivism or passive political actors. Especially Indigenous, peasant, and Black communities have led important anti-extractive struggles and filled extractivism with new and broader meanings. An example of this conceptual and political broadening is how different community leaders, especially women, and feminist scholar-activists have highlighted the patriarchal dimensions of extractivism and developed their own political proposals to confront the massive expansion of extractivism in their territories.

Finally, we learnt how the concept of extractivism has been further expanded in order to highlight the extractive logics in finance, green technologies, and digital platforms. Importantly, this recent expansion not only shows us how extractivism can apply to other forms of capitalist accumulation that are not directly resource based, but it also evinces how literal and apparently 'fictitious' forms of extraction are interconnected. Moreover, this recent expansion of extractivism highlights how extractive practices of exploitation and dispossession of nature and people are also characteristic of non-literal extractive practices in digital and financial capitalism, which generate new forms of injustice.

I close this chapter by mentioning a couple of post-extractive proposals coming from Indigenous, environmental, and feminist movements in Latin America. While this short overview is not reflective of the variety of post-extractive alternatives in the region, it is of ultimate importance and urgency to mention some of them. In the last years, several right-wing movements and figures have been elected or have taken over governmental power in countries like Brazil (Jair Bolsonaro), Argentina (Javier Milei), Bolivia (Jeanine Añez), Peru (Dina Boluarte), El Salvador (Nayib Bukele), and Ecuador (Guillermo Lasso and Daniel Noboa). While some of these governments are no longer in power, they have left indelible traces in terms of the regression of reproductive, social, economic, cultural, and environmental rights. Furthermore, many of these governments have expanded the extractive frontier in authoritarian fashion (through the militarization of vast territories or through presidential decrees), contributing to the rapid environmental degradation and spoilage of territories like the Amazon rainforest.

Post-extractive alternatives, developed before and during this moment of right-wing political ascendency, include political proposals for a just energy transition like the Pacto Ecosocial e Intercultural del Sur[4] or alternatives to the developmental model like *Buen Vivir* (Good Living) (Acosta 2017). These proposals not only seek to replace the extractive model but offer fundamental alternatives to the current capitalist world system (Lang 2013). While critical scholar-activists have been crucial at disseminating these proposals, they have been developed by Latin American Indigenous, environmental, and feminist movements.

In Ecuador, the Indigenous Movement – one of the strongest and best organized social movements in the region – has played a huge role in contributing to post-extractive alternatives. Since the founding of the Confederation of Indigenous Nationalities of Ecuador (CONAIE) in 1986, the Indigenous Movement has combined direct action strategies to halt the expansion of oil and mining projects with public declarations and proposals that underscore the colonial and capitalist dimensions of neoliberal extractivism and neo-extractivism. At the same time, the Indigenous Movement has contributed alternative proposals for post-extractive futures, like *Sumak Kawsay* – which means 'Good Living' and proposes new forms of relation between human beings and nature and among human beings – and the Rights of Nature – a proposal that recognizes nature as a legal entity, whose existence and regeneration of its vital cycles should be respected. Both proposals were adopted in Ecuador's 2008 Constitution, after years of political mobilization by CONAIE. The important role of Ecuador's Indigenous Movement can be seen in CONAIE's leadership of two nation-wide strikes in 2019 and 2022. These strikes forced Ecuador's right-wing government to retract several austerity and extractive policies.

Summing up, the Indigenous Movement and similar feminist and environmental collectives show the important role that social movements have played in expanding our understanding of extractivism beyond descriptive definitions that only focus on its operational characteristics. With this, I do not want to imply that intellectual work is superfluous or that theories of dependency or capitalist accumulation are not relevant to understand extractivism today. On the contrary, contributions from Latin American social movements and public intellectuals have been necessary to reveal and resist the continuity of regimes of colonial, capitalist, and patriarchal power that fuel environmental degradation and the climate crisis.

Notes

[1] https://www.merriam-webster.com/dictionary/extraction#:~:text=Etymology,words%20from%20the%20same%20century
[2] Abya Yala is term from the Kuna language, which means 'land in its full maturity', used by Indigenous and decolonial activists and scholars to refer to the American continent.
[3] Finance can be defined as 'an accumulation of drawing rights (droits de tirage) on the wealth to be produced in future, through private and public indebtedness, stock exchange capitalization, and a wide panoply of financial products' (Durand 2015, in Gago and Mezzadra 2017: 583).
[4] https://pactoecosocialdelsur.com/

References

Acosta, A. 2013. 'Extractivism and Neoextractivism: Two Sides of the Same Curse'. https://www.tni.org/files/download/beyonddevelopment_extractivism.pdf

Acosta, A. 2017. 'Post-extractivism: From discourse to practice—reflections for action' *International Development Policy*, 9.

Arboleda, M. 2020. *Planetary Mine: Territories of Extraction Under Late Capitalism*. Verso.

Burchardt, H.-J. and Dietz, K. 2014. '(Neo-)extractivism – a new challenge for development theory from Latin America.' *Third World Quarterly*, 35 (3): 468–486.

Cabnal, L. 2010. 'Acercamiento a la Construcción de la Propuesta de Pensamiento Epistémico de las Mujeres Indígenas Feministas Comunitarias de Abya Yala.' In *Feminismos diversos: el feminismo comunitario*, ACSUR-Las Segovias, 11–25.

Cabnal, L. 2015. 'Without Being Consulted: The Commodification of Our Body-Land Territory', in C. Papadopoulou and L.M. Carvajal (eds) *Women Defending the Territory. Experiences of Participation in Latin America*. Fondo de Acción Urgente America Latina y el Caribe, pp 41–56.

Cielo, C., Coba, L., and Vallejo, I. 2016. 'Women, Nature, and Development in Sites of Ecuador's Petroleum Circuit', *Economic Anthropology* 3(1): 119–132.

Colectivo Miradas Críticas del Territorio desde el Feminismo. 2014. *La Vida en el Centro y el Crudo bajo Tierra: el Yasuní en Clave Feminista*. Creative Commons.

Colectivo Miradas Críticas del Territorio desde el Feminismo. 2018. '(Re)patriarcalización de los Territorios. La Lucha de las Mujeres y los Megaproyectos Extractivos', *Ecología Política. Cuadernos de Debate Internacional*.

Collier, P. 2007. *The Bottom Billion: Why the Poorest Countries Are Failing and What Can Be Done about It*. Oxford University Press.

Coronil, F. 1997. *The Magical State: Nature, Money and Modernity in Venezuela*. University of Chicago Press.

Gago, V. 2020. *Feminist International: How to Change Everything*. Verso.

Gago, V. and Mezzadra, S. 2017. 'A Critique of the Extractive Operations of Capital: Toward an Expanded Concept of Extractivism', *Rethinking Marxism* 29(4): 574–591.

Galeano, E. 1997. *Open Veins of Latin America: Five Centuries of the Pillage of a Continent*. Monthly Review Press.

Gonzalez Casanova, Pablo. 1965. 'Internal colonialism and national development' *Studies in Comparative International Development* 1(4): 27–37.

Gudynas, E. 2010. 'The New Extractivism of the 21st Century: Ten Urgent Theses about Extractivism in Relation to Current South American Progressivism', *Americas Program Report*. Center for International Policy.

Kaldor, M., Karl, T.L. and Said, Y. 2007. *Oil Wars*. Pluto Books.

Karl, T.L. 1997. *The Paradox of Plenty: Oil Booms and Petro-States*. University of California Press.

Lang, M. 2013. 'Crisis of civilization and challenges for the left' In M. Land (ed), *Beyond Development: Alternative Visions from Latin America*, Permanent Working Group on Alternatives to Development, Transnational Institute / Rosa Luxemburg Foundation.

Lehuedé, S. 2022. 'Territories of data: Ontological divergences in the growth of data infrastructure' *Latin American Science, Technology and Society*, 5(1): 1–18.

Quijano, A. 2000. 'Coloniality of power, Eurocentrism, and Latin America.' In *Nepentla: Views From the South*, 1(3): 533–580.

Ricaurte, P. 2019. 'Data epistemologies, the coloniality of power, and resistance' *Television & New Media*, 20(4): 350–365.

Mezzadra, S. and Neilson, B. 2017. 'On the Multiple Frontiers of Extraction: Excavating Contemporary Capitalism', *Cultural Studies* 31(2–3): 185–204.

Riofrancos, T. 2020a. 'Extractivism and Extractivismo', *Global South Studies: A Collective Publication with The Global South*, https://www.globalsouthstudies.org/keyword-essay/extractivism-and-extractivismo/

Riofrancos, T. 2020b *Resource Radicals: From Petro-Nationalism to Post- Extractivism in Ecuador*. Duke University Press.

Rivera Cusicanqui, S. 2017. 'La Larga Marcha Por Nuestra Dignidad', *Cuestión Agraria* 4: 7–38.

Ross, M. 2012. *The Oil Curse: How Petroleum Wealth Shapes the Development of Nations*. Princeton University Press.

Svampa, M. 2015a. 'Commodities Consensus: Neoextractivism and Enclosure of the Commons in Latin America', *South Atlantic Quarterly* 114(1): 65–82.

Svampa, M. 2015b. 'Feminismos del Sur y Ecofeminismo.' *Nueva Sociedad* 256: 127–131.

Svampa, M. and Viale, E. 2014. *Maldesarrollo: La Argentina del Extractivismo y el Despojo*. Katz Editores.

Tait, M.M. dos Reis Peron, A.E. and Suárez, M. 2022. 'Terrestrial politics and body-territory: two concepts to make sense of digital colonialism in Latin America.' *Latin American Science, Technology and Society* 5(1): 1–16.

Ulloa, A. 2016. 'Feminismos Territoriales en América Latina: Defensas de la Vida frente a los Extractivismos', *Nómadas* 45: 123–139.

Vela Almeida, D. 2020. 'Extractivism', *Uneven Earth: Where the Ecological Meets the Political*. https://unevenearth.org/2020/08/extractivism/

Video lecture

Sempértegui, A. 2022. *Extractivism and Social Movements*, Connected Sociologies Curriculum Project. https://thesociologicalreview.org/projects/connected-sociologies/curriculum/environment-and-climate-change/extractivism-and-social-movements/

QUESTIONS

1. What is the relationship between the recent expansion of extractive projects and colonialism?

2. Why are so-called 'underdeveloped' countries the major exporters of raw materials like hydrocarbons, metals, and monocrops?

3. Why do so many peasant, Indigenous, and Black communities organize against extractive projects nowadays?

4. What is the relationship between natural resource extraction and contemporary forms of financial and digital capitalism?

Worksheet 26. Extractivism, Anti-Extractivism, and Post-Extractivism in Latin America

This worksheet is designed to support AS and A-level teaching on the topics of globalization and global development. This chapter and talk focus on the relationships between globalization and the environment, social power and stratification, and global inequalities.

Andrea Sempértegui introduces students to the concept of extractivism, drawing on two different approaches to the subject. Focusing on Latin America, a region that has experienced a recent significant expansion of extractive projects, Sempértegui sets out the role of extractivism and resistance to it within the wider colonial global economy. Sempértegui centres the role of social movements to highlight the importance of resistance in envisioning of post-extractive futures and sociologically understanding the climate crisis. This worksheet helps to expand students' vocabulary and understanding of the extractive and exploitative relations that underpin the colonial global economy. The questions are designed to prompt students to make connections between the ecological, social, and economic dimensions of global capitalism, and to think about the ways in which environmental harm interacts with global inequalities and injustices.

Time	Activity	Explanation
00.00–00.05	To warm up, answer the following question: *What do you think extractivism means?*	This warm-up activity introduces students to one of the key terms, 'extractivism', and encourages students to share what they already know about this concept. Students may also draw on their learning from the 'Colonial Dispossession and Extraction' topic.
00.05–00.10	Recap of understandings of globalization and global development	Students may be reminded of key concepts related to globalization, particularly the relationship between the environment and development.
00.10–00.20	Watch the talk from 2:12 to 3:50. *What is the definition of extractivism? What are some examples of resources involved?*	Sempértegui draws on Eduardo Gudynas' definition of extractivism – as activities that remove large quantities of natural resources from countries. These are not processed locally but are exported. Examples include monocrops such as soybeans, minerals like copper, and hydrocarbons such as oil and gas. By defining extractivism and starting to think about how it features in the global economy, this section helps students understand the relationship between globalization and trade, a key topic within the A-level Sociology curriculum.
00.20–00.30	Watch the talk from 5:40 to 6:36. *What is the relationship between capitalism and extractivism? How does colonialism fit into this relationship?*	Sempértegui explains that extractivism is viewed as a mode of accumulation that varies during different phases of capitalism, changing how resources are owned, accumulated, and invested at each phase. Colonial extraction is one of these phases. This activity prompts students to connect extractivism with colonialism and capitalism, building on their knowledge of the colonial global economy. Students may also draw on the 'Colonial Dispossession and Extraction' topic to help them to answer these questions.

Time	Activity	Explanation
00.30–00.40	Watch the talk from 8:12 to 11:01. *What is new extractivism? What are the main problems with this, according to Sempértegui?*	Sempértegui outlines a new form of extractivism emerging in the 2000s. This period saw the expansion of extractive processes to huge landscapes previously considered 'non-productive', and increased state investment and participation in these processes. Extractive practices expanded into landscapes which were previously unharmed by these processes, intensifying the ecological impacts. This period also saw an exacerbation of the colonial dynamics of dispossession, and a corresponding explosion of conflict over extractive projects. This activity asks students to summarize the features and problems with new extractivism in their own words. The activity also prompts them to start thinking about the roles of conflict and resistance within extractivism.
00.40–00.45	Watch the talk from 11:46 to 14:50. *Why are social movements important to understanding extractivism?*	A second, different approach to extractivism conceptualizes it as a discourse shaped by social movements, placing grassroots organizing and activism at the centre of its critique. A key example is the Indigenous movement in Ecuador, which has expanded understandings of extractivism beyond the descriptive definition, by proposing new forms of relations between human beings and nature. This question prompts students to consider the centrality of resistance and activism to understanding extractivism. In answering this question, students may draw on other chapters and accompanying talks which recover and emphasize the importance of resistance movements within the colonial global economy.
00.45–00.55	Watch the talk from 14:50 to 18:18. *What are the patriarchal dimensions of extractivism outlined by Sempértegui? What has been the role of Amazonian women in resisting extractivism?*	The Amazonian Women's March for Life was a collective act challenging the exclusion of Indigenous women's voices from government plans to expand extractivism in the Ecuadorian rainforest. Amazonian women have emerged as central actors contesting extractivism, highlighting the problematic masculinization of decision-making processes, the sexist hierarchical relations that define extractivism, violence enacted against women in extractive circuits, and deadly consequences for women leaders who have spoken out against it. These questions encourage students to understand the importance of centring social movements in discussions of extractivism. Students are invited to consider how gender inequalities intersect with the social injustices at play in extractive circuits, connecting to other talks and chapters which deal with intersectionality, and which take a feminist approach to studying global inequality.

Time	Activity	Explanation
00.55–01.00	Drawing on what you have learned throughout this talk, and from other topics, answer the following questions: *How are the climate crisis and the patriarchy interconnected? How would we study the climate crisis from a feminist perspective?*	Drawing on the previous questions, this concluding activity invites students to delve further and make connections between problems of extractivism and climate crisis, relating environmental issues to problems of patriarchal control and violence. Students may use their learning from this chapter and talk to think about the potential role of gender within other parts of this book. Students are encouraged to think about what methods might be used in a feminist sociological approach to studying environmental violence. In doing so, they may draw from other topics which centre marginalized women's perspectives, such as 'Black British Feminisms'.

This worksheet was developed by Isabel Sykes.

27

A Global Green New Deal? Signatures of Continuing Colonial Violence

Harpreet Kaur-Spannos

Objectives

- This chapter critically examines the limitations of mainstream Green New Deal proposals by analysing their failure to address global colonial histories.

- It explores the link between climate change and colonialism, demonstrating how contemporary climate vulnerabilities are shaped by historical and ongoing systems of extraction, dispossession, and exploitation.

- It analyses the role of climate debt, reparations, and global accountability in achieving climate justice, highlighting the disproportionate responsibility of the Global North and the mechanisms that perpetuate economic dependency and ecological degradation in the Global South.

- It interrogates the extractive foundations of the green economy by investigating how resource grabs, exploitative labour practices, and greenwashing in renewable energy sectors replicate colonial patterns of exploitation.

- It proposes pathways for a just and reparative climate transition, advocating for decolonial and redistributive policies that prioritize community-led renewable energy, Indigenous land rights, debt cancellation, and climate migration protections.

Introduction

Green New Deal (GND) concepts emerged as bold proposals for addressing the climate crisis *and* economic inequality in the Global North. Advocates in the United States and UK framed it as a transformative agenda that could deliver both sustainability and economic justice. However, mainstream proposals were grounded in state-led models that failed to reckon with the colonial roots of climate collapse. This chapter argues that climate change is not simply an energy crisis. Climate impacts – and neo-colonial climate 'solutions' – carry the signature of colonialism. The distribution of climate change's burdens reflects the colonial project's enduring significance. Any meaningful climate action must move beyond domestic policy frameworks and, instead, undo the structures of colonialism still in place.

Climate change is often framed as an unprecedented planetary crisis. Yet, such narratives mask a deeper historical continuity: the structures of colonial extraction and ecological dispossession that created the conditions for this crisis remain intact today (see Khoo, Chapter 3, this volume). This chapter locates the colonial roots of today's planetary distress.

Climate change is rarely discussed as a continuation of centuries-old extractivist cultures, political exclusion, or economies built on expropriation, dispossession, and deforestation. For centuries, colonial expansion was justified on the basis that both land and racialized peoples could be commodified and controlled – a logic that structured enslavement, forced labour, plantation economies, resource extraction, monoculture systems, and deforestation across the Caribbean, Africa, Asia, and Latin America (see Kaladeen, Chapter 4, Tyler, Chapter 5, and Sempértegui, Chapter 26, this volume).

Today's climate crisis is not a rupture from history but a continuation of these colonial legacies. The same regions that were historically mined, deforested, and plundered for European wealth are now the most vulnerable to climate shocks – rising seas, intensifying droughts, and devastating storms. At the same time, the nations and corporations that profited from centuries of ecological destruction continue to amass wealth through carbon markets, green extractivism, and financial instruments that entrench global inequalities.

Like the Haitian Revolution – whose radical break from colonialism was erased from dominant histories of modernity (see Bhambra, Chapter 1, this volume) – the voices of those most impacted by climate collapse are sidelined in mainstream climate discourse. This is despite the fact that 80 per cent of the world's biodiversity has been protected by Indigenous communities. Instead, the frameworks that dominate global climate policy remain rooted in colonial visions of technological innovation, state-led green growth, and financialized climate management that do not address the root causes of our crises, but further entrench their harmful practices. Any vision of climate justice must reckon with its colonial roots and demand a fundamental reimagining of power, ownership, kinship, and decision-making.

The chapter will examine:

- The limitations of the GND and how mainstream climate policies reinforce rather than dismantle extractivist economies.
- Climate debt and reparations, exposing how the Global North has offloaded the costs of climate breakdown onto the Global South.
- The extractive foundations of the so-called 'green economy', highlighting how renewable energy industries continue colonial patterns of dispossession.

A just climate transition must move beyond technocratic fixes and fundamentally challenge the global economic, political, cultural, and ecological systems that drive planetary crises and inequality.

Climate colonialism and the limits of the Green New Deal

The plethora of proposals that once defined the GND moment – articulated mainly in the UK and United States – are no longer in their ascendency. The political landscape has shifted. The visions of transformative climate action that were briefly mainstreamed by the GND frame have largely receded from public debate. Yet, while climate justice advocates grapple with articulating a new, cohesive banner under which to rally, the fundamental critiques of any climate proposal remain unchanged: responses to the climate crisis must be systemic and anti-colonial.

The GND was framed as a policy agenda capable of addressing the twin crises of climate change and economic inequality through green stimulus packages. While its advocates called for large-scale state-led investment in renewable energy, infrastructure, and social programmes, the proposals largely remained confined to domestic policy within the Global North. The GND echoed Roosevelt's original New Deal, which expanded public infrastructure and economic stimulus in the United States while deepening racial and colonial hierarchies (Podur 2021). Similarly, GND policies, while promising a transition away from fossil fuels, failed to confront the exploitation of labour, land, and resources from formerly colonized nations upon which green growth depends.

Hopes for systems change

In the late 2010s, GND frames, from movements and politicians in the UK and United States, captured imaginations for how fair economic, political, ecological, and social transformations – in energy, housing, transport, food, care, education, nature protection, and more – could drive rapid climate action while improving the lives of traditionally marginalized communities (IPCC 2018: 15). Proposals propelled hope that political leaders would heed the Intergovernmental Panel on Climate Change's (IPCC) warning that incremental policy changes would be insufficient to mitigate the worst impacts of the climate crisis. In its *Special Report on Global Warming of 1.5°C*, the IPCC made clear that limiting warming to 1.5°C above pre-industrial levels requires 'rapid, far-reaching, and unprecedented changes in all aspects of society' (IPCC 2018: 15). For many, GND proposals reflected the very scale of transformation called for by the IPCC.

GND frameworks pushed against mainstream proposals for addressing the climate crisis, which too often centred on market incentives, international cooperation, and technological experiments. Instead, given failures of such approaches to decarbonize, proponents of the GND pushed for understandings of how we live, move, collaborate, produce, and consume to inform justice transitions from fossil-fuelled food, fuel, and transport. Proposals featured large-scale public investment programmes that could transition industrial agriculture towards regenerative agroecology, shift from fossil fuels to renewables, and support public transport, energy efficient housing, low carbon care jobs, and much more. The proposals aimed to create hope in a climate transition involving millions of well-paid, secure jobs in renewable energy, infrastructure, and public services.

Advocates of the GND, particularly in the United States and the UK, positioned it as a necessary response to decades of austerity, stagnant wages, rising emissions, the failure of markets to incentivize decarbonization, and worsening climate disasters. The frameworks guiding it largely remained confined to domestic policy within the Global North, focusing on national-level economic restructuring rather than addressing the deeply entrenched global inequalities that shape who suffers the most from climate change and who currently benefits from international climate management.

The Green New Deal and the legacy of Roosevelt's New Deal

These concerns echo critiques made by Podur (2021) regarding President Franklin D. Roosevelt's original New Deal. Podur highlights how the New Deal was not a universal framework of justice but instead reinforced racial and colonial hierarchies. The original New Deal, implemented by Roosevelt in the 1930s, is often romanticized as a moment of economic transformation and social uplift. It expanded public infrastructure, created millions of jobs, and laid the foundation for the US welfare state; but it also systematically excluded Black and Indigenous communities from many of its benefits. Housing policies under the New Deal, for example, codified racial segregation, creating the conditions for entrenched wealth disparities between White and Black Americans.

Public works projects were largely concentrated in White-majority areas, while Indigenous lands continued to be expropriated for infrastructure and energy expansion. Labour protections prioritized White male workers, while Black and Latinx labourers were excluded from key social security benefits. Beyond the borders of the United States, the New Deal was financed through continued extraction from the Global South, including the expansion of resource extraction, industrial agriculture, and military interventions to secure access to raw materials (Podur 2021). The economic boom that followed did not challenge US imperial expansion but further embedded it. Much like Roosevelt's New Deal, GND proposals tend to position the state as the primary vehicle for economic and social transformation. However, they largely assume that the nation state can drive a just transition without reckoning with its foundational role in stewarding cultural, economic, and ecological domination.

The original New Deal helped consolidate US industrial power, but it did so at the expense of workers, ecology, and communities in the Global South, as well as through intensified exploitation of domestic racialized labour and land. In this sense, Roosevelt's New Deal serves as a cautionary tale: a large-scale state-led economic transition does not inherently produce justice and can, if not designed with an explicitly anti-colonial and anti-racist lens, reproduce the very inequalities it seeks to overcome.

Climate debt and reparations: who owes what?

Colonialism enabled countries in the Global North to accumulate the wealth that enabled only Europe to engage in a fossil-fuelled industrial revolution. From 1850 to 2002, the Global North was responsible for at least three times the greenhouse gas emissions of the Global South, despite housing a significantly smaller share of the world's population. By contrast, entire regions such as Africa, South Asia, and Latin America – home to most of the world's population – have contributed less than 10 per cent of total emissions. Yet, these same regions bear the brunt of climate-induced disasters, from devastating droughts to intensifying hurricanes. This historical imbalance forms the basis of climate debt – the obligation of the Global North to repair the damage caused by its emissions.

Colonialism's endurance is coded into today's global economy – debt regimes, unfair trade agreements, and exploitative financial institutions – meaning that formerly colonized nations remain the most vulnerable to climate shocks yet the least equipped to respond. However, rather than acknowledging responsibility and enacting systemic reparations, the Global North has transformed its climate finance promises into new mechanisms of control, further entrenching the systems that precipitated colonial violence and fossil-fuelled capitalism. The result is to reinforce dependency rather than provide meaningful redress and restructure.

The Intergovernmental Panel on Climate Change and the recognition of climate colonialism

In its *Sixth Assessment Report: Impacts, Adaptation, and Vulnerability* (IPCC 2022), the IPCC made a belated but significant acknowledgement: colonialism has exacerbated existing climate vulnerabilities, shaping the conditions in which communities today experience climate, health, and economic precarity. This long-overdue recognition echoes long-standing critiques from Indigenous groups and climate justice movements, which have consistently highlighted colonialism as central to both the *causes* of the climate crisis and the inequities in its *impacts*.

European colonialism was justified through racial hierarchies and the commodification of nature and non-European peoples, leading to the genocide of Indigenous populations, enslavement and forced relocation of millions, as well as cultural fragmentation and large-scale resource extraction and ecosystem destruction (see Khoo, Chapter 3, Kaladeen, Chapter 4, and Tyler, Chapter 5, this volume). Davis and Todd argue that the inception of the climate crisis can be found in European colonialism. For them, this requires a revaluation not only of our energy use, but also of 'our modes of governance, ongoing racial injustice, and our understandings of ourselves as human' given our relations with our 'other-than-human kin and the land itself' (Davis and Todd 2017; see Baldwin, Chapter 30, this volume).

Slavery, colonization, accelerated rural to urban population transitions, a racialized, gendered, and bonded workforce, and a nature/society divide allowed for some lives to be cheapened (Moore 2015). In addition to its mass ecocide and ethnocide (Voskoboynik 2018), colonialism silenced Indigenous systems of risk management to facilitate the outsourcing of food, fuel minerals, metals, and fibre to the North – regardless of whether they resulted in mass deaths from ruthless labour regimes or famines in the South.

Europe's wealth accumulation was built on plantation slavery, indentured servitude, colonial extraction, and the violent restructuring of economies in the South to serve Northern prosperity. Bhambra and Holmwood cite calculations by the Patnaiks that 'four-fifths of the export of capital from Britain went to developing continental Europe, North America, and regions of recent white settlement' such as Australia (2023: 170). This wealth meant that primarily colonizers and their places of White settlement had resources with which to engage in a fossil-fuelled industrial revolution. Colonialism with its mass violence of people and planet, therefore, marks the inception of climate change.

The expropriation of racialized people and environmental devastation of entire regions were central to this process. The dispossession of Indigenous lands in the Americas, the enforced monoculture economies of the Caribbean, the destruction of agrarian self-sufficiency in India, and the mineral exploitation of Africa all ensured that the Global North's industrialization was subsidized by colonial subjugation. While the Global North was able to consolidate wealth, fund the industrial revolution, construct resilient infrastructure, and develop social protections, the Global South was left with economic dependencies, ecological degradation, unfair trade practices, and financial instruments that perpetuated subordination.

Climate debt and the unequal impacts of climate change

The historic accumulation of wealth through colonialism and fossil capitalism has allowed the Global North to build resilient infrastructure, establish social safety nets, and develop emergency response systems to buffer its populations from the worst climate shocks. In contrast, in the Global South, decades of structural adjustment, resource extraction, and trade regimes – many of them direct legacies of colonial rule – have left governments with limited financial capacity to respond to escalating climate, health, and economic crises.

Colonialism is patterned into the fabric of today's economy (see Gilbert, Chapter 2, this volume). Public services are cut due to structural adjustment policies and unfair debt obligations. Trade agreements too frequently allow for extraction, and exploitation of communities in the South for the benefit of corporations in the North. They also facilitate tax evasion, leaving Southern governments ill-resourced. Aid and development prioritize investments in extractive industries – such as industrial agriculture, mining, deforestation, and tourism (see Sempértegui, Chapter 26, this volume). These realities create the context where climate change impacts hurt those least responsible the most.

While the wealthiest nations have the resources to protect their populations from climate shocks, Global South nations are left without the infrastructure, financial resources, or policy autonomy to facilitate just transitions, adaptation measures, or to repair loss and damage linked to climate change impacts (Kaur Paul 2021). Wealth is accumulated among a tiny fraction of the populations most responsible for emissions. Oxfam reports that the richest 10 per cent of the world's population were responsible for 52 per cent of the cumulative carbon emissions between 1990 and 2015. Around half of these are associated with the consumption of citizens of North America, the UK, and the European Union, and around a fifth (9.2 per cent of global emissions) with citizens of China and India. The poorest 50 per cent – almost 3.1 billion people – were responsible for just 7 per cent. Yet, when extreme weather events strike, it is these same communities that are most affected.

The richest 1 per cent (only 63 million people) alone were responsible for 15 per cent of cumulative emissions. They consume twice as much as the poorest half of the world's population (around 4 billion people), and their consumption has grown three times faster than that of the poorest 50 per cent of the global population. Doubling the per capita footprint of the poorest 50 per cent of the world's population from 1990 to 2015 would have increased total global emissions by less than the growth in emissions associated with the richest 1 per cent in this period. The consumption emissions of the world's super-rich 1 per cent between 2015 and 2019 could lead to 1.5 million excess deaths due to increased heat by 2120 (Oxfam 2023).

The concept of sacrifice zones – areas deemed expendable for economic or political reasons – has long been used to understand environmental degradation in racialized communities within the North. Today, entire nations are becoming climate sacrifice zones, as rising sea levels, intensifying storms, and desertification push entire communities to the brink of displacement. Nations like Bangladesh, where one in seven people is expected to be displaced by 2050, exemplify the reality of how climate change exacerbates existing inequalities, forcing the most vulnerable into cycles of loss and dispossession.

At the same time, climate change intensifies harms for already marginalized communities. Human Rights Council resolutions consistently highlight that the most vulnerable – based on geography, poverty, gender, age, disability, and minority status – experience the most severe climate impacts. Research reveals that:

- Women and girls face increased risks of gender-based violence, economic precarity, and lack of access to healthcare.
- Disabled individuals, particularly disabled women and girls, experience higher mortality rates during disasters due to inaccessible emergency response systems.
- Migrant and displaced children face growing threats to education, food security, and housing, with rising xenophobia preventing them from seeking refuge.
- Older people and incarcerated populations are often overlooked in evacuation and response efforts, leaving them highly vulnerable to displacement and disease.

Current climate solutions, then, continue to reproduce colonial dynamics, reinforcing who is protected, who is compensated, and who is left behind.

Climate reparations or market entrenchment?

The 1992 United Nations Framework Convention on Climate Change formally established the principle of Common but Differentiated Responsibilities, recognizing that industrialized nations must take the lead in both emissions reduction and financial support for climate action in Southern countries. However, these commitments have largely been replaced by voluntary pledges, carbon offset schemes, and exploitative financial instruments that maintain dependency rather than repair harm.

Instead of meaningful reparations, climate finance is largely provided in the form of loans, forcing already vulnerable nations to borrow money from the very countries responsible for their suffering. This creates a perverse system where climate disasters become financial opportunities for countries, banks, and development institutions, ensuring that those most responsible continue to accumulate wealth from the crisis they disproportionately created. Carbon markets have been similarly ineffective in addressing climate change. Under carbon offsetting schemes, corporations and governments in the Global North can continue emitting by purchasing credits from climate mitigation projects in the Global South. These projects, in turn, often lead to land dispossession, green grabbing, and further marginalization of Indigenous and local communities. Wealthier polluters can effectively buy their way out of emissions reductions while ensuring that the costs of mitigation are offloaded onto the poorest nations.

At the same time, carbon pricing mechanisms – and offers of climate finance – allow fossil fuel companies and financial institutions to position themselves as part of the solution, despite continuing to profit from extraction. Any climate finance provided is a drop in the ocean compared to the structural support for upholding existing reliance on fossil fuels. The Carbon Majors Report has established that just 100 fossil fuel companies are responsible for 71 per cent of all industrial greenhouse gas emissions since 1988.

BankTrack research reveals that world's 60 largest banks have collectively financed fossil fuels with US$6.9 trillion since the Paris Agreement. Financiers like JPMorgan Chase, Citi, and Bank of America invested US$705 billion in 2023 alone towards fossil fuel expansion. This cycle of investment ensures that new oil, gas, and coal projects continue, despite overwhelming scientific evidence that fossil fuel expansion is incompatible with the Paris Agreement's 1.5°C target. These same financial institutions greenwash their role by investing in carbon offset markets and voluntary sustainability pledges that lack accountability.

The maintenance of colonial forms of governance allows for the entrenchment of the very tools that have helped cause the climate crisis. As Bhambra and Newell (2023) argue, however, it is not enough to recognize colonialism as a historical event that sets the stage for modern capitalism's extractive tendencies. Colonialism remains structurally embedded in contemporary global inequalities, shaping who is most exposed to climate shocks and who has the resources to adjust to emerging impacts and redress accelerating loss and damage.

The extractive foundations of the green economy: green jobs, but at what cost?

GND formulations often focus on a transition to a renewable energy economy through good green jobs. This is often framed as an unambiguous good. However, this transition is far from clean. The push for renewable technologies – such as solar panels, wind turbines, and electric vehicle batteries – has triggered an aggressive race for rare minerals and metals, including lithium, cobalt, and nickel. These resources are primarily concentrated in the Global South, and their extraction mirrors the exploitative dynamics of past and present fossil fuel industries. Rather than breaking from an extractive economic model, green energy expansion risks entrenching new forms of ecological and social devastation, with multinational corporations controlling resource supply chains while local communities bear the environmental and human costs.

Mining

This pattern of green extractivism reveals a fundamental contradiction in mainstream climate action: while renewable energy is framed as a sustainable alternative to fossil fuels, it remains embedded in colonial-era resource extraction practices. Muñoz (2021) highlights the rush for lithium, cobalt, and nickel for electric vehicle batteries and solar panels is not only devastating local ecosystems but also exacerbating exploitative labour conditions, particularly in the Global South. This mirrors the same power dynamics that have long defined the fossil fuel industry – where corporations and states in the Global North dictate the terms of extraction, while communities in the Global South are left with environmental destruction, displacement, and economic precarity.

Muñoz argues that extractive industries tied to the green economy continue to destroy Indigenous lands and violate labour rights under the guise of sustainability. From lithium mining in Bolivia to cobalt extraction in the Democratic Republic of Congo, the same colonial patterns of land dispossession, forced displacement, and exploitative working conditions persist. In the Democratic Republic of Congo, for instance, cobalt mines – critical for electric vehicles – are often operated under conditions of child labour and severe human rights abuses, while revenues largely benefit foreign investors rather than local economies. This illustrates how, without structural changes, the transition to green energy can reproduce the very inequalities and injustices that fossil fuel dependency created. Mining focused transitions also assume it is possible to universalize the scale of consumption in the North. We do not have sufficient raw earth minerals and metals to do so. Change requires reconceptualizing well-being.

Resource grabs and displacement

Hamouchene warns that these extractive dynamics extend beyond economic dispossession – they also deepen political and territorial displacements. Large-scale renewable projects, such as solar mega-farms in North Africa, are being constructed with minimal regard for local communities, often replicating the colonial model of land grabs for export-driven resource exploitation. At the same time, the very people forced to migrate due to climate change and resource extraction find themselves confronted with fortified borders, militarized migration policies, and growing anti-migrant sentiment in the countries most responsible for the climate crisis. This underscores how, without a structurally anti-colonial and redistributive framework, the so-called green transition will reinforce rather than dismantle the inequalities that drive the climate crisis.

Hamouchene (2021) further critiques the rise of 'green' energy projects that displace Indigenous and local communities, particularly in North Africa, where vast solar farms are being constructed on occupied or communal lands without local consent. These projects are often designed to export clean energy to Europe, reinforcing colonial-era resource extraction dynamics where land and labour in the Global South are used to sustain prosperity in the North. Rather than empowering communities through decentralized, democratically controlled renewable energy, these projects further alienate them from their territories and perpetuate ecological injustice.

Migration

At the same time, climate-induced displacement is being met with border securitization. As climate change worsens and resource extraction intensifies, millions are being forced to leave their homes due to droughts, land degradation, and extreme weather. Yet, instead of recognizing climate migration as a crisis requiring global responsibility and reparative justice, wealthy nations are militarizing borders, reinforcing xenophobic immigration policies, and criminalizing those displaced by the very extractivist systems they profit from. The contradiction is stark: while the Global North accelerates the plunder of resources for its green transition, it simultaneously denies refuge and reparations to those whose lands and livelihoods are destroyed (Faciolince and Voskoboynik 2021).

The extractive foundations of the green economy reveal that simply shifting from fossil fuels to renewables is not inherently just or sustainable. Without addressing the underlying structures of exploitation, land dispossession, and global inequality, the transition to green energy risks becoming another iteration of climate colonialism. As climate justice advocates argue, a truly just transition must prioritize community-led energy systems, Indigenous land rights, and an end to the extractivist logic that fuels both environmental destruction and human displacement.

Conclusion

The GND emerged as a progressive framework for systemic change, challenging the market-driven and incremental approaches that have long dominated climate action. Yet, as this chapter has shown, proposals for a GND – like other large-scale state-led suggested transitions – risk reproducing the very inequalities they seek to dismantle. Climate action cannot be effective if it remains confined to national policies or relies on market mechanisms that allow the world's wealthiest nations and corporations to continue exploiting people and resources in the Global South.

A truly just transition must move beyond the extractivist logic that underpins both fossil fuel economies and mainstream renewable energy expansion. As this chapter has outlined, the rush to profit from loss and damage, and to extract minerals while impoverishing and polluting local communities, demonstrates how colonial patterns of exploitation persist within the so-called green economy. Without systemic interventions that prioritize resource sovereignty, Indigenous land rights, and community-controlled energy, the energy transition will become another frontier for accumulation rather than a pathway towards justice. Even climate change impacts can become spaces for accumulation through forms of climate finance that prioritize the payment of insurance premiums to corporate actors who may also fund (and profit from) fossil fuel projects.

The principle of climate reparations must underpin any systemic response to climate change, ensuring that wealth is redistributed to those who have suffered the most from environmental degradation and have contributed the least to emissions. The wealthiest individuals, corporations, and financial institutions bear a disproportionate responsibility for the climate crisis. Addressing the crisis requires changing the economic, political, ecological, and social structures that allow such actors to accumulate such wealth at the expense of people and planet.

As Bhambra and Newell (2023) caution, addressing climate change without acknowledging its colonial roots and contemporary structural injustices risks reinforcing existing global inequalities. The challenge is not merely technological but deeply political: Who controls resources? Who decides what a just transition looks like? Who benefits from climate policies? Without decolonial and redistributive policies, the transition risks becoming another mechanism for reinforcing North–South inequalities.

Moving forward, climate movements, scholars, and policy makers must push beyond the limits of existing frameworks like the GND and advocate for a global, reparative, and justice-centred climate response. This will change over time as climate change impacts accelerate in new and surprising ways. Nevertheless, some guiding ideas could include:

- shifting away from green extractivism and ensuring community-led renewable energy rather than corporate-controlled megaprojects;
- restructuring the economy for redistributions that enable climate reparations, and debt cancellation;
- recognizing climate migration as a justice issue, ensuring that those displaced by climate impacts and extractivism are provided with protection and reparations rather than criminalization and border militarization; and
- addressing social and cultural norms that deepen exposure to climate change harms, and facilitate extractive plunder.

Climate action cannot be separated from the struggles for economic justice, deeper democracy, or ecological, gender, and racial justice. The climate crisis cannot be fixed through the system that created it. Addressing it requires a transformation of global economic, cultural, ecological, and political systems, ensuring that those most affected by climate breakdown are not only compensated but also leading the transition. Anything less will simply reproduce the injustices that created this crisis in the first place.

References

Bhambra, G.K. and Holmwood, J. 2023. 'The Trap of "Capitalism", Racial or Otherwise', *European Journal of Sociology* 64(2): 163–172.

Bhambra, G.K. and Newell, P. 2023. 'More than a Metaphor: "Climate Colonialism" in Perspective', *Global Social Challenges Journal* 2(2): 179–187.

Davis, H. and Todd, Z. 2017. 'On the Importance of a Date, or Decolonizing the Anthropocene', *ACME: An International E-Journal for Critical Geographies* 16(4): 761–780.

Faciolince, M. and Voskoboynik, D.M. 2021. 'A Just Vision for Climate Migration', in H. Kaur Paul and D. Gebriel (eds), *Perspectives on a Global Green New Deal*. Rosa Luxemburg Stiftung, pp 113–117.

Hamouchene, H. 2021. 'Dismantling Green Colonialism', in H. Kaur Paul and D. Gebriel (eds), in *Perspectives on a Global Green New Deal*. Rosa Luxemburg Stiftung, pp 120–122.

Intergovernmental Panel on Climate Change (IPCC). 2018. 'Summary for Policymakers', in V. Masson-Delmotte, P. Zhai, H.-O. Pörtner, D. Roberts, J. Skea, P.R. Shukla et al. (eds), *Global Warming of 1.5°C: An IPCC Special Report*. Cambridge University Press, pp 3–24. https://doi.org/10.1017/9781009157940.001

IPCC. 2022. *Climate Change 2022: Impacts, Adaptation and Vulnerability. Summary for Policymakers*. IPCC. https://www.ipcc.ch/site/assets/uploads/sites/2/2022/06/SPM_version_report_LR.pdf

Kaur Paul, H. 2021. 'Towards Reparative Climate Justice: From Crisis to Liberations', *Common Wealth*. Available at: https://www.common-wealth.org/publications/towards-reparative-climate-justice-from-crises-to-liberations

Moore, J. 2015. *Capitalism in the Web of Life: Ecology and the Accumulation of Capital*. Verso.

Muñoz, S.O. 2021. 'No Worker Left Behind', in H. Kaur Paul and D. Gebriel (eds), in *Perspectives on a Global Green New Deal*, Rosa Luxemburg Stiftung, pp 18–21.

Oxfam. 2023. 'Richest 1% Emit as Much Planet-heating Pollution as Two-thirds of Humanity', *Oxfam International*. https://www.oxfam.org.uk/mc/qer7km/

Podur, J. 2021. 'Leaving Behind the Racist and Imperialist Baggage of the Original New Deal', in H. Kaur Paul and D. Gebriel (eds), *Perspectives on a Global Green New Deal*. Rosa Luxemburg Stiftung, pp 123–128.

Voskoboynik, D. 2018. *The Memory We Could Be: Overcoming Fear to Create Our Ecological Future*. New Society Publishers.

Video lecture

Kaur Paul (now Spannos), H. 2020. *A Green New Deal?*, Connected Sociologies Curriculum Project. https://thesociologicalreview.org/projects/connected-sociologies/curriculum/environment-and-climate-change/green-new-deal/

QUESTIONS

1. How does the Green New Deal reinforce or challenge historical patterns of colonial extraction and economic inequality?

2. In what ways does climate change function as a continuation of colonial violence, rather than a new crisis?

3. How can Indigenous and Global South communities lead climate transitions in ways that challenge North–South power imbalances?

4. What role does climate debt play in global inequality, and how could reparations be implemented in a just transition?

5. What would a genuinely decolonial climate transition look like, and what political, economic, and social changes would be necessary to achieve it?

Worksheet 27. A Global Green New Deal? Signatures of Continuing Colonial Violence

This worksheet is designed to support AS and A-level teaching on globalization and global development. This topic focuses on the relationships between globalization and the environment, and global inequalities. In her chapter and online talk, Harpreet Kaur Paul (now Spannos) explores the goals, motivations, and limitations to Green New Deals (GNDs). GNDs have captured much attention in the Global North, mobilizing state power to propose and enact policies that connect economic justice with climate action. Paul explains how these proposals have limitations for addressing the global injustices underpinning the climate crisis, including the ecological impacts of colonialism. This worksheet is designed to stretch students' critical thinking skills in assessing the political and economic aims of GNDs. Students are encouraged to examine why the Global North is failing in its duty to accept its 'fair share' of responsibility for the climate crisis, and to consider the challenges for reparative environmental justice. In addition to supporting A-level Sociology students, this session may be useful for students of related subjects such as Geography.

Time	Activity	Explanation
00.00–00.05	To warm up, answer the following questions: *What is involved in a Green New Deal? Have you heard this being discussed in the media?*	This activity introduces students to the topic, encouraging them to share what they already know about this subject. Students may have noticed political discourse surrounding GNDs during the July 2024 UK general election, for example.
00.05–00.10	Recap of understandings of globalization and global development	It may be useful to remind students of the key concepts related to globalization, particularly regarding the relationship between the environment and development.
00.10–00.15	Watch the talk from 0:00 to 2:19. *What are the main issues that GNDs seek to address?*	GNDs address fuel poverty and seek to reduce energy wastage in poorly insulated homes through 'green upgrades'. They also promote a democratic transition away from fossil fuels. Building on the warm-up activity, this question enables students to expand existing knowledge of GNDs. They may draw connections with the agendas of well-known political lobby groups and political party manifestos, following the point that GNDs are used to campaign for state power.
00.15–00.20	Watch the talk from 3:00 to 3:42. *What are some of the key problems with GNDs, according to Paul?*	GNDs promote environmental targets which are insufficient in tackling the climate crisis, often without acknowledging the Global North's heavier responsibility for climate change. They also promote potentially damaging schemes, such as 'dirty hydrogen', and support large corporations over community-owned green energy schemes. This activity encourages students to think critically about the aims and scope of GNDs, and to consider the question of responsibility within the climate crisis.

Time	Activity	Explanation
00.20–00.30	Watch the talk from 3:42 to 4:09. *How do we know what a country's 'fair share' is? What are the limitations of GNDs in addressing a country's 'fair share'?*	A country's 'fair share' is based on understandings that Global North countries have used up most of the world's carbon budget and should take on a greater share of responsibilities for tackling the climate crisis. Instead of prioritizing the greater responsibilities that countries like the UK should bear, GNDs focus on economic growth, assuming that the economy can continue to grow at the same unsustainable rate. Building on the previous activity, these questions encourage students to think about the importance of responsibility in global agendas for tackling the climate crisis. They are prompted to consider the role of capitalist growth and consumerism. Students may make links to 'Our Worlds of Palm Oil' and other chapters and talks in 'The Environment' section.
00.30–00.40	Watch the talk from 5:20 to 7:12. *What is the role of corporate power in GND proposals, and in the climate crisis more broadly?*	The lobbying power of corporations has impacted mainstream notions of GNDs, for example by the European Commission's hiring of BlackRock. Systemic corporate power is built into international treaties, debt, trade and investment regimes, as elements underpinning GNDs. This activity prompts students to think further about the intersection between corporate capitalism and environmental harm. It also encourages them to consider how corporate capitalism is built into agendas to tackle climate change.
00.40–00.50	Watch the talk from 11:19 to 13:20. *What are some of the challenges with pursuing global responses to the climate crisis? How can sociologists address these?*	National and local GNDs are not enough on their own to address the climate crisis. Instead, we need global visions that seek to promote equity both within countries and between them. It is important for Global North countries to recognize their historic responsibility for environmental harm due to the ecological injustices of colonialism. Students may identify challenges with recognizing responsibilities, and ensuring that Global North countries take responsibility for colonial injustices. Students might identify the importance of recovering hidden histories in bringing awareness about colonialism's enduring environmental impact. They might begin to consider how reparative responses could be implemented.
00.50–01.00	Drawing on what you have learned from this talk, and other associated topics: *What is the importance of responsibility in addressing the climate crisis?*	This activity encourages students to connect what they have learned about colonialism and the climate crisis from this session and other topics. By prompting students to think about globalization's impact on the environment and global inequalities, the question also connects to key A-level Sociology curriculum themes. Students may use their learning from the previous activity in identifying some potential challenges with ensuring that countries in the Global North take responsibility for the historical and enduring injustices of colonialism.

This worksheet was developed by Isabel Sykes.

28

Political Ecology: Critical Reflections

Mitul Baruah

Objectives

- This chapter presents a historical overview of political ecology, focusing on some of the key texts in the field and the historical circumstances in which these works came about.

- It posits the rise of political ecology as an antidote to apolitical ecology, examples of which include the Malthusian/neo-Malthusian 'eco-scarcity' thesis as well as the idea of 'ecological modernization'.

- It discusses and illustrates some of political ecology's defining characteristics by presenting a case study of flooding in Assam, a state located in the north-eastern corner of India in the Himalayan foothills.

- It explicitly takes up the issue of colonization to show how colonialism transformed nature and nature–society relations in much of the world, legacies of which continue today, inflicting violence, both materially and discursively, on the land.

- In calling for a decolonization of human–environment relations, this chapter foregrounds the critical and emancipatory role that political ecology can and ought to play.

Introduction

Imagine yourself visiting the beautiful state of Assam in north-east India – a state endowed with great biodiversity and a tropical monsoonal climate – in the months of June and July. You will most likely find yourself welcomed by torrential rain and deluge, with your movement severely curtailed by flooded roads and broken infrastructure. An otherwise scenic drive through Assam's countryside may now look apocalyptic, with villages and fields completely submerged, and displaced rural families along with their cattle and belongings camping on the highways for survival. Meanwhile, the TV screens will hold you witness to casualties, including that of one-horned rhinoceros and other wild animals. Given that these are recurring annual phenomena in Assam, they are invariably referred to, both in popular discourses and the media, as 'natural disasters' ('*Prakitik durjog*'). However, a closer examination of these phenomena will soon reveal that they are anything but 'natural'.

Located in the north-eastern corner of the country, in the shadow of the eastern Himalayas and crisscrossed by the braided channels of the mighty Brahmaputra river and its numerous tributaries, Assam is highly susceptible to monsoonal flooding. While flooding as a phenomenon is natural to Assam, over the years, various anthropogenic forces have turned these natural processes disastrous (Baruah 2022). There is nothing natural about the havoc wrought by flood year after year in the state. On the contrary, everything about the disaster – the causes of the flood, its impacts, and post-flood reconstruction processes – is socially produced (Smith 2006). I will return to this issue later but suffice it to say that the issue of flooding in Assam is a classic case of political ecology. It depicts how ecological processes, in this case, the highly potent north-eastern monsoonal regime and the abundance of rivers have interacted with the political economy of the state and its infrastructural projects, (re-)producing vulnerability and transforming a natural phenomenon into a calamity.

Political ecology: a brief history

Calling it 'a tree with deep roots', environmental geographer Paul Robbins (2004: 17–18) traces the genesis of the field of political ecology as far back as the turn of the 20th century when Russian anarchist philosopher Peter Kropotkin wrote his classic, *Mutual Aid: A Factor in Evolution*. *Mutual Aid* was a solid antithesis to social Darwinism – an idea, dominant at the time, that viewed the human world according to the Darwinian laws of natural selection that applied to plants and animals, where 'survival of the fittest' was believed to be the logic. Social Darwinism helped justify imperialism and racism, since some groups of people were believed to be inherently superior. Kropotkin challenged this notion by privileging cooperation over competition as the key to species survival.

Drawing on his in-depth knowledge of animal ethology, combining that with empirical data as well as a careful reading of histories of various societies around the world, Kropotkin showed the importance of 'inherent sociability' between species and between individuals within species. He acknowledged competition but argued that species had much more to gain from mutual coordination and support. Kropotkin's political project envisioned a society that was equitable, free from hierarchic tyranny, and in harmony with biophysical nature; and, in that sense, was political-ecological. For Robbins (2004), therefore, Kropotkin was one of the 'first real political ecologists'.

It was not until the 1980s, however, that political ecology emerged as a coherent body of work in the Anglophone world. While the 'Great Sahelian drought' swept through much of sub-Saharan Africa, resulting in severe famine and countless deaths, the Chernobyl and Bhopal tragedies of industrial radiation and chemical disasters not only shook the world but also laid bare the irresponsibility of both capital and the state. The destruction of the Amazonian rainforest foregrounded concerns of nature's commodification, the role of global capital and neo-colonialism, and environmental justice and activism (Hecht and Cockburn 1989; see Sempértegui, Chapter 26, this volume). At the same time, the Chipko movement in the Indian Himalayas drew worldwide attention as peasant women came together to hug trees ('*chipko*' means to hug or to cling to) that were central to their survival in the mountain ecologies, protecting them from the lumbermen. Even in a pre-digital world, the iconic image of rural women hugging trees, a rare form of environmental resistance, spread far and wide with huge significance for environmental activists and rural communities elsewhere.

Alongside these important events was an intellectual rising from the Global South which included the rise of peasant studies (the study of political movements and resistance among rural, agrarian societies in the face of coercive power and the incursion of capitalist relations) and 'dependency' theory (a theory that explained the underdevelopment of the 'Third World' as a direct result of the terms of trade established during the colonial period, which continued to shape the economies of these erstwhile colonies). These are examples of Southern Theory, which also revolutionized feminism, trade union and student politics. This new wave of scholarship brought concerns of social justice and political economy to the centre of analysing socio-environmental processes.

Michael Watts' (2013: [1983]) *Silent Violence: Food, Famine, and Peasantry in Northern Nigeria* is considered to be a foundational text in political ecology. In this classic, Watts examined the long-drawn famine in the Sahel region from a Marxist perspective and showed that at the heart of the famine was the incursion of capitalist economic systems into the Hausa society in Nigeria, changing their relations of production. *Silent Violence* showed that the pre-colonial Hausa society had practised a range of drought-coping mechanisms, including drought-resistant cropping, traditional irrigation mechanisms, and a 'moral economy' that privileged social obligations and reciprocity to economic values. However, once colonial capitalist relations established their roots, the pre-capitalist traditional systems were replaced by market economy, cash crops cultivation, and a system of heavy taxation on the peasantry, making them highly vulnerable to droughts (Watts 2013 [1983]). The famine in the Sahel region was thus a combination of prolonged droughts and political economic forces of colonial capitalism.

Piers Blaikie and Harold Brookfield's (1987) *Land Degradation and Society* is another important work that set the tone for future political ecological work. Calling land degradation a 'social problem', Blaikie and Brookfield argued that environmental processes alone, such as leaching and erosion of land, do not constitute 'degradation'; rather, degradation is when these biophysical processes impact actual or potential uses of the land. From a political ecology perspective, land degradation thus calls into question its social *causes* and *consequences*. For Blaikie and Brookfield, therefore, behind land degradation, the role of the 'land managers' – which includes farmers, agri-businesses, and the state – is crucial, and this itself has to do with the larger political economic processes. Once incorporated into the capitalist world economic system driven largely by surplus extraction from resources – in this case, land – peasants lose the ability to control their own lives, thus being pushed into a process of 'marginalization'. And it is, as they argue, the vicious cycle of peasants' socio-economic 'marginalization' and land degradation that maintains poverty and unequal social relations.

Indian environmental historian Ramachandra Guha's (2010 [1989]) *The Unquiet Woods: Ecological Change and Peasant Resistance in the Himalaya* and Hecht and

Cockburn's (1989) *The Fate of the Forest: Developers, Destroyers and Defenders of the Amazon* were two other pioneering works that helped shape the field of political ecology. As opposed to a simplistic interpretation of the Chipko movement as a purely *environmental* or *feminist* or *anti-development* movement, Guha's account situated it in the larger historical context of colonial and post-colonial forest management and agrarian relations in the region. The increased role of the market economy and a rising demand for timber made the mountain people and their forests vulnerable. This had to be understood in the specific contexts of the mountain ecologies that limited the possibilities of 'extensive' and 'intensive' cultivation in the mountains, thereby shaping a unique relationship between the peasants and the forests. In similar vein, Hecht and Cockburn (1989) offered a thorough account of the making and unmaking of the Amazonian rainforest by focusing on, among others, human interventions, global capital and the rubber boom, the role of fire and the Amazonian soil, and environmental activism and violence.

Set in widely diverse geographical contexts, these works viewed environmental phenomena as a combination of the natural world and anthropogenic forces; situated them within their specific histories, with a special attention to the role of colonial capital; and explained the so-called local processes by showing how the 'local' is always enmeshed in extra-local processes. The works discussed earlier also give us a glimpse into the genealogy of the field. In tracing the origin of political ecology, it is important to note that it emerged as an antidote to what may be called an 'apolitical ecology' – an approach that is technocratic and ahistorical and considers ecological systems as politically inert.

Good examples of apolitical ecology are the Malthusian and neo-Malthusian theses on population and scarcity, which find population growth to be the root of social problems. According to these theses, population growth far surpasses the growth of resources, resulting in resource scarcity and various problems associated with it. The neo-Malthusian approach not only naturalizes the impoverishment of certain nations and sections of the society but also holds the poor responsible for their poverty. A political ecological approach, on the other hand, views resource scarcity as being socially produced through unequal distribution of resources. Scarcity in this sense is relative, not absolute. In other words, a political ecological explanation of scarcity (or poverty) focuses on social relations of production and different kinds of inequalities and power imbalances that are produced and re-produced through historical processes of expropriation and unequal access to resources.

Political ecology: key characteristics

There are different approaches to political ecology, depending on the vantage point of a researcher. For instance, some political ecologists approach the field with a feminist perspective while some others come from the ecological sciences, or a Marxist position. This section outlines a four key defining characteristics of the field.

First, political ecology takes both *biophysical nature and politics* seriously. As Blaikie and Brookfield (1987: 17) put it, political ecology is '[an approach that] combines the concerns of ecology and a broadly defined political economy ... [thus] encompasses the constantly shifting dialectic between society and land-based resources, and also within classes and groups within society itself'. Political ecologists take nature's materiality seriously, with an acknowledgement that nature is not simply about objective facts and data that can be empirically observed, nor is it politically inert. Instead, for political ecologists, nature is inseparable from social relations of power.

Some political ecologists are more drawn to a constructivist approach that argues that the idea of nature is socially constructed through discourses, which in turn is a product of our cultural belief systems and practices. For instance, what comes to mind when we hear terms such as 'pristine', 'authentic', 'wild', and so on are all shaped by culture, media, advertisements, education, and the like – in other words, social processes. Some others approach nature more from a Marxist notion of 'production of nature', which is to say that nature is constantly being altered and re-produced through the labour processes. Nature, in this sense, is a product of particular modes of production. In short, political ecologists view nature as deeply embedded in social relations. This is not to say that nature's intrinsic value is not recognized; rather, political ecology situates nature within the context of the broader political economic processes.

The second important feature of political ecology is its engagement with *scale*. Blaikie and Brookfield (1987) note the importance of looking at environmental phenomena across scales. According to them, the complexity of human–environment interactions demands an approach that encompasses 'the contribution of different geographical scales and hierarchies of socioeconomic organizations (e.g. person, household, village, region, state, world)' (Blaikie and Brookfield 1987: 17). In other words, the so-called 'local' cannot be granted, a priori, inherent qualities, and must be understood through its relations with extra-local processes. Yet Blaikie and Brookfield conceptualized scale in a hierarchical fashion – a 'chain of explanation', to use their own term.

More recently, Zimmerer and Bassett (2003) stressed the centrality of both 'ecological scale' and 'social scale' to political ecological research. Unlike Blaikie and Brookfield, Zimmerer and Bassett consider scale not as ontologically given, but as socio-environmentally produced. Based on the nature of interactions between and within ecological and social processes, there can be 'a variety of scalar configurations that display vertical (hierarchical, nested) and horizontal (networked) patterns' (Zimmerer and Bassett 2003: 4). Swyngedouw's (1997) notion of 'glocalization' – that is, neither global nor local – draws our attention to the question of how 'scale' is produced and re-produced, and why we must pay attention to these processes, which are simultaneously social and biophysical. In a nutshell, scalar analysis of environmental processes remains central to political ecological scholarship, even as the idea of scale itself goes through different iterations.

The third defining characteristic of political ecology is its deep engagement with *power*. Political ecology draws on different versions of the idea of power, depending on the issue it is studying and the theoretical commitment of the researcher doing the study. Some engage with Marxian notions of power – that is, the ways in which capital deploys power to maintain the accumulation cycle, while others draw more closely on the Gramscian idea of 'hegemony' that shows how the ruling class exercises its power through coercion and consent. A lot of political ecology works also draw on the Foucauldian idea that power is all-pervasive. For Foucault, power permeates society through 'capillary' movement, affecting everyday life and social structures (Hall 1997: 77). Feminist political ecologists, on the other hand, put patriarchy at the centre of their analysis of socio-environmental processes. Irrespective of the specific conceptualization, by keeping power at the centre of its analytical lens, political ecology denaturalizes environmental processes and places them in the context of social relations of power.

Political ecology is grounded in 'methodological commitment to in-depth, direct observation involving qualitative research of some sort' (Perreault et al 2015: 7). The epistemic plurality of political ecology includes engagement with the role of the state, as well. I would however like to highlight one final characteristic of this field of study, and that is its 'normative *political commitment* to social justice and structural political change' (Perreault et al 2015: 8, original emphasis). From its very beginning, issues of resource degradation, conflicts over access to, and ownership of resources, and the concerns of socially marginalized communities have dominated the field. Thus, it has proven itself to be an explicitly normative project that strives towards social-environmental justice. It is in this spirit that Robbins (2004: 12–13) describes political ecology as a 'hatchet and a seed' and argues that political ecology is something that people *do* and not simply study.

Let me illustrate these features of political ecology by revisiting the case of Assam. Floods have been part of the natural landscape of Assam. Hence, the Assamese peasantry has, over the years, learned to live with and adapted their agrarian practices to the annual cycle of flooding. As have other rural communities whose livelihoods revolved around fishing, livestock rearing, pottery, boat making, and so on. The river, annual flooding cycle, and the sediments have been an integral part of life and livelihoods in the Brahmaputra floodplains. With colonization, however, Assam witnessed a proliferation of embankments along the Brahmaputra and its tributaries. This was because the colonial administration viewed floods as a calamity as they interrupted the flow of agrarian revenue. The embankments were supposed to protect colonial capital from the uncertainty of a natural disaster by separating the land from the water.

The post-colonial Indian state continued the project of embankment building with even greater fervour. Far from controlling floods, however, the embankments have rendered the river much more volatile, making flooding more disastrous. The embankments have significantly interfered with the natural courses and configurations of the river. They have confined the course of the river, turned it shallow by obstructing the natural distribution of sediments that floodwater carried, and deprived the wetlands of fresh water and fish. Periodically, these embankments have been breached as they could not withstand the force of these Himalayan rivers in the monsoon, creating havoc for the local population. In short, the embankments have turned what used to be a natural part of the local ecologies of Assam into a disaster. It is important to note that the embankments are not unique to Assam; rather, as part of the legacy of modernity, they have been deployed by state authorities across the world to control rivers so that the process of capital accumulation could be continued. But they have failed everywhere, producing more disasters.

In Assam, the flood crisis is also related with the failure of the state at many levels: the absence of timely flood forecasting and warning, absence of flood zoning, inadequate flood relief and rehabilitation measures, and non-incorporation of local, traditional knowledge into flood adaptation measures, to name a few.

What we have observed in this case study is that behind Assam's floods is a combination of natural and political economic processes. While a highly potent monsoon and the abundant river systems created the conditions for flooding, the colonial and the post-colonial state turned flooding into a disaster through specific hydraulic interventions, while failing to alleviate the plight of the flood-vulnerable population. The case of flooding in Assam also calls attention to the question of scale – both ecological and social. After all, the courses and configurations of the mighty Brahmaputra river and its tributaries and how they play out to reshape not just Assam's geographies but the Assamese society as a whole need to be situated in the context of changing Himalayan ecologies as well as the governance of these rivers across scales as they flowed down the terrains, meandering through different territorial regimes.

In short, then, the production of the flood disaster in Assam and associated vulnerabilities are very much about politics of scale. A scalar analysis of the crisis will help us gain deeper insights into it so that we can, perhaps, find ways to address it. A political ecological study of such an environmental disaster would also require paying close attention to the sufferings and struggles of the disaster-affected communities (see Baruah 2022) without which such research would not be able to contribute to better environmental governance, let alone social justice.

Political ecology, colonization, and perspectives from the Global South

That the natural process of flooding came to be considered a 'disaster' in Assam was primarily a colonial invention (Baruah 2022). For the colonial Raj, the vast fertile Brahmaputra floodplains offered great opportunities for revenue generation through cash crop cultivation, jute being the most lucrative. Second only to cotton as a fibre crop, jute was of tremendous significance for colonial capital. By the early 20th century, it was the highest export earner for the Raj and Assam was the second largest jute producer in the country after Bengal. Tea was another cash crop yielding colonial revenue in Assam. The massive conversion of the fragile riverine tracts into jute fields and tea plantations led to unprecedented reworking of their ecologies, rendering them highly vulnerable to flood and erosion.

At the same time, railway tracks also needed protection from regular inundation, as trains were the primary mode of transportation for goods, including tea, jute, and coal. Thus began an era of 'flood control' in Assam, mainly by constructing embankments. In controlling floods, the colonial state paid no heed to the fact that the peasantry in Assam was traditionally flood-dependent. Floods helped irrigate crops and replenished the fields with a regular supply of alluvium. Local knowledges about rivers, seasonal flooding patterns, and traditional adaptive measures were entirely ignored, replacing them with a technocratic approach to flood management.

Colonial flood control completely reconfigured the floodplains, producing new vulnerabilities by ignoring, even erasing, local knowledge-practices and replacing them with Western, 'scientific' practices. A political ecological study of flooding is therefore also about situating flood crisis in its colonial historical context. It calls for new material and discursive practices vis-à-vis floods that are democratic and emancipatory.

Colonialism occupies an important space in most political ecology research from/on the Global South. Colonization was part of the analytical optic of political ecology from the very beginning. Mike Davis' (2001) *Late Victorian Holocausts: El Niño Famines and the Making of the Third World* demonstrates much more explicitly the centrality of colonization to the political ecological explanation of the making of the 'Third World' (see also Ghosh 2021). Davis combined multiple domains – colonialism, capitalism, and climate – to talk about devastating episodes of famines and the deaths of hundreds of thousands in late 19th-century India, China, and Brazil. Davis particularly foregrounded the violence that colonial powers inflicted on the land, manifesting itself in the form of enclosures, robbery of the land, privatization, and what he called 'the modernization of poverty'.

The legacy of colonization continues to shape the environment in the Global South, both materially and discursively. On the one hand, much like neo-colonial forces, capital and the capitalist state continue to exploit and commodify nature, often violently and at cost of the native population; on the other, local knowledges and cultural practices are being sacrificed in the name of so-called 'scientific' knowledges and 'expertise'. Local people are often blamed for the miseries arising out of resource degradation without locating environmental crises in their colonial roots. The solutions that capitalist political economy puts forward for environmental challenges come from the ambit of 'ecological modernization', an *apolitical* and ahistorical thesis that is rooted in technological fix to deeper structural questions. What we need therefore is an alternative, decolonial approach to understanding nature–society relations in the Global South, and political ecology is one pathway towards this.

Many of the works cited here come from the Anglophone academy, even though the case studies are mostly based on the Global South. It bears mentioning that the Anglophone academy does not hold any patent on political ecology, nor is theirs the only model of political ecological scholarship. Recent years have witnessed a great deal of political ecology research coming out of the non-Western world covering a range of topics – from rural, agrarian issues to urban ecologies and new ecologies of waste, transgenes, viruses, and so on. Such has been the rise of political ecological research in the Global South that the 5th biennial conference of the Political Ecology Network, also known as POLLEN,[1] which has largely been Eurocentric, was held simultaneously in three locations: Lund (Sweden), Lima (Peru), and Dodoma (Tanzania) in June 2024. This author participated in POLLEN, Dodoma, and was overwhelmed by the numbers and varieties of papers that scholars and activists from different parts of Africa and Asia presented there.

The Global South's contribution to political ecology is not merely in the form of academic scholarship; it presents a new way of *doing* political ecology. And that is the kind of work that various activist-research organizations have been doing in these parts of the world. In India, for instance, the work of the People's Archive of Rural India,[2] the Centre for Science and Environment,[3] and Kalpavriksh: Environmental Action Group[4] are worth noting in this regard. These organizations carry out in-depth research on socio-environmental issues and often publish them in the form of short stories and reports. Without academic jargon and theories, these are much more accessible to ordinary citizens and policy makers.

The Centre for Science and Environment's fortnightly magazine, *Down to Earth*, for instance, has been a great resource for environmental scholars and activists alike. Similarly, Kalpavriksh's new initiatives such as 'Vikalp Sangam'[5] attempt to document and raise public awareness of range of alternatives that the grassroots offer. Examples of such activist political ecologies are found in Latin America as well. The Zapatistas of Mexico, for instance, undertake activities that help build autonomy in the mountains of southern Mexico, the Chiapas, and in the process, generate environmental knowledges. The Escuelita Zapatista or the Zapatista Little School is an attempt to fulfil such a project. The work of La Via Campesina[6] is another example of how attempts are being made, outside of academia, to produce an environmental regime that is inclusive and emancipatory.

Work of this kind holds great potential for political ecology scholarship: it is democratic, radical and serves to reinforce Robbins' call for 'doing' political ecology. To *do* political ecology is to bring together knowledge creation, resistance, and social transformation. It is about doing research with a direct political agenda of changing social relations and emancipation. It is this spirit of socio-environmental justice that characterizes the work of the activist-research groups discussed here. As Mexican radical scholar Enrique Leff (2015: 70) puts it:

> [T]he political ecology of the Third World is constructed as a discursive amalgam of academic and political actors, as a dialogue of knowledges between theoretical thought, participatory research and the social imaginaries of the people, in alliance with resistance movements and their political strategies for emancipation and reappropriation of their biocultural legacy.

Conclusion

This chapter presented a brief critical account of political ecology – a field of scholarship that is flourishing both in the Anglophone academy and the Global South, across disciplines within social sciences and the humanities. It began with a historical overview of the field, outlined some of its key characteristics, and moved on to discuss what political ecology looks like in the Global South, viewed from a decolonial, Indigenous perspective. A case study of flooding in the Indian state of Assam helped to explain the conceptual framing of the field with local details. The Assam case can also be viewed as a toolkit for how to conduct political ecological research, especially in a post-colonial context. Overall, the chapter provides the reader with a critical, historical, and global perspective on political ecology.

Given the planetary climate crisis facing us today, the salience of political ecology as an analytical lens to understanding nature–society relations cannot be overemphasized. We live in a world of deep, unprecedented social and environmental injustices, with corporate plunder of resources and commodification of nature in all its forms appearing to have become the world order. Now is the time to mainstream political ecology in environmental scholarship, for it is not enough to interpret the world – the point is to change it.

Notes

1. https://politicalecologynetwork.wordpress.com
2. https://ruralindiaonline.org
3. https://www.cseindia.org
4. https://kalpavriksh.org
5. https://vikalpsangam.org
6. https://viacampesina.org/en/

References

Baruah, M. 2022. *Slow Disaster: Political Ecology of Hazards and Everyday Life in the Brahmaputra Valley, Assam*. Routledge.

Blaikie, P. and Brookfield, H.C. 1987. *Land Degradation and Society*. Methuen.

Davis, M. 2001. *Late Victorian Holocausts: El Niño Famines and the Making of the Third World*. Verso Books.

Ghosh, A. 2021. *The Nutmeg's Curse: Parables for a Planet in Crisis.*, University of Chicago Press.

Guha, R. 2010 [1989]. *The Unquiet Woods: Ecological Change and Peasant Resistance in the Himalaya*. Twentieth Anniversary Edition. University of California Press.

Hall, S. 1997. 'Foucault: Power, Knowledge and Discourse', in M. Wetherell, S. Taylor and S.J. Yates (eds), *Discourse Theory and Practice: A Reader*. SAGE/The Open University, pp 72–81.

Hecht, S. and Cockburn, A. 1989. *The Fate of the Forest: Developers, Destroyers and Defenders of the Amazon*. Verso.

Leff, E. 2015. 'The power-full distribution of knowledge in political ecology: a view from the South' In Perreault, T.A., Bridge, G. and McCarthy, J. (eds), *The Routledge Handbook of Political Ecology*. Routledge, pp 64–75.

Robbins, P. 2004. *Political Ecology: A Critical Introduction*. Blackwell.

Smith, N. 2006. 'There's No Such Thing as a Natural Disaster', *Understanding Katrina: Perspectives from the Social Sciences* 11, https://items.ssrc.org/understanding-katrina/theres-no-such-thing-as-a-natural-disaster/

Swyngedouw, E. 1997. 'Neither Global nor Local: "Glocalization" and the Politics of Scale', in K.R. Cox (ed), *Spaces of Globalization: Reasserting the Power of the Local*. Guilford Press, pp 137–166.

Watts, M.J. 2013 [1983]. *Silent Violence: Food, Famine, and Peasantry in Northern Nigeria*. University of Georgia Press.

Zimmerer, K.S. and Bassett, T.J. (eds). 2003. *Political Ecology: An Integrative Approach to Geography and Environment-development Studies*. Guilford Press.

Video lecture

Baruah, M. 2023. *Political Ecology: Reflections from the Global South*, Connected Sociologies Curriculum Project. https://thesociologicalreview.org/projects/connected-sociologies/curriculum/environment-and-climate-change/political_ecology/

QUESTIONS

1. What should be the research agenda of political ecology in an age of neoliberal capitalism where a complex and ever-new set of processes, including genetic modifications, viruses, and artificial intelligence are constantly re-shaping human–environment relations? How should political ecology engage with these complex, multi-scalar issues?

2. What is at stake for political ecology in the recent call for decolonizing academia? Should political ecology be decolonized, too? If so, how?

3. How might political ecology as 'praxis' look like? What would it take for political ecology to be truly emancipatory while maintaining its theoretical rigour?

Worksheet 28. Political Ecology: Critical Reflections

This worksheet is designed to support AS and A-level teaching on the topics of social power, stratification and differentiation, globalization and global development, and sociological methods. In his chapter and online talk, Mitul Baruah introduces students to political ecology: an expanding and relatively new area of academic enquiry that can be traced back to the 1980s in the Anglophone world. Baruah gives students an overview of the key literature within the field, the central characteristics of this mode of enquiry, and some new directions in which the field is expanding. By providing a case study from Assam in north-east India, he highlights the key commitments of political ecological enquiry, and its growing importance in the Global South. The activities in this worksheet encourage students to think about the fundamental connections between humans' relations with nature, and our political, social, and economic structures of power. Students are invited to develop a critical understanding of the relationships between ecology and politics, and explore some of the methods and approaches employed by scholars in attempting to understand this relationship.

Time	Activity	Explanation
00.00–00.05	To warm up, answer the following question: *Can ecology be political?*	This warm-up activity is designed to get students thinking about the relationship between political and ecological issues, the central focus of the talk and chapter. The activity may work well as a group discussion.
00.05–00.10	Recap of understandings of globalization and global development	It may be useful to remind students of the key concepts related to globalization, particularly regarding the relationship between the environment and development.
00.10–00.15	Watch the talk from 0:56 to 2:10. *What is the problem with an eco-scarcity understanding of ecology?*	Baruah explains that, in an eco-scarcity understanding of ecology, the central message is that resource scarcity and population growth are fundamentally intertwined and dangerous. This discourse, he explains, is used to naturalize poverty in the Global South by blaming it on population growth. This section introduces students to different approaches to ecology, helping them to understand the theories underpinning the approaches, the political discourses they espouse, and the ways in which this chapter and talk challenge them. In doing so, students are encouraged to develop their critical thinking skills.

Time	Activity	Explanation
00.15–00.25	Watch the talk from 8:53 to 9:57. *What is a common critique of political ecology? How does Baruah refute this critique?*	Baruah states that critics of political ecology argue that it does not engage with ecological issues as much as it does with politics. Baruah points out that, as politics and ecology are fundamentally intertwined, it does not make sense to argue that one can be focused on without the other, and political ecology is committed to this idea. Building on the previous activity, these questions introduce students to one of the key critiques levelled at political ecology, and students are encouraged to weigh up this criticism alongside Baruah's defence of political ecology. This activity also allows students to build on the warm-up activity in developing their understanding of how politics and ecology are intertwined.
00.25–00.35	Watch the talk from 11:58 to 13:25. *What kinds of methods do political ecologists use in their work? What are some of the merits and challenges associated with these methods?*	Baruah explains that political ecologists share a methodological commitment to in-depth, direct observation. They favour qualitative research, and ethnographic methods are at the heart of a lot of political ecological work. This activity invites students to critically assess the methodological approaches of political ecologists. Assessing and comparing different sociological research methods is a key topic within the A-level Sociology curriculum.
00.35–00.45	Watch the talk from 14:20 to 14:58. *Why do we need to look beyond academia to understand the work of political ecologists? Why is it important to do this?*	As Baruah outlines, political ecologists share a political commitment to social justice and structural, political change. The emancipatory goal of political ecology is particularly important in the Global South, Baruah explains, where some of this work is expressed outside academia as knowledge claims, political practices, and radical political action by environmental groups. This activity pushes students to consider the limitations and boundaries of academic work. It encourages students to think about different forms of learning and knowledge that may challenge dominant academic ideas about how knowledge is produced and communicated.
00.45–00.50	Watch the talk from 19:22 to 20:44. *What does Baruah say was the central commitment of research into the hazardscape in Majuli?*	Baruah explains that the central commitment was to foreground the role of power. By underscoring the role of the state in the reproduction of the hazardscape, the research revealed it to be a social disaster and not a natural one. This question helps students to understand the significance of the case study Baruah includes in this talk, in that it illustrates the central role of power within global environmental disasters. Students are asked to draw on a key theme within the A-level Sociology curriculum in thinking about how social power and stratification play into global narratives of ecological change.

Time	Activity	Explanation
00.50–01.00	Drawing on what you have learned from this talk, answer the following question: *How might political ecology help us to better understand the relationship between nature and society?*	This concluding activity invites students to draw together what they have learned from this chapter and talk in illustrating the fundamental connection between politics and ecology. Students may take Baruah's cue in focusing on the case study of the Majuli hazardscape as an illustration of ecological disaster being socially produced. They may also draw connections to other topics in the book and associated talks. The activity may work well as a group discussion or pair work.

This worksheet was developed by Isabel Sykes.

29

Our Worlds of Palm Oil: A Tale of Colonialism, Consumerism, and Technology

Max Haiven

Objectives

- This chapter explores how people around the world have become dependent on palm oil for their everyday life, even if they don't know it.
- It explains how palm oil, which has been cultivated and used in West and Central Africa for millennia, was 'discovered' and exploited by European powers to (literally and metaphorically) grease the wheels of the industrial revolution.
- It draws on the history of 19th-century advertising for palm oil-derived products, notably soap and candles, to demonstrate how the European working class was conscripted into support for imperialism.
- It proposes that palm oil's story compels us to recognize that we are, today, a profoundly interconnected species with grave responsibilities for ecological, economic, and social justice.

The debate over palm oil

You and I are made of palm oil, at least in part. We eat it or products made from it every day. We use it to cleanse and care for our skin. It is in many of the products we use to clean our homes. It is fed to the animals on whose flesh or milk or eggs we rely for nutrition. It could be a part of the biofuels that power our vehicles or heat our homes. And the chemical derivatives of palm oil might be a component in the manufacturing of a wide range of the things that make up our lives, from paints and dyes to electronics to plastics (Robins 2021).

But unless you have lived in or visited a rural region in the tropics, it is unlikely you have ever seen *Elaeis guineensis*, the plant from which bunches of kernels are harvested to be processed into palm oil. And few even of the people who work on the massive, exploitative, and dangerous palm oil plantations have ever seen the factories that transform the fleshy orange fruits into the clarified, industrial-grade product that travels in barrels around the world to be used as cooking oil or transformed into soap or a million other products. This manufactured elixir is very different from the virgin palm oil that has been pressed from hand-harvested trees for millennia in *Elaeis guineensis*'s native West Africa and which is a core staple of the diet there to this day (Rodney 2018).

But perhaps you have heard of palm oil because, in recent years, it has become the target of a vociferous campaign by human rights and environmental non-governmental organizations (NGOs). This campaign that has been aggressively opposed by the powerful palm oil industry and its allies in the governments of palm oil-producing countries, especially Malaysia and Indonesia who, together, represent over 80 per cent of global exports (Dauvergne 2018).

NGO campaigns have tended to focus on the plight of 'charismatic megafauna', notably orangutans and tigers, whose habitat has been lost to deforestation driven by the conversion of tropical forests into monoculture palm oil plantations. The images and statistics are dramatic: between 2001 and 2017, Indonesia alone lost 24 million hectares of forest cover, almost equivalent to the entire area of the UK. Other NGOs have focused on the deplorable conditions of workers in the palm oil industry, many of whom are migrants who have been displaced from their ancestral homelands by other extractive projects or by colonialism.

Still others focus on how palm oil's artificial cheapness makes it a popular but profoundly unhealthy choice for poor people around the world (see Pye et al 2021). They rely on it as a staple cooking oil or ingest it in the form of inexpensive packaged and processed foods like instant noodles or fried snacks. NGO-led campaigns have been very successful in shifting laws, especially in the European Union, which has even sought to regulate palm oil imports (Pye 2019). These campaigns have also been successful in shifting consumer behaviours. These days, one can often see processed foods and cleaning products proudly boasting that they contain no palm oil, or only palm oil from 'sustainable' plantations (Dauvergne 2018).

The palm oil industry and its allies respond to criticism by noting that, in a world beset by climate change and a growing population, we need palm oil as never before. Though it takes several years to bear harvestable fruit, the mature *Elaeis guineensis* generates more edible oil per acre under cultivation and captures significantly more carbon than rival oil-giving plants like canola, soy, coconut, or sunflower (Robins 2021). The international Roundtable on Sustainable Palm Oil, an industry group made up of corporate and government representatives as well as some major environmental and human rights NGOs, has developed a set of voluntary guidelines on palm oil production (Pye 2019). But even so, only 20 per cent of companies exporting palm oil even claim to meet these guidelines, and only a tiny fraction of those is ever audited. 'Sustainability' in this case largely refers to the future growth of the for-profit industry, not to the conditions of workers or the planet.

What's missing from the debate

A few important things are lost in this debate. In the first place, the voices of those most affected by the industry itself: the workers on palm oil plantations; Indigenous people and peasants whose lands are seized or poisoned by the expansion of the industry; communities trying to find small-scale ways to grow and harvest *Elaeis guineensis* as part of a truly sustainable mix of agricultural activities (see Pye et al 2021). The complexity of the multiple and often contradictory interests in the palm oil industry can make the problem seem impossibly convoluted.

It's easy for us to imagine this problem is new, and that those of us far from the regions where oil palms are cultivated are not part of the story. And the second thing often lost in the debate is a longer view of the colonial history and legacy of palm oil. In this expanded history, people have consistently found themselves in a tangled global story of exploitation and profit, of ecological ruin and human ingenuity, a story that involves all of us (Rodney 2018; Li and Semedi 2021).

Ultimately, we can tell the story of palm oil in such a way that it reveals something profound about our human condition. We are a global species, one seemingly uniquely able to consider and change the world and ourselves. We have made a world held together by palm oil, in bodies made in part of palm oil (Gill and Taussig 2017). We have a power and potential to make a different world. How can we do so? And how can we come to recognize ourselves as a global 'we' and find new and different ways to collaborate to make a world, beyond all of us simply responding to 'the market'? Any chance we have will necessarily be based in understanding our shared history better, and the story of palm oil offers us a valuable approach to such a project (see Lowe 2015).

The origins of extraction

Elaeis guineensis has been cultivated by people in West and Central Africa for thousands of years and domestically produced products derived from its fruit and other parts have been, and continue to be, essential parts of rich, diverse, and innovative technological and cultural traditions (Robins 2021). Many of the empires and civilizations of that region made palm oil and palm wine such central parts of their world that they functioned as currencies. They were at the core of vast and complex systems of kinship, tribute, and trade. Palm oil was and is still a staple of the diet in that region. It remains an important cosmetic and medicine and is used in many religious and ceremonial rites. Families, ethnic groups, and nations throughout the region have a wide variety of ways to cultivate, harvest, process, store, prepare, use, and otherwise engage with red or virgin palm oil and palm kernel oil (both come from the same tree).

Today, the condemnation of palm oil by environmental and human rights NGOs headquartered in the Global North leaves a bitter taste in the mouths of many in Africa and elsewhere who know it as a profoundly life-giving and culturally rich product. This bitterness is deepened because such representations resonate with negative depictions of African civilizations. But in contrast to traditionally harvested and prepared palm oil, the commercial form of bleached, deodorized, standardized palm oil that circulates around the world today is the product of a history of colonialism and imperialism. This process not only uprooted and appropriated palm oil from its Indigenous context but also weaponized it against West African people. Palm oil was made into a tool of colonialism and empire (Rodney 2018).

Before the early 1800s, palm oil was extremely rare outside of West and Central Africa, and *Elaeis guineensis* itself was only transplanted to other continents a century later. It was with the gradual outlawing of the transatlantic slave trade in the early half of the 19th century that the global industry flourished. Liverpool trading companies, denied access to their profitable human cargo, went in search of new commodities (Robins 2021). At the time, Europeans and people in the Americas had little taste for palm oil. The customary culinary alternatives, animal fats, were then relatively cheap. But the dawning industrial revolution provided another global market for palm oil: it could be made into a lubricant that could maintain and cool the steam-powered machines that were becoming essential to European manufacturing, transportation, and war. By the 1850s, palm oil was quite literally greasing the wheels of empire: in the factories that churned out new commodities, and in the locomotives and steamships that brought those commodities to market.

As with the earlier trade in enslaved people, European merchants found it more profitable to anchor their ships off the West African coast near trading fortresses and obtain their cargo from local elites and traders in exchange for guns, shackles, trade commodities, and liquor (these, in turn, enabled the extractive process inland). But as the industrial revolution accelerated, the demand for lubricants increased. Many African empires and kingdoms had been ruled by a system of palm oil tributes for centuries, where families, servants, or enslaved people harvested fruit from local oil palm trees and sent the surplus to their rulers. In this context, oil palm trees were only one (very important) part of a mix of agricultural plants, and harvesting and processing its fruits was just one part of a spectrum of economic activities. But such artisanal systems could not keep up with export-oriented demand, and European traders became frustrated with the prices local merchants and intermediaries could impose. By the mid-1800s, Europeans began to take over African territory and establish monocultural plantations where *Elaeis guineensis* and workforces could be concentrated and exploited (Rodney 2018).

The uses of palm oil in the industrial revolution

The advent of European palm oil plantations in West Africa also came at a time when European powers began their extremely violent Scramble for Africa. This process was enabled by several imperial palm oil products. First, European industrialists had begun to use palm oil in the manufacturing of plated tin, including the cans that would be used to preserve foodstuffs. While eventually canned food would become a grocery staple, its first use was military: it allowed European troops to bring sustenance with them on colonial missions and thereby avoid relying on local suppliers that might be unreliable, or whose wares might be poisoned by imperial rivals or anti-colonial interests. As the 19th century advanced, canned food came to sustain the military and commercial agents of empire, but it also came to represent the empire to itself: the ability of middle-class consumers to purchase cheap(ened) canned tea from India and China, beef from Australia, salmon from Canada, and so on gave European consumers tangible access to the benefits of imperialism. These cans served as daily evidence of empire's technological progress (Naylor 2000).

Palm oil as an industrial lubricant was essential to the operation of the steamships and locomotives that could transport European troops inland into tropical regions to conquer and police new colonial territories, and to bring the extracted commodities (like palm oil) out from the hinterland to coastal entrepots. Palm oil as a lubricant was especially important in hot, tropical climates where alternatives like animal tallow could quickly become rancid and which was, in any case, becoming considerably more expensive (Robins 2021). The most certain military application of palm oil was the bonding of its extracted glycerin with nitrates to produce the highly explosive *nitroglycerine* which was later stabilized as dynamite. Not only did these explosives furnish European powers with devastating weapons of war, they also allowed railroad and mining engineers to blast through forest, rock, and many other obstructions to access new frontiers and return new resources to feed the industrial-imperial capitalist machine (Haiven 2022).

Technologies, commodities, and racism

'Innovation' has never been neutral. Palm oil importers in Liverpool, Bristol, and London eagerly hired and funded chemists to discover the substance's secrets and develop new industrial and military formulations and applications to drive market demand. Canned food, steam engines, and dynamite have all led to a remarkable transformation of the human experience and expanded humanity's powers immensely. But at whose cost? Who or what directed that process? And who benefited most?

Ultimately, the refinement of palm oil into so many products was led by the profit-driven needs of the market, not by genuine human or ecological concerns. The world we inherit today, with its many social and ecological problems, is the world built by imperial industrial capitalism (see Gilbert, Chapter 2, this volume). It is that system that still shapes what we call technological 'innovation', such that we see a new iPhone released every year, but at least 20 per cent of the world's children don't have access to safe drinking water and one in three children under five years old suffers from malnutrition.

Perhaps the greatest force that prevented any meaningful consideration of the broader human and ecological consequences of 'technology' and the palm oil question is racism. Throughout the history of capitalism, racism has been used to explain and justify why profound and deadly inequalities exist (see Baldwin, Chapter 30, this volume). Anti-African racism emerged from and helped to justify the horrors of the transatlantic slave trade, of which the palm oil trade was the direct descendant. Sometimes this racism was cruel and murderous, but other times it masqueraded as Christian benevolence. Many African kingdoms were destroyed in the name of 'liberating' their populations from supposedly (and occasionally actually) cruel and tyrannical rulers.

Racist benevolence was not merely the hobby of imperial elites – it was also marketed to working- and middle-class European citizens as their own duty. This was done, in part, through two key palm oil commodities: candles and soap. Before the industrial revolution, these products were largely manufactured from smelly and expensive animal fats and were out of reach of many poor European consumers. Palm oil offered a cheap source for both, and with that cheapness came profound cultural transformations.

Thanks to cheap candles, the night itself was transformed, including into a time for more work as poor pieceworkers (mostly women) could now toil late into the evening. Thanks to cheap(ened) commercial soap both working- and middle-class families could wash off the grime and soot of industrial cities. So, soap and candles became signatures of a new consumer subjecthood, first for the European middle classes, later the working classes. Enjoying a cheap candle's light into the night and using highly refined and scented soap became markers of social propriety and European 'civility' (Robins 2021).

Advertisements for soap and candles routinely depicted non-Europeans as dirty and benighted, locked into the predawn darkness 'before' civilization. By contrast, Europeans were represented as bearers of health, progress, and the en-*light*-enment. These tropes remain with us to this day and continue to animate racist fantasies, for example those that depict asylum seekers and other racialized migrants as threatening to introduce crime and public health menaces into European spaces, or that represent Africa and other areas of the Global South as morally, technologically, and economically dark, shadowy, and dangerous (see McClintock 1995; Haiven 2022).

Racism even more insidiously expresses itself in what can at first appear as benevolence. Prominent advertisements from the late 19th century, for example, suggested that buying palm oil candles could be a form of consumer activism. As part of imperial justifications at the time, it was widely reported in the press that slavery, whose trade had been abolished a generation or two ago in the British Empire, was still rampant within West and Central Africa, where local rulers, 'ignorant of Christian doctrine', were said to persist in this heinous practice.

Candles made from plantation-grown palm oil were advertised as a means to fight slavery because the plantations liberated African workers from bondage: on the plantation, they were wage-earners, not slaves (even if they were only paid a tiny fraction of the revenue the merchants gained). Even better, these were workers to whom the Christian faith could be evangelized. In the racist ideology of the day, forcing African workers to toil for a pittance on a prison-like plantation would teach maturity, thrift, hard work, and diligence to a people framed as childish, lazy, and unable to rule themselves. Such advertising used racism to conscript the European working classes into solidarity with empire and commerce, rather than with their fellow workers in Africa (Robins 2021).

This example might help us reflect on how we, too, in our own day, are so easily seduced by advertising and other messaging that encourages the erroneous belief that we can 'do our part' for the world and express our compassion for people 'less fortunate' than ourselves through our habits as capitalist consumers. Rather than imagine ourselves as, on some fundamental level, equals with palm oil plantation workers in South-east Asia, with whom we share a fate and a common struggle, we are instead easily beguiled by the messaging of industry and NGOs alike, which tells us we can be a 'part of the solution' simply by buying properly certified products. This framing inherently (if unconsciously) offers us a narrative where 'they', over there, dwell helplessly in a dark and unclean world of exploitation and degradation, whereas 'we', over here, are empowered and enlightened to make compassionate, clean consumer choices (Pye 2019). Who benefits from such a story?

Palm oil goes global

Demand for palm oil as well as for rubber (another African commodity) reached new heights in the late 19th century. This, combined with dramatic advances in transcontinental shipping and technology for the transplantation of oil palm plants, enabled Dutch, French, German and British traders to begin to establish *Elaeis guineensis* plantations in colonies in South-east Asia. By the 1920s, exports from colonies in South-east Asia (the regions that are now Indonesia and Malaysia) began to outpace those from West Africa. In this region, colonial wars and their aftermaths of genocide, dictatorship, and civil war provided palm oil capitalists with ample supplies of displaced people who could be exploited as an artificially cheapened labour force, and also vast areas of tropical forests that could be burned and converted into plantation land (Robins 2021).

Unfortunately, *Elaeis guineensis* grows particularly well in burnt landscapes, encouraging local landlords to incinerate forests, and palm oil exporters have been eager to buy from these suppliers of cheap(ened) oil (Patel and Moore 2017). By the second half of the 20th century the region was home to ever more acres of monocultures that would feed into a global export system. The process of formal decolonization and the establishment of the independent nations of Indonesia and Malaysia saw a local elite, working closely with these governments and foreign companies, expand their control of palm oil production. But European and American firms still, by and large, controlled the refining and export of palm oil to the world. Today they are still among the largest buyers of palm oil. This includes massive consumer product conglomerates like Nestle or Unilever. The latter of the two is the derivative of the Liverpool's Lever Brothers soap-maker, and still today one of the single largest buyers of palm oil, which is the basis of many of its food and cosmetics products that we use every day (Haiven 2022).

People always fight back. In West Africa, women of palm oil plantations led uprisings. In South-east Asia, struggles for national liberation forced decolonization on the British, Dutch, and other European empires. In the wake of formal independence, peasants and other poor people in Malaysia and Indonesia assembled around the dreams of communism or socialism, the desire to run their newly independent nations in the interests of the many rather than the profit of the few. Anti-communist regimes, backed by former colonial powers and the United States and their corporations, repressed these struggles brutally, with devastating consequences that haunt these nations to the present day.

During the era of the Cold War many movements for national liberation or communism adopted guerilla tactics, enfolding themselves in villages or jungles to avoid the direct attacks of a their much better armed foe. In this context, another even more infamous weaponized derivative of palm oil made its appearance: napalm. Originally developed in the United States during the Second World War, this jellied incendiary gasoline weapon was initially made with a derivative of palm oil, from whose name comes the weapon's portmanteau. Na*palm* would prove monstrously effective because it incinerated both the local people and landscapes that sheltered rebels and insurgents. The human and ecological consequences of the highly toxic napalm continue to leave lasting scars on the regions where it was deployed.

The fat of the world's poor

These scars are also economic. Napalm was a weapon of empire, used to slaughter people fighting for the right to determine their own economic futures in the wake of decolonization. Since 1989, no country on earth appears to be able to opt out of the global capitalist market and its pressures. In this context, even communist China turned, in the 1990s, towards capitalist principles. While 'economic development' since that time has transformed the lives of billions of people, it has also seen the world's largest ever migrations as displaced workers move from the Chinese countryside to coastal cities in search of livelihoods.

Around the world, the same disruptive capitalist forces that led to the concentration of *Elaeis guineensis* onto monocultural, export-oriented plantations have taken place in almost every other agricultural sector. This transformation has dramatically increased crop yields, but at great ecological and human costs. In contrast to older, traditional, and artisanal forms of agriculture, the high intensity export- and market-oriented plantation models, which typically benefit investors and landowners, tend to depend on burning and clearing, which drains the land of nutrients. They usually require imported fertilizers and demand the massive redirection of water systems for irrigation. They require complex mechanized farming implements, and attract insects and other pests that need to be controlled with chemicals. All of these factors tend to make agriculturalists dependent on external resources including specialized machines, fertilizers, and pesticides (and increasingly patented genetically modified seeds). These often require that agriculturalists gain access to debt, and are subject to expropriation when they cannot pay. This all means that, in order to be profitable, they must sell agricultural products to global markets, rather than feed local (poor) people. This tendency favours larger producers who can profit at scale, while small landholders and farmers go bankrupt. These technologies have also reduced the number of people needed to work the land to produce crop yields, and these workers by and large migrate to cities in search of work (Pye 2017).

This problem of what we might call *surplussed populations* should not be mistaken for the specious problem of 'overpopulation', which is a racist myth concocted and renewed over recent decades to insist that the Earth cannot support the growth of racialized poor populations. The Earth, in fact, has no definite, calculable capacity of humans – everything depends on *how* those humans live. Today, the ecological impact and resource consumption of a child born in the wealthiest of human communities of the Global North is equal to hundreds or thousands of times that of one born among the poorest. The problem is not the raw quantity of humans on planet Earth, but the way in which we humans live together on and with our planet.

Nonetheless, the problem of *surplussed populations* is very real: there are hundreds of millions of people who, denied access to land and the means to grow their own food, are *dependent* on global capitalism for the necessities of life. But for a growing number of these would-be workers, capitalism has no need of their labour and they are forced to rely on kinship networks, work in the informal economy, or carry out other forms of precarious economic activity to survive. They are thus condemned to scarcity (Hansen 2015). Here, palm oil once again appears, this time as the fat of the world's poor. Because of all the factors already listed, palm oil is artificially cheap. Its low price stems from the way the ecological and human costs are not fully accounted for: they are 'externalized' onto people and landscapes, who are made to pay the price. Corporations reap the rewards (see Patel and Moore 2017).

Ironically, this artificial cheapness puts palm oil within reach of many of the world's poorest people. This includes many palm oil plantation workers and many more who, like them, have often had their traditional or ancestral lands stolen or ravaged by poverty, war, pollution, or neglect. They find themselves, one by one or *en masse*, migrating to where they hope to find work. In India, for example, which has seen massive population movements in recent decades, many traditional cooking oils have been replaced in poor people's diets by palm oil imported from across the ocean, thousands of miles away, simply because it is incredibly cheap, but with terrible consequences. Not only are local oil producers driven out of business (with centuries of agricultural and manufacturing knowledge lost), easily accessible and cheap(ened) palm oil, with its very high proportion of saturated fat (relative to other plant oils) has contributed to a shocking spike in heart disease as people's diets gravitate towards what they can afford (Haiven 2022).

In China, prepackaged instant 'ramen'-style noodles (made of enriched wheat flour and palm oil) have fuelled the greatest migration in human history: since the 1990s, these noodles have become an emblem of the life of poor, migrant workers who have moved from the countryside to coastal cities to work in that country's factories, sleeping in dormitories and saving cash to send home to support their families or saving for a less precarious life. It is from those factories (where palm oil is eaten by workers and digested and converted into kinetic energy, and then transmuted into the production of things) that people around the world obtain most of the commodities we use every day. The computer on which I type these words, for example, is manufactured in factories where palm oil-powered workers sweat under intense and exploitative conditions to manufacture this modern-day 'necessity'. The world and we are made of palm oil.

Cooperating otherwise

What should we take away from all this? For those of us who have the privilege of studying in a university (and therefore might find themselves reading this book chapter), it is easy to imagine that palm oil's ills are someone else's problems. In the story we conventionally tell about palm oil, the human and environmental problems of the industry require of us, at best, more conscious, compassionate, and informed consumer choices. We feel some wealthy 'we' must do something for a poor 'them' somewhere far away. To some extent that's true. The consequences of palm oil's global story have many order of magnitude more impact on a displaced migrant worker on an Indonesian palm oil plantation than they do for me, a White, middle-aged, middle-class university professor who took a shower using palm oil-based soap this morning and (against the advice of his doctor) ate a delicious palm oil-heavy candy bar at lunch. And yet we are all part of the same system and the same story. Being thoughtful and sensitive to that story and its consequences is vital if we are to be a worthy part of rewriting it. To change the world, we will need to do more than just buy different products. We must change the way we, as a global, interwoven species, connected to a global web of life, cooperate and imagine ourselves and our world.

The reader is welcome to consult the hundreds of reports from environmental and human rights NGOs if they want to gain a fuller appreciation of the ecological and human impacts of palm oil plantations and the palm oil industry. My purpose here is not to convince you of their evils, though there are many. Rather, I hope this chapter has made it clear that engaging with the history of palm oil reveals something more complex about who we, as a global species, are. It is a story of racism, colonialism, and the devaluation of humans and non-humans alike. It is also a story of innovation, imagination, resistance, and becoming global, for good and for ill. The question is: who will we yet become, and how? How might we wrest our fate away from a global capitalist market that seems to be steering all our fates towards ruin? How will we become a 'we' that can make decisions for ourselves, collectively, as a species, that can benefit people and the earth of which we are a part?

References

Dauvergne, P. 2018. 'The Global Politics of the Business of "Sustainable" Palm Oil', *Global Environmental Politics* 18(2): 37.

Gill, S. and Taussig, M. 2017. *Becoming Palm*. Sternberg.

Haiven, M. 2022. *Palm Oil: The Grease of Empire*. Pluto.

Hansen, B.R. 2015. 'Surplus Population, Social Reproduction, and the Problem of Class Formation', *Viewpoint* 5. https://viewpointmag.com/2015/10/31/surplus-population-social-reproduction-and-the-problem-of-class-formation/

Li, T.M. and Semedi, P. 2021. *Plantation Life: Corporate Occupation in Indonesia's Oil Palm Zone*. Duke University Press.

Lowe, L. 2015. *The Intimacies of Four Continents*. Duke University Press.

McClintock, A. 1995. *Imperial Leather Race, Gender, and Sexuality in the Colonial Contest*. Routledge.

Naylor, S. 2000. 'Spacing the Can: Empire, Modernity, and the Globalization of Food', *Environment and Planning A: Economy and Space* 32(9): 1625–1639.

Patel, R. and Moore, J.W. 2017. *The History of the World in Seven Cheap Things*. University of California Press.

Pye, O. 2017. 'A Plantation Precariat: Fragmentation and Organizing Potential in the Palm Oil Global Production Network', *Development and Change* 48(5): 942–964.

Pye, O. 2019. 'Commodifying Sustainability: Development, Nature and Politics in the Palm Oil Industry', *World Development* 121: 218–228.

Pye, O., Fitri, A., Assalam, R., Haug, M., and Puder, J. 2021. *Just Transition in the Palm Oil Industry. A Preliminary Perspective*. Stiftung, Asienhaus, Sawit Watch, Transnational Palm Oil Labour Solidarity.

Robins, J.E. 2021. *Oil Palm: A Global History*. The University of North Carolina Press.

Rodney, W. 2018. *How Europe Underdeveloped Africa*. New Edition. Verso.

Video lecture

Haiven, M. 2022. *Palm Oil: The Grease of Empire*, Connected Sociologies Curriculum Project. https://thesociologicalreview.org/projects/connected-sociologies/curriculum/environment-and-climate-change/palm-oil/

QUESTIONS

1. How does the story of palm oil make us reconsider consumer activism and the idea that we can make the world better through our purchases?

2. How did racist advertisements for soap and candles work to conscript European working- and middle-class people into loyalty to Empire? Does this pattern persist in our present day?

3. Given that millions of people depend on the palm oil economy today, as both workers and consumers, how could we transition to a fairer, more just oil economy?

Worksheet 29. Our Worlds of Palm Oil: A Tale of Colonialism, Consumerism, and Technology

This worksheet is designed to support AS and A-level teaching on the topics of globalization and global development, focusing on the environment, social power and stratification, and global inequalities. This chapter and online talk introduce students to the global environmental, social, and economic consequences of the palm oil industry. Appearing in 50 per cent of supermarket products, Max Haiven explains how the conditions under which the fruits of the oil palm are cultivated, refined, and manufactured are defined by environmental violence and labour exploitation, particularly in South-east Asia and Latin America. Tracing the industry's historical roots in the transatlantic slave trade, Haiven reveals the centrality of palm oil within the history of colonial capitalism. Using a common commodity, students are invited to consider their own role as consumers and to investigate how more humane modes of trade may be developed. This topic may also be useful to students studying related subjects such as Geography and Economics.

Time	Activity	Explanation
00.00–00.05	To warm up, answer the following question: *How many products containing palm oil can you name?*	This warm-up activity encourages students to start thinking about how much palm oil features in their lives as consumers. Students may identify the use of palm oil in prepackaged foods, cleaning products, and cosmetics, for example.
00.05–00.10	Recap of understandings of globalization and global development.	It may be useful to remind students of the key concepts related to globalization, particularly the relationship between the environment and development.
00.10–00.20	Watch the talk from 7:48 to 9:48. *What does it mean to say that capitalism is built on the 'cheapening' of things?*	Haiven explains that capitalism 'cheapens' labour, care, nature, food, energy, lives, and money. Somebody or something is always paying the price for this 'cheapening' – from workers suffering inhumane working conditions, to destroying lands for plantations. This activity prompts students to think critically about the relationships between capitalist production, labour relations, and environmental crisis. Students may draw on other chapters and talks touching on how labour and resources were extracted to sustain the colonial global economy.
00.20–00.25	Watch the talk from 13:41 to 15:05. *What role did palm oil have to play in the industrial revolution?*	As the slave trade was gradually abolished during the early 19th century, palm oil was identified as a lucrative commodity to replace it. Palm oil was exported from exploitative West African plantations to grease the machines and railways of the industrial revolution. This activity encourages students to examine the role played by palm oil in making the modern world. In considering the exploitative labour relations involved in the industrial revolution, following slavery abolition, students may draw on broader discussions in the 'Making of the Modern World' section.

Time	Activity	Explanation
00.25–00.30	At 19:22 Haiven says that palm oil is often thought of as 'the fat of the world's poorest people'. *What social inequalities does the palm oil industry expose and exacerbate?*	While environmental campaigns implore people to make ethical choices, avoiding palm oil, the reality is that many consumers are too poor to make different choices, and are forced to depend on cheap palm oil products to survive. This question asks students to make connections between globalization, environmental harm, and global social inequalities, drawing on key themes within the A-level Sociology curriculum. In thinking about the unjust and unequal effects of environmental violence, students may connect to broader learning from the other chapters and talks in 'The Environment' section.
00.30–00.40	Watch the talk from 24:20 to 26:18. *What kind of sacrifices are made in the palm oil industry, and to what end?*	Haiven draws on Ruth Wilson Gilmore's argument that global capitalism is 'an era of human sacrifice'. In the palm oil industry, whole territories and groups of people have been sacrificed in the name of the 'beneficial' free market. Such sacrifices in the colonial global economy are often rendered invisible. This activity asks students to connect the themes of this chapter and talk with other topics that deal with the sacrifices and injustices of the colonial global economy. Students may draw on other chapters and talks such as on 'Global Supply Chains' to consider the exploited labour underpinning commodity capitalism, and how this is often made invisible.
00.40–00.50	Watch the talk from 27:58 to 30:50. *What challenges does the idea of a 'just transition' set for us?*	Haiven describes a 'just transition' as a shift that centres the perspectives and experiences of communities affected by palm oil production, rather than focusing on corporations and consumers. 'Just transition' requires us to think about our agency beyond being a consumer. 'Just transition' expresses the need for everyone to change, to develop new forms of global production and trade that are more ecologically sustainable and humane. This activity encourages students to critically assess campaign messaging by environmental groups focusing exclusively on consumer power. Thinking about our involvement in palm oil within the wider colonial global economy goes beyond purchasing choices. The question asks students to engage in the complex relationships between global inequalities, global trade, and the environment, answering to core themes within the A-level Sociology curriculum.
00.50–01.00	Drawing on what you have learned throughout this session, and from other topics, answer the following question: *What lessons can the palm oil industry teach us about the colonial global economy?*	This concluding activity prompts students to draw connections between this and other topics. The invisible 'human sacrifice' of commodity capitalism may be linked to the 'hidden histories' discussed in other chapters and talks. Students might consider how transforming the palm oil industry requires us to account for our own role within the colonial global economy, both as consumers and as responsible global citizens. This activity may work well as a group discussion.

This worksheet was developed by Isabel Sykes.

30

Remaking Race in the Crucible of Climate Change

Andrew Baldwin

Objectives

- To outline an important yet unconventional reading of the discourse on climate change and human migration.

- To demonstrate one of the ways race and racism are adapting to climate change.

- To show how the figure of the 'climate refugee' (sometimes called the 'climate migrant') is a racial category.

- To elaborate how this racial category plays a part in the adaptation of capitalism to climate change.

- To propose a new ethics of climate change, one that challenges how the political discourse on climate change and human migration is racialized.

Introduction

It is common nowadays to claim that the geophysical impacts of climate change are racialized. Consider a recent report by the Runnymede Trust, a London-based research institute, and the environmental organization, Greenpeace. It argues that 'Black people, Indigenous Peoples and people of colour across the globe bear the brunt of an environmental emergency that, for the most part, they did not create' (2022: 11). Claims like this are central to the political movement for 'climate justice'. They tell us that climate change is a form of racial injustice, and, in so doing, they situate race and racism at the heart of the planetary crisis. They make the point that systemic racisms have made the majority world particularly susceptible to the geophysical impacts of climate change and that this is largely the accumulated effect of British and European colonialisms. And, above all, they tell us that resolving the planetary crisis will be impossible without also resolving the legacies of empire, including racisms.

The idea that the effects of climate change are racialized is an important argument for anyone concerned with racial justice in the age of climate change and the Anthropocene. Yet, as important as this idea is, it contains a political risk that often goes unnoticed. By directing too much political attention towards the racialized impacts of climate change, those advocating for climate justice risk misunderstanding the protean quality of racism and, consequently, they risk overlooking how racism is being newly reworked within the political and scientific discourse on climate change, including that of climate justice. This chapter elaborates this risk and its implications. It argues that a form of racism unique to the planetary crisis is being articulated within the rapidly expanding policy discourse about migration and climate change. At the crux of this argument is the idea that the figure of the climate migrant and/or climate refugee is a powerful but often misrecognized signifier of racial difference. The chapter shows how this figure is invested with racial meaning, and how it can be understood to underpin the adaptation of racial capitalism to climate change.

The chapter proceeds as follows. The next section explains how the figure of the climate migrant/refugee is a bearer of racial meaning. The following section then explains how racial signifiers work in support of racial capitalism and also how the figure of the climate migrant/refugee, as a bearer of racial meaning, can be understood to do the same. The conclusion outlines a different kind of climate change ethics. Not one focused on rescuing or saving those who stand to be displaced by climate change, but an anti-racist ethics that challenges how poor and vulnerable populations of the Black and Brown majority world are being newly racialized as 'other' within the climate change imaginary.

Race and the figure of the climate migrant/refugee

When we read the headlines about climate change often what we encounter are stories about migration (see, for example, Lustgarten 2020; Khanna 2021). We are told, for example, that the geophysical impacts of climate change, such as flooding, sea-level rise, or extreme heat, are expected to force some of the world's poorest and most vulnerable people from their homes. Such stories leave us with the impression that those displaced by climate change will need to find shelter somewhere new or take refuge in a different country. Sometimes we are even told that when large numbers of so-called 'climate refugees' migrate from their homes and communities they will trigger 'climate wars' or large-scale humanitarian crises. Assumptions like these, that warn how climate change will force a new era of migration, are not unreasonable. After all, the science of climate change is clear: a warming planet threatens to render large areas of the world uninhabitable, leaving those who live in them no choice but to seek refuge elsewhere.

But even while this reasoning appears to make a lot of sense, there is good reason to be cautious about such seemingly self-evident truths (Baldwin and Bettini 2017). In fact, a substantial body of literature exists which challenges the climate justice orthodoxy that climate change will force people to relocate from their homes (see Farbotko and Lazrus 2012; Bettini 2013). As will be elaborated in more detail in what follows, central to this critique is the fallacy of causal reductionism. It is assumed that climate change will *cause* displacement or migration. But it is widely acknowledged in the field of migration studies and, paradoxically, even in the field of 'environmental migration' studies (see McLeman and Gemenne, 2018) that migration is irreducible to any one cause, including climate change.

Instead, migration is said to be 'multi-causal', which makes it impossible to talk meaningfully about something called 'climate migration', 'climate-induced migration' or 'climate migrants' and 'climate refugees'. What this means is that the political, scientific and legal discourse about 'climate change and human migration' is founded upon a fundamental paradox: climate change will adversely affect millions of people worldwide even while the fallacy of causal reductionism makes this almost impossible to prove. The result is that it becomes very difficult to sustain the notion that the displacement effects of climate change are a form of injustice. Surely, the geophysical impacts of climate change alone cannot account for such injustice. Inevitably, some other variable is also at stake.

In light of the foregoing paradox, how else might the relationship between climate change and human migration be understood? This section argues that the history of European colonialism is indispensable for understanding this relationship. This is both in the way colonial bureaucracies remade entire colonized landscapes through, for example, infrastructure projects like irrigation and transportation, but also in the way colonial difference would be represented within colonial and imperial discourse. Indeed, as many chapters in this volume attest, the practice by which Europeans sought to differentiate themselves from non-Europeans, such as the peoples of Africa, Asia, and the Americas, was an important aspect of the exercise European colonial power (see Kaladeen, Chapter 4, Murji, Chapter 17, and Narayan, Chapter 19, this volume).

For the Palestinian literary scholar, Edward W. Said (1994), Europeans often constructed racialized difference whether in art, literature, commerce, or military affairs, by depicting themselves as civilized, morally advanced, and peaceable, while defining non-Europeans as backwards, exotic, violent, or just simply different (see Fernandez, Chapter 23, this volume). Said argued that European imperialism was never simply imposed through violent military means but that it also involved claiming the right to define non-European peoples on terms set by Europeans themselves. Moreover, one of Said's core insights was that many of the same representational practices by which colonial difference was defined during the colonial period endure even in the period after colonialism.

Hence the field of post-colonial studies has been concerned with tracing the repetition of colonial power through such practices. Not surprisingly, then, what we find today is that many of the same racial tropes that Europeans used to represent non-Europeans during the colonial period are now being repeated in depictions of climate migration/forced displacement. Which in turn raises an important ethical issue concerning the discourse of climate mobility. Is climate change unjust simply because it stands to displace large numbers of people from their homes? Or is the real injustice to be found in the uneven relations of power by which such people are represented within the discursive context of climate change? In response to this dilemma this chapter argues for an anti-racist ethics and politics that acknowledges how the field of climate mobility studies is shaped by relations of power, most notably racism.

The most prominent racial trope organizing the discourse on climate mobility is that of naturalization. This is the well-documented notion that racial inequalities are often said to be a function of some underlying element of 'nature', whether biology or environment (Hall 2017). Thus, non-Europeans are routinely depicted in naturalist terms, which has also meant being pushed outside the order of history (McClintock 1995). Although different in important respects, the trope of naturalization resurfaces in discussions about climate change, where political economic phenomena, such as migration and war, are said be a function of nature, in this case, geophysical changes to the Earth system. According to this reasoning, the historical production of vulnerability is assigned secondary importance when explaining these phenomena. Bangladesh, which is often said to be 'ground zero' of climate change, offers a good example.

A recent report by the World Bank (Clement et al 2021) estimates, for example, that 13.3 million Bangladeshis will become 'internal climate migrants' by 2050. Without disputing the truth of this claim, the model used to arrive at this figure is limited in what it can do. Specifically, it de-emphasizes decades of aquaculture investment, which has adversely affected local coastal peasant communities, in explanations of internal migration, while at the same time it privileges geophysical phenomena like sea-level rise, drought, salinization, or cyclonic activity (Paprocki 2021). The result is that the history of capitalist investment is overlooked when explaining why people migrate in large numbers from coastal Bangladesh to Dhaka, Chittagong, or further afield. Instead, migration is wrongly attributed to climate change. This is not to say that the geophysical impacts of climate change do not matter. Just that they are not the only variables at play when peasants decide whether or not to migrate. Such accounts also risk producing misaligned policy, whereby policy makers may end up seeking to manage future migration rather than regulating or curtailing underlying drivers such as maladaptive investment or inequality.

A second trope is the denial of political subject-hood. This trope comes from the transatlantic slave trade, which involved robbing Africans of the 'right to have rights', to borrow a phrase made famous by the political philosopher Hannah Arendt (1967). In order to be bought and sold as commodities, Africans were imagined not to have any rights whatsoever, especially not to their own bodies let alone sovereignty or self-determination. During the era of the slave trade, European empires were sustained by suspending the political and legal subject-hood of enslaved Africans and Indigenous peoples (see Bhambra, Chapter 1, and Kaladeen, Chapter 4, this volume).

Paradoxically, we find a similar racial trope at play in the discourse on climate refugees. We might use the term 'climate refugee' as a well-intentioned shorthand to describe someone victimized by climate change. Yet, it is well documented that there is no legal basis to the concept of 'climate refugees'. This is a category for which there is no commensurate set of rights. Thus, to invoke this category to describe those who stand to be displaced by climate change is to repeat the trope of the denial of political subject-hood. It is to place those deemed as climate refugees into a legal non-space, in effect suspending whatever rights a person may already have. To make this point is not to attribute malign intentions to those who invoke the 'climate refugee' category. It is simply to acknowledge how suspending the political rights of those deemed different is a long-standing political practice associated with European colonialism.

A final trope concerns notions of excess and ambiguity. It is widely acknowledged that it is impossible to define the categories 'climate migrant' or 'climate refugee' in any definitive or comprehensive way. As in the case of Bangladesh, for example, how can we say that *climate change* is the reason people are migrating if we also know that migration in the region is driven as much by historical forces, such as investments in destructive land-use practices? How can we disaggregate the forces of climate change from the forces of history? The truth is we are unable to, which raises profound questions about the explanatory value of climate change, leading some to caution against the ideology of 'climate reductionism' (Hulme 2023). This also makes it impossible to define someone as a *climate* migrant or *climate* refugee, if climate is not the sole factor explaining migration. The result is that these categories are defined, paradoxically, by their lack of definition. And so they are, in this sense, excessive categories; they exceed our ability to define them and as such they are by definition 'other'.

A great deal more can be said about each of these tropes and the foregoing analysis. What it points to, however, is that the figure of the climate migrant/refugee cannot be taken for granted. If anything, there is good reason to challenge the widespread use of these terms and to ask instead, why, in spite of their problematic nature, they continue to occupy such a privileged location in the climate change imaginary. Or we might simply ask: for whom is the category of the 'climate migrant/refugee' important? One answer to that question is that the figure of the climate migrant/refugee plays an important part in masking the adaptation of racial capitalism to climate change.

Racial capitalism and the management of surplus populations in a warming world

Racial capitalism is the subject of considerable discussion within the social sciences. It refers broadly to the idea that capitalism cannot exist without racism. This means that as the production of value under capitalism adapts to changing historical circumstances, so too racism must also adapt as part of the same historical process (see Thompson, Chapter 24, this volume). A good illustration of this can be found amid the transformations that racial capitalism underwent in the mid-20th century, as geopolitical might shifted from Europe to America.

Through much of the 19th and early 20th centuries race was largely said to be biologically and/or genetically based. However, by the mid-century, after the horrors of the Nazi Holocaust, race would be explained culturally. Under the former regime, race was imagined as a biological fact, but under what would later become known as the 'new racism', race was said to be a cultural fact. This transformation in the logic of race coincided with broad mid-century shifts in the organization of political economy, most notably the advent of the welfare state in North America and Britain, but also the advent of Fordist production, large-scale post-war suburbanization and the decolonization of former European colonies. The new racism was adopted as a means of managing labour relations, especially non-European migrant labour in America and Europe, under these new conditions of production (see Anitha, Chapter 8, this volume).

Arun Kundnani (2021) documents a more recent shift in the history of racial capitalism. He shows how the advent of neoliberal capitalism in the 1970s and 1980s also entailed a fundamental reworking of race and racism. Central to his thesis is that this reworking of racism arose in response to a fundamental political anxiety synonymous with neoliberal rationality. The promise of neoliberalism lay in universalizing the market economy, but it would also fail to deliver on its promise, generating instead a mass of global surplus labour that was of little or no value for capital. This surplus labour would then be viewed as a political threat to the political authority of neoliberalism, symbolic of neoliberalism's failure to achieve its ambition.

For Kundnani, racialized language would be used to define surplus populations as a means for managing this fundamental contradiction. In his words, it would provide 'a means of coding and managing the material boundaries between different forms of labour under neoliberalism: citizen and migrant, waged and "unexploitable", bearers of entitlements and bare life' (Kundnani 2021: 53). So, for example, the neoliberal state would use racist terms like '"welfare queens", "Muslim extremists", "illegals", "narcos", "super-predators", and so on' (Kundnani 2021: 65) to characterize surplus populations. While these figures were not racial per se, they became so as they were made to represent threats to the economic orthodoxy of neoliberalism, which the neoliberal state would then police, often through quite violent means (see Thompson, Chapter 24, this volume).

This divisive strategy allowed the neoliberal state to ward off the possibility of cross-race worker solidarity, pitting low-paid White workers, who had experienced decades of wage declines, against workers of colour and migrant workers who would be blamed for stagnating wages. Indeed, as Kundnani puts it, '[b]ehind the images of the Black woman on welfare, the radical Muslim and the violent immigrant lie fears of actual Black radicalism, of the actual Palestinian national movement, and of the actual politicization of working classes induced by migrant workers' (2021: 65). No wonder these terms would acquire such symbolic significance. They were necessary for resolving neoliberalism's most fundamental contradiction: its failure to universalize wage labour.

But what does the racialization of surplus labour have to do with climate change and migration? Climate change is not simply a planetary crisis. Through investments in energy-efficient technology, re-valuing forest carbon and carbon sequestration and transitioning away from an over-reliance on fossil fuels towards more renewable energy, climate change also signifies a wholesale transformation in the organization of capitalist political economy. In this context, and given what we know about racial capitalism, it is entirely reasonable to expect that the green energy transition will also entail the reworking of race and racism.

Enter the figure of the climate migrant/refugee, which, we have already seen, is a bearer of racial meaning. We can start to imagine how it plays a role similar to that of the 'welfare queen', 'terrorist', and 'Muslim extremist': resolving a fundamental contradiction inherent in the process by which racial capitalism adapts to climate change. Much as neoliberalism's racist figures would be used to manage actual threats to neoliberal authority, the figure of the climate migrant/refugee is a racial figure used to manage the political gap between the global proletariat and the global surplus population in the context of a rapidly warming world.

As in the neoliberal context, surplus populations in the context of climate change are viewed as inherently threatening, inasmuch as they represent a fundamental alternative to capitalist hegemony. Thus, the figure of the climate migrant/refugee is used to codify this threat in terms of geopolitical instability or humanitarian crisis such that it might be actively policed by militaries or development agencies; meanwhile, capitalism and technology are imagined to be morally good and the rightful saviours against climate crisis. But, to paraphrase Kundnani, behind this imagined threat lie fears that global surplus populations may stage actual challenges to the hegemony of global capital. Lives made disposable by the forces of history and climate change may seek to transform the very political economies that have brought the planet to the brink of ruin.

A whole suite of political technologies has emerged in recent years for policing the so-called climate migrant/refugee. Certainly, militaries and humanitarian agencies are imagined to play a part. But so has migration itself. The progressive argument is that migration is a basic human attribute, central to what it means to be a human being. Migration should therefore be a legitimate means for adapting to climate change rather than being treated as a failure to adapt, which is assumed when the figure is said to be a security threat or humanitarian crisis. It is now common, for example, for international institutions like the World Bank, International Organization for Migration, and Intergovernmental Panel on Climate Change to advance the idea that workers living in places threatened by climate change should be encouraged to use circular and temporary migration to adapt to climate change. Examples of which might include South Asian migrant labour (recall that poor Bangladeshis are often codified as 'climate migrants/refugees') providing the labour needed in cities like Dubai and Qatar.

Computational modelling is also now being used to anticipate future migration under climate change, which may be useful for incentivizing workers to migrate to places requiring labour. Such future modelling could be used to facilitate the resettlement of workers in a way that meets the market demand for labour in a warming world. More broadly, both of these governing strategies can be understood as counter-transformational. If surplus populations in the context of climate change are imagined to threaten unwanted transformations, state-led strategies that encourage adaptive migration can be construed as counter-transformational, on a political continuum with counter-revolutionary or counterterrorism strategy. Which is to say they seek to reverse the problem before it materializes. For some people, this may be desirable. For others, though, such strategies would be viewed as another episode in a longer history of state intervention that undermines the principle of autonomy or self-determination.

All of that said, it remains unclear how precisely labour migration will be managed in the context of a rapidly changing global climate. Global labour policy has yet to really catch up with the problem. So what I want to emphasize, instead, is that at least for the time being the figure of the climate migrant/refugee can be understood as yet another figuration of 'race' that codifies the gap between the global proletariat which would include waged workers of all kinds – education and healthcare workers, unionized workers, waged managers, industrial workers, and so on – and the global surplus population that coincides with the Black and Brown majority world (see Narayan, Chapter 19, this volume). In this way, the figure of the climate refugee works to resolve a fundamental contradiction at the heart of the climate change imaginary.

Capitalist modernity in general, and its post-war liberal democratic manifestation in particular, have utterly failed in their promise to improve the living conditions of the world's poorest. Meanwhile, processes of extraction, exploitation, and dispossession have merely intensified in the three decades since United Nations Framework Convention on Climate Change came into force. And it is this fundamental contradiction that the racial figure of the climate migrant/refugee works to resolve. If climate change signifies the need for a wholesale transformation in the way capitalist modernity is structured, then by scrutinizing the figure of the climate migrant/refugee as a racial concept we can start to appreciate how labouring surplus populations will not be fully incorporated into the emerging green global economy (see Kaur-Spannos, Chapter 27, this volume). And in this sense, we start to grasp how the figure is used to govern the material boundaries in the global division of labour.

Conclusion

So where does this leave us? For some readers, the foregoing argument will feel very counterintuitive, especially for those who, quite rightly, view climate change as a significant global injustice foisted upon those who have contributed very little, if anything, to the problem. For those wishing to give assistance to those who stand to be displaced by climate change the foregoing argument may even appear to undermine those efforts. These are legitimate concerns which I also share. Indeed, the tension between a genuine concern for those who will experience the worst effects of climate change and the representational politics I have sketched in this chapter has been a source of discomfort for me over many years. Still, I think it is important that students, scholars, and activists remain mindful that race and racism are not static phenomena but ever-evolving logics that have always been used to manage boundaries in the division of labour.

Yes, the impacts of climate change are racialized. But this is not the end of the story on climate change, race, and racism. The theory of racial capitalism tells us that racism is continuously adapting as capitalism's labour needs shift and change depending on how value is produced. We can certainly expect that this will continue to be the case in the coming decades as capitalism adapts to a rapidly changing global climate. The point I want emphasize in this chapter is that when those advocating something called 'climate justice' focus too much political attention on the racialized effects of climate change, they risk inadvertently overlooking the fluidity of race and racism. And, consequently, they risk overlooking how race and racism are being re-articulated within the political and scientific discourse on climate change and human migration.

Perhaps, then, what is needed alongside an ethics and politics of climate justice that recognizes the racialized impacts of climate change is a new anti-racist ethics that challenges the relations of power at stake in constructions of 'climate mobility' discourse. Such an anti-racist ethics is one that would recognize the relentless adaptability of racial capitalism, especially in the context of a rapidly changing global climate. This is an ethics less concerned with saving or rescuing the other of climate change than one concerned with holding powerful institutions accountable. Such an ethics questions the discourse on climate migration on the basis that it is racialized and can be used to manage the global division of labour for capitalism.

References
Arendt, H. 1967. *On the Origins of Totalitarianism*. George Allen and Unwin.
Baldwin, A. and Bettini, G. 2017. *Life Adrift: Climate Change, Migration, Critique*. Rowman & Littlefield.
Bettini, G. 2013. 'Climate Barbarians at the Gate? A Critique of Apocalyptic Narratives on "Climate Refugees"', *Geoforum* 45: 63–72.
Clement, V., et al. 2021. *Groundswell Part 2: Acting on Internal Climate Migration*. The World Bank.
Farbotko, C. and Lazrus, H. 2012. 'The First Climate Refugees? Contesting Global Narratives of Climate Change in Tuvalu', *Global Environmental Change* 22(2): 382–390.
Hall, S. 2017. 'Race: The Sliding Signifier', in K. Mercer (ed), *The Fateful Triangle: Race, Ethnicity, Nation*. Harvard University Press.
Hulme, M. 2023. *Climate Change Isn't Everything*. Polity Press.
Khanna, P. 2021. 'Migration Will Soon be the Biggest Climate Challenge of Our Time', *Financial Times*, 3 October. https://www.ft.com/content/415f4a8c-cab4-4f95–99aa-b347bb510365
Kundnani, A. 2021. 'The Racial Constitution of Neoliberalism', *Race & Class* 63(1): 51–69. https://doi.org/10.1177/0306396821992706
Lustgarten, A. 2020. 'The Great Climate Migration Has Begun', *New York Times Magazine*. https://www.nytimes.com/interactive/2020/07/23/magazine/climate-migration.html
McClintock, A. 1995. *Imperial Leather: Race, Gender and Sexuality in the Colonial Contest*. Routledge.
McLeman, R. and Gemenne, F. 2018. 'Environmental Migration Reseasrch: Evolution and Current State of the Science', in R. McLeman and F. Gemenne (eds), *Routlege Handbook of Environmental Migration and Displacement*. Routledge.
Paprocki, K. 2021. *Threatening Dystopias: The Global Politics of Climate Change Adaptation in Bangladesh*. Cornell University Press.
Runnymede Trust and Greenpeace. 2022. *Confronting Injustice: Racism and the Environmental Emergency*. Runnymede Trust and Greenpeace, pp 1–78.
Said, E. 1994. *Culture and Imperialism*. Vintage Books.

Video lecture
Baldwin, A. 2022. *Climate Change, Migration, Race*, Connected Sociologies Curriculum Project. https://thesociologicalreview.org/projects/connected-sociologies/curriculum/environment-and-climate-change/climate-migration-race/

QUESTIONS

1. Climate change is expected to result in more migration. What kinds of actors and institutions, for example, universities or media, make this claim? Why do you think they make it? In whose interest is this claim being made?

2. What are the various ways 'race' and climate change are related? This chapter provides one perspective. What are some others? How do they differ? What do they have in common?

3. How are the legacies of European imperialism and colonialism implicated in (a) climate change and (b) the discourse on climate change and human migration?

4. How would you describe the voice of the 'climate migrant' or 'climate refugee'? What do they say about their lives? What do they leave out? How is the voice of the 'climate migrant' or 'climate refugee' socially constructed?

Worksheet 30. Remaking Race in the Crucible of Climate Change

This worksheet is designed to support AS and A-level teaching on social differentiation, power and stratification, and globalization and global development. This chapter and talk focus on the relationship between globalization and the environment. Andrew Baldwin challenges widespread assumptions about how climate change relates to problems of migration. Building on the theoretical arguments of Edward Said and Dipesh Chakrabarty, he argues that the international political discourse around climate change and migration is a form of racial rule, with the figure of the 'climate migrant' used to indicate racial difference. The activities in this worksheet encourage students to draw on their knowledge from across the other topics in this section and other chapters on migration, borders, and diaspora. Bringing together themes of migration, racial 'othering', and environmental decline, this session provides students with tools to think critically about media portrayals of 'climate migrants' and the climate emergency.

Time	Activity	Explanation
00.00–00.05	To warm up, answer the following question: What do you think the term 'climate migrant' means?	This warm-up activity introduces students to one of the key terms within the chapter and talk, encouraging them to think about where they might have heard or seen it before. Students may be able to think of examples from media headlines. The activity may work well as group work.
00.05–00.10	Recap of understandings of globalization and global development.	It may be useful to remind students of key concepts related to globalization, particularly regarding the relationship between the environment and development.
00.10–00.20	Watch the talk from 1:15 to 2:34. How is the relationship between climate change and migration typically portrayed in the media? Can you find any examples of headlines that do this?	Recent news media headlines show how climate change is presented in international political discourse as a problem of migration. Migration is portrayed as being caused by environmental events such as rising sea levels, extreme weather events, and droughts, which displace people from their homes. This activity gets students thinking critically about subtler messages within media portrayals of climate change and migration. By finding examples on their own and looking for these messages, students are encouraged to practice analysing sources independently.
00.20–00.30	Watch the talk from 5:50 to 8:10. What is the relationship between climate change and humanism, according to Dipesh Chakrabarty? How does Baldwin draw on this argument in the talk?	Referring to Chakrabarty, Baldwin explains how the 'human' is destabilized by climate change, and can no longer be understood as separate from nature. Given this destabilization of the 'human', the international discourse around climate change and migration tries to re-stabilize this figure or category, constructing 'others' in the process. This activity familiarizes students with central theories and arguments about racialization. Students are encouraged to think critically about the category of 'human', including how it is constructed, who is included, and who is excluded from its boundaries.

Time	Activity	Explanation
00.30– 00.40	Watch the talk from 10:43 to 13:38. *How does the naturalization of migration also de-historicize it?*	Baldwin explains that, when the figure of the climate migrant is understood exclusively in terms of climate change, this erases the historical conditions that made these people vulnerable to climate change in the first place. In the example of coastal Bangladesh, decades of Western intervention, including the expansion of the shrimp farming industry, have transformed the coastal landscape, causing its inhabitants to be dispossessed of their land and rendering them economically vulnerable. This activity encourages students to think about how the concept of the 'climate migrant' is built on historical 'silences' about colonization, displacement, and dispossession. Students may draw connections between this talk and other topics in the book considering the colonial contexts that underpin the climate crisis.
00.40– 00.45	Watch the talk from 14:05 to 16:30. *How does the status of 'climate migrant' or 'climate refugee' change a person's citizenship?*	Baldwin explains that the category of 'climate migrant' signifies a loss of political status, positioning people outside the boundaries of the law. He connects this to the long history of stripping 'othered' people of their legal status, for example within the context of colonialism. This activity asks students to delve further into the connections between climate change and colonialism. Students may draw on their learning from other chapters and talks in considering how notions of citizenship and political legitimacy are constructed.
00.45– 00.50	Watch the talk from 22:04 to 23:03. *What does the term 'racial futurism' mean?*	'Racial futurism' imagines the 'other' as a potential future problem that must be governed and intervened upon, in order to mitigate future consequences. The technology used to govern the 'other' is adaptation: teaching individuals how to adapt to climate change so that they do not become a problem for the Global North or 'West'. This activity introduces students to a useful key term for understanding the relationship between climate change and migration. Students are invited to consider how political discourses of migration represent these notions of governance and adaptation, and they may reflect on how the media examples discussed at the beginning of this talk illustrate these points.
00.50– 01.00	Drawing on what you have learned from this talk, answer the following questions: *What purposes do the terms 'climate migrant' and 'climate refugee' serve? For whom are they useful?*	This concluding activity is designed to ensure that students have a strong understanding of the main arguments discussed in this talk, and that they are able to put these into their own words. Students are encouraged to recall the three tropes of the 'climate migrant' outlined (naturalism, loss of political status, and recognition) and discuss how they construct migrants as signifiers of racial difference. Students are invited to follow Baldwin's assessment of these tropes in recognizing that they are used to shore up a particular, Western, notion of 'the human'. The activity may work well as a group discussion.

This worksheet was developed by Isabel Sykes.

Conclusion: Remaking the Social Sciences After Colonialism

*Paul Robert Gilbert, Gurminder K. Bhambra, Ipek Demir,
Su-ming Khoo, and Lucy Mayblin*

Objectives

- To consider arguments that have been made to 'open up' the social sciences.
- To consider the social sciences in the context of the arguments presented in the chapters that make up this book.

Introduction

The chapters in this volume provide detailed analyses of issues that are of central concern to contemporary sociology and the social sciences more broadly. The five parts of the book have addressed a variety of questions about the origins of modernity; class, inequality and labour movements; immigration, asylum, and human rights; racism, citizenship, and multiculturalism; and climate change and ecological injustice. The distinctive contribution of this book is to explore these issues from a perspective that foregrounds how British and other Western societies were shaped by colonial relations and connections, even as standard social scientific concepts and approaches have rendered those colonial connections invisible.

We cannot understand the modern world without recognizing that colonial trades in enslaved and indentured people, wealth extraction, and the establishment of plantation economies shaped modern patterns of labour, citizenship, and ecological relations. Equally, however, we cannot grasp the patterns of urban development and 'gentrification' that led to the Grenfell Tower disaster, for example, without situating local histories of racism, migration, and policing within Britain's colonial management of its borders, policing, and citizenship eligibility. Similarly, analyses of modern slavery will never be sufficient if they focus only on 'bad actors' and criminals, rather than systemic patterns of labour exploitation that are enabled by structures of the global economy that were established in the historical processes of European colonialism.

As noted in the Introduction to this book, early sociologists were preoccupied with understanding the emergence of the modern world from the vantage point of

19th-century Europe, where the social sciences were first institutionalized as formal disciplines. In a context in which the European world appeared to itself as 'culturally triumphant', it was perhaps inevitable that the social sciences were established with a Eurocentric approach to their object of study (Wallerstein et al 1996: 51). The Nigerian political scientist Claude Ake (1982) described classical social science as both *parochial* (that is, rooted in a limited, local worldview) and *teleological* (or shaped by an idea of linear progress). In other words, the classical social sciences framed contemporary Europe as the ideal, advanced society against which others should be measured. Such an approach by necessity builds its concepts and frameworks on a denial or erasure of the colonial connections through which Europe – and its former colonies – were made.

Recognizing the parochialism of the social sciences has been the starting point for previous efforts to 'open up' or remake sociology and its neighbouring disciplines of anthropology, politics, history, and economics (Wallerstein et al 1996; Burawoy 2005). For example, the Gulbenkian Commission on the Restructuring of the Social Sciences, chaired by Immanuel Wallerstein, recognized the limitations of disciplines with a European heritage, that claimed to have universal lessons, even while their frameworks and concepts excluded significant aspects of global social and political structures. The Commission recognized the need for 'decolonization', which would involve examining the theoretical premises of social science disciplines which were shaped by their emergence in 19th-century Europe. Michael Burawoy (2005), for his part, has called for 'provincializing' sociology and the other social sciences by making explicit the participation of these disciplines in the worlds they claim to describe and understand and the limited perspective from which they derived; for him, this involved understanding that the so-called 'centre' was no less provincial than the places it presented as 'peripheral'.

A great deal of discussion about opening up, remaking, provincializing, or decolonizing the social sciences has operated at a fairly high level of abstraction. What this volume has sought to do is to work towards remaking the social sciences by providing chapters that address specific issues of sociological concern: whether that involves understanding the lives of British elite migrants ('non-doms' and 'expats'), or the weaponization of the Prevent programme, Islamophobia, and right-wing think tanks against Muslim teachers in the Trojan Horse affair. In each of the chapters, the authors show that social life in contemporary Britain, and more widely, cannot be adequately understood by analytical categories or frameworks that fail to respond to the colonial connections through which the modern world and understandings of the modern world were forged.

The collection focuses predominantly on contemporary Britain and the colonial connections through which it emerged. This is deliberate, precisely because it is impossible to make sense of modernity without taking colonialism seriously, whether that be in former colonies or the former colonial metropole. As much as the application of parochial, teleological Eurocentric theories to the study of the Global South has been critiqued as a misguided, imperialistic endeavour (Ake 1982), it would be entirely inadequate to study European modernity itself using frameworks and concepts that deny the role of colonial connections in shaping that modernity. The chapters can be read separately, but together they establish a comprehensive and substantive exemplification of what it means to take colonialism and its legacies seriously.

The making of the modern world

The chapters in Part I broadened our understanding of the historical processes that contribute to the making of the modern world. From a simple account of economic and political transformation associated primarily with events within Britain and France, this section provided a richer account of globally located processes. It addressed the political contribution of the Haitian Revolution in its own terms as well as thinking through its implications for how we should understand citizenship in the present. It provided a globally oriented consideration of the economy that takes colonial histories seriously in examining its contemporary contours and ongoing implications in the configuration of global inequalities. The section also made central the processes of resource extraction and colonial dispossession without which what are presented as the advances of the modern world would not have been possible.

Alongside a consideration of histories of slavery, this section examined the historical processes of indenture which contributed so significantly to the development of unequal labour regimes globally. This was accompanied by a consideration of the ways in which land and territory were enclosed and privatized as part of a process of dispossession which happened both domestically within the West as well as more widely across the colonized world. The similarity of the processes outlined here points to the need, always, to consider what happens 'here' in relation to what happened 'there'. This was a common point across many of the chapters in this book. Part I ended with a consideration of decolonization – a process that often is seen as bringing to an end the period of colonization. However, here questions were asked about the longevity of colonialism and the extent to which decolonization completed that earlier process or is perhaps better understood as another stage within which it still requires further work.

The chapters in Part I, together, drew attention to the range of global processes that contributed to the making of the modern world, and which are rarely addressed within standard accounts of modernity. They set out the various forms of domination central to the modern world, their accompanying and ongoing inequalities, and the ways in which these were contested and resisted, historically and into the present. While decolonization was primarily a social, political, and economic process oriented to the dismantling of the structures of European colonial role, it has also, in recent years, been associated with the challenge posed to the forms of knowledge production linked to European colonialism. This book provides resources with which to think about the ways in which colonial histories have shaped our world and structured the ways in which we know it. Starting from a perspective that acknowledges global colonial processes as significant provides us with richer understandings of the contemporary complexities of the world as the following parts also go on to highlight.

The politics of inequality

The chapters in Part II all provided a challenge to frameworks for understanding inequality which take individual nation states as the 'container' for their analyses. It is common in sociology (as in economics, and other social sciences), to take the nation as the unit of analysis, and to think about class relations, say, as playing out within a given national context. But the chapters in this section showed that whether you are attempting to understand modern slavery, labour unions, or the super-rich, class relations and patterns of inequality are forged in and through colonial connections. This is true for how the complexities of class inequality have developed within Britain, with workers' bargaining power shaped by European settlement in the colonies. It is likewise necessary to situate our understanding of deep and persistent food poverty within the contemporary UK in light of the features of a colonial global economy. To say that inequality in Britain is shaped by historical and present forms of unequal resource extraction is not to deny that local inequalities exist; it instead highlights the alarming fact that poverty in contemporary Britain would be far deeper and more widespread without the global inequalities that shape food consumption in the UK.

The first section of this book examined in detail the processes of dispossession, forced labour, indenture, and transportation that were integral to the making of the modern world through European colonial administration. One of the consequences of these patterns of dispossession is a 'surplus' labour force that often lacks the power to collectively bargain for better wages and conditions. This underpins the production of cheap food that is imported, purchased, and distributed through 'emergency' food banks in Britain. But contributors to this section also highlighted how this colonial inheritance shapes the vulnerability of people to incorporation into modern forms of slavery. A lesson of Part II – as in chapters across the book – is that a failure to understand the colonial contribution to these kinds of vulnerabilities will always lead to misguided policy recommendations that focus on 'bad actors' and narrow histories, rather than the deep structural drivers of inequality that arise from colonial histories.

Contributions to Parts III and IV addressed the colonial connections that underpin the contemporary politics of citizenship and belonging in Britain. But these are of course connected to the politics of inequality. The chapters in Part II, therefore, also highlight that many issues of central concern to sociologists – from trade union disputes to struggles against gentrification – cannot be fully understood without reference to histories of migration from British colonies, and the struggles around citizenship and belonging that emerged in the face of racist responses to the mobility of colonial subjects and their descendants. The authors in this section reminded us that there is an obligation to depart from methodologically nationalist studies of inequality and re-tell stories of class (struggle) in a way that takes colonialism seriously.

Migration diaspora and asylum

Part III draws our attention to how colonialism has shaped who can move where, and on what terms. This is, in part, through the emergence of key tangible regimes like those of citizenship and the asylum system, and in part through tacit understandings of, for example, who *belongs* where, and what a *real* family looks like. Ideas of race and racial hierarchy were a strong recurring theme across the section. These ideas emerged as a way of legitimizing colonialism and later governing colonized peoples. The idea of White supremacy and Black and Brown inferiority was fundamental to colonialism and was globalized over 500 years. We should not be surprised to find, then, that racism influenced the development of citizenship and immigration policies in Britain. In fact, immigration policy emerged as a way to control the movement of racialized peoples both within and across colonial territories and into the metropole.

What the chapters in this section traced was how the pervasive logic of race, embedded within citizenship and immigration policy, continues to affect the lives of people today. It is not simply in the past, a relic of history, and nor is it only identifiable via faint 'traces'. The legacies identified are manifest in the present, and demarcate who belongs and has rights, and who does not. Racialized ideas of an idealized 'family life' are also used in the organization of immigration and border regimes in contemporary Britain. Legal status, an integral mechanism of migration governance, can also be provisional and contingent on contemporaneous geopolitical dynamics as well as long-standing racial logics. But the legacies of colonial thinking about racial difference is not only to be found in the formalized regimes of citizenship and immigration. It can also be traced from past to present in the wider rhetoric and representation of migration in the public sphere.

As well as sharing these continuities in inequality, exclusion, and dehumanization, the section dealt with resistance and transformation. When people move, they bring ideas with them, they build alliances, make connections, discuss how to resist ill-treatment, and ultimately change the places where they now live. Anti-colonial resistance has shaped the modern world, and when people move, they share thinking and experiences of such resistance, including to former metropoles. If we appreciate this capacity and potentiality for resistance, we can imagine different futures in the social sciences, and also in wider society.

Multiculturalism and anti-racism

The chapters in Part IV addressed the anxieties, effects, and repercussions of the inclusion and exclusion of previously-colonized-and-now-minoritized populations in the Global North. They did this by making anti-racist activism, research, and multiculturalism central to their analyses. However, the chapters also made us go beyond and rethink what we might learn about these histories if we were to consider them simultaneously, and vis-à-vis each other. This is important as research on anti-racism and multiculturalism has often examined them as separate entities and with different histories. They are even, at times, understood as opposed to one another, despite both anti-racism and multiculturalism having being part of the resistance of racialized and minoritized communities in the Global North. By bringing them together here, we note how a naïve uncoupling of anti-racism and multiculturalism is problematic.

Today's anti-multiculturalism (Demir 2022) is deeply related to a broader anxiety about ethnic and religious minorities in the Global North, their anti-racism demands and their inclusion as equal citizens. This uncoupling is, to some extent, an outcome of how these movements and ideologies have been studied and taught in academia, often at the expense of seeing their intertwined – though not fully overlapping – development and histories. Part of it is also to do with the fact that multiculturalist policies were often instrumentalized, essentialized, and also used for tempering the radicalism of anti-racist policies by those in power. But it is also to do with how anti-racist mobilizations have not always made sufficiently central the exclusions and othering that those from minority religions have faced.

This section, then, also builds on multiculturalism and anti-racism to demonstrate the consequences of the increased hostility Muslim populations have been facing across the Global North. Anti-multiculturalism is one of the main ways in which anti-Muslim racism/Islamophobia is being channelled in contemporary times. In fact, we might have moved to a more dangerous time than the classical age of European Orientalism and colonialism that Edward W. Said studied and problematized. As Hamid Dabashi (2018) writes, the problem is even more acute: 'Today, Arabs and Islam are no longer subjects of knowledge and understanding, but objects of hatred and loathing.' Anti-racist struggles, together with multiculturalist ones, make demands on ethnic and religious minorities and the majority populations to make significant shifts and accommodations. Neither multiculturalism nor anti-racism should be reduced to uttering tepid platitudes about diversity and the celebration of difference. These traditions and associated mobilizations need to be understood in the context of their role undoing and challenging the racialized hierarchies consequent to colonialism, and the fight they have taken towards inclusion and equality and against discrimination.

The environment

Part V encompassed different geographical starting points, beginning with the analysis of extractivism in Latin America, situating the origins of palm oil in West Africa, and explaining political ecology through flooding in India. Pollution and palm oil show how people are materially connected on a planetary scale, yet environmental impacts remain uneven, unequal, and unjustly racialized. The 'Global North' and 'Global South' are not simply geographical hemispheres; they are nuanced concepts that connect disadvantage, including 'sacrifice zones' located within the geographical north. North–South ambiguities are further explored within the section in the (largely Northern-focused) discussions of the Green New Deal and the problematically racialized figure of the climate migrant.

Climate change tends to be presented as the single, unprecedented, and overwhelming environmental challenge facing global society. However, this section reframes climate change as part and parcel of wider historical-structural problems of colonial dispossession, extraction, exploitation, and racialized discrimination. These problems continue to shape and haunt both contemporary environmental problems and their proposed solutions. Climate change is more than an 'environmental' or energy crisis in any simple sense, while pollution poses an equally disastrous, but less-noticed transgression of the global 'safe operating space for humanity'. This section illustrates historical imbalances resulting in some people in some places being responsible for the lion's share of global environmental damage, while others suffer from the displacement of harmful effects.

The chapters point towards a need for differentiated approaches to prevent, remedy, and repair environmental damages, but they also show that fundamental structural changes are needed to stop certain places and people from being treated as mere 'taps' for raw materials and labour, or as 'sinks' for wastes and toxic pollution. Latin

American perspectives highlight the joint importance of feminist, decolonial, and Indigenous resistance efforts. Anti-colonial and anti-patriarchal critiques mesh in the fight against the occupation of bodies, communities, and territories. These situated perspectives emphasize women's key role in environmental struggles and common opposition to masculinized and patriarchal forms of extractivism, which involve sexualized and disproportionately gendered violence. The deep connections between ecological and feminist struggles explain the salience of women's resistance, the leading role of women, and the disproportionate costs to women in countering extractivism, pollution, and environmental injustice.

Much of the discussion highlighted the material impacts of the industrial age, imperial war, and global markets in creating novel substances, commodities, and pollution, spreading them worldwide. These phenomena of colonial and capitalist development are also racialized. West African societies, for example, were the first to use red palm oil, before colonialism and imperialism appropriated and uprooted it from its original context, and directed its industrial development against its original Indigenous users. Technologies that claimed to represent moral and technological superiority, cleanliness and 'civilization' ultimately served to embed racism, discrimination, and ecological damage. Across the section, the chapters questioned how both states and markets fail to reckon with the colonial roots of environmental collapse. Without a clearer understanding of these processes, it will remain impossible to realize just and reparative approaches to environmental problems. A global, connected, and decentralized approach helps us to think differently about how the social sciences might approach, conceptualize, and narrate knowledges, theories, and problems.

Conclusion

A better contextualized, materially grounded social science re-situates the analysis of the modern world in colonial histories and their aftermaths. A more thorough evaluation of the past allows for a renewed approach to teaching and learning about modernity as globally constituted and points to different future options for living together on a shared planet. This book is a collective intervention in rethinking not just the making of the modern world, but how we have come to think of that world as modern. That is, it is also an attempt to open up new spaces within the disciplines of the social sciences such that they are themselves more effective in their responses to the challenges that shape our contemporary world. This is, of course, not the first volume to seek to 'open up' the social sciences (Wallerstein et al 1996). But it is distinct in that it offers a concrete set of resources for opening up and remaking the social sciences after colonialism.

The chapters here, and the associated teaching resources, speak to 'foundational' concepts in the social sciences (class, race, migration, the family) and widespread issues of concern (economic inequality, racism, populism, climate change, housing, labour rights). But they approach these issues in a way that does not rely on conceptual frameworks which fail to take colonial connections seriously. This means 'demythologizing' how we teach about the emergence of modernity. As students of the social sciences go out to face a world beset by climate injustice, populism, racism, exploitative labour practices, hardening borders, and restrictive citizenship, it is more important than ever to address this sustained colonial amnesia. This book offers a set of resources to do just that.

References

Ake, C. 1982. *Social Science as Imperialism: A Theory of Political Development*. Ibadan University Press.

Burawoy, M. 2005. 'Provincializing the social sciences', in G. Steinmetz and J. Adams (eds) *The Politics of Method in the Human Sciences*, Duke University Press, pp 508–525.

Dabashi, H. 2018. 'Edward Said's Orientalism: Forty Years Later', *Aljazeera*. https://www.aljazeera.com/opinions/2018/5/3/edward-saids-orientalism-forty-years-later/

Demir, I. 2022. *Diaspora as Translation and Decolonization*. Manchester University Press.

Wallerstein, I., Juma, C., Fox Keller, E., Kocka, J., Lecourt, D., Mudimbe, V.Y., et al. 1996. *Open the Social Sciences: Report of the Gulbenkian Commission on the Restructuring of the Social Sciences*. Stanford University Press.

Using the Lesson Plans for the Connected Sociologies Curriculum Project

Isabel Sykes

Objectives

- This chapter explains the rationale behind, and purpose of, the worksheets associated with the Connected Sociologies Curriculum Project and reproduced in this volume.
- It talks through the design and creation of the worksheets, including how they fit into the national A-level curriculum.
- It outlines how the worksheets can be used for both A-level and undergraduate study, using the Haitian Revolution worksheet as an example.

Introduction

The Connected Sociologies Curriculum Project brings to the fore histories, theories, and perspectives that are too often absent from standard sociological accounts of the modern world. The talks centre key sociological events and voices that have previously been overlooked or ignored by dominant, Eurocentred narratives of modernity. In doing so, the Project invites us to see the importance of 'rethinking' how we understand Sociology and 'reconstructing' the way in which it is practised (Bhambra 2007, 2014).

If we are to 'reconstruct' Sociology, how does this change the way we teach it? One way is through transforming our curricula. Curricula introduce students to important cultural and intellectual discussions (Dennis 2018). They also help us to produce standard accounts and widely understood forms of knowledge (Shahjahan et al 2022). 'Reconstructing' Sociology curricula involves interrogating these existing forms of knowledge and centring histories and theories that have been rendered 'alternative, optional or invisible' (Elliott-Cooper 2018: 293).

However, 'reconstructing' does not end with introducing new perspectives into existing modules and lesson plans; the recovery and centring of marginalized understandings should be at the centre of how we teach Sociology. This is the rationale behind initiatives to decolonize higher education, such as the 'Rhodes Must Fall' and 'Why Is My Curriculum White?' movements (Peters 2015; Chantiluke et al 2018; Elliott-Cooper 2018). In order to contribute to the goal of 'reconstructing' Sociology, then, the content of our curricula must be transformed, and so must the way in which they are taught. As Dennis writes in her essay on decolonizing education: 'a decolonized pedagogy thinks alongside, from and within knowledges that have been rendered invisible' (2018: 199). This is the starting point for the Connected Sociologies Curriculum Project worksheets.

To aid teaching that supports the 'reconstruction' of Sociology, this chapter introduces the Connected Sociologies worksheets. Each worksheet corresponds to a talk in the Project, and they have been designed as a learning tool to help A-level teachers and university lecturers or seminar leaders to teach the topics covered. As I explain in this chapter, the activities in each worksheet have been created with a focus on critical thinking. As such, they are intended to support A-level and undergraduate students in thinking 'alongside, from and within' perspectives and forms of knowledge that are too often elided from standard sociological discourses.

In the following section, I detail how the worksheets were designed, using the core requirements from the A-level Sociology curriculum as a jumping-off point, and expanding outwards to new topics and wider subjects in order to encourage a 'connected', interdisciplinary way of thinking. The subsequent two sections take the reader through an example of how one of the worksheets might be used for both A-level and undergraduate study, demonstrating how the activities could be adapted for differing levels of sociological understanding and skill. In the conclusion I bring the focus back to the overall purpose of the Connected Sociologies Curriculum Project and its transformative potential with regards to how we understand and teach Sociology in schools and universities.

Designing the Connected Sociologies worksheets

As per the latest guidance set out by the Department for Education, AS and A-level Sociology specifications should focus on 'the development of critical and reflective thinking', with a focus on developing students' awareness of sociological debates in 'contemporary society' and forming evidence-based arguments pertaining to these debates (Department for Education 2014). The Connected Sociologies worksheets have been designed with these aims in mind, drawing upon several compulsory topics and themes within national A-level Sociology syllabi.

In the 'Theory and Methods' core module of the AQA curriculum, for example, the topic 'concepts of modernity and post-modernity in relation to sociological theory' directly pertains to the focus of the Connected Sociologies Curriculum Project on theories and narratives of modernity, such as those outlined within the modules 'The Making of the Modern World' and 'Modern Social Theory' (AQA 2016). Similarly, 'Globalization' is a core topic within the OCR curriculum, and underpins many of the sessions within the Connected Sociologies programme, for example within the 'Colonial Global Economy' module (OCR 2024).

Furthermore, the topic of 'Crime and Deviance' features as a compulsory topic in the AQA syllabus and as an optional topic in the OCR syllabus. With a consistent focus on interrogating connections between crime, policing, and social control, as well the relationship between crime and the media, and theories surrounding the social construction of crime and deviance, the Connected Sociologies Curriculum Project module 'Policing "Crime" and "Deviance"' offers a rich, challenging insight into this topic.

As well as aligning with A-level curricula on subject matter, the talks on the Connected Sociologies Curriculum Project feature varied methods of sociological research, including a variety of qualitative methods with which students can familiarize themselves. Each worksheet points out explicitly where there are connections to be made between the talk and the A-level Sociology curriculum to aid session leaders in integrating the worksheets into their teaching.

While the Connected Sociologies worksheets purposefully make links to the core A-level curriculum, then, the central purpose of the worksheets is to develop students' critical thinking skills in order to furnish them with the tools to think beyond their syllabus. As bell hooks describes it, critical thinking 'involves first discovering the who, what, when, where, and how of things ... and then utilizing that knowledge in a manner that enables you to determine what matters most' (2009: 9). When students watch the talks, they are introduced to 'the who, what, when, where, and how of things', with a focus on new perspectives, marginalized voices, and hidden narratives.

As a supplement to these talks, the worksheets are designed to enable students to put the knowledge they have gained from them into practice by investigating sociological questions. As such, the activities in the worksheets consistently prompt students to think beyond the material presented in the talks. Rather than memorizing and recounting the content of the talks, the worksheet activities are intended to provide a space for students to process the information presented there and put it to use for their own purposes. Focusing on the combined practices of 'synthesis, evaluation and criticism', the activities are intended to help students to develop an authoritative authorial voice which will aid them in producing nuanced arguments and generative work (Fitzgerald 1994: 381).

While these skills are useful to students studying Sociology and other social science subjects, the application of the worksheets could also extend more broadly. Emphasizing the 'connected' nature of Sociology as a field of study, the talks in the wider Project, and their corresponding worksheets, highlight the ways in which Sociology can be brought into dialogue with other fields. In terms of A-level and undergraduate study, for example, there are connections to be made to subjects including History, Geography, and Anthropology. This reflects the aims of the overall Project to emphasize the connectedness and plurality of the field of Sociology (Bhambra 2014).

To summarize the rationale behind these resources, the Connected Sociologies Curriculum Project worksheets have been designed to enable students to critically assess their existing knowledge of the modern world and challenge dominant social narratives. This in turn is intended to help them to stretch their learning beyond compulsory curriculum material. Given the level of critical thinking the students will engage in by completing these worksheets, the activities are not only suitable for A-level study but may also be beneficial for bridging the gap to undergraduate level. The following section sets out a guide for how this could be put into practice.

The Haitian Revolution: for A-level study

As I have established, the Connected Sociologies Curriculum Project worksheets map onto several core and optional modules in the A-level Sociology curriculum. In this section, I break down each of the activities in a worksheet, explaining how they might be used as a learning tool in an A-level Sociology classroom. For a case study I have chosen the Haitian Revolution worksheet, which corresponds to Gurminder K. Bhambra's chapter with the same title. The worksheet is available on pp 28–29 in this volume. I discuss the rationale behind its different parts.

This topic is an ideal example of how the Connected Sociologies programme centres marginalized historical perspectives with the view to challenging dominant narratives of modernity. Furthermore, the session's focus on critical thinking with regards to concepts of modernity firmly embeds it within the core A-level Sociology curriculum. It may also be useful to A-level students studying related subjects such as History, and particularly modules related to the history and legacy of colonialism.

The warm-up activity for this session asks students to consider the following questions: 'What is democracy? What are the features of a democratic society?' This activity is designed to introduce students to thinking critically about 'modern' societies as they know them and prompts them to begin interrogating the features of a 'modern' society, such as democracy. As well as connecting to the core A-level topic of 'concepts of modernity', the activity introduces students to the central rationale underpinning this talk in order to prepare them for undertaking the subsequent activities in the worksheet.

The next activity in the worksheet invites the session leader to spend five minutes recapping the students' previous learning on the topic of 'globalization'. This is a core topic within the OCR curriculum. Teachers may find it useful to utilize online resources – such as ReviseSociology,[1] for example – to re-familiarize students with the definition of globalization, and some relevant theories related to global development, such as 'modernization theory'. As this is only designed to be a short activity, keeping the theory light-touch at this stage may be helpful. The recap activities are designed to help students to situate the topic of the talk within their wider learning rather than detract from the main focus of the session.

For the next five minutes of the session, the worksheet prompts students to use a short snippet of the talk as a starting point to begin synthesizing their learning from the talk. Students are asked to consider the significance of the fact that the abolition of slavery in Haiti happened as a result of events *within* the island, rather than in the metropole. As Bhambra details in the talk, and in her chapter in this volume, abolition is often thought of as being brought about by events happening in the metropole (in this case, Paris). The Haitian Revolution, she explains, demonstrates that calls for the abolition of slavery were happening within the colonies at a time when there were no similar initiatives anywhere else in the Atlantic. This activity is intended to draw students' attention to the significance of this fact at an early stage in the session. This has been done to encourage participants to start thinking critically about accepted narratives of democracy and modernity. Fostering this kind of thinking and prompting students to begin questioning the validity of dominant sociological narratives is the central objective of this worksheet.

The subsequent two activities, intended to be carried out during the following 15 minutes of the session, ask students to watch a few minutes of the talk, digest the information, and synthesize the key points in their own words. By building on the knowledge they have gained from the talk, and going beyond 'the who, what, when, where, and how of things', students are encouraged to exercise their skills in 'synthesis, evaluation and criticism'.

Furthermore, as the worksheet indicates, these activities encourage students to draw thematic connections with other talks on 'The Making of the Modern World' module and the wider programme. By prompting students to exercise these skills, the tasks aim to aid students in producing high-quality written work at A-level. As such, these activities may work well as short, timed writing tasks.

Halfway through the session, the worksheet prompts students to reflect on their learning thus far. The activity asks students to think back to the first questions they answered at the start of the session, encouraging them to consider if and how their thoughts on the definition and features of a democratic society have changed. Reflection activities are placed at the end of most of the worksheets. They are intended to allow students to consolidate what they have learned throughout each session and promote reflective thinking, which is a key foundation of the A-level Sociology curriculum (OCR 2024).

The final two activities in this worksheet provide an opportunity for students to put their critical and reflective thinking into practice. Inviting students to reflect on the phrase 'the silences of history' from the talk, these tasks ask students to tap into a key theme across the Connected Sociologies Curriculum Project. Students are prompted to think about how and why sociologists should contribute to recovering the silenced understandings of the Haitian Revolution, and what some consequences of this 'reclaiming' might be. These activities push students to connect their learning to challenging questions about the scope, methods, and purpose of sociological inquiry. This level of critical thought may help advanced A-level students to approach undergraduate levels of thinking and working.

In sum, the activities in this worksheet, and in all worksheets within the Connected Sociologies Curriculum Project, are designed to support A-level teaching, with the primary aim of fostering critical and reflective thinking among students. The themes in each session map onto modules within the A-level curriculum, but the activities are also designed to challenge students to go beyond their syllabus. In doing so, worksheets such as the Haitian Revolution may be useful to students hoping to bridge the gap to studying Sociology at undergraduate level.

The Haitian Revolution: for undergraduate study

Following on from the previous section, here I detail how the Haitian Revolution worksheet could be adapted for use at undergraduate level, for example for a Sociology or History seminar group. The primary difference between using the worksheets for A-level study and for undergraduate study is that, at degree level, the activities may be used less prescriptively and more as guidelines or prompts. For example, the questions may be used by a session leader to spark a seminar group discussion or set up a breakaway group activity. Furthermore, degree-level students may be more likely to independently draw connections, from their wider learning, between the topics covered in the Connected Sociologies Curriculum Project.

In the warm-up activity, as I have explained, the questions 'what is democracy?' and 'what are the features of a democratic society?' are designed to prompt students to question dominant perceptions of modern societies. At university level, this activity may be used to instigate a short group discussion, giving students the opportunity to demonstrate their existing abilities to think critically about dominant Eurocentred narratives of democracy and modernity.

The next activity prompts the session leader to recap previous sessions on the topic of 'globalization'. To adapt this for undergraduate study, students could be prompted to lead this section themselves, discussing what they already know about the relationship between globalization and modernity. Students may start to consider how the Haitian Revolution fits, or does not fit, into the narratives of global development and the making of the modern world with which they are already familiar.

In the subsequent three activities, taking the session up to the halfway mark, there are more opportunities to adapt the questions for a degree-level seminar group or study session. At undergraduate level, as the students progress through the activities that prompt them to synthesize what they have learned in the talk and put it into their own words, there are opportunities for them to go a step further. The session leader may find it beneficial to place more of an emphasis on how students can mobilize what they have learned about the Haitian Revolution to think critically about dominant narratives of abolition and modernity more broadly. They may have studied abolition in other modules, subjects, or at previous academic stages, and could be encouraged to consider which perspectives have been prioritized in these historical narratives, which voices have been absent, and why they think that may be. This line of enquiry could facilitate a more sophisticated understanding of why the Haitian Revolution, and its significance, has been elided from dominant sociological accounts.

In the penultimate activity, which asks students to consider what Bhambra means by the phrase 'the silences of history', undergraduate students may be able to engage more thoroughly with the implications of this phrase for sociologists, rather than just for historians or academics more generally. Undergraduate students may be able to situate this phrase within the wider context of the Connected Sociologies Curriculum Project, including aims such as 'reconstructing' Sociology and transforming curricula. Students may also be able to apply these ideas to completing the final activity, which asks them to articulate how sociologists can contribute to 'reclaiming' the Haitian Revolution, and what some potential outcomes of this might be. This activity may work well as an independent writing exercise and could also be adapted for use as an essay question.

Finally, undergraduate students are especially encouraged to make use of additional resources provided at the end of the chapter. At undergraduate level, these additional readings could provide a solid starting point for further independent research into the Haitian Revolution.

In sum, while the Connected Sociologies worksheets are primarily designed with A-level students in mind, the scope of the activities is such that they may be adapted for more advanced academic levels, such as the early stages of undergraduate study. At this level, the activities may be a useful support for independent research, provide inspiration for essay questions, or act as prompts for seminar discussions.

Conclusion

In this chapter I have detailed the purpose, design, and suggested application of the Connected Sociologies Curriculum Project worksheets. As I have explained, these worksheets aim to support efforts to transform curricula, drawing on theory and practical initiatives that recognize the need to 'reconstruct' Sociology as a subject. While these worksheets have strong links to the national A-level Sociology curriculum, I have detailed how they may also be adapted for use at undergraduate level, given that their central focus is to develop students' critical thinking and reflective learning skills. Regardless of academic level, this chapter has made clear that the Connected Sociologies Curriculum Project worksheets are designed to challenge standard accounts of modernity in society, and to encourage students to do so in their own thinking and writing. In this way, these worksheets aim to support the pedagogical dimensions of 'reconstructing' Sociology; recognizing that there is a need to transform how we teach Sociology as well as how we study it.

Note

[1] https://revisesociology.com/

References

AQA. 2016. *A-Level Sociology*. https://www.aqa.org.uk/subjects/sociology/a-level/sociology-7192/specification/subject-content

Bhambra, G.K. 2007. *Rethinking Modernity: Postcolonialism and the Sociological Imagination*. Palgrave Macmillan.

Bhambra, G.K. 2014. *Connected Sociologies*. Bloomsbury.

Chantiluke, R., Kwoba, B., and Nkopo, A. 2018. *Rhodes Must Fall: The Struggle to Decolonize the Racist Heart of Empire*. Zed.

Dennis, C.A. 2018. 'Decolonizing Education: A Pedagogic Intervention', in G.K. Bhambra, D. Gebrial, and K. Nişancıoğlu (eds) *Decolonizing the University*. Pluto Press, pp 190–207.

Department for Education. 2014. *GCE AS and A Level Sociology*. https://www.gov.uk/government/publications/gce-as-and-a-level-for-sociology.

Elliott-Cooper, A. 2018. 'Free, Decolonized Education: A Lesson from the South African Student Struggle', in J. Arday and H.S. Mirza (eds) *Dismantling Race in Higher Education: Racism, Whiteness and Decolonizing the Academy*. Palgrave Macmillan, pp 289–296.

Fitzgerald, M. 1994. 'Why Write Essays?', *Journal of Geography in Higher Education* 18(3): 379–384.

hooks, b. 2009. *Teaching Critical Thinking: Practical Wisdom*. Routledge.

OCR. 2024. *AS and A Level Sociology – H180, H580*. https://www.ocr.org.uk/qualifications/as-and-a-level/sociology-h180-h580-from-2015/

Peters, M.A. 2015. 'Why is My Curriculum White?', *Educational Philosophy and Theory* 47(7): 641–646.

Shahjahan, R.A., Estera, A.L., Surla, K.L., and Edwards, K.T. 2022. '"Decolonizing" Curriculum and Pedagogy: A Comparative Review Across Disciplines and Global Higher Education Contexts', *Review of Educational Research* 92(1): 73–113.

Index

References to figures appear in *italic* type; those in **bold** type refer to tables. References to chapter endnotes show both the page number and the note number (65n1).

A

Aba Women's War (1929) 87
Abasindi Women's Co-operative 281
Aboriginal Australians 50–51
Acemoglu, Daron 37–38
Acosta, Alberto 359, 360
Acuña, Máxima 361
Advani, Arun 171–172
advertising 404–405
Afghan refugees 189, 254
Afghan women 319
African Union 199
Ahmad, Babar 320
Aitlhadj, Layla 322
Ake, Claude 425
Alam, Tahir 307
Ali, Nadya 322
Ali, Taj 235
Ali, Tosir 266
Amin, Idi 118
Anderson, Clare 75
Andriessen, Thirza 146
Angelo, Anne-Marie 266
Ansari, Humayun 318
anti-colonial resistance
 and 20th century decolonization 87–89
 Demerara Uprising 62–63
 Haitian Revolution 17–20, 21–22, 23–26, 24–25
 India 25, 88–89
 Palmares 24–25
anti-racism 263–272
 and anti-imperialism 266–267, 270
 and class struggle 267–268, 270–271
 influence of US movement 264
 legacy of British Black Power 270–271
 neoliberal approaches to 269–270
 and political Blackness 264–267, 277
 women's organizations 277–278
anti-slavery movement 63–64, 65
Arboleda, Martín 363
archives 279, 280, 281–282, 283
Arendt, Hannah 181, 415
Ashiagbor, Diamond 59

Asian Youth Movement 269
Assam, flooding 390–392
assimilation 291–293, **292**
asylum in Britain 194–202
 and 1951 Refugee Convention 195, 196, 197–199
 border controls 195–196
 child refugees 227–228
 colonial and racial dynamics 159–160, 197–202
 political rhetoric 227
 refugee statistics 195
 terminology 195
 see also British citizenship; British immigration policy
Australia 50–51, 58, 62
authoritarian populism 234, 237, 241
Azadian, Anahita 144
Aztec Empire 47, 48

B

Bailey, Guy 115
Bakali, Naved 318
Baker, Baron 131
Bales, Kevin 154–155
Bangladesh 197, 377, 415, 416
Barbados 36, 58, 61, 76–77, *76*
Barber, Miles 77
Bartle, John 238
Bassett, Thomas 389
Bauman, Zygmunt 239
Bayly, Christopher 18
BBC Bitesize website 65n1
Beaumont, Joseph 64
Bechu, Indian indentured labourer 64
Beck, David J. 143
Beckert, Sven 167–168
Beckles, Hilary M. 61, 63
Belgian Congo 88
Bellay, Jean-Baptiste 19
Benjaminsen, Tor A. 51
Benson, Michaela 189
Berbice Slave Rebellion (1763) 62–63
Berg, Joel 143

440

INDEX

Berlin Conference (1884–1885) 87
Bermudans 186
Bhabha, Homi K. 3, 208–209
Bhagat, Ali 159
Bhambra, Gurminder K. 2, 3, 4, 12, 33, 107, 108, 166, 248, 375–376, 378, 381
Bhattacharya, Gargi 227
Birmingham Trojan Horse Affair 302–311
Black, Richard 188
Black British feminism 275–284
  development of movement 277–278
  gaps in narrative 279–282, 283
  specific organizations 277, 280, 281, 282
Black Liberation Front (BLF) 264, 266, 268, 277
Black Panther Movement (BPM) 264, 266, 267, 268
Black Power *see* British Black Power
Black Unity and Freedom Party (BUFP) 264, 266, 267, 268
Blackness 20–21, 264–267, 277, 283n1
Blaikie, Piers 387, 388–389
Blair, Tony 317
Blue Planet II (BBC documentary) 344
Bockman, Johanna 129
Bolívar, Simon 22
border controls 195–196
Bouchareb, Rachid 214
Boyd, David R. 345
Brah, Avtar 117, 208–209
Brexit 122, 127, 128, 227, 238–239, 253–254, 271, 322
Bristol Bus Boycott (1963) 115, 213
British Black Power 263–272
  anti-imperialism 266–267, 270
  contemporary relevance 270–271
  contribution of women 276, 277
  influence of US movement 264
  and political Blackness 264–267
  reconceptualization of class struggle 267–268, 270
  see also Black British feminism
British citizenship 181–190
  colonial citizenship regime 182–186
  Hong Kong residents 186, 188–189, 250–256
  national citizenship regime 186–187
  post-colonial citizenship 187–189
  see also asylum in Britain; British immigration policy; integration; Windrush scandal
British counterterrorism policy
  pre-emptive policing 319–321
  Prevent Duty 302, 311n4, 317, 320, 321–323
  Prevent Strategy 321
  Schedule 7 searches 319
British education policy 308–309
British elites 166–173
  aristocracy 167, 168–169
  fortunes from commerce and finance 168–169
  golden visa programmes 172–173
  industrial capitalists 167–168
  international connections 166–167, 171–172
  and non-dom tax status 172
  and race 170–171

  transnational dynamics 167
  use of term 167
British Empire
  colonial economic model 34–35, 75–77
  colonial laws 50–51
  control of mobility 222–225
  indentured labour 57–65
  land enclosures 76–77
  role of British elites 167, 168
  rule in India 25, 34–35, 51, 87, 88–89, 390–392
  slave trade 59
  sterling as global currency 49
  uprisings against 62–63, 87
British immigration policy
  border controls 195–196
  Commonwealth Immigrants Acts 183–185
  'foreign national offenders' 220
  hostile environment policy 127–128, 132, 187–188, 196–197, 210–211, 254
  national citizenship regime 186–187
  No Recourse to Public Funds 132, 145
  patrials and non-patrials 265
  and political Blackness 264–267
  post-war policy 236
  resettlement schemes 188–189, 250–256
  role of family and intimacy 224–228
  see also asylum in Britain; British citizenship
British Nationality Act 1981 (BNA 1981) 186, 188, 249, 250–252
British values 303, 304, 311
British Virgin Islanders 186
Brixton Black Women's Group 278, 280
Brookfield, Harold C. 387, 388–389
Bryceson, Ian 51
Burawoy, Michael 425
Burnard, Trevor 76
Bush, George W. 316, 317
Butler, Rab 184

C

Cabnal, Lorena 362
Cáceres, Berta 361
Cain, Peter J. 168
Callaghan, James 120, 185
Cameron, David 304, 305
Canada 159, 182, 294, 345
Cannadine, David 167
capitalism 101–109
  basis of system 102
  and class structure 102–106
  communal economies contrasted 102–103
  emigration and 104
  Eurocentric accounts 44
  extractivism and 359–360, 361, 362–363
  industrial and commercial elites 167–169
  mercantile capitalism 107
  palm oil industry 403–407
  and race 106–107
  racial capitalism 107, 157, 160–161, 329–332, 416–419
  roots in colonialism 107–109, 156–161

surplussed populations 407
transformation process 103–104
see also colonial global economy; colonial resource extraction; extractivism; neoliberalism; plantation system
Caraher, Martin 144
Carby, Hazel 278, 279
CARICOM Reparations Commission 36
Carmichael, Stokely 264
Carson, Rachel 345
Centre for Science and Environment (India) 392–393
Césaire, Aimé 89
Charles III, King 295
Charles X, King of France 22
child labour 79
child refugees 227–228
Chimni, B.S. 200
China 48–49, 344–345, 406, 407
Chinese indentured labourers 58, 60
Christophe, Henri 22
citizenship *see* British citizenship; universal citizenship
cladding scandal 128–129, 134–135
Clark, Lindsey 307
Clarke report (2014) 305–307, 308–310
class
 capitalism and 102–106
 and economic inequality 106
 and ethnicity/gender 105, 106
 formative role of enclosure movement 74–75, 103, 107–108
 hierarchical models 105–106
 Marxist ideas 102–106, 109, 168, 268
 social mobility 105
class struggle 267–268
Clayton, Matthew 310–311
climate change 371–381
 colonial dynamics 373–380
 economic impacts 36
 Green New Deal (GND) 371–372, 373–374, 378, 380
 little ice age 47
 pathways for future action 380–381
 and pollution 343, 344
 and racial injustice 412–420
climate migrants 380, 381, 413–416, 417–419
Cochrane, Kelso 131
Cockburn, Alexander 387–388
Cohen, Robin 208
Cohen, Stanley 303
Collins, Patricia Hill 222
Colombia 195
colonial archives 279, 282
colonial capitalism, use of term 155
 see also capitalism; colonial global economy; colonial resource extraction; extractivism; plantation system
colonial global economy 30–38, 156–161
 climate change impacts 36
 economic sociology 32–34

Eurocentric accounts 33–34, 37
Keynesian macroeconomics 31
legal origins approach 37
methodological nationalism 31–34
new institutionalism approach 37–38
use of term 156–157
 see also capitalism; colonial resource extraction; extractivism; plantation system
colonial racial capitalism 157
colonial resource extraction
 Columbian exchange 46–48
 economic model 34–35
 materialist approach 48–49
 ongoing impacts of 92
 palm oil 400, 401, 402, 405
 precious metals 48–49, 60
 role in modern slavery 155
 see also extractivism; plantation system
colonialism, origin and use of term 46–47, 156
Columbian exchange 46–48
Columbus, Christopher 46, 47, 86
combat breathing 333
Commonwealth Immigrants Acts 184–185
compensation and restitution
 injustices of slave trade 35–36
 loss of slave trade 22, 35
 native title 51
Confederation of Indigenous Nationalities of Ecuador (CONAIE) 365
Conservative governments 122, 127, 183–184, 185–186, 189, 227–228, 235, 237, 239, 240, 253, 254, 265, 322
Conservative/Liberal Democrat coalition 304
continuity doctrine 51
Convention relating to the Status of Refugees (1951) 195, 196, 197–199, 255
Cooper, Anna Julia 17–18
Corbyn, Jeremy 127–128
Cortés, Hernan 47
cosmopolitanism 291–293, **292**
cotton mills 78–79
counterterrorism *see* British counterterrorism policy
COVID-19 pandemic 141
Cox, Oliver Cromwell 106–107
Cragg, Timothy 78–79
Crewe, Ivor 240
Crosby, Alfred W. 47–48
Crowley, Robert 73, 80
Cuffy (Kofi), Guyanese rebellion leader 62

D

Dabashi, Hamid 429
Dadzie, Stella 282
Daffarn, Edward 129
Daily Mail 227
Davies, Thom 345
Davis, Heather 375
Davis, Mike 392
De Genova, Nicholas 239
de Haas, Hein 200
decolonial theory 3–4

INDEX

decolonization 85–94
  impact and significance of 90–92
  Indigenous peoples 93
  meaning of term 85
  ongoing legacies of colonialism 92–93
  resistance movements as drivers 87–89
  Vietnam (case study) 89–90
Demerara Uprising (1823) 62–63
democracy
  anti-immigration sentiment in 236, 238, 265, 304, 332
  Haiti and the code-noir 23–24, 28
  and the idea of the modern nation state 2, 17, 23, 101, 292
  and multiculturalism 293–295, 303
  and policing 328
  and pro-democracy in Hong Kong 252
  and self-determination 85, 88–91, 104, 249–250, 357, 415, 418
demographic transition 104
dependency theory 359–360
Des Voeux, George 63–64
Desai, Jayaben 118, 119, 120
Dessalines, Jean-Jacques 20
diasporas 207–215
  colonial and imperial axis of 209–211
  contributions to modernity and globalization 211–214
  founding theories 208–209
  methodological nationalism and amnesia 209–211
dispossession
  Aboriginal Australians 50–51
  Columbian exchange 46–47
  extractivism and 361–362
  Haitian constitution 20
  legal doctrines 50–51
  restitution of lands 51
  scientific conservation practices 51
  see also enclosures
Dolphyne, Samuel 333
Dominica 36
Dorling, Danny 135
dos Reis Peron, Alcides Eduardo 363
Douglas, Flora 145
Du Bois, W.E.B. 88, 266
Dubs Amendment 227
Dufay, Louis-Pierre 19
Duggan, Mark 318, 332
Dummett, Ann 252
Dutch Empire 62–63, 64
Dutt, R.C. 34

E

East London Black Women's Association (ELBWO) 282, 283
ecological imperialism 47–48
ecology *see* political ecology
Ecuador 365
  see also Latin America
El-Enany, Nadine 225

elites *see* British elite
Elliot-Cooper, Adam 320
Empire *see* Aztec Empire; British Empire; Dutch Empire; French Empire; Ottoman Empire; Portuguese Empire; Roman Empire; Spanish Empire
Empire Windrush, HMT 183, 249, 275
  see also Windrush scandal
employment *see* labour practices
enclosures 70–80
  connections to colonialism 75–77, 78
  formative role of enclosure movement 74–75, 103, 107–108
  impact on landless 45–46, 70–71, 73, 74
  methods used 72–73, 74
  resistance against 73, 74–75
  revocation of common rights 72
  in Wales, Scotland and Ireland 71–72
epistemology 3–4
Eurocentricity 33–34, 37, 44, 279
extractivism 356–365
  as capitalist accumulation 359–360
  data extractivism 363
  feminist resistance to 361
  financial extractivism 362–363
  in green economy 374, 376, 379
  green extractivism 362–363
  greenhouse gas emissions 378
  Latin America's dependency on 357–359
  as mode of dispossession 361–362
  neo-extractivism 360
  neoliberal extractivism 360
  palm oil 400, 401, 402, 405
  patriarchal dimensions to 361–362
  post-extractive alternatives 364–365
  use of term 356–357
  see also colonial resource extraction; plantation system
extremism
  accusations against schools 303, 306–307, 308, 310–311
  pre-emptive policing 319–321
  Prevent policy 302, 311n4, 317, 320, 321–323
  Schedule 7 searches 319

F

Falkland Islanders 186, 251
family 219–229
  colonial ideals of 220–222
  and current immigration practice 225–228
  imperial controls on mobility 222–225
Fanon, Frantz 330, 333
Farage, Nigel 227, 241
Farah (Park View pupil) 311
FareShare 141, 144
fascism 89
feminism 275–284
  and Afghan women 318–319
  colonial dynamics 277–278
  development of Black British activism 277–278
  and extractivism 361–362

gaps in Black British activist narrative 279–282, 283
Ferguson, Roderick 221
Fernandez, Shereen 322, 323
feudalism 102–103
Fiji 58
First World War 88
Fischer, Sibylle 21
Fisher, Andrew 143
Fitzgerald, David 196
Floyd, George 333
food banks 140–147
  corporatization of 143–144
  effectiveness of 143
  extent of provision 141, 142
  gratitude and deservingness 143, 145, 146
  institutionalization of 142–143
  potential alternatives to 145–146
  use of term 140–141
forced labour 153–161
  campaigns to curb 154
  colonial dynamics 155, 158–159, 160–161
  incidence of 158
  legal definition 153–154
  racial dynamics 158–161
  scholarship/dominant accounts 154–157
  where occurs 154
Foucault, Michel 329, 389–390
France 22–24, 333, 334
  see also French Empire; French Revolution
Fraser, Nancy 107
freedom of speech 294
French Empire
  Haitian independence 19–20, 22
  indentured labour 64
  response to decolonization demands 89
  sale of Louisiana 22
  slavery 19–20, 23–24
  Vietnamese independence 89–90
  wartime contribution of colonial troops 214
French Revolution 17–18, 22–23
Friedman, Sam 169–170
Furey, Sinead 144
Fyfe, David Maxwell 183–184

G

Gago, Verónica 362–363
Gama, Vasco de 46, 86
Garner, Eric 333
Geggus, David P. 23
gentrification 129
Germany 195, 332–333, 334
Gibraltarians 186, 251
Gibson, Angelica 143
gig economy 122, 144
Gilmore, Ruth Wilson 331
Gilroy, Paul 208–209
Gladstone, William 79
Glass, Ruth 129
Global North
  ecological impact 406–407
  economic system 33–35
  and green economy 376, 378, 379–380
  greenhouse gas emissions 374–375
  and pollution 349–350
  see also diasporas
Global Solidarity Alliance for Food, Health and Social Justice (GSA) 145–146
Global South
  and green economy 376, 378, 378–380
  impact of Roosevelt's New Deal 374
  political ecology 392–393
  and pollution 345, 349–350
  as price takers for Global North 33–35
  see also colonial resource extraction; extractivism; plantation system
Goldthorpe, John H. 105
Gorrie, John 64
Gove, Michael 304, 305
green economy 371–381
  colonial dynamics 373–380
  extractive foundations 374, 376, 379
  Green New Deal (GND) 371–372, 373–374, 378, 380
  pathways for future action 380–381
greenhouse gas emissions 374–375, 376–377, 378
Greenpeace 412
Grenada 36
Grenfell Tower fire 127–136
  cladding and insulation 128–129, 134–135
  demography of residents 132
  government responses 133
  history of area 130–132
  importance to social history 130
  political context 127–128
  public inquiry 134–135
  role of fire service 132, 134–135
  undocumented status and 133–134
Griffin, Carl 75
Griffith, Sian 304
Grovogui, Siba N. 24
Grunwick strike 114–123
  background to strike 117–119
  mass picketing 119–120
  policing of 120
  previous historiographies of 115, 116
  significance of 120–122
Guadeloupe 64
Gudynas, Eduardo 359, 360
Gueye, Ama 282
Guha, Ramachandra 387–388
guild system 102–103
Gulbenkian Commission 425
Guyana 60–61, 62–63, 64
Gwilym, Hefin 143

H

Habermas, Jurgen 32, 33
Hafez, Farid 318
Haiti 17–26
  compensation to France 22
  constitution 20–21

economic blockade 21–22
independence from France 20, 22
renaming from Saint-Domingue 20
revolution 17–20, 21–22, 23–26
Hall, Catherine 76
Hall, Stuart 135, 186, 208–209, 234, 235–237, 238, 331
Hamouchene, Hamza 379
Hansen, Randall 183
Harding, Thomas 65n4
Hartman, Saidiya 157
Hayes, Nick 75
Heath, Edward 185
Heath-Kelly, Charlotte 320
Hecht, Susanna 387–388
Henderson, Russ 131
Hickel, Jason 345
Higgins, Katie 170–171
Hillyard, Paddy 319–320
Hinde family (case study) 77–79
Ho Chi Minh 90
Hoad, Neville 221
Hobsbawm, Eric 18
Hochschild, Arlie 119
Holmwood, John 375–376
Honduras 361
Honeyford, Ray 311n3
Hong Kong residents 188–189, 247, 250–256
hooks, bell 222, 434
Hopkins, A.G. 168
hostile environment policy 127–128, 132, 187–188, 196–197, 210–211, 254
human rights
  family life 219, 228
  refugees 198, 200, 201
human trafficking 59

I

Immigration Act 1971 185, 186, 265, 268, 276
immigration policy *see* British immigration policy
Imperial Typewriters strike (1974) 115
Ince, Onur Ulas 37
indentured labour 57–65
  Chinese indenture 58, 60
  European labourers 61–62
  Indian indenture 58–59, 60–61, 64–65
  omitted in national histories 58
  in plantation system 58–59, 60–64
  resistance to 63–64, 65
  slavery distinguished 59
  uprisings against 62–63
Independent Food Aid Network (IFAN) 141, 145
India
  colonial resource extraction 34–35, 51
  cooking oil use 407
  flooding in Assam 385–386, 390–392
  forced labour 158–159
  independence 89
  Indian indentured labourers 58–59, 60–61, 64–65
  political ecology organizations 392–393

post-colonial dispossession 51
resistance to British Empire 25, 87, 88–89
Indigenous communities
  claims for decolonization 93
  Ecuador's Indigenous Movement 365
  forced labour 158–159
  resistance to extractivism 362
individualist integration 291–293, **292**
Indonesia 400, 405
industrial action 74–75, 78–79, 119, 120
industrial revolution 35, 36, 74, 167–168
integration 288–297
  four modes of 291–294, **292**
  levels of 291
  and the national 295–297
  and neoliberalism 269–270
  and religion 294–295
  use of term 289–290
Intergovernmental Panel on Climate Change (IPCC) 349, 373, 375
International Labour Organization 153–154, 158
intersectionality 121–122, 160–161
Iran 195
Ireland 71
Irish republican movement 88, 267, 319–320, 320
Islam *see* Muslims; Trojan Horse affair
Islamophobia 241, 294–295, 318–319, 322–323

J

Jackson, Robert H 91
Jadhav, Sushrut 317
Jaeggi, Rahel 107
Jamaica 36
James, C.L.R. 18, 19–20
James I, King 73
Jenrick, Robert 227–228
Johnson, Boris 241
Johnson, Simon 37–38
Johnson, Walter 80
Jones, Claudia 131
Jonsson, Terese 276

K

Kalpavriksh 392–393
Kalra, Virinder S. 239
Kelley, Robin 157
Kempadoo, Kamala 59
Kenyan Asians 184–185, 251
Kenya–Uganda railway 64
Kershaw report (2014) 305–306, 311n6
Kerslake report (2014) 304
Keynes, John Maynard 31
Khan, Imran 134
Kropotkin, Peter 386
Kundnani, Arun 417, 418
Kymlicka, Will 297n3

L

La Via Campesina 393
Labour governments 172, 184–185, 186, 235, 265, 303, 304, 321, 322

Labour Party in opposition 127–128
labour practices 115–116, 118–119, 275–276
  see also forced labour; indentured labour
Lancaster, UK 77
land enclosures *see* enclosures
Las Casas, Bartolomé de 60
Laslett, Rhaunne 131
Latin America 356–365
  colonial dependency on extractivism 357–359
  data extractivism 363
  feminist resistance to extractivism 361
  financial extractivism 362–363
  green extractivism 362–363
  neo-extractivism 360
  neoliberal extractivism 360
  post-extractive alternatives 364–365
  scholarly approaches to extractivism 359–360
Leff, Enrique 393
Lehuedé, Sebastián 363
Liboiron, Max 348, 349
Liverpool, UK 77, 78, 224, 402
Lockhart, Judith 282
Louisiana 22
L'Ouverture, Toussaint 20
Lugones, Maria 4, 221
Lung theatre company 311

M

Machung, Anne 119
Magellan, Ferdinand 46, 47
Mahmud, Tayyab 63
Malaya 34
Malaysia 58, 400, 405
Manchester, UK 168
Māori people 22
Marcos, Ferdinand 267
Márquez, Francia 361
Martinique 64
Marx, Karl 70–71, 102, 103–104, 105, 109, 168
Marxism 102–106, 109, 168, 268
Mauritius 58–59, 61, 65
May, Robert 350
May, Theresa 127, 128, 135, 187
Mayblin, Lucy 209
McLaren, John 64
media reporting 120, 154, 155, 227, 235–236
Melamed, Jodi 157
Melhuish, Francesca 239
Merzouk, Nahel 332
methodological amnesia 209–211
methodological nationalism 5, 31–34, 166–167, 209–211
Mexico 393
Midland Revolts 73
migration
  border controls 195–196
  climate migrants 380, 381, 413–416, 417–419
  colonial settlement 104
  and displacement 400, 406
  enclosures and 71, 74, 75
  family migration 225–228
  gendered representations of 116–117
  as multi-causal 414
  ongoing colonial dynamics 92, 159, 246–256
  and urbanization 74, 407
  women's agency 117
  see also diasporas
Mills, Jean-Baptiste 19
modern slavery 153–161
  campaigns to curb 154
  colonial dynamics 155, 158–159, 160–161
  incidence of 153, 158
  racial dynamics 158–161
  scholarship/dominant accounts 154–157
  types of 153–154
modernity, understandings of term 2–4
Mongia, Radhika 5, 223
Montagu, Sir Edward 73
Moore, Jason W. 44, 52
Moore-Bick, Martin 134
moral panic 236, 302–303
Morris, Julia 159
Mujeres Amazónicas 362
multiculturalism 290–297
  key characteristics 290, 291–294, **292**
  levels of 291
  and the national 295–297
  and neoliberalism 269–270
  and religion 294–295
  see also Trojan Horse affair
Muñoz, Sebastian Ordoñez 379
Muslims
  impact of Prevent Duty 322–323
  and multiculturalism 294–295
  Muslim diaspora 212
  othering of 241, 318–319
  see also Trojan Horse affair

N

Nafafé, Jose Lingna 25
Nagdee, Ilyas 269
Naoroji, Dadabhai 34
napalm 406
Napoleon 20
National College of Teaching and Learning (NCTL) 308, 309–310
naturalization 415
neoliberalism 269–270, 320, 331, 360, 417
Nepal 158–159
Neptune, H. Reuben 36
Netherlands *see* Dutch Empire
New Deal (Roosevelt) 373, 374
New Zealand 22
Newell, Peter 378, 381
Nicol, Andrew 252
9/11 294, 316–318
Nkonde, Mumbi 281
Nkrumah, Kwame 88, 266
Non-Aligned Movement 91
North Kensington, London 130–132
Notting Hill Carnival 131
Nyhagen Predelli, Line 282

O

Obama, Barack 323
Ofsted 304–306, 307
Organization for African Unity 199
Organization of Women of African and Asian Descent (OWAAD) 277, 278, 280
Orientalism 211, 318
Osterhammel, Jürgen 18
Ottoman Empire 86, 89

P

Pakistan 195, 198
palm oil 399–408
  development of market 402–405
  in foodstuffs 399, 400, 407
  in household products 399, 404
  impact of production 400, 405
  importance to empire 402–403
  origins of production 401–402
  resistance to 400, 405–406
  traditional vs commercial products 400, 401–402
  uses of 399, 400, 402–404, 405–406, 407
Palmares 24–25
Palme, Olof 346
Parekh report (2020) 303, 304
Paris, liberation of 214
Park View Educational Trust (PVET) 302, 305–311
Patel, Raj 44, 52
Patnaik, Prabhat 33, 33–34, 108, 375–376
Patnaik, Utsa 33–34, 34–35, 108, 375–376
Paul, Kathleen 250, 252
pesticides 343, 344, 345–346
Phillip, Matthew 131
Phillips, Nicola 159
Piketty, Thomas 166–167
planetary boundaries model 342–343
plantation system
  economic model 75–77
  indentured labour 58–59, 60–64
  palm oil 400, 401, 402, 405
  Saint-Domingue 19
  sugar plantations 49–50, 58
  see also colonial resource extraction; extractivism
Podur, Justin 374
policing 328–335
  abolitionist approaches 334–335
  pre-emption 319–321
  public disorder 120
  and racial capitalism 329–332
  resistance to 334
  and un-breathing 332–333
Policing the Crisis (Hall et al) 234, 235–237, 331
Policy Exchange 130, 310
political Blackness 264–267, 277, 283n1
political ecology 385–394
  brief history 386–388
  defining characteristics 388–390
  flooding in Assam (case study) 385–386, 390–392
  legacy of colonialism 391–392
  perspectives from Global South 392–393

Political Ecology Network (POLLEN) 392
political economy *see* economy
political rhetoric 122, 227, 235, 238–241
pollution 341–350
  colonial dynamics 348, 349, 350
  common but differentiated responsibility (CBDR) 345, 347
  and economic efficiency 342
  forever chemicals 342
  industrial development and 341–342, 347
  planetary boundaries approach 342–343
  polluter pays principle 345, 347
  regulation 346, 347, 348–349
  technical definition of 348
  types of 342, 344–345
  uneven distribution of harm 343, 344, 347
Polverel, Étienne 19
populism 234–242
  authoritarian populism 234, 237, 241
  diasporas and 214
  nationalism and 239
  political rhetoric 122, 227, 235, 238–241
  race and 235–237, 238–242
  rise of 106, 238–239
  use of term 238
  Vote Leave campaign 227, 238–239, 271
  and White resentment 235–237, 238–241
Portuguese Empire 24–25, 89
post-colonial theory 3–4
Powell, Enoch 122, 185, 186, 237
Power, Madeleine 141
Prescod, Colin 132
presentism 4–5
Prevent Duty 302, 311n4, 317, 320, 321–323
Prevent Strategy 321

Q

Quijano, Anibal 4, 247
Qurashi, Fahid 321

R

race
  in 1970s Britain 235–237
  and asylum 159–160, 197–199
  and British elite 170–171
  and capitalism 106–107, 157, 160–161, 329–332, 416–419
  and climate migrants 413–416
  and colonialism 157
  and forced labour 158–161
  and Grenfell Tower fire 134–135
  and labour practices 115–116, 118–119
  use of term 157
Race Relations Acts 213, 265, 276
race-thinking 157
Rajina, Fatima B. 239
Redclift, Victoria M. 239
Rees, Marvin 213
Reeves, Aaron 169–170
Reform UK 228, 322

refugees 194–202
  border controls 195–196
  climate refugees 415–416, 417–419
  colonial and racial dynamics 159–160, 197–202
  Refugee Convention 195, 196, 197–199, 255
  refugee statistics 195
  scholarship/dominant accounts 194–195, 200
  use of term 195
religion and schooling 308–309
renewable energy *see* green economy
reparations 35–36, 63
restitution *see* compensation and restitution
Réunion 61
#RhodesMustFall 92–93
Ricaurte, Paola 363
right-wing populism *see* populism
Riofrancos, Thea 358
Robbins, Paul 386, 390, 393
Robinson, Cedric 157
Robinson, James A. 37–38
Rodney, Walter 57–58
Roman Empire 46
Roman law 50
Roosevelt, Franklin D. 373, 374
Roundtable on Sustainable Palm Oil 400
Rubinstein, William 168
Runnymede Trust 412
Russian Revolution 88

S

Sabir, Rizwaan 321
Safran, William 208
Sahagún, Bernardino de 47
Said, Edward W. 318, 414, 429
Saint-Domingue *see* Haiti
Sarr, N'deye Mariame 332–333
Scarman Inquiry (1977) 120, 269
Schumacher, Patrik 130
Schwundeck, Christy 332–333
Scotland 71
Second World War 88–89, 213–214
Shafi, Azfar 269
Sharp, Granville 63
Shawcross report (2023) 322
Shilliam, Robbie 129
Sigona, Nando 189
Silvasti, Tiina 144–145
Sinha, Satyendra Prasanna 170
Sista Mimi 333
Sivanandan, Ambalavaner 129, 132, 265
Skinner, Benjamin 154
slavery
  abolition in Haiti 19–20, 22
  anti-slavery activists 63–64
  compensation paid 22, 35
  denial of subject-hood 415
  escapees 78
  impact on family and intimacy 222
  indenture distinguished 59
  operation in Saint-Domingue 19
  palm oil as successor to 402
  police power and 329–330
  rebellions against 21–22
  reparations for 35–36, 63
  restoration by Napoleon 20
  revolts 21–22
  slave trading families 77–79
  transportation 59, 60–61, 77–78
  wealth derived from 76–79
  see also modern slavery
Smith, Daniel 169
Smith, John 62–63
social media 240
Sonthonax, Léger-Félicité 19
South Africa 58, 92–93
South Asian migration 116–119
South Sea Islands 58, 62
Southall Black Sisters 277, 280
Spanish Empire
  colonization 19, 47, 48
  encomienda system 60, 61
  trading currency 48–49
Spillers, Hortense 222, 224–225
Spivak, Gayatri Chakravorty 3–4
Spring, Charlotte 144
Sri Lanka 64
Stampnitzky, Lisa 322–323
Stoler, Ann Laura 253, 279, 282
Stovall, Tyler 23
Streeck, Wolfgang 32, 33
Suárez, Marcela 363
Sudbury, Julia 280, 280–281
Sunak, Rishi 235
Sunday Times Rich List 171–172
Surinam 64
Svampa, Maristella 359, 360, 361
Swyngedouw, Erik 389
syndemic 48
Syrian refugees 159, 189, 211, 238–239, 254

T

Taino Arawak people 20
Tait, Márcia M. 363
Táíwò, Olúfẹ́mi 93
Táíwò, Olúfẹ́mi O. 93
Taylor, Charles 290
textile mills 78–79
Thatcher, Margaret 186, 235, 237, 241, 269
Thompson, E.P. 71, 74–75
Todd, Zoe 375
Torres Strait Islands 51
trade unions
  approach to migrant labour 115–116, 119–120, 121, 122
  endorsement of colour bar 213
  indifference to anti-racist struggle 268
  industrial action 119–120
transportation of convicts 61–62
Traoré, Adama 333
Trinidad 60–61
Trojan Horse affair 302–311
Trouillot, Michel-Rolph 26, 279, 280

Trump, Donald 106, 238
Trussell 141, 142, 144, 145
Tuck, Eve 93
Tugendhat, Tom 189
Turkey 195, 211
Turner, Joe 209
Turner, Nat 22

U

Ugandan Asians 118
UK Independence Party 238–239
Ukrainian settlement schemes (UK) 189, 200
Ulloa, Astrid 361
Unilever 405
United Coloured People's Association (UCPA) 264, 266, 268
United Nations 89
United Nations Conference on the Human Environment 346
United Nations Environmental Programme 347, 349
United Nations Framework Convention on Climate Change 377–378, 419
United Nations High Commissioner for Refugees (UNHCR) 199
United States
  American Revolution 17–18, 21
  Louisiana's 'Cancer Alley' 345
  purchase of Louisiana 22
  revolts against slavery 21–22
  Roosevelt's New Deal 373, 374
  Vietnam War 90, 346
  War on Terror 316–319, 320
  welfare system 108
universal citizenship 22–24

V

Valluvan, Sivamohan 239
Vesey, Denmark 21–22
Vietnam 89–90
Vietnam War 90, 346
Vote Leave campaign 227, 238–239, 271

W

Wales 71
Wallerstein, Immanuel 425

Walvin, James 63
War of the Pacific (1879–1884) 50
War on Terror 316–319, 320
Ward, George 120
Watts, Michael 387
Weber, Max 102, 103
White abolitionists 63–64
White feminists 284n2
White servitude 58, 61–62
White working class 240, 268
Whiteness 106, 240
Who's Who 169–171
Williams, Eric 36, 38, 57, 61, 76
Williams, Wendy 188
Wilshaw, Sir Michael 304, 304–305
Wilson, Amrit 117, 226
Wilson A. (Zurich) 333
Windrush (HMT *Empire Windrush*) 183, 249, 275
Windrush scandal 131, 132, 187–188, 210–211, 254
women migrants 104, 116–117, 118–123, 275–276
Women's Liberation Movement 276, 277–278
women's rights 87, 119–123
  see also feminism
Wootton, Charles 224
workers' rights *see* Grunwick strike
World Bank 37, 360, 415, 418
World War I 88
World War II 88–89, 213–214
Wynter, Sylvia 198

Y

Yang, K. Wayne 93
York, Peter 171
Young, Arthur 74
Young, Iris Marion 294
Younge, Gary 235
Younis, Tarek 317, 322

Z

Zambelli, Elena 189
Zapatistas 393
Zedner, Lucia 319
Zimmerer, Karl S. 389

Printed and bound by CPI Group (UK) Ltd, Croydon, CR0 4YY
07/04/2026
14856151-0001